Essays in Bibliography, Text, and Editing

Essays
in Bibliography, Text,
and Editing

Thayer

Fredson Bowers

Published for the Bibliographical Society
of the University of Virginia
by the University Press of Virginia
Charlottesville

THE UNIVERSITY PRESS OF VIRGINIA
Copyright © 1975 by the Rector and Visitors
of the University of Virginia

First published 1975

Library of Congress Cataloging in Publication Data
THE UNIVERSITY PRESS OF VIRGINIA

Bowers, Fredson Thayer.
    Essays in bibliography, text, and editing.

    "Fredson Bowers: A checklist of publications to
1976:" p. 529
        1.   Bibliography—Collected works.   2.   Bowers,
Fredson Thayer—Bibliography.   I.   Title.
Z1005.B68   016.081   74-18055
ISBN 0-8139-0586-9

Printed in the United States of America

Foreword

THIS VOLUME is published by the Bibliographical Society of the University of Virginia in honor of Fredson Bowers, the founding editor of its *Studies in Bibliography*, who since 1948 has presided over the twenty-eight volumes that the Society has issued annually to this time. The *Studies* have received their proper share of high praise in bibliographical and literary circles, praise due not only to the high worth of the contributions but as well to Mr. Bowers' controlling judgment and editorial skill. Many contributors, I am sure, have benefited from his rigorous and thoughtful criticism. The Society, honoring him in the year of his retirement as the Linden Kent Memorial Professor of English Literature at the University of Virginia, is pleased that he will continue as its editor.

These essays in bibliography—analytical, descriptive, textual—have been selected and a few slightly revised by Mr. Bowers from his publications, extensive in length and versatile in range that, omitting his lost juvenilia, begin in 1928. They have been arranged to start with some general observations on bibliography, to move to specific methods and problems in descriptive and analytical bibliography, and to conclude with principles of textual criticism and editing. They show—as do all his writings—the perceptiveness of his approach and the thoroughness of his method. The readers of those essays who wish to explore other of his publications have as their guide an appended checklist where, I may suggest, they will find some surprisingly varied subjects.

We are grateful for the permission of those who hold the copyrights to reprint these essays; specific acknowledgments are made elsewhere in this volume. The styling used in the text of these publications has been generally retained in reprinting, despite the resulting minor inconsistencies in British and American punctuation and spelling. Only a few changes have been made by Mr. Bowers: any substantial new material has been placed in brackets; notes newly added are marked by asterisks; some minor deletions have been made.

The official announcement of the publication of these essays was made at a dinner on October 26, 1974, in Charlottesville given for Mr. Bowers by the doctoral graduates of the University of Virginia and of the University of Chicago whose dissertations he directed or codirected. They join with the members of the Society in gratitude and affection for his services to the world of bibliography, a world that has felt—and will continue to feel—his creating and forming hand.

IRBY B. CAUTHEN, JR.

University of Virginia
Summer 1975

Contents

Foreword by Irby B. Cauthen, Jr.   v

The Bibliographical Way

Bibliography and the University (1949)   3
Some Relations of Bibliography to Editorial Problems (1949)   15
Bibliography, Pure Bibliography, and Literary Studies (1952)   37
The Bibliographical Way (1958)   54
Bibliography and Modern Librarianship (1966)   75
Four Faces of Bibliography (1971)   94

Descriptive Bibliography

Purposes of Descriptive Bibliography, with Some Remarks
    on Methods (1952)   111
Bibliography and Restoration Drama (1966)   135
Bibliography Revisited (1969)   151

Analytical Bibliography

The Headline in Early Books (1941)   199
An Examination of the Method of Proof Correction in
    King Lear Q1 (1947)   212
Elizabethan Proofing (1948)   240
Running-Title Evidence for Determining Half-Sheet
    Imposition (1948)   254
Bibliographical Evidence from the Printer's Measure (1949)   258
Motteux's *Love's a Jest* (1696): A Running-Title and
    Presswork Problem (1954)   269

Textual Criticism and Editing

Current Theories of Copy-Text, with an Illustration
    from Dryden (1950)   277
Old-Spelling Editions of Dramatic Texts (1957)   289

Textual Criticism and the Literary Critic (1958)   296
The Folio *Othello*: Compositor E (1959)   326
Established Texts and Definitive Editions (1962)   359
The Text of Johnson (1964)   375
Old Wine in New Bottles: Problems of Machine Printing (1966)   392
Practical Texts and Definitive Editions (1968)   412
The Facsimile of Whitman's Blue Book (1969)   440
Multiple Authority: New Problems and Concepts
        of Copy-Text (1972)   447
Remarks on Eclectic Texts (1973)   488

Fredson Bowers: A Checklist of Publications to 1976   531

Chronology   549

The Bibliographical Way

Bibliography
and the University

I AM CONSCIOUS that I am speaking not only to my colleagues in the English department, but to various other schools of study as well. I should therefore make my apologies if I seem to deal most directly with English studies, for these are what I know best. Yet I think that the general principles I have in mind actually are of wider application. No matter what the field of study, the basis lies in the analysis of the records in printed or in manuscript form, frequently the ill-ordered and incomplete records of the past. When factual or critical investigation is made of these records, there must be—it seems to me—the same care, no matter what the field, in establishing the purity and accuracy of the materials under examination, which is perhaps just another way of saying that one must establish the text on which one's far-reaching analysis is to be based; and in order that one may not be misled, one must know the accurate publishing history of the material so that false assumptions may not be made based on old editions which are not correctly dated, on forgeries, on an inability to distinguish reprints from originals, or confusion between reset textual editions, standing type, and simple reissues of old material with a new false face.

I am minded of a tempest in a teapot that occurred a while back between two Spenserian scholars, because precisely this sort of thing could happen in any field. These gentlemen had it hot and heavy at each other in print about the respective accuracy of what they had written concerning what was found in a certain eighteenth-century edition of Spenser; and it was some time before the discovery was made that each had thought he was using the same edition but in fact one was using a large-paper copy and the other a trade or small-paper copy, and it so happened that, unknown to everybody concerned, about one-third of the small-paper edition was in a completely different typesetting with a variant text from that of the large paper. This is an excellent case of what can happen to critical or historical

An address delivered before a group of members of the faculty and administration of the University of Pennsylvania, May 13, 1949. Printed in *The Library Chronicle of the Friends of the Library of the University of Pennsylvania*, 15 (1949), 37–51; reprinted with permission of the University of Pennsylvania Library.

scholars when they base their research on material which has not been examined bibliographically.

I rather suspect, indeed, that precisely the same sort of controversy could develop among historians using seventeenth-century newspapers as source material. Last summer while going through the Harvard file of the newspaper *Mercurius Politicus* in search of book advertisements, I found several duplicate copies. In such cases my reflexes are as well conditioned as any Pavlov dog; I compared these promptly, and found the duplicate copies of the same date actually to be different typesettings with some variance in their text. Duplicate typesetting in early newspapers is not, I think, commonly recognized as a possibility—perhaps even as a normal probability when we consider the large number which had to be printed in short order on a relatively slow hand press. Hence it seems that historians relying on these newspapers can never be entirely sure of their ground until a very large-scale bibliographical job is done with this material.

But first I had better define just what it is I am talking about, for "bibliography" is a loosely employed and much abused word. First let me utterly cast aside the kind of gossiping about books which is written by and published for amateur collectors and which reaches its nadir in some so-called bibliographies of modern authors or in book-collectors manuals. This sort of thing is usually quite incompetent or irrelevant from any professional point of view, and since it is often in the public eye it has given a bad name to the whole subject, especially as bibliography may concern rare books or collected items. There is no reason why scholarship cannot be applied to bibliographical work with modern books, although there are very severe difficulties in the way; but what is usually produced by and for collectors comes under no definition of scholarship with which I am acquainted.

On the other hand, I have respect for what is perhaps the commonest idea of what constitutes bibliography. This is the compiling of lists of books for the basic purposes of information. We are all familiar with the two fundamental categories. First, the recording of original material, such as lists of scientific incunabula, which any historian of science must know about; early editions of Euclid; or the Short-title Catalogues of books printed before 1640 and before 1700; the listing of the English and continental early editions of the historian Gibbon, of the scientist Boyle or the theologian Fuller. Second, the listing of research done about this original material, as in the annual bibliographies in various learned journals in history, American literature, Renaissance studies, and so on.

As I shall indicate later, students must be familiarized with the vast growth of such bibliographical material, and in order to familiarize themselves with the material, they may properly be assigned problems in it or be made to work up checklists as a kind of study associated with their particular research. Whatever their nature, these lists or "bibliographies" are in some sense a collection of library cards conveniently assembled in one place and bearing on one subject. They are, of course, the very foundation of scholarship, for unless one knows where to turn quickly and conveniently for all available material on any subject, infinite hours are wasted in desultory search. All fields of study combine in their needs for such collections. We are particularly rich in these resources for English, but I have heard friends in other fields complain bitterly about incompleteness in theirs and the resulting difficulties of research. I think that if departments would accept such lists in annotated form as masters theses, we should accumulate the necessary material more rapidly.

Every student must therefore know something about the subject, but the compilation of such purely enumerative bibliographies is not an operation of scholarship on a level with the forms of scholarship which make up graduate instruction for the doctorate. In its teaching on an over-all basis the library schools have properly specialized, and there seems little need for duplication of such instruction on any wide scale outside of these schools, and to any greater extent in a university than is necessary for a research student to know how to do his own work. In this connection, however, I specifically except the field of descriptive bibliography as represented by W. W. Greg's work with the Elizabethan drama, a certain number of very closely analyzed author bibliographies, such projects as Mr. Alden's researches in Rhode Island imprints, or the forthcoming Pennsylvania imprints bibliography. For reasons which I hope will shortly become clear, these are properly scholarship, for they cannot be achieved except by scholarly investigations.

What I have in mind as a most strikingly neglected field for university study is a kind of bibliography which is almost entirely a product of twentieth-century scholarship. This is analytical bibliography, sometimes called critical bibliography. In the words of W. W. Greg, its most noted living practitioner, it is the study and analysis of a book as a material object which has been created by the mechanical process of printing. This sounds not only like a very narrow subject, but one scarcely of much concern to the humanities. Yet in truth it is of the most vital concern, because starting on this narrow basis the study broadens out until it penetrates—or should penetrate—every aspect of human thought set down on printed pages or in manuscript. And I am myself convinced that either by pursuing this subject itself, or by directly and consciously utilizing its results, a new trend in scholarship is developing in the light of which a great deal of past work needs re-examination and correction.

I find it of considerable significance that the appreciation of this new scholarship comes most strongly from scholars who are normally at opposite poles of thought: on the one hand from the traditional academic researcher with his markedly factual leaning, but on the other from the so-called higher critics, the present liberals and new interpreters of literature. For a time I was somewhat puzzled by this latter interest, but now I think it derives from the strong trend in this criticism towards the minute and searching examination of an author's language for its meaning in image after image, phrase after phrase, before beginning the process of the full estimate of his literary status. This close though often speculative examination into imagery and symbol in poetry, for example, has led to a recognition that for valid results one must have purity of text, so that assumptions are based not on an eighteenth- or nineteenth-century editor's highly personal and selective idea of what, say, Shakespeare or Donne wrote, but instead on a rigorous and even scientific enquiry according to definite principles into a recovery, in as close a form as is possible, of the author's original composition.

Only an analytical bibliographer can begin this enquiry, for it needs a special knowledge to follow in the most minute detail the operation by which a handwritten manuscript or a printed text, possibly with authorial annotations, is set in type by a compositor, the type-pages arranged for the press and then printed on a series of sheets of paper, with these sheets (sometimes altered and revised from their initial form) being sorted, stored, and finally bound into a finished book which will probably differ in certain respects from many others in the same set of bound and finished books.

The only reason why this close and painful study should be undertaken as a branch of humanistic investigation is that it may ultimately become textual or historical criticism, or—as I prefer to believe—that it may provide a sounder and more informatory basis for textual and historical criticism than has existed in the past. When Greg, in what is to me a ringing phrase, declared that bibliography is the grammar of textual criticism, he was being as literal and as accurate as he could possibly manage. Before a critic can speak with any authority about the works of an author, whether he is analyzing his imagery, his metrics, his language, his facts, or in certain cases his over-all literary art, he must have settled for him what were the actual words which his author penned in manuscript insofar as these can be determined from a scientific study of the printed result. Until we know, as nearly as we can come to it, what an author actually wrote, or intended to write, we are often spinning critical pipe-dreams or working under factual misapprehension based on the second-hand report of a printed text which, with all its possible corruptions, we must accept in lieu of the author's own manuscript at first hand.

It is the duty of the bibliographer to help the critic or the historian to arrive as close as he can to a first-hand report; or, to put it more negatively, it is his function, by his technical knowledge, to help the critic to evaluate the second-hand printed report more accurately. As an example of this new trend to get back to the original documents and to estimate them as accurately as possible, I originally found G. B. Harrison's paper at the 1946 MLA meeting of considerable significance. There he offered what seemed to be a most convincing attack on editors who had re-lined *Coriolanus* to suit their preconceived ideas of metrical regularity, and he affirmed the original and irregularly lined Folio text as the one which accurately represents Shakespeare's conscious lining. If, then, he asserted, we want to read the lines of *Coriolanus* with the distributed emphases, the dramatic cadences that Shakespeare had in mind when he wrote, we cannot take the Globe text or any text based on similar principles. [The only difficulty with this purely literary argument is that it is completely wrong. At the time I did have some uneasy queries how an Elizabethan actor under the repertory conditions of the theatre could memorize and retain an intricate system of short lines as a guide to emphasis and cadence, but I subdued these doubts under the spell of Professor Harrison's eloquence and what I believed was an admirable effort to restore meaning from the original documents untainted by the regularizing of eighteenth-century editors. My instincts were right, of course, but my credulity was too elastic. C. J. K. Hinman's work some years later on Compositor B in the First Folio showed that he especially (and occasionally other of the Folio workmen) on occasion used this device of dividing a regular pentameter to form two short lines either to waste space when the cast-off copy was insufficient to fill the column but more often to avoid a turn-over or turn-under when the line was too long to set in the relatively narrow Folio measure. True bibliographical evidence, thus, established the purely mechanical reason for the phenomenon and replaced Harrison's speculative and quite erroneous literary guesses with the hard daylight of fact. As a consequence we do not need to revise our conventional notions about Shakespeare's metrics because of Compositor B's short lines.]

This is not the occasion to go into the intricacies of editing texts according to bibliographical principles, and so I can only mention the fact that Greg has on various occasions pointed out the confusion which results from trying to reconstruct an author's correct reading from English printed texts on principles which apply more properly to the determination of the Latin and Greek text from manuscripts of classical authors. But there has been another kind of editing which has come down to us from the eighteenth and nineteenth centuries in which a critic decides between two possible readings purely on his personal estimate of the feel, the tone, the language, the poetic insight, sometimes the smoothness.

Now actually I am not decrying this kind of editing completely, but I regard it as the ultimate stage when all other means have failed. I studied under Kittredge at Harvard, I shall always think of him as one of the truly great men whom I have known, but he inherited this method and it sometimes failed even him. I remember that Kittredge came down to the University of Virginia once to deliver a lecture, and one of my students, Charlton Hinman, now a famous bibliographical scholar, was at the time midway into his searching examination of the text of *Othello* which has rather altered the traditional views of this play. He asked Kittredge a question on some point about the Boston Public Library copy, and Kittredge said rather grandly that he was just then writing the notes for *Othello*, and after determining in that process what Shakespeare had said, he would make up his text. Now Hinman went on to take the text apart line by line and to study its transmission; and by a chain of bibliographical evidence which could be taken into a court of law, he succeeded in demonstrating the relation of the Folio to the First Quarto, and of the heretofore puzzling Second Quarto to both, in such a way that every single variant of consequence in this late Quarto was shown to have been derived from states of its printed copy before it was proof-read, and hence no single one had any authority. Yet Kittredge, like every other editor of *Othello*, when given the choice of these variant readings, chose on literary grounds some corrupt ones and inserted various completely unauthoritative Second Quarto readings into his text as representing the true recovery of what Shakespeare had written.

Now Kittredge worked on what Greg calls *metacritical* evidence, which does not rely on bibliography, the grammar of criticism, to establish the precise derivation of texts. I was once very badly burned on such a matter when I was a bibliographical novice, and ever since I have had a peculiar interest in the problem.* In the last few years I have run across several dozen cases of partial resetting in books, and in each I have tried to amuse myself by estimating which was the earlier, this estimate being made purely on critical grounds, before tackling the bibliographical evidence. It is no longer astonishing to me that in the majority of these cases my metacritical reasoning led me to a conclusion which my bibliographical completely reversed. Very possibly my critical faculties may seem rather suspect after this confession, but I would gladly give these same problems to any group of editors and make money at odds of two to one against them.

The most dangerous kind of criticism incidentally is when a metacritical writer attacks a problem with a false semblance of bibliographical reasoning which superficially disguises the real basis of his approach. It takes a real analytical bibliographer to unmask this pseudo-bibliography, as Greg has

---

* In my first fumbling approaches to the text of Thomas Dekker, on pseudo-critical evidence I decided that one state of the partially reset inner forme of sheet I, with variant readings, was the earlier and another the later. On strictly bibliographical evidence based on the analysis of the running-titles, Dr. J. G. McManaway demonstrated the reverse in *The Library*, 4th ser., 19 (1938), 176–179. This and another salutary shock of the same nature assisted me to become a bibliographer.

often done, but the confused distinction between what is bibliographical evidence, and what is not, is too large a subject to engage us now. It is, however, of prime importance in the sometimes difficult task of deciding the order of two editions printed in the same year.

I have digressed a bit, too, and I should return to a more precise explanation of just what an analytical bibliographer does. Well, in the first place, he studies books as material objects. He tries to uncover what printing evidence they contain about every step in their process of manufacture. If he is preparing a book for close textual study, he wants to know whether one or else two or more compositors were engaged in the production, whether one or two or more presses printed it. He wants to know whether the book was set and printed continuously or in sections simultaneously. Whether it was proofread and corrected or not. He wants to know in each case which side of every sheet of paper was printed first, because this has an intimate relation in some cases as to whether we may assume that one side or the other has been proofread. He especially wants to know whether they were printed with one, or two, or three, or four skeleton-formes because this evidence may unlock the secret of much of the above. He wants to know what evidence he can adduce from spelling tests or certain technical type measurements to separate different compositors within the same book and to determine just which pages each composed. Different compositors will have different habits which affect the authority of the text. He wants to study watermarks to see if they can help date undated or falsely dated books, and also, as we are slowly learning, for what they can sometimes tell about the printing process. He wants to know that each leaf is an integral part of the whole sheet on which it is printed, and whether all the leaves are present, or whether some leaves are later substitutes which contain revisions. He wants to know about types and where they came from, ornaments and ornamental initials, for what these matters can sometimes tell about the order in which certain books were printed, or for their aid in identifying anonymous or falsely named printers, or misdated books. He wants to make studies which will identify the printers of certain periods and will analyze their methods of composing, printing, and proofreading for what this evidence can supply about the true relations of the publishing history of books and the authenticity of their texts.

Now all this is technical knowledge about a technical process. How is it justified in graduate study in the humanities? The answer is in several parts, I think. First, the humanities deal more often with printed transmission of human thought than with oral transmission, and if criticism or history is to be put on an absolutely sound basis it must rest on an accurate estimate of the nature of the original documents with which it deals. On the theory of setting a crook to catch a crook, you set an analytical bibliographer to catch the printer and see what he has done, since your documents are derived second-hand to you through this printer. No matter how technical and seemingly unrelated to any literary use some bibliographical investigation is, all of it is some time applied. And even if a bibliographer were never anything else, he would justify his existence and his technical studies by serving as the OK'er of basic documents. Yet why bring him into a university? For the simple reason, I feel, that only in universities is there the tradition of scholarship on a professional basis which will support this specialized work as the scholarship which it is, which will keep this work out of the market place and will encourage it and direct it to its proper ends. Only in the universities is there encouragement for purely theoretical studies without immediate practical aims; yet, as every scientist knows, without such abstract research, the practical appliers soon run out of material. If critics want the services of bibliography, they must bring it to them, and work closely with it. By a mutual understanding of the problems involved, the work gains a rationale which might otherwise be lost.

This brings me to my second part, which is the use of a university library and its rare books. I do not know a great deal about library schools, and so I hope I shall not give offence if I remark that so far as I can observe they handle other functions admirably, but they do not know enough to teach analytical bibliography as I understand it, and this deficiency sometimes also means, unfortunately, that books cannot be recorded accurately in libraries. As scholars turn more and more to a re-examination of the original documents, the rare book collection of a university assumes its place as the heart of the most significant research activity. As I have tried to indicate, old books are highly variable in their structure and contents, and unless those who have charge of them are technically trained to deal with them analytically, and to assist by their own bibliographical work in the huge task of correctly and completely determining all these variants and their inter-relationship in the original documents, the library in my opinion is failing in its duties to the critical and historical scholars who work with these documents.

For my third part, I should say that a Ph.D. candidate is indeed too naive to be a critic, let alone a research scholar, if he does not understand by practical experience the processes by which the printed books with which he works came into existence. My experience is that the average graduate student takes printed editions as if they had been typeset on Mount Sinai; and he has no idea of any principles by which he can determine whether a text in his hand is good or bad regardless of whether it is an old or new text, or whether one early edition on which to base his work is more trustworthy than another. I deplore this separation of those who depend on modern edited texts or early reprints from any practical idea of how such texts are constituted. This ignorance leads to naiveté and a basically unprofessional approach to literature or history. I say this because such students must constantly be taking other scholars' word for their basic material and they cannot have enough knowledge to sift the frauds from the true men. Time after time, therefore, they will be misled.

Moreover, it has been my practical experience that if analytical bibliography is properly approached as the grammar of criticism, even its necessarily technical foundation can be made interesting to superior literary students; and as they see that here is a wide-open field in which one's productiveness really leads to making original contributions to the sum of human knowledge, they may turn to it to give them a foundation for their research. Many students I have taught have, very properly in my opinion, combined in themselves the bibliographer and historian or critic and have put their technical information to use by applying it to literary study. But though I feel that this application justifies the teaching of analytical bibliography in universities, I warn my students that they are going to have to earn their living as professors of English first. Bibliographical studies may become their special field of research and they may continue if they choose to do nothing but technical research which simply prepares the ground for textual critics to take over; but for their teaching they must be literary men.

Yet they are literary men with a difference. They have had the training so that they do not have to take the specialists' word for any textual matter but can evaluate the interpretation of the technical evidence which is offered in argumentation. They do not need to rely on boiled down and popularized accounts of the most complex transmission of some of Shakespeare's text from quarto to quarto to Folio, or from independent manuscripts. They can follow and criticize the validity of specialist studies in these matters and interpret them to their students with first-hand authority. They learn a kind of professionalism, a scholarly discipline in testing and evaluating evidence on logical grounds which I myself think is the equal of other hurdles, chiefly linguistic, which we set up for advanced students. They learn what is the hardest thing to instill in a graduate student—confidence in their own conclusions based on never taking anybody's word for anything, but knowing enough to test any statement made. I was rather amused, but pleased, when a student this year who has been working on the much debated *Troilus and Cressida* problem and who has solved by completely demonstrable evidence what has only been guessed at before, when this student said rather bewilderedly—"You know, there wasn't really any problem there—all these people had to do was to look at the two texts." This was, actually, a rather over-simplified statement; but I think he had learned a most important thing—to work logically on primary evidence and not to bow down to authority. Most graduate students believe, of course, that if a thing is in print, it's true. Bibliography is constantly taking big names apart and demonstrating that the scholarship they have printed is not true; and that is rather healthy work for a research student, until he needs taking down in turn.

Analytical bibliography finds another justification as an integral part of university study in its preparation of scholars for the task of editing, a job which is, I think, becoming more and more important in present-day scholarship. At one time I hoped that the functions of bibliographer and textual critic could be separated and that one could simply prepare the material for the other. Now I am sure that any such separation would constitute a positive danger: whereas every bibliographer certainly is not and even should not be a textual critic, yet textual criticism is becoming more and more dangerous to engage in unless one has had rigorous bibliographical training. Far too much unnecessary metacritical thinking is being put into scholarly editions when bibliographical was actually available. There is really no need for an editor to attempt to demonstrate on purely textual grounds that a sixth Dryden edition was typeset from an annotated copy of the fifth collated and marked by an editor (perhaps even Dryden himself) with the fourth to correct certain readings, when one can easily demonstrate that two compositors set the sixth edition in relay, one using a copy of the fourth and another the fifth, and hence the sixth edition has no authority since there was no editorial intervention. There is really no need on pseudo-bibliographical or on textual grounds to argue which of two editions printed in the same year was the earlier. The case can almost always be demonstrated not by argument and inference but by facts that one could take into a court of law for a decision.* This holds true for the relation of any two editions one to another, whether editorially annotated or not; the derivation of one can almost always be demonstrated by bibliographical evidence beyond the shadow of a doubt whether it was printed from a specific earlier edition or from an independent manuscript. These are larger questions, but in detail after detail in choice of variant readings or of whether to emend, the editor without first-hand bibliographical training is faced with problems that he can solve only by guesswork. I do not assert by any means that bibliography is all there is to textual criticism, for it certainly is not, but it must be the foundation on which the editor's linguistic knowledge, his taste, and literary insight into meaning are based.

Rigorous bibliographical training first on the techniques and then on their application seems to me—to sum up—to be an integral part of a university's graduate program because the new bibliography is as much concerned with the basic elements of the humanities as is, say, philology.

* An illustration may be drawn from "The First Edition of Dryden's *Wild Gallant*," *The Library*, 5th ser., V (1950), 51–54, summarized in "Some Relations of Bibliography to Editorial Problems" in pp. 28–32 of the present collection.

In the increasing complexities of research it is one of the few studies which offer a basic analysis of the composition and transmission of the tools of research, the original documents. Testing evidence by sound bibliographical fact and not by the speculation of half-knowledge will remove a considerable part of the cloud of unreality which to my mind hangs over certain areas of criticism, editorship, and historical studies.

Now much of what I have said has been rather specifically directed at English studies, but there are wider applications. Any field in which work is done with early books needs to have these books closely examined, sorted out systematically, their relationship established, and their publishing history determined. The purity of text of the original documents seems to me to be of as much concern to the field of history, for example, as to English. And with history there is an even greater need for bibliography to sort out and systematically analyze this mass of source material in a way which certainly has not been done. A Virginia friend of mine tells me, for example, that there is enough material in the Historical Society of Pennsylvania to fill a bibliographical journal on American history and literature for the next twenty years if it were properly worked over. Until seventeenth- and eighteenth-century American printing history is worked out—printers and papermakers dated and identified, books collated in all their editions to establish their line of descent and correct relationship, their place and date of publication established—for all any historical student may know the text he is using for his work may be a corrupt reprint in which certain essential facts are misprinted or even missing. Any other field, such as philosophy, sociology, art, science, once it begins dealing with the original source books of the past is in the same fix until bibliographical examination has established the facts about these books. I can say with confidence that library cataloguing or the compilation of checklists is only a partial answer to the problem; bibliographical analysis in a way largely unknown to cataloguing, analysis that ends in true descriptive bibliography, is the only means to provide the answers and to bring some degree of order out of what is often a chaotic field, especially in Americana. If the universities do not train men to do this essential and basic work, I don't know who will; and the field will be left to the amateurs, as it has been largely in the past, with some rather dreadful results.

I think that to strengthen the research techniques of its graduate students, every department in a university should have a required course to acquaint these students with the tools of their trade, specifically with the materials of enumerative bibliography, to enable them to find their material quickly and accurately, to investigate it systematically, and to write it up logically. But over and above this, in view of the crying need for specially trained men, it is rather horrifying that few American universities offer formal instruction, at least at the research level, in analytical bibliography in spite of the magnificent new fields for research in humanistic studies which this science provides. Moreover, if ever there is a subject which requires instruction it is this. Mere reading and dabbling is not enough to learn this trade. The research student must work over books in process after process to acquire by actual and repeated experience the technique, the imagination, the feel, and the logic of bibliographical investigation. This is a field requiring rigorous discipline, a considerable amount of time for research, and rigorous instruction based on special knowledge which itself has been acquired and is constantly being enlarged by research. These men may, according to their special interests, turn out to be active teachers, practising bibliographers, or really knowledgeable rare book librarians who are more than simple custodians of locked-up treasures. But whatever they may be, we are in America training too few of them for the future.

And I put the emphasis on training, because all my generation were self-taught, and I know from bitter experience how enormously one can waste one's time in false starts and undirected research, how half-baked one's work is for years when one is forced by necessity to learn only by private experience and wasteful trial and error, lacking the trained direction which can produce good work by students from the start. I know that I am not alone in the conviction that Philadelphia's magnificent resources make it the logical place to be the bibliographical training and producing center of this country if you will welcome and foster this new basic scholarship among you.

Some Relations of Bibliography to Editorial Problems

BIBLIOGRAPHY CONCERNS ITSELF with editorial problems not as a usurper of the functions of legitimate criticism, but instead as the necessary foundation on which, in certain investigations, textual criticism must be based and to which criticism must constantly refer for more or less definitive judgments. Bibliography, in W. W. Greg's acute phrase, is the grammar of literary investigation. This position was strikingly advanced in Greg's classic address on the relations of Bibliography to literature which appeared some time ago in *Neophilologus*, and, again, in his "Bibliography —An Apologia" (*The Library,* 4th ser. XIII [1932], 113 ff.). Any attempt merely to restate Greg's views here would be quite superfluous. For some years, at least among scholars, the inferential identification of bibliography with textual criticism has been so firmly established that to talk about the contribution of one to the other might appear to be like a solemn discussion of the usefulness of the arm to the hand.

Nevertheless, it is possible to suspect that, as more and more scholars have come to deal with these twin methods, the popularizing of their disciplines may have led, by subtle degrees, to a rather over-simplified view of the basic provinces of bibliography and textual criticism, especially as applied to editorial problems. Certainly the theory that every bibliographer is professionally qualified to be a full-fledged textual critic and editor is quite wrong. Correspondingly, there are a number of distinguished textual critics whom, according to any strict accounting, we might hesitate to call bibliographers.

Some fortunate scholars like Pollard, McKerrow, and Greg may happily combine in themselves both functions, although perhaps in unequal proportions; but this two souls in body one is certainly the exception rather than the rule. On the other hand, the most prominent Elizabethan textual critic now living—I refer to Mr. Dover Wilson—often operates in that dark region of the ur-state of a text which McKerrow rightly hesitated to identify with bibliography. One should comment, however, that not all of Wilson's readers—or his critics—are completely aware of the distinction.

Read before the English Institute at Columbia University on September 9, 1949. Printed in *Studies in Bibliography,* 3 (1950–51), 37–62.

It is somewhat perturbing, for example, in Hereward Price's admirable "Towards a Scientific Method of Textual Criticism in the Elizabethan Drama"[1] to find his chief whipping boy, Dover Wilson, consistently referred to as representing the bibliographical school. Save for his impatience at various of Wilson's well-known aberrations, Mr. Price—no more than the rest of us—would, I should think, completely discount such investigations. But we may agree with McKerrow and Greg that this scholarship is not usually bibliographical in any sense in which we should be prepared to use the term.

Bibliography is likely to be a vague and misused word because it has come to be employed for too many different purposes. For the present discussion we may rule out enumerative bibliography—the making-up of finding or reference lists of books on various subjects—and use the term to mean analytical bibliography, the investigation and explanation of a book as a material object. Yet even within this narrower limitation there are various strata and subdivisions of research. For example, we have such forms of bibliographical spadework as the identification and recording of typefaces by Haebler, or of *STC* printers' ornaments now in progress by F. S. Ferguson, with their dates and history.

But when we move from such essential preliminary investigation, and from the recording of material data as a part of publishing history, to another sort of bibliography, more specifically of the kind we designate as *analytical*, we come to a field in which all our accumulated knowledge of printing practice and history is devoted to the examination of individual or related books as material objects, with a view to determining the facts of their production. Is there or is there not a cancel in a certain gathering; were the various sheets of a book printed *seriatim* or simultaneously in two or more sections; did one or two compositors, one or more presses, work on this book, and if so which parts did they do; was a cancel title-page or a cancel in the text printed later or as a part of the continuous printing of the book. Are variants in the sheets of the book the result of different impressions, or do they result from different typesettings or from simple correction at the press. If some of the sheets are of a single impression but certain others exhibit variant typesettings, which setting is the original, and why was the resetting made. If there are variant imprints, which was first through the press. And so on. It will be seen that correct answers to some of these questions depend not only on the simple discovery of the facts themselves, but more particularly on the satisfactory explanation of the ascertained facts. From specific analyses of this kind, some speculatively minded bibliographers may endeavor to evolve new techniques for bringing

---

1 *Journal of English and Germanic Philology*, XXXVI (1937), 151–67.

to light yet further secrets in printed books, techniques which may enable us to attack successfully some general problems which have heretofore been thought insoluble.

Such technical examinations of individual books for their own sake are proceeding very swiftly these days, and they are being matched step by step by the parallel development of techniques for determining with greater precision the relation of the printed book to its underlying manuscript.[2] No textual critic can afford to ignore the results of these investigations. From Willoughby's and Hinman's explorations of spelling tests,[3] assisted in certain cases by evidence from the varying length of the compositor's stick,[4] we are now able to distinguish with some certainty in the *STC* period and the following years the precise pages of a book set by different compositors. By an equation of these compositors' habits we can thereupon make certain assumptions about the characteristics of the manuscript from which they were setting. The cooperative efforts which have been made in the analysis of the evidence of headlines[5] have opened up possibilities, in combination with this compositor evidence, for determining sometimes quite minute but necessary questions of the presswork and proofreading. To these may be added—among many other investigations —the classic Carter and Pollard examination of paper and type which exposed the Wise forgeries, Hazen's use of identified paper to detect Strawberry Hill forgeries, and Stevenson's technique for aligning watermarks with presswork.[6] The unexpected uses of bibliography have been demonstrated in Bond's assignment of authorship to certain doubtful *Spectator* papers, the whole argument resting ultimately on type left standing in advertisements and headings.[7]

2 In this connection one must always recall W. W. Greg's searching monograph on *Orlando Furioso* and *The Battle of Alcazar*.

3 E. E. Willoughby, *The Printing of the First Folio of Shakespeare* (1932); C. J. K. Hinman, "Principles Governing the Use of Variant Spellings as Evidence of Alternate Setting by Two Compositors," *The Library*, 4th ser., XXI (1940), 78–94; see also P. Williams, "The Compositor of the Pied-Bull *Lear*," *Papers Bibl. Soc. Univ. Virginia* [*SB*], I (1948), 61–68.

4 *Studies in Bibliography*, II (1949), 153–67.

5 For a number of references, see J. G. McManaway's footnote in *Standards of Bibliographical Description* (1949), pp. 88–89. See also *The Library*, 4th ser., XIX (1938), 315–38; 5th ser., II (1947), 20–44; 5th ser., III (1948), 124–37; *Papers Bibl. Soc. America*, XLII (1948), 143–48; XLIII (1949), 191–95.

6 J. Carter and G. Pollard, *An Enquiry into the Nature of Certain Nineteenth Century Pamphlets* (1934); A. T. Hazen, *A Bibliography of the Strawberry Hill Press* (1942); A. H. Stevenson, "New Uses of Watermarks as Bibliographical Evidence," *Papers Bibl. Soc. Univ. Virginia*, I (1948), 151–82.

7 D. F. Bond, "The First Printing of the *Spectator*," *Modern Philology*, XLVII (1950), 174–77.

Astonishing results have recently accrued from certain research on eighteenth-century press figures, which had been earlier dismissed by Mc-Kerrow as of little bibliographical significance. Knotts[8] has added a chapter to the work of Sale, Chapman, and others; and W. B. Todd's latest interpretation of the evidence of these figures in a number of books demonstrates some most exciting things one can learn of printing.[9] From this evidence a whole new area of research has been opened up of such importance for distinguishing impressions, partial re-impressions, and editions, as well as various other important textual matters, that we may well believe in many cases press figures alone will come to be the most valuable tool for penetrating the extreme difficulties of textual problems in frequently reprinted popular eighteenth-century authors.

I should be less than candid if I tried to pretend that the immediate or even the chief aim of these and of many other bibliographical scholars was to serve as the sons of Martha to textual criticism. Without question, a number of bibliograpical investigations which eventually proved invaluable to textual criticism were not undertaken with this end immediately in view and almost by accident arrived at their textual applications. Thus a real difference from textual criticism must always be felt, I suspect, in bibliographical research in its purest aspect. To defend themselves against doubters, bibliographers are accustomed to argue that the ultimate aim of all bibliographical research, and therefore its justification, is the definitive account of books in a descriptive bibliography, or the direct application of their findings to textual criticism. But I make bold to say that—at least as I view it—the *immediate* end of a great deal of research is no such thing. Although I believe that the conventional justification is valid for the ultimate aims, and that this rationale is deeply felt by almost every bibliographical student, nevertheless, even though eventual application is the ideal, ordinarily textual criticism has not provided the immediate spur to the investigation and no specific textual use is often anticipated, at least in the early stages of the work. This attitude develops, in part, because many technical studies that are absolutely necessary yet require no interest in textual criticism on the part of the investigator. In part, because various of these studies are concerned only with a fragment of some total problem, the whole of which must be unraveled before any of it can be made of practical use to textual criticism.

Nonetheless, in spite of the various legitimate reasons which may be ad-

8 W. E. Knotts, "Press Numbers as a Bibliographical Tool: A Study of Gay's *The Beggars' Opera*, 1728," *Harvard Library Bulletin*, III (1949), 198–212. See also, P. Gaskell, "Eighteenth-century Press Numbers: Their Use and Usefulness," *The Library*, 5th ser., IV (1950), 249–61.

9 "Observations on the Incidence and Interpretation of Press Figures," *SB*, III (1950–51), 171–205.

vanced to explain the rationale for much technical work in bibliography, the point of view does in fact serve to separate many bibliographers from textual critics; indeed, it would be tempting to say *most* bibliographers were it not an increasing tendency for a number of analysts, with or without due training, to cross over the line and to concern themselves directly with the editing of texts. Others, though not editors, may develop so great an interest in textual questions that they direct their research specifically towards bibliographical problems which do have an immediate textual application and thus underlie accurate criticism. The record, while respectable, has not been one of unalloyed success, perhaps, and when bibliographers have concerned themselves with matters of textual criticism that were not primarily bibliographical, they have sometimes floundered pitifully if they lacked the training and the qualities of mind which are necessary for textual criticism in *its* purest state.

I use this statement of a point too often overlooked, in our current tendency to exalt the bibliographer, as an aid towards a cursory glance at the nature of textual criticism, a subject on which I can speak with little authority and on which I shall anticipate correction. It is perhaps absurd to set up too sharp a distinction between textual critics and textual bibliographers. Anyone, we may suppose, who is concerned with the origin, derivation, authority, and correctness of a text, in whole or in part, is a textual critic, no matter what his method of approach. Some scholars tackle problems through bibliography, some through what Greg has called metacriticism, some through an attempted or actual combination of bibliography and criticism. For purposes of distinction I must deal in blacks and whites more starkly than is perhaps realistic. Nevertheless, I am sure that when we distinguish between a McKerrow and a Dover Wilson, both brilliant examples of different schools, we are in fact implying a greater fundamental difference than exists between the conservative and speculative wings of the same method.

Greg—and in this he is frequently misunderstood—insists that the bibliographer must view a book only as a material object.[10] This is a far cry from the aims of a textual critic. Historically, textual criticism developed long before analytical bibliography; and it evolved its own rules, especially for dealing with manuscripts, both classical and vernacular, according to certain principles which are outside the strictly bibliographical range, if for our purposes we continue to limit the definition of bibliography to analytical bibliography. These principles, or something like them, were also applied to printed books, again before bibliography was more than a gleam in the eye, and—as Greg has shown in his "Rationale of Copy-Text" read before this meeting in his behalf by Mr. Osborn—they

10 "Bibliography—An Apologia," *op. cit.*, pp. 121 ff.

are still in part applicable to certain problems. Thus there has been established in the past a firm tradition for dealing with texts; and it would be foolish for us to believe that analytical bibliography has displaced this tradition, or even that in many cases it could. Nevertheless, analytical bibliography has demonstrated that in some circumstances the classical tradition is not completely self-sufficient. We may put it, therefore, that bibliography is neither a usurper nor a poor relation in the field of textual criticism, but rather its foundation, the grammar of the subject.

If, in the interests of brevity, we pass over the important field of manuscript texts and concern ourselves with textual criticism based chiefly on printed books, we may, perhaps, discern three main but by no means mutually exclusive lines of endeavor. The first concerns itself with the authorship, origin, and characteristics of the lost manuscript behind a printed book both in whole and in part. I am thinking first of various studies in the attribution of anonymous works, or of the solution of problems in multiple authorship as in the Beaumont and Fletcher plays, Massinger, and Dekker; and secondly of such studies as Mr. Duthie has made in the bad quarto of *Hamlet* and more recently in the Pide Bull *King Lear*. Dover Wilson's reconstructions of the manuscript copy for *Hamlet* and other texts should be placed here, as also various studies such as Hoppe's of *Romeo and Juliet* but especially Greg's of *Doctor Faustus*.* As with the *Faustus* and *Lear* investigations, according to the circumstances this division may merge imperceptibly with the second, which I take to be concerned with the critical analysis of texts in known manuscripts or printed exempla. Here we might place studies like Grierson's on the text of Donne, Wolf's on commonplace books, Shaaber's on 2 *Henry IV*. The determination of the order and authority of printed texts after the first also applies, and we must certainly include the very difficult task of separating from compositor's, proofreader's, and printing-house editor's alterations those true revisions from an authoritatively corrected copy used as the basis for a later edition. The relation of the variants in the Quarto and Folio of *King Lear* or *Troilus and Cressida* is such a problem. In all of these divisions various special studies may enter in one form or another. I list as examples a few of the inquiries which Mr. Price sets up as among the subjects for textual criticism: vocabulary tests of authorship, and also of plagiarism, metrical tests including study of broken lines, deficient lines, redundant syllables, feminine endings, prose as blank verse, and so on, applied to form an opinion of a text.

Finally, perhaps we may assign as a third general division the orderly bringing together of all this information in an editorial capacity, and the

* For an initial acceptance of Greg's views on *Dr. Faustus* and then a rejection, see my "The Text of Marlowe's *Faustus*," a review article in *Modern Philology*, 49 (1952), 195–204, but then "Marlowe's *Doctor Faustus*: The 1602 Additions," *SB*, 26 (1973), 1–18, and the textual introduction in volume 2 of the Cambridge *Marlowe* (1973).

consequent evolution of a modern critical text designed to represent the intentions of the author more faithfully than any single preserved manuscript or printed copy. Whereas the findings of analytical bibliography may or may not be applicable in the first two divisions, the claims of analysis enter full force in the editorial third.

In the first two divisions, it is true, the investigations lead hopefully towards the ideal of a definitive text, but, as with pure bibliography, much textual criticism is undertaken either for its own sake or else to attack only a fragment of the total problem, so that the immediate end of the research may not be the formation of a text. For example, Mr. Duthie did not edit *Hamlet* after he had solved the problem of the bad quarto. It will be convenient, however, to treat textual criticism and its relations to bibliography in its narrower application to the evolution of an edited text and to the various delicate problems that arise before this text can eventually be fixed. Moreover, the limitation may be extended to cover only the specific problem of old-spelling critical texts, for—as Greg's paper has shown— these are subject to certain criteria which do not always apply to modernized versions, even though the basic problems are shared in common.

At the start one should distinguish certain editorial problems that have no necessary connection with bibliography. An editor of the literature of the past must have considerable linguistic attainments, or ready access to professional advice. Through long familiarity he must grow to be a native in the characteristic thought, usage, speech patterns, and customs of his period. Although bibliography may occasionally assist in the solution of some problems, or offer a convincing after-the-event confirmation, much emendation—or refusal to emend—much estimate of authenticity, must be made quite independently of bibliographical considerations and instead on a philological basis. This aspect has no relation to bibliography, and it requires a discipline and study which leave little time for bibliographical investigations not concerning the problem immediately at hand. Moreover, if we speak of only one characteristic, the great emendations have been inspired art and not systematic science. One can give a rational palaeographical explanation to derive "a table of green fields" set in type from the crabbed script of "a' babld of green fields," but I beg leave to doubt that this famous emendation would to the present day ever have been arrived at by strictly palaeographic reasoning. Greg, I believe, has no very high opinion of palaeography as giving more than a hint for emendations,[11] although its confirmation is often most valuable. Usually, I suspect, one arrives at an emendation of any subtlety by inspiration, memory, and a strong sense of analogy, and then one brings in palaeography if possible to justify one's conclusions.

11 "Principles of Emendation in Shakespeare," *Proceedings of the British Academy*, XIV (1928), 154–55.

Many other considerations of text are too frequently confused as soluble by bibliography. For example, bibliography can establish that edition *B.* was printed from edition *A.*, and not from an independent manuscript; but if revisions appear in *B.*, there is no bibliographical technique for determining except in isolated cases whether they derive from the author himself, a scribe revising the text of *A.* from a manuscript, or an editor of some kind. Such problems in one way or another involving emendation or the acceptance of variant readings fall to the lot of the textual critic once bibliography has cleared his way to the limit of its ability.

This critical acumen, which we cannot value too highly as applied to text, is, of course, the product of a keen and imaginative mind; but, again, it is materially aided by a very close acquaintance with one's period in general philological considerations. This acquaintance gradually develops an opinion about speech and imagery which, in mature and thoughtful hands, has its own authority not only in questions of emendation but in any division of textual criticism. We may note that even the conservative, bibliographical McKerrow does not disdain in certain circumstances to write about the authority of variants between editions which best seem to have the greatest internal harmony with an author.[12]

This strong and subtle imagination necessary for close inquiries into texts may apply itself to studies in attribution, plagiarism, or multiple authorship, or to studies in an author's speech and metrical characteristics, or it may be found in Dover Wilson's various attempts—whether rightly or wrongly—to discover layers of revision in the pre-printing history of a manuscript, or it may be utilized in the scrupulous examination of the sources and methods of corruption in a text which Duthie has demonstrated in *Hamlet* and in *King Lear*. Such striking deductions as those Duthie makes about the composition of memorial texts from tag ends of general recollections exhibit a critical virtuosity which has its own discipline and rigorous training.

If I were a textual critic concerned with such matters as I have been sketching, problems involving my total powers as a critic, I fancy I should be rather impatient with a bibliographer who insisted that I should be all this and McKerrow too. And I should be strongly inclined to reply: you are a technician—you do the technical part of this business and I shall apply your findings, taking care that I have studied the principles and general methods of your craft seriously enough so that I can follow your arguments and understand the applicability of what you are saying.

This is roughly what has happened, and as a consequence something like the following rationale is commonly accepted. The bibliographer's func-

12 *Prolegomena for the Oxford Shakespeare* (1939), p. 18.

tion is to prepare the general material of the texts, when bibliographical investigation is necessarily involved; and the textual critic, in the light of bibliographical findings, can then proceed to apply the discovered relationships, and to add his own art, to achieve the finished, definitive result.

Since we are an age of specialists, this separation of function seems reasonable to us. Indeed, in various cases it may work very well, and in some it may even be positively necessary. Yet I must confess it is a position I held with more conviction in the past than I do today, and I anticipate holding it with even less conviction in the future, especially if certain far-reaching bibliographical speculations and experimental techniques for dealing with the accidentals in an old-spelling text ever reach success. This change in attitude, I am conscious, may have been dictated too much by various experiences with amateur editors, from whom the good Lord deliver us, by a tendency to over-emphasize the importance of a close reconstruction of accidentals, and by allowing the special problems of distinctly unusual texts to bulk too large in my mind so that the uncomplicated, run-of-the-mill variety is obscured.

Whatever the cause, I have here what is only a selection of examples to illustrate that a textual critic, when he is himself incapable of applying advanced bibliographical techniques to every detail of an old-spelling text, can seldom achieve absolute authority in his results, and may indeed be led into serious error through the false confidence induced in him by the notion that bibliography has sufficiently prepared the way before his labors have begun.

This hypothetical critic can ordinarily be prepared only to follow and apply bibliographical arguments: his training has not prepared him to evaluate their correctness on technical grounds. A small but rather interesting example occurs in Thomas Southerne's *Disappointment* of 1684. Here the case for a cancel to abridge a censored scene was very plausibly advanced in 1933, and in 1946 was vetted by a good bibliographer who made some necessary modifications but in no way questioned the central thesis. Yet in the last sixteen years if any textual critic had treated the scene in the light of this apparently authoritative evidence, without testing it bibliographically for himself, he would have been quite wrong, for no cancel exists and the scene is not abridged.[13]

Secondly, this critic may often be forced to enter upon subjects where rigorous bibliographical investigation has not yet been made, although he may not be aware of that fact. A really egregious case of false bibliography has only recently been corrected by W. B. Todd's study of *The*

---

13 *The Library*, 4th ser., XIII (1933), 395–98; 5th ser., I (1946), 67–69; II (1947), 64; and finally "The Supposed Cancel in Southerne's *Disappointment*," *The Library*, 5th ser., V (1950), 140–49.

Monk.[14] The full story is very involved, but the point is brief. If between 1935 and 1949 any critic had blindly relied on the accepted ordering of the publishing history which pseudo-bibliography had set up, he would have been led to evolve a text which treated Lewis's revisions as the original readings, and the readings which Lewis had discarded as in fact his later revisions. *Q. E. D.* Don't trust all the bibliographers.

This is a pretty fix for a textual critic, since he is damned if he does and damned if he doesn't. And in fact, in many cases no solution for his dilemma is possible unless he is himself also a trained bibliographer who is capable of re-examining technically a fouled-up problem. Yet he must do something. One course is to trust only *some* bibliographers. The very best butter. Nonetheless we may well remember in this connection Curt Bühler's favorite quotation of the observation made by A. W. Pollard on his colleague Robert Proctor, a great pioneer in incunabula studies, "that in matters of bibliography he would not have taken the results of an archangel upon trust." As an example we may survey two specific but fortunately minor instances in which Mr. Duthie in his new edition of *King Lear* was misled by untested bibliography. A small part of his arguments concerning certain peculiarities of the quarto rests on Greg's speculation that two compositors with different habits might have been engaged with the book. Now in this case Greg was not speaking *ex cathedra* as the result of a detailed bibliographical examination, but only in terms of possibilities. Fortunately the point was of no very great consequence for Duthie's conclusions, because he accepted the speculation on trust and did not test it. We know now, however, from a recent bibliographical study, which can be confirmed by even stricter bibliographical evidence,[15] that only one compositor set the book. These peculiarities, therefore, require another explanation.

In the second instance the point of discussion is the mislining of the verse at the opening of Act III, Scene 2, the great storm scene. Greg took the view that the early part is mislined because the compositor was setting the text as prose, and it was not until he reached a certain point that he recognized he was dealing with verse and thereafter proceeded to line correctly. Duthie, naturally, accepted Greg's explanation as 'bibliographical,' and quite properly added that of course the compositor must have gone back to insert capitals at the beginning of each line in the prose section to give it the appearance of verse that it assumes in the printing. However, a single piece of bibliographical evidence demonstrates the mechanical impossibility of such a procedure. Throughout *Lear* the compositor of the quarto used a short stick for verse and a longer stick for prose; and he never sets prose

14 "The Early Editions and Issues of *The Monk*," *Studies in Bibliography*, II (1949), 3–24.
15 P. Williams, *loc. cit.*; see also *Studies in Bibliography*, II (1949), 164.

in his short or verse measure.* Since the opening lines of this scene were set in the verse measure, not the prose, the explanation for the mislineation must be sought elsewhere, for from the start the compositor intended to set verse. But other consequences resulted from this failure to see the bibliographical evidence. Because the implications of the short measure were not recognized, in these lines Duthie over-conservatively retained a corrupt lack of punctuation which succeeds in destroying, almost completely, not only a successful flower of rhetoric but also one of the mightiest images of this great storm scene.[16]

If the critic finding himself thus abused hurls a curse on this treacherous science of bibliography and betakes himself to his own estimates—to what Greg calls metacritical evidence—he may find himself in a rather vulnerable position. A simple, though typical, case occurs in *The Dumbe Knight* of 1608 which is preserved with either one of two title-pages, the major difference between them being that one gives the author's name whereas the other does not. Metacritics worked up a pretty romance about this play, conjecturing that Gervase Markham, the author, was so disgusted when he found his play printed with an inferior under-plot by another hand that he withdrew his name from the title. On the contrary, bibliography demonstrates that the title with the name is the true cancel leaf so that the name was added rather than excised.[17]

Vulnerability increases when the problem is one of any complexity. Here is a small problem yet one in which an old-spelling editor must make a decision. The inner forme of text sheet A of George Sandys's *Christs Passion*, a translation in 1640 from Grotius, was reset in the course of enlarging the edition. One typesetting of this inner forme agrees largely with the invariant outer forme in making up capital W's from two V's, whereas the other uses regular W's. Aha, says the critic, I'm not so bad at bibliography myself: obviously the setting of inner A which is consistent with outer A must be the original for me to reprint. The only trouble is, he is wrong. A rather technical interpretation of the evidence of the headlines demonstrates that this setting must have been printed a sheet or so later.[18]

---

* In a notable use of bibliographical evidence, D. F. McKenzie has now shown that the differences in measures were not caused by composing sticks of two lengths but instead by the use of special indenting quads: see his " 'Indenting the Stick' in the First Quarto of *King Lear* (1608)," *PBSA*, 67 (1973), 125–130. So far as I can see, the point being made above is still valid, however, regardless of the means by which the variant measure was secured, and the effect of it on the typesetting.

16 For a detailed consideration of this passage, see G. W. Williams, "A Note on *King Lear*, III. ii.1–3," *Studies in Bibliography*, II (1949), 175–82.

17 W. W. Greg, *A Bibliography of the English Printed Drama to the Restoration*, I (1939), no. 277.

18 *Papers Bibl. Soc. America*, XLII (1948), 146–48.

The inconsistent forme is the authoritative original which must be taken for the copy-text, and it is probably inconsistent because we may be dealing with two compositors casting off copy and setting by formes in order to get the book started in a hurry.

We do not need the example of nineteenth-century editors basing Shakespeare texts on the Pavier Quartos to indicate some of the larger dangers of inferences about the relations of texts made on purely meta-critical grounds. But lest we feel too confident about our present abilities to cope with matters more properly the province of textual criticism, such as our ability to construct a correct family tree of editions on the basis of their readings alone, we may consider the case of the ninth edition of Dry-den's *Indian Emperour* in 1694. Certain of its readings are drawn apparently at random from those which are unique in the seventh edition and are not found in the eighth. Others derive from equally random readings unique in the eighth and not found in the seventh. There are three reputable critical interpretations of this phenomenon: (1) the ninth edition comes from an independent manuscript; (2) the seventh and eighth editions were collated at the printing house and the conflation of readings thus results from editorial intervention—or one might even introduce collation of one of these editions against a prompt copy or other manuscript; (3) the ninth is set from a lost edition which may be placed in between the seventh and eighth and on which the eighth is also based. This last would be a favorite with critics accustomed to dealing with manuscripts, and it is certainly the most plausible.

At least the first two of these quite reputable explanations might cause some critical perturbation, since fresh authority could have been introduced into the text, and the various new readings in the ninth not found in either the seventh or eighth might demand critical acceptance on their merits. However, when analytical techniques are applied, the answer is not hard to find. Two compositors were employed on the ninth edition, but—perhaps because only one press was available—instead of chopping the reprint up into two sections to be set and printed simultaneously, they set the book *seriatim* but working in relay. One would compose from four to five type-pages, or only one or two, and then be relieved by the other while he distributed his type, and so on in turn. Since the eighth edition was a paginal reprint of the seventh, what actually happened was that one compositor set from a copy of the seventh, and the other from a copy of the eighth, and so they worked merrily along in relay to the confusion of scholarship, conflating the two editions to form the ninth. The answer is very easy after bibliographical analysis.[19]

19 J. S. Steck, "Dryden's *Indian Emperour:* The Early Editions and their Relation to the Text," *Studies in Bibliography*, II (1949), 147.

I do not wish to infer that in all cases bibliographical evidence is applicable. To be properly bibliographical, evidence must concern itself with only certain relations between preserved printed or inscribed pieces of paper. For example, a form of textual criticism linked with bibliography can usually decide on an over-all basis whether variations in a later edition are compositors' variants or editorial revisions; and pure bibliography can demonstrate whether or not this later edition was otherwise set from a copy of an earlier. But whether these revisions were the author's or someone else's can never be decided by bibliography under ordinary circumstances; that is for textual criticism pure and simple. The case is usually not demonstrable by any form of bibliographical evidence. Some critics may deal extensively with evidence which is probably bibliographical at bottom because it is founded on the peculiarities of printed inscriptions on paper; but the inferences they draw may have no relation to the laws of bibliographical evidence. As I shall indicate in a moment, strictly bibliographical deduction is not always possible from bibliographical facts. It is this common confusion about the difference between the strictly bibliographical and the metacritical interpretation of the evidence offered by a book as a material object which places, wrongly I believe, a number of Dover Wilson's ingenious arguments in the field of bibliography. Larger examples may be cited. The *Taming of the Shrew* problem can have no bibliographical basis, for whatever relation existed between *A Shrew* and *The Shrew* antedates their printing, and the manuscripts behind the printed copy of each have no bibliographical relation. Somewhat less clearly, perhaps, the construction of a critical text of *Hamlet* is not exclusively a bibliographical problem: it is bibliographical to the extent that there are bibliographical links between the editions, but the fact that the manuscripts behind each of the editions differ introduces elements that go beyond the reach of bibliography.

But when pure textual criticism concerns itself with problems in which bibliographical investigation is possible, it can seldom be equally definitive as in this other field, for critical interpretation of evidence is at best inferential, and the logic of the argument is frequently reversible. Until the problem was directly tackled by bibliographical methods, the question of whether *Troilus and Cressida* in the Folio was set from an annotated copy of the quarto or from an independent manuscript had yielded no convincing answer from the critical approach. Yet Mr. Williams has made the problem seem like child's play,[20] and we may find his study very illuminating for the relative validity of bibliographical and critical methods in such situations. Similarly, Mr. Hinman's authoritative study of *Othello* and its second

20 P. Williams, "Shakespeare's *Troilus and Cressida:* The Relationship of Quarto and Folio," *SB,* III (1950–51), 131–43.

quarto contains a most ingenious bibliographical solution of another long-vexed critical problem.[21]

There are other problems involving the relations between editions. Greg, I think, has remarked that given two editions only, the critical method could never satisfactorily establish their relationship or indeed, if they are similarly dated, as with certain of the Pavier quartos, their priority. I may be making this more positive or detailed than his original statement, but when we realize that Greg is not thinking in terms of inferences establishing high probability but instead of absolute proof, then we must admit that true demonstration is impossible because of the reversibility of the critical evidence. Is a variant a correction or rationalization in one edition, or a corruption in the other—frequently the case may be argued either way.

An example is Dryden's *Wild Gallant,* which has two editions in 1669, the year of its first appearance in print. One is clearly a paginal reprint of the other, but the question is—which? On the one side we have Macdonald setting up his number 72a as the first edition, whereas Griffith, backed by Osborn, argues for 72b, or Macdonald's second edition. As a part of a fresh bibliographical examination of this play I have elsewhere tried to show in detail too lengthy to be summarized here that while the basic fact on which each hinges his argument is bibliographical, the arguments from this fact are only inferential and therefore do not conform to the strictest requirements of bibliographical reasoning, that is, to a mechanical demonstration for which there is no possible alternative save in the realm of purest fantasy.[22]

It will be pertinent, however, to consider more fully in this play certain kinds of evidence which, for a very good reason, have not been published. The exposé, I hope, will offer an enlightening example, though at my own expense, of what bibliographical evidence is and what it is not. I can speak very feelingly on the subject because when I came to the problem as an editor I was completely booby-trapped, and at first I arrived at certain conclusions on grounds which I gullibly persuaded myself were bibliograpical only to have the whole argument blow up in my face (fortunately before publication) when at length the true evidence became apparent.

A textual collation of the two editions quickly established that there had been no real rewriting between them, but that in a score of places—if 72a were first—corrections, possibly even revisions, had certainly been made in 72b, a few of which could have come only from the author himself. On the other hand, if 72b were first, in various readings the text had undergone a corruption rather more serious than one might expect in a first

21 C. J. K. Hinman, "The 'Copy' for the Second Quarto of *Othello*," *Joseph Quincy Adams Memorial Studies* (1948), pp. 373–89.

22 "The First Edition of Dryden's *Wild Gallant,* 1669," *The Library,* 5th ser., V (1950), 51–54.

reprint. Mr. Osborn in his notes to Griffith's argument had confidently pronounced *B.* the first on the evidence of this textual degeneration in *A.*[23] This is a critical touchstone which experience has shown to be sound, provided the further inference is made that the author had no part in producing the reprint. However, I approached the *Gallant* fresh from a study of *The Indian Emperour,* in which without question Dryden had directly concerned himself with revising not only the second but also the third edition, the year before and after *The Wild Gallant* respectively. With this example before me, I felt hesitant to accept Osborn's conclusions without further inquiry, for the second inference could not be automatically applied. Indeed, I came to feel that there was just about as much chance that the careless errors of *A.* had been rectified in *B.* by an errata list sent to the printer as that *A.* represented a careless and unauthoritative reprint of *B.* And I still do not think that the priority of one or other edition can be positively demonstrated on the readings alone. Whether one is corruption or the other correction is not demonstrable in the very strictest sense once we know that Dryden had concerned himself at this date with correcting reprints of at least one other play.

I approached the two editions, therefore, not on the basis of the respective 'goodness' of their readings, but in search of some material evidence that one had been printed from the other. Here are some of the highlights of the preliminary case I evolved for the priority of *A.*

In the *A.* edition, the shortened name *Will* is almost invariably followed by a period to indicate that it is an abbreviation for *William,* and this period substitutes for other necessary punctuation such as commas, semi-colons, or even question marks. In *B., Will* is treated as a simple familiar name and no period is ever found except once—and significantly this once is the first time the name appears. Inadvertent following of copy by *B.* in this single initial instance seemed the best answer.[24] Given this hint, I continued looking for what one might describe as fossils in *B.* of strong characteristics present in *A.* but not in *B.* Twice in *A.* one compositor set the extreme contraction *h's* for *he's,* and, once later, *h'll* for *he'll.* In *B.* the two *h's* are normalized to the conventional *he's,* but the fossil *h'll* retained. More evidence appeared of what was apparently inadvertent following of copy. For example, the two compositors of *A.* spelled the conjunctive adverb *than* indifferently as *then* or as *than.* In *B.* the invariable spelling is *than,* even when *then* appears in *A.,* except for two cases, and one of these turned

---

23 J. M. Osborn, "Macdonald's Bibliography of Dryden," *Modern Philology,* XXXIX (1941), 83–85.

24 The reverse seemed, and still seems to me, almost incredible. With *A.* the reprint, both compositors of *A.* (for two compositors can be readily established) agreed in treating the name as an abbreviation and in substituting the abbreviating period for other punctuation found in *B.,* their copy, perhaps rigidly following the single hint of the initial abbreviation of the name in *B.*

out to be in the uncorrected state of a press-variant forme in *B.* where the *A.* spelling *then* originally appeared in *B.* but was changed by the proof-reader to *than.* There were various other instances in which the isolated appearance in *B.* of marked characteristics in *A.* seemed significant, especially since the two pairs of compositors were different in each edition. Moreover, on the textual principle that the 'harder' reading is the original, there were at least two cases which seemed to point to the priority of *A.* In the first, the form *wall* in the phrase in *A.* "she wall write" seemed to derive more plausibly from a manuscript colloquialism *wall* or *wull* than from a misprint of *B.* "she shall write." In the second, Constance is deceiving Lord Nonsuch that she is with child, and when he demands the name of the father she responds that she does not know. He exclaims, "Not know! went there so many to't?" and in *A.* she answers, "So far from that, that there were none at all, to my best knowledge, Sir." In *B.* the repetition *went* substitutes for *were,* and it seemed a plausible hypothesis that the 'harder' reading was *were,* and that memorial failure in the *B.* compositor carried over the repetition of *went* from Nonsuch's line. That the *A.* compositor in such a circumstance, where the repetition seems most natural, saw *went* in his *B.* copy and set *were* seemed more difficult to believe.

There is not time to go into this next evidence, but in the light of general experience that irregularities between catchword and following word in an original edition usually tend to be normalized in reprints, it seemed to me at first highly probable that certain irregularities in the *A.* catchwords were much better explained on the belief that it was the first edition rather than the second.

Finally, I attacked the gap of eight pages in the pagination which appears between sheets G and H in both editions. In one edition this identical error could have resulted only from slavish following of copy. Hence if I could establish a reason for the gap in one edition, but no reason in the other, I felt I should have my original. Analysis disclosed that edition *A.* was set by two compositors in sections of one or more full sheets and that their respective sections can be identified not only by the different lengths of their sticks but also by the difference in the use of skeleton-formes which is associated with each.[25] In *B.* there is no evidence for any interruption in the presswork between sheets G and H, and indeed it seems likely that one compositor set the last pages of G and continued over into the first pages of H as part of his stint. On the contrary, in *A.* the gap in pagination occurs between one of the clearly marked sections where the compositors shifted, and it seemed a reasonable inference that when the compositor of sheet H returned to duty and came to make his first impositions, he forgot the system under which he was working and miscalculated the pagination.

25 One identifiable compositor used only one skeleton to impose both formes of his sheet; the other, seemingly the quicker workman, used two.

I had, then, among various other pieces of evidence, the apparent survival in unique forms in *B*. of strongly marked compositorial habits manifested in *A*., among such fossils being the abbreviation of *Will*, the survival of the form *h'll* and of a random *then* spelling. I may also mention a few cases in *B*. of the very common practice in A. of using a semi-colon for a question mark, the setting in *A*. of a period in over a dozen cases where a necessary question mark was used in *B*., and a very odd but marked use of the full -*ed* ending in *A*. for the elided form *apostrophe d* in *B*., an expansion difficult to account for with such frequency in a reprint. Then there were such cases as this. The colloquial form *u'm* for *them* is absolutely consistent throughout both editions except for one single late use of *them* in *A*. where *u'm* appears in *B*. The probability seemed much higher that *B*. had normalized *A*. than that *A*. had wilfully departed from its copy *B*. There were also two cases where proper names were found in italic in *B*., as customary, but in roman in *A*., a reversal hard to account for. Finally, the evidence of the catchwords possibly, but almost certainly that of the mispagination, seemed to point to *A*. as the original.

I hope I have made this case reasonably convincing, even in an incomplete and digested form, because I am ashamed to confess that initially— before I began to prepare the text for an edition—it had me thoroughly convinced. Yet I hasten to point out that all these conclusions are quite wrong, that Griffith and Osborn are right. Edition *B*. indeed precedes *A*.; and this case I have presented for Macdonald's order, though based mostly on 'bibliographical' facts, has been one only of inference and probability but never of true bibliographical demonstration.

This, briefly, is the real evidence for *B*. as the first edition which my subsequent investigation revealed. Only one press-variant forme emerged from collation of eleven copies of *A*., but from ten copies of *B*. I finally turned up seven formes which had undergone stop-press correction. Of these, two are indifferent since the uncorrected state agrees with *A*. for one, and the other is the variant act-heading noticed by Professor Griffith in the apparently unique Texas copy. Of the remaining five, all—in their significant *B*. readings—have an agreement between the *corrected* state of the formes and *A*. There is no need to elaborate the bibliographical argument here.[26] Almost inevitably, *A*. must have been set from *B*.

Finally, to clinch the case, this next evidence developed. On one occasion in *A*. the verb *tells* in the phrase *she tells me* is misprinted as *tel's*. We can

---

26 The full argument is provided in the article mentioned above in fn. 22, but no bibliographer will need the details. If *B*. were set from *A*., we should have to believe that in these five corrected formes in *B*. the proof-reader made only changes in minutiae which helped to bring the reprint into conformity with its copy, and no other alterations. Moreover, an error in the uncorrected state of one forme in *B*. could under no circumstances have originated in a misreading of *A*.

demonstrate the source of this misprint in *A.* when we find that in the corresponding place in *B.* the second letter *l* in *tells* inks so very slightly in all observed copies that only its tip is visible without a magnifying glass; and since this inked tip would almost inevitably be taken as an apostrophe, the compositor of *A.* read it as one and faithfully followed what he thought was the spelling of his copy. Correspondingly, in three places in *A.* where rather essential punctuation is missing, we find that the actual commas are so lightly inked in some copies of *B.* as scarcely to be seen. The evidence of the *tel's* alone is sufficient on which to rest one's whole case for the order of the editions; but especially when so powerfully confirmed by the evidence of the press-variant formes in *B.* followed by *A.*, one could take the dispute to a court of law and secure a judgment for the priority of *B.**

From this detailed example I draw a moral which applies to much of what I have been trying to say in this paper. Textual and pseudo-bibliographical evidence can seldom if ever afford more than a high degree of probability, and this is essentially different from positive demonstration. A very plausible chain of inferences can be built up, if the person is as stupid as I seem to have been; and if only the same line of evidence is employed to attack such a case, nothing but an indecisive stalemate can result. On the contrary, strictly bibliographical evidence such as that about the *tel's* and the press variants—evidence which usually appears in texts if one digs deep enough—crosses the line of probability into something close to the field which in science would be regarded as controlled experiment capable of being reproduced. Instead of high probability we have, in fact, practical demonstration on physical evidence of a mechanical nature, demonstrable by a mechanical process, evidence like the prose and verse measures of *King Lear*, and this is what Greg means by bibliography's treatment of a book as a material object. To every point in my construction of the case for 72a as the first edition, alternatives could have been suggested, and therefore any credibility it possessed depended on the cumulative bulk of the inferences. Yet when actual bibliographical evidence enters the scene, one little *tel's* sweeps all before it.

I draw the further moral as this applies to editing. Such minute yet crucial evidence on which the case hinges would normally be discoverable only by an editor. For example, the ordinary tests which a descriptive bibliographer would apply could not determine the truth; hence, if a textual critic, faced with the problem of corruption versus correction, felt that the standard bibliography of Dryden had sufficiently set up the material for him to proceed with 72a as his copy-text (and he could very well

---

* Similar evidence from the misreading of broken types settles the vexed question of the order of the two undated octavos of Marlowe's *Certaine of Ovids Elegies*: see "The Early Editions of Marlowe's *Ovid's Elegies*," *SB*, 25 (1972), 152.

do so), he would be most seriously misled if he failed to come upon the bibliographical points which destroy Macdonald's case.

In this paper I seem to have given a considerable number of examples where bibliographers were wrong. I have not intended to cast doubts on the validity of bibliographical findings, or to speak in a way to discourage the faint-hearted from depending upon bibliographical evidence. Quite the reverse. What has been paramount in my mind is, first, that bibliography may sometimes be imperfectly practised; and unless a textual critic is himself enough of a bibliographer to make his own discoveries independently, or else to submit existing bibliographical conclusions about his material to the acid test of his own bibliographical re-evaluation—unless he can do this, in many cases he will be living in a fool's paradise, either believing that there are no bibliographical problems, or else that the bibliographers have authoritatively worked over the material for him and he can go ahead on his own line without further consideration.

Secondly, this principle seeps down from the very top, or the choice and treatment of the copy-text, to the very bottom of the last, minute detail of an old-spelling critical edition which must be exhausted bibliographically before pure criticism can properly operate.

Thus I think we may freely say that the bibliographer's text is by no means always the best that can be contrived if the editor has not got the mind of a true textual critic—only perhaps that such a text does the minimum of harm. On the other hand, as a practising bibliographer I do object mightily to critics who often nullify the brilliance of their substantive text by failing to observe bibliographical principles when they engage themselves to an old-spelling edition. I should be inclined to set up four operations which an old-spelling editor should perform, for the interpretation and application of the evidence discovered by these investigations lie at the heart of a sound edition. It is astonishing to a bibliographer to find how often various of these have been omitted by an editor who otherwise has exhibited every desire to be scrupulous in the details of his work. First, the determination of authority in all early editions and, on this evidence, the proper choice and treatment of the copy-text as we have heard it described by Greg. Second, the collation of multiple copies of each authoritative edition to disclose proof-corrections for analysis. Third, the analysis of running-titles for the interpretation of the presswork, a matter which is closely linked with the fourth, or compositor analysis, this last being positively essential, at least in Elizabethan texts, for any consideration of the variants between two or more authoritative editions in a direct line of derivation.

These few demands are not especially severe and need not require any extraordinary technical training. But I place them as the basis for any bibliographical preparation of an individual text by an editor once the larger questions have been settled. And until they become standard procedure, at least in cases of any complexity where their chief value is found, our old-spelling texts are not going to be definitive in any real sense. Critical brilliance can settle many a substantive crux, although by no means all of them; but if these excellent major substantives are placed in a semi-substantive old-spelling background which is not itself accurate, then the reason for old-spelling texts degenerates into sentimentality or ostentation. Moreover, by an accurate background of accidentals and minor substantives, much more should be implied in many cases than the mechanical ability to copy and then proofread accurately from an old edition. If we are to learn to reconstruct the accidentals and minor substantives of an author's manuscript with as much care as we labor over reconstructing his correct major substantives, a whole new and delicate biblio-critical art is involved in which criticism by itself can never be a sufficiently scientific instrument.

I shall try to summarize the main points at which I have glanced. First, both textual criticism and analytical bibliography in their purest states are, in my opinion, independent arts which have no necessary relation in their disciplines, or frequently in the subjects with which they concern themselves. Textual criticism must deal with words and their meanings, with stylistic and linguistic considerations, and with the basic questions of authority in texts, both in whole and in part. Pure analytical bibliography, on the other hand, deals with books as material objects formed by the mechanical process of printing. In many investigations it is not concerned with texts as such; but when it does approach texts it endeavors to treat them not from the literary or critical point of view, which is that of the 'goodness' of readings, but instead as pieces of paper mechanically impressed with certain symbols. The mechanical relation between these sets of symbols is thereupon its chief concern.

Second, although the two methods are essentially independent, textual criticism cannot controvert accurate bibliography in its findings when the subject is one on which bibliography can properly operate. However, the two often join in attacking certain problems of texts. These problems are by no means limited to editing, but nevertheless the construction of a critical text is most commonly the point at which the two methods cross.

Third, even though the first and the last approach to a text must be the bibliographical one, neither method can achieve definitive textual results in any detailed manner if utilized without reference to the other. On a broad scale it is bibliography which establishes the physical facts of the derivation of texts from one another and which wrings from a given book every last drop of information about the mechanical process of its printing that may be of service in determining the relation of the printed result to the manuscript or printed copy used by the printer. Still on a broad scale, it is the function of textual criticism to evaluate the authority of this manuscript and then to proceed to the correctness and the authority of the words in the text in the light of the ascertained physical facts which bibliography has furnished. Thereupon, in the process of fixing the text of a modern critical edition in every possible detail, the two methods are often so closely conjoined that an attempt to separate their respective functions would be futile.

When we come to criticize the average edited text produced today, we find that the usual source of error lies in the insufficient bibliographical training of the editor. Either he has little concept of textual problems, and —scornful of the minutiae which sometimes concern the bibliographer—is content to have any kind of a text, because what he really wants is only a peg on which to hang his annotations; or else he is overconfident in his purely critical abilities to solve any problems which may arise. In either case he has ventured on a delicate literary task without knowing his grammar, and hence his results can seldom be definitive. Sometimes even greater harm is caused by a little knowledge than by none. It is enough to make the angels weep to find Saintsbury, for example, throwing out various correct readings in Scott's text of *The Wild Gallant*, derived from edition 72b through the Folio and a later edition, to substitute absolute corruptions from 72a under the illusion he was restoring the purity of the text from the first edition. Or to find Davenport in the new edition of Joseph Hall's *Poems* declining the editorial responsibility to make a choice of readings, and basing his text on the derived reprint of 1598 for the first six books of *Virgidemiarum*, even though it was slightly revised, rather than the purer 1597 first edition.[27] It is really the hardest job in the world for a bibliographer to convince a critic who is beginning to be conscious of old-spelling problems that an author did not set his own type, seldom proof-read his book and if he did cannot be taken as approving every minute detail of its accidentals, and that a printed book is a fallible second-hand report of the author's manuscript, not a facsimile of it set in type.[28] One of the chief functions of textual bibliography is to try to pierce this veil of the printing process and to restore, however imperfectly, the authority of the manuscript, which we know only through its printed and thus secondary form.

On the other hand, a bibliographer who tackles the problems of text with insufficient critical and philological training is also in danger of false

27 Davenport's theory of editing and its contradictory results are touched on in my "Current Theories of Copy-Text, with an Illustration from Dryden," *Modern Philology*, 48 (1950), 64–68.

28 Apparently this unbibliographical view is held by Richard Flatter, *Shakespeare's Producing Hand* (1948), and the error succeeds very thoroughly in turning his textual criticism into absurdity. For an analysis of his position, see my review in *Modern Philology*, August, 1950.

judgments in decisions which are not material and are therefore not strictly the business of bibliography. The usual result is that he may retreat to the narrowest conservatism to avoid having to face up to problems which are not wholly factual. And this timidity is as unbalanced as a critic's rashness in proceeding without the counterweight of bibliography. Such critical uncertainty may lead to good reprints of a single authority for a text but by no means to a true edition of the best text of an author.

It seems to me that for an ideally definitive work an editor must combine in himself the knowledge of both methods, and the training to put both into practice, or else he must resort to an almost impossible attempt at collaboration. Collaboration can be effective between a bibliographer and a literary critic who will handle all problems of biography, attribution of authorship, literary estimates, and who will write the critical introductions and illustrative notes. In such a case each has his relatively independent responsibilities; and indeed Greg is inclined to recommend this procedure for many editions. But I find it harder to imagine save in the most exceptional circumstances an effective collaboration of bibliographer and critic on the minutiae of the text.

I disclaim bibliography as the usurper of editorial privilege, and indeed I am concerned to aid the textual critic against the increasing pressure which editor-bibliographers are exerting on him. But if this potentially most valuable kind of an editor is to produce texts which in every detail will stand up under the increasingly exact and rigorous standards which are now being applied to this form of scholarship, he must learn his bibliography with a thoroughness not previously thought necessary. Only by this wider extension of scholarship can texts be achieved which will not need to be done all over again by the next generation.

Bibliography, Pure Bibliography, and Literary Studies

THERE IS SOME VALUE for any scholarly method periodically to examine its principles, its aims and methods, with a view to determining whether it has lost sight of its original objectives and experienced a change of values. The necessity to define, or to re-define, the methods and aims of a field of research is also useful for any individual toiler in the vineyard, for it may serve to raise him, at least momentarily, from concentration on the detailed minutiae to which he must ordinarily apply himself in his research, and by bringing an added consciousness of the purport of what he is engaged in, give to his work a fresh sense of direction. On some occasions it may enforce a recognition that routine has worn ruts which are too deep. But above all, in this specialized society of scholars today when in numerous fields we are coming to know less and less of what our fellows are doing, and why, it is almost incumbent once in a while to try to gather together certain principles of the craft of which we are members for translation into general theories of scholarship. It may be that the statement in plain terms of the objectives of a method or field of research will serve to clarify its position not only to its practitioners but also to those scholars whom it may in one manner or another affect. It may be, also, that a statement in plain terms will arouse such critical objections as to force a reconsideration of the position and thus lead to a valuable reorientation of principles.

I am not concerned with explaining or defining the validity of the bibliographical approach to appropriate literary problems. That battle was fought and won many years ago, and there is no value at this late date in adding a 'me too' to the clear expositions of Sir Walter Greg and R. B. McKerrow. It seems to me, however (or rather I should say, perhaps, it has been forcibly brought to my attention), that the almost incredibly rapid strides which have taken place of recent years in some special areas of bibliographical research have brought into being not a resistance but rather a sym-

Based on a paper read on May 9, 1952, before the Bibliographical Society of the University of Virginia in joint meeting with the Bibliographical Society of America in Charlottesville, Virginia. Printed in *Papers of the Bibliographical Society of America*, 46 (1952), 186–208; reprinted by permission of the Council of the Bibliographical Society of America.

pathetic fear that bibliography is in process of developing into something quite different from its original intent. This is worth examining, even with an enforced brevity, for the objections come as well from within as from without the camp and are concerned with a most significant matter, whether bibliography is losing touch with literary study.

As an example I quote from a review of the third volume of *Studies in Bibliography* by an English bibliographer for whom I have a particular respect (*TLS*, March 23, 1951). I am afraid the subject relates to some statements of mine on the relation of bibliography to editorial problems in a paper read before the English Institute and printed in the *Studies*. On what was the major argument of my paper, that the present-day editor of an early text must learn his bibliography with a thoroughness not previously thought necessary, the reviewer writes, "Thus far, though one may unreasonably yearn to put the clock back, [the] thesis is not controversial." However, I then let slip the leash a bit, and tried to explain how, in my opinion, if one dealt with the two disciplines as absolutes, the practitioners of analytical bibliography should not be restrained by the practical requirements of textual criticism from pushing their researches to the farthest possible boundary. On this matter the reviewer continues with a warning which merits careful attention:

The immediate and chief aim of bibliographical scholars, [B.] says, is not "to serve as the sons of Martha to textual criticism," and [B.] makes the same point more forcibly elsewhere—"Textual criticism and analytical bibliography in their purest states are, in my opinion, independent arts which have no relation in this disciplines, or frequently in the subjects with which they concern themselves." If it were pushed too far, this thesis would seem fraught with certain dangers. [A] flair for the solution of technical bibliographical problems could lead able technicians, who lacked . . . literary judgment, to regard analytical bibliography as an end in itself and the solution of such problems as worthwhile for their own sake. Such work, it could indeed be argued, was designed to evolve techniques which might possibly have some ultimate practical application. Bibliography may, of course, legitimately concern itself with other things than textual criticism: for example, it may be applied to the definitive description of books and to numerous aspects of *Kulturgeschichte*, such as the evolution of printing, binding and bookselling. In the past, however, it has always been the servant of the humanities. We seem now to be approaching a conception of pure bibliography, written by bibliographers for bibliographers. This is new and rather disquieting, not only to those who lack the ability or the leisure to master strange and highly complicated techniques.

The second quotation, I am afraid, also concerns some of my opinions about bibliographical method, and comes from another distinguished English scholar:

The danger of such elaboration [in bibliographical description] is that it may so widen the division between the bibliographer and the student of literature that it will be impossible even for the textual critic to use without difficulty some of the technical devices now employed in the analysis of the physical makeup of a book; and the expert bibliographer will be tempted more and more to devote himself to the detection of all the possible aberrations of the printer whether they have any effect on the text of the book or not.[1]

When we survey these very temperately stated objections, we see that they both rest on one main point: a fear that bibliography may push itself to such arcane reaches that it will become an end in itself. If this occurs, it is argued, the usefulness of bibliography to literary or humane investigation will be seriously lessened by the gap that will develop to separate the two fields, hitherto allied. The result will be: (1) bibliography in becoming an end in itself, or a pure science, will tend to concern itself more and more with investigations which have no ultimate application to research in the humanities, thus breaking an established tie; (2) as bibliography tends to become more and more a pure science, the complex techniques that are developed will grow less and less comprehensible to the literary scholar and will eventually reach beyond his ability to utilize; (3) the special language and formulas of highly developed bibliography will preclude the possibility of the use of its results by literary students, who cannot be expected to learn a complex system of technical devices in order to read and understand bibliographical writing.

These objections will strike a responsive chord in many hearts, and hence they must be considered seriously. They are doubtless representative of too large a body of opinion to be brushed aside lightly; and it may be that they are so valid as to create the necessity for bibliography to re-examine its present course and possibly even to modify its future.

However, I hold to the belief that though this critical word of caution is a useful check on possible bibliographical excesses, it is not so basically irreconcilable with the ideals of advanced bibliography as may appear at first sight. I take it, also, that some of the distress exhibited here—to discount the frankly admitted nostalgia for the good old days before the tabby cat of bibliography grew into a tiger—may rest upon some slight misapprehension of the internal divisions within bibliographical research. As a consequence, it is possible that certain technical fields of bibliography are being confused with those whose main purpose is to deal directly and critically with literature or to serve as an immediate foundation for such study. In other words, whether we are arguing for or against the present

1 H. J. Davis, "Bibliographica," in *The Year's Work in English Studies: 1949*, ed. F. S. Boas, XXX (Oxford University Press for the English Association, 1951), 238.

course of bibliographical research, it is necessary to understand what we mean by *bibliography*, for a view applicable to one of its branches may have small pertinence applied to another. In fact, *bibliography* is now too general a term to attempt to discuss as such without confusion. We can find common ground only by specifying what branch of bibliography is in question.

With some deliberate simplification, therefore, let me suggest that the major, but by no means mutually exclusive, compartments within the far too general term *bibliography* are these:

(1) The construction of lists of books and writings on various subjects. This common and extremely useful form of bibliographical endeavor I should like to distinguish as *enumerative* or *compilative bibliography*, and thereafter to drop it from consideration since it has no bearing on our present enquiry and has not been brought into question.

(2) Enquiries into the evolution of printing (including typefounding and paper-making), binding, book ownership, and bookselling. I distinguish this as *historical bibliography* and suggest that we limit this field as much as possible according to its historical intent. That is, I take it we should include here all biographical and historical studies of printers, papermakers, binders, typefounders, engravers, publishers, booksellers, and anyone else in any way concerned with the materials and the production of the book and its subsequent dissemination. Under the history of such I should also include studies of costs and prices, methods of sale and distribution; studies of the meaning of imprints, colophons, copyright entries, and of advertisements; all aesthetic studies of printing and its materials as an art; all studies of sizes of editions from the collateral evidence of publishers' records or other external material; all investigation into the circumstances of literary composition which have any relation to the physical form of the literary work, the transmission of literary documents, and the relation of authors to the commercial process of publication. It is difficult to limit this grouping narrowly, but let us say very much in general that it concerns itself chiefly with the discovery and interpretation of external evidence.

In between this section and the next there is an intermediate group about which opinions as to the placement may well differ. I refer to such studies as Hodnett's of woodcuts, McKerrow's and Ferguson's of printer's devices, or Miller's of ornaments,[2] the purpose being to identify ownership, establish dating, and trace deterioration, recutting, and copying. Studies of watermarks, their forms, places, and dates, such as by Briquet, Churchill, Heawood, and Stevenson are analogous, as are the type studies

2 C. W. Miller, "Thomas Newcomb: A Restoration Printer's Ornament Stock," in *Studies in Bibliography*, III (1950), 155–170.

of Isaac. In one sense these are historical studies; in another, the investigation may verge on the analytical. But some idea of what I assume to be an essential difference, at least in their pure states, may be exhibited if one compares the largely historical and compilative study of watermarks in A. H. Stevenson's "Watermarks are Twins"[3] with his earlier and strictly analytical investigation of the bibliographical evidence afforded by watermarks for determining the order of sheets through the press, the use of one or of two presses, and the size of an edition-sheet.[4] Another example would be the establishing of the date of a book by the historical method of aligning it with publishers' advertisements versus the more analytical method of placing its ornaments on evidence of wear or fracture within a dated series of books in which they also appear.

(3) This distinction may serve to introduce the third major grouping, covered under the term *analytical bibliography*. In general I define this as technical investigation of the printing of specific books, or of general printing practise, based exclusively on the physical evidence of the books themselves, not ignoring, however, what helpful correlation may be available with collateral evidence.[5] It is possible to give only a selection of the various lines of investigation that have developed, such as the detection and explanation of cancels and of reprinted sheets of all kinds; the detection and explanation of any departure from normal printing practise within a book; determination of the order of the formes through the press and of the number of presses engaged on a book at any one time, with an identification of the formes and sheets printed by each; the analysis of press-figures, running-titles, and watermarks as bearing on the above, as well as the evidence for different compositorial activity; identification of the date of

---

3 *Studies in Bibliography*, IV (1951), 58–91.

4 "New Uses of Watermarks as Bibliographical Evidence," *Studies in Bibliography*, I (1948), 151–182.

5 It is a feature of bibliography that in practise the methods of its different disciplines frequently overlap. Thus *critical*, or *textual bibliography* will often call on the help of *analytical*, as will *historical*; or *analytical* will merge with *historical*, and *descriptive* with both. As an example, my recent identification of Robert Roberts as the printer of the first section of the Shakespeare Fourth Folio rested exclusively on the identification of his ornamental initial letters. The investigation was historical insofar as this was necessarily related to the records of his printing with and without his sometime partner Anne Maxwell and his relations with a certain group of publishers. But it was analytical in respect to the attempt to claim these initials exclusively for Roberts, despite the fact that they had appeared in a book with a Thomas Newcomb imprint, by showing that the book in question was printed in two sections. Analysis based on physical evidences of the printing process was also necessary to show that the Folio was also not printed as a continuous operation in the same shop, and thus to limit that part printed by Roberts, with the further object of showing that he also printed the preliminaries as well as the first section of text. See *Shakespeare Quarterly*, II (1951), 241–246.

undated or misdated books by such internal physical evidence unrelated to the readings of the text, including the evidence of its materials (as in the Carter and Pollard study of the Wise forgeries); identification of the printers when more than one participated in a book; and so on.

It is worth emphasis that this analytical method operates only on the physical evidence of the book, and generalizes from that. It is far from true, however, that a book with blank leaves would serve as well, except for the most elementary of analytical operations. What is important is that the impressed symbols which are letters and words are treated in a physical and not in a literary way. (I think it was Sir Walter Greg who once remarked that it should make little difference to analytical studies whether a book were printed in Sanskrit or in English.) Without regard for the meaning conveyed by these symbols, the method of typesetting the text may provide evidence for analytical procedures, in revealing the presence of one or more compositors from typographical characteristics, without any consideration whatever for the significance of the words or for their correctness.*

An illustration may be helpful. In *The Manuscript of Shakespeare's* HAMLET (I, 98) Dover Wilson assigns only one compositor to the Q2 *Hamlet* "because the imperfections of this text are so uniformly distributed throughout that it is hardly conceivable that they belong to two different workmen." This is not a bibliographical statement, for the imperfections chiefly cited are omissions of words, and misreadings, which have been assigned as imperfections on purely literary evidence, such as their effect on meaning in Q2 or their inferiority to the corresponding reading in the Folio. Strict analytical bibliography, on the contrary, would endeavor to ascertain whether the pattern of the running-titles indicated the possibility that more than one press printed the book. The answer to this question could have a direct bearing on the matter of its composition. If only one skeleton-forme were employed throughout, we should never expect two

---

* Insofar as it concerns studies like the folding of the sheets to form quires, the presence of inserted leaves or of substitute cancellans, the analysis of running-titles, the evidence of variant measures, and even the tracing of identifiable imperfect types in handset books through setting, distribution, to resetting, with what this may tell us about seriatim versus setting by formes, Greg's statement is accurate enough once its shock effect has worn off. But other forms of physical evidence that he did not envisage would require a knowledge of the language. Chief among these is compositor identification through the analysis of variant spellings, of course. Greg would perhaps have denied the inclusion under analytical bibliography of what may now be distinguished as textual bibliography which may attempt on occasion far-reaching conclusions about the nature of the printer's copy and its relation to the author, depending upon the analysis of physical features of the text, including spellings, that also requires an understanding of its purport.

compositors setting in alternation to speed the work, but the pattern would not necessarily preclude the possibility that another workman took over composition at any point. On the other hand, if we found that the book were divided into two sections marked by differences in the settings of the running-titles, and thus by new skeleton-formes, we should expect two workmen each setting a part simultaneously; and we might be able to confirm the evidence of the running-titles by detecting a difference in the length of the printers' measure used in each section. Or we might find such an alternating pattern of four skeleton-formes as to be inexplicable if only one compositor and press were employed. If, thereupon, we verged on another possible form of bibliography and showed by spelling tests the real assignment of one or more compositors, we should have a bibliographical case utilizing evidence of a completely different nature from that which Wilson customarily employs.[6]

(4) This pure form of analytical bibliography lies in back of and leads directly into two other divisions: *descriptive bibliography* and what I should like to distinguish as *critical* or *textual* bibliography.[7] The function of *descriptive bibliography* is to examine a book by all the methods of analytical bibliography in order to arrive at a total comprehension of the maximum physical facts as a preliminary to writing these up in set terms as a definitive physical description of the book, its external appearance, and the internal evidence bearing on the details of this external appearance. There is some need to emphasize that descriptive bibliography which is not based on analytical is practically useless, for it is as important to explain the reason for the peculiarities as it is to give the external facts about them; and, truly, the external facts often cannot be properly described until analytical bibliography has provided the reasons for their existence.[8]

6 The bibliographical gap in Wilson's evidence is that he makes an initial non-bibliographical assumption that the 'imperfections' are compositorial and then uses this assumption, with circular logic, to argue that only one compositor set the text. He does not demonstrate that, in fact, the 'imperfections' were not in the copy, for if they were, they could have been uniformly distributed throughout the text even though more than one workman was engaged in the typesetting. What the truth is in the Q2 *Hamlet* I do not know, for the matter has not been investigated. My only concern is to indicate certain differences in the method of attack between the literary and the bibliographical approach to a problem. [The printing of *Hamlet* Q2 with two compositors and two presses was later studied in "The Printing of *Hamlet* Q2," *SB*, 7 (1955), 41–50; 8 (1956), 267–269.]

7 *Critical* is often applied, especially in England, to what I have called *analytical* bibliography.

8 An elementary example would be the fact that a descriptive bibliographer must discover whether an odd number of leaves in a gathering is the result of excision or of addition before he can construct an accurate collational formula for the book.

(5) I shall try to define *critical* or *textual bibliography* as the application of the evidence of analytical bibliography, or at least of its pertinent methods, to textual problems where meaning of some sort is involved and where it does make a difference whether a book is printed in English or in Sanskirt. The analytical basis for critical bibliography is usually the bibliographer's experience with the details and characteristics of the printing process interpreted in terms of its specific application to text. This process can take many forms, but a few typical illustrations may serve to indicate what I mean. When Dr. Williams demonstrated on the physical evidence for the method of printing the book, chiefly its pattern of running-titles, that the cancellans fold in the 1609 *Troilus and Cressida* containing a new title-page and an added foreword was not a later substitution as commonly thought but instead that it was printed at the same time as the rest of the book, and as an integral part of the final sheet,[9] he was engaging in pure analytical bibliography. When, on another occasion, he demonstrated that the Folio used as copy an annotated 1609 quarto and not an independent manuscript,[10] he was dealing with critical bibliography since his evidence was the form of the text itself insofar as it related to common typographical features in the two editions which could be explained rationally only by the fact that one was printed from the other. A similar investigation was that of Sir Walter Greg, who demonstrated that the Folio printer's copy for *King Lear* was the Pied Bull quarto on the evidence that it followed certain uncorrected states of the quarto's press-variant formes.[11] As a further example one can cite the evidence based on the physical facts of typesetting used by Dr. Hinman (with no regard for the goodness or badness of the readings) to demonstrate that Q2 *Othello* had merely reprinted the Folio for the added lines not found in Q1 and had not utilized an independent manuscript.[12]

I have suggested some major differences elsewhere between textual criticism and analytical bibliography,[13] and therefore need not belabor the point again except by summarizing my belief that textual criticism concerns itself with words and their meanings, with stylistic and linguistic considerations, and with basic questions of authority in text both in whole

9 "The Second Issue of *Troilus and Cressida*, 1609," *Studies in Bibliography*, II (1949), 25–33.

10 "Shakespeare's *Troilus and Cressida*: The Relationship of Quarto and Folio," *Studies in Bibliography*, III (1950), 131–143.

11 *The Variants in the First Quarto of* KING LEAR (London, The Bibliographical Society, 1940), pp. 18–39, expanding and confirming the earlier discovery by P. A. Daniel.

12 "The 'Copy' for the Second Quarto of *Othello*," *Joseph Quincy Adams Memorial Studies* (Washington, D.C., Folger Shakespeare Library, 1948), pp. 373–389.

13 "Some Relations of Bibliography to Editorial Problems," *Studies in Bibliography*, III (1950), 37 ff.

and in part. Pure analytical bibliography, on the other hand, deals with books and their texts as material objects and forms manufactured by the mechanical process of printing, and therefore has no proper concern with meaning in texts. The two may join, and even become inextricably mingled, in certain reaches of textual bibliography. Again, an illustration or two may be useful. If a scholar collates a series of editions and on the basis of their readings alone decides their genetic relationship and order, I take it that he is engaging in simple textual criticism. That is, edition B is derived from edition A and not from an independent manuscript. Edition C follows various unique readings in B and therefore derives from B, not A. Edition D follows the unique readings of B, but not the unique readings of A or of C, and therefore derives from B, and so on. Ordinarily a study of this sort can be made with no bibliographical training whatsoever.[14] But when, as with Shakespeare's *King Lear* or Dryden's *Wild Gallant*, the genetic relationship is in fact indeterminate from the readings in this manner and the evidence rests on the fact that one physical state of a given variant edition was followed in certain readings rather than the readings of another physical state (again with no regard for meaning), we have a different order of evidence which is within the province of critical bibliography.

The above is a most incomplete and sketchy account; but I must pass on to the main point of this paper. If the five major divisions, as I understand them, are generally valid within the field of bibliography—even though admittedly they are not watertight—then I hope that recognition of the functions of these divisions will somewhat help to clarify the relation of bibliography as a whole to literary studies. Each one of these divisions may have some ultimate application to literary problems, but the relationship is much more intimate for some than for others. It would seem, then, to be an unduly narrow view which would lump all these different disciplines together and to demand that each be as immediately applicable as the others. I fancy Mr. Hodnett when he was engaged with the lengthy process

---

14 In this statement there is, of course, a weak link, in that readings alone could never positively demonstrate that edition B derived from A and not from a manuscript. The exact demonstration must always be made on such bibliographical evidence as the fact that one is a page-for-page reprint of the other, or demonstrates precise typographical links with the other. In some complex cases readings alone, without a bibliographical explanation, may prove an uncertain guide. For instance, a late edition of Dryden's *Indian Emperour* is not clearly derived from either of its two immediate predecessors but takes over unique readings from each. The ordinary solution of pure textual criticism would be to posit a lost intermediate edition. Bibliography, however, demonstrates that two compositors alternated in setting the text, one using one edition and the other the other. See J. S. Steck, "Dryden's *Indian Emperour*: The Early Editions and their Relation to the Text," *Studies in Bibliography*, II (1949), 147.

of collecting the materials for his historical account of English woodcuts
would have felt it somewhat beside the point to justify his labors by their
usefulness in any immediate application to study of the humanities. Dr.
McKerrow and Mr. Ferguson were intent on adding a contribution to the
clarification of publishing history, and nothing else one would think, when
they collected and analyzed ornamental devices. They could not have been
unaware, of course, that on some rare occasions by a tortuous chain of
circumstances their results could assist in some general problem of text.
But I am inclined to suspect that this vague eventuality was not a very
important inspiration to their investigations. May we not, perhaps, admit
quite reasonably that pure historical bibliography should pursue its research into publishing and printing history without our worrying whether
it is becoming an end in itself which mistakes the solutions of its peculiar
problems as worthwhile for their own sake?

Let us, then, look at analytical bibliography. Now if my attempt to
delimit this field is at all legitimate, it may follow that some of the fears
that analysis is becoming too pure to have a general usefulness stem from
a failure to distinguish analytical from textual, or critical, bibliography. If
I am at all right, I should like to view analytical bibliography as by definition a pure method, and critical bibliography as its application to immediate
and specific problems. If this view be accepted, it must follow that analytical bibliography should be allowed to pursue its own investigations
in its own way without being forced to justify itself, at least as a principle,
by the necessity for practical application in the service of humane studies.
So long as its results filter down through critical bibliography to assist in
literary study, as they most certainly do, we should not worry whether it is
becoming an end in itself, for in the course of time every fresh conquest of
knowledge finds its application. When one is dealing with pure research
and trying to find the principle behind assorted and apparently disparate
pieces of evidence, it seems to me quite impossible to distinguish between
technical problems the solution of which is worth while only in itself as a
kind of virtuoso performance and those in which the value consists of a
clearly perceived ultimate literary application. In fact, from what experience I have had in this matter, I should deny that any such distinction
exists. To a research student a problem is a problem; and a human being
fortunately being an animal afflicted with acute curiosity, a true research
student cannot rest until he has solved a problem which confronts him. I
have a great respect for pure curiosity: if we are to believe our folklore,
such curiosity led to the discovery of the law of gravity. Astronomy is no
less a respectable science and its concern no less pertinent with whether
we are involved in an expanding universe because, as Raphael pointed out
to Adam, the application of such information to human affairs is rather
obscure.

But this is mere dialectic. Let us instead try to face certain facts without self-deception. It has always been a cornerstone of belief that bibliography is the servant of the humanities. I believe this is true and demonstrable. Yet we are only confusing ourselves if we fail to see the obvious fact that certain branches of bibliography are more related to pure research than other branches which have a nearer degree of immediate and practical usefulness. If we are willing to face the truth that no knowledge or love of literature is of material assistance (except as a spur) to the solution of the technical problems which analytical bibliography in its pure state has always set itself, we shall come to the accurate conclusion that it is not itself essentially a literary study no matter how applicable its findings prove to be in the solution of literary problems. The full implications of Sir Walter Greg's remark that [analytical] bibliography is exclusively concerned with the book as a material object have never been properly recognized. If one thinks of a book as a material object, for the purposes of analytical bibliography there is not the slightest difference between a unique first-edition quarto of Shakespeare and the most worthless ephemeral pamphlet of the time.[15] In fact, for the analytical evidence it yields, the pamphlet may be much more valuable than the Shakespeare.

I am talking now in terms of absolutes, for anything less can lead only to confusion. It has been in general true in the past that those who engaged themselves to analytical investigations had earlier had a primary concern with literature, or at least busied themselves as much as possible in turning their analytical results into practical application to literary studies. So far as I can see this is still the case; moreover, I know of no analytical bibliographers who are not either professors of English literature or at least professed students and admirers of literature. But it must be emphasized that this has come about only through certain historical circumstances and need not of necessity be the rule for the future. The discipline is a technical study of a material object divorced from its content, and as such might easily fascinate anyone with a logical turn of mind no matter what his opinions about the humanities. There is nothing we can do about it, and nothing we need do, for it is not a dangerous situation so long as we have critical bibliography to translate the results of pure research into practical application to literature. No scientist would dream of fearing that pure research would become an end in itself, for by its nature it cannot do otherwise; hence I fail to see why literary men should be concerned about the natural course of analytical bibliography, which by its nature is truly written for other bibliographers and not for literary students. Moreover, I think it true that just as the advances of applied science have usually been predicated on the discoveries of pure science, so

15 One must handle the first rather more carefully, of course.

the astonishing new methods by which critical bibliography can attack problems of text have descended directly from the complex and non-literary work of the analytical bibliographers.

Why, then, has the future of analytics become disquieting even to clear-sighted scholars? There is, I think, at least a partial answer. Analytical bibliography finds its practical application in, first, descriptive bibliography and, second, critical bibliography, which is now a necessary supplement to textual criticism. By using the resources of historical and of analytical bibliography, descriptive bibliography attempts to set in order the basic materials for literary scholarship not only by the discovery of their maximum extent but also by establishing their proper relationship, their internal variants, and last by defining all these matters within the formula of a description. The major justification for this applied scholarship is undoubtedly its usefulness, indeed its necessity, for accurate results in humane studies. So far as this is true, it is certainly an obligation on the part of the bibliographer to state the immediately essential results of his findings in terms that can be understood by a literary student willing to make a reasonable attempt to comprehend them. On the other hand, if a literary student is unwilling to read his McKerrow to achieve an elementary knowledge of the basic printing processes which are being described as part of the procedure of adequately defining a volume under scrutiny, then he has no business coming to such a bibliography for this definition and should content himself with the more general information purveyed in it.

I rather imagine that the greatest uneasiness concentrates on the apparent complexities of the collational-formula system for describing the makeup of a book first proposed by Sir Walter Greg[16] and successfully used by him in his great *Bibliography of the English Drama to the Restoration.* The more immediate source of discomfort, however, may well be my own efforts, as a disciple, to fill-in and slightly elaborate certain features of this system to take account of various bibliographical peculiarities which might be met with by a descriptive bibliographer. The only question, then, is whether this system is too complex to be understood with reasonable effort by those literary students who are competent to make use of the information which it endeavors to crystallize. On this one can only say that time alone will tell. I myself feel that the apparent horrors vanish on slight acquaintance with the few logical principles and symbols underlying the system, and I will guarantee to teach any student in under two hours, no matter how slight his bibliographical knowledge, to read the most tolerably complex collational formula he is ever likely to encounter in the normal course of events. It takes rather longer, however, to teach one to write these

16 "A Formulary of Collation," in *The Library*, 4th ser., XIV (1934), 365–382.

formulas, but that is not the point of criticism. Thus I am still inclined to stand by a statement earlier made, "In actual truth the characters employed in standard description are very few and readily learned; the various shortcuts are so clear in principle and construction that no extraordinary intelligence is needed to decipher them correctly after only the briefest acquaintance, provided the reader has a minimum knowledge of the makeup of books."[17]

The technical devices which may cause difficulty for the literary student need not be confined to the collational formula, however, although it is a little difficult to think of others, outside of the running-title and type-identification analysis, perhaps. On this ground I should be willing to lock horns with critics, whatever the devices are, for though it may be the major purpose of a descriptive bibliography to serve the students of literature, it is surely confining a bibliography's usefulness excessively to insist that it have no other purpose. I have elsewhere given various arguments why it is necessary and even essential for bibliographies to be written in part with bibliographers in mind,[18] and so shall not press the point save to remark that in such portions of a description as come in this category, the literary student is missing nothing of immediate importance to him if he quite sensibly skips it. He has been served, and the ensuing analysis is aimed at a different audience.

I do not really like to debate these matters, but the concluding portion of Mr. Davis's remarks call for comment since they do him less than justice; he writes that if the tendency towards elaboration in descriptions persists, "the expert bibliographer will be tempted more and more to devote himself to the detection of all the possible aberrations of the printer whether they have any effect on the text of the book or not."

Here opinions may well differ, but I should like to clarify the point. So far as I understand the principles of bibliographical description as narrowly applied to a single book, it has three main purposes: (1) It attempts to describe the physical characteristics of an edition of a book within a conventional framework of detail and precision in order to distinguish that particular edition from every other edition; (2) Having established the distinguishing characteristics of the edition as a whole, it then attempts to describe every variant form of this edition, as issue and state, in order to prevent internal confusion of minor characteristics; (3) Whenever possible it thereupon attempts to analyze the printing process which produced the internal variants described within the edition. It is worth pointing out that some of the bibliographically very important variants within an edition such as cancellation or press-alteration of a

17 *Principles of Bibliographical Description* (Princeton, N. J., Princeton University Press, 1949), p. 28.
18 *Ibid.*, pp. 9–15.

title-page have little or no effect on the text as such, though they are emphasized even by the most elementary bibliographer.

When we come to the aberrations of the printer, in all possible forms, I have no clear idea of what Mr. Davis has in mind. Hence I must resort to two generalities. First, as with the description of variant title-pages, at least some part of bibliographical description is not concerned with the state of the text but instead with the publishing history of the volume. Second, it is also necessarily concerned with the printing history, for without a prior analysis of this an accurate description cannot be written. The details of the printing history may or may not ultimately be brought to bear on textual considerations by an expert (the direct application is no part of the descriptive bibliographer's duties), but if there is the slightest chance that any detail of this history, as known only to the bibliographer of the book, could have such an application, the bibliographer is surely derelict to his duty if he suppresses the information.

Now we come to the nub of the matter. If, as Mr. Davis appears to suggest, the bibliographer takes it upon himself to decide which printing peculiarities can be utilized for textual studies and which not, and on that basis provides some information and suppresses other, he will be constructing a bibliography sure to be superseded in the future, for it is given to no man to know at any stated time what evidence is pertinent and what not. One reason why we have so many bad descriptive bibliographies is that the compilers omitted much information because they did not see its usefulness, and the techniques for bringing this evidence to bear on text had not yet been invented. With sixteenth- and seventeenth-century books there is perhaps no single piece of bibliographical evidence of more concern to textual critics than the evidence for composition and for proof-correction afforded by the running-titles. In the eighteenth century there is no single piece of evidence more valuable for differentiating mixed and closely similar editions and, within them, their variant impressions, than press-figures.[19] Yet McKerrow in his *Introduction* ignored the first and remarked of press-figures that they seemed to have no bibliographical significance. Since even so great a bibliographer in these matters could not be ahead of his time, we who follow cannot have the presumption to expect that we are ahead of ours and that we shall not provoke the impatience, or the pity, of future generations for our incredible failure to see the significance of evidence in front of our noses. Mr. Davis would encourage us to take too complacent a view of our omniscience, but I fear that in this specific matter he is mistaken. In fact, I can give an example. Until A. H. Stevenson

19 The revolutionary series of studies in this matter by William B. Todd begun in his "Observations on the Incidence and Interpretation of Press Figures," *Studies in Bibliography*, III (1950), 171–205, have effectively demonstrated the primary value of this evidence.

with startling ingenuity showed the direct application of watermarks in paper to the bibliographical analysis of the printing of a book,[20] I shared with other bibliographers some knowledge of the more elementary uses to which the evidence of watermarks might be put but thought it of insufficient account to warrant the recording of these watermarks in descriptive bibliography. Now, in spite of the enormous difficulties I see in the process of such recording, I am convinced that it will be a future necessity for any really detailed bibliography, for we are only on the threshold of knowing how this new method may be used in the future. Similarly, the researches into the evidence of press-figures by W. B. Todd should show us the way to enjoy the blessings rather than the curses of future generations by being copious in our descriptions of "all possible aberrations of the printer" no matter how little we may understand their bibliographical (which is only to say their future textual) significance in our limited moment.

If, then, we may dismiss a fear of technical descriptive bibliography, which is in course of absorbing some of the lessons from its analytical progenitor long overdue, may we not bring equal confidence to charting the future of critical bibliography, the second derivative from analytical. Here I must restate my prime assumption that it is the chief purpose of critical bibliography to translate the pure end-in-itself findings of analytical bibliography into direct application to literary study. This will, of course, chiefly be in connection with problems of text both of a general and of a specific nature. It is clear that this translation can be achieved only by those among the analytics who are interested in both divisions of bibliography or else by the pure textual bibliographers constantly keeping pace with analytical methods not as an independent field of research for them but as a necessary understanding on which to develop their own method. In practise there need be little reason to fear a lack of communication. Since analytical bibliographers do not work by ratiocination in a void but instead with material books, they often cannot help solving textual problems in the simple course of analyzing the printing history of a book.[21] In fact it is

---

20 *Studies in Bibliography*, I, (1948), 151–182.

21 If I may be forgiven an example from my own experience, I came upon the fact in the course of investigations for a descriptive bibliography that John Banks's *Cyrus the Great*, 1696, had three sheets which existed in two quite different typesettings. Since I hold that a descriptive bibliographer must not only record but also classify, order, and explain, it was incumbent on me to demonstrate which setting was the initial one. Before I had finished doing this to the best of my ability, I was forced to run the gamut of a particularly complex and technical explanation of the printing which made use of various bibliographical arguments which could only be incomprehensible to a literary student. The end result, however, was—I hope—a determination of which setting was made from manuscript and which was a mere reprint, without which information an editor could not properly tackle the text. Any

almost impossible to stay away from text in pursuing evidence to its ultimate conclusions. Hence even the most arrant technicians of the future will be unable to avoid applying their findings to text on many occasions, since that often represents the most complex technical problem for ingenuity to solve. And critical bibliographers, since it is their only excuse for existence, will need to be peculiarly apt in picking up hints in this direction. It does not really seem that we have much to fear if analytics sometimes appears to be going off on its own. Its primary concern is not with text, but somehow it can never for long avoid the problem.

Where the danger lies, in my opinion, is in quite another direction. In my paper on bibliography and editorial problems I attempted to comment on this, and so shall be brief here. I have a great respect for the possibilities, still largely unexplored,[22] of applying critical bibliography to knotty textual problems, but some practical experiences as an editor have convinced me that, though it is the only basic method, it is not an invariably complete one. In other words, critical bibliography does not comprise in itself the whole of textual criticism by a long shot, and any claims that it is more than a basic approach to textual criticism should be vigorously combatted. On the other hand, pure textual criticism as such, without a basis in critical bibliography, is no longer a discipline to inspire utter confidence.

It follows that to produce the best texts critical bibliographers must learn as well as they can the highly developed methods of textual criticism to implement their own work when they turn editors. Correspondingly, textual critics must learn their essential bibliography in a manner not previously thought necessary if their results are to stand up under any searching scrutiny. There are times when after the most scrupulous bibliographical examination, only refined textual criticism can lend authority to a decision.[23] But decisions of textual criticism made without reference to bibliography may too often be exposed as futile guesswork. One may not

---

pure analytical technician—which I am not—would have been forced to follow the same course and eventually end with the text. See, for the horrid example, *Studies in Bibliography*, IV (1951), 174–182. As a similar instance, the bibliographical investigation of the evidence of running-titles, with which I have been in part connected, began purely for the technical problem they posed. Shortly, the research led in direct path to the application of the printing process they revealed to the textual question of proof-reading.

22 Some suggestions as to lines of exploration were made in my paper "A Definitive Text of Shakespeare: Problems and Methods" recently read before the Shakespeare Conference at the University of Miami and printed in *Studies in Shakespeare* (University of Miami Press, 1952), pp. 11–29.

23 In this class I should place the *sallied-solid flesh* crux in *Hamlet*, since the strict bibliographical argument for *sallied* may be very slightly suspect. [In 1956 it seemed stronger and this footnote out of date: see "Hamlet's 'Sullied' or 'Solid' Flesh: A Bibliographical Case-History," *Shakespeare Survey*, 9 (1956), 44–48.]

unreasonably yearn to turn the clock back to simpler days, before the complexities attending the definitive treatment of a text were recognized, but to do so is to invite the dodo.

I take this view the more seriously because, though I welcome scientific method where it is applicable, I am distressed by the overweening claims which are made for it when it comes into conflict with the higher values of the humanities. The methods of critical bibliography at least parallel the scientific method and to that extent partake both of its strength and of its weakness, with the latter powerfully reënforced on occasion by the inescapable fact that critical bibliography must deal with a text which was both written and printed by a human being, and therefore subject at every step in its path to the unknowable and aberrant human equation, no matter how material the form of the text, in a manner denied to neutrons and protons. This is where the higher values of textual criticism must not be lost if we are to avoid mechanical texts of which the best that can be said is that they do least harm. But if we are to continue to receive saving grace from the higher values of textual criticism, it must be on different terms than before, and in that respect the pressure is on textual criticism to understand and to utilize where applicable the newer scientifically related method.

Insofar as critical bibliography, stemming from analytical, is a scientific method,* it can secure good results within its natural limitations. Nevertheless, as scientific method, if too sweepingly applied it cannot fail to ignore certain higher values which only pure textual criticism can preserve, and these are values we should not willingly forfeit. The scientific method should have its valued place in humane studies, but as a servant, not the master. The current exaltation of the scientist in other fields should not lead to his domination of the humanities. Yet the processes of logical and material demonstration which the more scientific bibliographical methods bring to literary studies cannot be idly surveyed from an ivory tower or they will eat away its foundations and topple it. A new form of scholarship is reaching its majority. Literary students must now make the necessary efforts to understand it and thus to absorb it into the larger stream of the humanities.

* For an exhaustive analysis of the claims made for bibliography as a science and an indication that I was well advised to treat the subject gingerly here, see G. T. Tanselle, "Bibliography and Science," *Studies in Bibliography*, 27 (1974), 55–89.

The Bibliographical Way

A WELL-AGED SLICE OF AMERICANA goes something like this: "There's the right way of doing a job; there's the wrong way; and By God, gentlemen, there's the Navy way." I would suggest that there is also the bibliographical way. This *way* is a method, a state of mind if you will; it is also one road to truth. I should not dare to assert that it is the only road, for manifestly it is no such thing. I should be content even to have the bibliographical way described as the low road to truth, and the way of literary criticism as the high road. Those of us who—fictively—plod along this somewhat dull and unadventurous low road may comfort ourselves, however, that without the distractions presented by the variety of scenery and the precipitous dangers of the path, we shall arrive safe in Scotland before our more intellectual colleagues.

Of course, I really do not believe in the terms of this over-elaborate metaphor, for which I apologize. The bibliographical way has its unexpected twists and turns, its ever-present dangers, and I may say its excitements. For myself, I find the discovery of demonstrable truth to be an exciting venture, worth all the drudgery that the bibliographical way normally entails. Too often, it seems, the uninitiate confuse the means with the end. No more serious error could be made. That bibliography depends upon ascertained fact and like the whale must strain some sea acres of plankton to build up a dinner does not mean that the results are dull and insipid because the method has superficially seemed to rely more on doggedness than on intellect. There are many mansions in the house of bibliography, many levels of truth. Some, I grant, are modest and inconspicuous in the extreme. The turrets of others may rise to gleam in the sunlight. I propose in this lecture to examine, with more brevity than they deserve, some of the means by which the bibliographical way leads to literary truth. My purpose is to explore various aspects of the bibliographical method and to try to analyze something that I can describe only as the bibliographical state of mind.

The Sixth University of Kansas Annual Public Lecture on Books and Bibliography, delivered in Lawrence, Kansas, on November 14, 1958, and printed as No. 7 in the University of Kansas Publications: Library Series (1959); reprinted with permission of the University of Kansas Libraries.

Incidentally, and for illustration, I shall consider a few relations of its discipline to that of conventional criticism, but only for the sake of clarifying the peculiar methods of bibliography.

That bibliography concerns itself with books treated as tangible objects is a truism. But, truism or no, the baldness of this statement has led to various misconceptions. In my discussion I must pass over the Enumerative form. The general usefulness of arranging the titles of books systematically for certain purposes requires no words from me. What I am concerned with is Analytical Bibliography, or the examination of books as tangible objects in order to recover the details of the physical process of their manufacture. This general method starts with what may be called historical study: What can be gathered about the printing process from external evidence such as printers' manuals, contemporary references, craft records, and so on. Then by an independent study it endeavors to recover exact details about printing methods in general from the scientific analysis of the physical evidence of the books themselves. Next, it may endeavor to apply the knowledge thus gained in order to interpret—from specific evidence in any given book—the effect of the production process on the physical characteristics of the book as a whole, considered as part of an edition, and of any of its variant copies that comprise issues and states. Finally, this analysis of the effect of the production process on the physical characteristics of a specific book may be developed in one of two ways, either as the foundation for descriptive bibliography, or as the foundation for textual bibliography, both of which serve as intermediaries between the book and the literary critic. In a nutshell this is the method, and the process, that I am concerned with today.

The determination of the physical, external appearance of a book in terms of the technical analysis of its production, which is the function of analytical bibliography applied to description, does not collide in any direct manner with other forms of analysis that go by the name of criticism. But the relation of analytical bibliography to textual bibliography, and thence—immediately—to textual criticism, is subject to misinterpretation, principally because analytical bibliography thereby invades a field that has customarily been preempted by some form of literary criticism. The examination of a book as a tangible object, consequently, applies to something more than the easily understood concept of its description as a dimensional object without relation to its contents. If we take it, in addition, that analytical bibliography is as much concerned with the contents as with the external form of a book, we may see its application to textual criticism. The peculiarity of the approach to textual bibliography, however, is this. The contents—the author's words—are not thought of primarily as symbols instantaneously to be resolved into meaningful concepts in the mind. Instead, at least at the start, the words and punctuation are thought of primarily as simple inked shapes, imprinted on paper from pieces of similar-ly shaped metal selected and arranged according to a system by some human agent, the compositor. This comprises another and perhaps less familiar notion of the book as a tangible object. Accordingly, the function of analytical bibliography is to treat these imprinted shapes, their selection and arrangement, without primary concern for their symbolic value as conceptual organisms but, instead, as impersonal and non-conceptual inked prints. Thus the general laws governing the selection and arrange-ment of the pieces of metal and their transfer of tangible inked impressions to paper are the concern of bibliography. Yet these general laws must always be related by analysis to the peculiarities of the evidence at hand in the specific book, and indeed to any specific copy of the specific book.

To determine the exact details of the mechanical process that produced the sequence of these inked shapes, and the selection and the order of each shape within an arrangement, therefore, is the primary end of textual bibliography. In other words, the heart of the technique consists in supply-ing a mechanical explanation for all phenomena whenever such an ex-planation can be arrived at on the available evidence. Since the transfer of inscribed symbols in an author's manuscript to the forms of impressed symbols in a book is a mechanical process, any explanation that can be made within the terms of the mechanical process for phenomena relating to these transferred symbols is to be preferred to explanations that ignore the process and seek some other terms of reference. This is the simple difference between a bibliographical and a critical explanation. However, such a statement does not go quite far enough. Bibliography has its own laws of evidence that must be observed, else its way is being violated.

It will sometimes happen that a critic will use a conjectural method proper enough for his own discipline, but improper for bibliography, within the terms of the mechanical printing process, and the results may too easily deceive the innocent. For instance, John Dover Wilson—who is a constant offender in this respect—makes certain statements about the text of *Hamlet* resting on a conjecture that the proofreader misconstrued the original compositorial typesetting and altered a word for the worse during the course of printing. In the known copies we have the misconstruction, he argues, but the lost original may be conjecturally restored. This sounds very 'bibliographical' since it appears to explain a phenomenon in terms of the mechanical process; but actually it is no such thing. Wilson is violating here a primary doctrine of bibliographical scholarship that con-jectures based on our general knowledge of printing as a process cannot be applied without specific evidence in the book itself from which inferences can be drawn in the light of general practice. Wilson's hypothesis is the product of pure guesswork, without a shred of evidence in its favor, and therefore it has no more validity because it is cast in language that refers to printing than if he had framed it in critical terms of value-judgment. It takes more than bibliographical language to achieve the bibliographical method. The bibliographical way is not the critical way with a vocabulary sea-change.

Analytical bibliographers must use as source studies the various contemporary accounts of the printing craft in different periods, but the evidence of the books themselves is the more detailed and valuable, at least in earlier times. An example that is perhaps not wholly typical—though certainly not unique—may be drawn from the process of proofreading. We know from historical accounts that can be checked from the evidence of the books, as McKerrow showed, that in Elizabethan days type was not set into long galleys, with the ensuing process of hand-pulled galley proofs, correction, page proofs, correction, and printing. Type was set directly into pages, and all proofreading was done at this advanced stage. Moreover, owing to the stiffness of the ink, proofs could not be pulled by hand but required the considerable pressure exerted by a press.* The earliest English printer's manual, written by Joseph Moxon in the Restoration, describes the mechanical part of the proof-correction process as follows. When the compositor has prepared and locked up a forme (that is, the type-pages that print one side of a sheet of paper), he takes it to the pressman, who is obliged to stop printing, to remove the forme on the press, to substitute the forme to be proofed, with this forme to print a few sheets on one side that can be used as proofs, to remove the proofing-forme, substitute the forme he had been in process of working, and resume printing. After the proofs are read, the compositor will correct the type and in due course the forme is sent to the press. From this period we also have references to proofing presses, old presses no longer fit for active service but good enough to use for pulling proofs. If one of these were present in a shop, the pressman need not be interrupted in his work in order to secure proofs from a forme just composed.

It must be obvious that if either of these methods were employed, the proof-correction of a book would be concealed as it is in modern times, and any variants would come—as in modern times—from the emergency repair of errors. However, on the evidence of the books themselves, Moxon's description appears to have been largely theoretical, for many—perhaps most—earlier seventeenth-century books exhibit variants within their sheets that are too numerous and too systematic to result from second thoughts alone. Instead, from the books themselves it becomes clear that a quite normal method of proofing was to start printing, to send an early

---

* Evidence is beginning to accumulate that whereas this statement about hand proofs may be true in general, exceptions could be made in special cases.

sheet to the proofreader, but to continue printing with the uncorrected type until the marked proof was returned; whereupon the press was stopped, the type corrected, and printing then resumed with the corrected state of the type.

It is clear that such press-variants are of prime interest to an editor, who must embalm his choice from among them in a fixed text, and they are occasionally of import to a textual critic. Any process that alters the details of what the compositor set while looking at the author's manuscript must always come in question. When their existence in books was discovered, these press-variants were almost automatically equated with the several accounts we have preserved of authors attending the press to read their own proofs; and hence the corrections were at first assigned the highest authority. It is only after many years that soberer evaluation has prevailed and we have come to realize that though author correction is not unknown—as witness Ben Jonson's Folio, Herrick's *Hesperides*, and Dryden's *Indian Emperour*—the burden of proof is now on the critic who assigns such variants to the author. Positive evidence from the nature of the variants themselves in favor of authorship is now required, and negative inference based on external evidence will no longer serve. The change in attitude now means that an editor should view any alteration in press with suspicion instead of trust, for it has become evident, on the face of it, that most press-variants represent the proofreader's own ideas, which may readily differ from those of the author; and that the proofreader seldom bothered to consult the author's manuscript when reading proof. Hence the authority of most such alterations is nil, and though some may correct compositors' mistakes, many succeed only in sophisticating the text and placing it at one further remove from the authority of the lost manuscript.

This new view of the variants has been arrived at by literary as well as by bibliographical evidence (as from posthumous books), and it may be useful therefore to contrast briefly the two methods as applied to the general problem. Literary judgments ought to derive from evidence, of course, and thus should ultimately refer back to a factual basis even though the major test for the interpretation of the fact is the intellectual satisfaction gained from the explanation that will lead to common acceptance. A literary critic, for instance, can read this dialogue in Dekker's *Match Me in London* (1631):

King. Whom hast thou poyson'd?
Doctor. The Queenes Father.

And when the proofreader alters 'Father' to 'Father in law' (a character that does not exist), such a critic is certainly justified in believing that the wrong meaning is sufficient factual evidence for a hypothesis that someone other than the author made this change. But suppose, as often happens, that the corrections in a forme appear to be minor and so relatively indifferent as to meaning that no evidence can be gathered whether the author or the proofreader was the agent. In such a case the fact of alteration is still present but the critic is helpless, for the evidence is insufficient to support a value-judgment that can be offered to the test of general opinion. Hence a discussion of the origin of the alterations can be only speculative, whether thinly disguised as an appeal to common experience or as some other proposition.

Analytical bibliography may not always be able to solve a specific problem either; but occasionally its peculiar technique will yield results that are demonstrable in a manner impossible for critical methods. Suppose, for instance, that an alteration in press occurs on page 1 of an early book, and another on page 2. The non-bibliographical critic might assume that any hypothesis he can make about the first variant will apply equally to the second, because of its proximity; and he might be tempted to appeal to similarity in his values-judgment as confirmation. On the contrary, the bibliographer's insistence on founding a case (at least at the start) only on some assured fact from tangible printing evidence—the bibliographical way—demonstrates not by opinion but by the requirements of the printing process that there is no necessary connection between the variants on pages 1 and 2. If the pages are part of a full sheet, they will have been physically separated in the printing and proofing process because page 1 will be in the outer forme (or the series of pages that locked up together as a unit printed one side of the paper) and page 2 was in the inner forme (or the series of pages that as a separate unit printed the other side of the paper at a quite different time). Separate printing is ordinarily the cause of separate proofreading. The same agent *might* have read proof on both pages, but there is no physical evidence resident in the printing process that he did. No necessary connection can be established between the two pages without further specific information.

Still treating these two pages and their variants with no regard for the derived meaning of their symbols but only as physical objects that have received markings in ink on one side and then on the other, the bibliographer may continue his examination. He knows that proofs can be pulled only on a press, and not by hand pressure. Moreover, to imprint one side of a sheet of paper the type-pages must be correctly arranged in relation to one another and firmly locked up in a frame, called a chase, a process that we loosely call imposition. To a critic seeking further physical information about the possible relationship of the variants on pages 1 and 2, the bibliographer can say this. If only one set of materials, what is called a skeleton, were made up to impose the type-pages for all formes in a book, it is very clear that this skeleton cannot have been used to lock up one

forme of a sheet for proofing until the other forme had altogether finished
its printing, Moxon to the contrary. When a bibliographer from its running-
titles identifies such a single skeleton, he can tell the critic that at least
five or six hours separated the proofreading of page 1 from that of page 2.
Thus the agent may have been the same but there is no physical requirement that he should be, and any assumption must rest exclusively on
literary evidence. Nevertheless, if two different skeletons can be identified
as imposing the formes of this sheet, the critic can be told with some
positiveness that—under the conditions of normal printing—if there is a
variant on page 1 no variants will ordinarily appear on page 2, and the
type of page 2 will have been corrected by the same agent who proofread
page 1.

On the other hand, if the pages were 2 and 3 in, say, a folio in 2's,
and in some copies alterations were found in these pages, the bibliographer
can guarantee the critic that there is a necessary physical connection between these two pages in the same forme, and that the odds are the alterations were ordered by the same agent in both pages. Even if in some copies
changes were made on page 2 but not on page 3, and in other copies the
page 3 alterations appeared beside those of page 2, the bibliographer could
describe the process by which proof might be read and corrected one page
at a time (as occasionally in the Shakespeare First Folio and in Dekker's
Magnificent Entertainment) so that a provisional inference could be
drawn that the proofreading of the two pages was actually continuous
even though the correction in the type was performed in two parts. However, it would not be the bibliographical way to assume this continuous
reading on general information about printing practice alone: general
knowledge of procedures must always be used only to confirm the specific
evidence of the book in question. Thus if the bibliographer collated twenty
copies of the book and found no variants on either page 2 or 3 in five
copies, alterations on page 2 but not on page 3 in one copy, and changes
on page 3 added to those on page 2 in the remaining fourteen, he would
be justified in the inference that very few copies of the singular alterations
on page 2 were printed before the press was stopped once more to correct
page 3. Hence it would be a reasonable hypothesis that the reading of the
proof was continuous and performed by the same agent. On the other
hand, if he found, say, five invariant copies in the original state, ten copies
with the alterations only on page 2, and the remaining five with the added
page 3 variants, the proportions would suggest by extrapolation that about
one-half of the whole time required to print this forme had elapsed between
the two stages of press-correction, or perhaps about three hours, and therefore the reading was very likely not continuous. In such a case the agent may
have been the same, or a different person: the interpretation of the press-

work can have any affirmative bearing on this problem only when continuous proofing is indicated.

This illustration could be carried forward into areas of some complexity. For instance, if two skeletons were utilized to print the sheets of the book, the situation would be quite different and would call for changed sets of time-schedules owing to the marked difference in the details of the printing process. In turn, such inferences would differ according as the bibliographer was able to analyze the evidence to see whether the book were printed with the compositor setting each page in order, or whether he used cast-off copy and skipped so that he set the diverse pages that make up one forme before returning to fill in the gaps with pages of the other forme. The discovery, made only recently, that this method of typesetting was commonly used in Elizabethan times has quite revolutionized the interpretation of bibliographical evidence, and we are still trying to find our bearings as a result.

In another situation that the bibliographer would recognize—but the critic would not—if the pages 1 and 2 with their variants were part of a half-sheet gathering, there might be as close a connection between them as between pages 2 and 3 in a full-sheet forme; yet if the half-sheet type-pages were imposed according to an alternative method, there would be no connection at all. These technical issues illustrate how improper it is for critics to deal with evidence according to their literary standards until the absolutely basic facts have been determined by informed bibliographical analysis. How helpful, indeed how crucial, such technical investigation may be has been illustrated in the conclusions that have been drawn in the second volume of the Cambridge Dekker about the authority of the text of *The Magnificent Entertainment.* Here analytical bibliography furnished the textual critic with the necessary information for a series of reasonings that led to the view that Dekker himself had corrected the proof for a few specific pages and that the variants in the other pages were unauthoritative. Moreover, when a revised second edition was printed, the bibliographer could determine largely on mechanical evidence which revisions were Dekker's and which were not.

The Honest Whore is another Dekker play in which once the mechanical facts were determined and logically interpreted to relate to general printing procedures (a process not always so simple as it sounds), purely critical inference about Dekker's revisions was almost completely confined by bibliographical facts, and the lot of the editor was made surprisingly easy.

For example, when in 1933 Hazelton Spencer came to Dekker's *Honest Whore,* Part I, in his *Elizabethan Plays,* an anthology that for its day was most conscientiously edited (far in advance of conventional practice for anthologies at the present time, as a matter of fact), his use of the then newly discovered second edition was eclectic in the old-fashioned sense, since he had not solved the bibliographical problem of the exact printing relationship between the two editions, the retention of standing type from the first in the second edition, and the differing relationship of the variants in the standing type from those in the reset type. Thus he could not define the respective authority of each edition, page by page, and so could not explain why in some places the second edition seemed inferior but in others patently superior. Failing here, he had no possible criterion other than personal, critical taste to guide him in the choice of readings from among the numerous variants, and it was inevitable that he should not be correct in all cases. (In truth, there is no indication in his introduction or notes that he was aware of the existence of any bibliographical problem in the relationship of the two texts.)

In comparison, present-day bibliographical techniques distinguish the use in this second edition of corrected standing type from the first, and of reset type; and then proceed to analyze the textual characteristics of the variants in each according to the bibliographical units of the different sheets printed in three different shops. The bibliographical explanation of the evidence suggests why in the work of only one shop the reset formes contain authoritative revisions and corrections, although the standing formes in all shops were authoritatively corrected. Thus the problem of authority of the several classes of variants is solved according to the mechanical evidence of the printing process. Consequently, editorial eclecticism in the choice of variants now from one and now from the other edition becomes quite automatic, completely demonstrable on physical grounds, and not subject in the least to differences of critical opinion.

It cannot be repeated too often that when the evidence of analytical bibliography is available, critical judgment must be limited by bibliographical probabilities and must never run contrary to bibliographical findings. Another simple illustration may be given. Suppose we have a sheet in an Elizabethan book that shows press-alterations in both formes, that is in the pages on each side of the unfolded sheet of paper that was the printing unit. The problem is—which are the original readings and which the altered in each set of pages. Often there will be little difficulty in deciding about the changes in one forme, for the printer usually took advantage of proofreading to correct literal errors such as a turned piece of type, transposed letters, obvious misspellings, and so on; and hence the direction of the changes will be clear. But on other occasions the variants may be so indifferent as to give rise to legitimate doubt, especially when they are few in number and therefore not cumulative in their evidence. In such cases when the order of change in one forme can be determined, the order of the variants in the other forme can usually be demonstrated on incontrovertible mechanical evidence that has no need for critical conjecture. For instance, in Dekker's *Match Me in London* (1631), a quarto, there are thirteen press-variants in the inner forme of sheet G, and only two inconsequential punctuation changes in the outer forme. The literary world will not come to an end if the order of these latter cannot be proved; but any poor devil of an editor must know which is which before he can have a reasonable basis for deciding what to accept for his text.

The solution is quite elementary. Under most conditions when the press had finished printing one side of the pile of paper that comprised an edition-sheet, the pile was turned over so that the first sheets printed, say, with the inner forme would now be on the top of the pile and would become the first sheets, also, to be printed on the other side by the outer forme. When this happens, the earliest sheets will always represent both formes in their original, unaltered state, and an overlap will later occur in which the corrected state of the type of one forme will back the original state of the other, and then the printing will continue so that the corrected state of the laggard forme will appear in connection with the corrected state of the other. Among the thirteen variants of the inner forme in the *Match Me* sheet are four corrected literals that show beyond question which was the order of change. We may then observe that of the twenty-five collated copies only five show the original readings of the thirteen variants, and these five plus seventeen examples of the revised forme are backed by the uncorrected state of outer G whereas the three known copies of corrected outer G appear in connection with the revised pages of inner G. This is evidence that could be taken into a court of law to show that those readings in the outer forme of G that were printed on the same sheet with the original readings of the inner forme represent the first examples of outer G to go through the press, and thus only the three copies with the altered readings contain the proof-corrections.

One more example may be taken from *Match Me*, since it is so rich in illustrations of the way in which analytical bibliography applied to textual problems can produce findings that limit very severely the areas in which criticism can operate independently. The first and the last gatherings of this play are half-sheets, and each gathering exhibits press-variants made at two different times. Analysis can demonstrate that these two widely separated parts of the book were actually printed together as one sheet before being cut apart for binding at front and back, and therefore that each of the two stages of proof-correction in one half-sheet can be associated with the corresponding stage in the other half-sheet as performed at the same time and hence presumably ordered by the same agent. Thus when the critic finds some suggestive evidence that Dekker himself made one of the sets of proof-corrections within the preface, in the first half-sheet, the bibliographer can guarantee the critic that the corresponding set of alterations in the final half-sheet should also be authorial. An editor need not consult his private judgment in such a case, for if he accepts one group of changes as Dekker's, he is bound to accept the other in toto as well, and he need not be concerned about the literary evidence. The bibliographical evidence is inexorable.

The point I want to make is this. Impersonal judgment is to be preferred to personal judgment. The mechanical interpretation of analytical bibliography based on physical fact is always to be preferred to the interpretation of the critical judgment from values. When bibliography and critical judgment clash, the critic must accept the bibliographical findings and somehow come to terms with them. Critical assumptions can never be so valid as strict bibliographical evidence. Indeed, this is not a question of degree: when a clash develops, strict bibliography must be right since step by step it rests on the impersonal interpretation of physical facts according to rigorous laws of evidence; and, correspondingly, criticism must be wrong since its interpretation of evidence can rest only on opinion.

Opinion that was largely based on false critical grounds decided that one of two editions in the same year of John Dryden's *Wild Gallant* (1669) was the first edition, since what seemed to be obvious errors in it were corrected in the other. But one single piece of quite impersonal evidence was sufficient to destroy the pseudo-logic of this reasoning and to show that the reverse was true. Whenever possible the bibliographical way shuns the interpretation of readings and tries to find evidence that does not depend upon assumed literary values. In this case such evidence was found when it was observed that in some copies of one edition in a particular word the letter 'l' inked fairly clearly but in other copies only its tip inked so that it closely resembled an apostrophe. And as a real apostrophe it appeared in the other edition. To reverse the order that mechanical evidence demonstrates, one would need to argue that a compositor, seeing an apostrophe in his copy, deliberately imitated it with an imperfect 'l'; or else that the whole concurrence was mere chance. A question of legal sanity might well arise about anyone disposed to uphold such a case. Nor do I need to cite the familiar story of the Pavier piracies of Shakespeare quartos and the fallacious literary judgment by which the Old Cambridge editors upheld the piracies of *King Lear* and *The Merchant of Venice* as the superior original texts, or thought that the bad quarto of *Richard III* was superior to the corrected Folio text. Too many other examples of the like exist for the point to need belaboring.

On the other hand, a note of caution must be struck. Just as the hypotheses of theoretical science are constantly being revised, so the findings of theoretical bibliography need revising from time to time as further information comes to hand. What a bibliographical fact is needs constant testing. In reference to some of the examples I have cited, let me say that the assumption of normality that is basic to bibliographical reasoning can be very dangerous if too little information has been recovered about the variety of procedure possible in the printing process. Thus, pages of type are not always set in sequence, as we have usually imagined, and an assumption based on an incomplete general knowledge of printing practice that any specific book was type-set and machined in 'normal' order instead of by formes from cast-off copy may lead to quite false conclusions. Just so, there are known cases in which the pile of sheets printed on one side was not turned so that the printing of the other side was performed in exact sequence according to the original order of the sheets through the press, and these irregular examples can produce results quite different from those normally anticipated. All such cases come under the preliminary qualification I have tried to make that general hypotheses about printing practice must always be tested by the specific evidence of any book under examination. The bibliographical way is inductive, not deductive, when properly employed.

Moreover, there is a hidden danger difficult for laymen to detect, the ever-present danger of bad bibliography. This danger may come from insufficient general examination of evidence as well as from the misinterpretation of specific evidence. For example, in Macdonald's bibliography of Dryden, the most important edition of *The Indian Emperour* is not recorded because the bibliographer failed to compare enough copies to see that there were three editions in 1670, not just one or just two. Yet in this unrecorded edition Dryden first introduced a major revision of the text of the play. Misinterpretation of evidence (or rather the building of a hypothesis on a fact that was not truly evidential) is present in Macdonald's assignment of the second edition of *The Wild Gallant* as the first. Similarly, Sir Geoffrey Keynes chose precisely the wrong order for the first two editions of Sir Thomas Browne's *Religio Medici*.

These were serious errors because they purported to have been derived from bibliographical evidence and were affirmed by men who should have known their business. As a consequence, critics—whose judgment must always rest on the precise details of a given text—were seriously misled for some years. The wrong order was assigned to *The Wild Gallant* editions by hinging the major case on the presumed bibliographical evidence of an ornamental initial letter. When the initial in one edition was seen not to fit the space so tightly as a slightly smaller initial in the other, and the editions were observed to be line-for-line duplicates, the theory was born that the apparently ill-fitting initial belonged in the second edition since the area of the surrounding type had been dictated by the first. This was an example of false bibliographical reasoning, for the assumed poor fit was actually a typographical convention, as should have been known. Two fallacies were present here. First, what was actually a neutral fact was used as the basis for reasoning that did not conform to bibliographical laws of evidence. Second, no attempt was made to confirm the suppositions by any further bibliographical examination, and Macdonald was content to rest his case on a very narrow band of evidence that played him false.

The Keynes error was the result of even faultier bibliographical method, and his erroneous conclusion was reached from evidence on which nobody would hang a dog: the assumed order of alterations in a plate that was not even an integral part of the printing of the editions in question. In both cases it was bad enough to have a number of collectors and libraries bilked with second editions bought at fancy prices as the first; it was worse to have critics misled for years by incompetent bibliography into using corrupt texts as the basis for critical analysis. Both men were led astray because they were satisfied to do what little they could with the evidence of external features of a book and made no effort to develop the bibliographical evidence waiting in the text itself that would easily have settled the question. That neither investigated fully enough was almost certainly due to a feeling that after all both editions had been described so that a library or collector could acquire them. This attitude—which seems to have produced a certain jauntiness in Sir Geoffrey's later references to his error, as in his presidential address to the Bibliographical Society—is the very reverse of scholarly. It reduces the importance of descriptive bibliography to catalogue proportions because it overlooks the fact that the critic is the ultimate consumer, and the purchaser (whether collector or library) is only the intermediary.

This is a point I cannot labor too strongly. Of course, the librarian must have the tools of his trade, and he requires some published basis, whenever possible, to guide him in his purchases and to identify (even if in an elementary fashion) what he has bought. Nevertheless, books are (or should be) bought not just for the sake of buying, but because they are to be put to critical use; and therefore it is the critic at whom the descriptive bibliographer must always aim.

Some of the things a critic wants to know may be summarized. He needs the information found in the systematic arrangement of books and their description in a bibliography to tell him what is the correct order of editions so that he can go to a primary edition and not base his evaluation on the inevitably corrupted text of a derived secondary edition. Moreover, when he holds an example of this primary edition in his hand, he wants to know whether it is complete in every respect, and whether different copies have physical variants such as cancels or substituted sections of text; in which case he wants the features of these to be identified and the order ascertained. He wants to know, in short, all the details of what is known technically as 'ideal copy.'

Since it is not always possible for the descriptive bibliographer to inform the critic about revisions in later editions unless they are announced in the book, the critic expects a full account of the editions after the first and a correct arrangement, with falsely dated editions, piracies, and so on, all identified and securely placed. Even after the death of the author and the end of very much possibility that fresh authority can enter the established text, the critic cannot be indifferent to the history of an author's work in later periods. The study of Restoration and of eighteenth-century adaptations of Shakespeare, for instance, is one of literary importance.

But if a critic is wise, he still wants to know more. First, he wants to know that the account of any book in a descriptive bibliography has been made up from the direct comparison of enough copies to assure him that the odds are small that a copy he holds in his hand will have textual variation from another of the same described state, issue, and edition—at least, no variation beyond presumptive press-correction. I can assure you from my experience with the collation of multiple copies of Restoration plays that this is no idle requirement. A somewhat surprising number of books will be found in which one or more sheets are printed from a completely different typesetting from that in most copies of the same edition. Almost always these represent remainder copies in which a few sheets have been reprinted, perhaps years after the original, to perfect the last sets of the sheets to be bound and sold. Always a present danger, moreover, is the sophistication in rebound volumes whereby owners insert sheets from a different reprint-edition in order to round out an imperfect copy. These are usually sold in good faith and bought in good faith, and some of this country's best libraries own such dangerous copies. (I am not referring to the Thomas Wise sophistications, either.) These generally distributed made-up copies are deadly traps for scholars, who do not realize that librarians for the most part are helpless to detect such variants and that even the fullest bibliographical descriptions may be insufficient to reveal the falsities. Of course, the more 'bibliographical' the description, the more it concentrates on the features of the book in which printing variation might produce identifiable anomalies; and the better chance there is for the detection of sophisticated copies from comparison with the bibliographical account. However, if a scholar is so fortunate as to hold in his hand a copy of an edition from a library recorded in the bibliography, he has an absolute right to demand that in no respect save press-variation should the text of this copy differ, without remark, from other copies of the same state, issue, and edition that are also recorded. Not many bibliographies are capable of meeting these demands, it must be confessed; nevertheless, it is the bibliographical way. It is also the bibliographical way, if I may interpolate, for a library to emulate The

University of Kansas in its ownership of a Hinman Collating Machine and thus to be able to check its duplicates to know precisely why it is keeping certain copies that in fact are not precisely identical.

But the deficiencies of descriptive bibliography when aimed only at the assumedly limited demands of the collector and librarian and not at the scholarly critic are too long a subject to expatiate on here. It is a false assumption that bibliography is indifferent to literary considerations. On the contrary, this method requires criticism constantly to refer the 'facts' on which its findings are based back to bibliography for validation. When Delmore Schwartz does not know how to identify a misprint, and thus interprets Yeats's poem "Among School Children" in two ways, depending upon whether one reads 'solider Aristotle' or 'soldier Aristotle,' he is making a mockery of criticism because he has not referred to the necessary bibliographical arbiter what wrongly seemed to him to be a critical problem. When F. O. Matthiesen goes into metaphysical ecstasies about the famed misprint 'soiled fish of the sea' in Melville's *White-Jacket*, he is betraying his own discipline by his ignorance of bibliography, just as surely as does Empson, who rests his whole critical theory about the point of T. S. Eliot's poem "Whispers of Immortality" upon two misprints in a late edition. The misconception that criticism and bibliography are not intimately connected goes back to that truism already cited, that bibliography deals with books as tangible objects. But since the shaped forms of inked impressions are tangible objects, and since they produce responses in a critic that flash the picture of 'solider' or 'soldier,' of 'coiled' or 'soiled,' the bibliographer is very much concerned with which is which. Unlike the critic he does not care from the point of view of the interpretation of the Yeats poem or of the detection of early metaphysical elements in Melville's style. His concern is much more narrow. He simply wants to know whether 'solider' or 'soldier,' whether 'coiled' or 'soiled,' is right; and he wishes the critic would consult him when these questions arise, since he can very often report back with the correct answer.

So far I have tried to illustrate various cases in which bibliography by means of its particular methods can determine, analyze, and interpret facts in a manner that leaves no room for critical option. Such situations may concern large problems, such as the order of editions like the Pavier Quartos, the first edition of *The Wild Gallant*, or even the determination of the printer's copy for the Folio version of Shakespeare's *Richard III* as the third quarto or the sixth (although Mr. Walton, the New Zealand scholar who has recently attempted this, failed to develop the bibliographical method for discovering the really demonstrable truth about this interesting problem). Sometimes, however, the situations may be reduced to relatively small and narrow problems, like the determination of the authority of certain press-variants in *Match Me in London*, the Yeats reading 'solider' or 'soldier,' or the Shakespeare reading 'sullied' or 'solid' flesh.

Yet there still remains an important area in which bibliography competes with other methods to offer an explanation for phenomena that is not demonstrable by the ordinary tests for truth that bibliography can often meet. In these cases a plausible bibliographical—that is to say, a mechanical—explanation for an aberrancy must match itself against an explanation offered from conjectures based on literary or historical interpretation of the same phenomenon. It is of the utmost importance for critics to be able to distinguish the two cases—those in which bibliography can speak with absolute authority, and those in which it can offer only an alternative suggestion.

In some respects the more closely bibliography turns its application to specific and detailed textual matters, the more it is likely to enter the area of probability and to leave the area of demonstrable fact. I have some hopes for the future that this no-mans-land of probability will more and more be gathered into the realm of logical demonstration, and I see this happening, actually, in the newest and most advanced methods of applying compositor analysis, a method sure to bring many dim areas now subject only to twilit conjecture out into the daylight of ascertained physical fact. But even when we have extended our future knowledge into many matters that are now very much a mystery, it will doubtless still remain true that superior possibility can be shown by bibliographical reasoning in some textual matters but not absolute demonstration. An interesting case in point has not been discussed in public before, and I am happy to be able to refer to it.

In Shakespeare's *Richard III* in Act IV, scene ii, some 18 lines present in the first and subsequent quartos are omitted in the Folio, which offers for the whole play a revised and much improved text. These lines are part of a scene in which Buckingham gags at Richard's proposal to slaughter the young princes, and—unconscious that he has sealed his own fate—returns to beg in vain for his promised earldom of Hereford. Although not necessarily Shakespeare's in every detail, since the only authority is the corrupt first quarto, the lines as a whole have not been questioned by modern critics, and the problem has become only that of accounting for their absence in the Folio.

The literary explanation—which in my opinion is pure romance—is summarized in the notes to the recent New Cambridge edition of the play (p. 159):

The deletion . . . of . . . some twenty lines, towards the end of 4.2 we may probably put down to the influence, direct or indirect, of the censor on the political side. The lines in question, which comprise the famous 'clock' passage at 4.2.96–114, are not, as Patrick has shown, a piece of actors' gag introduced into Q, as some conjecture, but have been cut out of the copy from which F. was printed, seeing that they refer to matter in two separate passages of Holinshed, while Richard's line (115)

Thou troublest me, I am not in the vein,

which appears in both F. and Q, is undeniably connected with 1. 113,

I am not in the giving vein today.

which appears in Q1 only. Patrick was unable to explain the cut; but a year later W. J. Griffin and R. B. McKerrow pointed out that the deleted lines might well have been considered dangerous at the time when F. was published, since the reference to the unlucky castle at Richmond (11. 100–4) would have sounded inauspiciously in the ears of King James who possessed a palace of that name, while a Buckingham whose demands upon his sovereign were repeated like strokes of a clock might seem to reflect upon James's favourite, who like 'his predecessor in the title was ambitious, grasping and importunate', and whose monopolies Parliament had actually attempted to curtail in 1621.

If we examine this reasoning carefully, we see that it is based on pure assumption without a single shred of evidence. Possibly, the audience of the time would equate the Jacobean Buckingham with the Yorkist, but we have no evidence that it ever did so or that such an equation was customary in history plays. Indeed, if history plays had been used in such a manner, scarcely a one might have escaped censure. That King James—who did not frequent the public theatre—would have objected to a reference to a castle because he had a palace of the same name is mere daydreaming. English monarchs owned the Tower of London, too, which comes in for few words of praise in the drama. If the literary critics had been able to show that the text as represented in the Folio was immediately derived from a playhouse prompt book that had been specifically cut for court performance, they might have had the shadow of a basis for conjecture, provided that similar cuts could also have been shown, but no such argument is possible. What we have, therefore, is the most insubstantial speculation applied with an air of specious confidence to try to explain a stubbornly inexplicable fact.

Here, instead, is a bibliographical explanation, and I think it legitimate to ask whether any thoughtful man would not prefer an answer such as this that has some evidence in its favor. The passage in question bridges the foot of one page and the head of the next in both Q3 and Q6, either one of which must have served as copy-text for the Folio. Thus it is not susceptible of any such rationalizing pseudo-bibliographical conjectures as compositorial eye-skip, a torn-off part of a leaf in the printer's copy, or some other elementary mechanical explanation. This would be applying general printing procedures to a specific problem without the concurrence of evidence from the book itself. Baffled, the bibliographer might notice that in the

Folio the lines come very close to the foot of the second column of signature s3ᵛ (the equivalent of a page 6 in a Folio gathering), but this would at first sight appear to have little significance. Even when the bibliographer applied spelling tests and discovered that signature s3ᵛ was set by Compositor A, and the next page s4 (the equivalent of page 7) by Compositor B, no immediate explanation would occur to him. It would not seem possible that the cut was somehow caused by the transfer of copy from A, finishing his stint, to B, just beginning his, because on the evidence Compositor A in his portion had resumed the scene after the gap and set nine lines of text to complete the column and the page. The change of compositors between two pages might have seemed significant if the break in the text had corresponded with the break between the pages; but it does not.

Actually, all the necessary evidence is present here, and the distinction between these two particular pages in the gathering set by different compositors is indeed a crucial one. What is lacking is an appeal to general printing practice to make the specific evidence of the book susceptible of interpretation in a rational manner. Without this information the matter would rest in troubled uncertainty, the scholar dissatisfied with the historians' fanciful reconstruction but unable to offer any positive alternative. However, Dr. Hinman has recently advanced our knowledge of Elizabethan printing in general, and of the precise printing of the Shakespeare First Folio in particular, in a quite sensational manner. We now know, thanks to his bibliographical discoveries, that the Folio was not typeset page after page in a regular order, with s4 (or page 7) succeeding s3ᵛ (or page 6) in temporal sequence. Instead, the copy was estimated and marked off according as it was supposed to fill a Folio page, and on the basis of these paginal estimates the compositors typeset by formes; that is, the order of setting the pages in a gathering was not 1 through 12 in sequence but instead pages 6 and 7 first, then 5 and 8, then 4 and 9, 3 and 10, 2 and 11, and finally 1 and 12. This means that the amount of material assigned each page was strictly predetermined; and if the space assigned were insufficient, something had to give. This something would always be the text.

In this particular case if Compositor A had set both pages s3ᵛ and s4 (pages 6 and 7), page 7 would have come after page 6, and adjustments might have been made if the text assigned for page 6 had been too great for the space. But since, as it happened, Compositor A started to set page 6 at approximately the same time that Compositor B started to set page 7, if towards the end of the second column on page 6 Compositor A had found that he had more lines in his copy than he had space to set them in, he would have been helpless to make adjustments because he positively had to join the text at the bottom of his second column to the text of B's heading the first column on page 7 that had been set several hours previously. Something would have to give, and it would be the text. Hence if the amount of text assigned Compositor A for signature s3^v had been miscalculated, cuts would need to be made as he neared the end of the second column and recognized his predicament. From the literary point of view this 'clock passage' is most important, but from the point of view of the play's action it can be omitted without interfering with the course of the narrative. Hence, if as I speculate the passage was excised for such mechanical reasons, the omission was selected with some intelligence.

We have this situation, then. The excised lines cannot be explained as a theatrical cut: they comprise the most extensive omission in the play and there are no other certain signs of cutting in the Folio text. The theory that they were omitted because of censorship difficulties rests on a very flimsy line of argument quite without evidence of any validity; in fact, without any evidence at all. If, instead, we seek a mechanical cause, we have the suspicious circumstance that this self-contained passage occurs near the end of a page that had to link with the beginning of the following page set several hours previously by a different compositor. We have the general knowledge that copy could be cast off and printed by formes. We have the specific knowledge that this method of printing was the invariable method used to print the First Folio. If the same compositor had set both pages, some doubt might arise whether—despite the cast-off copy—he would not have tried so to adjust his future pages that the extra lines could have been absorbed. But, instead, it can be proved that the very circumstances obtained that would make this absorption impossible: the division of the copy at pages 6 and 7 between Compositors A and B. It is obvious that what we lack here is the specific evidence from the book itself on this page, although our information about the printing of this page is more detailed than usual. No power on earth, therefore, can demonstrate that the agent who cast off the Folio copy here had miscalculated to the extent of eighteen lines. Nevertheless, if the success of an explanation may be judged by whether it does or does not satisfy, I should be content to rest the case on this bibliographical possibility rather than on the quite speculative historical if's and and's about the hypothetical reactions of a Jacobean audience and of King James. This is only to say that a plausible mechanical hypothesis in matters involving the transmission of a text ought usually to be preferred to a plausible (or, in this case, implausible) literary or historical conjecture.

This is a situation that we are likely to find occurring more and more as analytical bibliography extends its methods into the problems of textual criticism. In some cases the new techniques, when properly evaluated, will produce results attainable by no other form of scholarship. Several generations of critics have haggled on inconclusive evidence over whether, for instance, the Folio *Hamlet* was set from an independent manuscript or from an annotated copy of the Second Quarto. Until this problem is satisfactorily answered, the very foundation for a scholarly edition of the play is lacking. I have some definite expectations that the new bibliographical technique of applying compositor analysis to transmission problems will eventually lead to the solution and thus enable editors to tackle the numerous individual textual problems on the basis of a sound hypothesis about the exact relationship of the two substantive texts, Quarto and Folio.

Textual criticism dealing with the transmission of texts has heretofore used only readings as evidence, but these are subject to value judgments. Much of the confusion that has previously attended the discussion of the source of the Folio *Richard III* text has come from the exclusive use of readings as evidence. Thus one finds that at IV.iv.536 the first five editions of *Richard III* read

Is colder tidings, yet they must be told,

but the sixth edition reads

Is colder news, yet they must be told,

and the Folio agrees with Q6 in the substitution of *news* for *tidings* and reads

Is colder news, but yet they must be told.

If readings alone must be evaluated, the critic is faced with estimating the odds whether (1) this is a quite fortuitous similar corruption made independently by two compositors. (2) whether the similarity of error means that the Folio was directly dependent upon Q6 at this point, or (3) whether no connection exists between the two editions, but the Folio alteration was the result of an authoritative annotation made by the scribe fixing up Q3 for the printer and the earlier Q6 similar reading was merely a chance compositorial corruption that happened to correspond to the true reading. Whatever conclusion he comes to here will be controverted by just the same sort of evidence from other readings in these texts pointing in the opposite direction. But once the bibliographical way is established in textual studies and the analysis of compositorial characteristics of spelling, capitalization, punctuation completed for the specific workmen who set the Shakespeare texts, it will be a blessed relief to escape from value judgments that carry little conviction in such matters and to arrive at the truth by impersonal evidence of a mechanical nature that does not lean so much weight on the unpredictable human element, as at present.*

The conclusion we may come to, then, is a hopeful one. The bibliographical way is not only a technical manner of dealing with complex material. It is a logical method of analysis that inevitably prefers physical facts to immaterial speculations, but it is quite prepared to combine with any other form of criticism in whatever proportion is needed to solve the problem at hand. If a value judgment is the last brick needed to support the arch, the bibliographer is I daresay prepared to make, or to accept, this value judgment provided it fits into the one place left vacant by bibliographical logic. Once analytical bibliography began to extend its usefulness beyond the confines of the library and to take an active part in the affairs of academic scholarship, especially in this country, it broadened and developed its methods and vastly extended the material on which it could properly operate. This increased influence is not to be measured alone in terms of the positive results that have accrued in new fields by the application of bibliographical analysis to material not previously thought to be subject to such examination. The influence has been, and will continue to be, more widespread. Once a scholar has tasted the intellectual pleasures of a bibliographical solution to a given problem, some part of bibliography's rigorous treatment of evidence is inclined to rub off on him. Under the pressure for novelty, much academic literary criticism is growing increasingly slipshod in its logical method, especially when it comes to deal with the interpretation of evidence. It may be that the discipline that will return us to an intellectually bracing critical vigor will come from the extension of the kind of reasoning mind that is now sweeping clean the bibliographical way.

* Indeed, bibliographical evidence can be applied to this particular problem to suggest that at this point, at least, the Folio was following Q6. See *Shakespeare Quarterly*, 10 (1959), 543–544.

Bibliography and
Modern Librarianship

W HAT IS A LIBRARIAN, one may ask, and possibly not stay for an
answer. It may be that the great days of librarianship are over,
that the total operation has become such a rabbit warren that no longer
can a single man put his impress on the whole complex of operations.
Indeed, one wonders whether the specialization required to staff the
different sections of a large institutional library these days must not
necessarily produce men and women trained in such various skills that
there can be as little identification, or communication, among them as
there is in a university faculty between, say, the engineers and the art historians. This is an exaggeration, no doubt. But the technicians charged with
the treatment and preservation of precious and fragile manuscripts may
have little understanding of, or concern for, the process of cataloguing
serials. The specialist at the reference desk need never cope with the
peculiar problems that hover menacingly above the rare-book librarian
in his dimly lighted cave.

It is odd to consider that of all forms of librarianship, the training of
the rare-book librarian has been most neglected. Perhaps this neglect may
be rationalized, but for myself I can only speculate. It seems to me
possible that the simple lack of congregation in a rare-book room, the
generally limited demand for the use of its materials as against the active
traffic in consultation, withdrawal, and return of books from the general
collection, funnels the attention, and indeed the main concern, of those
in library corridors of power to the more obvious busyness of the beehive.

I am far from asserting that all the time the queen bee, surrounded by
her drones, is hidden in the rare-book room, the quiet center of this turning
world, this humming activity, while elsewhere the workers go about their
constant tasks of regulating the economy of the hive, building up the
combs, and getting the world's business done. I can conceive of working

Delivered on May 9, 1966, as the Zeitlin–VerBrugge Lecture in Bibliography at the
University of California at Los Angeles, and on May 10 as the Howell Lecture at the
University of California at Berkeley. Printed by the University of California (1966);
reprinted with permission of the Graduate School of Library Service, University of
California, Los Angeles.

libraries without a single rare book in them that might serve quite adequately some special academic or intellectual communities. Indeed, when years ago discussions were going forward about the planning of the Brandeis University Library, the original practical intention was to allot little or no space to rare books. I have not inquired, but I suspect that indulgent donors have long since forced a rare-book library upon this university. Status symbol, tax-loss repository, or whatever, the accumulation of some form of rare books is almost inevitable, and indeed is highly desirable— if we are willing to adopt a somewhat unconventional notion of what constitutes rare books.

Nonetheless, the cathedral hush of the traditional rare-book room may tempt the more worldly minded librarian to deposit there as custodian some outworn cataloguer, or some shell-shocked delivery-desk attendant, as a reward for faithful service where the world will pass her peacefully by and no extraordinary demands will interfere with her equable latter years.

I recall vividly once taking up temporary residence in a great mid-Western university, and being offered luncheon by its librarian. When we were seated he took a sip of water and as a prelude to our conversation he leaned across the table and said to me, with deadly emphasis, "Mr. Bowers, I want you to know that we are not interested in rare books here." I believe he had risen to his eminence from a beginning in one of the more mechanical divisions of the library, a fact that might explain his oddly cloistered attitude. Yet the truth of his statement was apparent when I started to work in the rare-book room, which, despite his disclaimer, housed a very respectable collection, though not one that was then being increased at any great rate. In those days the official custodian busied himself with light housekeeping tasks on another floor and left the conduct of the working quarters to a she-dragon who had demonstrated her incompetence so successfully in every other division of the library that by the process of natural selection she had finally gravitated to the rare-book room. I think her feet hurt, since she detested seeing anyone come in the door in search of a book she would need to fetch from the locked cases.

At first we did not get on at all well, since I required about ten books an hour for my project, and I also had the nasty habit of dropping by after a late seminar for the last half hour of the day, precisely when she wanted to close up early and catch an uncrowded bus home. But all was forgiven one day when she learned I came from Virginia. It developed she was a devoted genealogist, whose researches always seemed to lead her back to the Tidewater country, and so she had an enormous respect for my state even though she had never set foot in it save in her fantasies. One day she asked me in a conspiratorial whisper if I didn't miss all that wonderful Virginian culture in the midst of this crass mid-Western city. To keep my credit, and insure the steady flow of my ten books an hour, I was so venal that I never divulged I was born in the relatively uncultured confines of New Haven, Connecticut—that is, if one discounts Yale's benign influence on the town, which in my youth, as I recall, was limited chiefly to football.

At any rate, my other fond memory of this she-dragon goes back to the day I had to check a bibliographical description of an incunable and wanted to know if another library within reaching distance had the book. I asked, "Do you have a copy of the Newberry catalogue of incunabula?" She was flustered, pawed about her desk, put through a call to the librarian two floors below, and then looking desolately about, said, "He says it's on my desk, but all I've got is the Catalogue of Fifteenth-Century Books in the Newberry Library." I managed to make do with that invaluable reference work.

It was in this library, too, that I came upon a unique copy of the Dryden *Sir Martin Mar-all* of 1691 with the original title-page, all others being cancels. Since the cancel provided Dryden's name on the title for the first time in the history of the publication of this play, I had always suspected that the original title had followed the earlier editions in omitting the name, but I had looked years for the proof. Here it was, catalogued as a normal edition, just a few weeks before I arrived, completely without reference to the available Dryden bibliography and hence completely in ignorance of the extraordinary bibliographical rarity of the copy, not to say the literary value of its evidence.

Quite otherwise is the attitude I detect at Harvard, say. (If I draw my illustrations from the East, please forgive my provincialism; I'll tell stories about California next time I talk back home.) I suppose the reading room at the Houghton holds fewer than forty people. I think every scholar who has ever worked there is inclined to regard it as the living, beating heart of the whole magnificent Harvard library complex. I recall that its late librarian William A. Jackson, a lecturer in this present series, once re-marked with quiet pride that he had been ordered by the President of Harvard University to suspend for several months his normal activities in raising funds for book purchases because he was interfering seriously with a multi-million dollar endowment drive in which the University was then engaged.

The glory that is Harvard, or Yale, or Texas, or the Clark Library, or the Huntington, or the Folger, or the Barrett Library at Virginia, stems from the aristocratic fact that when scholars congregate and, as usual, talk shop, they meet in these places as in a private club, where they do the work that writes the books that make them and their universities famous.

The main reason is, undoubtedly, that the rare-book division houses the primary materials for scholarship. The secondary books, the reprints, the critical works, the files of learned journals, the reference series, can be found almost anywhere, especially in these days of offset printing. But the only true source for fresh research on the frontiers of knowledge lies in the special collections housed in the rare-books division, and every scholar knows it. That five hundred may busy themselves in the general collection for the one who reads in the rare-book room means little when quality, not quantity, is the criterion.

For this reason I address myself not to the multitude but to the rare-book librarian and his wrestlings with the cloven-hoofed demon of bibliography. I am conscious that technology will soon disseminate the transferred images of rare books to every hamlet in the nation in some form of microfiche, xerox, television, or what not. Yet this dissemination, paradoxically, will only aggravate bibliographical problems and increase the difficulties facing the librarians of great collections. Though the images may multiply, the books remain, and their collection and organization will prove to be even more of an art when the consequences of misinformation are multiplied by the forthcoming wave of popularization.

Indeed, if the rare-book librarians do not protect innocent students and scholars of the future from the snares of microfilm or its successors, who will? A great organization like University Microfilms, concerned with the reproduction of every book in the *Short-title Catalogue* to 1640 cannot engage itself to check each exemplar for bibliographical completeness and authority. If the British Museum catalogue entry agrees with the *STC* description of number so and so, then the copy gets filmed, regardless of whether the title-page is a substitution, leaves are missing, pages are cut into, or whether the book is one or another issue, or even the edition it is supposed to be. Mass production stays for no question, for no refinement of accuracy, and not for many facts.

For instance, I nearly jumped out of my chair a few years ago when in Virginia I was collating some microfilm ordered from the library of a prominent Eastern university, since it seemed that I had come upon a whole reset sheet in the second edition of a Dryden play, never previously noticed. But checking my films of the third and fourth editions indicated that the sheet was actually from the fourth. Inquiry then established not that the sheet had been bound in to make up a defective second edition. Instead, the rare-book curator, knowing that the copy of the edition was defective, had very kindly (in his view) requested the film laboratory to fill the gap from the next edition he had in order that I should be able to read the whole text. Possibly the Kingdom of Heaven is made up of such innocents, but I hope not.

I grant that scholars should know their business, but the fact is that the average literary scholar has little idea of the methods of bibliography and its findings, and he is therefore almost completely dependent upon those whom he must regard as the experts—the rare-book librarians—correctly to organize the primary materials with which he works.

How well trained for this function is the average rare-book librarian? In an article in *The Times Literary Supplement* for October 14, 1965 (p. 928), John Hetherington describes some of his experiences with trying to locate and identify pre-1662 quarto editions of *The Book of Common Prayer*. In one library he came upon over twenty quartos that had been reported to the *STC* as octavos, and were so listed (usually as unique editions) in that widely consulted checklist. For another incident, I quote:

"I reported a quarto Prayer Book to the *STC* editor as being the only copy of that edition known to me. She replied that a copy was recorded as held at YZ College. The college librarian confirmed this. As there were two widely differing formats for the quarto Prayer Book, I went along to see it. He had some other quartos ready when I arrived. It was a pleasant little array—of handsome folios! They were not without interest to me; but I felt that I ought to explain the technical differences, for which I was thanked.

"An important university library reported a sixteenth-century quarto of the metrical psalms. After some years I had to say that the collation differed from that of any other contemporary editions, and from a copy now found of the same date. I added that certain indications suggested a resemblance to a somewhat later 16mo edition in my own collection. While my guess as to size was confirmed, I fear that the librarian was rather hurt that it should come from a man who had never seen the book. This copy was recorded for the new *STC* as a quarto."

My own experience has not been unlike. I recall some years ago writing to the Library of Congress Rare Book Room to ask for a check on the press-variant formes of two copies of the same edition of an early seventeenth-century book by George Sandys. I supplied the signature identification and the variant words. When the reply came back, it was evident that the person charged with answering did not know how to find a page (as in the latter half of a quire) on which the signature was not printed. Moreover, the answer revealed that all the time he believed he was checking two different editions. That he had never heard of press-variant formes was bad enough. What seemed impossible was that he could fail to notice that except for a few words the pages were in the identical typesetting.

At the very start of my investigation of Restoration plays, I asked the Union Catalogue for the holdings of American libraries that reported their acquisitions of rare books. The results were so jumbled and inaccurate as to be worse than useless. Facsimiles, even microfilm copies, were listed as regular editions. Dates were meaningless. Ghosts abounded. It was evident that most libraries reporting to the Catalogue their rare-book acquisitions scarcely knew how to identify a book in the most elementary sense. Perhaps the worst came when I asked for a special advertised search for some uncommon editions, all listed by date. The standard reply, with every good intention to be helpful, referred me to edited texts in nineteenth-century collected series.

I am minded also of the summer I spent some years ago collating Restoration plays in a great Eastern university library. I noticed that many volumes of the various composite collections bound together in the eighteenth or nineteenth centuries were tied up by library red tapes to hold together the bindings after plays had been abstracted. Occasionally a left-over catalogue card referred me to one of these broken volumes for a play that proved to be missing. Noticing my concern, the custodian explained that to save space on the shelves all duplicates had been removed from these several collections and sold to the local bookseller. With only the minimal necessary double-take I asked how it had been demonstrated that these were indeed duplicates, and was answered that they had been compared. This was in the early days of the Hinman Collating Machine, but I knew this library did not possess one. (Indeed, though immediately approached when the first orders were being made up, the head librarian had referred the description of the machine and its uses to the Art School, and there the matter had dropped—permanently, so far as I know.)

So I asked how the comparison was made and was answered that the title-pages had been compared side by side.—What then constituted a variant that would cause a duplicate to be kept?—Why, different title-pages, of course, or any indication of added material in the contents.—A press-variant imprint?—Yes.—I agreed, certainly, any variation that concerned the book's publishing history was valid ground for preservation to attest to the fact. But suppose there were a misprint somewhere in the title, like "Pirnted" for "Printed." Would this be a variant that would cause a duplicate to be kept?—Yes, of course.—I remarked I was glad even for that, but since the chief reason for preserving books lay in their contents, how was it known whether or not textual variation existed, as by proofreading during the printing that might or might not be authorative?—There was no way of finding textual variation, of course, before deciding whether the book was to be sold.—Was the library, then, prepared to keep a duplicate because it had a simple misprint in the title, of no significance at all for literature or for publishing history, but prepared to sell it and take a chance it was not textually variant in a manner important to scholars concerned with the author's own words?—What other choice was there?—After all, the great collections at the Bodleian, the British Museum, or the Folger were not based on that principle.—Finally the custodian could take no more. "Mr. Bowers," she exploded, "I wish you would give me one good reason why a library should keep a duplicate!" Well, I was not employed by that university, I could give only a scholar's reason, not a custodian's, and so I returned to my comparison of the remaining plays in the collections, page by page, for typographical identity, against my control microfilms. Life is short and art is long to learn. The incident did stay in my mind, nevertheless, as an example of the distance that so frequently occurs between the custodial cares of a rare-book librarian and his knowledge of what a scholar wants of the rare books he is preserving—or not preserving as in this case.

It is this distance that should concern us all, for it lies at the heart of the problem of rare books and the literary, as well as the bibliographical, knowledge required of the superior rare-book librarian.

In a talk given before the American Library Association in July 1965, Cecil Byrd, the Indiana University Librarian, remarked that in the past there have been no organized programs for training rare-book librarians. "We have drawn them," he continued, "from the book trade and from the ranks of private collectors and printing enthusiasts. They have come to us self-trained men with a knowledge derived from personal experience rather than formal training. It can be, and frequently has been, argued that there is no background for rare-book work comparable to experience in the trade or as a collector—but the fact remains that these sources cannot supply the number of rare-book librarians which we now require. New sources of experience and training must be developed."

Mr. Byrd then described the one-year experimental training course developed by the Lilly Library for students who wanted to become rare-book librarians.

I am no authority on the library schools of this country, but on Mr. Byrd's word there is no such institution that takes upon itself the task of preparing students for rare-book work. Nor does there seem to be much interest in these schools and their students in filling the vacuum except on a very amateur basis. For example, the English Department at the University of Chicago teaches several excellently conceived courses in analytical bibliography that would be at the very core of a rare-book librarian's preparation, but few visitors seem to drift over from the Library School to train themselves, as well as to discover what the scholars are working at and what their next demands will be.

Possibly the problem is insoluble, at least in terms of library-school training or personnel, since their varied backgrounds do not give all librarians either the preparation or the interest to deal with rare books as the tools of scholarship instead of as venerable objects of a certain monetary value. In the Lilly program the fellows were selected only from candidates holding degrees from library schools, and in the space of a year they were introduced in broad terms to the extremely intricate "management of, use, preservation and acquisition of rare books and manuscripts. Additionally, they were exposed to the antiquarian book trade and expected to become competent bibliographers, capable of analyzing and describing the anatomy of a book using the scientific methods enunciated by W. W. Greg...."

"Our program," Mr. Byrd continued, "was not designed to train chief rare-book librarians, curators, or any particular specialist in the rare book profession. We hoped to familiarize the Fellows with all the operations involved in running the Lilly Library, a fairly typical rare-book operation."

This most interesting program, as further elaborated, seemed to concentrate on what might be described as the managerial aspects of the rare-book room; and in the time available there could scarcely have been room, perhaps, for much instruction except in this operational end. Under such circumstances it may perhaps be churlish to wonder how thorough or deep-grounded was the instruction that was mentioned in making competent descriptive bibliographers out of the students, since the knowledge necessary to analyze a book—that is, a grounding in analytical bibliography—which must precede the description is rather more than I can teach in an intensive semester with highly selected Ph.D. candidates.

The fact is, this basic form of bibliography, the analytical, is available with formal instruction in any sort of depth in only a handful of places in the United States and England combined; and its practitioners remain largely self-taught. There is no harm in being self-taught—my generation was completely so—but it is a very time-consuming process and one peculiarly difficult to get right.

Two points may need emphasis. First, where and when is the rare-book librarian going to acquire the knowledge of analytical bibliography that will enable him to assess independently what he reads in bibliographies and bibliographical articles and books so that the organization and recording of materials in his collection is not based upon inadequate, false, or misleading information? Second, where and when is the rare-book curator with his B.A. and his library-school degree going to acquire the expert knowledge of literature and of history—to choose the main subjects of research in rare-bok collections—that will enable him to understand the needs of scholars even as applied to the purchasing and the recording of the materials in his collection?

These two questions are, in fact, so intertwined that a real distinction is difficult between them. Modern librarianship must go far beyond the merely custodial with which it has been too often content in the past. If rare-book curators do not understand the needs of scholars, and so cannot meet scholars on their own ground of interests, the already wide gulf between the two will broaden until it can never be bridged. Bibliography alone is not the only ground of understanding, but it is a significant and perhaps even the basic ground, and from it springs much of the philosophy of rare books.

What is this philosophy? I do not know enough to give anything approaching a satisfactory answer, but I would suggest a consideration or two. If rare books are the primary material of scholarship, they are so in two senses. First, there is the scholarship devoted to improving methods for investigating the composition and printing of books in general, from which methodology it is often possible to select lines of investigation to apply to the special problem posed by any individual book. This is analytical bibliography, and it requires for its scholarship books not only in number but in depth. From this scholarship eventually springs on the one hand textual criticism and on the other descriptive bibliography, this latter a necessity if the books of the past (or even the present) are to be sorted out, correctly arranged, and identified as to printer and date, and their physical relationships traced.

Second, only after books have been identified and arranged and their relationships established is the literary scholar in a position to read them with intelligence. If properly directed, especially by rare-bookroom assistants, a typical historian can be persuaded to use first editions of early basic books instead of the late and corrupt texts to which he inevitably tends. A literary man can understand that in certain books, for instance, authorial revision may alter his view of authorial art. A critic like Leavis, for instance, need no longer put himself in the position of arguing for an early influence of Dickens on Henry James's *Roderick Hudson* because he was unaware that the New York edition of 1907 (which was the only text he had read) had considerably altered the original of 1874. Editors of popular editions of George Meredith's *The Ordeal of Richard Feverel* (as I have been informed) need not reprint the 1878 edition as the revised text when in fact the revision dates from 1875, and there was a further revised edition in 1896, which only the Everyman editor seems to have known and utilized.

I am far from arguing that faulty scholarship of this nature can be prevented by enlightened librarianship, but it can be diminished; and I do suggest that if in all humility a critic were to approach a librarian to ask for advice about the best edition to use for a stated purpose, the librarian should know enough to answer the question with some intelligence. And, at least in his own institution, a knowledgeable librarian can help to bring up the young scholars who use his materials in the paths of bibliographical and textual rectitude.

To answer such questions, to be in a position where one's influence can guide the users of one's books, to select and organize the raw material for scholars, requires some understanding of the scholarly process. It is, therefore, no accident that among the great rare-book librarians I have known in the East, John Quincy Adams was a former professor of English, William Jackson had his professorship, and William Bond, his successor, is a Ph.D. in English, as is James Thorpe, now of the Huntington. The librarian of the Folger, as of the Newberry and the Clark, may be addressed as Doctor, and each has been an active historian. I myself feel that preparation like this, even if on a lesser scale, is perhaps of better ultimate use to a modern librarian than some training as a private collector or as a bookseller. If there are the technicians on the one side, and the scholars on the other, mutual exacerbation will continue.

No course in the care of bindings, the lamination of manuscripts, the preparation of exhibits, or even in the care and feeding of booksellers can prepare a modern librarian for some of the decisions he must make. For instance, J. Q. Adams, I am told, practically mortgaged the Folger to buy the Harmsworth Collection, which became the cornerstone of that great library. If it had gone elsewhere, or had been dispersed, what the Folger would have become is difficult to conceive. This enormous purchase, up to the limits of foreseeable resources, required an imaginative grasp of the uses to which these books would be put, a concept beyond the range of the simple custodian.

His successor, Louis B. Wright, though criticized at the time for his decision, proved himself a man of equal foresight and imagination when he turned the Folger's acquisitions in a major way to the later seventeenth century and well into the eighteenth century. This acumen was more than financial—that such books were then cheap and would not long remain so. Indeed, they have climbed so steadily in price that if the Folger were today to engage itself to the same purchasing program, its resources would be inadequate. Instead, what Dr. Wright saw was the need to relate literature, as such, to the whole complex of the philosophy, the science, the theology, the history, the social institutions of its day. That he directed purchases so as to encompass this grand plan has made of the Folger not just a collection of rare books but a magnificent working library, one of the greats of the world, for scholarly investigations of a staggering variety of purposes.

Nor is the time for greatness past. One of the central problems of today, for instance, is the selection of what will be of significant value to future scholars from among the unsorted higgledy-piggledy raw materials available from contemporary writers. In this process of selection for the future, Harry Ransom of Texas, a former professor of English despite his present eminence, has been particularly knowing, as time will tell. William Jackson made it his especial business to match his own literary taste and foresight against such problems to assure himself that, when reputations were sorted out in the future, Harvard would have more than its share of the basic documents for scholarship devoted to still-living literature.

Moreover, Jackson knew what he wanted. He knew that first editions were precious documents, but he knew that manuscripts were more precious, and that the more these were the working manuscripts, the rough drafts, the notes, the trials, the more valuable they were for the future scholar. Only a few months before his death by chance I was discussing this very question with him, and he was illustrating his policy. He thought that E. E. Cummings was going to be a writer of considerable importance in the future, and he described his efforts to acquire all that he could of Cummings' work. As I recall, I remarked that we at Virginia, in the Barrett Library, had a very considerable collection of Cummings manuscripts. "Ah," said Jackson triumphantly, "but I have the whole set of his notebooks!" He always had such an ace up his sleeve: one of the numerous reasons why he was a truly great scholar-librarian.

Another way in which Jackson and his kind stood head and shoulders above the crowd was in the extent of their personal knowledge. No great librarian has ever been content, like the rank and file, to take checklists, bibliographies, or the tradelore of booksellers as the ultimate authority. I do not believe it is any accident that, even after the *STC* period, Harvard seems to have more examples of unrecorded Restoration play variant issues than any other library. Clearly, some knowledgeable persons were watching, comparing, and buying. Strickland Gibson, Keeper of the Books at the Bodleian, had made the history of the Bodleian shelfmarks so much his province, among many other things, that when a private collector brought to him a copy of the Shakespeare First Folio, he identified it—in a thrilling moment—as the long-lost Bodleian copy, originally presented by the Stationers' Company on publication in 1623. Jackson made his extraordinary researches into the revision of the *Short-title Catalogue* the vehicle for Harvard's purchases as well as for the ordering and identification of library collections throughout England and America. Lars Hanson, the late Keeper at the Bodleian, was authority on early newspapers. The constant activity of members of the British Museum staff, not in the simple, mechanical preparation of the public catalogue but in the scholarly bibliographical labors of the special BM published catalogues, as in the classic incunabula series, makes them highly trained beyond the qualifications of most of their profession.

Such scholarly activity, indeed, seems to me to be the most desirable attribute, since in it the modern librarian joins with the scholar in the use of books and thereby gains the broader vision that can come only from firsthand experience. Indeed, such activity serves as the link not only between the librarian and the critical or historical scholar for whom he is building his collection, but also between the librarian and the bibliographer.

It is something of a paradox that even ill-trained librarians know the general uses to which criticism and history may put rare books, but have little insight into the needs of bibliography and its adjunct, textual criticism. This distinction was forcibly brought home to me once when in an endeavor to sort out and establish the very difficult bibliography of Christopher Marlowe's translation of Ovid's *Amores* I brought my microfilm rolls to a famous private collection in a metropolitan center of the Eastern seaboard, and found that the collection had two enormous safes, or strong-rooms, magnificent carpets, and easy chairs, but no microfilm reader. The custodians of this collection throughout its history had never considered that an outsider might want to use these books for something other than reading, or checking against notes, and hence were not equipped to deal with a visitor like myself who brought with him the only positive means of comparison and identification that exists for strict bibliographical investigation—a complete run of editions of a book on film. After that I learned to take my portable reader with me wherever I went, and I have often needed it.

Such experiences only confirm one's misanthropy, or in some cases one's misogyny. The British Museum has numerous microfilm readers on a balcony in the North Library where the rarest of the books are consulted. But in the university library in this country that I mentioned earlier, where the custodian had sold off all the duplicates, the microfilm readers were located in the ordinary stacks adjacent to the newspaper files; and once when I had neglected to tote my own small reader it required an earthquake of effort before I was allowed to take a rare book out of the collection, cross the lobby, and descend to the film readers in the stacks in order to make a comparison with my filmed copy.

No rare-book librarian has any knowledge of the ways of bibliography if he does not put a film reader in his rare-book room for the use of bibliographical scholars. The librarian of the future will need a Hinman Machine for the same purpose. This machine, as we all know, by an optical process of superimposing two images, can make an exact comparison of a page in two different copies of the same typesetting, whether type-metal or plates, and at a glance the user can detect the slightest variant. The uses of this machine are manifold. On the practical level, it will pay for itself in comparing duplicates of early books and, if both are identical, thus permitting a librarian to dispose of actual identical copies, of little or no use to keep together except for a study of their paper—an investigation not to be despised, however, as Dr. Allan Stevenson has repeatedly shown.

When a library's duplicates have not been so surveyed, a visiting bibliographical scholar may ascertain printing and textual variants for himself at small expenditure of time in comparison to the weary labor of detailed sight collation. Indeed, it seems probable that a visiting scholar can secure carefully controlled photographs and be able to compare them in a Hinman Machine against a book in the library's collection, thus enormously expediting and extending the range of textual collation that an editor of early books, especially, must undertake in search of press-variants. Or a descriptive bibliographer who now can make only rough and ready comparison of copies against a control microfilm, in the available time ascertaining little more than that any given page of type is in the same setting, can record textual variants not possible to ascertain by any other system of examination. By such means any book in a library's collection may be compared with any other copy in the world.

Originally the Hinman Machine seemed to benefit mostly the scholars of hand-printed books, but it is likely that more use will be found for the Collator in the future in connection with machine printing than with hand printing. A modern librarian must become aware of what scholars are doing in the investigation of plated books both for descriptive and for textual bibliography. Only when he is abreast of current research can he plan a purchasing program that will be realistic in the light of modern needs. For instance, book collectors are bemused by the cult of the first edition, although for many nineteenth-century plated books which was the first edition may be seriously in question. But collectors, and in this case scholars also, want to be able to identify the first printing made from these plates.

Collectors may concentrate on this 'first of the firstness' for sentimental reasons, which often have a quite false basis. The late John Hayward once asked me to tea to seek advice on a problem that had arisen about T. S. Eliot's *The Cocktail Party*. The publishers had sent to Mr. Eliot 'the first copy off the press,' which he in turn had presented to Hayward. A short time later Donald Gallup of the Yale Library cabled asking if a misprint were present on such and such a page, as in his own copy; but the 'first copy off the press' had the correct reading. How had this occurred? There was some memory of this variant in a rather late proof. Had there been a confusion in the printer's shop whereby the reading had been corrected and printing started, only to have an anterior proof turn up with the error, mistaken for a final proof, and the press stopped to make the change under the illusion it was a required correction?

Speculation of this nature can have no bounds. I felt the problem very likely was much simpler. In brief, how did the publishers identify the first copy off the press? Did they instruct the pressman to isolate the original sheets, one by one, as the formes were changed on the press, and then were these segregated sheets put through the bindery as a special job apart from the regular piles of sheets? No evidence was forthcoming of such unexampled care. At the most the publishers may have requested the first copy through the binding machine to be isolated as a presentation copy. But the first copy from the bindery was a very different matter from 'the first copy off the press,' for almost inevitably the last sheet to be printed from any forme would be on the top of the pile of sheets sent to be bound, and thus the first copy bound would contain the very last printed sheets. Hence it seemed inevitable that Mr. Eliot's 'first of the firstness' copy would contain the correction of an error, mended in press, since it was in fact the 'last of the lastness.' Of such soap bubbles are collectors' dreams made.

The collectors' passion for the 'first of the firstness,' when applied to the distinction of separate printings made from standing type, or from plates, has a legitimate origin if properly evaluated, nevertheless: important changes can be made in plates or in standing type and thus a textual scholar is closely concerned to trace the history of the text as it is altered in successive printings. Here two main considerations apply. If a librarian is bookcollector oriented, he will pay handsomely for a first edition, so-called, and bother little about collecting later editions in depth. For many books, however, he has paid first-edition (that is, first printing) prices for quite another article. As an example, many collectors and libraries that record the possession of a 'first edition' of Hawthorne's *The House of the Seven Gables* have instead either the second, third, or fourth printing made in the same year, 1851, or else a fifth printing made in 1852 but with the 1851 date unchanged, all of them superficially identical with the first printing. In this book, as a matter of fact, no textual changes occur in these five printings, but their distinction is not entirely an academic matter, since to identify the number of concealed printings of a book is to secure detailed evidence in respect to its publishing history, a not unvalued part of descriptive bibliography. Even the biographer and critic may be interested in the physical facts of popularity or nonpopularity as evidenced by the number of printings that can be distinguished on the Hinman Machine from the evidence of type-batter, and sometimes from the alteration of the plates. And if a collector is prepared to pay for his 'first of the firstness,' he should be prepared to see that he is getting his money's worth.

Certainly, in purchasing *The House of the Seven Gables* before scrupulous bibliographical attention was given to these first-edition plates in the preparation of the Centenary Edition, a scholary enterprise, many collectors have paid their money for the wrong printing. And it is distressing to contemplate that all the Hawthorne collecting did not disclose the presence of some duplicate typesetting with minor textual variation in the first-edition plates of this book. Similarly, the attention that collectors and librarians for a hundred years have given to acquiring the famed *The Scarlet Letter* first edition of 1850 failed to disclose that duplicate typesetting also existed in this first edition, though without textual variation. Moreover, the lack of interest in anything but the first edition effectively concealed the fact that a large portion of the second edition, though reset in the earlier pages, was printed from the standing type of the first edition, with some interesting textual alterations made in this standing type. Whether or not the second edition of *The Scarlet Letter*, in the same year, or even the third edition, also of 1850, contained any authorial revisions among their textual variants never concerned a single book-collector or librarian (or scholar of American literature) so far as any preserved record attests.

The Centenary Hawthorne may fairly claim to be the first scholarly edition to utilize the full powers of modern analytical bibliography applied to the text of a nineteenth-century American author. If modern librarians would read the textual introductions to the three volumes published to date, they would learn to modify their purchasing and collecting theories by what is represested there as the demands that present-day advanced textual and bibliographical scholarship makes on rare-book collections. Certainly something of a revolution in the collecting of nineteenth-century American books was started by the Ohio State University Libraries in preparation for this edition.

Indeed, the lessons of the Hawthorne Centenary Edition are revolutionary in their import. If a library is to serve advanced bibliographical scholarship applied to machine-printed books, it must collect broadly what appear to be duplicates of the 'first edition,' else the evidence will never be assembled for the detection of concealed printings that cannot be distinguished by the conventional evidence of binding-variation or of so-called 'points,' but by the expert use of the Hinman Collator. In addition, it must forsake the collector-fostered cult of the first edition in favor of the assembly of every ascertainable later printing or edition, even—I assert—down to the twenty-fifth printing in paperback form.

The reasons are twofold. When scholars investigate the transmission of a text, all editions within an author's lifetime are hypothetically significant and must be recorded. But the experience of the Hawthorne editors has been that nothing is so unrecorded, uncollected, and elusive as later editions after the first, since even if they are randomly present in libraries our modern rare-book custodians have banished them from companionship with the first editions and have sent them to the general stacks, where they may be lost, read to death, dismembered, or mislaid. The lesson is plain that if a rare-book librarian has a first edition of an author, he should retain in immediate proximity all purchasable copies of later editions, regardless of their scarcity of price, right down to the paperbacks. If he does not, he is failing in his duty to the scholar who will someday investigate the text, or else the scholar who needs the evidence that has been drawn together of the detailed publishing history of an author's work not alone for its intrinsic interest for the critic and biographer—although that should be considerable—but also for the historian of literary and cultural tastes and trends. As a result of the lack of understanding on the part of librarians about how books are used by bibliographical scholars and by those literary scholars who depend upon bibliographical findings for quite other purposes, an artificial distinction has arisen in nineteenth- and twentieth-century books whereby they are collected, or not collected, according to 'first of the firstness' or price. If the library as a whole owns a collection of an author it is likely to be split up among different sections, not all of which are equipped to preserve the various editions. This is slovenly librarianship in these modern times. It would not occur if our rare-book custodians were active in any scholarly way, and thus aware that all editions may differ in significant ways and hence must be collected in quantity and tested by bibliographical techniques before being passed on as duplicates. *Some* librarian ought to have discovered the duplicate typesettings in *The Scarlet Letter* and *The House of the Seven Gables* before the editors of the Centenary Hawthorne. None did.

Textual criticism and the investigation for critical purposes of publishing history do not end with the first edition. The challenge that bibliographical scholarship presents to our modern librarians is to recognize that rare books are rare in another sense than their value at auction, or their simple scarcity regardless of price. Rare books are the primary materials of scholarship. This is true when an obscure seventeenth-century sermon throws light on a disputed passage in Milton or furnishes a footnote for a study of theological controversy in the period. This is true when newspaper files of the nineteenth century yield another version of a poem by Poe, or articles that can be attributed to Stephen Crane. The whole complex of historical and critical investigation depends upon the accumulation of the most varied texts, even down to dime novels that at least can reveal something about public taste at a given period and the formation of certain reading habits or even of certain sociological attitudes. This is the customary view of the value of rare books, and in general the custodial position will serve for these so long as they are identified and organized within the framework of existing enumerative information.

However, when enumerative information fails, the scholar-librarian must take over. Only if he understands the uses that textual scholars will make of primary documents will he devote more effort to tracking down and buying the magazines in which an author's work appeared for the first time than the commonly sought-after first editions in book form, which may represent only unauthoritative reprints of the magazine texts, as is true in general of Hawthorne's or of Stephen Crane's tales. Even if an author had concerned himself with the transition from magazine to book, the variant forms of the text are of the highest interest to literary critics, and the earlier, even though seemingly ephemeral, version may remain of prime authority to the textual critic and editor. It is ridiculous that the serial of a novel in a set of magazines will sell for practically nothing, whereas the later form, first published as a book, may be bid up and up to the sky.

Price is not my concern, however, but the preservation of scholarly documents by those charged with their collection. Too often the uncollected is of more importance to the scholar than the collected. An extraordinary example of the result of fashions in book collecting, customarily followed by bibliographies of modern authors and thus by many rare-book librarians, is the distinction of what is the first edition of a book when it is published more or less simultaneously in two countries. If the author is an American, the English edition may in fact be published ahead of that in the United States, but it will bring a markedly lower price and will go relatively uncollected, because it will not be considered the 'first' edition.

If there were a sound textual reason, as that the English edition was set from American galleys, some common sense might inhabit this paradox. But mostly collectors and librarians have no means of ascertaining the textual relations of the two editions, even if they were interested, and for all they know may be preserving the inferior authority. Certainly, anyone who buys the two-volume first American edition of Hawthorne's *The Marble Faun* in preference to the three-volume English edition called *Transformation*, is for scholarly purposes preserving the wrong edition. The English was set directly from Hawthorne's manuscript, and the American edition, set from the English galleys, has little or no independent authority, and is more often in error in its reprinting than right.

Yet the case goes beyond the question of first editions, important as these may be for the textual scholar. It is not too much to say that any English edition of any American author should be collected as systematically as all the American printings. We know now, because a scholar looked into the matter, that James Gould Cozzens corrected and revised the text of the American editions of some of his books when they were printed in England. If one wants the superior text, one must seek out these English editions. Until collections are made of these now unregarded books, for all American authors, the whole textual case for a great deal of American literature must go unresolved. These books could be of prime importance, but they have not been bought and preserved for scholarship. Most bibliographies and checklists either ignore them, just as English bibliographies are sketchy about the American printings of English books; as a result, modern librarians have not independently gone beyond available enumerative information (or have not often taken advantage of what information there was). The scholarly uses of these editions are not understood; hence they are not collected.

This question, now neglected, will assume an ever larger importance in the future. When researchers in the twenty-first century come to write the history of scholarship in the twentieth, I prophesy that outside of certain interesting critical movements worth tracing, they will end by calling the latter half, at least, of our century the age of textual criticism, of editing, in which a new methodology was introduced, new standards that broke sharply from the past, with results of a higher order than had previously been attainable. If the history of our culture is ultimately the history of the writings of our great men, whether they be literary authors, statesmen, philosophers, theologians, economists, or scientists, then we should have a passionate concern to make sure that we are reading them aright and not in corrupt texts that in hundreds of cumulatively important ways distort, blunt, obscure, modify, or contradict what in fact they were saying.

To preserve the written record of our culture in this manner is the duty of the textual critic, ending ultimately in the establishment of an author's text by the most advanced methods of scholarship, whether it involves, as it may, the preservation and analysis of magazines, newspapers, books, phonograph records, moving pictures and their scripts, magnetic tapes, or whatever medium of communication has been used. Modern librarians have sadly neglected this second aspect, which in the end rests on bibliographical investigation, chiefly because they have made too little effort to acquaint themselves with the demands of this new and peculiarly twentieth-century scholarly discipline, which is far removed from the enumerative bibliography taught in their profession.

If training is needed, as it certainly is, especially in this country, here is where the emphasis must fall. It is not too much to say that scholarship among librarians is more highly valued in England than here, because they have kept to a tradition from which we have fallen off. In the great days of English librarianship the librarians were often better scholars than many of the persons whom they served. This was the British Museum tradition, and the Bodleian, and that it has not wholly died out abroad we may be thankful. Various of the British Under-Keepers I have met in recent years have been extraordinarily knowledgeable men in their field of analytical and descriptive bibliography as applied to literature.

However, the tendency of librarians not brought up in the humane tradition to become managers and technicians who have dissociated themselves from active works of scholarship has had a most unfortunate effect. Even such an original and useful program of training as that undertaken at the Lilly Library seems to make little or no reference to scholars or to scholarship and to presuppose that most rare-book librarians will be drawn from the ranks of library-school graduates without advanced degrees in literature, history, or other disciplines, or else from the body of collectors and booksellers who, it is stated, have furnished most of the rare-book librarians of the past.

The results of the American tradition are already apparent in the failure of rare-book libraries to rouse themselves from their sixteenth, seventeenth, and eighteenth-century somnolence and to adjust to the demands of modern scholars, working bibliographically, and thence textually or historically, especially with the machine-printed books of the present, or indeed of the nineteenth century. When *Studies in Bibliography* or *The Library*—to name the two most analytically minded bibliographical journals now being published—are as popular reading in library circles as *The Antiquarian Bookman*, then we shall know that the future will not cry out against us who suffered our librarians, in direct contrast with the past, to fall behind our practising scholars in erudition but chiefly in the understanding of what books are collected for and how they are to be used as something other than sterile artifacts under glass in an exhibition case.

Four Faces of Bibliography

M Y SOMEWHAT CINEMA-MARQUEE TITLE, "Four Faces of Bibliography," came to me with some vague idea of the four points of the
compass, but then the notion of the Greek masks worn according to the type
of drama and the persona of the characters began to seem pertinent. I leave
it an open question which is the tragic or the comic mask of bibliography,
the tragical-historical, or the tragical-comical-historical-pastoral; whether
it is bibliography individable, or bibliography unlimited, how far the
law of writ runs and how far liberty.

I gather that this colloquium may become an historical event, a seminal
attempt to systematize the field of Canadian bibliography. I hope so. I
hope that with the exercise of that noted Canadian rigour and thoroughness
you can furnish an example to other regions, not least that area that lies on
your southern borders. But systematizing implies that one knows where
one is going, and why—that the principles are fixed and accepted, and that
it is only the implementation of these principles that needs setting in order
and a logical extension. In certain areas of bibliography I am not certain
that, in fact, the principles are understood or accepted. There may be some
excuse, then, for an attempt on my part to bring the four masks on the
stage, with some few comments and illustrations that will touch on their
nature and distinctive expressions.

I conceive of bibliography as separable into four major fields: enumerative, descriptive, analytical, and textual. Each field can be ploughed separately. A scholar can spend his whole life within one boundary. That is a
virtue, but it is also a virtue that each field is not separated from the other
by stone walls. We must not forget that Robert Frost was ironic when he
made us of the old saw that good walls make good neighbours. Each of
these four areas of bibliography is, in fact, interdependent, and each merges
—sometimes almost imperceptibly—into the other. A scholar, then, may
concentrate, but he should always be conscious of his place in the whole

Read on November 5, 1971, before a Colloqium on Nineteenth-Century Canadian
Bibliography sponsored at Massey College, the University of Toronto, by the Bibliographical Society of Canada; printed in *Papers of the Bibliographical Society of Canada*,
10 (1971), 33–45; reprinted by permission of the Bibliographical Society of Canada.

spectrum and aware that he holds hands with his neighbours to the right and to the left. I will not say that the order I have stated for these divisions —enumerative, descriptive, analytical, and textual—is necessarily an ascending one in any aristocratic sense. I do not propose to make value judgments that could scarcely be defended. I do remark that there is something of a pyramidal effect, however. I am minded of the medieval belief in the ascending order of all created things in the world, each rising category containing within itself all the elements of those below as well as the new element that it contributed. Objects like stones had substance; vegetation had substance and growth; animals had substance, growth, and sense; man had substance, growth, sense, and soul.

This expanding comprehensiveness is also true for bibliography. The base of the pyramid is surely enumerative bibliography, the systematic collection and preliminary identification of specimens of the printed and written word. The more detailed and accurate identification and investigation of such materials as seem worth the effort occupies descriptive bibliography. Analytical bibliography faces two ways. Accurate and meaningful description cannot be written unless the books have first been subjected to analytical examination, at least in their externals. To that extent, one cannot be a good descriptive bibliographer without first having had some training as an analyst. On the other hand, the application of analytical bibliography to textual problems differs in proposed results from the aims of description, even though eventually many of the analytical findings about text prove to be of service to description. Textual bibliography may not be, like mathematics, the queen of the sciences but it cannot be practised until the ground has been cleared by enumeration, clarified and ordered by description, investigated by analysis. There may also be a rising scale of difficulty in these areas: at least—whether because of popular requirements or of natural selection—there are more enumerative bibliographers than descriptive, and more analytical than textual. I should, of course, mention a fifth area although I am not prepared to discuss it. This is historical bibliography, the study of the history of the implements of printing like type, presses, paper, inks; or of the records of printing like the accounts kept by the seventeenth-century Cambridge University Press, the eighteenth-century publisher Strahan, or the nineteenth-century Ticknor and Fields. The products of this research may sometimes have the most intimate application to any of the four methods I have cited. And, of course, we must not neglect that subdivision of the historical that might be called aesthetic bibliography, the history of type and book design as an art.

It is not my purpose to give a text-book analysis of the four or five divisions in which I am most interested. I am aware that I am preaching to the converted, to an audience that is more knowledgeable than I am in certain of these tools of the trade and thus in its understanding of the disciplines. Instead, within my categories I propose to touch briefly on certain special problems in the nineteenth century that come crowding to my mind from personal experience. They are problems because they are sometimes overlooked or undervalued and hence have received insufficient attention. They are also problems that I hope will have a special pertinence to any systematic proposals that may arise in the future from this colloquium.

My experiences in editing two nineteenth-century American authors—Hawthorne and Stephen Crane, with an excursion or two into Walt Whitman—have shown me the particular weakness that exists in the simple collection level of enumerative bibliography. I fancy that the problem arises because few attempts have been made towards organizing the efforts of individual scholars. In Evans and in Blanck we have comprehensive listing of books, in Blanck with detailed descriptions. But I am concerned with the much more difficult problems of periodical publication. Scholars are likely to tackle the collection of serialized publication on an author-by-author basis. This strikes me as a wasteful and inefficient method. The same newspaper and magazines that are searched to find the periodical appearances of Stephen Crane's stories and journalism must be gone over by another scholar concerned with W. D. Howells, say, or Edgar Saltus. This is a sad duplication of effort. Moreover, in my experience it is done very badly on an author basis because most scholars do not have the facilities or the financial support (which is the same thing) to be sufficiently comprehensive. As a result, enumerative lists of periodical publications of individual authors are seldom if ever complete. Indeed, few efforts have been made toward completeness except, say, to secure an example of one periodical appearance, at least, for every serialized or syndicated work. This last is usually thought to be sufficient to provide scholars with the necessary text, but I assure you it is not. Historically, it distorts the picture of the popularity of particular works, of the audience that they received. In the Williams and Starrett *Bibliography of Stephen Crane*, which by conventional standards is an admirable compilation, ordinarily only one newspaper publication is listed. This selectiveness has obscured some vital historical information. The reader would never know from the listing that only the *Nebraska State Journal* seems to have printed on May 22, 1895, the first of Crane's Mexican fables, "The Voice of the Mountain." At least forty-one other newspapers my assistants have searched never ran this or its successors. On the other hand, an impressionistic sketch of his daily-life observations in Mexico, syndicated only three days earlier, was run by at least nine newspapers of the forty-two examined, although the bibliography lists only a single appearance also. One sketch of New York Bowery life entitled "In the Tenderloin," on November 1, 1896, was confined to the *New York Journal*. One month later a similar sketch, "In Minetta Lane," appeared in the *New York Herald* and in six other newspapers throughout the country. These variations are important critically for his American audience's knowledge of what Crane wrote besides *The Red Badge of Courage*; and they are also important as standards of taste— why did one newspaper accept a particular Mexican sketch and reject another? They are biographically important as they reveal his associations with different syndicates, not always mentioned in the newspapers listed in Williams and Starrett. It is not at all unusual to find the clue to whether an article was a McClure or a Bacheller syndication in only one newspaper out of eight or ten, and often in quite obscure journals.

For textual critics, any enumerative bibliography that does not list all known appearances in multiple form is misleading and dangerous. Editors of Crane's journalism have not had the private resources nor the curiosity to pursue printings other than the single newspaper listed by Williams and Starrett. But when with resources supplied by the federal government and the curiosity of a textual bibliographer I was able to have forty-two newspapers searched, the results were usually of the highest importance. It frequently turned out that the New York newspaper text listed in the standard bibliography was either incomplete or else was the most corrupt of all the versions. In the Spanish-American war dispatches my assistants recovered several thousand words of Crane's writing, previously unknown, scattered through his recorded reports but cut in the New York newspaper though printed in full in Chicago, or Kansas City, or San Francisco, or Omaha. In various war dispatches but also in some of his city-life sketches, the *New York Sun* customarily rewrote his articles; yet these sophisticated texts have been accepted as Crane's true text because editors did not bother to search out other newspaper printings when the information was not available in the standard bibliography. To get down to the ultimate refinement, let me add that we discovered not only in New York but also in Philadelphia and no doubt in other cities that the text of a Crane war dispatch might vary according to whether it was printed in the city or in the out-of-town edition. This is a possibility not envisaged in any enumerative bibliography I happen to have seen, but it exists as an ever-present danger. Four or five hundred words of his most famous Spanish-American war dispatch on the taking of San Juan Hill had never been reprinted in edited texts because they were present in the city edition but cut in the out-of-town edition of the *New York Journal* that is most commonly on file, especially at the Library of Congress. In fact it takes some doing to locate a file of the *New York Journal's* city edition in 1898. For some obscure reason, the Minnesota Historical Society seems to have the best. Even more disturbing, we found that in Crane's most famous Graeco-

Turkish war dispatch, the battle of Velestino, the text was rewritten in two completely different versions, one for the city and the other for the out-of-town *Journal* edition. The relationship of both of these to Crane's actual cable, as it could be reconstructed in part from other appearances of the same story in still somewhat different versions in Chicago, Philadelphia, Kansas City, and Omaha, was of singular importance to the editing of an authoritative text. Newspaper syndicated texts can vary considerably between New York and other cities, and not just in simple cuts. The *Journal* received Crane's Graeco-Turkish war cables and many of his Spanish-American war dispatches and would ordinarily put these on the wire to subscribing newspapers in earlier stages of editing the typescript than that represented by its own final published version. Thus to recover the purer Crane text with the least amount of *Journal* rewriting, the *Chicago Tribune* was usually more authoritative than the originator, the *New York Journal*.

These are enumerative problems that might never have been uncovered had it not been for the requirements of textual bibliography. They serve to highlight the need for comprehensive newspaper enumeration of literary works. This must be a co-operative enterprise, government or foundation funded, and destined for preservation in a computer bank. And it must be started soon, newspaper by newspaper, year by year, through the whole nineteenth century before these newspapers crumble to dust. The files are becoming mutilated by time and by use, there are not many files extant, and these are often of mixed or unidentified editions. Canadian literary study will be the poorer if your newspapers are not systematically searched and indexed for poems, essays, articles, stories, and reviews about and by Canadian authors. Time is running out, I warn you. These newspapers are disintegrating and they have immensely valuable material locked up in them, unknown and untouched.

Is there a comprehensive index of material in Canadian magazines in the nineteenth century? If so, you are more fortunate than we in the United States, who have nothing of the sort. One New York magazine called *Truth* in the late nineteenth century that printed several Crane stories as well as work by other important authors exists to my knowledge in only one major file, that at the University of Idaho, and even it is incomplete. Nor is it available on microfilm. We had to send in a camera crew from Minneapolis to have films made of the years when Crane was writing for the magazine so that we could check the accuracy of the Williams and Starrett listings.

There is another aspect of this textual need for comprehensive listings in enumerative bibliographies. When an author's works are syndicated, the syndicate has them put into type and proofs are pulled from this typesetting and dispatched to member newspapers for publication on a fixed date. Each newspaper sets up its own type using the common proof as copy. As a result, any individual newspaper text is one stage removed from the proof, which in turn is one stage removed from the manuscript. No single newspaper text can be trusted to be authoritative, therefore. From a composite collation of as many texts as possible an editor can attempt to weed out errors and ultimately to recover from the various imperfect documents the purer readings of the lost common proof. His edited text, thus, will usually differ from that in any individual newspaper, for all compositors will depart from their copy in various respects. But an editor cannot recover his author's texts from these multiple witnesses if the enumerative bibliographer has not told him where to go to secure the raw material for his analysis.

Somewhat similarly, when an author's work is printed in two or more magazines the texts may perhaps not derive one from another but instead may radiate independently from a common typescript and its carbons. In such cases no one magazine text has a superior technical authority to any other, and an editor must undertake to recover the lost typescript text from the evidence of the two or more magazines. This is a technique of editing that is almost invariably ignored, but it is an important one, and its advanced methods of editorial analysis are completely dependent upon adequate enumerative information about magazine text sources. Even derivation of one magazine text from another may have evidence of editorial significance. For instance, the English editorial changes from Crane's manuscript of "The Scotch Express" as distinct from his own typescript alterations may be discovered from the fact that the American *McClure's Magazine* text was set from an early proof of the English *Cassell's Magazine* before these unauthoritative changes were made. Correspondingly, the book edition of Crane's *Great Battles of the World* was set from the uncorrected proofs of *Lippincott's* magazine texts, and thus offer here and there the opportunity to recover what Crane actually wrote instead of what the magazine editor thought he should have written.

Just so, even when the transmission of a series of texts within journals is not in question, the relation of any periodical to book publication is usually significant. Again, editors have overlooked the value of what they have regarded as comparatively ephemeral and preliminary publication, and they have tended to regard the book as the only authority. This textual blindness has created a situation in which practically every nineteenth-century English and American novelist who was serialized needs to have his works re-edited. It also means that libraries and private collectors cannot put too much emphasis upon the accumulation not just of first editions but of the more difficult to come by magazine and newspaper versions of an author's text, and that bibliographers must give these texts their fullest attention. Indeed, whenever there is international publication textual problems of particular significance are likely to arise. Kathleen Tillotson found a stretch of the most authoritative text of *Oliver Twist* in an obscure Philadelphia edition. Unknown to his American publishers, James Gould Cozzens was in the habit of revising the proofs of his English editions so that in many respects they offer a more authoritative text than the original American publications, which have still not been revised.

I have taken a disproportionate amount of time on this problem of indexing newspaper and magazine publication for material of literary and historical interest because I take it to be the most pressing and certainly one of the most fruitful tasks for an enumerative bibliographer of the nineteenth century. It goes without saying, however, that every prominent nineteenth-century Canadian author deserves a full-dress descriptive bibliography. The records of this detailed form serve as a particular stimulus to book-collecting and thus to the dissemination of fresh information, until finally what one hopes will be a definitive study for historical, biographical, critical, and textual purposes can be built up. And it is not to be overlooked by librarians that book-collectors are prone eventually to generous impulses.

The general formula for the presentation of material in full-fledged descriptive bibliographies is by this time tolerably well established. But it should not be allowed to harden into dogma. David Foxon has queried the usefulness and certainly the practicability of detailed description for vast eighteenth-century compilations. Something of the same sort of problem may well face nineteenth-century Canadian bibliography. In some respects the questions of practicability do indeed begin to enter as one goes down the pecking order of authors and arrives at relatively minor figures unless, as I urge, bibliographies are as much a part of publishing history as they are the technical biography of a man's literary efforts. Yet I must emphasize that we cannot rest on our oars in nineteenth-century descriptive bibliography. As the hand-press gives way to power, as printing from type-metal is modified by the use of stereotype plates, and as in the latter years the linotype machine produces its peculiar revolution, it might superficially seem that the need for comparison of multiple copies would diminish because the kinds of variants that delight the bibliographer of the seventeenth century are rare indeed if not non-existent under the changed conditions of the nineteenth. Yet nothing could be farther from the truth. Complexity is still present, though in a different form. If it is unlikely that the presses will be stopped to insert authorial or shop press-corrections as in Elizabethan days, it is not unlikely that changes in stereotype plates will be made within a series of well-concealed small printings, sometimes of no more than two to three hundred copies. The most scrupulous attention needs to be given to minor binding variants in the cloth, stamping, and endpapers as a clue to possible printings, even though often these variants represent only different bindings-up of identical sheets. Yet they may start one off on the search for other evidence that will prove rewarding. One must pay attention to the weight and quality of the paper, to variant gathering not always in agreement with the signatures, and even to the wear of the plates and the evidence of progressive batter, the purpose being to distinguish and if possible to order concealed printings that are so very characteristic of the nineteenth century, printings that may need textual examination for variation that might or might not be authorial. Even if the textual examination is negative, the number of different printings is a matter of importance for the full record of an author's publishing history. In some respects, then, the evidence for variation that in the Elizabethan age knocks at one's consciousness for recognition, conceals itself very quietly in the nineteenth century. If anything, the standards required of the investigative stage of nineteenth-century descriptive bibliography are more rigorous and scrupulous than those for earlier periods.

In this connection I urge a continuing dialogue on the usefulness of the different items conventional in descriptions. Is there more virtue in a small line cut of a title page than in a quasi-facsimile transcript? Are detailed lists of contents necessary? Is the signature collational formula still meaningful or is the pagination formula sufficient? In the pagination is it of any real use to list every unnumbered page whenever the omission of the page numbering is conventional, as on section titles and their blank versos or on pages that begin chapters? Is it worthwhile to transcribe all headings in quasi-facsimile? I must say some years ago I was horrified to see a bibliography of a nineteenth-century poet that down to the last reprint faithfully transcribed every heading, yards and yards of them. What about the value of the description and measurement of type? Is it necessary to have a gadget that will measure the thickness of a leaf of paper to within a thousandth of a millimetre? The list of queries is a long one that should be re-examined not merely on an opinionated basis but after experience and from an informed point of view of their practical value. My own experience is that the discussants of this problem are sometimes confused because they have not come to a broad enough conclusion about the purposes of bibliographical description. It is quite true that identification is important. That when a collector or a librarian holds a copy of a book in his hand and compares it with a bibliographical description he is concerned to be given enough detail to enable him to decide whether the book he holds is physically identical with the copy the bibliographer held when he described it, or that it differs in certain specific ways according to the bibliographer's record of variance, or even that his copy differs in ways unknown to the bibliographer who wrote the description. It is legitimate to ask, in this connection, what are the differences normally to be expected between copies of nineteenth-century books and then to enquire whether the details of the description are actually suited to identify them or whether modification or substitution of other details would be more useful than the standard set. After all, what *are* the major problems of identification in the nineteenth century? Are they likely to be previously unknown editions, close reprints, piracies, press-variant imprints, reprinted gatherings, cancelled leaves with substitution, and so on, as in the days of hand printing, or are they more likely to be concealed impressions or printings than unknown editions, modified plates, remainder issues, and so on? According to the problems, what can be done to adjust the details of the description in the direction of greater usefulness for the detection of variation? Can they be better adapted, or are the problems of a nature not susceptible of detection by any terms of bibliographical description unless the bibliographer has himself recognized and noted them? Unquestionably, a more subtle and often more searching examination is needed by a bibliographer of nineteenth-century books if we are to require of him the record of replated pages than if we do not. To give one practical example that I shall illustrate in a moment, should we begin in this century to add as a standard item the gutter-measurements of books—that is, the distance between the two typepage in an opening? This is a measurement which does not necessarily differ when plates are put back on the press for a new printing, but it may. Many new questions, and possibly new techniques to solve them, arise in the nineteenth century.

However, the confusion I spoke of comes, I believe, when the sole criterion applied to the value of any item in a description is its usefulness in identifying different copies of a book. I take it that a descriptive bibliography has other purposes in addition to the simple one of identification as a guide to collection, and that certain of its items record facts that are of historical importance primarily. This importance may be of two kinds. It may concern chiefly the publishing history of the author who is the subject, and it may record facts and details that bear on this matter without regard for their value as an identifying factor in the detection of variation. But there is a larger publishing history to which each individual descriptive bibliography contributes. This concerns the details of printing and publication as they change from year to year. What about the rise and fall of the popularity of certain typefaces? Of recent years we have seen a tendency in book designers to give us longer and narrower pages (a design that personally I detest). When did this start—how common is it—is it confined only to certain categories of books and not to others? Do certain printing-houses or publishers favour it and others not? As a matter of curiosity, I should myself like to know more about the selection of paper that was customary in the house of Appleton in the 1890s. Is it significant when they use laid paper for one author and wove for another? Is it significant if one printing of the same author is on laid and another on wove?

I have seen various nineteeth-century books where the signing bore no relation to the actual imposition. How customary was this anomaly? One could make up quite a long list of items which might be of comparatively little practical value in some cases for identification but which, when accumulated in the records of descriptive bibliographies, are illuminating for the history of printing and book-production. I grant that the process of accumulation of these details so that they can be used by scholars is a lengthy one if we must rely exclusively on author bibliographies, and I urge your attention to the rewards of descriptive bibliographies of individual Canadian publishers. By the way, what efforts are being made to see that these publishers' records are preserved? In sum, any new formulation of standards of bibliographical description should not be undertaken on a narrow front even when specifically directed toward the special problems of the nineteenth century. The needs of the collector or accumulator, important as these are, must not be allowed to overshadow larger purposes of history to which descriptive bibliography contributes.

It is true that absolute accuracy in bibliographical description is dependent upon the knowledge of analytical bibliography, that art or science of determining from the physical evidence of a book how it was printed and then the application of this knowledge on the one hand to the details of bibliographical description and on the other to the editing of texts. It goes without saying that a descriptive bibliographer who does not have an adequate knowledge of how a book is printed can scarcely write an accurate description when the facts are not truly revealed by the appearance that meets the eye. Description is not simply a mechanical process of recording certain external data: it has its roots in analysis because the external data may be false, as when the signatures do not in fact correspond to the gathering. Hence the greater the analytical knowledge of the printing process, the better the bibliographer will be able not only to recognize irregularities that lie under surface appearances but also to explain them, put them in their proper sequence, and evaluate their importance for collection and for textual scholarship, and sometimes for printing history. In this process the Hinman Collator, or one of the several substitutes now coming on the market, has proved itself to be an important contributor to knowledge. Without its use, for example, Professor Bruccoli could very likely not have distinguished fully and ordered the different early printings in the United States of Hawthorne's *Marble Faun* and thus determined not only their relative importance to the collector but also to the textual critic. It is textually significant that the third prepublicaion printing suddenly changes certain of the plates in order to incorporate variants that seem to have come to the attention of the publisher from the belated arrival of a set of revised English proofs. It is more interesting that the important question of the variant text of Hawthorne's added Postscript, or Conclusion, and the priority of his writing of the English or the United States version, in part may rest on the identification and dating of the exact Boston printing in which it made its first appearance.

The Collator was designed to detect press-variants in the Shakespeare First Folio; but it has come to be the chief analytical and textual tool of the bibliographer of nineteenth and of twentieth-century books because of its ability rapidly to detect plate changes and sometimes to isolate separate printings not only on this evidence but also on that of progressive plate deterioration. The descriptive bibliographer of Hawthorne, for instance, could not write a definitive account of *The House of the Seven Gables* without the evidence furnished by the Hinman Collator. Ordinary methods of examination short of complete textual collation by hand would not reveal that a textual variant occurs in half-sheet 22, depending upon the presence or absence of a comma after the word 'solitude'. Yet even if he saw it, if the describer were not an analytical bibliographer he could readily misinterpret this evidence in a manner that would affect his description. This is an excellent example, although of a tiny point, to illustrate the principle that recording without interpretation simply is not enough. Was the comma removed from the plate or added? If the bibliographer were working only with two copies that showed the variant he might be puzzled if his knowledge of printing did not come to his aid to whisper in his ear that in the typesetting a place must be left for the comma, so that it is unlikely a comma could be added without something of a squeeze, not present in that line. Was the comma removed, then, leaving a blank space? That could be the natural inference and it might satisfy an unwary or an inexperienced investigator. A difficulty arises in that the comma is more desirable than not. Moreover, in this case if the bibliographer thought to check a photograph of the manuscript he would see that the comma was written there and hence ought to have been set. Why should a useful and certainly inoffensive comma be removed? If the book had been printed from type-metal the answer would be easy: it was loose and fell out during the course of printing, the way a useful exclamation point fell out during the first printing of *The Scarlet Letter*, leaving a blank space that was filled by an unauthoritative comma in the second edition and in all editions thereafter. But *The House of the Seven Gables* was printed from plates, and to remove the comma someone would need to have cut a hole in that plate and solder in a space instead. No other changes were made in the line, the page, the forme.

Nevertheless, if the investigator had some notion of the printing process —that is if he were an analytical bibliographer—he would accumulate more copies, and he would find that eventually by the use of the Collator he could distinguish four different printings of this first edition, partly from plate repair in other places and partly from type batter. He would then discover that in each of these four printings some copies would have the comma and some not. Any hypothesis for plate-revision is therefore shown to be impossible, and only one answer results: half-sheet 22 was machined for economy and speed with two identical formes made up of duplicate plates, as one might well have anticipated anyway if one were an analyst. Still, what about that comma? Priority of printing cannot account for it, because the plates were bolted on the press side by side and hence printed the same sheet of paper at the same time. Priority of manufacture of the plate seems to be the only answer; and from that hypothesis it is only a step to an explanation that the typesetting with the comma was the authoritative original, but when the first flong for plate-making was removed from the type-page it carried with it the loose comma so that the second flong from which the duplicate plate was manufactured did not have it. Hence the description of this book can record, accurately, that half-sheet 22 was printed from duplicate plates, and it can identify them and assign the order of their manufacture, of some interest to the collector and to the editor.

Yet this particular little piece of analytical bibliography produced a second dividend. Each of the four concealed printings in 1851 can be identified for a collector by precise details of plate repair or of type batter. By this means a collector who understandably wants a copy of the first printing of the first edition can recognize it and buy it, instead—in his ignorance—of paying the price of a so-called 'first edition' for a superficially identical copy of the second, third, or fourth printings in 1851. However, over and above this desirable identification and ordering so that collectors and libraries may know what they have got, the bibliographer can accurately describe still one more feature. The Ticknor, Fields *Cost Books* list these four printings in 1851, and a fifth printing in 1852. What was this like? But correspond as widely as he can, the bibliographer will not turn up a copy of *The House of the Seven Gables* dated 1852. The Collator will not help here, because its evidence reveals only four printings. But an alert analytical bibliographer looking for special evidence appropriate for nineteenth-century books will find that the presumed fourth printing that can be identified by three reset lines on page 57 varies within itself in the gutter measurements between pages. This difference cannot be produced by alterations within the manufacture of each gathering of the same printing, but it can be produced in a different printing when the pressman arranges the plates on the press with somewhat different standard spacing between them. Now the description can be completed. The 1851 date on the plate of the title page was never altered for the 1852 printing, but the gutter measurements identify it. The publishing history is now finished and the description is accurate.

As for the application of analytical bibliography to text, on the one hand

analytical investigation applied to the recovery of the printing process
and its interpretation as concerns textual problems is still alive and kicking
in the nineteenth century if one adjusts one's techniques to the different
sorts of problems. I am told that some scholars have taken too seriously
as discrediting the whole methodology the strictures on some claims of
analytical bibliography so persuasively argued by D. F. McKenzie in his
well-known article "Printers of the Mind." For myself, I am unpersuaded
and although I acknowledge the usefulness of this article in warning us
to beware of extending hypotheses too thinly without supporting evidence
of some kind (not necessarily publishers' records), in my opinion the
basic soundness of analytical bibliography as a method remains untouched
by Professor McKenzie's attacks. That the interpretation of its evidence
by a few scholars has not been impeccable is of no more consequence
than the occasional misinterpretation of the evidence of Strahan's ledgers
in the eighteenth century has been for the soundness of the methods used
in Professor McKenzie's own field of publishing history. However, the
questions raised by McKenzie have pertinence only for the earlier period
and so far as I can see should not trouble the analytical bibliographers of
the nineteenth century. I will not pretend that the results in the nineteenth
century are as rich as they are in Elizabethan printing, but analysis cannot
be ignored. The anomalies in the text of Stephen Crane's short story "A
Little Pilgrim" can be resolved only by a curious analytical explanation
for simultaneous setting of the story in both the magazine and book versions, one half of each typesetting being made from the uncorrected proof
of the other and the opposite half of each from the typscript. The identification of certain peculiarities of a Heinemann printer's compositor named
in the manuscript of "Five White Mice" can be applied to textual problems in the book version of the story "Death and the Child," set in part, one
may conjecture on the evidence, by this same compositor. The variable
punctuation system in "The Clan of No-Name" in the collection *Wounds
in the Rain* can be related to the printing shop and not to the copy or the
author by the identification of three different compositors who were concerned with the typesetting. And instead of following this anomalous and
unauthoritative printed copy an editor has some foundation for principles
of emendation that restore a close approximation of what the lost typescript
that was the printer's copy must have contained in these respects. In another story a series of puzzling little omissions of words and phrases here
and there that might have been authorial pruning are revealed to have
had a mechanical and unauthoritative origin when a textual critic notices
that they all occur in the final line of a paragraph that was a short line,
and thus represent a subtle means of shortening the story by small alterations. These save enough lines and sacrifice relatively few words so that
the end of the story can coincide with the foot of the page, plus an illustra-

tion, without reducing the size of the illustration—already manufactured—
or running the story a half dozen or more lines over on the succeeding
page.

In other cases textual bibliography diverges in the nineteenth century
from traditional techniques of analytical bibliography, especially when a
critic undertakes to trace and to evaluate the authoritiy of the transmission
of a text through a number of different versions. By applying logical
principles of textual bibliography the complicated and apparently random
verbal differences in four different authorities for "Death and the Child"
can be reduced to two lines of the text, each stemming from two different
typescripts, with their respective carbons, made at different times from the
original manuscript. With this information the editor can reduce the
scores of variant readings to a dozen that diverge according to the two main
textual traditions and he can then deal with this dozen as best he may
instead of with fifty or sixty. Textual bibliography testing the evidence can
decide in the case of Crane's short story "A Self Made Man" that the
later book collection *Last Words* was not set up from a clipping of the
earlier magazine appearance but instead from a carbon of the typescript
from which the magazine text derives. Hence the book text is of equal
authority with the magazine. In addition, a typescript that has been
preserved can be shown not to be related either to the magazine or book but
instead to be a document made up at another time from the manuscript
to serve as printer's copy for an abortive American edition of *Last Words*.
The editor has three equal authorities to deal with, not two, although
arranged in two different independent derivations from the same manuscript. If he does not know what to do with the verbal variants under this
situation, he had better turn in his union card.

It took the Universities of Oxbridge a long time to recognize that the
study of literature later than the Anglo-Saxon was really a substantial
discipline and not something that a gentleman picked up in his own library.
Somewhat the same attitude has until recently set off the nineteenth
century as so familiar and recent that it could scarcely contain problems
worthy of intensive scholarship. All that is changed in the universities
now, of course. But the position of nineteenth-century bibliographical
studies has not perhaps kept up with the advances of other forms of scholarship in the period. You are to be congratulated on this colloquium and
on the results that may reasonably be anticipated. May I offer two brief
suggestions, in conclusion. First, do everything in your power to encourage
all forms of bibliography as reputable and indeed necessary parts of
post-graduate liberal arts training. Do not make the mistake of unconsciously trying to confine bibliography to the libraries, simply because it is
always welcome there, and appreciated. And recognize that the most
valuable kind of bibliography for the training of academic scholars is

textual. Second, do not tacitly confine the study of bibliography in its different forms only to those who have begun to be sympathetic to its promise, the students of literature. The most bibliographically benighted scholars in the universities these days are the historians, who will not even encourage the training of archivists as a legitimate subject for the doctorate. A real effort must be made to show these scholars not just the advantages of enumerative bibliography, with which they are acquainted, but instead the necessity of descriptive and particularly of textual, the importance of pure texts, and the fatal innocence that accepts the authority of the details of any document without having traced its textual transmission and the effect of this process on its words. Send missionaries to the heathen. Convert the historians!

Descriptive Bibliography

Purposes of Descriptive Bibliography with Some Remarks on Methods

O N THE PRINCIPLES which lie behind any form of scholarly endeavour depend the methods. Common experience shows that no discussion is more fruitless than that which is concerned with methods when there have not first been clearly outlined into areas of agreement and of disagreement those purposes which the methods are supposed to implement. Since I propose to deliver a few comments on methods, specifically on the methods I have adopted for the investigation and the writing-up of a descriptive bibliography of Restoration drama, some generalizations about purposes had better be introduced.

Among the interested persons who consult a descriptive bibliography, three major categories may be discerned.

1. Booksellers, private collectors, and librarians need the specialized information of a bibliography to aid them in their joint task of accurately collecting for preservation the printed records of our civilization.

2. The analysis and ordering of books in a descriptive bibliography is of assistance to all persons, whether literary or textual critics, who make direct use of the books concerned. However, there are indirect users, who may come to the descriptions in lieu of the books themselves for information about contents and physical characteristics, and even for the circumstances and forms of publication.

3. General bibliographical students may be greatly assisted by the detailed recording of a considerable quantity of bibliographical data.

My purpose in proposing to compile a descriptive bibliography of the Restoration drama to 1700 is briefly stated: it is, within all practicable limits, to offer the maximum amount of information to all three groups, maintaining such a balance as will, I hope, over and above this specific usefulness create an independent work of scholarship in its own right. The methods I am employing both for the original investigation of the books, and then for the subsequent recording in descriptive form of their characteristics, have been designed with this ultimate independent aim in

Read before the Bibliographical Society in London on November 18, 1952; printed in *The Library*, 5th ser., 8 (1953), 1–22; reprinted with permission of the Council of the Bibliographical Society.

view, but also, on a more specific plane, to maintain a desirable balance in treating the demands of the users. I should say with some emphasis, however, that in my opinion a balanced method of bibliograpical description, which will adequately treat the needs of the three major groups concerned, cannot be achieved by concessions and compromises. I take it as a principle that it is wrong to expect all parts of a bibliographical account of a book to be of identical use to each of the three main groups of ultimate consumers. And I believe that any bibliographer who tries to make his descriptions be all things to all men will end by effectively cancelling out the positive virtues of his work.

Let us be a plain about this matter. Most users of a descriptive bibliography will come to it only for their own specific purposes. Some may have no comprehension of the requirements of different classes of scholars; others' sympathy may prove limited when different requirements seem to come in conflict with their own. This is understandable and inevitable. There would be no harm in it if the situation did not create pressure groups which tend to operate powerfully on bibliographical thinking. Let me illustrate. I hold that bibliography is properly an advanced form of independent scholarship,[1] which is not necessarily subsidiary to other forms; and as such that it has as much right to express itself in its own technical terms as any other independent form of advanced scholarship. I have every sympathy with the literary student, and every wish to encourage him to understand and to make use of bibliographical description; but if we are to confine bibliography and its expression, as I have seen it suggested,[2] to the level of a university student who has listened to eight lectures on the subject and passed a satisfactory examination, then I must say in all candour that I can see no future for bibliography as a scholarly discipline, dependent or independent. But I have expressed myself at such length elsewhere on this subject that it would be tedious to repeat the arguments here, and especially before a bibliographical society. The nub of the matter is, surely, that if one has not had the training to understand moderately advanced bibliographical expression, then one has not had the training to understand the basic information purveyed, no matter how it

1 At the risk of pressing an unpopular point of view I had better make it clear that throughout this paper I depend upon the tacit thesis that bibliography is indeed a form of scholarship and that it is essentially an independent form, despite the fact that in certain of its branches, such as descriptive and textual bibliography, it is of direct service to other disciplines of scholarship. Much still remains to be said, but I have glanced at the subject in 'Some Relations of Bibliography to Editorial Problems', *Studies in Bibliography*, iii (1950), 137–62; and recently in more detail, in 'Bibliography, Pure Bibliography, and Literary Studies', *Papers of the Bibliographical Society of America*, xlvi (1952), 186–208, I have tried to explore some of its implications.

2 *Modern Language Notes*, lxvi (1951), 569.

is expressed. The technical part of a bibliographical description, therefore, is of no interest to the literary student until he understands enough to make use of it. There are plenty of others matters in the description which he will find to his purpose, however; and he should be satisfied with those until he reads and understands his McKerrow and Greg, and comes to some comprehension of the printing process and of the methods that have been adopted for describing analytically its results in the form of a book. This applies not only to the literary student but to every diverse member of perhaps the most important pressure group the bibliographer has to resist, a group which in the last analysis is attempting to prevent him from becoming an independent scholar by the insistence that he must address himself to the lowest common denominator of his readers.

Within the camp, however, there is also a strong opposition between two points of view, each of which would mould bibliography in its own image. I can illustrate again from discussions which, being directed at some of my own work,[3] have the advantage for our purposes of a common focus, however dubious. A distinguished textual critic and scholar for whom I have a warm admiration writes that in the principles and rigorous methods I have advocated for bibliographical description, I do not always 'remember that the new method of bibliographical investigation—however fascinating to those studying the ways of printers and publishers or to certain collectors and booksellers—will be useful to the student of literature only in so far as it is of assistance in solving problems connected with the transmission of the text. Analytical bibliography has proved its value to the textual critic and the editor: but it must continue to remain adaptable to their varied requirements, and its methods of description must be those that will best serve their purpose.'[4]

On the other side, the cudgels are taken up by a distinguished bookman who has always been very active in explaining the interests of collectors and of booksellers and, to our profit, in following the ways of publishers and readers:

Professor Bowers's thesis is that 'if bibliography of machine-printed books is to take its place in scholarship beside the best work devoted to older books, it must be conceived and executed for scholarly purposes'. This is unexceptionable; but he sometimes reacts from 'the excesses of undiscriminating commercialism' to a position in which it almost seems that collectors and their interests are outside the pale of scholarship. Scholarship, in this context, surely does not end with the mere text: it embraces book-structure, publishing practice, copyright regulations and the remuneration of authorship, distribution methods and

3 *Principles of Bibliographical Description* (1949).
4 H. J. Davis, in *R.E.S.* New Ser., iii (1952), 297.

reading habits. And these can sometimes be illuminated by bibliographical evidence of a kind which gets short shrift from Professor Bowers.[5]

It is a little hard, perhaps, to be simultaneously accused of paying too little and too much attention to text, and too much and too little to publishing history in its various manifestations. I should certainly feel more acutely conscious of serious deficiencies in my methodology for bibliographical description if it did not seem that, apparently being in the middle, I must accept fire from port as well as from starboard. I have quoted from these divergent opinions not from any sense of virtue, however, or in any hopeful belief that they might cancel each other out, but rather to illustrate the strength of opposing claims to the main services of descriptive bibliography, and the difficulty, seemingly, of satisfying one without alarming the other. In fact, I myself believe that each has expressed a legitimate aspiration and has erred only in the ardour of statement of his own particular interests without a full understanding of the case for the other side.[6] In my own view, publishing history and literary history are often too closely connected to have searching inquiries into the publication background dismissed as the sport of collectors and booksellers. I grant that to a serious literary student some manifestations of an exclusive interest in publication problems may seem rather trivial,

5 John Carter, 'Some Bibliographical Agenda', in *Nineteenth Century English Books* (University of Illinois, 1952), p. 80.

6 Since this matter will be taken up from time to time, no full discussion need be given here. I should perhaps say, however, that being a pedagogue, like Professor Davis, I share his esteem for text and hold in highest estimation that form of bibliography which is intended to illuminate textual problems. On the other hand, as I have tried to explain in my paper on 'Bibliography, Pure Bibliography, and Literary Studies', referred to above, I am unwilling to see analytical bibliography limited only to a direct application to textual problems. I must say, however, that I have not observed, at least as common experience, any great fascination with analytical bibliography among collectors and booksellers, as he suggests. If so, the organs devoted exclusively to their special interests have effectively concealed the fact. Mr. Carter's strictures on my overly narrow concept of scholarship are perhaps just, even though I had thought to have given the evidence of which he speaks somewhat longer shrift than he allows me. Perhaps it is proper to define scholarship more by method than by subjects suitable for its attention and to take our chance on ending with angels dancing on the point of a pin. A difficulty is, if in my academic provincialism I do not exaggerate, that persons trained in scholarly method are most often actively associated with the universities. This being so, they come under the influence of university authorities in regard to the direction of their research and its dissemination in teaching; and as a general academic discipline these authorities take a conservative view about the close study of publishing history in connection with demonstrating one's ability to instruct students in a critical view of literature. The difficulty seems to be, then, to find the persons sufficiently trained in method who can be professionally interested in such investigation, and who can thus—to reverse the adage —drive out the bad money.

as in earnest discussions of the priority of this or that state of the binding. But evidence that can be evolved from such matters can sometimes be applied to the sheets and may thus be of service in helping to reveal concealed impressions of a book, by this means throwing considerable light on the author's popularity with his public. I should not wish, however, to defend publishing history only as it may have direct literary implications. It is a legitimate field for inquiry in its own right. But legitimate as it is, the fact that it is most often pursued apart from literary study in a period of printing when the text is less affected than with earlier books by publication problems should not, I think, lead to dismissal of the heart of our interest in any book, as 'mere text'. Definitely, both these interests are legitimate and must be served in a descriptive bibliography. I suggest, however, that the clash of interests would be materially simplified if it were clearly recognized by both sides that much of what they are demanding cannot be contained in the formal bibliographical description itself, which places on record the physical characteristics of the sheets of a book and their contents. Rather, both are in part confusing the requirements and methods of this description with what is in fact ancillary to the description proper; that is, the information contained in illustrative notes on collateral as well as on analytical material. My own view is that the basic form of a standard bibliographical description that a careful bibliographer would contrive supplies both parties indifferently with close to the maximum information which either wants from the details of the description itself. The interpretation of these details and the summoning up of allied evidence is another matter.

The printed description of a book in a bibliography is like the visible tip of an iceberg, the submerged four-fifths corresponding to the unseen investigation which underlies and supports the description. To a certain degree—as I shall try to bring out when I come to the question of identifying copies from a description—the form of the description is often in part dictated, or at least should be dictated, by the nature and extent of the research. By this I mean that if the bibliographer has been deficient in the number of copies he has examined, or in his method of examination, then clearly a reader will feel safer with a fully detailed description than with a condensed one which lacks sufficient data to identify and isolate forms of the book that the bibliographer may readily have overlooked. On the other hand, if both in extent and in method the bibliographer has emphasized range and exactness, some condensation in description may safely be allowed if this is confined to such detail which has as its chief purpose the identification of unrecorded forms of the book.

Since in some respects my descriptions of the plays will be condensed, I have tried to examine all copies in about thirty collections in the United States and in England. Many of these plays being of no great rarity, and some libraries possessing duplicates, I shall have seen an average of twenty to thirty copies of many editions, and for the scarcer items at least all the copies recorded which are not in private hands.[7] I do not list any copy which I have not personally examined either by direct handling or on microfilm. By the generosity of my university and of the Richmond Area University Centre, I possess and travel with a complete microfilm of every edition and issue of the plays with which I am concerned, these films serving as a series of control copies. When I go to a library to record its collection, I utilize its Recordak projector, or else a portable projector of my own which can be set up anywhere and used in daylight. Every copy of every play which I record is compared page by page against my control microfilm by checking its salient typographical features to ensure that the typesetting of each page is the same as in my control and that it is printed from the same imposition. I also use additional microfilm in some quantities, since I have had filmed for deposit in my university's library the entire collection of every important United States library to which it was impossible for me to travel, in cases where loan of books was prohibited by the terms of foundation or by a narrow application of the principle of 'the full reading room'.

This method of comparison is not only, curiously, faster than the conventional way of comparing copies against one's notes, but it is to the highest degree more accurate.[8] I need hardly say that in this process I have

7 Except when books are of great rarity the bibliographer is perhaps best advised to confine his records to those copies which are in a place of permanent deposit and therefore always available for scholarly research.

8 There is, of course, nothing esoteric about this method: all it does is to reproduce the conditions to infinity of a duplicate set of copies in one library, which under any system a bibliographer would carefully compare page by page. As for speed, with practice one learns quickly to flick one's eye down the page, comparing the copy in one's hand against the film-image for identical alignment and composition of headline in relation to the type-page, one or two prominent typographical peculiarities in the type-page itself including alignments, and the alignment of any signatures. Different impositions are most readily detected by comparing the relation of the running-title or of the headline pagination to the type-page. The typography and alignment of running-titles may thus be seen at a glance rather than painfully disentangled from a series of notes and drawings, page by page. One may compare two title-pages in this manner, also, faster than one can read and collate against notes. Accuracy resides not only in the detection of untranscribable matters but also in relation to many matters of concern to the investigtion and writing-up. For example, except for notes on variants it would be possible not to write up descriptions until one is ready for the press, since all the essential facts are stored on film. This saves time, since as comparisons progress one must often modify considerably an early written description, and then retype it for press. Moreover, it is almost inevitable that as one's investigations continue, early conceived methods of description may require modification on experience. It is very difficult to be consistent in revising one's notes and descriptions to take account of a newly developed change in method; and often when one can see copies only in libraries

been able to discover reimpositions, partial resettings, new closely re-printed editions, and miscellaneous variants to an astonishing number and to an extent which, according to my experience, would have proved impossible by any other method.[9] Not the least valuable, I estimate, has been my ability to detect the making up of copies from sheets or leaves of various editions and thus to warn my readers where they are and of what they are composed. Conversely, if no record to this effect is found in my listing of the copies, the user of any recorded copy can be assured that it is the assigned edition for every leaf. I believe this method of comparison against a constant control is good scientific bibliography and is, in fact, the only safe method to employ.[10] I can guarantee that it is practicable and indeed time-saving. From my experience with the method as applied to books of no great rarity, I think I can state that though it is not impossible that an unknown edition of a recorded Restoration play-title may be turned up somewhere after the bibliography is published, the odds against this happening decrease materially with every copy over a dozen or so that

----

a considerable amount of rechecking is necessary. But when one has every edition and issue on film, one has a constant and convenient check whenever desired. Finally, film enables one to check one's final description back against the originals without difficulty; and even to read proof against the originals without stirring from one's own study. The fearful uncertainty that often assails a bibliographer relying on notes and title-page photostats as to his accuracy can never trouble the possessor of a library on film.

9 A bibliographer who has only a series of notes and photostats of title-pages is helpless to detect many such variants unless he is so fortunate as to find them in duplicate copies in the same library. With a film control copy they are always detectable, and immediate collation of the text can be engaged in for any purpose. For example, so far as I know at present, the fact that sheet F in part 2 of D'Urfey's *Massaniello*, 1699, exists in two settings could not be discovered from duplicate holdings—and certainly not from notes.

10 It is, of course, expensive and on any really large scale cannot be engaged in without subvention. Yet when one surveys the history of scholarship and sees the number of faulty publications on important subjects which by the very fact of their existence inhibit a fresh attempt with proper methods and resources, a question arises over the ethics of pre-empting a major bibliographical subject unless one has assurance of financial grants sufficient to permit one to adopt a method which can lead to definitive results. Discussion of the place of money in producing scholarship is a more ticklish subject in the arts than in the sciences, but we shall gain nothing by looking daintily the other way whenever the subject is broached. My scientist friends are by no means so diffident. Moreover, it would seem that conditions in the arts are already in process of change for this generation, and I suspect will accelerate for the next. Whether we like it or not, the attack of scholarship on large-scale projects these days can be made only from well-financed bases. Whether such resources are available will more and more in the future, I am afraid, dictate the subject (since treatment ought not to be affected if it proposes to be scholarly) to which one can most fruitfully devote oneself. I am happy to be informed that at least the newer British universities as a general rule, like their American counterparts, recognize the need to assist with the expenses for research in the humanities on which members of their staffs are engaged.

one can examine; and I have set twenty to thirty as my ideal when they are available. I do believe, however, that I can guarantee that in the copies I list as examined there will not be hidden any unrecognized edition, impression, or issue, and I hope no variant state of the kinds that I record.

The accuracy of investigation which this method promotes has, I believe, important implications The first affects the form of the description, and the second the amount of information which can be provided for the users of the bibliography. As concerns the form, there are three specific matters to which it is worth calling attention. First, although my description of the earliest edition and its issues is relatively full, the fullness and precision, however useful for the purpose, are not aimed primarily at offering identifying details to enable the reader to detect editions which were unknown to me. However, since the variant states of parts of the book may be more numerous than I shall have had opportunity to view and record,[11] the possible detection of such variants from my description has carried some weight. Secondly, the opportunity to make a far-reaching and minute examination has helped to solve one of the most vexing problems in descriptive bibliography, the question of what form to give the descriptions of editions after the first. From a strictly bibliographical point of view, which considers all books only as they are tangible objects, the twentieth edition is just as interesting and even as important as the first, since it is a part of the total publishing and textual history of the author, without regard for the authority contained in the text. The textual critic, concerned only with these questions of authority, will have small opinion of this twentieth edition and would view an elaborate description of it as quite out of proportion. Yet for the student of publishing history in general, or of the specific publishing and literary history of this author in particular, the form taken by a late edition may be just as significant as that of an earlier.

However, I have followed the general custom of giving a less detailed description of the form of a book in editions after the first, and have done so with more confidence because my own examination of these late editions has been just as scrupulous and wide as for textually more important editions. Hence elaborateness is less needed for reasons of identification; and I have been able to refer back to the detailed description of the first

11 A tolerable number of variant states which have analytical or textual interest are for some plays known to me in only a single copy. The rewritten text in sheet H of Dryden's *Albion and Albanius*, 1685, is a good example; the important cancellandum in the preliminaries of his *King Arthur*, 1691, is another. A third concerns a most interesting series of reimpositions in the last of the 1696 editions of *The Indian Emperour* made to avoid having to throw away a very small quantity of misprinted sheets. I have perhaps half a dozen or more similar examples in my notes. Many such variants must have been produced in relatively small numbers and hence may not turn up among copies seen in even a scrupulously wide range of examination.

edition, usually in a simplified manner, for whatever description was necessary to help bring an absent book before the mind's eye.

The third way in which my method of investigation has affected the form of the description is in lending an authority to quasi-facsimile transcription, a feature of description which it is becoming increasingly fashionable to attack. I wish I had more opportunity to inquire into this matter, for it is one of considerable importance. So far as I can see the basis for the attack on quasi-facsimile transcription, it represents the feeling that such transcription provides an imperfect means for identification. The argument needs examination. Before books can be used, they must be acquired. They can be systematically acquired only when differentiated. The demands of the acquirer on the bibliographer, therefore, fall into two parts as concern identification. First, the bibliographer must by his own investigation identify all different forms of the book. Depending upon the scholarly minuteness of his study, he should not only differentiate each edition, but within each edition the one or more impressions which comprise the edition; then within each impression the one or more identified issues; and finally, within each issue, the variant states conventionally found worthy of mention.[12] Not all acquirers need such a complete breakdown of the total information, but each will need some of it. Ordinarily the acquirer is not interested in the bibliographical processes by which this family tree of identification and differentiation has been constructed, or with the textual or publishing history associated with it. All that is required is that a differentiation be made between the major forms of the book, and suitable information be given of what constitutes minor forms. The second demand is that the points of difference in each form of the book be so recorded as to enable the acquirer to identify any copy in his hand as definitely from a certain edition, impression, and issue—and occasionally state—of the book described. Nothing else concerns such a consultant but ascertaining this single fact. Identification pure and simple.

The important, indubitable fact that descriptive bibliographies are of major service to systematic acquisition of books by collectors and libraries has led, in my opinion, to some fallacious thinking about the form that description should take, by giving undue prominence and false complexity

12 Ordinarily we may expect a bibliographer, at a minimum, to record variants to any feature of the book which he lists or transcribes. In the first category would certainly come variants within the collational formula for a book, including anything to do with the register of the signatures or the numbering of the pages. A transcript is usually made of the title-page, frequently of the head-title and running-titles, and sometimes of the headings to parts of the book including such information as inscriptions and subscriptions. We cannot expect the bibliographer to record all proof corrections within the text proper made in press, for he would have no means of determining these short of full textual collation except for such as accidentally call themselves to his attention.

to quite simple problems of identification. For example, some bibliographical theorists are so concerned with the problem of identification that
they believe ordinary methods of description cannot ensure sufficient accuracy; and hence, whenever practicable, photographic reproductions of
title-pages should replace the familiar compromise represented by quasi-
facsimile transcription.[13]

Under certain conditions I have no quarrel with this school, although
the most recent writer in its favour has given me one by wrenching out of
context to relate to photography a sentence from my book which was
written to apply specifically to the superiority of quasi-facsimile to simplified transcription, photographic facsimile excluded. Nevertheless, this
facsimile principle is so very important—since if adopted it would change
the face of every descriptive bibliography—that it is worth considering
in some detail. In my opinion photographic facsimiles of title-pages may be
useful supplements to transcription, but they are no such cure-alls that we
can set up their utilization as a necessary or even as a generally desirable
principle. As I see it, the theory on which they are advocated has a major
fallacy. First, let me emphasize that the positive identification which they
are supposed to give is not to assist the user of the bibliography to identify
his copy as belonging to one of two or more known and identified editions.
This simple identification can be managed much more conveniently and
accurately by standard descriptive methods.[14] Please notice that what is
in question is the whole book, and not just the title-page as the sole
source of identification. That there has indeed been some confusion about

13 This view was recently argued in some detail by Philip Gaskell, in a letter printed
in *The Library*, 5th series, vii (1952), 135–7.

14 It will often happen that the typesetting of a reprint is so close that a very careful
and time-consuming examination must be made to separate the two title-pages. Very
often, some small point, but one easily overlooked, can be emphasized in a transcription
to serve instantly as the point of separation between two identified and described titles.
Thus the two 1669 editions of Dryden's *Secret-Love* are perhaps most quickly distinguished in their titles by whether or not *Maiden-Queen* begins with a display or a
regular-fount M. One of the three 1670 editions of *The Indian Emperour* has its title
most quickly identified by whether the spelling is *Emperor*. When points like these are
properly emphasized by special notation in a transcribed title, the reader can make his
identification faster than by poring over two greatly similar titles in search of identifying
details. However, a reader seeking the fastest and surest method of identifying any
given copy is better advised to skip the title-page and to check off certain invariable
points that should be listed within a book. For example, if he held a copy of Buckingham's *Rehearsal*, the 1687 edition, with imprint so shaved as to destroy the date, this
edition could be most readily distinguished from the 1683, of which it is a close reprint,
by looking at the running-titles. These are regular throughout the 1683 edition; but
a description of the 1687 edition would list the fact that no stop was present after the
running-title on CF1, BE2, GH3, and that a plain italic R was found, instead of the
usual swash, on B3, DF4. Incidentally, these are not only superb identifying points but
also very illuminating pieces of information about the press-work for this edition.

precisely what it is that is being identified by a photograph is in my opinion due to the curious fallacy that the title-page is the most important single feature of identification that exists for a book. Thus, it is argued tacitly, if we photograph the title-page we have in some major substance identified the book.

I feel that this is a rather naïve point of view. Nothing is more detachable than a title-leaf. The majority of imperfect copies of plays I have encountered, for example, have lacked this leaf and sometimes the whole of the preliminaries. Moreover, it is not unknown that the title-leaf alone, or the whole of the first preliminary gathering (sometimes including one or more text gatherings for good measure) can be transferred from an imperfect copy of an early edition to make up a superficially perfect example though chiefly composed of sheets of a later edition. If we place such confidence in our ability to identify books by their title-pages that we fail to describe other matters in the more important body of the book, we are misleading a reader by providing him with insufficient information to identify an imperfect copy lacking the title, or by recording in a bibliography the presence of such and such an edition in a library when in fact it is a dangerous made-up bastard copy.[15] If we are sincere in desiring to record the true details by which to identify books, let us deliberately describe books as if they had no title-leaves, and choose, rather, variants in running-titles,[16] measurements of type-pages,[17] measurements of the gutters be-

15 It has been very correctly suggested to me that the use of a photograph for the title does not preclude careful description of the body of the book. In theory this is right, but I have not observed it in practice. The question is in part one of emphasis. The employment of unusual 'scientific' means like photographic facsimiles of titles places so much emphasis on this feature as to lead, so far as I have observed, to a false confidence in its efficacy. Indeed, the advocates of facsimile are often those who are foremost in arguing for a reduction of the detail of descriptions in the body of the book— who query, for example, on the grounds of expense, the usefulness of transcribing minute running-title variants, and so on. Even bibliographers who examine collections armed only with a photostat of each title and notes for the body of the book are, I feel, victims of this conventional thinking. Conventional investigative methods would not disclose that a presumed copy of the first edition of Etherege's *Man of Mode*, 1676, held by a great library in this country and sold to it by a famous bookseller in good faith, is in fact composed of the first three sheets of the 1676 edition but thereafter of the second-edition gatherings of 1684. A scholar using this copy in all innocence might be seriously misled in various textual points. If the cult of the title-page persists so strongly among the investigators, we cannot expect a lesser emphasis among the users of bibliographies. The less emphasis a descriptive bibliographer gives to the employment of distinctive means for identifying any single feature of a book, the more he is likely to provide a harmonious method for over-all identification.

16 Before 1700 running-titles, when present, are perhaps the most valuable single item for identification in a description, only type-page measurement being a serious rival.

17 Since it lacked running-titles and was a line-for-line and page-for-page reprint of

tween the imposition of the type-pages, but not the tender and variable title-leaf. That the title has assumed so much prominence in bibliographical thinking is in part because it is of course convenient (if one is unaware of its dangers), and because it has sometimes a literary importance[18] and almost always an importance for publishing history.

Since with proper investigative and descriptive methods the identification of known editions of a book can be managed for the benefit of the reader in much simpler and less expensive fashion by ordinary means, what then remains of the argument that the photograph is superior to transcription for the purposes of description? There is something, certainly, to the fact that a picture gives us an image which transcription can only adumbrate. But, essentially, and for any scholarly uses, how important is it to have this precise image of only one feature of the book? I have heard it said, also, that a photographic facsimile is easier reading than a transcription. This I do not understand except for modern brief titles and a reader who is such an amateur that he is not used to the conventions of transcription. But for earlier books, to read in photo-facsimile form— usually rather less satisfactory than the original—lines of small type and uncertain inking which may cause trouble even in the document itself to determine questions of accent, pointing, and spelling, when these can be avaliable in transcription in large-size legible modern type seems to me somewhat old-fashioned, to appropriate a phrase I have heard applied to quasi-facsimile transcription.

The true argument can only be that a photo-facsimile title will identify for the reader a copy of the book in his hand which differs from any that the bibliographer has seen and reproduced.[19] Within certain limits I agree. Mr. Gaskell gives as an instance the 1757 Virgil in two editions, the title-pages of which could not be differentiated in quasi-facsimile transcription. From my knowledge of Restoration plays, I can add half a dozen or so more examples. The third and fourth editions, in 1670, of Dryden's *Indian*

---

the first edition, the second edition of the Etherege mentioned above could be distinguished as a made-up copy only by typographical measurements unless one were comparing it against a control copy.

18 In fact, the head-title is more likely for early books to reflect any title found on the manuscript. That books like incunabula without title-pages require for identification a more elaborate description than books with title-pages was one of the cardinal points of Madan's theory of degressive bibliography. I am afraid I may have paid lip-service to this theory in the past; but if so, I disown it now, and would prefer to substitute for all books the principle that they should be described as if no title-page were present..

19 Since the distinction between known and recorded editions, or the title typesettings, by no means requires the assistance of the photographic facsimile, the strongest argument in its favour becomes this of recognizing the unknown. I wish to emphasize this matter because I fancy most advocates do not appreciate the precise and narrow basis on which the photo-facsimile for any practical purposes has the advantage.

Emperour and the 1695 editions of Jevon's *Devil of a Wife* come first to mind. But these do not trouble me greatly, for there is more to description than identification, and more to identification than the title-page. Let us look at the two 1670 editions of the *Emperour* with differently set title-pages identical in every transcribable point. Suppose by criminal negligence I had seen and described only the fourth edition and not the third, and a user of my bibliography had a copy of the third in his hand. He would find no difference in my transcription of the title. I transcribe the heading to the first act in my description of the first edition, and thereafter indicate any alternations. The reader ought to see, therefore, that the word 'Country' is spelled differently in the heading for the copy he holds from that which I have indicated for the edition. If I had noted typographical differences in the dating of the dedication, he would also see a difference, but I might not do this. At any rate, when he came to compare the collational formula, he would see that the edition I was describing mispaged the whole inner forme of one sheet, whereas the copy in his hand did not. If this made him suspicious, as well it might, and he was encouraged to measure a typical type-page to compare with my figures, he would see beyond a doubt that he had a different edition in his hand. Heading, pagination formula, type-page measurement—here were three points of difference despite similar title-pages, and in spite of the fact that my bibliography treats more briefly editions after the first which have not been thoroughly recast.

If we were to put all our money on the title-page in descriptive bibliography, and as a result were inclined to reduce our account of the rest of the book, as usually happens, I too should insist on photo-facsimiles of title-pages. But for every example of similar titles not to be differentiated by quasi-facsimile, I know of differentiating points in the body of the book which in any normally full description would show variance. Moreover, for every example of similar titles I know of an instance where a photo-facsimile could be misleading. A typical example is Banks's *Cyrus the Great*, 1696, in which the first three text sheets exist in two different settings, but the two varieties have the identical title-page setting. Two editions of Southerne's *Maids Last Prayer*, 1693, have the same title-page, as do two distinct 'first' editions of Congreve's *Love for Love*, 1695, and three 'first' editions of Ogilby's coronation entertaiment of 1661. Until very recently the second edition of Lord Lansdowne's *Heroick Love*, 1698, was not distinguished from the first, in spite of the fact that it ends on sig. K4 instead of L2, since the titles of the two editions are in the same setting of type.

I do not wish to decry unduly the argument for identification, since some small part of my preference for liberal transcription of headings in the first edition stems from a desire to increase the odds in favour of identification of previously unknown forms. But these forms, I believe, are much more likely to consist of variant states of the edition under description than of new and previously unidentified editions which the reader has turned up. And for identifying most of these states, transcription is quite as satisfactory as photography, and is not confined to the title. Since there are various economic as well as mechanical difficulties with photo-facsimile, it is legitimate to inquire how serious in fact is the identification problem before we engage ourselves to considerable expense in the creation of a new requirement for bibliography.[20] In my view the answer lies almost completely with the standards by which the bibliography in question has been performed.[21] If it has been done, as far too often, by the bibliographer merely visiting two or three great libraries and looking through their copies to see if they agree with his notes, then I should favour every mechanical means for identification we can invent, in order to protect the user. Bibliography of this—to me—imprecise and elementary sort should not be excused on grounds of insufficient finances to do better work. The scholars who may be seriously misled by trusting to imperfect results obtained by half-methods will not be inclined, I should think, to accept good intentions alone as justifying the production of an over-ambitious piece of work. Check-lists, the 'bibliographies' of enumeration, may be expected to betray faults; but one would wish descriptive bibliography to be definitive.[22] As I

20 The expense may be twofold: the reader of the bibliography will be charged a higher price to cover the more expensive process, and the compiler of the bibliography may be required by his publisher to provide the photographs. Expense is not, I believe, a legitimate argument to employ to excuse bad bibliography, as is sometimes done; but the whole process of bibliography is certainly so costly in comparison with other forms of scholarship that each detail must pass some scrutiny for its usefulness and pertinence to the whole.

21 Under this head should come, of course, questions of the nature of the material. Material scarcely investigated before and tricky by nature may well need more safeguards than commonly surveyed and familiar material. It is possible that in some respects machine-printed books, because of the minuteness of evidence which may obtain for resetting, need photographic helps for identification more than the average hand-printed book, although popular authors in the eighteenth century surely present serious problems. There are certainly times when conditions are such as to put an imposing burden for identification on normal bibliographical description. In such cases it would be absurd not to make full use of mechanical aids.

22 The difficulties encountered by a bibliographer in his investigations vary, of course, not only with his material and the extent of his field but also with conditions in different countries. I am not qualified to speak of the special difficulties which face British scholars. Some account of problems when working in the United States will be found in my 'Certain Basic Problems in Descriptive Bibliography', *Papers of the Bibliographical Society of America*, xlii (1948), 211–28. Distances between collections compose only one of these problems, but a serious one. Even under impossibly ideal conditions, to have made the circuit of the collections in my own country which I am recording would have involved travelling at least 7,000 miles and perhaps two years away from home.

have mentioned, I do not in fact think that proper exactness can be guaranteed in descriptive bibliography unless a control is established for the whole volume, in the form of a private copy, photostats, or the very convenient and relatively cheap microfilm, with which I have had considerable experience.

If then we use proper methods to examine and compare copies in the investigative stage of a descriptive bibliography, it seems to me that the expensive photo-facsimile of a title-page is an unnecessary precaution, and even a confession of weakness, if it is inserted to enable the reader to continue further the bibliographical investigation, which should, of course, have been performed definitively by the original scholar. If this is so, the sole legitimate purpose of the photo-facsimile is to assist the acquirer in identifying an edition which he holds. I am sure this simple matter can be handled much more cheaply by other means so long as we can trust the bibliographer to have performed his researches according to proper scholarly standards. I am not sure that the advocates of photography as a cure-all, or even as a generally desirable thing, have always thought through their position. It would seem that in part they are influenced by the pleasure they receive from looking at a series of title-pages. This is understandable, but aesthetic enjoyment must not be allowed to interfere with methods of bibliographical scholarship when the two do not happen to coincide.[23]

My own specific position is this. I should think rather highly in most respects of a bibliography employing photo-facsimiles, first, if the problem were solved of relating the plates closely and conveniently to the appropriate printed part of the description; second, if these facsimiles were not reduced;[24] and, third, if they were not retouched. I should prefer facsimiles to be accompanied by quasi-facsimile transcription to serve as a standard and to clarify doubtful points, but one could not reasonably

---

Clearly, some travel must be supplemented by the borrowing of books through one's own library and by the extensive use of microfilm.

23 For example, a bibliographer might seriously consider whether the extra money required for photo-facsimiles of titles would not, for his material, be better spent in providing more details of description, not for the purposes of identification but to increase the general bibliographical usefulness of his work. More detail, or more precise detail, will sometimes, on practical grounds, assist a user to discover sophisticated copies, in my experience a far more common occurrence than unrecorded editions. More detail will, also, increase the bibliographical depth of the work by making it useable for research into printing practices.

24 Reduction can well be allowed for machine-printed books in a period when the title-page is not cluttered; but I do not think that reduction is at all practicable for most periods of hand-printing. [Of course, large folio titles would ordinarily require reduction.] Throughout this paper I have had most specifically in mind the problems of descriptive bibliography for early books. I am sorry for this, but exigencies of time and space left no alternative.

insist on this perhaps. However, unreduced facsimiles are very difficult to work in with the rest of the printed description without a great deal of wasted space, accompanied by a marked increase in the expenses for extra paper and presswork as well as for the cut itself. And my own experience in dealing with manufacturers of line, or zinc, cuts is that they cannot reproduce satisfactorily many a sixteenth- to eighteenth-century title-page without retouching.[25] Once retouching is admitted, it becomes basically uncontrollable by the bibliographer; and it is always, from any scholarly point of view, a form of faking. I feel strongly on this point. Mr. Gaskell has suggested that it is quite practicable to reduce title cuts to 4 by 3 inches. Doubtless this would do for modern novels (where I should gladly admit it); but from experience I believe I can state that many a crowded title of an early book would be unreadable at that or at any reduction. Possibly by the alignment of types someone could identify a variant major resetting from such a reduced cut; but the cut would often be useless for any other purpose. Advocates of reduced title-cuts for early books do not seem to take account of the fact that some users of the bibliography will actually want to read the title-page; and that with a 4 by 3 inch cut a transcription will need to be provided for this worthy purpose. If both cut and transcription must be used, then we are faced with considerably greater expense, and some duplication. I myself think it is the ideal method: I wish I could employ it. But if I must make a choice between cut and quasi-facsimile transcription, I should take the transcription, always provided the rest of the description is sufficiently full and provided the investigation has been made according to scholarly standards. May I repeat: no mechanical process can act as a substitute for such standards.

A good descriptive bibliography should assist directly the users of the books it lists, and indirectly those who come to it merely for certain kinds of information which may not require consultation of the books themselves. I cannot hope to indicate all the possible uses, apart from simple identification, that can be applied to descriptive bibliography. A bibliography—to mention only one—can specify to a literary critic, within some

---

25 As an example, line cuts were first ordered to illustrate the imprints in W. B. Todd's article on Shakespeare's Second Folio in *Studies in Bibligraphy*, v (1952). A good firm refused to make these cuts under the instructions not to retouch, and insisted on the use of more expensive offset. Unless the individual bibliographer controls every step in the process of making a cut—and usually this is impracticable—he cannot guarantee that retouching has not taken place, since its use is so normal in cut making that it is taken for granted by the manufacturers. In order to control the process the bibliographer would need to demand to see the photographs from which the negatives were to be made before passing them as suitable provided these prints were not themselves retouched; and he would need to demand assurances, much more difficult, that the negative had not been doctored subsequently.

limits, the most suitable edition, or that best form of the most suitable edition for him to utilize. I qualify this statement, for I do not see how, ordinarily, a descriptive bibliographer can be responsible for collating the texts, which is the only way he could discover in some cases without notice that a particular edition after the first has been authoritatively revised; or that a title-page claim to revision is in fact untrue. I happen to know that Dryden revised the second edition of *The Indian Emperour* in 1668, and the third edition in 1670, and no other edition thereafter.[26] But I know this from having edited the play, not from having described it bibliographically. Nevertheless, in my bibliography the critic will at least find three editions listed and differentiated in 1670 instead of the previously recorded two, and he will find them in their right order, which has previously been confused. So much, I hope, will be found for every play I treat. In such cases the descriptive bibliographer must collate text provided this is the only means for deciding or for confirming the correct order of editions. From collation alone can one confirm that the three 1696 editions of *The Indian Emperour* have commonly been listed in reverse order of publication. From collation alone can it be known that of the three 1684 editions of Dryden's *State of Innocence* the commonly listed fifth edition is in fact the third, and the commonly esteemed third is in fact the ninth, a late misdated piracy. Or that the eighth and ninth editions as commonly described are in fact the eighth and seventh, in reverse order.[27] To this extent a descriptive bibliography can prepare the ground for criticism by accurately differentiating editions and assigning them their right order. It can also help criticism by determining and recording the full and ideal form of the various editions listed.[28] It can warn not only of major alterations in press but also of cancels, and indicate, when discovered, the characteristics of the two forms of uncancelled and cancelled leaves. Any biographer must consult a bibliography, for the history of the author's brain-children is part of the biography of that author. The publishing history of the author may be illuminated; and in some circumstances his

26 'Current Theories of Copy-Text, with an Illustration from Dryden', *Modern Philology*, xlviii (1950), 12–20.

27 M. H. Hamilton, 'The Early Editions of Dryden's *State of Innocence*', *Studies in Bibliography*, v (1952), 163–6; and my 'The Pirated Quarto of Dryden's *State of Innocence*', ibid., pp. 166–70.

28 For example, some important alterations were made to the text of Crowne's *City Politiques*, 1683, while sheet K was going through the press. Since the second edition of 1688 follows the expanded form, a critic who knew only the unaltered state of sheet K in 1683 would believe that fresh authority had entered the text in 1688, whereas in truth the second edition is a mere reprint. Yet if a critic took it that in this place the 1688 edition had been authoritatively revised, he would be bound to give some possible authority to other variants elsewhere in the second edition, whereas these are in fact printer's corruptions.

textual history may be clarified. A record of the location of copies of the various forms, and of their completeness or imperfection, is of enormous assistance to students. It is difficult to limit the uses which can be found for the analytical determination of ideal copy within a series of correctly arranged editions, the relation of all variants to this ideal copy, and everything in the editions that in a printing and publishing way happened to the book within its life.

I do not maintain that a descriptive bibliographer should do all of a textual critic's work for him; but I do suggest that any editor or critic of Restoration drama can be somewhat fortified if he knows that a bibliographer has gone over his material first and will guarantee that every page of every listed copy is in the same setting and imposition unless specific exceptions have been made. And that bibliographical determination has been made of all known problems, such as the separation and the order of the two unrecorded editions of Betterton's *Prophetess* in 1690 and of Buckingham's *Chances* in 1692, the three 'first editions' of Ogilby's *Entertainment* in 1661, the two recorded editions of Southerne's *Fatal Marriage* in 1694, of Shadwell's *Psyche* in 1675, and so on. Or if, say, he is editing Lee's plays, and wants to collate for variant readings all the seventeenth-century editions, that the piracies of three plays will be outlined for him, which otherwise he might never discover and separate from the legitimate editions.[29] It should be of some comfort to know which of two leaves in Lee's *Princess of Cleve,* 1689, was intended for cancellation;[30] that the ideal copy of the cancel leaf in Congreve's *Double Dealer,* 1694, can be found in only one recorded example but can be reconstructed bibliographically from others;[31] that there is no cancel in Southerne's *Disappointment,* 1684;[32] that the order of the first two editions of Dryden's *Wild Gallant,* 1669, is such and such and not the reverse;[33] that bibliographical demonstration can be made of the order of the two settings for sheets B–D in Banks's *Cyrus the Great,* 1696;[34] that there are two different type-settings of the single leaf g1 which bridges the two-section printing of Crowne's *Country Wit,* 1675; that the cancelland leaves containing the original ending for the second act of Payne's *Morning Ramble,* 1673, may be found, so

29 'Nathaniel Lee: Three Probable Seventeenth-Century Piracies', *Papers of the Bibliographical Society of America,* xliv (1950), 62–66.

30 'A Crux in the Text of Lee's *Princess of Cleve,* 1689, II, i', *Harvard Library Bulletin,* iv (1950), 409–11.

31 'The Cancel Leaf in Congreve's *Double Dealer,* 1694', *Papers of Bibliographical Society of America,* xliii (1949), 78–82.

32 'The Supposed Cancel in Southerne's *The Disappointment* Reconsidered', *The Library,* 5th series, v (1950), 140–9.

33 'The First Edition of Dryden's *Wild Gallant,* 1669', ibid., 51–54.

34 'The Variant Sheets in John Banks's *Cyrus the Great,* 1696', *Studies in Bibliography,* iv (1951), 174–83.

far as I know at the moment, only in copies at Lincoln College, Oxford, and the University of Michigan; that there is a unique completely reset forme in the Worcester College, Oxford, copy of D'Avenant's *Man's the Master*, 1669; that there is a reimposed sheet in Dryden's *Spanish Friar*, 1681; that there are more editions of Vanbrugh's *Aesop*, 1697, than have been listed, and more of Jevon's *Devil of a Wife*, 1695, than have been recorded; and so on.

These are all problems which lie in the bibliographer's own work of identification and ordering before he even comes to making up his descriptions. It has been suggested that the descriptions themselves should be written in a form best suited to assist the textual critic, and that details of interest chiefly to the analysis of the printing and publication should be condensed or omitted. I do not really understand this point of view, for the descriptions themselves, as descriptions, and distinct from the collateral notes, are of no use to textual criticism; it is the bibliographer's prior identification and interpretation of his evidence which is of importance.[35] But the bibliographer has recognized these variant forms I have been listing by just the process of comparison (except in a more refined way) that presumably anyone with an unrecorded copy checking it against the description would use to discover variants calling for investigation. Hence to demand that the details of a description be condensed so that the textual critic may use them is in my opinion to confuse the wider purposes of bibliographical description and indeed to assist in removing all possibility for the discovery of further variants in copies not seen by the bibliographer. I cannot emphasize too strongly that all detail about printing practice is of textual concern, since any abnormality anywhere in the book may have textual repercussions. It is strange to have these printing variants, the raw material for analytical bibliography, named as of interest only to collectors. Does a bibliographer list a book with a variant page number at a certain place? If the forme were unlocked to alter the pagination, possibly textual alterations were made at the same time: an editor had better collate the text of that forme very carefully in the variant copies. Is a book printed simultaneously in two sections? Either the listing in the description of typographical differences in running-titles or of differences in the type-page measurements should reveal this important fact for textual criticism, since the text will be affected by the characteristics of more than one compositor.[36] Every minute piece of the printing history of the book is of crucial

35 One may query of what use to textual criticism were the bibliographical descriptions of the two 1669 editions of Dryden's *Wild Gallant* when they were given in the wrong order. The descriptions themselves could reveal nothing of the correct order; yet if an editor had followed the bibliographer's misassignment of these two editions he would have used a derived edition for his copy-text and would have reprinted some important errors.

36 I myself treasure such titbits as the following: in George Granville Lord

textual concern; and if the bibliographer, who is in the best position to work out this history, is prevented from making such evidence known, it will very likely become permanently lost. Textual students may reasonably expect a certain amount of bibliographical pre-digestion for their benefit; but they must not try to influence either the presentation of evidence on which conclusions are based, or the simple presentation of evidence without conclusions, for sometimes the conclusions can be appropriately drawn only by the textual critic or the generalizing analytical bibliographer. What is important is to recognize that one simply cannot separate any operation of the printer from its possible textual consequences.[37] I could

---

Lansdowne's *She-Gallants*, 1696, the printer's measure in the preliminaries is 116 mm. The text starting on sig. B1 is set to a measure of 111 or 112 mm. on B1 and B1^v but thereafter between B2 and F4^v changes to 116 mm. From G1 to the conclusion on L2^v, the measure reverts to 111 or 112 mm. I propose to print this information in my bibliography and shall be disappointed if any textual critic of the play ignores its implications, for if he knows his business he will see that he has been given important information about the compositors. I am not engaging in bibliographical virtuosity in purveying such information based on the listing of minute detail: I am trying to assist the critic who may not be aware, before he comes to descriptions, that such evidence can exist. So far as I have had experience in my own work both with analytical and descriptive bibliography and also with textual criticism, my feeling is that a textual critic would be better advised to demand from a descriptive bibliographer the maximum of detail rather than the minimum. It is not beyond all possibility that an advanced textual critic will know better than a descriptive bibliographer (who may not have had editorial and critical experience) how to apply bibliographical evidence to textual problems. Correspondingly, some detail in a bibliographical description may excite the interest of a textual critic to find its application in cases—not wholly uncommon—where the descriptive bibliographer knows more than he does. Thus if I were an editor and were engaged on the text of *She Ventures and He Wins*, 1696, the information that the preliminaries in sheet A and the first text sheet B were set to a 123 mm. measure, sheet C to 120 mm., whereas D–G to 130 mm., might save me from some unwarranted assumptions about the applicability of evidence from sheet D, say, to a crux in sheet B. And if I were a textual bibliographer searching in bibliographies to improve my acquaintance with printing conditions in the period affecting text, I should find this evidence useful. Finally, if I were an analytical bibliographer reading bibliographies to assess evidence about printing practices, I should be glad to find in those measurements confirmation for the fact that in some first editions the preliminaries might be set first, not last. I might have suspected it, of course, if the bibliographer had pointed out—as he ought—that the catchword on A4^v was 'He' for head-title 'She' on B1, even if the bibliographer had not seen and recorded the unique copy at the University of Illinois in which the head-title reads, in error, 'He Ventures, and She Wins', and this error is found uniquely in the running-titles of the outer forme, demonstrating also that in this case the outer forme passed first through the press, from which fact certain assumptions can be made about the rate of compositorial to press speed and thus about the number of copies printed. Reduce the details of description indeed!

37 Moreover, one must recognize that bibliography and text are interrelated for *all* editions, not merely for textually authoritative editions. In order to deal properly with all details of an authoritative text a critic must have an intimate knowledge of how text

illustrate this point at length, but I must pass on to a swift survey of two other matters before I close.

The first I must simply state and then move on. The mass of bibliographical detail contained in a good bibliography may superficially have no direct textual or publication bearing; but it will eventually be used somehow by the bibliographer. A late seventeenth-century quarto of Shakespeare may be of no consequence whatever to the textual critic of Shakespeare, although the information about who printed it, and how, may unexpectedly illuminate a similar problem in Dryden of extreme textual pertinence. (I hasten to add, this is a hypothetical example, only.) If one rules out from descriptive bibliography the recording of interesting detail because it seems to have no pertinence, one will be calling down on one's head the curses of the next generation, which may have found a most ingenious use for the evidence. As I have remarked elsewhere, if even McKerrow, whom I venerate, could write of press-figures only that they seemed to have little bibliographical significance, a view which Dr. Todd has shown to be shortsighted, it is difficult for us lesser students to feel fully capable of estimating the value for the future of some kinds of bibliographical evidence merely because at the moment we do not see how to apply it. Moreover, some of this evidence is always applicable, at least to the analytical bibliographer in search of material. For bibliographies are also, I maintain, written to assist that neglected scholar the bibliographer, who seldom seems to be envisaged as a user. Bibliographies, I hold, should be written to advance bibliographical knowledge. The fact that they often have such important mundane uses as assisting the acquisition of books, or helping a textual critic about his business, should not blind us to the fact that they are also independent works of bibliographical scholarship which need to be consulted by research bibliographers. To insist that description be so denuded of bibliographical detail that whenever a bibliographer wants to ascertain some fact about printing, like the uses of running-titles and of press-figures for analysing presswork, he must order up from his library a miscellaneous group of books without knowing what they contain to his purpose, and that he should never be able to secure such evidence from a bibliography is a singularly shortsighted view which can cause much harm. But at present I cannot elaborate this subject.

I shall close with a few hasty generalizations about degressive bibliography,* a phrase increasing in popular esteem at the moment. Madan popularized this phrase not quite fifty years ago,[38] although I think almost

is corrupted by the printing or copying process. This he can best learn by working closely with tracing the mutations of text through unauthoritative editions, with due regard for the bibliographical information which can be extended to these editions.

* A fuller discussion may be found, later, in "Bibliography Revisited."

38 F. Madan, *Transactions of the Bibliographical Society*, ix (1906–8), 53–65.

nothing has been done with it since his day. To Madan degressive bibliography meant varying the description according to the differences in the period treated or the importance of the work to be described. There was no conflict for him between these two essentially divergent criteria, since it seemed self-evident at the time that *incunabula* for period, and for importance, required a very full description, and a late machine-printed book practically no detail. Those who are now advocating the theory of degression as applied to bibliography are the first to disclaim Madan's own interpretation and practice;[39] but so far as I am aware they have offered little but generalizations to fill the resulting vacuum, and are still forced back on the basic inconsistency in practice which degression would permit. One critic, it is true, agrees substantially with Madan in the proportions of detail he assigned to incunables and on up to machine-printed books; and would apply the degressive principle (which in practice always seems to mean *less* detail) to books of no textual significance. Another believes that the formula for description which I advocate is unnecessarily elaborate even for the books for which it was designed;[40] and that for later periods more elasticity (i.e., degression)—nature unspecified—should be permitted.[41]

39 In practice, only incunables would receive what we should now call a bibliographical description. Books of the sixteenth and seventeenth centuries, and perhaps of the eighteenth, would receive what would approximate to a full catalogue entry. The short entry, which 'befits modern literature', would correspond roughly to an enumerative check-list form. In theory, Madan did not provide any definition of what is to guide a bibliographer in estimating the 'importance' of a work. Right or wrong as the chonological practice may be, it at least produces consistency. But if within a coherent subject or a coherent period some books are amplified in description and others condensed according to 'importance', some very inconsistent results are going to be secured; and critics had better begin to define what is 'important'. I wish them joy of the worm.

40 This I deny.

41 I should speculate, instead, that the bibliographers of the future dealing with machine-printed books with any minuteness will find that more elaboration of detail, rather than less, will be found necessary if the central problem of identifying unmarked impressions is to be solved. I suspect that the attempt to solve the problem will take the form of extremely technical detail of measurements, paper study, study of damage to plates in storage between impressions, and so on. If this is to apply the principle of degressive bibliography according to the nature of the material treated, to bring up and to emphasize appropriate evidence in place of less appropriate evidence, then I am for it, and always have been even to the extent of separating in my book the problems and methods of bibliographical description for hand-printed and for machine-printed books. But my impression is that for later-printed books (perhaps the most complex and baffling form of printing one can deal with) present views imply by degression the right to deal with less detail than for relatively simple earlier printing, perhaps for fear of alienating the general reader by too much technical evidence. If this is the way of degressive bibliography, to throw out evidence without substituting at least an equal amount of more valid evidence for the changed conditions, then I am not for it and do not

I am hesitant to advocate any method which relies on the bibliographer's own decision as to what is significant and non-significant evidence, or on which edition is textually significant or not. I do not hold that the bibliographer is an ignorant mole burrowing his way under literature without regard for the sunlight of the content. I merely wish to point out that definitions of what is significant vary according as the definer is a textual critic, a literary historian, a recorder of publishing history, or an analytical bibliographer. There can be no common agreement between these as to what is significant to preserve, according to the degressive principle, and what to discard; and in fact there can only be conflict since each ultimately would like to be bibliography's sole master. Under these circumstances I am hesitant about attempting to discern any general principles which one can reasonably apply to clarify the workings of degressive bibliography, other than the two stated below, without unbalancing the nature, purposes, and methods of bibliographical description.

In practice I see a rough and ready form of degression working itself out in accordance with the amount and the acuteness of investigation which descriptive bibliographers have devoted to their subject within the range of their abilities; but I should hesitate to offer this Darwinian natural selection as a principle. The only two degressive principles that I really know, and that I attempt to apply myself, are: (1) changes in the mechanical processes by which books are printed should have small effect on the general amount of detail offered in a description but should certainly affect the nature of the detail according to the period and the art treated; and (2) a full description of one edition, which by convenience and convention is ordinarily the first, may relieve the bibliographer from offering equally full detail in later editions when this is chiefly repetitive. The loss of significant detail is not therefore very great, and the descriptions of editions after the first may be materially simplified so long as they remain relatively similar reprints. But since this particular form of degressiveness is only a matter of commonsense convenience, if some key late edition underwent a change in form and itself became the copy for a subsequent series of reprints, thus requiring detail in its description to which they could refer, I should myself feel it necessary on purely bibliographical

---

prophesy a bright future which will attract many scholars to such a debased and vulgarized procedure, no matter how directly the principle may stem from Madan's restricted views on the value of dealing bibliographically with late printing. As a matter of fact, when the technicians really get to work on the problems of machine-printing, I rather suspect that the general reader and the bibliographer who has catered to him are due to suffer a shock. For an interesting start in generalizing about evidence which can be drawn from a study of plate variation and machine printing, see C. R. Coxe, 'The Pre-Publication Printings of Tarkington's *Penrod*', *Studies in Bibliography*, v (1952), 156–7.

grounds to revert temporarily to my original fullness of description.[42] These two categories, as I take it, represent allowable degressive bibliography on bibliographical principles, not on principles brought to bibliography from outside by the special interests of historian or of textual critic.

Until his discipline is better understood than it is at present, the bibliographer—it seems to me—will always, perhaps, fail to satisfy completely each class of user of a descriptive bibliography. It is inevitable that each will make such demands for its own special interests that to give way to any school would seriously unbalance a bibliography. As I stated at the beginning, I advocate as desirable and necessary the service which descriptive bibliography can perform to various fields of conflicting interest. But in this process I believe that bibliography will suffer if it falls under the domination of any other discipline and is thus untrue to its own principles. I am conscious that the concept of bibliography as a means to an end, as the servant of literary and historical studies, is one which is popularly held and will not readily be relinquished. I must, I am afraid, place myself in opposition to this view. Bibliography in its several essential forms is, I hold, an end in itself and not a means to an end; it is an independent discipline of scholarship and not merely an ancillary technique to literary investigation.[43] Textual and literary criticism, and literary history, may draw on its findings, as they necessarily must; but this does not mean that the reservoir of bibliographical knowledge and its future development should run through only one set of pipes to end in a faucet that can be turned on or off at will. I believe we are in a period which is witnessing bibliography coming of age: the sooner we all adjust our thinking to this new concept, the better bibliography we shall have—the immediate concern of this society—and, I make bold to say, what is our broader concern, the better criticism and history.

42 This is substantially what I had in mind in my remarks in *Principles*, pp. 383 ff., about 'parent' editions and their subsidiaries.

43 Arguments in favour of this view will be found in *Papers of the Bibliographical Society of America*, xlvi (1952), 186–208, referred to above.

Bibliography and
Restoration Drama

IN A LIBRARY that houses one of the country's great collections of Restoration plays, it is certainly suitable for me to discuss the bibliographical problems posed by a large-scale survey of the Restoration drama. The heart of the matter is, of course, what contribution can the methods of bibliography make to an orderly account of these plays, and for what purpose? Then, perhaps the question may intrude whether the results have been commensurate with the effort, the expenditure of time and of money.

One may as well state clearly at the start that any bibliographical inquiry into the Restoration drama would scarcely rise above the level of a hobby if it did not have a precisely defined end in view. It is not enough to say that the end is the discovery of all available information: if information remains indefinitely in one's card file as a source of private satisfaction, of occasional disbursement through articles and notes or in answer to personal queries, one is still operating at the level of a hobby. Instead, the end must be the public dissemination of all collected information in the form of a descriptive bibliography, no matter how painful or expensive is the process of putting together the raw material of research in an organized manner for public use.

At this point, certainly, something of an obligation exists. Admittedly, this is a free country. If a person wants to spend his life making notes about Restoration plays and their physical characteristics, that is his private affair. But if he attempts publication of a descriptive bibliography, he will be pre-empting the field. No one else is likely to engage himself to a competitive effort, nor will more than one press undertake the costs of publication of such a document. In short, one bibliography is enough, presumably forever; hence, it behooves the prospective bibliographer to devote some thought to the coverage he proposes of this literature cast in dramatic form. Particularly, a decision is required as to the amount of information that

Read at a Clark Library Seminar on May 7, 1966, in Los Angeles, California; printed in *Bibliography*, by Fredson Bowers and Lyle H. Wright (William Andrews Clark Memorial Library, University of California, Los Angeles, 1966); reprinted with permission of The William Andrews Clark Memorial Library, University of California, Los Angeles.

should be printed, and the form that this should take, in order to benefit the maximum number of users, who will certainly come to the bibliography for a multiplicity of reasons.

These considerations force a bibliographer to an attempt at definitiveness of research. That is, although no way exists to protect oneself against the unique copy of a variant in a private collection, or in some out-of-the-way small library which one would not ordinarily consult, one's coverage should be so wide as materially to reduce the odds that an unknown variant will turn up later to dim one's hopes for completeness. (The number of variants I have already seen in unique copies does not give me any great confidence, however, that an equal number still does not lie in wait, unknown and unsung, waiting for my book to be printed.)

Moreover, the method by which the known information is published should be so calculated as to serve the widest range of users that will come to the work, so long as their quest for completeness and accuracy of information is legitimate, within the reasonable limits of a descriptive bibliography's form and basic purposes. As something of a bonus, if the descriptions have been made full enough to satisfy this broad spectrum of ultimate consumers, one hopes that the information provided will enable the fortunate possessor of variants the bibliographer has not himself seen to identify these as authentic differences, and thus to make public such supplementary information as will maintain the bibliography's usefulness as a definitive work, even though annotated here and there.

Mind you, mere fullness of description without wide coverage of copies examined is scarcely enough. That is, one is hardly doing one's duty only to provide an account of some readily observable norm, with the friendly expectation that anybody can then identify variation from that norm when it occurs. Completeness of research is essential, else several major classes of users will be slighted. Analytical bibliographers interested in records of printing variants, students of publishing history, textual scholars, and finally the booksellers, collectors, and librarians who nourish these various scholarly disciplines—all these will scarcely be satisfied by any bibliography that puts the burden of investigation on them and does not itself make public the maximum information that truly comprehensive research can provide.

The bibliographical investigation of Restoration drama, therefore, is no limited subject: the problems raised not only apply to but indeed require the assistance for their solution of various kinds of bibliography, including the enumerative and historical as well as the analytical and descriptive. As a consequence, my paper attempts to give a conspectus of these problems and some account of an attempt at their solution as required for the preparation of a large-scale descriptive bibliography of Restoration plays. I

shall not confine myself simply to an account of the bibliographical variation that exists within these plays, although that matter will be touched on.
In short, method must come before results, and I shall be concerned much
with method and its rationale as applied to a concrete set of problems.

The initial problem is to define a Restoration play. The first part—the
Restoration—is more easily answered than the latter. By common consent,
a literary period that can be called "Restoration" after the first years of its
inauguration exists in a fairly homogeneous state between 1660 and 1700.
The dates are arbitrary but convenient. I have no disposition to quarrel
with them.

The second half—what is a play?—is rather more difficult to answer.
Anything that had seen the stage, or some manner of presentation like an
opera or entertainment, presents no problem. About 480 of these titles
exist in about 750 editions between 1660 and 1700, although not all of
these can be firmly distinguished from the sixty or seventy additional closet
dramas that were printed, ranging from plays by the Duchess of Newcastle
to translations of the classics not intended for stage performance. Also,
there was a handful of collections, as well as separate titles in foreign
languages. Finally, the inclusion of political pamphlets written in dramatic
form presented the most difficulty. On what may have been somewhat
subjective criteria I have selected about twenty of these as qualifying for
description.

Thus the drama that seems to merit notice in a descriptive bibliography
is far from a unified literary form. It might be argued that a bibliography
should be restricted only to those titles which evidence suggests were
actually presented in public or in private; but the evidence in this respect—
though sufficiently complete for the public stage, perhaps—could not ordinarily be extant for private performances or readings. It seemed best,
therefore, to be comprehensive in regard to all manifestations of what
might be called dramatic genre and, hence, to include reprints of classical
or European plays in their own languages as well as in translation, manifest
closet dramas, political controversies masquerading in play form, and such
public entertainments at gratulatory receptions and lord mayors' shows.

Before descriptive bibliography can operate, the titles must be identified
and collected. This process calls for enumerative, or systematic, bibliography, best illustrated by the brief notations of check lists. In theory, a descriptive bibliographer could perform the main enumerative preparation
himself. This would certainly be practicable for an author bibliography;
but for a large-scale genre bibliography like Restoration plays I take it
that the enumerative must precede the descriptive and that some check
list constructed by an expert in that form of investigation is a desideratum
before the descriptive bibliographer should attempt to operate. Obviously,

the more searching investigation that descriptive bibliography requires will turn up editions and issues of known titles unrecorded in even the best of check lists. This is to be expected. On the other hand, if a descriptive bibliographer did not have enumerative information readily available, as in Allardyce Nicoll's list of plays in his *Restoration Drama* history, the time spent in searching out political pamphlets in pseudodramatic form, for example, would seriously interfere with his ability to cope with his main job, which is the analysis and description of works already ascertained by experts as belonging in the genre selected for investigation.

For Restoration drama, the appearance in 1945 of *A Check List of English Plays 1641–1700*, compiled by Gertrude Woodward and James G. McManaway, made possible the start of my own attempt over the course of years to produce a sequel to Greg's massive *Bibliography of the English Printed Drama to the Restoration* that would carry forward the descriptive listing of plays to 1700. This Woodward and McManaway *Check List* was compiled with unusual care and thoroughness, and with a detail not ordinarily found in its kind. Its scope in the admission of titles was somewhat less comprehensive than my own, but, within its own rules, only one title of a stage play, and that an undated one assigned to 1700, proved to be omitted. That it had not uncovered all editions of known titles, that editions were sometimes mistaken for issues, and issues for editions, that the determination of what constituted an issue was sometimes arbitrary—these flaws, inevitable in any check list, can by no means dim the gratitude that all libraries and collectors must feel for the information brought together in this work, often not previously recorded. It has been invaluable in stimulating the collection of Restoration plays on a more knowledgeable basis than was previously possible, and in many ways it has proved to be the almost required foundation for the larger attempt at a descriptive bibliography of the drama of the period.

A descriptive bibliographer must formulate what may be called a philosophy of his craft that will apply to the construction of the descriptive method most suitable for dealing with the particular kind of material he encounters. I am far from advocating Madan's discredited theory of "degressive bibliography," despite its attempted revival by a recent reviewer in the *Times Literary Supplement* for March 24, 1966. Instead, I am suggesting only that each element of a bibliographical description must pass a rational test, according to the general nature of the material, before it is uniformly applied to all works described. This test is of two kinds: first, what material should be included in a description, and why; and, second, what form should it take if it is to be included.

No philosophy can animate the first criterion—the details to be included —which does not justify the rationale in terms of the uses that will be made of the parts of the description. Very briefly, let me mention what seem to me to be the main purposes of descriptive bibliography, as opposed to the simply enumerative or check-list variety. The first is surely to establish for all scholarly and practical uses the form of the 'ideal copy' of each edition and issue of a book. Only in this manner can a norm be set up to determine the nature and direction of variation. The second is to describe this norm and its known variations in terms sufficiently full and detailed, though without prolixity, so that comparison of any actual copy with the description will establish its identity with some one or more recorded copies or else reveal that this compared copy contains unrecorded variation.

What is variation? A variant within an edition may be as small as a departure from the norm and established ideal in the misprinting of a word in the title-page, of a signature, a running-title, a paginal number; or it may represent some resetting of a part of the book; or it may comprise the planned addition or subtraction or substitution of material. Or, indeed, the difference between copies may be so marked as not to be covered by the possibility of internal printing change and to require the hypothesis that a previously unrecorded edition is in hand.

One of the prime purposes of descriptive bibliography, then, is to provide sufficient information in such necessary and practicable detail as will serve for exact identification in part as well as in whole. By this means, book collections of various degrees of scope and of depth can be built up for the ultimate uses of scholarship. That this information needs to be organized, and the correct order and relationship established between variation, running from printing states to new editions, if the physical descriptions are to be put to any further use than accumulation, is a matter to be remarked later.

Restoration plays are relatively simple books whose contents are organized in a generally standard way. As with all other books, the title-page and its information is of considerable importance, and variation is often found. Sometimes this variation has little practical significance except to indicate some care taken with proofreading, whether initial or secondary, as when a simple misprint like "Pirnted" is corrected to "Printed" during the course of the impression. Some information about typographical standards may occasionally be secured from seeing attempts made to improve the appearance of a title-page, as in the subtitle of Dryden's *Spanish Friar* of 1681 set either in black-letter or in roman type. Theatrical history may be corrected or amplified if the title statement about the company and the theatre acting the play is altered.

Literary history may also be affected. It is of more than casual interest, possibly, that only in 1691, and then by the cancellation of the original title-leaf that had copied preceding editions, was *Sir Martin Mar-all* claimed for Dryden by the insertion of his name on the title.

Title-page variation in the imprint is a rich source of publishing history, as when the imprint is altered by press-variation or by cancellation to include or exclude different booksellers or publishers.

Since even minor typographical changes have their points of interest and should be collected for the purpose of recording and explaining, the system known as quasi-facsimile transcription must be employed, since only it will take account of minor variation that might show up between the official bibliographical transcript and a copy held in hand. Some bibliographies substitute photographic facsimiles for the quasi-facsimile transcript as a means of even greater accuracy. This method of exhibiting the title-page has its virtues as well as its troubles, but the expense is seldom warranted for Restoration plays, since few editions have such similar title-pages that only spacing, not some transcribable difference, would reveal the fact of variation. Exceptions do occur, of course. For example, no system of quasi-facsimile can illustrate the difference between the third-edition and the fourth-edition title-pages of Dryden's *Indian Emperour* in 1670 or the title-pages of the three editions in 1695 of Thomas Jevon's *Devil of a Wife*, only two of which have previously been recognized. In each case, transcribable differences normally noted elsewhere in the book would reveal the fact of variation, but I grant that a made-up copy might pass muster with the wrong title-page if one gave it so casual an examination that the lack of conjugacy of the leaf was not observed and investigated.

The next item for identification I prefer to place as the collational formula. This line in the description records first the format of the book, whether quarto, octavo, or folio, or (in complex cases involving the printing with special paper) whether quarto-forme octavo, for example, as when a double sheet has been cut in half and each half machined with quarto imposition. The account of the number of gatherings in the book and the register of their signatures follows, accompanied by a note on the system of signing (whether customarily of one-half of the leaves or of one over one-half) together with any variation in the system or any errors. In turn, this is succeeded by the formula for the pagination, including variation or errors.

So far as concerns the printings, this formula line as a whole is the heart of the description, since it records the mechanics of the book's production. Often its details are crucial for identification. Makers of check lists and cataloguers before Woodward and McManaway failed to distinguish the first two editions of Lord Lansdowne's *Heroick Love* (1698) because the two have the same setting of type for the title-page despite the fact that the first ends on sig. L2 whereas the second condenses to end on K4. The third and fourth editions in 1670 of Dryden's *Indian Emperour* have been confused, although the third has correct pagination and the fourth mispages one forme consistently. In either case, the checking of a copy against a collational formula would have given notice that the variance should be investigated.

Next come the transcription (in quasi-facsimile, for easier identification of typographical differences) of the head-title and the running-titles. The first has a literary significance, chiefly, but any difference in its form from that of the title-page needs critical investigation, since the odds favor the reproduction in the head-title of the form found in the manuscript: title-pages of plays are seldom written out by the authors. Thus it is of more interest than the simple fact that a variant exists to learn that in the anonymous *She Ventures and He Wins* of 1696 the head-title and title-page agree in the name of the play except for a unique copy in the University of Illinois where the head-title reads "He Ventures, and She Wins," a form that coincides with the constant catchword "He" on sig. A4^v of the edition's preceding sheet, and with the also variant running-titles in the outer forme of the Illinois copy that follow the wording of the head-title.

Usually, as suggested by the running-title concurrence in the Illinois copy of *She Ventures,* these headings merely confirm the form in the head-title and, hence, have no independent authority of their own. However, the transcription in quasi-facsimile of these running-heads offers a rich source for identifying copies owing to the common differences in typography that result when these heads are set, the more especially if the bibliographer will note the presence of such irregularities as swash versus regular italic capitals.

We come then to the notation of the contents, which in these plays is usually fairly standardized. The contents list has a literary value in that it should contain information about dedications and the name of the dedicatee, the titles and signatures of commendatory poems, the existence of prefaces by author or publisher. Not to lose the opportunity for such detailed description as might reveal variation in copies, I transcribe in quasi-facsimile the titles of all such material and the subscriptions, including dates. I note the appearance of prologues and epilogues, including the number of lines for each, and add a transcript of the heading and also of the opening line, with indication of the indentation required by any heading capital. To get the play itself started, since the head-title has already been noted, I transcribe the first act-scene heading and the opening stage direction. Finally, the form of the finis is transcribed, and the contents list is complete except for the epilogue and the noting of book or other advertisements that may fill up space at the end, the number of titles always specified.

The listing of selected catchwords in these plays does not prove to be significant enough as a means of identification to warrant the space. A recent writer has argued for the usefulness of noting the alignment of leaf signatures to the text line above, since resettings or reimpositions are likely to vary the relationship. This is an excellent idea, but the evidence does not seem readily susceptible of formulation in a condensed system of notation, and I have not utilized it except in notes where observed evidence of variation may be cited.

The description closes, then, with the abbreviated signs of the libraries where copies are located that I have actually examined, each arranged according to the already noted variants. Except in cases of extreme rarity, I have not examined copies of plays in private hands, since they may not be permanently placed and are often not available for examination by the general scholar. In all, over thirty significant collections in this country and in Britain are listed, complete as to the holdings at the particular time that I examined them. However, the purpose of this listing of libraries is not to serve as a census of holdings, for libraries will add to collections, or subtract sometimes, and no bibliography could keep up to date in this respect. Instead, the list informs the scholar where he may go to consult copies that I have seen and it furnishes the precise evidence on which my description of the ideal copy of the edition has been based. For American scholars who want photocopies of prominent British holdings, I furnish the shelf-marks of the examined books in the British Museum and also in the Bodleian Library.

A series of notes concludes the entry. These concern themselves with the publishing history in that they list the newspapers or journals, with dates, in which advertisements of publication appeared, as well as appearances of the entry in book advertisements in other play volumes. Any other information about the printer or publisher is gathered together, including what may be gleaned from a study of the ornaments or initials. Further notes may point out the significance of bibliographical evidence about the printing. For instance, I have regularly kept a record of the appearance or nonappearance of watermarks in the two half-sheets whenever a quarto play begins and ends with two-leaf gatherings. From this evidence, and sometimes from the evidence of running-heads, a statement can be made that the two half-sheets were or were not machined together, a matter that has some textual and bibliographical significance but cannot be shown in the collational formula. Evidence in the description that ought to be readily interpreted by any knowing reader is not usually subject to comment, such as the fact that the variant running-titles of sheet B in *She Ventures and He Wins* indicate that the outer forme of this sheet was first through the press. But when, as often, a play has been simultaneously typeset in two or more parts, the fact is noticed according to the evidence.

An attempt is made in these notes to give a few significant facts about the typography, including the standard formula for the number of text lines per typical page, together with the vertical and horizontal measurements of the type-page with and without the running-heads, and the measurements of twenty lines of type. These figures must be used with caution as an identifying device, since the shrinkage of the paper will vary, and my own measurements of the same page in different copies may differ as much as 2 millimetres. However, the statistics may have two functions other than that of identification. When, for instance, the width of the measure varies in different parts of the book systematically, or the number of lines per page, this is useful bibliographical evidence about the number of compositors and the method of printing. Second, the accumulation of evidence of this sort may eventually result in useful information about typographical styles of different years within the period, and possibly even of different printers.

The notes will always offer evidence for the history of the textual transmission whenever one edition was not printed from its immediate predecessor, whenever false dates occur, or there is a suspicion of piracy and, thus, of illegitimate printing. Full discussion will be provided of facts that have any textual significance, such as the duplicate typesetting of the early text sheets in John Banks's *Cyrus the Great* (1696), the unique reset forme in the Worcester College copy of D'Avenant's *Man's the Master* (1669), or the previously unknown rewritten text in sheet H of Dryden's *Albion and Albanius* (1685). When bibliographical problems have been worked out in detail, as in the extent and intention of the cancel in Lee's *Princess of Cleve* (1689), reference is made to the publication of the information. Whenever the method of my comparison of copies reveals the presence of press-variants, these will be indicated in the notes, but on the understanding that no attempt has been made to collate the texts in a manner to asure the reader that all, or even a majority, of such variants have been noticed. In short, the notes will contain whatever information bears on publishing history, textual transmission, or the method of printing the edition under examination. Manuscript markings that represent a significant date of purchase or price, as in the Luttrell copies, will be remarked, and also the presence of manuscript actors' lists or of prompt-book markings. I propose to list the songs printed in the play, together with the number of lines they contain and a transcript of the first line. Separately printed prologues and epilogues will be recorded.

Further to make the information in the bibliography useful to a wide group of readers, I have determined on several conventions. The first concerns the arrangement of the plays, in which I shall follow Greg's principle of listing the titles by number so far as possible according to the date of publication of the first edition, followed in order by all subsequent editions to 1700. Collections will be described as a whole, but their individual play titles will be included, with appropriate description, in the general chronological listing.

Each carved ornament and initial letter will be reproduced in an appendix, and identified by assigned number in the separate play descriptions. I expect that this process will result in the identification of various printers of plays, and will also serve as something of a source of supply for bibliographers concerned with the investigation of ornaments in nondramatic works. Occasionally a small bibliographical point may be served by this identification, as when one initial is substituted for another in press.

Indexes will provide immediate access to a considerable fund of information about the persons connected with the drama of the period and its printing, as well as the associated literature. Separate indexes will list the names of all publishers and printers found in the imprints or conjectured from other evidence, internal or external; the names of all dedicatees; the names of all writers of forewords and commendatory poems; the names of all actors listed in the dramatis personae; and the names of writers of prologues and epilogues; and separate first-line indexes will be provided for all prologues and epilogues, songs, and all commendatory verses.

Not to be separated from the information purveyed in the description is the method of examination from which the information derives. From the start, I determined that notes accompanied by photostats of title-pages were insufficient for the ideal bibliography that I was contemplating, which would contain a range of detail not previously envisaged. Hence, I secured a control microfilm of each play in all its editions and issues for a total in all of about 6,000 feet of film. Some libraries, I decided, I would be able to visit for periods long enough to work through their collections: these were chiefly the Folger Shakespeare Library, the Library of Congress, the Boston Public Library, and the collections at Harvard, Yale, Illinois, Chicago, Williams, Columbia, the British Museum, the Bodleian Library, and the various colleges at Oxford and Cambridge, as well as the Dyce collection in Victoria and Albert Museum and the Eton College collection. For the rest, I ordered duplicate microfilm of all holdings from the Huntington, the Clark, and the Newberry libraries, as well as the collections housed at Northwestern, Michigan, Cornell, Claremont, the New York Public Library, Princeton, Pennsylvania, Texas, and the National Library of Scotland. A scattering of valuable copies were consulted in such smaller collections as the Pierpont Morgan, and the libraries of Ohio State, Lehigh, Virginia, Duke, and Cincinnati, partly by borrowing, partly by film, and partly by travel.

Since I travel with my own portable microfilm projector, I can set up shop in any library and compare its copies systematically against the control microfilm for each edition, issue, and major variant. Not much practice is required to scan various points on each page of a book back against the projected control image. Thus I check each title-page scrupulously, and each head-title and running-title and all other material that I shall be transcribing. In the text for each page I check the alignment of the running-title and of the signature against the first and last text lines, and I also check the alignment of the type in at least four different places on each page. Catchwords, of course, are checked, and so is each ornament and initial. This system, if carefully carried out, will disclose all transcribable variants, and some not normally transcribed, and it will guarantee at a minimum that in the listed copies each detail of the description is precisely accurate, unless a special note is made of variance. It will further guarantee what I think no other bibliography has yet been able to claim, that each page of every copy listed is in the identical typesetting, press-variants excepted. Indeed, even the occasional reimpositions of the same type in a forme or sheet can usually be noticed, as in the last of the 1696 editions of Dryden's *Indian Emperour.*

Not only have hundreds of small printing variants been discovered by this special method of comparison, but various copies made up from sheets of different editions, or pieced out by leaves from another source, have been noted so that scholars consulting them may be duly warned.

Some idea of the trivia, as well as of the more important variants, can be had from the following notes, which I have copied as I leafed in alphabetical order through my records.

In John Bancroft's *Henry the Second* (1693), sig. E1 is missigned as D1 in two out of the twenty-seven copies examined. On sig. G2 the heading for Act V is set immediately below the running-title without a space in a majority of copies, but with a desirable white space between the two in a minority. The text in this inner forme of sheet G is identical, however; in this case a typographical disturbance produced or resulted from no textual alteration.

In two copies of Bancroft's *King Edward the Third* (1691), sig. B2 is not signed. Only two of twenty-eight copies examined had an important seven-line errata slip pasted in. In seventeen copies, an inserted dedication leaf to Captain Richard Savage is present, but it is absent in eleven.

In John Banks's *Cyrus the Great* (1696), sheets B, C, and D exist in duplicate typesettings which can be placed in their correct order by bibliographical evidence.

In Banks's *Innocent Usurper* (1694), five of the twenty-nine observed copies still contained, unexcised as sig. A4, the Bentley title leaf for the 1694 nonce collection of Nathaniel Lee's *Plays,* an interesting oddity useful for dating the binding up of the collection.

Woodward and McManaway record the presence of two issues of Banks's

Rival Kings (1677), according as the imprint reads "Printed for Langley Curtis" or "Printed for L. C." It could not describe the interesting printing of this variant, whereby the title-page with the name is sig. A1, and the form with the initials, otherwise in the same setting of type, is sig. A2, and thus the cancellation of one or other leaf would create the desired issue. Woodward and McManaway list nine copies with the name and only three copies with the initials; but of the twenty-five copies I have examined seven had both title-pages preserved, twelve had the name title-leaf on sig. A1 cancelled, and only five cancelled sig. A2 and, thus, were issued with the imprint containing the name. The remaining copy, unique at Harvard so far as I know, cancels A1, but on A2 has the press-variant imprint not of Curtis but of William Cademan, a piece of publishing history one is glad to have recorded for the first time. The comparison of the outer forme of sheet F revealed typographical disturbances due to press-variants that an editor would want to know about. Other press-variants may be seen in inner D.

In Banks's *Island Queens* (1684), type disturbance reveals a significant textual variant on sig. A1^v in only two of the twenty-one copies examined. On sig. F4^v, the catchword may be (correctly) "Read" or incorrectly (in five copies) "As," a reading that agrees with the first word of the second line on sig. G1. It seems probable that some rearrangement of the lines between pages was undertaken in proof and that the failure to alter the catchword, as a consequence, was not seen until printing had started. Watermark evidence demonstrates that the single-leaf title was printed originally as K4, the final leaf in the book, which would otherwise have been blank.

In Banks's *Unhappy Favourite* (1682), sig. D1 is correctly signed in only three of the twenty-two copies examined. In the same author's *Vertue Betray'd* (1682), press-variation occurs in the outer forme of sheet C and the inner forme of sheet E. The uncorrected state of the first I have seen in only a single copy. In the 1692 edition of *Vertue Betray'd*, the number of page 19 may be absent, as in three copies of the fourteen observed, and in one copy page 31 is misnumbered as page 35. The Newberry and Pennsylvania copies have manuscript actors' lists that differ slightly in the assignment of parts.

In Aphra Behn's *Amorous Prince* (1671), the catchword 'PRO-' may be improperly present on sig. A2^v (since the Prologue is actually on sig. A2 recto), or it may have been removed. Watermark evidence shows that the half-sheet of preliminaries and the half-sheet of final text were printed together as a full sheet and then cut apart.

In Aphra Behn's *Debauchee* (1677), one copy (the Folger) out of twenty-seven examined has the title-page variant 'As it is ACTED at the | Dukes Theatre.' instead of the conventional 'ACTED at his Highness | The

Duke of *York*'s THEATRE.' In Behn's *Dutch Lover* (1673), the address to the reader ends on sig. a2 in twenty-three plays with a rule and catchword, but in the unique Princeton copy the rule and catchword are missing. The Clark copy has a manuscript actors' list.

Behn's *False Count* (1682) has a cancel title-leaf in twelve copies examined, but in the thirteenth and fourteenth (Harvard and New York Public) the previously unrecorded original cancellandum title-leaf is preserved. In the original, the title reads, 'A | FARCE | Call'd | The False Count', but in the cancellans the title begins simply 'THE | FALSE COUNT' (with a turned *N*). Oddly, the licensing notice of the original, signed Charles Killigrew and dated July 21, 1681, is omitted on the cancel title. And, curiously, the Princeton copy is dated by Luttrell on December 17, 1681. Clearly, a problem in publishing history is present here, whether publication approximated the original licensing notice or the Luttrell purchase. For what it is worth, the type of this cancel was printed, in large part, from the standing type of the cancellandum and must, therefore, have been machined very close in time to the original.

The original title of Behn's *Feign'd Curtizans* (1679) contained only the name of Jacob Tonson at the Judge's Head in the imprint, but an unrecorded press-variant imprint in the Lehigh and Harvard copies adds the name of Richard Tonson in Gray's Inn Lane, another nice bit of publishing history. An incorrect catchword on sig. A4, though not a variant, may indicate some rearrangement of the type between sigs. A4 and A4^v before printing started.

The two forms of the heading in the dedication of Behn's *Roundheads* (1682) to Hery Fitz-Roy have been noticed in the Woodward and McManaway check list, but other interesting variants occur. In what must be the earlier state of the title through the press, the unique Newberry copy reads 'As it was Acted', but all other copies advertise 'As it is Acted'. The uncorrected state of this same forme signs the dedication 'Ann Behn', but the corrected reads, properly, 'A. Behn'. Some copies of the uncorrected state have the offending double *n* of 'Ann' deleted in ink as a special hand correction. In the Clark, the Folger, and the Illinois copies, sig. G2 is incorrectly signed F2.

Of the twenty copies examined of Behn's *Young King* (1683), five lack the inserted dedication to Philaster signed Astrea, and thus it is likely not that these are imperfect, but instead (as suggested by its signing in lower-case inserted in an upper-case signed half-sheet) the leaf is almost certainly an addition not originally planned. In this edition, page 7 is numbered in only two copies. In Behn's *Younger Brothers* (1696), the copies of sheet B with page 5 unnumbered are the later, not the earlier, state, since others show the figure in the process of coming loose and wandering off into the margin.

The Bodleian copy of Reuben Bourne's *Contented Cuckold* (1692) contains an unrecorded press-variant imprint advertising Walter Shropshire as the seller instead of R. Taylor, another piece of publishing history. In Roger Boyle Earl of Orrery's *Two New Tragedies* (1669), more than half of the examined copies lacked the cancel slip on sig. R2ᵛ of *The Black Prince* whereby the error in the heading 'PROLOGUE' was emended to the correct 'EPILOGUE'. In *Tryphon,* in the same volume, both sigs. C1 and N2 are cancels, with textual alterations from the originals preserved by pure chance in only a copy or two. In Orrery's *Herrod the Great* (1694), leaf M2 is missing in many copies and blank in some, but in the unique St. Johns College Cambridge copy the leaf holds the title for the nonce collection *Six Plays* (1694). In Orrery's *Guzman* (1693), the two-leaf gathering signed lower-case *a* and containing a puff of Orrery by Nahum Tate, and also the dramatis personae, is missing in enough copies to confirm that it is a late addition. In four observed copies, page 16 is misnumbered 14, and in more it is misnumbered 15. In the 1690 edition of Orrery's *Henry the Fifth,* a printer's error placed the notation 'his Son' after the Duke of Burgundy in the cast of characters instead of after 'Chareloys' in the line below. This was altered by press-correction, but in the uncorrected copies the two words were cut out and 'his Son' was stamped in by hand at the right place.

This recital does not even finish with the records of the *B* authors, but it will give some idea of the kinds of variants that commonly appear in Restoration plays, all of some interest for studies of printing procedures, some that concern publishing history, and some that provide vital information to a prospective editor. An indication of the valuable textual information that may accrue can be given by the unrecorded facts about Congreve's *Love for Love* (1695). The most common form of the first edition remains constant in its setting and imposition, without variation. But, in fact, there are two forms of this first edition, undoubtedly the result of increasing the size of the printing, in which every sheet is either reimposed in whole or in part, or reset, usually with textual variation in either case. Copies of this variant form are likely not to remain constant but to represent a mixture of common sheets with the rarer variation. Thus, the alternate textual state of this important play must be built up from the comparison of three or four copies, and the account of the method of the variant printing and its relationship to the standard text, whether earlier or later, poses a bibliographical problem of remarkable complexity. Neither editors nor collectors seem to have come upon this significant state, or to have recognized it if they have.

I can give a hint here. If line 2 of sig. B1ᵛ reads 'damm'd' instead of 'dam'd', if line 7 of sig. C4ᵛ reads 'white——' (no comma) instead of 'white,—', if line 34 of sig. D2 reads, in error, 'hid' for correct 'did', and if in line 31 of sig. E1 'excuse' is found with a lower-case *e* instead of a capital, then you have in hand the very rare supplementary printing that reset sheets B, C, D, and the outer forme of E, and reimposed the standing type of at least one forme of all other sheets.

The text of Congreve's *Mourning Bride* (1697) was most interestingly revised in its early printings in a manner not yet recognized in full by any editor.

Even so commonly collected an author as Dryden yielded some gold to bibliographical investigation. Although he had been the subject of a descriptive bibliography by Hugh Macdonald, and a further close study to correct this bibliography by James Osborn, dozens of small unrecorded printing variations appeared in the large-scale comparison from film controls that I undertook. Moreover, such not wholly negligible information was secured as the identification of the piratical printing that upset the customarily assigned order of editions of *The State of Innocence*; the reversal of the commonly accepted order of the two editions in 1669 of *The Wild Gallant* and the establishment of the true first; the discovery of an unrecorded but textually important cancel leaf and its original in *King Arthur*; a textually reset and variant sheet in *Albion and Albanius*; the correct rearrangement of the three 1696 editions of *The Indian Emperour* from their previously accepted order; and, finally, the discovery that there were three editions in 1670 of *The Indian Emperour*, not two, and that Woodward and McManaway 417 covered two separate editions, one of which represented the highly significant first printing of the text in its finally revised form.

These concrete details offer some answer to the question that was posed at the start of this paper: what contribution is it that the methods of bibliography can make to an orderly account of the drama of the Restoration, or to any other form or period of literature? What needs emphasis is that the ordering of the material in a descriptive bibliography cannot be undertaken without the services of analytical bibliography. That is, simple description is not enough, for simple description cannot decide the order of the first and second editions of *The Wild Gallant*, trace the order of the printings of Ogilby's *Relation of his Majesty's Entertainment* (which has more editions than have been recorded), detect piracies in the editions of Nathaniel Lee, analyze the complex printing problems in the production of Mary Pix's *Spanish Wives* (1696), reverse the order of the first two editions of Sir Robert Stapylton's *Slighted Maid* (1663), or determine the priority of the two issues of d'Urfey's *Cynthia and Endymion* (1697) and of the reset first three text sheets in Banks's *Cyrus the Great* (1696). Even such small details as the choice of the ideal form of title-page to print as the basic transcription, with differences in a press-variant state listed separately beneath it, all these may require the services of informed, expert, analytical bibliography.

The answer, then, is a simple one. Without the bibliographer who can determine the printing relationships of variants and of editions, the descriptive bibliographer alone would be helpless to provide an orderly and correct account of the Restoration drama or of any other form of literature. The two kinds of bibliography cannot be separated.

Whether the results have been—or, rather, will be—worth the effort is perhaps only personal opinion. If we are to study Restoration drama as a literary form we must have all the facts about its printing and publishing history. Private collectors and librarians cannot collect these plays systematically without an account of the normal forms of the plays and the variants that a wide-ranging search has turned up. Without full and complete collection in depth, and without the bibliographical facts revealed by the analytical method, the publishing history of the period cannot be written nor can editors be made aware of sources of textual variation and relationships that will inevitably affect the nature and authority of the texts that they select to work with. Bibliographers can find a mine of information to investigate in the descriptions about printing variation and methods. A properly investigated and then written-up bibliography can serve as a model for future bibliographers to build their own work on, according as they study the virtues and deficiencies that time will reveal in any massive work of this nature.

If, then, one can have the personal satisfaction of engaging in a work that, one hopes, may be supplemented but not superseded in the foreseeable future, and can combine this with the satisfaction that comes from being of service to a host of scholarly and general users of the information one has collected, analyzed, and finally organized, then surely the only answer is a resounding Carlylean Everlasting Yea. Albatross as it has often seemed about my neck, horrible as is the prospect of redoing the descriptions destroyed a few years ago in a fire (perhaps a third of the total), distressing as is the fact that of recent years my personal interests have changed from descriptive to textual bibliography and the problems of establishing and editing both Elizabethan and American texts, the answer still is—Yes! The drudgery of comparing page by page between fifteen and twenty thousand copies against microfilm, of evaluations, of typing, of checking and rechecking, cannot be concealed. And proofreading lies ahead, perhaps to be undertaken as Jackson did the Pforzheimer Catalogue, letter by letter backwards. But underlying this drudgery has been a generative excitement of exploring the unknown and bringing some order, and of drawing some maps of terra incognita. The answer is—Yes!

Bibliography Revisited

ANY LARGE MOVEMENT whether in scholarship or in the arts progresses in spurts of energy followed by periods of rest, consolidation, and re-examination. This fallow time, if the movement is on the right track, leads to a further outpouring of energy generated by fresh critical insights, a clearer sense of purpose, and a grasp of the more refined techniques by which problems of principle as well as of method may be solved.

So with bibliography. I am no historian of this art, or science—which-ever one wishes to call it. But I would suggest that its development may be followed with some exactitude in the pages of *The Library*, the printed transactions of our Society. The early series were almost exclusively his-torical and enumerative in content: biographies of printers, essays on the appearance in print of major early books or groups of books, discussions sometimes of early type-faces and their origin, almost wholly within the incunabula years, that period of eminent respectability like the teaching of Anglo-Saxon in the English programmes of the universities. Looking back, one seems to see, whether conscious or not, a search for a rationale of purpose and then of method. To repeat, I am no historian; and it might have been better if you had selected for today's speaker one who could have analysed the growth, not specifically of our Society or of its practical accom-plishments, but of what bibliography has come to stand for in the history of scholarship as represented in microcosm by the developing concerns of the Society's members. An essay, in short, that would perform for biblio-graphical scholarship in the round what the late F. P. Wilson so brilliantly accomplished for Shakespearian textual scholarship in the *Retrospect* volume published by this Society to mark the fiftieth anniversary of its existence. It is no digression to pay special tribute to this essay as an example of a kind of creative scholarship that I am not equipped to emulate. The hundredth anniversary, and—as actuarial tables suggest— a different speaker, will have to be saved for this much-needed critical

An abridgement of this paper was read before The Bibliographical Society on 17 Octo-ber, 1967 as a part of the seventy-fifth anniversary celebration. Printed in *The Library*, 5th ser., 24 (1969), 89–128; reprinted with permission of the Council of The Bibli-ographical Society.

synthesis such as Sir Walter Greg offered before the Society at several important points in its history.

Choosing the smaller goal and the wiser conduct, therefore, I propose to narrow my discourse to a second look at two major tenets that have developed from the particular spurt of energy in bibliographical inquiry for which we may chiefly credit both the theories and the practices of three giants in scholarship: Pollard, McKerrow, and Greg. The first is the tenet of descriptive bibliography which will occupy my main attention, and the second the tenet of textual bibliography.

In the past year *Times Literary Supplement* reviewers of several bibliographical ventures have raised serious doubts about the individual status of these two disciplines, and have even queried the soundness of their relationship. Perhaps this has been only a passing flurry, and indeed the subject was dropped with rather less discussion than one sometimes encounters in the correspondence columns of the *Times Literary Supplement*. However, I am inclined to take seriously certain of the questions that were raised. Descriptive bibliography has reached something of a point of stasis, if that is not too quiet a phrase for what may prove to be a growing loss of belief in the practicability of the discipline to encompass the goals that have been traditionally assigned to it. The questioning goes beyond that of method (although methods are under attack) and strikes directly at the ends, at the very heart of principle. I have no neat solution, but this occasion would seem to be an appropriate one to consider in as practical and objective a manner as possible the present situation in descriptive bibliography.

Textual bibliography, on the other hand, seems to me to be already engaged in a fresh upward movement of surprising dimensions, not I think fully appreciated in this country. The problem here is quite different from that facing descriptive bibliography, and in the end a less serious one, since in my view it centres chiefly on the gap that exists between the perplexed understanding of the audience at whom are aimed texts formulated by modern bibliographical principles and the sophistication in their discipline of the scholars who are producing these texts.[1] However, the future of

---

1 I am thinking mainly of the literary texts of the nineteenth and twentieth centuries. The movement toward the scholarly editing of Elizabethan texts, which we may properly credit to the appearance of Tucker Brooke's *Marlowe* in 1910, has steadily developed without a great deal of controversy except between the advocates of old spelling and of modernization wherein an accommodation seems to be in process; hence the virtues of bibliographically edited texts in this period, of either form, are now accepted by scholars with little dissent. Although there are still amateur textual critics of the eighteenth century, as is perhaps suggested by the ill-informed remarks on old spelling, its purposes and methods, in a recent review in *RES*, xvii (1967), 207–10, of Professor Bond's *Spectator*, the naïve attitude of scholars is beginning to be modified. But the age of innocence still prevails in the nineteenth and twentieth centuries, with especial reference in my country to many students of American literature as an independent phenomenon.

descriptive and of textual bibliography may be more related than is thought, since in their modern developments a difficulty sometimes appears in assigning clearcut demarcated areas of responsibility to these two forms, springing whether from the right or the left forehead of analytical bibliography.

What might have been a major issue was raised in the *Times Literary Supplement* review on 7 July 1966 (p. 604) of Dr. William Todd's *Bibliography of Edmund Burke,* and in the ensuing correspondence, although, I think, no final agreement was reached. The reviewer remarked that Dr. Todd's degressive principles (being motivated by literary considerations) had led him to treat with great fullness the early editions of textual significance but to reduce to handlist proportions the reprints and the post-humous and automatically unauthoritative editions that followed. Although the reviewer accepted this distinction as a necessary concomitant of an author-bibliography—in which, he held, textual considerations offer the primary impetus—he suggested that the bibliographical usefulness of such author-studies is beginning to be challenged, and called for a new rationale of degression.[2]

2 'Historical studies in bibliography may be likened to a web in which the careers of the various authors form the parallel threads of the warp, interlacing themselves with the cross threads which represent the activities of printers and publishers of the author's works. Thus the author bibliography tells only part of the story and touches upon important aspects of the history of the trade only in references to a series of individual books. Thus in Professor Todd's account of Burke's *Philosophical Enquiry into . . . the Sublime and the Beautiful* (no. 5, pp. 33 ff.) the inevitable variations in printing practice between the first edition of 1757 (*5a*) and the fifteenth London edition of 1812 (*5o*), or between that of the London printers (*5a–o*) and of printers in Dublin (*5p* and *r*), Berwick (*5q*), Oxford (*5t*), Montrose (*5u*), and Philadelphia (*5v*) are ignored because these editions are textually unimportant: but all are books, and from a strictly bibliographical point of view one book, considered as the physical product of a particular process carried out by particular persons in a particular place, is as interesting and significant as another. It may be that the days of the author-bibliography are already numbered.'

When on 4 Aug. (p. 716) Mr. John Carter protested that this position altogether negated the degressive principle and would result in extremely bulky and expensive bibliographies 'if every Penguin reprint is to be deemed, for descriptive purposes, "as interesting and significant" as the *editio princeps* or the last edition to be revised by the author', the reviewer took a somewhat more extreme position. The difficulty with author-bibliographies, he wrote in reply, is that the selection of a single book for analysis from the whole series of productions of a press distorts conclusions about book-production. The book was not produced in isolation, and 'after all the business of bibliography is to relate the finished article to the means of production'. He continued: 'The "degressive principle" which is the main defence of the author-bibliography is probably a necessary factor in its preparation in order to keep the size and price of the result in reasonable bounds, but if such bibliographies are, as I suggest, distorted in their approach, then this "principle" must be suspect. It seems to be founded on a pretty evident *petitio principii* in that the slight descriptions accorded to the "less important" editions are very likely

The reasons stated in the review and in a reply to a protest in the letter columns on 4 August (p. 716) are interesting. For example, the business of bibliography (it was suggested) is to relate the finished article to the means of production. By its selection of an isolated example for no other motive than a literary one, an author-bibliography distorts the picture of book-production at various periods by drawing conclusions on insufficient evidence about book-production in broad and general terms. When Professor Todd ignores the inevitable variations in printing between the first edition in 1757 of Burke's *Philosophical Enquiry into . . . the Sublime and the Beautiful* and the fifteenth London printing of 1812, or between the productions of the London printers and those of Ireland and Scotland because these editions are textually unimportant, he negates the principle that all are books.

On the one hand, then, is placed what the reviewer would regard as the false and arbitrary principle that leads a bibliographer to select from literary motives alone a group of books to analyse, order, and describe, and the purer technical motive to illustrate historically the relation of the finished article to the means of production. The literary motive, it is stated, leads to the author-bibliography, whose days are perhaps numbered. From the only illustrations given, one is led to suppose that the book-production bibliography would lead to the opposite—the study and description of books produced by a single press.

I suggest that this is a false opposition. It is quite true, as Professor Tanselle reminded us in a judicious communication in *TLS* on 22 September (p. 884), that 'there is no reason why a bibliography conceived of as an *historical record* of the physical forms in which an author's work has appeared cannot continue to be as useful as in the past'. He comments that obviously it would be ideal 'to have detailed studies of the output and habits of all publishers in a given period first and only then to attempt specialized bibliographies of the major authors in that period, drawing upon this accumulated information'. But, he adds politely, 'historical knowledge rarely advances methodically'; although 'it may be true that the literary or cultural significance of a writer is irrelevant bibliographically', yet in the interval author-bibliographies 'generally provide excellent opportunities

---

to ensure their continued insignificance. At its worst, despite the Newtonian and Einsteinian claims, it looks very like the rationalization of laziness or ignorance, and at best it is a defence of prejudgment.'

In *TLS* for 11 Aug. 1966, p. 732, Mr. Carter disagreed with the assertion that 'the business of bibliography is to relate the finished article to the means of production'; and on 1 Sept. (p. 781) Professor Todd by a *reductio ad absurdum* example attacked the premise that it is possible for descriptive bibliography to pay equal attention to printing production.

for examining representative cross-sections of the publishing practices and problems of their times'.

The justice of this position is unexceptionable. It would indeed be useful to have some publishers' bibliographies to serve as the basis for more comprehensively knowledgeable author-bibliographies. For example, in the late 1890s the New York house of Appleton might print one impression of a book on wove paper and another on laid paper, with or without a seal watermark, and with vertical chainlines, as it did with Stephen Crane's *Maggie* in 1896. A bibliographer of Stephen Crane would remark this irregularity and on some rather slim evidence of type batter could conjecturally assign the two papers in *Maggie* to two different impressions. Because three other Crane books happened also to be printed by Appleton he would notice that at least one printing of *The Red Badge of Courage* (1895) was on wove paper and another on laid paper with horizontal chainlines. He would observe that *The Little Regiment* of 1897, on unwatermarked laid paper, is found with a printing that is bound with wove endpapers, another with laid endpapers with vertical chainlines like the text but watermarked with the Appleton seal, and still another with laid endpapers having horizontal chainlines. *The Third Violet*, later in 1897, appears to be printed exclusively on wove paper. These books alone provide inadequate evidence from which to generalize whether the use of wove versus laid paper had anything to do with sales expectations, whether batches of watermarked and of unwatermarked laid paper might be used (except to make up copies) within any impression of an Appleton book, including its fly-leaves and endpapers in the binding process, or whether the distinction indicates a true difference.

No doubt a bibliographical survey of all Appleton books from the technical point of view would furnish some basis for analysing the use of wove and laid seal-watermarked papers in *Maggie*, and so on. Certainly under such ideal conditions the author-bibliographer of Crane would be spared the unpleasant dilemma of merely recording what he saw in respect to the papers, without knowing whether there was any significance to the evidence; or else dropping his work on Crane in order to plunge into a study of the paper used by Appleton in 1895–97 (and no doubt in years before and after), a task that would multiply, with each publisher so investigated, to massive proportions.

Paper alone is not the only problem posed in the Appleton editions of Stephen Crane. An author-bibliographer finds also that in *Maggie* the laid-paper printing is accompanied by a resetting and replating of the title-page whereby a modest black-letter typographical layout is replaced by a very bold layout in roman capitals. On the evidence that *The Red Badge of Courage, The Little Regiment,* and *The Third Violet* have the same form of black-letter title-page as *Maggie,* a bibliographer might speculate that the black-letter was the standard form of Appleton title. But it would be mightily convenient to know from an Appleton bibliography that this was true, and that the typography was not instead a device to put the Crane books into some sort of uniform series. He would also like to know how peculiar was the change in the *Maggie* title-page or whether Appleton was in the habit of replating title-pages to emphasize the names of popular authors and their successful books, as in the roman title-page of *Maggie.* He would also like to know about Appleton's habits in respect to altering advertisements in the final text-gathering of a book, as occurs in *The Red Badge of Courage* and *The Little Regiment.* Specifically, would Appleton confine such changes to separate printings or might it order alterations during the course of a press-run? This question is an important one in the consideration of an unrecorded substitution of one advertisement for another in the laid-paper 1896 *Maggie,* since the evidence of batter does not certainly distinguish this as a separate impression of the whole book. He would also like to know what was the usual practice with Appleton about plating books. No stereotyper's notice appears, but *Maggie*—like the others—was presumably plated. Yet *George's Mother,* published also in 1896 by the firm of Edward Arnold, may have been printed from type-metal, on the doubtful evidence of some worked-up types. Did Arnold customarily plate his books? If so, is the fact that he did not plate *George's Mother* (if this is true) any indication of an estimate that it would have a small sale? A bibliography of Arnold books that would note printing from plates or type-metal would be useful.

What have been described as 'advance copies' exist of the Appleton *Maggie, Little Regiment,* and *Third Violet.* These are all in wrappers instead of cloth. *Maggie* has a different imposition of the preliminaries that omits the Publisher's Note found in the trade edition. Also, the trade final gathering in 8s with integral advertisements in the last six leaves appears as a two-leaf fold of text without advertisements. Are these true advance copies, and if so what purpose did they serve? Why are the publisher's notices on the verso of the half-title missing in this state of *Maggie* and of *The Third Violet* but not in *The Little Regiment?*[3] Why is the front wrapper of *The Little Regiment* copy blank; the front wrapper of *The Third Violet* printed with the complete title-page

3 To be precise, these advertisements are present in the wrappered copy in the Barrett Collection at the University of Virginia, which has the original conjugate New York title-leaf. They are absent on the verso of the cancellans Heinemann title-leaf in the previously unnoticed issue for copyright purposes of the American sheets deposited in the British Museum on 30 October 1896 and unfortunately rebound with the consequent destruction of the original binding. The Williams and Starrett bibliography of Crane is untrustworthy on this point.

setting, including the imprint; and the front wrapper of *Maggie* with the title-page in the same setting but without the imprint? Was the imprint in this case omitted so that Heinemann in London could put his imprint on the wrapper by rubber stamp, as in the wrappered deposit copy in the British Museum? Was the tipped-in cancellans title-page with a Heinemann imprint, but with typography (though in a different setting) imitating the Appleton roman title, printed in America for the Heinemann copies used to establish copyright, or in London? What other examples of Appleton books used for copyright deposit in England have such cancellans titles, and what other Heinemann books have them though printed by other American firms?

The advertisement on the verso of the half-title of *The Little Regiment* states that *Maggie* was in its fourth edition, which would have been by October 1896, after initial publication in June. Only three printings can be identified, one on wove paper and two on laid (provided a change in advertisements is a satisfactory identification of a different impression, as seems likely). But a copy at Harvard of the wove-paper printing represents an unrecorded issue wherein the roman-type title-page on laid paper cancels the black-letter title-page on wove. Would Appleton have been likely to count this sort of issue as an 'edition'? Was Appleton likely to exaggerate the number of 'editions' of its books, as did some publishers, in order to give a false notion of their popularity? What evidence is available?

Although these questions are bewildering in their number and variety, they all concern the publishing history of *Maggie* and are certainly matters that an author-bibliographer would feel bound to discuss, if he could. Yet it is clear that several of these problems would require extensive research into the practices of at least two publishers merely in order to write proper notes to a bibliographical description of a single edition of one book, research so far-reaching and minute as to make almost prohibitive the production of an author-bibliography if such demands for authority are to be met without the assistance of publishers' bibliographies put together according to the highest standards of comprehensiveness.[4]

So far the *TLS* reviewer has a point; but his insistence (if seriously advanced) that the main purpose of descriptive bibliography is to illuminate printing production I find preposterous, although I should certainly accept it as one of the minor purposes, and it is not a bad capsule definition of the purposes of analytical bibliography. It is all the harder to swallow because by its nature the requirement would limit the production of bibliogra-

---

4 Whether the answer to all these questions could be encountered by a wide reading in other author-bibliographies of the period which also examine representative cross-sections of printing problems and practices, as Professor Tanselle hopefully remarks in his letter, is doubtful, although some useful information might be found that could be applied to illuminate a few.

phies not only to printing-houses, or publishers perhaps, but also merely to some printing-houses and publishers. That is, a bibliography of books from Jaggard's press is perfectly practicable, as was D. F. McKenzie's extraordinarily valuable study of certain years of the Cambridge Press. It is perfectly practicable, also, to study the production of a modern private press. Even the operations of a nineteenth-century publisher like Appleton or of a house like Heinemann within a certain time-span is possible. But what could be done with an active publishing house of the present day, and for what rational purpose? The enormous output each year if fully analysed would soon demand very bulky volumes when extended over any useful length of time. And even so, a time-limitation would fail, because what then would one do about the endless series of reprints and paperbacks extending beyond the cut-off point for the production of what must be described as the *editio princeps* and its immediate derivatives? Isolated from their context of general printing production in the later years, these would offer as little evidential basis for proper generalization as the late Burke editions about which the reviewer complains.

And if we are to forsake publishing houses and concern ourselves with bibliographies of modern commercial printers, we would record details such as the typographical design, the quality and make of the paper, and so on, that are decided for the printer by other agents. Under these circumstances I wonder how useful or illuminating a bibliography would be of the annual output of today's conventional job printer of books, working for a number of publishers according to rigid specifications set by each house, and indeed not always the manufacturer of the entire edition. For example, in the United States in order to save freight and distribution charges over our considerable distances, and to promote expedition, publishers of best-sellers (especially of book-of-the-month club volumes) may print them regionally, perhaps in as many as four or five shops, from duplicate plates. To track these printings down is, in my view, a legitimate duty for an author-bibliographer since obviously such regional printing is an integral part of the book's publishing history and thereby evidence of an author's popularity. A study of a printing-house would legitimately inquire into these operations, as well, though for a slightly different purpose. But the significance a record of such matters would have as part of a bibliography of one of these job printers does, I confess, escape me.

It would appear, then, that this particular controversy has proved a red herring except in so far as it has usefully concentrated attention on what is at least a potential source of weakness, especially when a subject is treated according to rather summary degressive principles. This is a matter I shall discuss before I close. In the interval I may remark my sympathy for the reviewer's position in so far as he does point up the one-sided emphasis found in some of the descriptive bibliographies published, and the resulting lack of information about technical matters of real concern that have never been analysed as a result.

In my view it is a real defect in our scholarship that we continue to produce—although on a diminishing scale—the old-fashioned essay biographies of Elizabethan printers in terms of the titles and the kinds of books they printed, their difficulties with each other and with the Stationers' Company, and so on. Whereas the *true* biography of such a printer is a bibliography of his products, which can scarcely be written until we know the number of founts he owned, and their size, year by year; the width of the measure, the number of lines per page, in relation to the size of the type he would select for books of certain kinds; the paper that he bought. How he employed his compositors, especially in relation to more than one press and more than one book. What are the distinguishing traits of these compositors, as by spelling and typographical evidence? Do they impose books customarily with one forme, with two, with three, or four? Are books divided between two presses fore and aft, or do two presses print alternate sheets, or does one perfect for the other, or do both print white paper and then perfect the same sheet? What about cast-off copy? What stock of ornaments and initials did the shop have, and how constant did it remain? How many books were shared between shops?

Matters like these comprise the essential technical biography of an Elizabethan printer, and they can be presented as readily in descriptive bibliography as in a formal biography. Such information can lead to the further identification of books printed in the shop but not assigned because external evidence has been wanting. Moreover, a textual critic can approach a book printed in this shop from a new position of strength and with the facts available on which to rest studies about the nature of the copy and the fidelity of the typesetting to copy-characteristics according to the differentiated habits of the several compositors. Finally, what can be learned from one shop by an analysis in such depth will be pyramided by study even of a second shop, and can be extrapolated in some part to still other shops for testing of similar evidence. Cumulatively, a series of such studies in a period of important literary history, such as the Elizabethan age,[5] would supply a foundation for textual study that is

5 Although I have taken my example from the Elizabethan period where compositorial analysis is a feasible investigation from the evidence of the printed texts, the nineteenth century should not be neglected. For example, Hawthorne's *Fanshawe* (1838) proved susceptible of compositorial analysis almost as if it had been an Elizabethan text; two compositors can occasionally be distinguished in the *Harper's Magazine* printings from manuscript of Crane's Whilomville stories in 1898. A glorious project would be the various compositors in the Hobart and Robbins shop in Cambridge, Massachusetts, who in 1851 and 1852 set the manuscripts of *The House of the Seven Gables and The Blithedale Romance*, leaving their marked stints in the preserved manuscripts for the analysis of fidelity to copy that played an important part in the establishment of the

now sadly lacking and is at best but hit or miss according to any professional scholarly standards. These blessings are not inconsiderable. It is true that in small part some general information is purveyed by searching author-bibliographies or by bibliographies of literary genres that cut across the printing history of an era, like Greg's great *Drama to the Restoration.* Yet I for one would be willing temporarily to dispense with the immediate literary benefits of some bibliographical research in progress if the corresponding energy could be diverted to the technical study of specific printers in certain important periods of literary activity. That these studies would inevitably have a narrower public and a limited sale, and that they do not conform to the standard requirements of academic literary research, does not remove the responsibility of scholars and of university presses —and bibliographical societies—to engage themselves to filling this gap in the technical basis for textual criticism and thence for critical literary study.

Something like this broader ground, I take it, might have provided the reviewer of Professor Todd's *Burke* with a better stance for argument and saved him from the extreme and even doctrinaire position that bibliography ought to be so concerned with technical matters of printing that it should ignore all literary concerns and be indifferent to ultimate critical application,[6] a point of view that seems partly to have been espoused by the earlier bibliographical writer 'Of Text and Type' in the *TLS.*

Centenary Hawthorne texts of these two books. If other manuscripts are preserved marked by these compositors, the Centenary investigation can be carried forward with profit, especially since Hobart and Robbins merely set and plated books, the actual printing being done by other printing shops for various publishers.

6 Thus I should certainly approve whole-heartedly of his statement that 'the business of bibliography is to relate the finished article to the means of production' if instead this was to define the purpose of analytical bibliography and not to be extrapolated to delimit the final purposes of descriptive bibliography as such. There is nothing in this statement that goes contrary to the literary interest which may be derived from an author-bibliography—whether from the illumination of the text or of the publishing history of a book—if this 'business of bibliography' is confined to that part of the description and its notes that is the proper province of analytical bibliography. Indeed, if one chose one could apply the axiom even to a discussion of the condition of the text and the history of its transmission for any book in a descriptive bibliography since textual disruption when not editorial is always directly related to the printing process and its immediate agents. This being so, I think I may say that I fail to understand another bibliographical reviewer in the *TLS*, the writer on 24 March 1966 'Of Text and Type', when (p. 234) he mentions cancels for four leaves in an octavo Dutch piracy of the London 1710 collected edition of Farquhar, discusses the collational formula that would record them, and then remarks 'but the lack of interest which the collational statement induces in a feature only indirectly associated with the text might lead the bibliographer, in a similar case, to miss an important *textual point.*'—I am afraid this baffles me. Any bibliographer who failed to see the textual significance of alterations to the text performed by cancellations recorded in a collational formula had better turn in his union card. This applies as strongly

If this narrow view were to prevail, all cultural agents ranging from book collectors through the great libraries to the literary critics of academia would drop any interest in bibliography, and it would become a branch of the study of the craft of printing, not of literature. As such it would attract few disciples and wield small influence. Fortunately, there is no danger that the printing technicians will take over the guidance of bibliographical investigation, for the history of bibliography, again as reflected in the pages of the transactions of this Society, demonstrates that bibliography's remarkable activity in late years, and the respect that is accorded it as a scholarly discipline, rests on the converts it has made as a new method of literary investigation. Bibliographers are no longer confined to persons professionally concerned with books, like librarians, the more scholarly printers, and a group of active booksellers and collectors. What has firmly established bibliography as a dynamic force in the present scholarly world is its association with the universities and their courses of instruction in literature. This is a fact, especially in the United States, and its impact on bibliographical scholarship by bringing in an entirely new breed of researchers can be traced directly back to the appearance in 1927 of McKerrow's *Introduction to Bibliography for Literary Students*. The title alone is a sufficient indication of the change in direction that bibliography was thereafter to take in appealing to a broader public and receiving thereby a broader participation in its discipline.

However, I take it that the case for querying the present value of descriptive bibliography is not so easily disposed of as all that. Let us grant what Sir Walter Greg was never tired of hammering home—that literary study *is* the final goal of bibliography (although not, I may add, the

---

whether the alteration by cancellation occurs in the *editio princeps* or is a piracy. In the one the editor of a definitive text must necessarily search for the cancellanda in order to evaluate (and record) the changes made in the text as originally set from manuscript, and also to return the edited text to the accidental texture of the cancellanda. In the other, the establishment of the text will not be of concern, but its transmissional history will be vitally affected, the more especially if the edition in question was itself used as the copy for subsequent editions. Hence any editor would wish to see the cancellanda in the piracy, too; and surely a descriptive bibliographer would feel compelled to illustrate the reasons for cancellation when he discovered the cancellanda. On the other hand, if the writer had in mind the patent fact that no collational formula by its nature can record the printing together as a full octavo sheet in a 16-page forme of four pages of preliminaries, four of text, and eight of cancels, and feared that this deficiency in the formulary would conceal the actual technical facts, he has too low an opinion of the duties of a descriptive bibliographer, who should certainly investigate the watermarks of various copies to see if the π^2 and G^2 gatherings were not indeed printed, in an octavo, with the four cancellans leaves, as one would normally expect, and to record the conclusions in a note to the collational formula. Such notes are often a necessity and must always be envisaged in any discussion of the ability of collational formulas to convey all the facts about printing.

immediate goal of all of its investigative parts). Let us repeat that this axiom by no means prevents a considerable value being placed on technical bibliographical investigations that may be gibberish to the literary critic but some day, in some manner, will be brought to bear as part of a broad attack on literary problems for which he will be grateful.[7] Too much has been made of the gap between the bibliographer and the critic by emphasizing the purely technical side of bibliography and underplaying the accepted material benefits that it confers upon criticism. To quote another *TLS* writer on bibliography ('Of Text and Type', 24 March 1966, p. 233): 'The critic is apt to stare in bewilderment at the bibliographer's algebra, wondering whether, and if so where, it contains a clue to his text. Sometimes he can hardly be blamed if he begins to feel that he is looking through a microscope at a life so minute that it can have no bearing on his own activities.' Surely this is an over-simplification. It strikes me as a fantastic proposition to expect a literary critic to have studied the analysis of running-titles in their transfer with the skeleton-formes from sheet to sheet so that he could follow with ease and sympathy the technical explanation why

7 Bibliography for its own sake is another red herring. I must confess that the intellectual pleasure one receives from the successful solution of a bibliographical problem is not always directly related to its literary application. No more, we may say, is the impetus that leads a theoretical mathematician to solve problems to be related to his interest in 'applied science'. Virtuosity may well be its own reward and I think we would be wrong to deny this satisfaction, for theoretical studies need no immediate application to justify their existence. I have in the past suggested, and I see no reason to alter my opinion, that it is a mistake to demand that every bibliographical investigation have a clearly delimited literary end. Much technical bibliographical investigation in that sense does exist for its own sake, as a pure printing or historical problem and nothing else. But before hands are lifted in pious horror at this plain fact, another proposition, also based on experience, should be mentioned. It is this. No matter how technical the study and seemingly far removed from critical application, I know of no practitioner who does not recognize that ultimately a way will be found to bring the technical information to bear on practical ends. The most immediate motivation, then, may have no literary purpose whatever, and purely technical interest may lead a person to engage in bibliographical research for its own sake in the sense that he may never (or not for years) have either the interest or the opportunity to seek in his own person a literary application. But experience shows that sooner or later (and especially these days if the researcher is in academic life) he moves like McKerrow and Greg toward the editing of texts where his expertise gives him a peculiar advantage over non-bibliographical scholars, especially if it is combined with some critical discrimination. That not everyone in this situation proves automatically to be a successful critical editor is not necessarily evidence demonstrating the limitations of a bibliographical background. Textual criticism, and its practical application in the form of an edited text, is not purely a mechanical operation. An insensitive mind will produce inadequate textual criticism whether the owner has been bibliographically taught or is the product of an advanced critical training school. As Greg once pithily remarked, 'No one can prevent fools from behaving after their kind', and Housman required a textual critic to have something other than a pudding for his brains.

certain text sheets of Crowne's *Darius* (1688) can be assigned by demonstration as original setting and as reprint, or one setting of certain pages in Dekker and Middleton's *Roaring girl* (1611) as authoritative and the other not. When this past year a revival of the controversy about the circumstances and meaning of the quarto preface to Shakespeare's *Troilus and Cressida* appeared in the correspondence columns of the *Times Literary Supplement*, with complete disregard for the well-established bibliographical facts about the printing of these two cancellans leaves, a simple statement of the bibliographical position was immediately accepted, although it was perhaps agreed to more on faith than on understanding. However, blessings should not be too closely scrutinized.

In short, no more need exists for the critics to read the bibliographical theoreticians than for the bibliographers to read the critical theoreticians. The point of communication lies in the area of application, and it is only here that we should be concerned about occasional ignorance and insensitivity on the part of the critic. The application of bibliographical theory to literary problems is itself a necessary act of intermediation. For instance, in the absence of a descriptive bibliography of Crowne, it would be absurd to ridicule a critic who, consulting a first edition, quoted from what he thought to be an authoritative source but by bad luck happened upon the less authoritative resetting of the early sheets.[8] Are we to expect every literary critic to collate for variants several copies of any first edition from which he wants to quote? If the facts are not readily available in normal reference books, a critic does the best he can.[9] All one can reasonably ask is that he does not make a virtue of laziness and quote from the most convenient source which he should be sophisticated enough to evaluate as an inferior authority, like Matthiessen in the famous case of 'soiled' versus 'coiled' fish of the sea.

Difficulty may easily arise when bibliographical facts with a literary application stay buried from the critic in bibliographical journals. It is true that the facts about the foreword to *Troilus and Cressida* had been in print for a number of years in a bibliograpical journal and had not gone unremarked thereafter. That the recent contestants had not done their homework is quite true. I take it that it would be an excessive demand on Professor Empson's time and patience to require him to read *Studies in Bibliography* each year; whether it would be excessive, however, to expect

8 I speak here of the casual critic, of course. If instead a critic were engaged on a full-scale study of Crowne and had neglected to keep abreast of published scholarship on the plays, even in bibliographical journals, we should have reason to believe him to be a careless scholar.

9 Indeed, in this hypothetical example we should be prepared to congratulate any critic who distrusted the edited text of Crowne and concerned himself to seek out the first edition, instead, as a source of accurate quotation.

him to have consulted Greg's *Shakespeare First Folio* or the annual Shakespeare checklists to make sure that he was aware of factual developments about plays that he proposed to write upon is perhaps more debatable. But if a descriptive bibliography of Shakespeare had been available that provided the evidence in the case, then I think one would have cause for some mild indignation at a failure to consult a commonly recognized source of interpretation of bibliographical evidence.[10]

I do not myself fancy the image recently proposed (*TLS*, 1966, p. 233) of bibliographer and critic stalking each other on different sides of the same hedge, each nervously glancing down from time to time to see if a pair of yellow stockings, cross-gartered, have found their way on to his legs. I yield to no one in my contempt for critics to whom intermediaries like descriptive bibliographies and bibliographically edited texts are available yet who ignore them and babble that 'it was great pity, so it was, This villanous saltpetre should be digg'd Out of the bowels of the harmless earth Which many a good tall fellow had destroyed, so cowardly'. I am especially concerned not so much at any indifference but indeed at the positive resistance to the new methodically edited texts one encounters sporadically, at least in my own country, from practising scholars who should know better.[11]

The point to which I am leading is the obvious one that any chasm between technical bibliography and literary criticism needs bridging from both sides. The bridge that bibliography can thrust out across the void consists on the one hand of good descriptive bibliographies and on the other of good editions. The two are, indeed, very closely linked since if the textual situation of an author is at all complex an edition cannot be formulated without the amount of preliminary investigation that would be the proper business of a descriptive bibliographer.[12]

10 Unfortunately, no up-to-date source like this is available, except for Greg's *Bibliography* (which was in print before the facts were known). On the other hand, the bibliographical solution of the printing of the foreword was made public in *SB*, ii (1949) and was referred to on p. 339 n. 3, of Greg's standard reference work *The Shakespeare First Folio* of 1955. It has been common knowledge, since, among scholars who are concerned with what bibliography has contributed to Shakespearian studies.

11 See, for instance, *American Notes & Queries*, i (June 1963), 159–60, and *American Literary Scholarship: An Annual*, 1965, Duke University Press, 1967, pp. 21–7.

12 That a good edition not only may contain a great deal of the same material but also may carry it forward so much farther toward completeness of fact and interpretation as to replace the usefulness of the descriptive bibliography, at least in certain respects, is a question not necessary to pursue here since it involves most complex relationships between textual and descriptive bibliography. The proposition is by no means always true since most editions do not see the need to continue the account of the publishing history much beyond the author's lifetime; moreover, the fullness of bibliographical detail characteristic of introductions in modern attempts at definitive editions is usually forced on the editor by the lack of adequate descriptive consideration to which he can refer the

I think a major and potentially dangerous misunderstanding that needs to be challenged has quietly become prevalent about descriptive bibliography. The most dangerous aspect, to my mind, is the narrow insistence that descriptive bibliographies have only one purpose which must shape and even excuse the governing of their methods by the degressive principle. For author-bibliographies this purpose is taken to be, in rather vague words, a literary one. We may perhaps make this more concrete by calling it literary in the specific terms of the identification and analysis principally of those editions that must be construed as substantive, or authoritative, in their texts. The reviewer of Professor Todd's *Burke* protested against this literary principle and the degressive features of the bibliography that were consonant with its purpose.[13] The critic who a few months earlier had published 'Of Text and Type' seemed in some part to agree that a literary pre-occupation is an unduly limiting and even a distorting factor in bibliographical description. He wrote, for instance: 'The aim of bibliography is not just

---

reader. Moreover, it would be foolish to reject the proffered virtues of descriptive bibliography while waiting for the uncertain appearance of editions that are truly definitive. None the less, if descriptive bibliographies were to become too textually oriented, as has been alleged, they might run the risk of replacement by the very editions they had fostered.

13 The protest was not, perhaps, logically organized. After very properly remarking that Professor Todd had concentrated his attention upon editions of textual significance and had reduced to handlist proportions the entries for most of the reprints and translations of the works surveyed, the reviewer then deplored that as a result the inevitable variations in printing between 1757 and 1812, and between books produced in different countries, were ignored under the degressive method because all the editions were considered to be textually unimportant; nevertheless, they were all books (see footnote 2 above). On the other hand, in his rejoinder to Mr. Carter on 4 Aug. the reviewer made clear that even an author-bibliography dedicated to fullness of description throughout, without degression, would not have satisfied him since any 'procedure which selects a single book [i.e., title] for analysis from the whole series of the productions of a press, and on the basis of that exemplar draws conclusions about book-production in broad and general terms', produces distorted emphasis. I do not myself understand that the usual author-bibliography does attempt to draw conclusions about book-production in these broad and general terms, and I take it that what conclusions a reader draws are beyond the competence of a bibliographer to control. However, this really turns out to be a side-issue. It becomes evident that the reviewer was not truly concerned with the inadequacies of the degressive method in an author-bibliography to yield the kind of comprehensive bibliographical information that he wanted. Believing in the pre-eminence of trade bibliographies, he would have felt obliged to object to any author-bibliography as not fulfilling the true purpose of description because of the principle involved in the selection of the books. It is perhaps proper to say, for the sake of the record, that the issue raised in this review between degressive and non-degressive bibliography was unduly coloured by this other and more powerful consideration, and some confusion of motive was the consequence. It was not perhaps wholly sporting to decry Professor Todd's use of the degressive method when a non-degressive method would have been logically subject to the same strictures. Unconsciously, it would seem, the reviewer was arguing

to serve textual criticism; further, restriction to the study and analysis of those aspects of printed books which refer directly to the text may inhibit the study of other aspects which may in the end prove the more useful.' The degressive principle, although not necessarily its methods, is then given implicit approval, but the statement follows that a 'rationale of degression' is still very far off.[14] On the other hand, the practical necessity for degressive bibliography cannot be put more pithily than in Mr. Carter's words: 'If every Penguin reprint is to be deemed, for descriptive purposes, "as interesting and significant" as the *editio princeps* or the last edition to be revised by the author, then future Soho bibliographies (and not they alone) will be as fat as Debrett and as expensive as a case of whisky. Must they be?' (*TLS*, 4 August 1966, p. 716).

God bless, of course they must not be! That we might need to make a choice of this nature is to be avoided at all costs. Just the same, I think it is time to take a look at the supposed relation to textual criticism which has been deplored by two knowledgeable reviewers as a distorting factor in descriptive bibliography, and in the process to examine whether—especially in the popular author-bibliographies—we are blindly following some ancient tribal rite that has lost its meaning and should be given a fresh rationale and method, some new steps for the dance, some new rhythms for the gourds. In the process I hope not to lose sight of the

---

on the basis of half a loaf is better than none; but this regret that in the *Burke* he did not receive all the printing information he would have liked got confused with the axiom that author-bibliographies cannot furnish this information in a satisfactory manner anyway. As a result, the ensuing discussion about degressive bibliography got off on the wrong foot and never quite recovered its equilibrium.

14 'Closely linked with the exclusiveness that demands the omission of what is irrelevant to the text [F.B.: This is a strange doctrine to me.] is the inclusiveness that demands a uniform treatment for all the works dealt with.' This is taken to be contradictory to the necessity of varying description according to the purpose of the bibliography and the date of its books as enunciated by Greg and Pollard in 1906, whose 'views were crystallized in the "degressive principle" defined by Madan in his appendix as "the principle of varying a description according to the difference of the period treated or of the importance of the work to be described". The modern bibliographer is admirably equipped to deal with works of equal textual importance, but confronted with a vast amount of material of varying importance he has only the most primitive means of providing the necessary variation in the technique of description. A "rationale of degression" is still very far off. Time spent on studying the printing and bookselling practice of the time and relating it to what one sees is always better spent than on forcing the evidence of one's eyes to fit a predetermined set of values. This is not to deny the value of subjecting each copy of every edition seen to the same set of questions; but it is not necessary always to record all the information thus derived, nor should it be thought that all the relevant information will be known once the questions are answered' (*TLS*, 24 March 1966, p. 234). That Greg and Pollard approved of the degressive method as enunciated by Madan (which is not to say of the principle itself) is incorrect, however.

question of degressive bibliography, which occasionally seems to resemble King Charles's head in these bibliographical discussions.

As a member of the editorial board for the Soho bibliographies, Mr. Carter speaks with some authority in his cautionary letter to the reviewer of *Burke*: 'When he says that "textual considerations are the primary impetus of author-bibliographies" he is perhaps over-refining the objectives of the Soho series, which is designed not only for the scholar and the literary critic . . . but also for book-collectors and librarians.' Of late years I must confess that I do not regularly curl up in bed with a good bibliography, and so my information is more limited than it should be—yet I am at a loss to name a single bibliography that is so oriented as to appeal, even in the main, to the textual critic and not to be of equal service to all other classes of users excepting only, perhaps, the printer-technician. Is it not obvious that the collecting instinct is inbred in the human race? If one does not collect books, one accumulates paintings, statuary, glass, furniture, vintage automobiles, stamps, theatre programmes, match-box covers, and in some spectacular cases, beloved of newspapers, wives.

Bibliographies are guides to collection first and foremost, and if they fail in this purpose, as many do in the ultimate refinements, they fail for all other purposes as well. The collection of books of literature, and especially of creative writing in the English language, has fostered more guides than the collection of medical books, of historical books, books about the history of science, or of any of the crafts like printing, for a single reason. This is the simple one that since literature is the most popular preserver of our cultural heritage, the amount of money that private and public collectors are willing to spend to accumulate works of literature, as well as books collateral to literary study, is in the aggregate considerably greater than the amount of money that collectors are prepared to spend to accumulate books on other subjects.

However, it would be naïve to assert that questions of text in any deliberate and immediate sense dictate the pattern of collecting. The value placed upon objects of historical interest as such is no doubt predominant, as much in the collection of Shakespeare as of cook-books, and this means that early editions that are closest in time to the date of a work's composition are taken to be more valuable for collection than editions that are comparatively late in the author's publishing history or in the history of printing in general. That the earliest editions are the more likely to preserve the text in a form closest to the original composition is fortunate for textual and literary scholars, but it is a highly dubious proposition that the average collector is moved to spend his money for this especial reason.[15] The

15 One cannot, of course, ignore the streak of sentiment that runs through book collecting and often seems to provide its chief impetus, as when a copy demonstrably handled by the author because he has inscribed it though with no more than his name

world gets on well enough with only one copy of the first edition of *Titus Andronicus* in existence; we should like more copies to compare duplicates in order to resolve possible doubtful readings and also to detect any press-variation, but these cannot begin to compare in importance with the information that this single copy gives us as the first edition set against what we should possess if, as for so many years, only what proved to be the second edition had been in existence. Scholarly investigation does not require the preservation of scores of copies of the first edition of Hawthorne's *Scarlet Letter* or of Crane's *Maggie.* Hence when collectors continue to purchase copies of commonly preserved first editions, some other motive than an overwhelming love of textual purity must lie behind their actions.[16]

I have no quarrel with the collector who is prepared to pay more for the first edition of Dryden's *Indian Emperour* (1667) than for the revised second of 1668, and certainly more than for the finally revised third of 1670 which is verbally the most single important authority for the text,[17] although I would quarrel with him if he confined his collecting activities merely to the 1667 edition and did not pursue this interesting book up through the editions in the 1690s and beyond. The historical fact of the initial form taken by a literary work (or of a non-literary work) may itself be a legitimate enough consideration often to override other considerations like the relative textual importance of subsequent editions. The best example I know that demonstrates how little collectors or librarians may care for textual value concerns Hawthorne's *Marble Faun* of 1860. Here the holdings of rare-book rooms in American libraries demonstrate a rather lukewarm interest in *Transformation,* the authentic first edition printed in England and placed on sale several weeks before the American first. This compares with a lively interest in acquiring a copy of the Boston edition.

---

is valued considerably more than uninscribed copies. From a scholarly point of view, the value of a presentation copy lies not in the autograph but only in the biographical fact of the name of the recipient or on the bibliographical fact of an inscribed date which may be useful (as in deposit copies) in setting straight obscure details of the printing history. And it is a paradox that first editions of posthumous books, even though textually as important as the firsts of books published in the author's lifetime, seldom command equal auction prices. To rationalize collectors' motives as textual is a serious over-simplification.

16 The products of a particular press (like the Kelmscott or Golden Cockerel) for historical or artistic reasons may also be thought more desirable than ordinary editions that are textually purer, but this is of course a special case and does not bear on the argument.

17 Amusingly, the collector of the first is partly right even on a textual basis, although he is not usually familiar with Greg's 'Rationale of Copy-text' (*SB,* III 1950–1), 19–36. Even in revised editions verbal corruption may take place; but more important perhaps for questions of authority is the fact that when a manuscript copy-text is wanting, the first edition retains pre-eminent authority in the texture of its accidentals even when in the matter of substantives it must bow in general to a revised edition.

Yet *Transformation* was set from Hawthorne's manuscript and is a true substantive text of prime authority, whereas the Boston *Marble Faun* has mere reprint status and is of concern to a textual critic only because it was set up in part from uncorrected English proofs, as the most recent editors were the first to discover.[18] When for collecting purposes the arbitrary decision was made (as it may still be in some circles) that without regard for priority of publication or of the history of textual transmission the edition first printed in an author's native country is to be considered the first on an absolute basis, one can see how little book collectors and librarians weigh considerations that are of primary concern to the scholar.

Much as scholars may regret the lemming tendencies of collectors and librarians, especially the exaltation of the first edition above the balanced accumulation of editions that will preserve the full publishing history of an author, the hard fact remains that the collection of materials must precede their study. There would be small market for descriptive bibliographies if the collectors of literary materials were not interested in them; and we had better reconcile ourselves to the necessities of collectors, and this reality, when proposals are made to improve the rationale of degressive bibliographies.[19] For these reasons it is perhaps improper to blame Professor Todd's use of the degressive principle on his paramount concern for literary, which is to say textual, values. Mr. Carter's statement covers the ground: the Soho *Bibliography of Burke* used the degressive method because it was intended to appeal to collectors and to librarians as well as to scholars, and these collectors and librarians are less interested in

18 A rhetorical question may also serve to illustrate the natural importance of historicity in collection. If one were the curator of a rare-book collection and were offered either the first-edition 1893 *Maggie* or the revised 1896, which would one choose? The answer is fairly obvious, I expect, even without consideration of monetary value. I should also expect the choice to be made without pondering the difficult question whether in its censorship of the language of 1893, the revised edition is on the whole superior or inferior in literary quality or in fidelity to what Crane might or might not have wanted as a writer.

19 Oddly enough, some features of bibliographies that by tradition appear to concern the collector alone, and to be of small interest to scholars, in the long run may serve both audiences. Professor Tanselle is quite correct when he remarks: 'Surely the time is already past when a list of the "points" necessary to identify first impressions of an author's work can be thought of as a "bibliography"' (*TLS*, 22 Sept. 1966, p. 884). It is still possible, of course, to satirize the frequent ignorance of book collectors, both private and public, about the bibliographical reasons for the points they are paying premiums to secure, especially since the priority may actually be the reverse of what is assumed. On the other hand, the more refined techniques fostered by the Hinman Collating Machine for determining the existence of discrete unmarked printings within nineteenth- and twentieth-century books demonstrate the occasional validity of these minute collectors' 'points' as evidence of different impressions. Difference in impression may sometimes produce textual variation (as by the correction of plates) that is the proper business of textual scholars.

identifying and purchasing comparatively late Burke items in preference to the earlier historical monuments. Thus the practical need did not exist to describe late editions with the minuteness that was thought useful for the early.

I cannot speak for Professor Todd, of course, but I suspect that the fact that the historically significant Burke editions which demanded and received the most thorough inquiry were also mainly of textual significance was more or less fortuitous, and the degressive method of handlist entry was applied to late editions in considerable part because of their lack of intrinsic historical importance as documents close in time to the origin of the works. To imply that Professor Todd compiled his bibliography chiefly with a textual critic or editor in mind is, in my view, to imply nonsense if by 'chiefly' we mean 'immediately'. Any bibliography, it seems to me, must be compiled with the immediate purpose of guiding the collection of materials—whether literary, historical, scientific—although the ultimate benefit will be to scholarship once the collection has been made and is opened for study. However, if the bibliography is to be a well-rounded and truly valuable exemplar, it must have secondary motives to aid scholarly research in the collected items; but until the collection is made there can be no scholarship, and hence the primary purpose of a bibliography is to ensure comprehensive, accurate, and efficient collection. First things must come first. Indeed, I should say that if a bibliography fails to be an adequate guide to collection, any secondary virtues appealing to literary students cannot save it.

If we will hold in suspense for the present the question of degressive bibliography, it would be hard to demonstrate any conflict of interest between the collector and the scholar that need affect any feature of descriptive bibliography. Let us put the case on the inclusion or the exclusion of detail and take it as an axiom that no one is hurt by the inclusion of matters that do not directly interest him, but someone is indeed hurt if matters are excluded that are of considerable usefulness to him. Obviously, the matter that is sacrificed most frequently in bibliographies is that which is of no direct aid to the comprehensive collection of all forms of a book, including its variants. This may be precisely the information that a scholar wants most after the collection has been completed, for it would be foolish in the extreme to suggest that descriptive bibliographies automatically lose their usefulness, like bingo cards, once the game is over.

A well-balanced bibliography, then, must supply what discoverable detail will be of service to the comprehensive collection of the described materials. In this respect the value of the guide is in two parts. First, it provides positive information about identification so that a collection may be made as complete as the knowledge of the bibliographer has extended. Here the *agreement* of all books in the collection with the bibliography is the desideratum. Second, it provides in its description as much detail as practicable in order to give the collector a sporting chance to identify *disagreements* with the guide, to confirm that they are significant, and thus to increase the collection beyond the scope of previously discovered evidence. Unless the bibliography is cast in a form that permits this extension of its usefulness, its method is surely faulty. This is, of course, the main difficulty with the degressive principle.

If one could be certain that the positive information already ascertained was complete, paradoxically for collecting purposes—even for the *editio princeps*—no need would exist for the traditional full description but only for a series of notes to handlist entries, something like the late entries in a degressive bibliography except that these are never so thoroughly investigated as to permit such treatment.

If for the moment we are to treat only the form in which to reproduce the positive information already ascertained for agreement, it is obvious that the farther the bibliographer's investigations have progressed toward what is hypothetically a definitive knowledge of the physical characteristics of an edition in its various forms, the less need there is to reproduce these details for the collector save in a list of 'points'. For example, the editors of the Centenary Edition of Nathaniel Hawthorne went so deeply into the history of the first edition of *The Scarlet Letter* and applied so many tests beyond the normal duties of a descriptive bibliographer, such as the machine-collation of eight copies and the spot-checking of revealed details against ten more, that one may be as confident as a world of mutability permits that if a collector will purchase two copies with clearly defined characteristics in the duplicate typesetting of signature 21, he will possess every variant form that this edition took outside of a dropped exclamation point and a few displacements of type. Secondly, if he will check such and such readings, he will be able to distinguish this first edition of 1850 from the second and the third editions in the same year (if they have been sophisticated). In all practical terms, therefore, a simple notation—*The Scarlet Letter*, first edition, Boston, 1850—with perhaps four lines of type beneath it fully suffices for all purposes of collecting. Since in this case impression and edition are known to coincide, no distinction of printings within the first edition is required.

A more complex case concerns Hawthorne's *House of the Seven Gables*. Unlike *The Scarlet Letter* which was printed from type-metal in only one impression, *Seven Gables* was plated from the start and went through a large number of printings, of which the first five (though otherwise undifferentiated) are dated 1851. The Centenary editors put six copies through the Hinman Machine and spot-checked the results against twenty-one additional copies. The evidence thus assembled was found to agree with the publisher's records noting four printings in 1851, although there was still a surprise in store. Given a bibliographical analysis of this search-ing kind, all one needs for the purposes of collection is the title and date, 1851, followed by the evidence from type-batter that differentiates the two pre-publication printings and then the remaining three dated 1851, the last with a note that it seems to represent a printing in September 1852 recorded by the publisher but not otherwise identified. This fifth printing, falsely dated, can be distinguished from the fourth, incidentally, not by type-batter but by gutter-measurements that vary four to five millimetres. A complete collection of all forms of the first edition would consist not of these five printings, of course, but of all subsequent printings up to the four impressions of the New Fireside Edition first published in 1886. But completeness is not yet. All printings from these first-edition plates exist in two states resulting from the use of duplicate plates to print half-sheet 22. Since in the production of the duplicate a comma at 343.31 was jerked out when the flong was removed to make the cast of the first plate, the second plate is readily distinguished by the absence of this authoritative comma; and a determined collector if he is not content with purchasing two copies of the first printing may continue his duplication of copies with the variant plates in gathering 22 all through their publishing history.[20]

What may be called this quantitative recording of available informa-tion in a well-wrought bibliography can scarcely be distinguished from the qualitative. One of the reasons why collectors' manuals of points have been largely displaced by rigorous bibliographical investigations is that the relationship between the noticed variants was not always indicated, or, if so, was not always accurate. That is, if a collector was advised to secure a copy of a book with a misprint on one page, and another copy with the correct reading, and by the law of scarcity the misprint was thought to be the more desirable, one would be bound to infer that the misprint identi-fied an early printing of the book and therefore a more desirable historical condition for collection. I know of no tip-sheet manual of this kind that customarily pursues the matter to its ultimate conclusion by adducing bib-liographical evidence from collation on the Hinman Machine. For in-

20 In this particular case, the binding evidence of the five states of the stamping of 1851 copies recorded in the *Bibliography of American Literature* is an untrustworthy guide when compared with the evidence of type-batter revealed by the Hinman Ma-chine. A spot-check of the large collection of thirteen 1851 copies held at Ohio State University kindly made for me by Professor Bruccoli reveals that, of three copies of *BAL* binding A, one is the first printing and two are the second. The single OSU copy of binding C is the fourth printing. One copy in the B or E binding is the first printing but two are the fourth, and so on. The B and E states could not be clearly distinguished owing to the difficulty of measuring a difference of $\frac{1}{32}$ of an inch on a curved surface. Thus a truly determined collector apparently could amuse himself by securing each one of the four actual 1851 printings in at least several binding states.

stance, if the book was printed from type-metal a correction of a misprint might be made in the type either during the press-run or else between impressions. On the other hand, the misprint might as readily have resulted from a disturbance in the type during the course of the initial impression or between impressions when formes were unlocked, so that the error could represent a later state than the correct reading. Other tests need application since the evidence of the misprint is itself perfectly neutral. Similarly, if a book was plated the good reading might have resulted from a correction of the plate between printings, as often happens; but on the contrary the error might well have been created during a partial resetting to repair a plate so that the correct reading is the earlier.

Qualitative method begins the process of interpreting the quantitative evidence that has been supplied as the raw material for collection, and is the second requirement for a good bibliography. In some cases the description of a book can scarcely be written until the physical evidence is interpreted in terms of priority. The transcript of a variant title-page of a second printing obviously must be put in a subsidiary position to the transcript of the title found in the first printing, which must form a part of the central block of the description. This being so, a bibliographer of Crane's *Maggie* of 1896 must assess the partly contradictory evidence and make up his mind to select the black-letter title of the wove-paper printing as his norm, and the roman title-page of the laid-paper printings as his later variant before he can write the description.[21] And unless all bibliographical evidence has been exhausted a reader should not be satisfied merely by a statement of probability that a previously unrecorded copy with *The Three Musketeers* advertised on the last page instead of *The Story of the West* series identifies a later instead of an earlier printing of *Maggie* on the laid paper.

In a more extreme case, a bibliographer would certainly be responsible for determining beyond all doubt the priority of the two separate editions of Dryden's *Wild Gallant* in 1669 before he could assign a number and describe the *editio princeps* in the place of honour. In most cases physical, which is to say bibliographical, evidence is available if one is prepared to

21 The physical evidence in favour of the black-letter title and wove paper as characteristic of the first printing is overwhelming, but the evidence of type-batter is not systematic and indeed two pieces of this evidence would point to the reverse. Fortunately, these two are not confirmed by other batter evidence, some of which favours the wove with real positiveness, and the two mavericks can perhaps be explained as resulting from the different pressures of the makeready in the two printings, whereas no explanation is possible for the other evidence, such as the offset of the black-letter title on the verso of the half-title in the British Museum wrappered American copy deposited by Heinemann to secure copyright, even though this copy has a tipped-in cancellans Heinemann title that imitates the Appleton roman title-page.

dig deeply enough. Because the Ticknor and Fields Cost Books listed four 1851 printings of *The House of the Seven Gables*, a scrupulous bibliographer would have been alerted to put enough copies on the Hinman Machine to discover the evidence of type-batter that identified these printings and, as a bonus, offered him the 'lost' printing of 1852.

On the other hand, in rare cases physical evidence may be completely wanting in the usual bibliographical sense. Stephen Crane's story 'His New Mittens' was published simultaneously in the November 1898 numbers of *McClure's* in the United States and *Cornhill* in England. The subsequent reprint in the collection *The Monster* has no textual authority. Priority in this case in terms of which magazine appeared a few days before the other is of little consequence. What a collector who is accumulating historical documents needs to know—and for a literary critic the point is crucial because of some textual differences—is what is the first in terms of relationship to the lost manuscript. Was one magazine text set from proofs of another—and if so, which? If not, is there still a chance that one is derived from the other in its textual transmission, as if one was set up from a typescript copied from the original typescript? Or is the relationship not linear but one of radiation? That is, was one set from the original typescript and the other from its carbon, or was each typed independently from the holograph? Even if one has a derived copy-relation to the other, did Crane perhaps go over the subsidiary copy and make authoritative alterations not present in the primary copy? These are questions of some delicacy that can be answered by no external evidence (so far as is known), and they are not susceptible of bibliographical analysis (since it would appear that one was not directly derived from the other), and perhaps only tentatively of solution by textual criticism. One could scarcely blame a bibliographer of Crane who gave up and merely recorded the facts of roughly simultaneous periodical publication without attempting to adjudicate priority. But he would not be of much help to the collector *or* to the literary scholar consulting his work.

In both categories of quantitative and qualitative bibliography it strikes me that the collector and the literary student are equally involved since the same evidence as it is assembled and interpreted is needed by both. A literary student may grow impatient at the attention paid to finicky little points, of interest only to a collector and of no literary significance, he thinks, as in a solemn discussion of the three types of paper found in the fly-leaves and endpapers of Crane's *Little Regiment*. But this is a fault in the interpretative analysis, for he would rapidly change his tune if these were to occur in a book in which the differentiation of printings by such means put bibliographical order into alterations in the text that needed to be evaluated for authority. Hawthorne's *Marble Faun* is such a case. Any collector's point may or may not end by having literary significance. One can never tell ahead of time.[22] What is clear is that the real value of such small matters of record is usually obscured by the failure of the bibliographer to discuss them qualitatively, that is, to determine with precision whether—especially in modern books—they are clues to the fact of different printings, and, if so, in what order. From then on it is up to the literary student, who can examine whether textual variation is involved or else just the author's publishing history, which after all is a literary fact too since it is an index to the reception of his works by the public. The most serious deficiency in bibliographies of machine-printed books is this lack of knowledge, or of interest, in how to go about the business of qualitatively interpreting the quantitative information.

With the exception of this frequent fault in qualitative interpretation, so far at least a bibliography aimed squarely at the collector is equally satisfactory to the scholar up to the point where the degressive principle enters. Yet there are other features of ideal bibliographies that have nothing to do with the strict purposes of the collection of facts and their ordering and assessment, and thus are not an integral part of a simple guide to collectors. In this area alone, I suggest, the method of a bibliography may be affected by a purely literary or by some other motive, and I hope that collectors will learn to be patient at the space this material may occupy. Although it will not directly aid collecting, it may often prove instructive and perhaps even helpful in establishing a rationale of accumulation.

This material is so rich that I must restrict myself to only two major examples.

No bibliography, unfortunately, and no editor before the Centenary Hawthorne, noticed that the latter third of the second edition of *The Scarlet Letter* was printed from the standing type of the first. This fact has nothing to do with collecting, except perhaps to stimulate a person to

22 For instance, if a bibliography of Crane pointed out a series of typos in the 1893 *Maggie*, a literary student might query the usefulness of listing 'amirable' for 'admirable' and 'oblgied' for 'obliged' on p. 67, 'raking' and 'trash' on p. 68 for 'racking' and 'thrash', and so on through 'now, door' for 'door, now' on p. 80. It is clear that at least partial pie may have occurred in sheet 5, which takes in these pages, with resetting; or else the original careless setting was not proofread by Crane for this sheet. A spot-checking of a number of copies does not turn up any variation; nevertheless, a descriptive bibliographer would be delinquent if he did not supply a sufficient number of these errors so that any future owner of an 1893 *Maggie* could see if he has hit the jackpot with another state of sheet 5. The recovery of the original setting, if a pie indeed occurred, would be of considerable textual interest because any reset text in this 16-page forme would be, in general, less authoritative than the original setting elsewhere. This is as true for the seemingly correct readings, and for all 'accidentals', as it is for the crux whether 'raking his brains' on p. 68 is an error and the 1896 'racking' a correction, or the reverse. Naturally the bibliographer would point out the printing evidence furnished by the presumed pie about the work-and-turn printing in a 16-page forme since egregious errors are found in both formes of the octavo gathering.

acquire a copy of the second edition to pair with his first. The fact applies to all copies of the second edition, the textual variants in the standing type are not needed to identify the two editions correctly, and it produces no internal variance or multiple states of the second edition. It simply is a fact about the second edition. But what a fact! Textually it identifies all the changes made in the standing type as ordered by a publisher's reader, not by Hawthorne. This being so, the variation in the reset pages must be equally unauthoritative, and an editor may be saved from making an ass of himself by accepting some very tempting variant readings in the second that are mere sophistications. Of all bibliographical facts about *The Scarlet Letter* that are of literary concern this is the most important.

The usefulness of this single piece of information is not exhausted by the text, however. From the uneven pattern of distributed and standing pages when the order was received for a second edition, one can determine what would not otherwise be apparent: the first edition was printed by work-and-turn in 16-page formes. That the first edition of *The Scarlet Letter*, moreover, was printed from type-metal as shown by the distribution is an interesting commentary on the publisher's judgement of its probable lack of popularity, a pessimism that was not modified even by the rapid call for a second edition: the second edition, also, was printed from type-metal in one impression; and it was not until the third edition, in the same year, that the publisher plated the book. A collector had better have a copy of this third edition, therefore, since it has some historicity as the first plated edition.[23] The textual scholar wants to see this edition to discover whether Hawthorne took the opportunity to revise the text before its type was set. Finally, of course, these third-edition plates by their use for any number of editions over the course of more than thirty years fixed the pattern of the textual history of the book, unfortunately in a rather corrupt form. The date of the last printing from these plates is of interest as well (it is in some post-1886 reprint of the New Fireside Edition), and should be recorded for the benefit of the enlightened collectors who, quite correctly, might see the historical importance of this impression. The textual scholar, also, would like to see this printing in order to put it on the Hinman Machine against a copy of the first printing from the plates, thereby to recover a list of all the textual changes made by alteration or repair of the plates during their long career. The printing historian, as

23 Mr. John Carter would allow a violation of the degressive method in special cases, although I am not certain he would agree with this one. 'I am sure Falconer Madan would approve an entry by the putative bibliographer of the works of Mr. Eric Linklater for the 1957 edition of *Private Angelo* privately printed for Sir Allen Lane, on the ground of its claim to be the first book to be filmset in Great Britain (by the Intertype Fotosetter)', *TLS*, 11 Aug. 1966, p. 732.

well as the textual scholar interested in the transmission of the text, can thereby identify simply by inspection the impressions for which the various changes were made.

My second example will be briefer but no less important. I suggest that the student of publishing history and the literary scholar deserve to have recorded in a descriptive bibliography all available facts about the financial arrangements of a book as well as everything to do with its publication and subsequent history with especial reference to its popularity as evidenced by sales. Thus a bibliographer of Crane's *Great Battles of the World* (1901) should be obliged to track down and to print the pertinent data about the sale of this book from the letters of Cora Crane; of Alfred Plant, the solicitor for the Crane estate; the agent, and the publisher. The lengthy correspondence with the literary agents James Pinker and G. W. Perris that concern the proposals for and finally the posthumous collection of *Last Words* (1902), or the arrangements for the completion of the manuscript of *The O'Ruddy* and then its sale and publication in two countries, are the legitimate concern of bibliography even though they have no application to the guided collection of these books. One can only applaud those bibliographers who search publishers' records to reproduce contracts, correspondence, and especially to provide the number of copies ordered for each printing of an edition down to the last Colonial issue.

Earlier I remarked that bibliographical descriptions were designed for two purposes: first to provide positive information so that a collector could know he had exhausted the bibliographer's expertise when he had acquired all examples of a book that agreed with the description and its notes; and second by the selection and the method of reproduction of significant detail to identify copies that are variant from those recorded by the bibliographer since they disagree with the details of the description. In opening this matter I may remark that I do not follow the complaints of the *TLS* bibliographical reviewer that the details commonly chosen for notice in descriptions are governed by the literary motives of the bibliographers. Of course, if one is to kill two birds with a single stone it is more efficient than with two stones. The literary divisions of a book have an independent interest in description that would alone justify their recording. A reader of a Crane bibliography should be informed that the 1896 revised *Maggie* has a Publisher's Note to the reader that concerns the work, and the first English edition of the same year an Appreciation by W. D. Howells. Whether the author has a foreword himself, or not; to whom the book is dedicated; whether its head-title agrees with the title-page—these are legitimate concerns of readers interested in the use of collections and therefore employing bibliographies as the reference books they should indeed be about an author, a genre, a period. It is as legitimate for an

investigator of prologues and epilogues to go to a bibliography of Restoration drama for a record of non-authorial examples as it is for a student of
Prospero's farewell to skim through Greg in search of other examples of
l'envoi. The alternative would be to read the corpus of Elizabethan drama.
The more multiple uses to which descriptive bibliographies may be put,
the more valuable they become.

The indicators of literary divisions of a book have a peculiarly important
value in themselves, therefore, but they also are very handy for technical
purposes because their form may change in an identifiable manner in
different editions. Thus if a bibliographer of hand-printed books chooses
to use quasi-facsimile transcription to reflect the exact form of the typography of a title-page, a head-title, the heading to a preface, and even the
exact form of a *finis*, he is doing so not simply for antiquarian, and surely
not for literary, purposes, but in the hope that if a variant copy turns up it
will be revealed for what it is by the differences from the details chosen
for the exact description.[24] I would not argue with any critic who pointed
out that some technical details of printing not associated with conventional
literary divisions might be even more valuable for identification, such as
type and paper, and even evidences of imposition and machining. For in-
tance, it would be helpful to note the evidence that the first printing of
The House of the Seven Gables was machined work-and-turn with 16-page
formes for its gatherings in 8s whereas double paper came to be used
starting with the second printing and thus 32-page formes were utilized.
A bibliographer should certainly deploy every weapon in his armoury
within practicable limits to serve the collector on the one hand by offering
full and explicit description of known evidence for identification and on

24 It may happen that the notation of details that superficially has a literary motive
may be associated more vitally with questions of printing and thence with identification.
For example, the form that a title takes in the running-heads of a sixteenth- or seventeenth-century book may have a strong literary interest if it differs from the text of the
head-title or of the title-page. However, the exact recording of the typographical details
of the running-titles according to form and position recommended in *Principles of
Bibliographical Description* is basically aimed not only at permitting an analysis in some
books of the method of printing but also at listing evidence for checking in one of the
most likely areas for variation in cases of partial resetting or of concealed editions. On
the other hand, since the running-heads of modern books do not vary, normally, notation
of these could be a formality for identification and aimed instead at establishing the title
in its different appearances within a book, as in half-title, title-page, head-title, running-
heads. That this description is not always idle may be illustrated by the first English edition of Hawthorne's *Marble Faun* under the title of *Transformation* on the title-page
but with the sub-title 'The Romance of Monte Beni' in head-title and running-heads.
This difference reflects the fact that printing was started before a title was firmly agreed
on and before Hawthorne had capitulated to the publisher's insistence on 'Transformation'.

the other by casting this description in such form, with such appropriate selection of detail, as may most probably reveal the existence of variation unknown to the bibliographer when a copy is compared against the bibliographical entry.

In this matter each period will have its peculiar details that are of the most service. Typographical detail is often useful in early books where the variant use of roman, italic, black-letter, or of capitals, lower case, swash letters, and so on, in headings of various kinds, especially in running-titles, offers a significant series of points for checking agreement or disagreement. It is good that we seem to be edging toward a more exact method for the description of type than the standard measurement of twenty lines, which I have not found to be very satisfactory. Paper in early books may or may not be significant for identification. The usual job-lots mixture found in Elizabethan commercial printing is quite impossible to describe in any useful manner. On the other hand, in the eighteenth century the growing equation of impression with a uniform lot of paper begins to offer reliable evidence which becomes a positive necessity to record in the nineteenth and twentieth centuries. From the very little bibliographical work done on Crane to date, for instance, it seems clear that the Appleton use in the 1890s of wove versus laid paper may prove to be significant. Moreover, the Appleton laid paper must be described as with or without the seal watermark and with vertical or horizontal chainlines, or valuable evidence will be overlooked.

None the less, as McKerrow remarked about the need for a conservative adherence to the old-spelling forms of texts, we insist on certain conventions of bibliographical description through a recognition of our ignorance. As I have suggested earlier, for simple purposes of identification if we could be sure that the circumstances were such as to permit it, we could scrap as useless rigmarole all conventions of quasi-facsimile transcription of titles and headings, the elaborate construction of collational formulas, the description of typography, paper, contents, and so on. Should they then be abandoned on a new degressive principle in which the fullness of description would vary for each entry according to the confidence of the bibliographer in the definitiveness of his investigation? I am afraid that this would prove unfeasible, and besides it would slight the non-technical users of bibliographies as reference books for more purposes than a bibliographer can perhaps conceive. Still, it would be amusing to contemplate this carrying of the degressive principle to its logical conclusions (or confusions).

In our state of innocence, then, I suggest two main points. First, the kinds of variation that are encountered are likely to alter from period to period, and thus the details of description must remain appropriate to the problem by altering in conformity. The scrupulous transcription in quasi-facsimile of headings in early books on which I place so much reliance[25] is of little or no value in much nineteenth- and twentieth-century printing. Early books printed from type-metal have few problems of impression but many of issue and edition. But when plates enter the picture one of the most delicate responsibilities of a descriptive bibliographer is the differentiation of concealed separate printings within an edition. This poses problems that most bibliographers of modern books have been unwilling or unable to face.

The simple fact is, the kind of detail that is required in modern books to replace the kind of detail appropriate for Elizabethan can be staggering in its demands on the investigation and sometimes on a reasonable brevity of description. For instance, it was a devoted book collector, Professor Bruccoli, checking a personal copy of the 1896 laid-paper *Maggie* against a library copy, not against the three available bibliographical descriptions (which would have proved unhelpful), who found an unrecorded impression characterized by a change in the advertisement on the last page. So far inquiry in the standard rare-book collections in the United States has disclosed only one other example (not catalogued as a variant), and so we may take it as probable that even a most scrupulous bibliographer of Crane, were it not for this alert collector, might have been unable to record the existence of this impression. Yet advertisements are known to change with impressions, as evidenced by two other Appleton editions of Crane. Foreseeing, as he ought, the possibility that variant copies could come to light in the future, should the bibliographer of the 1896 *Maggie*, and of all other such books, list the titles of each advertisement in an integral gathering? In *Maggie* these integral advertisements take up twelve pages of a 16-page quire. Just the same, a bibliographer had better make up the list if he expects his description to be sufficiently detailed to reveal further variants than he has himself observed in an area where they are to be anticipated.

But the question of detail, at least in plated modern books, goes deeper. No description that can be conceived would enable an owner checking his private copy against a bibliography to detect that he had a variant setting of gathering 22 in *The House of the Seven Gables* if the bibliographer had not noticed it from a machine collation. I am interested in the impact of the Hinman Machine on descriptive bibliography. I do not see how any future definitive bibliography of modern books can be issued that has not made extensive use of this machine-collation. We have just had published early volumes of one of the great bibliographical enterprises of this

25 For the bibliographical reasons for a choice of descriptive detail in the latter half of the seventeenth century, see my 'Bibliography and Restoration Drama' in *Bibliography*, Clark Memorial Library, 1966, pp. 9–16.

century, Jacob Blanck's *Bibliography of American Literature*. The scrupulous sight comparisons against extensive notes, and of duplicate copies when they existed in the libraries visited, the recording of highly technical evidence beyond previous experience for use in the constant checking of new copies seen, all this took the energies of one or more experts headed by a singularly accomplished bibliographer for a number of years. As a result we have a record that is unsurpassed to date for its completeness and its recording of minute detail never before recognized. Yet this truly extraordinary investigation, performed according to standards that I think we may fairly say were unexampled in modern bibliography as applied to a task of such scope—but without utilizing the Hinman Machine—failed to disclose the duplicate typesettings in *The Scarlet Letter* and *The House of the Seven Gables*; the third edition of *The Scarlet Letter* in a new typesetting was listed as a second printing of the second edition; the five printings of *Seven Gables* dated 1851 were not identified and ordered except wrongly by binding states set against the four Cost Books entries, nor were all of the concealed printings in 1860 identified of *The Marble Faun* (except for those with different make-ups), at least one of which contains textual information of some import. Somehow the Harvard issue of the 1896 *Maggie* with cancellans roman title-leaf replacing the black-letter original in a wove-paper copy escaped notice, and so on.

Since more and more the differentiation of modern variants depends upon the recording in bibliographies of extremely minute evidence, some of which can be discovered only by machine-collation and its expert interpretation for descriptive purposes, I predict that a revolution is about to to take place in the bibliographical description of nineteenth- and twentieth-century books if the public that buys these reference guides learns to demand scientific results. If I were a collector who had paid well for a first edition of *The House of the Seven Gables* and had ended, it is true with a first edition, but with a misdated copy of the fifth printing a year later (in an alleged first-printing binding state), I think it would occur to me that something is wrong with a discipline like bibliography that fails to keep up with the newest scientific instruments for investigation, whether they be Dr. Stevenson's methods for photographing paper or the now common use of the Hinman Machine for the editing of texts.[26]

26 Much will depend upon the reaction of booksellers, who are supposed to educate book-collectors. These are too often unaware, however, of what scholars are doing with books that are their stock-in-trade. For instance, it is now six years after the appearance of the Centenary *Scarlet Letter* with its information about the duplicate typesetting in the first edition; yet no bookseller seems to have picked up this information and identified a copy in his catalogue as one or the other settings. It is an open question, also, how many rare-book libraries have altered their catalogue cards to identify their *Scarlet Letter* holdings.

It is a cause for some private amusement, then, to read that bibliographies are being unduly canted toward the uses of textual criticism. In my
experience in editing two nineteenth-century authors I have found quite
the contrary: that available descriptive bibliographies have been of little
more value than enumerative handlists. The truth is, modern textual criticism has progressed so far beyond descriptive bibliography as to be an aid
to description, not the reverse. If a definitive Hawthorne or Crane bibliography is written, as proposed, it will be as the result of the searching editorial investigation of these authors. The editor's work, it is true, would
have been materially lightened if scientific bibliographies of comparable
technical expertise had been available. They were not only not available—
they and their like had not even been dreamed of. Let me state another
hard truth. Descriptive bibliographers of nineteenth- and twentieth-century
books are hopelessly old-fashioned and out of date in their aims and
methods compared to the modern breed of editor—at least the breed that
is developing under the spur of substantial government grants for the
production of definitive editions of American authors planned on the
model of the pioneering Centenary Hawthorne.

This has been my second point. It has, I think, something to do with
the current discussion about the form of descriptive bibliography, and even
the basic usefulness of the discipline. We may put aside from any further
present notice, then, the relation of form to content and of both to the new
methods of technical investigation that are bound to affect descriptive
bibliography and, one hopes, not only the more informed collection of
books but also their more informed scholarly use. This is the wave of the
future, and it cannot be commanded to retreat. The effects will be far-
reaching, of course, and will have much to do with the rationale of descriptive bibliography as a whole, perhaps in quite unpredictable ways. My own
gazing into the clouded crystal ball produces only one or two suggestions.
The first is that of all aspects of descriptive bibliography, its contribution
to the publishing history of an author or of a literary form has been the
most neglected. In part I put the neglect down to the not always clear connection between this aspect and the immediate purposes of bibliographies
to guide collection. In part, also, it may be the victim of what I am inclined
to regard as a falsely puffed-up concept of the somehow mysterious literary
value of bibliographical description as such, especially the full description
of the *editio princeps* and allied substantive editions as against the neglect
permitted editions of less concern for the narrow purpose of establishing
the definitive form of the text.

In my view this last represents less than complete textual scholarship.
Obviously, if one is playing the desert-island game and dealing on an
either-or basis, no doubt can exist which is the more important—prece-

dence must be given to the textual history of a book within the range of its composition and authoritative revision as against the subsequent history of its transmission beyond the range of demonstrable or of possible authority. But if the life of an author is bound up in the total history of his text—as I should assert—an author is what his text represents to any generation one wishes to select. Scholars have found a quite independent interest in tracing the taming of Shakespeare's Elizabethan vigour and originality of language in the eighteenth century and beyond and in the then reversed trend of a gradual recovery of a respect for the texts of the early editions as the nature of their peculiar authority began to be more precisely understood. This history of the transmission of Shakespeare's text is not a mere academic exercise, however, but a generative form of scholarship. The state of the text in some part reflects the critical views of a period, and sometimes has assisted in forming them; and since all literary criticism is a continuum, we are in the end as affected by Morgann's essay on Falstaff as by Dover Wilson's, by Goethe's view of Hamlet as by Stoll's. The case is even more pointed, however. Modern texts of Shakespeare still depend excessively on the eighteenth- and early nineteenth-century versions, and even the most recent editions have not always succeeded in weeding out traditional non-Shakespearian readings the origin of which has long since been forgotten—like 'a rose by any other *name* would smell as sweet'.

It is of the utmost critical importance, therefore, to track down and to differentiate beyond degressive handlist standards of accuracy the complete list of Shakespeare editions from Rowe to the present. For instance, it is only in comparatively recent times that three different editions of Rowe, with somewhat different texts, have been recognized so that the origin of certain Shakespeare emendations could be correctly assigned. The case of Shakespeare, as of the black-letter Chaucers, may be an extreme example, but its principle marches on. And this principle is the importance to the total critical view of an author's publishing history as most broadly interpreted.[27]

27 Although much of the publishing history gains its importance from textual considerations since in it is established the tradition—often corrupt and misleading—of an author's text, it also contains more, some of use as a guide to collection, some to students of technical printing and binding matters, and so on and so on through the history of book-manufacture and sales. For instance, if one were to ask what would be the value of a Hawthorne or a Crane bibliography after the textual history had been wrung dry by definitive editions, the answer is reasonably clear. First, a full descriptive bibliography would bring together between two covers and in readily ordered and usable form material widely scattered over perhaps ten volumes containing textual and historical introductions. Second, a definitive edition is not a variorum. The editors of Hawthorne collated all editions and printings within Hawthorne's lifetime, and continued this collation through the Riverside edition of 1883, edited by Hawthorne's son-in-law

The immediate question I take it is whether degressive bibliography is in a satisfactory position to perform this function. In my own opinion it is not when it is practised as in the present day. For a moment, however, let me pay my respects to the phrase itself and what it has come to mean as against its original signification. I shall do so briefly, and certainly arbitrarily, because the whole question is one that would take almost an essay in itself thoroughly to analyse.

In its origin, as a memorandum attached to Pollard's 'Some Points in Bibliographical Description', Madan argued for four degrees of fullness in the description of books 'according to the difference of the period treated or of the importance of the work to be described'.[28] This difference he was to suggest over ten years later in his Presidential Address in 1920 to this Society as 'the view of books in proper perspective'. To Madan, it is very clear—especially from the generally overlooked commentary on the Memorandum contained in his Address—the importance of a book was roughly to be equated with its date. This is to be expected as the general view of the time: in great part Pollard's 'Points' focus on the basic problem of describing incunabula as if this was the most important question

---

Lothrop, which fixed the textual tradition up to the appearance of the Centenary volumes. However, one lesser strand of the tradition radiates from the derived Autograph edition of 1900 and its various printings usually offered under various guises as 'editions'. The Autograph was therefore added to the collation list, and its variants recorded in the Historical Collation of the textual tradition. On the other hand, once the textual derivation was established, the Centenary editors did not list by date and number of copies printed each impression made from the third-edition plates, or of derived 'editions' from the fourth edition 'Little Classics' plates of 1876, some of which lasted beyond 1900. Nor, once the lack of authority was established of the first English edition by Bohn in 1851 followed in the same year by another edition from Routledge, both piracies, was the English textual history pursued. Hence the literary historian is completely ignorant at the moment of the publishing history of *The House of the Seven Gables* in England and thus of the reception and modification of the text in Britain. Finally, the Centenary introductions do not concern themselves with states of the binding, the kinds of paper, and so on, in the considerable history of this book's publication, though they are a part of publishing history comprising book manufacture as well as literary history. In short, a descriptive bibliography that adequately traced the publishing history of *The House of the Seven Gables*, even if generally confined to the United States, would hold a great deal of material information not so directly of textual concern as to occupy an editor intent upon establishing the text and delineating its major textual history. When these matters are looked into from the point of view of pure descriptive bibliography, not simply of textual authority and tradition, one may confidently anticipate the discovery of much fresh publication information not turned up, or recorded, by the Centenary editors in their own searching investigation of the text.

28 The 'Memorandum' appeared in *Transactions of the Bibliographical Society*, First Series, ix (1906–8), 53–65; the Presidential Address 'Some Experiences of a Bibliographer', in *The Library*, IV, i (1920), 129–40.

in description instead of—as would be generally thought today—a subsidiary one. In his Address, for instance, Madan suggested that all books up
to 1660 deserve considerable attention, from 1660–1800 careful but less
attention, and from 1800 ordinary attention, 'merely as a matter of date
and speaking quite generally'. However, the historic importance of books
may also be considered as cutting across the general assignment of importance by date. In his view the great Oxford *Corpus statutorum* of 1634
obviously demands 'special attention and description—it is a curiosity
as well as an important book'. But a 1634 Proclamation about the Market
of the City with lists and prices, or John Scot's *Foundation of the University*
printed at Cambridge, and so on, would deserve only intermediate treatment. The books which deserve to be registered as being products of the
Oxford Press may be awarded 'sufficient but not over-flowing detail'.[29]
It is indicative of the changed attitudes of the last fifty years, and the
vastly expanded audiences for bibliographies, that various groups today
would each object with vigour and with justice to any such relative estimate
of the 'importance' of these books. I suggest this is a useful object lesson
in the dangers of modifying bibliography by an estimate of the 'importance'
of books and ordering some as first-, some as second-, and some as third-class
citizens on the basis of an arbitrary set of values sure to be overthrown in
the passage of time. I suggest also that the indifference to the bibliographical
interest of books after 1800, typical of the early years of this century and
thus of degressive bibliography, is not precisely the way we look at the
matter today.

I fancy it is of little present concern to argue whether Madan contemplated applying the degressive principle only to different *kinds* of bibliographies but not *within* a single bibliography. I am altogether positive that
a recent writer in the *TLS* (27 April 1967, p. 362) who so cordially
noticed the twentieth-anniversary volume of *Studies in Bibliography*, is
mistaken in his belief that Madan's intention was to illustrate uniform
entries in different possible kinds of bibliographies, and not adjusted
fullness of description within one bibliography according to the date and
nature of the books.[30] What is of concern is that we are saddled with the
word 'degressive' although its sense has changed as much from Madan as

29 It is indicative of the changing audience for bibliographies that economic historians would consider this pamphlet on prices as a more 'important' book than the *Corpus
statutorum*! With D. F. McKenzie's work on the Cambridge University Press in mind,
one may smile at the placement of the products of the Oxford University Press at the
foot of the class.

30 From the Presidential Address it is sufficiently evident that Madan was thinking of
the bibliography of Oxford books that occupied his interests for some years and that he
drew his examples not from a hypothetical series of bibliographical entries but from
actual problems that faced his own work on a single subject.

T. S. Eliot's sense of the phrase 'metaphysical poetry' has altered from Dryden and Doctor Johnson. Madan's degressive casting into outer darkness of all post-1800 books has combined in a curious way at the present time with his principle that for various reasons some books are more 'important' than others in relation to the subject of a bibliography. I take it that these days the selective principles he enunciated for *books as entities*, that is as independent works—as different titles—has come to be applied to *later editions of the same books versus the earlier editions*, a switch of considerable importance in its implications and effect since it is one never contemplated by Madan. In utilizing Madan's phrase 'degressive bibliography' to apply to a book's later editions, present-day critics have completely misinterpreted his actual purposes.

Partly as a consequence, this question of 'importance' on its altered grounds seems to be uneasily divided in current thinking. On the one hand we have the view of books as 'important' to a collector because they are the traditional foundation-stones of the structures of author, period, or genre collection. These are conventionally the earliest editions of a work that are in most immediate context to the historical span of the author's life. Customarily these represent first editions, taken to be of supreme importance. Compromises may occasionally need to be made. For example, since the floating supply of Shakespeare first quartos is not inexhaustible, a collector may need to content himself with what he can get that is nearest to the first—that is, with second, third, fourth, or fifth quartos so long as they are pre-Rowe. After the date of the first formal edition of Shakespeare, most private collecting interest is likely to cease on the ground that what may (although with some dubiety) be called the original documents have been exhausted. Whether professional scholars are confused about the traditional bases for collecting or are unconsciously upholding some of their own standards amidst the alien corn, it is true that simultaneously with this value placed on the simple historicity of documents has come to be acknowledged the desirability of full treatment to be given editions of textual importance as if the two categories of historicity and text were indeed identical. (Sometimes they are; sometimes they are not.) This is accompanied by a willingness to accept handlist entries for editions that are not in an area where they could be 'important' according to this hypothetical textual standard.

In my own cynical view both reasons for accepting the degressive principle are faulty, especially the second, which with time and further experience I fancy will become as outmoded as Madan's own quite different reasons for degression now appear. Since the first is based on sentiment bonded to the law of demand and supply, it is likely to be semi-permanent. Collecting standards have already endured for a long time, whereas the textual rationalization for degression is a johnny-come-lately.

One reason for my distrust of the textual rationale, when too narrowly applied as it always seems to be, is the quite practical one that it is not and cannot be made to be consistent. If a descriptive bibliographer must rely upon secondhand information—or upon no information at all—as a guide to the principle of degression, he is going to make any number of serious errors. For instance, before the Centenary Hawthorne how was a bibliographer to know whether or not the second and third editions of *The Scarlet Letter* were revised and thus of immediate textual significance demanding full description? Yet according to the degressive principle usually advocated, his treatment of these editions would have been dictated by precisely the information he did not know. How far indeed are we justified in demanding that a bibliographer ascertain textual authority when the information is not available? What degressive bibliographer, until the present year, would not have assigned a handlist entry to the 1801 *Pamela* in blissful ignorance that it contains—curiously enough—Richardson's final textual revisions? [31] Must a bibliographer of Stephen Crane collate the text of the 1896 Heinemann *Maggie* before he can decide on the fullness of description to award it? Because this first London edition, on examination, turns out to be of no immediate concern for the establishment of the text,[32] should it be given a handlist entry instead of full description? Here the textual principle clashes with the historical-document principle, for ordinarily without regard for textual significance the first appearance in England for an American, or in the United States for an English, book is taken to be of sufficient importance to warrant some interest in collection. It follows that more often than not a demand develops for a description suitable for detailed identification—that is, a full description—on a scale that cannot be justified by the immediate textual importance of the document. One wonders, for example, if a fresh Shakespeare bibliography were to be written whether the public would be satisfied with a handlist entry for the third quarto of *Romeo and Juliet* or the second quarto of *Titus Andronicus* because they are textually without authority?

Thus the textual rationale for degression is something of a cheat when alleged as a literary reason for a reduced scale of entry. It is not, and it cannot be, consistently applied even within its own assumed principle unless we are prepared to demand that a descriptive bibliographer must collate every text he treats when reliable information is not available

31 T. C. Duncan Eaves and B. D. Kimpel, 'Richardson's Revisions of *Pamela*', *SB*, xx (1967), 78–88.

32 It is of historical concern, however, since the standard edition of Crane edited by Wilson Follett is 1925–7 relied heavily upon this edition or its Heinemann derivative. Thus certain erroneous readings have got into the Crane textual tradition which can be determined when the matter is viewed historically as a problem of transmission, i.e. of publishing history.

about its transmission.[33] Moreover, in any case of conflict it bows to the central collectors' standards of 'importance' as a justification for full description. If collectors' standards ever had a true textual reason as an important consideration, it had to be applied in ignorance, naturally. That is, a collector might well feel that pending solid information he ought to have a first London edition of *Maggie* in case it was ever shown that Crane had taken the opportunity to revise the text. This is a sensible attitude. However, the convention once established that certain editions are 'important', such as the first editions in each country, it continues in fossilized form without regard for whatever virtue may have been present in its beginning. No doubt the price might go up if it could be shown that Crane had supervised the production of the first London edition of *Maggie* (I am advisedly using language as appealing as possible to a collector); but we may be sure that every collector of Crane will still want this edition, for other reasons, even when he learns the sad truth that Crane personally had nothing to do with its text or other details. That this is a normal edition to collect within the charmed circle of traditional desirability means that it must be given a full description without regard for its textual significance. So much for textual criticism in its usual form as an effective rationale for degressive bibliography. It will not work, and of the two the usual collectors' criteria may do the least injustice to the author.

However, where criticism and publishing history join, a broader concept of textual criticism emerges that may be used as a rationale. No one can deny the paramount value of the true substantive editions (the only ones with any authority) when it comes to establishing an author's text. Nevertheless, I should regret the imposition on bibliography of any criteria of a book's 'importance' that disregarded the further principle that there are also editions that can be taken as substantive for the *history* of an author's text even though not authoritative for the actual *establishment* of

33 The amount of information about the textual history that a descriptive bibliographer should feel bound to provide in his notes is a difficult problem. Working with brief texts and at a time when determining transmission is not overly troublesome, I have felt impelled in my bibliography of the Restoration drama to cite the copy for each edition. Some author-bibliographies, like one of Stephen Crane, would offer so few problems and occupy so little time as to make it feasible to trace the family tree of each text, at least in a generally accurate manner. (It would be expecting too much for the bibliographer to discover minute points such as the fact that whereas the copy for the collected *Whilomville stories* [1900] was the text as printed in the *Harper's Magazine* appearances, part of the last story in the book, because of the time element, was set from manuscript and the *Harper's Magazine* text was derived from it.) If a modern edition of an author with full collations has been prepared, a bibliographer can apply these and carry them forward with little difficulty. On the other hand, if a bibliography precedes an edition the textual ancestor of each entry is surely one of the most valuable pieces of information that can be provided for literary students and is worth a major effort to discover.

that text. That is, if what has been for over forty years the generally received text of *Maggie* goes back (as it does) not to the authoritative American but to the English line of transmission, does a descriptive bibliography have the right to reduce to handlist entries the key English editions in the formation of this tradition simply because the first happens to be an unauthoritative reprint (with some editorial tinkering) of the 1896 American text? Would a descriptive bibliography of Shakespeare's *King Lear* assign a one-line entry to Tate's version in 1681 when the tradition established there represented the acting version, as against the literary, that held the stage for a hundred years? Should the Globe edition, perhaps the most influential text of Shakespeare ever produced, its effects still powerful a hundred years later, be given a handlist entry as of its appearance in 1866 because it was in major part a derivation of the Old Cambridge edition; and should the Globe modification of 1893 be ignored when, although almost unknown to scholars, its form constitutes the modern Globe tradition for scholarly reference?

I do not argue that the bookseller's and collector's standard of 'importance' is anything but artificial, arbitrary, and often so ill-informed that in disregarding the critical principle as applied to the foundation of a text, as well as disregarding the publishing-history or textual-transmission principle, its results can be frustrating to the scholars who want to use the collection and find gaps precisely where their interests lie.[34] Let us be under no illusions about a set of criteria for collection that places primary importance for simple firstness upon the book form of a text and neglects the earlier periodical publication set directly from an author's manuscript, and thus the only suitable copy-text for an edition, as in Crane's *The Monster* or *The Little Regiment*. If the argument is made that the author no doubt oversaw the production and revised his text for book publication, and therefore it is the more important form to collect, the burden of proof is upon any person who asserts this for Crane, no matter how applicable to Dickens or to Henry James. Moreover, if textual criteria are thus to be introduced, why is it that the collectors so concerned with authorial revision have not run down the later printings of F. Scott Fitzgerald's novels with their altered plates? Why is a textually deficient American first edition like Hawthorne's *Marble Faun* collected more vigorously than its substantive English first which was set from manuscript? Why did we wait

34 For example, no more than a handful of American research libraries seem to own copies of the second and third English editions of *Transformation*, nor do English libraries (because this is an American author) seem to be better provided with anything but the first edition. Yet Hawthorne did see that several corrected readings were introduced into the second edition, and a knotty bibliographical problem exists about the relationship of the second and the third that can be subject only to hypotheses at present owing to the lack of a sufficient number of collected and thus preserved copies to serve as evidence.

until 1967 to learn that certain obscure American editions of Thomas Hardy's *Woodlanders* contain authoritative readings not known in the received tradition?[35]

No rationale can be found in these matters to act as a guide to a new principle of degression such as has been called for. On simple grounds of expediency I suggest only that *sometimes* a collector's standards of collectability, and thus of full entries in a bibliography, are more comprehensive and therefore to be preferred to a logically applied rationale of immediate textual importance—even provided a bibliographer were prepared to engage himself to discover the facts necessary to set up a scale of degressive description on this principle. My distinction here of the immediate textual importance of certain documents in establishing a text versus the scholarly importance of the history of a text's transmission, even in unauthoritative form, must not be forgotten, however. In rejecting the textual principle I refer only to the authoritative sources of text, not to what may be called the substantive documents in its transmission.

In the search for a rationale, perhaps we had better revert briefly to the question of the usefulness of full description as against partial, or even a handlist entry form. If certain editions of a book are to be assigned a position of such considerable importance as to merit full description and others not, it is vital for us to agree not only on the criteria for 'importance' that govern this distinction but also on the value of full versus partial description.

Let me repeat my personal convictions. If we narrow the discussion only to that of the problem of identification, the value starts with A. W. Pollard's minimum requirement that a description be at least sufficient to show whether a copy is perfect.[36] We progress from there to the fullness of description that enables a collector (*a*) to identify a copy in his hand as among the variants observed by the bibliographer, or (*b*) to identify, with

35 Dale Kramer, 'Two "New" Texts of Hardy's *The Woodlanders*', *SB*, xx (1967), 135–50.

36 'Some Points in Bibliographical Description', *Transactions of the Bibliographical Society*, First Series, ix (1906–8), 52. This requirement is amusing, these days, in context since it is enunciated after comparing the problem of describing an incunable with the problem of Burton's *Anatomy of Melancholy*. The sentences read: 'In the *Anatomy*, which has no bibliographical interest, and which belongs to a period when books were too common to make identification by the beginning of leaf 11 generally practicable, the information given is reduced to the minimum necessary to show whether a copy is perfect. But for special reasons any of the details appropriate in the description of a fifteenth-century book may be introduced into that of a more modern one.' There follow three degrees of fullness recommended for description. The first is merely an enumerative entry quite inappropriate in a descriptive bibliography; the second would enable a collector to know if a book was complete only if the pagination formula were sufficient. Only in the third, or full-fig, description is a collational formula required.

luck, a variant in his copy that has not been observed and recorded by the bibliographer. The fuller the description the better both of these aims are fulfilled, and the better—to broaden the usefulness of descriptive bibliography, as we must—the entries meet the varied requirements of readers other than collectors. On the other hand, it is proper to enquire what scholarly magic rests in the simple fact of a full description after it has satisfied the collector's needs. The answer reverts to the needs of these other readers, who will be concerned with the literary contents, with the technical production details, or with the publishing history, including textual transmission.

Candour compels us to recognize that in some considerable part an interest in the contents of a book requires a full description of its form as first produced; but thereafter, if the contents and their headings remain the same (independent of differences in textual authority and transmission) the full transcriptional form of description becomes of no importance to anyone but the collector and occasionally the student of typography. If the contents alter, then the original form of the altered publication demands the full treatment once more. On the other hand, as editions with similar contents succeed the first, the concerns of the textual critic and of the literary critic who need to follow the publishing history (and, of course, the needs of the printing technician) do not decrease, if we accept my broader notion of textual criticism as occupied with the transmissional history of the text as well as with the establishment of its most definitive form. In so far as small variation is often evidence of altered textual and publishing history (as when in early books a piracy or some other separate edition is detected that previously had been confused with its model; or in modern books when type-batter, paper changes, and so on, distinguish different printings), the needs of collector and scholar are identical. Unfortunately, this happy union dissolves when the collector begins to lose interest in such details and to be content only with sufficient information to determine the completeness of a book, and not always that. This interest is lost at varying stages in different periods, and sometimes even with different authors and the publishing conditions that affected the forms of their work. All one can say is that just about the time the form of a book ceases to be fluid in respect to its contents and in respect to its publication in countries ordinarily regarded as of major interest for collection, the collector becomes satisfied with considerably less than full description since he grows indifferent to minor variation.

I suggest that this general rule is a sensible enough one in most circumstances for an average good bibliography if the decrease in detail offered in the description is not accompanied by a corresponding decrease in the bibliographer's investigation of the form represented by the entry. Such a decrease in research can be injurious in two ways. Most obviously, if it contracts the scope of the bibliographer's comparison of multiple copies to establish the exact form represented by the entry, it contracts the authority of whatever quantitative information is provided. That is, the more a bibliographer abridges description that would serve to assist in the collector's identification of unobserved detail, the more he should be obligated at the very least to maintain the standard of his own investigation guaranteeing comprehensiveness of research behind the omitted part of the description that implies lack of variation. Here is where the great deficiency appears, of course.

If I may draw on my experience, I have certainly used the degressive principle in respect to fullness of description in the bibliography of Restoration drama that has occupied me from time to time over the past twenty years. From the very beginning I never proposed to write quasi-facsimile transcripts of headings, or even simplified transcripts, after the first edition when the material remained the same. For example, I was prepared to transcribe exactly in facsimile form the heading of a preface, to indicate whether an ornamental initial or a type capital was used, and the number of indented lines this occupied, together with a reference by number to a photograph of the initial and of any engraved ornament associated with the heading, and finally a transcript of the form of any subscription including numbered reference to any engraved ornament or a verbal description of type-ornaments at the conclusion. For a second edition, and others that repeated the same material (which would also imply the same text of the heading), I proposed merely to provide the word 'Preface' without transcription in any kind of the heading so long as the heading and the text remained constant; however, the typographical details of ornamentation I proposed to retain as an assistance to proper identification and as a contribution to the knowledge of printing history. This truncated form of secondary description in some part increases the odds against the identification of variants from the description itself. It seemed to me, therefore, to be a point of bibliographical honour to make the same scrupulous investigation of these late editions as of the earlier, comparing them page by page against a control film for typographical identity, and in the same large numbers as earlier editions to the limit of the holdings of the libraries I proposed to visit in person or by a complete filming of their holdings.[37] The form of the description, hence, had no effect whatever upon the form of the investigation, or vice versa.

Under these controlled conditions I see nothing wrong with degressive bibliography as applied to a reduction in the detail awarded a description

---

37 Collecting being what it is, later editions of most Restoration plays are much rarer, usually, than first editions if the holdings of the most prominent libraries in England and the United States furnish an accurate criterion, which doubtless they do not.

of the same features in each edition as in the original full description. That is, it seems to me unnecessary, particularly in modern books where the typography of reprints is likely to be uniform in respect to the reduced detail, solemnly to reproduce in quasi-facsimile or even in simplified form the identical text of the identical headings for the identical contents in edition after edition. I trust this is not heresy. But I do not find it unnecessary to indicate that the same contents are present, and that they may be found on such and such pages. This latter seems to me to come under the head of Pollard's recipe for a description that will indicate the completeness of a volume, even though I am admittedly carrying it forward from the limited sense in which he defined completeness, as the presence in a book merely of so many numbered pages.

On the other hand, I think we must insist that the practical considerations which move us toward a reduction in the presentation of detail in the described features must not affect the original research. That is, simply because a collector and some scholars are likely to lose interest in editions the farther they progress in point of time away from their fully described original, we are in danger of moving away from descriptive bibliography toward enumerative if the bibliographer himself shares this relaxation of interest. For instance, if a bibliographer of Shakespeare decreases his standards of wide and minute comparison of copies after the Fourth Folio so that he fails to discover Rowe 2 and 3, as well as Rowe 1, or to confuse them with each other and with Rowe 1, he is no descriptive bibliographer and his book would be a fraud. Moreover, I think we should insist that whatever abridgement we may accept in the details that come under the quantitative part of the description should affect not one jot of the qualitative interpretation of the omitted detail, since any diminution in this important aspect of bibliography strikes at the very heart of the scholarly application of description to other purposes than identification.

May we not, then, accept in a sense quite different from Madan's[38] the general principle of degressive bibliography and move toward some future rationale according to the following statements of principle modified as necessary by experience and the peculiar problems of the period of the bibliography? The exact details of method, adapted to varying circumstances, will always fall into place if the principles are sound.

38 We should not forget that Madan's suggested method (which he equated with the principle, an error that has continued to trap critics to the present day) was rejected by his contemporaries and thereafter. An interested reader should count the number of official objections recorded in footnotes to the 'Memorandum'. As late as the Address of 1920 Madan remarked that the idea of degressive bibliography 'seems not yet to be taken seriously' (p. 134). He is still talking, however, about 'the view of books in proper perspective, and the treatment of them accordingly', not of later and 'less important' editions of books that have already had full description, as is the present theory of degression.

1. A distinction must be made between descriptive and enumerative bibliography. When the abridgement of a bibliographical description moves into the area of a checklist entry,[39] simple enumeration has replaced the analytical purposes and methods of description. At this point a descriptive bibliographer either should halt his work or he should proceed (if he is interested) under a different section, and with clear recognition of the changed conditions behind his investigation of entries since he has now forsaken descriptive bibliography as completely as if he had appended to his list of descriptions an enumerative handlist of scholarship devoted to the books he has treated.[40]

2. Following this distinction between the descriptive and the enumerative parts of a bibliography, the bibliographer should guarantee the same standards of methodical investigation both in respect to scope and to minuteness of examination for all entries listed under the descriptive sections of his bibliography.

3. These conditions being observed, a bibliographer at his own discretion may after the *editio princeps* reduce the detail pertaining to the description of any literary part of the book that in its contents—applying both to the initially transcribed material and to the material identified by this transcript—agrees with the fully described form.

4. A descriptive bibliographer will usually find it advisable to provide a relatively full description for any seminal form of the book in a historical sense, as for example the first American edition of an English book or of any other foreign editions selected for description, not for enumeration; or for any marked changes in the presentation of the text such as the

39 It is not that at this point description takes the form of handlisting: instead, description under these circumstances has *become* handlisting, or simple enumeration, and is description no longer either in standards or in form. There is more to descriptive bibliography, of course, than the form taken by the act of description. The fullest description ever compiled would be a mere catalogue entry if based on the examination of only a single copy. It is the matter of standards of examination, quite apart from the differing forms of the entry, that distinguishes descriptive from enumerative bibliography.

40 Thus the reviewer of Professor Todd's *Burke* (*TLS*, 7 July 1966, p. 604) remarks: 'This is an important bibliography, perhaps more important to the bibliographer than to the Burkean who may well regret that the opportunity was not taken to gather together other material relative to the author. A handlist of surviving manuscripts and a record of Burke's library might well have come within the purlieus of a study such as this. . . .' As he was well aware, the reviewer was wishing that when the bibliography had completed its descriptive function it had added enumerative sections on more general subjects of interest to students of Burke. Surviving manuscripts of printed entries properly belong in notes to the entry, of course, as a matter of the keenest possible literary and textual interest, not isolated in a separate list unless unpublished. The general value of other appendices cannot be denied; yet one may only query whether a scholar trained in descriptive bibliography will be willing to devote his research time to the collection of all ancillary enumerative material to his author before he can be prepared to publish the bibliography.

appearance in a collected edition, the first paperback edition or other cheap form, and so on, that marks the start of a new tradition in the presentation of the text.[41]

5. If the true purposes of descriptive bibliography are not to be controverted, the qualitative, or interpretative, part of the entry material should not be affected by the application of the degressive principle to the details of the description itself.

These are proposals for a new rationale of degressive bibliography. I offer them with some modesty since I have not been able to test them in my mind for a very long period, and certainly not by the extensive practical experience which alone can show their efficacy. However, with some immodesty, perhaps, I can hope that they will prove to be a more logically motivated and trustworthy guide than the tacit assumptions, or rather misassumptions, that I have tried to analyse in this paper as prevalent today among the critics of bibliographers if not among the bibliographers themselves.

41 Certainly to be considered here are newly plated editions in their first and last printings that have a significant influence on the transmission of the text and the sale of the book in different forms to the public.

Analytical Bibliography

The Headline in Early Books

IN THIS PAPER I am concerned with a method for bibliographical investigation and with a method only: specifically, the method of examining the headlines of a book for what they can tell about its printing. I feel justified in calling to your attention the importance of the headlines in any book under bibliographical examination, since it is only in comparatively recent times that their usefulness has been recognized. Indeed, the subject receives no mention in McKerrow's classic, *An Introduction to Bibliography*, and there is scarcely any literature on the subject. Today, largely as an introduction to Mr. Hinman's paper,* I wish to sketch very briefly a few of the basic methods for a study of headlines and to illustrate what information may often be discovered about books by these methods. Mr. Hinman has with great originality pushed ahead in certain explorations which show what can be done if more bibliographers will study the subject. At the moment we are barely beginning to see what is possible in a fascinating field for research.

At the start, a few definitions are necessary. By the word 'forme' I mean not only one side of a printed sheet of paper but also, more technically, the type-pages which would print this one side, plus the chase which surrounds them, the crossbars which separate them from each other, the headlines, and the furniture (pieces of wood or metal below type height) used to secure them in the chase, the whole locked up by quoins, or wedges, and ready to be put on the press. When I use the word 'skeleton' I mean the skeleton of such a forme: in other words, all the material which surrounds the type-pages. It is a common practice to use the words 'running-title' and 'headline' as synonyms. I wish to differentiate these in the following manner. 'Running-title' is applied only to the letterpress of the headline, that is, the actual type which prints the words of the title across the top of the page. The headline I consider to be the letterpress of the

Read on September 9, 1941, before the English Institute at Columbia University; printed in *The English Institute Annual 1941* (1942), pages 185–205; reprinted with permission of Columbia University Press.

* C. J. K. Hinman, "New Uses for Headlines as Bibliographical Evidence," *The English Institute Annual 1941* (1942), pp. 207–222.

running-title on any single page plus the quads on either side of it which, extending out to the margins of the type-page, may include the type used for foliation or pagination. I advocate this firm distinction because of its precision. For example, when the title of a book is split between the two pages, there is properly only one running-title, but there are two head-lines. Moreover, although I have not time to deal with this question to-day, the numerals for pagination or foliation are sometimes just as important as running-titles, and we must think of them as part of the headline, thus emphasizing the fact that the running-title is only a part, too. Finally, the quads in a headline are sometimes of importance, and it would be impossible, of course, to speak of them properly as the quads of a running-title.

The basic principles of the printer's use of headlines did not differ mark-edly in any period when books were printed by hand. Thus I have inter-preted my subject "The Headline in Early Books" very liberally and I have drawn examples both from incunabula and from books of the six-teenth and seventeenth centuries. The first point which must be understood is of crucial importance. This is, the headline was treated as an integral part of the skeleton; and since a skeleton was used over and over again in successive formes, we may identify any skeleton by the headlines it contains. According to Moxon, after a forme is removed from the press and rinsed, it is brought to the distributing bench where the quoins are removed, the chase lifted off and placed about the type-pages of the forme which is to be prepared for printing. The crossbars are then lifted out and placed be-tween these new type-pages, then the furniture, and finally the quoins to lock it up. Moxon specifically warns the compositor to place each article in precisely the same position in the new forme that it occupied in the old, and we learn later that the chief reason is to preserve the correct register which the pressman has adjusted on the first use of the skeleton. Thus the same skeleton is transferred piece by piece to the new type-pages, and this process is repeated throughout the printing of the entire book.

Now Moxon does not mention them specifically, but it is certain that the headlines were transferred as part of the skeleton.[1] Hence we may see the same sets of headlines appearing in forme after forme, usually, although not invariably, in the same position. And I make bold to say that nobody can assert he has made a thorough bibliographical examination of a book unless he has identified the sets of headlines used in its printing and has followed them in their various appearances throughout the book, ex-plaining all variations of position and all variations of content.

Before the Restoration it was fairly common for only one set of headlines to be used in printing a book. For instance, if a book were a

[1] For the details of this proof see my "Notes on Running-Titles as Bibliographical Evidence," *The Library*, fourth series, XIX (1938), 318–22.

quarto, which would mean four type-pages to a forme, the identical set of four headlines will often appear in every forme of the entire book, that is, twice in every sheet. Obviously, when only one set—which always means only one skeleton—was used, the press was idle while the forme just off the press was being washed and stripped and its skeleton was being transferred to the type-pages which were next to be printed. Mr. Hinman has some very interesting things to say about this delay and the reasons why a printer would suffer it. I merely point out the fact that a delay in presswork is inevitable when only one skeleton is used for all formes. Some printers used two skeletons, each with its own set of headlines. Thus while one forme was on the press, the skeleton was being stripped from an already printed forme and imposed about the type-pages next to be printed. Since the transfer of this second skeleton could take place while the press was printing the first, there was no delay at all between the time a forme was removed from the press and the time the new one was planked down on the bed. Rarely, and I think only for special reasons, three skeletons could be used in more or less regular alternation.

It is essential, of course, to identify the sets of headlines which represent different skeletons. Variations in spelling, or punctuation, or capitalization; variation in the fount, such as swash forms; actual broken or bent letters (and I say 'actual,' because bad inking can be very deceptive)—all these are of considerable use. Mr. Hinman has discovered another method of identification which is often extremely useful, especially in dubious cases. Normally this consists of measuring the distance between the left-hand margin of the type-page and some fixed point in the first letter of the running-title. Since it is highly unusual for a printer to construct the headlines of a set with precisely the same number of quads and spaces placed before each running-title, the distances will usually vary sufficiently to be used for constant identification, accidents such as pieing excepted.* A special technique must be used, however, for measuring headlines which contain foliation or pagination.

Identification may be speeded by knowing where to look for the next appearance of each headline in a set. One should try to spot a real peculiarity in a running-title in one forme of a sheet and then to see whether it is reproduced in the other forme. If it is, and if the other running-titles check, we have a sheet printed with only one skeleton. Since the pieces of a stripped skeleton were normally always placed exactly in the same position about the type-pages being imposed, a graph of the imposition of the

* The spacing between words in different running-titles may also vary; hence it is usually most convenient to line a card up with the left type-margin of a page and to tick off for comparison and identification a series of ascenders or descenders in all the different words, including any punctuation. Professor Gerritsen has had success with the use of tracing paper, I believe.

two formes of a sheet will ordinarily show where each headline should reappear. The imposition of a quarto is given below as an example. This, incidentally, is the correct relation of one forme to another on the imposing stone, a point to be emphasized, since McKerrow illustrates them in an incorrect relation to each other.[2]

TYPE-PAGES IN QUARTO

Inner Forme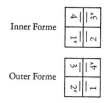

Outer Forme

Thus it can be seen that a headline stripped from B1 verso of the inner forme should normally appear again on B2 verso of the outer forme if only one skeleton were used. When two skeletons were used for each sheet, usually the skeleton which printed the inner forme of the first sheet printed the inner forme of each succeeding sheet; and so with the skeleton for the first outer forme. Hence the headline of B1 recto should normally be found on C1 recto, and so forth.[3]

In making a bibliographical examination of a book one cannot simply carry through the identification of a few prominent running-titles in a set and trust these to suffice for the identification of the skeletons. It is essential that every headline in every set be checked throughout the whole book for possible variations. All sorts of variations in headlines from the normal process may provide evidence as to the manner of the printing. These variations may be of three major classes: (1) changes from normal position, either of the headlines within a set in relation to one another or of the whole set in relation to the normal alternation with other sets; (2) the introduction of new sets within the body of the book; (3) variations in the letterpress of individual running-titles or in the structure and mea-

2 The imposition given here is that illustrated by Moxon. That it is correct is shown by the usual relations of the headlines in successive formes; moreover, only by such an arrangement can the printed sheet be perfected by turning it end for end so that the pins in the tympan will go through the identical holes, a necessity for correct register.

3 The most usual variation occurs when a forme returned from the press to the imposing stone is turned end for end. In such a case the headline on B1 verso will appear on B4 verso, and so forth, if only one skeleton is being used; if two skeletons, the headline on B1 recto would appear on C4 recto. Occasionally irregular variation occurs in which two headlines in the set will exchange position diagonally in the skeleton; this appears often enough to warrant the conjecture that at least some compositors stripped the quarters of a forme diagonally.

surements of individual headlines owing to accidents in transferring from forme to forme, or for other reasons.

Of the many facts that can be told about a book from its headlines I select only a few prominent ones to present here. They are all concerned with printing with only one press, as have been the remarks above, since the behavior of headlines in a book printed with two or more presses is a very complex subject.

The first is the order in which the formes went through the press. A fairly typical case is the 1563 edition of Baldwin's *Mirror for Magistrates*, a quarto in 8's. Here both formes of the two sheets in gathering B were printed from only one skeleton. On B5 recto of the outer forme of the inner sheet we find the spelling "Magisstrates" in the running-title, but this misspelling is not found when the otherwise identical letterpress of this headline appears again on B6 recto, the inner forme of the same sheet, or in either forme of the outer sheet of B or later gatherings. Thus we may assume that when printing of the book started, and this was with the text beginning on B1 recto, the initial state of the skeleton contained a running-title which was misspelled and that this skeleton was used for the first forme through the press. Then when the skeleton was stripped and transferred to the other forme, the error was corrected. We can infer from this evidence not only that the outer forme of this gathering was first through the press but also that printing started with the inner sheet.

The above example could be explained in another, although less reasonable, manner, but the type of evidence found in Wood's *Conflict of Conscience* (1581) is crystal clear. This book is a quarto which is printed throughout from only one skeleton. In gatherings B, C, and D a spelling error 'Conseience' appears in a running-title consistently in its proper place in the skeleton. This error is also found on E3 recto of the outer forme, but it was corrected on E4 recto of the inner forme; and the appearance of this correction in the otherwise identical headline throughout the remainder of the book proves that the outer forme was first through the press. In the 1622 quarto of *Othello* the head-title which appears on B1 recto of the outer forme was split in two and the first part was used for the running-title on B1 verso, the second part appearing on B4 recto —both pages of the inner forme. This tiny economy by which the printer saved himself the trouble of setting another headline for his next forme (only three headlines, of course, are present in the outer forme, while four are necessary for the inner forme) clearly indicates to the investigator that the outer forme went first through the press.

Still another method of determining the order of formes is found in *The Tragedy of Darius* (1603), by William Alexander. This book is a quarto which concludes on gathering K, a half-sheet of two leaves. Each gathering has been printed from two skeletons, one for the outer and one for the inner formes, although in the body of the book there has been an exchange. When we come to half-sheet K, however, we find that the four headlines of inner I are used to print the four pages of half-sheet K. Since K would normally be imposed for half-sheet printing while the last forme of sheet I was being machined, the inference is that inner I was first through the press, since only then could its skeleton be available for transfer to half-sheet K while the other forme of I, the outer, was on the press.

Headlines may also be useful to show what sheet of a quired gathering was first printed. An example has already been given for Baldwin's 1563 *Mirror for Magistrates.* Another occurs in Caxton's *Confessio amantis,* of 1483. Here several errors show that Caxton printed his folio in 8's from the inside out; that is, he printed the inmost sheet of his quired gathering in 8's first, and moreover he used two skeletons for every sheet. On A7 verso of the outer forme the 'i' dropped out of 'Liber' in his running-title 'Liber Octauus', and this same headline without the 'i' appears also on outer A8 verso and then on outer B5 verso and outer B6 verso, but was corrected on outer B7 verso and all subsequent outer formes. The error does not appear in any of the inner formes and therefore indicates that two skeletons were used for each sheet. More important, this error suggests that the inmost sheet of gathering B was first printed, and the case is clinched by an error in the preceding gathering, gathering A. Liber Septimus had concluded on signature &7 verso, and Liber Octavus, with its changed headline, had begun on signature &8 recto, the two adjacent pages of the outer forme of the outermost sheet. The correct headline 'Liber Octauus' is found on all pages of the next gathering A except for A4 recto, the outer forme of the inmost sheet, where we find the error 'Liber Septimus' printed so far as can be told in the identical type of the running-title 'Liber Septimus' on &1 recto. Clearly the printer forgot to change the headline from the last printed outer forme of gathering & when he imposed its skeleton about the type-pages of the first printed outer forme of gathering A. And since this particular error was immediately corrected, it seems certain that the inmost sheet containing page A4 recto was therefore first through the press.

CONFESSIO AMANTIS, 2° (8's)

Liber	Liber		Liber	Liber		Liber	Liber		Liber	Liber		Liber	Lber		Liber	Lber
7	7		7	8		7	8		8	8		8	8		8	8
&2	&7ᵛ		&1	&8ᵛ		A4	A5ᵛ		A3	A6ᵛ		A2	A7ᵛ		A1	A8ᵛ

Liber	Lber		Liber	Lber		Liber	Liber		Liber	Liber
8	8		8	8		8	8		8	8
B4	B5ᵛ		B3	B6ᵛ		B2	B7ᵛ		B1	B8ᵛ

Headlines may sometimes determine more clearly than any other evidence the earlier and later states of a variant forme. When in Lodowick Lloyd's *Pilgrimage of Princes* (1573) the press was stopped while printing the outer forme of gathering A and for the running-title 'The Paradice of Princely Histories' was substituted the running-title 'The Pilgrimage of Princes', which appears on inner A and throughout the rest of the book including the title-page, we may be certain not only that outer A was first through the press but also that the correct running-title gives us the later state of the forme. Not all cases are so clear. For example, in Dekker's *Roaring Girle* (1611) one state of the inner forme of gathering C has the running-title spelled 'Girel' on C2 recto. Another state of inner C, with textual variants, has the correct spelling 'Girle' in the identical type, and this correct spelling in this identical type had already appeared on B2 recto of the inner forme, C1 recto of the outer forme of the same sheet, and later on D3 verso and D4 verso, the inner and outer formes of gathering D. One's first impulse would be to declare that the state with the corrected spelling was the later, and indeed in this book the textual variants show that this assumption is correct. However, in principle the correction of a running-title during the printing of a forme is no certain proof of a later state. The error might have been caused by an inkball jerking out the type, in which case the state with the error would be the later. Or if the forme were unlocked for correction, the running-title might have been disturbed and the error made, to be corrected when the skeleton was stripped for the next forme. Here again the later state would contain the error.

There are cases, however, in which the evidence of headlines is clear. I still remember with considerable ruefulness another gathering in *The Roaring Girle* where an accident during the printing had pied parts of two pages of the inner forme of sheet I and there had been the necessary resetting. Guiltless at that time of a knowledge of headlines, I decided on what seemed decisive internal evidence in favor of one state as being the later, only to have Dr. McManaway expose my ignorance by showing that the resetting of the pages in the inner forme had also included the resetting of the headlines and that these new and different headlines appeared not only in the outer forme of sheet I but also in both formes of sheet K. Thus the state with the altered two headlines which printed the next forme and the next and following sheets (the original two headlines disappearing completely) must be the later state, and by bad luck it was the state which I had thought was the earlier. This example furnishes an object lesson in the need for checking 'internal evidence' by bibliographical evidence whenever possible.* Incidentally, the inner forme of this sheet must have been first through the press.

* If I may interject an autobiographical remark, it was this salutary correction of my error (which had been printed) coming on top of W. W. Greg's correction of

Cancels—so important to textual critics—may almost always be detected by altered headlines which do not appear in subsequent formes. Sometimes, indeed, when we have only one copy to examine and no previous knowledge of the existence of a cancel in the book, and when the cancel is so cleverly done that it defies detection otherwise, headlines are the only means to discover the cancel. For example, we are checking through a set of headlines which printed all the inner formes of a quarto, and we find that the headline on G2 recto differs in its setting from the headline on F2 recto, although the other three headlines in both sets are identical. This is suspicious, but if we find that the new headline appears also in inner H, then it is only a simple case of an accident necessitating a substitution. But if the old headline which had printed F2 recto also appears along with the other three in the set in inner H instead of the new headline found on G2 recto, then we are almost certainly in the presence of a cancel, which can be confirmed by seeing whether the headline on G2 verso is of a different setting from the appropriate headline of outer F and outer H. If it is, a cancel is definite.[4]

One of my students, Miss Irene Mann, who is working on an edition of the plays of Robert Wilson, found that one set of headlines printed both formes of all sheets before and after gathering F in the quarto *The Cobblers Prophecy* (1594). Both formes of sheet F, however, were printed from a different set of headlines which appeared nowhere else in the book. This in itself was a suspicious circumstance, and she examined sheet F with extra care. She discovered that this sheet had been set by a different compositor from the regular compositor of the rest of the book and that there was definite evidence that he was trying to space out the sheet as much as possible. Since the play dealt somewhat dangerously with contemporary affairs, she came to the conclusion, and I have no doubt that it is the correct one, that sheet F is a cancel sheet with a considerable amount of material removed. Miss Mann will shortly publish the full details of her interesting discovery.* I mention it here because it is a rare example of the discovery of a sheet cancel made when no copy of the cancellandum

---

another bibliographical mistake I had made about Dekker's *Magnificent Entertainment* that first suggested to me I had better learn something about bibliography if I were going to edit Elizabethan plays.

4 Of course, cancels might be printed after the completion of the text as part of the final gathering or of the preliminary gatherings, in which case a skeleton containing the headlines of the rest of the book would be found. The chances are that the cancel could nevertheless be detected by duplication of identical headlines in one forme and such other impossibilities in normal printing.

* Irene Mann, "A Political Cancel in *The Coblers Prophesie*," *The Library*, 23 (1942), 94–100.

is known and because it was the study of the headlines of the play which gave Miss Mann her first clue.

Headlines may often be of use in determining unusual methods of printing. I offer this next example with some hesitation, because I have just started to investigate the book, which presents many difficulties, and until my investigation is completed I cannot guarantee the facts. At the moment, however, I think there is a chance that in Caxton's edition of Higden's *Polycronicon* (1482), a folio in 8's, the same headline may appear in at least some instances on the two pages of a single forme. Since this is an impossibility with normal printing, if true it would show that the book was printed at least in part page by page. Even if with this particular book I eventually find that the headlines of these formes are in fact different, the method exists for detecting page by page printing when headlines are present and when the same skeleton was used for each page-forme.*

I am a little proud of my last example for determining unusual printing by the examination of headlines, since it shows a method (which can be varied to suit the circumstances) for doing something that Dr. McKerrow said could not be done;** that is, it checks half-sheet imposition in a normally printed book. The book is *The Picture of a Papist* by Oliver Ormerod, printed by R. Bradocke for N. Fosbroke, London, 1606, with the collation 8° (4's), A–Z⁴, ¶², ²A–I⁴. An interesting bibliographical problem is to determine whether this book was printed by half-sheet imposition, as would normally be expected, or by some other means.

A printer imposing an octavo in half-sheets had his choice of two methods. With the first, and more common, he would impose both the inner and outer formes of a gathering in 4's in one chase and print and perfect from this one forme of eight type pages, cutting the sheet in two on conclusion to obtain two identical gatherings in 4's.

SINGLE HALF-SHEET IMPOSITION OF 8° (4's)

ᴧ2	ε	ᴧε	2
1	4ᵛ	4	1ᵛ

* For reasons that escape me, I never have pursued this promising lead. Perhaps some interested bibliographer will have a look at the problem (and let me publish his results in *SB* if it turns out to be printing by single pages, in fact).

** Reflecting his general distrust of analytical evidence, Dr. Gaskell in his *New Introduction* (1972), p. 106, states that it is 'normally' impossible to distinguish work-and-turn (or single half-sheet imposition) from twin half-sheet layouts. For a demonstration to the contrary, see "Running-Title Evidence for Determining Half-Sheet Imposition" (1948–49), below.

When this method is used, it is obvious that two sets, each of four headlines, must be employed, one for the outer and one for the inner forme of
the 4's gathering; and therefore no single set of headlines could print both
the outer and inner formes of any gathering. Moreover, any individual
headline found in one forme cannot appear in the other forme of the
printed gathering. Hence when we see in the graph below of *The Picture
of a Papist* that only one set of headlines printed both formes of gathering
B and in addition that the identical headlines numbered V and VI appear in
both formes of gathering C, although the remainder of the set are different,
we can immediately discard the possibility that this method was used to
print the book. Other gatherings with this duplication are D, E, F, G, L, N.

There was another method of half-sheet imposition, however, by which
the inner formes of two consecutive gatherings in 4's were imposed together in one chase and printed, and the sheet was perfected by another
large forme containing the type-pages of the outer formes of the two
gatherings. In examining the diagram of this imposition one must remember that the sheet of paper was turned end to end when it was perfected.

TWIN HALF-SHEET IMPOSITION OF 8° (4's)

	Inner					Outer		
B1ᵛ	B4	A3ᵛ	A2		A2ᵛ	A3	B4ᵛ	B1
B2	B3ᵛ	A4	A1ᵛ		A1	A4ᵛ	B3	B2ᵛ

By such a method each gathering would also contain two sets of headlines,
even though the same large skeleton was transferred from one forme to
another. However, in case the forme were turned before it was stripped,
only one set of headlines would appear in each gathering. Since such
turnings do sometimes occur, one would sometimes find a book printed by
this method which had two sets of headlines in some gatherings and one
set in others. Moreover, the stripping of a skeleton and its transfer to
another forme is not always a regular process; that is, a quarter in the
skeleton is not invariably placed in precisely the same position in the
other forme. Hence a single headline may sometimes appear to wander
and could perfectly well appear in both formes of a gathering, even
though the others in the set differed. It is obvious that such wanderings
provide a method for distinguishing books printed by the first method and
by this second method. Some such wanderings do appear in *The Picture of
a Papist*, but other evidence proves that the book was not printed by this
second method of twin half-sheet imposition either.*

* It seems to be at least theoretically possible that the Elizabethans could have imposed, say, inner B with outer C, and outer B with inner C for 8⁰ in 4's. McKerrow

The evidence is this. Since the inner formes of two gatherings are imposed together, and the outer formes of two gatherings together in this second method, we must always take the two gatherings so printed as a unit. It therefore follows that in any two gatherings forming a unit the method of printing the headlines must be similar. If gatherings B and C compose one unit through being imposed together, and gatherings D and E another unit, it would be quite possible for both B and C to be printed with only one set of headlines in each gathering, provided it were a different set in each, and for D and E to be printed with two sets of headlines appearing in each gathering, provided the same two appeared in both gatherings. But it would be a physical impossibility for gathering B to appear with only one set of headlines, and gathering C with two. Therefore when in *The Picture of a Papist* (the printing of which began with gathering B) we find that gatherings K and L constitute one unit if this second method is employed, but that gathering K is printed from two sets of headlines and gathering L from only one, we must discard altogether any theory that this book was printed by half-sheet imposition, especially when the same situation is found in M-N. Moreover, gatherings H-I could not be imposed inner with inner and outer with outer without an impossible duplication of running-titles in each forme.

We conclude, therefore, that the paper must have been cut in half before machining, and that the formes were imposed for actual printing as a quarto in 4's, although we must, of course, still label the book an octavo in 4's. Only by conjecturing this method can the irregularity in the headlines be explained, whether one or two presses were used for the printing. What would lead the printer to the relatively cumbersome method of cutting his paper before machining instead of printing by half-sheet imposition must remain a matter of conjecture. Since the octavo is a rather large one, I believe that he had bought some particularly large paper which could not be accommodated in his press, and so was forced to resort to cutting.

I have sketched in only the broad outlines of my subject today and have suggested only the more prominent and clear-cut methods of adducing evidence when one press was used. There are many abnormalities, both com-

---

(Introduction, p. 68) recognizes that this was the usual imposition for later printing with large sheets but believes that in early days inner was imposed with inner and outer with outer, and he offers an example from a 16mo in 8's printed in Basle in 1575 which would be decisive evidence if it is a unique copy. Gaskell (*New Introduction*, p. 90) illustrates a quarto in 2's with inner A and outer B imposed together, and vice versa, but on p. 94 provides only the layout for an 8^0 in 4's with inner and inner perfected by outer and outer. The reasons for one but not the other are not discussed. It is possible that this is a matter requiring more attention from bibliographers. However, the conclusions below about *The Picture of a Papist* are not affected, whatever the exact method of twin imposition. Each form runs into impossibilities.

plex and simple, that I have not referred to, since we cannot yet be sure of all the answers to the problems they raise. We may, for example, sometimes guess why headlines occasionally change their positions within a set and why the relations of complete sets of headlines are sometimes so curiously irregular.

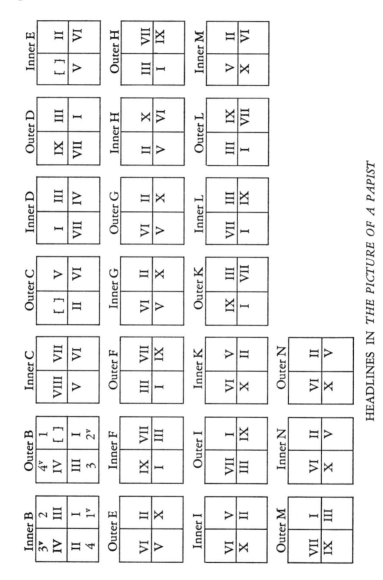

HEADLINES IN *THE PICTURE OF A PAPIST*

But we urgently need a larger body of information about all deviations from the norm; and once we get this and understand it, I think we shall be able to follow the early printer in certain details of his work with a clarity we have not previously thought to be possible.

An Examination of the Method of Proof
Correction in King Lear Q1

IN HIS MONOGRAPH on the printing of the Pide Bull *Lear,* Dr. Greg[1] has suggested the employment of a method of proofing not previously envisaged by students of Elizabethan printing practices. Briefly, this significant and interesting theory is as follows. From sheet D to the end of the book, a forme (*I*) was placed on the press and a pull or two was made to secure a proof. Forme *I* was then removed; the second forme (*II*) was placed on the press and printing of the white paper begun. While forme *II* was printing, the proof-reader was correcting the proofs separately, first that of forme *I,* and then that of forme *II* for which an early printed sheet would serve as proof. The proof of forme *I* was returned to the compositor, who corrected the type of forme *I.* At this point the printing of uncorrected forme *II* was suspended. Proof-corrected forme *I* was placed on the press. This forme *I* began its impression by perfecting those sheets which had been immediately before printed by forme *II;* on completion of this perfecting it continued printing by running-off the remaining white paper of the edition-sheet. On removal from the press, forme *II* was corrected from proof. Then when forme *I* had entirely finished printing and was ready to be taken from the press for stripping and distribution, forme *II* in its corrected state was replaced on the press and finished the machining of the edition-sheet by perfecting those sheets which had been printed on white paper by forme *I.*

This hypothesis solves the following difficulties. (1) It explains why, in each sheet of *Lear* that underwent stop-press correction, only one forme is variant. Logically, therefore, the invariant forme of a sheet always represents a proof-corrected state since it was machined by forme *I* which never printed uncorrected type. (2) It offers a practical method of proofing which avoids all unnecessary idleness of the press while proof corrections

Printed in *The Library,* 5th ser., 2 (1947), 20–44 as "An Examination of the Method of Proof Correction in *Lear*"; reprinted with permission of the Council of the Bibliographical Society.

1 W. W. Greg, *The Variants in the First Quarto of 'King Lear': A Bibliographical and Critical Inquiry,* pp. 40–57.

are being made in the type of a forme. (3) It explains the 'consequential' correction of the catchword on K4^r of the inner forme to coincide with the stop-press correction altering the first word on K4^v of the outer forme.

The logical reasonableness of Dr. Greg's theory for *Lear* has secured for it a very general acceptance, and indeed it has recently been taken as representing the normal practice in Elizabethan printing-shops with one press. Hence the implications of the *Lear* hypothesis go far beyond the single case of *Lear* (which was all Dr. Greg was concerned with) and have now assumed such importance as to affect general bibliographical research.[2] In such circumstances it is incumbent to check this theory by every piece of available evidence to determine its accuracy.

The evidence which headlines can furnish about the printing of a book has not previously been tested in connexion with the proofing of *Lear*.[3] The results of such a study are, I think, most instructive since they cast serious doubts on certain important details in Dr. Greg's reconstruction of the proofing and printing.

The following is a list of the headlines and their various appearances in *Lear,* the variant formes being braced.

OUTER FORME	INNER FORME	
B1 —head-title	B1^v—VII	
B2^v—II	B2 —VI	
B3 —III	B3^v—IX	
B4^v—IV	B4 —VIII	
C1 —X	C1^v—V	
C2^v—XI	C2 —I	
C3 —XII	C3^v—IV	B(o)
C4^v—XIII	C4 —III	B(o)

2 F. R. Johnson, 'Press Corrections and Presswork in the Elizabethan Printing Shop', *Papers of the Bibliographical Society of America,* xl (1946), 276–86, accepts the theory and applies it to the printing of all two-skeleton books. C. J. K. Hinman, 'New Uses for Headlines as Bibliographical Evidence', *English Institute Annual,* 1941 (1942), modifies the theory slightly and reconstructs the printing of the 1622 *Othello.* In the same *Annual,* R. C. Bald, 'Evidence and Inference in Bibliography', pp. 171–2, writes of it approvingly.

3 As a part of some general notes on headlines and their bibliographical importance ('Notes on Running Titles as Bibliographical Evidence,' *The Library,* 4th series, xix [1938], 326–31') published before the appearance of Dr. Greg's monograph, I offered the tentative suggestion that *Lear* might have been printed on two presses and that the breaking-up of the quarters of its formes might be explained as the result of a 'pool' of stripped skeletons. It seems clear now that *Lear* was printed on one press, and I hope to show below that there is a more reasonable explanation for the curious behaviour of the running titles. The list of these titles given below corrects three errors made in my article.

Outer Forme			Inner Forme		
D1	—VI	B(i)	D1ᵛ	—VIII	B(i)
D2ᵛ	—IX	B(i)	D2	—VII	B(i)
D3	—V	C(i)	D3ᵛ	—III	C(i)
D4ᵛ	—IV	C(i)	D4	—I	C(i)
E1	—XII	C(o)	E1ᵛ	—XIII	C(o)
E2ᵛ	—XI	C(o)	E2	—X	C(o)
E3	—VIII	D(i)	E3ᵛ	—V	D(o)
E4ᵛ	—IX	D(o)	E4	—IV	D(o)
F1	—VI	D(o)	F1ᵛ	—VII	D(i)
F2ᵛ	—III	D(i)	F2	—I	D(i)
F3	—XI	E(o)	F3ᵛ	—XII	E(o)
F4ᵛ	—IX	E(o)	F4	—VIII	E(o)
G1	—V	E(i)	G1ᵛ	—IV	E(i)
G2ᵛ	—XIII	E(i)	G2	—X	E(i)
G3	—III	F(o)	G3ᵛ	—VI	F(o)
G4ᵛ	—XI	F(o)	G4	—IX	F(o)
H1	—VII	F(i)	H1ᵛ	—XII	F(i)
H2ᵛ	—I	F(i)	H2	—VIII	F(i)
H3	—XIII	G(o)	H3ᵛ	—III	G(o)
H4ᵛ	—XI	G(o)	H4	—V	G(o)
I1	—XI	H(o)	I1ᵛ	—I	H(o)
I2ᵛ	—IX	G(i)	I2	—X	G(i)
I3	—IV	G(i)	I3ᵛ	—VI	G(i)
I4ᵛ	—XIII	H(o)	I4	—VII	H(o)
K1	—XII	H(i)	K1ᵛ	—IX	I(o)
K2ᵛ	—VIII	H(i)	K2	—XI	I(o)
K3	—V	H(i)	K3ᵛ	—III	H(i)
K4ᵛ	—I	I(i)	K4	—X	I(i)
L1	—XIII	I(o)	L1ᵛ	—VI	I(i)
L2ᵛ	—XII	K(o)	L2	—IV	I(o)
L3	—I	K(o)	L3ᵛ	—IX	K(i)
L4ᵛ	—blank		L4	—XI	K(i)

According to Dr. Greg's reconstruction, the errors discovered in inner C, which necessitated two separate stop-press corrections, led to the start of a new system of proofing with sheet D. Hence, to follow his hypothesis, we put inner D (I, III, VII, VIII) on the press and pull a proof. We then remove inner D, replace it with outer D (IV, V, VI, IX), and begin printing. When the corrected proof of inner D is returned and the type-pages corrected from it, the press is stopped. Outer D is removed to be replaced by inner D, which starts by immediately perfecting the sheets already printed by outer D and then continues without interruption by printing the remaining white paper sheets. When it has finished, outer D (which in the meantime has been corrected) is again put on the press and concludes the machining of the edition-sheet by perfecting those sheets which it had not previously printed. Thus inner D is invariant and is ready for distribution earlier than outer D, which is variant and was last off the press.

When the printer came to impose the two formes of sheet E simultaneously, he had ready the skeleton of outer C (x, xi, xii, xiii) and he should have had the inner forme of D which had been wrought-off earlier than outer D. We find, however, that the forme of inner E, which must be imposed and placed on the press first for a proof (it being invariant), takes over two headlines from outer C (x, xiii) but also two from outer D (iv, v). Outer E, imposed next immediately, takes the remaining two headlines from outer C (xi, xii), one headline from outer D (ix), and one headline from inner D (viii).

It is clear that the press must have been idle during the time that outer D was rinsed, stripped, and parts of its skeleton imposed about the type-pages of inner E. Since such delays would cost Okes money if they happened during the printing day, we should expect them to be cut to a minimum. Moreover, there was no apparent reason for a delay here since inner D was ready and sheet E should normally have been imposed from the skeletons of outer C and inner D. One such occasion is of little importance, but if it reappears frequently (and especially when there is no apparent reason), the system of proofing which demands such an order of imposition and of passing the formes through the press must be scrutinized to see whether there is not an alternative explanation.

When we continue to print according to Dr. Greg's reconstruction, we see that inner E (invariant) is wrought-off first and outer E (variant) concludes the printing of sheet E. Thus, when the printer came to impose both formes of sheet F, he had available one quarter with its headline from outer D (vi) [4] and three quarters with their headlines from inner D (i, iii, vii). If inner E had been stripped, as we should expect, while outer E was bringing to a close the machining of the sheet, he also should have had ready the skeleton of inner E (iv, v, x, xiii). We find, however, that outer F (first imposed for proofing) instead takes two quarters from outer E (ix, xi) which was last off the press, as well as the remaining one quarter from outer D (vi) and one from inner D (iii). Inner F takes the remaining two

---

4 How these quarters detached themselves from their skeletons will be shown later. For convenience in this present description I am writing as if each forme was imposed as a unit at one time. This is not true since there seems to have been partial imposition (in the sense that quarters of skeletons were laid about some type-pages) before the final quarters were laid in and the forme locked up. The point is immaterial for the present argument, however.

quarters of outer E (VIII, XII) and the remaining two of inner D (I, VII). As a result of the use of the skeleton of outer E to impose outer F, there is a second inexplicable delay.

Outer F (invariant) is finished first on the press and inner F (variant) last. Sheet G is imposed without delay since inner G (first imposed for proofing) takes two quarters from inner E (IV, X) and two from outer F (VI, IX). Outer G (variant and last off the press) takes the remaining two from inner E (V, XIII) and the remaining two from outer F (III, XI).

Since inner G (invariant) was first wrought-off, there should have been available to impose sheet H the stripped skeleton of inner F and inner G. We find, however, that outer H (invariant and first imposed for proofing) takes two quarters from outer G (XI, XIII) and two from inner F (I, VII). Inner H is imposed from the remaining two from inner F (VIII, XII) and outer G (III, V). As a result of the use of outer G to impose outer H, there is a third delay before proofing can be started.

Sheet I is imposed without delay since inner I takes over two quarters from inner G (VI, X) and two from outer H (I, VII). Outer I uses the remaining two from inner G (IV, IX) and from outer H (XI, XIII). Since in all known copies both formes are invariant, Dr. Greg does not conjecture which forme was printed first and which last, and as a matter of fact the point proves of no consequence for this present inquiry.

When sheet K was to be imposed, there was ready the skeleton of inner H (III, V, VIII, XII) and, depending on the order of formes, either the skeleton of inner I (I, VI, VII, X) or of outer I (IV, IX, XI, XIII). Inner K was first imposed for proofing, and we find it taking over one quarter from inner H (III), two from outer I (IX, XI), and one from inner I (X). Outer K was imposed from the remaining three quarters of inner H (V, VIII, XII) and one from inner I (I). Since parts of the skeletons of both formes of sheet I were used to impose inner K, there must have been a fourth delay.

Inner K (invariant except consequentially) was printed first and outer K (variant) last. Thus when sheet L was imposed, the printer had available two quarters each from inner and outer I, and he should have had the skeleton of inner K. Since sheet L is invariant in all known copies, Dr. Greg does not conjecture the order of the formes which printed it. We find that inner L takes one quarter from inner I (VI), one from outer I (IV), and two from inner K (IX, XI). Outer L, however, draws two from outer K (I, XII) as well as the one remaining quarter from outer I (XIII). L4^v is blank, and only seven headlines are used. Since sheet L uses headlines from both formes of sheet K, there is between the printing of sheets K and L a fifth delay.[5]

5 It might be held that inner L was first imposed for proofing and thus made use without delay of the quarters available; then by the time outer L came to be imposed,

If, then, *Lear* was indeed printed in the manner Dr. Greg conjectures, we find that between the printing of those eight sheets where his theory would apply there were five delays of some duration to continuous press-work, all of them seemingly arbitrary and unnecessary. We can only guess at the time needed to spread and rinse the type as related by Moxon, partially lock it up again, and then transfer it to the distributing bench, and afterwards carefully transfer the skeleton to the type-pages next to be printed. Whatever the precise time, it must have been considerable enough to delay seriously the continuous operation of the press, and there seems no reason why Okes should willingly have suffered this loss if he could have avoided it. If printing had been managed as Dr. Greg describes but with only two skeletons, there would necessarily have been a lesser delay in continuous presswork; but the three skeletons of *Lear* hypothetically provide for simultaneous imposition and no delay whatever.

Certain delays of this nature can be explained. If the end of machining a sheet coincided with the close of the work day, we may believe that the wrought-off forme would be rinsed before the compositor went off duty. Thus, if he began the next day by imposing the next forme for the press, the last forme off the press would be available on an equal footing with the others for this imposition and there would be no actual delay. Obviously this situation cannot explain all the delays in *Lear*.

When Dr. Johnson transfers the *Lear* method to printing with two-skeleton books, he recognizes that there is a delay in the imposition of the second forme of a sheet, but minimizes its importance by holding that various necessary duties about the press covered the interval in which the last wrought-off forme was rinsed, stripped, and imposed.[6] Possibly these duties have an application to the delays in *Lear* itself, but I am inclined to doubt it on the evidence of the irregularity as shown by the running titles. In *Lear*, moreover, we should need to believe that the compositor five times did not take the short-cut of utilizing already-rinsed formes which were available but went out of his way to rinse immediately a forme just off the

---

outer K could have been removed from the press, rinsed and stripped, and made available. On the face of it this seems improbable. There were enough quarters still remaining from already stripped formes to impose outer L without the labour (and certainly some delay) of immediately rinsing and stripping outer K, especially since this final imposition concluded the book except for the half-sheet preliminary which contained only the title-page. If these extra quarters had already been distributed, then simultaneous imposition of L was not planned. On the other hand, if outer L was first imposed, the question arises why the printer did not use the four quarters already waiting on the bench and delayed imposing the first forme of L until the last forme off the press (outer K) had been rinsed and stripped. Whichever forme of L was first on the press, it seems reasonably certain that as with the imposition of sheet K (probably a precise parallel) there was a fifth delay.

6 Op. cit., p. 283.

press and to strip its skeleton to the new type-pages before completing his imposition. It seems doubtful that the duties about the press would actually cover the time interval necessary to treat a wrought-off forme and re-impose its skeleton.

It might also be held that if the compositor were behind the press, there must necessarily by a delay while he composed the last type-pages for the forme about to be printed, and that in this period some helper could rinse and strip the forme for him. If this situation obtained, we should expect the inner forme to be first imposed to save time. Yet, after the delay necessitated before sheet F, outer F was first imposed and proofed; although there was a delay before sheet H, outer H was first imposed. When, as with *Lear*, there is no consistent order of the formes through the press but the outer forme is imposed first as casually as the inner, we have excellent proof that the compositor was ahead of the press and had completed setting all the type-pages of a sheet before imposing his first forme.

There is one other piece of evidence in *Lear* which indicates that, in sheet I at any rate, the compositor had set his full eight pages before he was called on to impose the first forme. This evidence is bound up with the explanation for the curious shifting about from forme to forme of the quarters of the skeletons, and hence it is appropriate to consider this special problem here.

So far as I am aware, *Lear* is highly unusual in the manner in which, beginning with sheet D, the skeletons lose their unity in imposition and no one skeleton is transferred as a unit from one forme to another.[7] I emphasize this point because the system of stripping a forme for transfer of its skeleton to another forme, as described by Moxon and demonstrated as normal practice by an examination of a number of Elizabethan books, does not obtain here. According to Moxon's description the compositor imposes the type-pages of a forme on the imposing stone. He then takes a forme which has been printed from and subsequently washed, rinsed, and placed on the distributing bench, and transfers its skeleton piece by piece to his newly imposed type-pages. In this process the skeleton is preserved as a unit, especially since Moxon warns the compositor to take pains to place each part of the skeleton in precisely the same position about the new type-pages that it occupied about the old. The point of interest here is that this process can be followed by tracing the running-titles in their various appearances, and that the compositor would never have stripped a forme until he was ready to impose a complete new one for the press.

7 I have examined a number of Elizabethan plays but have not seen another like it. However, a group of plays which I am investigating in 1661 seem to exhibit roughly parallel characteristics.

The washed and rinsed wrought-off forme, therefore, would have reposed untouched on the bench awaiting his convenience, providing the rinsing had not been delayed to the period immediately preceding the stripping.

Waiting on the bench, the type in this forme could not ordinarily be distributed until its skeleton had been removed. Apparently this was no hardship to the compositor, since the evidence of the running-titles shows that in normal Elizabethan printing he was content to delay distribution of the type of a wrought-off forme until he was ready to impose the first forme of the next sheet. This is of considerable interest, for it meant that in a two-skeleton quarto the compositor would have a minimum of fifteen type-pages standing without replenishment of his cases. If his cases could not stand this strain, it follows that he would print with only one skeleton where a minimum of only eleven standing type-pages was required.[8] If, however, he wished to retain the more efficient two-skeleton method of printing, when the time approached that he needed to break in on the waiting forme to secure type for distribution, he could remove as many quarters from this as there were type-pages on the stone and thus partially impose the furniture and headlines of the forme which he was working on.[9]

This seems to be precisely what occurred in *Lear*, beginning with sheet D. The customary way in which the type-pages for $1-2^v$ are imposed from a wrought-off forme of a sheet once removed in printing, indicates that when the compositor had set 2^v he customarily stripped an available rinsed forme and imposed its quarters about the first two pages of both formes which had been set and placed in imposing position on the stone. Thus $D1-2^v$ are imposed from the skeleton of $B(i)$; $E1-2^v$ from $C(o)$; $G1-2^v$ from $E(i)$; $H1-2^v$ from $F(i)$.

The most obvious and, I believe, the correct explanation is that Okes ordinarily needed the type in the wrought-off forme before he composed

8 I do not recall having seen this matter mentioned previously. Dr. Hinman (op. cit., pp. 207–12) makes out an excellent case for an equation between the size of the edition-sheet and the number of skeletons used; I think his findings are correct but that this matter of the available type must be added as an equally important factor, at least in small printing shops.

9 On the almost invariable evidence that skeletons are retained as units, a compositor performing this action could free no more than two, at the most three, type-pages for distribution without wasting time in what amounted to double imposition; that is, if he is stripping his inner forme and partially imposing its skeleton about the incompletely set inner forme on the stone, he would need to transfer the furniture from $4 and possibly 3^v to the stone, piece by piece, without there being type-pages ready for these quarters. When the type-pages were set, the furniture would again be lifted piece by piece and imposed about them. That this practice of partial imposition did not ordinarily obtain may be shown by the manner in which running-titles normally keep their regular position in relation to one another; but more importantly by the fact that what happened in *Lear* because of early stripping and distribution is not commonly found.

type-page \$4, and that he adopted this unusual expedient to free it for distribution. As against the fifteen standing type-pages required as an absolute minimum for two-skeleton printing, three-skeleton work with imposition delayed until \$4 is set requires a minimum of nineteen standing pages. By freeing a wrought-off forme for distribution when \$2^v was set, Okes reduced the number of standing pages to sixteen, the precise number required for two-skeleton work if imposition is delayed until \$4^v is set.[10]

This valuable evidence may be used in various ways. It shows us clearly what rinsed formes were available at an earlier time than would otherwise have been required, and thus may help us to trace the crucial order of the formes through the press in relation to the proofing. In a more limited manner, to conclude the conjecture that the compositor of *Lear* did not consistently fall behind the press, it may show that all eight type-pages of sheet I were composed before it was necessary to start their final imposition.

Sheet I is one of the several exhibiting variance from the normal pattern. I1, 1^v, 4, and 4^v are imposed from the quarters of outer H whereas I2–3^v utilize the quarters of inner G. The explanation for the fact that ordinarily \$1–2^v are imposed from one skeleton seems to be the theory that only these four type-pages were ready on the stone to receive the stripped quarters when the compositor regularly undertook distribution of the wrought-off forme after setting his sixteenth standing type-page. On the other hand, with sheet I we can explain the curious pattern by supposing that precisely six type-pages were lying on the stone, in the position illustrated by Moxon, but with the incomplete formes side by side instead of one beneath the other, in which case I2^v, 3, 3^v, 2 would have formed a central block comprising the only four type-pages about which the skeleton of inner G could be imposed as a unit. If so, this would indicate that composing had progressed as far as I3^v before imposition of the two formes was begun. Furthermore, if the compositor had been at all rushed by the press, he could have waited until I4 was set and then imposed inner I from inner G to send to the press without delay for proofing. That he took the time to strip inner G about these particular type-pages of I when lacking only one type-page to complete his inner forme would seem to indicate that he was in no hurry. According to Dr. Greg's reconstruction, outer H

10 It is possible to argue that if the compositor were falling behind the press, a helper could save him time by taking over certain elementary procedures such as the transference and re-imposition of the quarters of a skeleton and that this assistance would have its greatest value if performed at the period indicated by the evidence. I have tried to show above that there is some evidence that the compositor was apparently keeping abreast of the press without difficulty, and the evidence below about sheet I, and later about sheet E, may perhaps strengthen this conclusion. Nevertheless, this helper is a possibility, although the need to distribute type must have been the major factor.

which was used to impose the remaining pages was first off the press, but the time taken to strip it even partially to fill up the first forme of I to be delivered does not lead us to suppose that the compositor was under pressure to keep the press supplied.

The evidence of the headlines shows that in eight sheets there were five delays in the continuous presswork that could be expected with three-skeleton printing, these delays being caused by the imposition of the first forme of a sheet to be delivered to the press (the proofing forme) not from a forme or formes which should have been rinsed and available on the bench but instead partly from the skeleton of the wrought-off forme which had just been taken off the press. Since no combination of plausible reasons will, in my opinion, explain all of these curious and seemingly arbitrary delays, we must face the possibility that the problem of the printing of *Lear* has not been fully solved.

Any alternative theory should, I think, satisfy two major requirements: (1) it must be based on the evidence of the headlines and must reduce the series of inexplicable delays; (2) it should ideally be a system which we may suppose was the standard, not an exceptional, Elizabethan printing practice, and within that framework must satisfactorily explain the peculiarities present in *Lear*.

At the start it must be emphasized that the simultaneous imposition of two formes for proofing and printing as envisaged in *Lear* requires three skeletons and hence on the evidence could not have been normal Elizabethan printing practice since most Elizabethan books utilize only one or two skeletons. Dr. Johnson's recent attempt to transfer the major points in Dr. Greg's hypothesis to two-skeleton printing is not, in my opinion, successful.

If we search for what must have been the *basic* method of Elizabethan proofing, we find it in one-skeleton books where press-correction can be managed in no other way than by stopping the press and keeping it idle during the time of correction. Two-skeleton printing was an extension of one-skeleton, devised to secure relatively continuous presswork by avoiding the major delay at the press which occurred when a new forme was imposed for printing. If delay is avoided in the imposition of formes, we should expect the two-skeleton printer to modify the traditional method of proofing in a manner which would be the simplest and most obvious extension to the changed conditions.

With one-skeleton printing there is nothing for the press to work on when the forme is removed for correction. The most obvious thing to do with two skeletons is to plug this gap by putting the second forme on the press and pulling its proofs so that correction in the type can be made at leisure without further halting the press. Hence we arrive at a theoretical system for the normal proofing and printing of two-skeleton books, and one which I hope to demonstrate probably printed *Lear*.

As with one-skeleton books, forme *I* was placed on the press and printing was started. The first pull was sent to the corrector, who marked the proof and returned it. Again as with one-skeleton books, the forme was only then removed from the press for correction,[11] to be replaced on the press by forme *II* from which proofs were pulled. We have extant too few copies of *Lear* to do more than guess, but if we can trust the evidence of only twelve copies out of perhaps a thousand, this forme *II* was placed on the press only for proofing and did not print any sheets in its un-corrected state. Corrected forme *I* was returned and finished printing the white paper. In the meantime forme *II* was corrected from its proofs; hence when it perfected the edition-sheet as one operation from start to finish, it was correct and invariant. It will be noticed that strictly simul-taneous imposition of two formes of a sheet is not required (an impossi-

11 If we may believe the evidence of only twelve copies of *Lear*, the time before the proof was returned must have varied considerably. Outer D, for example, has six corrected states and six uncorrected; outer E eleven corrected and one uncorrected; inner F nine corrected and three uncorrected; outer G six and six; inner H and outer K each four corrected and eight uncorrected. Even allowing for the wide margin of chance in basing statistics on only one per cent. of the edition-sheets, surely the uncorrected state of the forme must in certain sheets have printed many more copies than in others. In comparison we may profitably compare Thomas Dekker's *Satiromastix*, printed with two skeletons. I have collated nine copies of this play and find that inner B has eight corrected and one uncorrected; inner E four corrected and five uncorrected; outer F eight and one; outer H seven and two; outer I eight and one; outer L six and three; inner M three and six; outer M four and five. In contrast to *Lear*, I think there is some evidence that the author himself corrected the proofs, and the markedly low number of un-corrected states in general might show that he was fairly prompt in his attendance at the press. Basing our evidence only on nine copies, and including invariant sheets, we may perhaps see that when proof correction was prompt, rather less than ten per cent. of the number of copies of a forme need be in the uncorrected state, or something over a half-hour's work for the press; and I suspect that further collation of this play will lower the percentage of uncorrected states. Therefore, most of the corrected formes of *Lear* seem to have been on the press for several hours before the proofs were returned, and with sheets H and K the time may have been extended. There are two explanations which may be reasonable. Firstly, the manuscript was difficult to read and the proof-reader on occasion must have been appreciably slowed by his attempts to decipher it. Secondly, since Okes could scarcely have had a full-time proof-reader, the duty of read-ing proof would perhaps fall on himself or on someone else in the shop who was not always immediately available when required. Thus the combination of difficult manu-script and part-time proof-reader may perhaps explain the comparatively large number of uncorrected states in some formes of *Lear*. It may be pure chance that sheets H and K which have the highest percentage of uncorrected states are followed by sheets which are invariant in both formes; on the other hand, if there is actually a connexion between these conditions the fact would have considerable significance in a reconstruction of the proofing. The headlines, however, offer no suggestions to be followed.

bility with two-skeleton printing) and that the time taken to proof-read forme *I* covers satisfactorily the operation of rinsing and stripping the last wrought-off forme of the previous sheet and the imposition of its skeleton about forme *II*. It will also be noticed that presswork was not perhaps always continuous, since the time necessary to correct the type of forme *I* would presumably be greater than that necessary simply to proof forme *II*. This matter will be discussed later. The operation of proofing is similar to that required by one-skeleton printing except that the un-economic delay with one-skeleton work while the first forme through the press is being corrected, supplemented by the delay in stopping the press to correct the second forme, is for the first satisfactorily filled and for the second obviated.

It is my position that the third skeleton in *Lear* was introduced (since it is abnormal) for a special purpose connected with only one forme of sheet C, and, that purpose satisfied, was retained only as a convenience. It follows that this third skeleton then could have had nothing to do with altering the basic method by which *Lear* was printed and therefore is not consequential upon any method of proofing adopted for the book as a whole.[12] If this is true, *Lear* was not printed by any special system but by the standard method for two-skeleton books, a method which, according to sheet B, it was intended to follow.

The evidence of the headlines, which in my opinion casts doubt on Dr. Greg's hypothesis, must now be called on to examine whether the different system which I have sketched above is possible and even probable. For the moment we may see how the evidence works for the book, leaving until later the difficult question of sheets B and C.

Outer B would have been first through the press, followed in order by inner B, inner C, and outer C. It will be noticed that inner C is imposed, as normally in two-skeleton printing, from the skeleton of the first forme of the preceding sheet to be printed. In their perfectly correct positions, B3 is transferred to C4, B4^v to C3^v. A new running title (1) is necessarily constructed for C2; and since running title II never appears again in the book we may suppose that it pied in the transference from B2^v to C1^v and was replaced by v. A new skeleton is constructed for outer C. When composing of sheet D began, the skeleton of inner B was available, and inner C should have been ready shortly if not immediately. When D2^v is set, inner B (VI, VII, VIII, IX) is imposed about D1–2^v; on completion of D4^v,

<hr>

12 This third skeleton, I have tried to show, was used beginning with the imposition of sheet D only as a convenient way of securing distribution of type earlier than could otherwise be managed. Without going into the various details, I think it would have been difficult to distribute the type of an imposed forme unless the surrounding furniture were first removed. Since it must be removed, time is saved not simply by placing it somewhere else but by imposing it about any available type-pages next to be printed.

inner C (I, III, IV, V) is imposed about D3–4^v. Both formes are available, and which is put first on the press is therefore of no consequence. Outer D is selected and begins printing. Its first pulls are read as proof, and when the corrected proof is returned the forme is removed from the press and corrected. Inner D, which has been locked up in the meantime, is then placed on the press, possibly given a rough make-ready, and a proof or two pulled. Outer D (corrected) is then returned and finishes machining the white paper of the edition-sheet. As a final operation, inner D (invariant and corrected) perfects the edition-sheet.

When composition on sheet E is advanced, the skeleton of outer C was available, and that of outer D shortly after. Outer C (X, XI, XII, XIII) is imposed about E1–2^v. If sheet E followed the pattern set for D, outer D should have been used for E3–4^v, but instead we find that only three quarters from outer D (IV, V, IX) impose E3^v–4^v, with VIII from inner D used for E3. Although by this imposition inner E could immediately have been placed on the press, we find in fact that variant outer E must have been first printed. As a consequence, the first delay in continuous presswork is encountered.[13]

When composition had proceeded at least as far as F2^v, the remaining three quarters of inner D were stripped and imposed about F1–2^v; subsequently, the next available skeleton, that of outer E, completed the imposition of F3–4^v. Inner F (variant) is first locked up and starts the printing. Outer F (invariant) is last off the press.

13 The implications of this significant delay are helpful. On all the evidence, inner E was available to continue presswork immediately. That, instead, outer E was first on the press indicates a delay so serious and unnecessary that it would not be tolerated if it actually wasted time. The answer would seem to be that the only occasion arose in which no time would be actually wasted: the press must have ended its working day with the completion of perfecting sheet D. Inner D was therefore rinsed before the imposition of sheet E was concluded. Moreover, there must have been sufficient leisure before starting to print E to impose outer E fully so that it was indifferently chosen to start the next day's printing. It follows that imposition of outer E must have been completed that night or while the press was being prepared the next morning.

I do not pretend to have a positive answer to why E3 was skipped when the skeleton of outer D was imposed about the remaining type-pages of E, but I do offer this suggestion which fits the conjectures above. At the time it was decided to strip outer D, composition had progressed beyond E4^v, and F1, at least, was lying on the stone. In some manner the imposer overlooked E3 (perhaps it was misplaced) and imposed the four quarters of outer D about four type-pages on the stone, including F1 by error. That night after rinsing inner D the compositor saw the unimposed page (or checking his imposition for the morrow discovered the misplaced F1), and to forestall subsequent error, took a quarter out of inner D to complete the imposition of the two formes of E on the stone. The next morning, by chance, outer E was locked up and delivered to the press to start the day's printing. It seems necessary to posit the inclusion of F1 by error, followed by the repairing of the omission to E3 during a period when the press was normally at leisure.

As normally, the ready inner E skeleton is imposed about G1–2^v, and inner F should have completed the two formes. Instead, we find outer F (last off the press) imposed about G3–4^v. Since, therefore, no forme of G could be printed after the last forme of F without a delay in rinsing outer F, a second and apparently complete[14] break in continuous presswork is found at this point.

Outer G is first through the press and inner G last. The first four type-pages of sheet H are imposed from the ready skeleton of inner F, with the last four imposed from outer G following its removal from the press. Inner H was first printed and then outer H.

The probable reasons for the curious imposition of the pages of sheet I have been given above. In essence the sheet is similar to sheet G in that a ready skeleton is imposed at an early stage (in sheet I after more type-pages had been set than with G) about four pages but the remaining four are imposed from the last forme off the press of the previous sheet although another skeleton (here inner H) should have been available. Hence another marked break in continuous presswork occurred between the printing of sheets H and I, probably for the identical reasons which caused the break between F and G. There are no variants in either forme of sheet I to indicate positively which forme was first impressed, but from the evidence of the headlines it is likely that inner I was first locked up and printed, with outer I last off the press.

Sheet K exhibits a slight change in the manner in which the compositor had up to this point imposed a skeleton about four sequential type-pages of the two partially set formes on the stone. Outer K is the first forme to use more than two quarters from any one skeleton; probably as a result of this procedure it is the first sheet (except for E) in which a part of one skeleton is utilized to impose one forme but not the other: two quarters from outer I appear in inner K but no quarters from outer I in outer K. What probably happened is not, I think, too difficult to reconstruct. If

14 That inner F had not been rinsed by the time it became necessary to finish the imposing of sheet G and hence that outer F was indifferently chosen to be rinsed, stripped, and imposed while the press waited cannot be believed. Such a circumstance would require the compositor to have fallen so far behind the press that he could not perform his normal duties, and there is no significant indication of that fact. The simplest explanation that presents itself is that presswork for the day had ended with the completion of sheet F and that outer F had been rinsed and placed on the bench beside inner F before the remaining imposition of G was undertaken. When the final imposition was made that night or the first thing in the morning, outer F was indifferently chosen for stripping, as being most convenient on the bench. This hypothesis does presume that inner F was not imposed about G when G4^v was completed for the reason that (1) distribution of inner F had not been immediately required, or (2) there was a slight delay and G4^v was not set until outer F had come off the press. The circumstances can be understood if the printing day ended with sheet F, and hence the compositor was under no pressure to impose G.

a skeleton is stripped when only $1–2^v$ are lying on the stone, there is of course, no possibility of any variation: inner B, for example, can be imposed only about $D1–2^v$. If, however, there is no need to get at the type of a wrought-off forme for distribution until type-pages beyond 2^v of the sheet being composed are lying on the stone, then we should expect variation in the type-pages chosen for partial imposition. Moreover, in such a case we should expect in general a reversion to the standard method of re-imposing a skeleton about a unit of four type-pages; in conventional printing these four type-pages would, of course, represent a complete forme. When, however, as with *Lear*, the pages of no complete forme are ready on the stone to receive the skeleton as a unit when it is stripped and re-imposed before the conventional time, the compositor is free to choose what he will consider his unit if there are additional pages. With sheet I, it was conjectured that when inner G was re-imposed, the type-pages of $I1–3^v$ were prepared on the stone and the compositor transferred the complete skeleton to the only block of four pages which was available, which would be $I2–3^v$. In sheet K it seems clear that when the time came to distribute the type of inner H, setting of K had also progressed as far as $K3$ or $K3^v$. Two or three pages of the inner forme were on the stone, but here the compositor imposed as much of a complete outer forme as he could from the skeleton of inner H, with the fourth quarter placed casually about $K3^v$ (the formes being in such a relative position that $K3^v$ was immediately next to $K3$).[15] He must have been under no immediate pressure from the press since he was able to set $K4^v$ before he completed the imposition. However, he must have received a warning call from the press after $K4^v$ was set but before he had begun the process of placing the quarters about the remaining four type-pages of both formes. The forme which was readiest was outer K, with three quarters already imposed. Hence the available skeleton of inner I was broken into and one quarter transferred to complete the imposition of outer K, which was thereupon delivered to the press. There was now no great hurry about imposing inner K; as a consequence, the compositor must have rinsed the wrought-off forme of outer I and placed it on the bench before he turned to complete inner K. Why he did not utilize the remaining three quarters of inner I to fill up inner K is explicable only on the supposition that there

15 With sheet I it was conjectured that the imposed type-pages of each forme were placed on their sides in the relation to each other as shown by Moxon except that the formes were side by side, not one above another. If the inner forme were to the left of the outer on the stone, $I2–3^v$ would form the only block of four type-pages about which a skeleton could be normally imposed. This relation of the pages in K would mean that $K3^v$ would be immediately to the left of $K3$, and it would be natural for the compositor to impose the extra quarter about it. If $K3$ but not $K3^v$ had been composed, the empty quarter might have been laid in that position to be filled by the next type-page set.

was an interval between the imposition of outer and of inner K during which outer I was rinsed and placed on the bench.[16] However, what is of immediate consequence is that with outer K (variant) first on the press, there was no break in continuous presswork.

If type were required from the remaining pages of sheet I after L2 had been composed but before outer K was off the press, we should find—as we do—that L1–2 were imposed by the remaining two quarters of outer I (which conjecturally were now the lowest quarters on the bench) and one quarter of inner I just above them. Possibly L2^v had been set but the headline of the remaining quarter (VII) of inner I pied and the quarter was not transferred. Possibly only the pages to L2 had been completed, in which case the quarter for I4 was never utilized and was distributed. At any rate, if outer L was first on the press, its final imposition (like that made originally of outer K) was handled by taking quarters from outer K to get it to the press without delay. Hence inner L was not simultaneously imposed, and quarters were not placed about L3^v–4 until after inner K had been wrought-off, rinsed, and placed on the bench, with its bottom quarters (IX and XI) of I^v, 2 perhaps lowest and most conveniently to hand. The evidence against simultaneous imposition would thus indicate that outer L was first printed.

By Dr. Greg's reconstruction which conjectures the start of a different system of proofing with sheet D from that earlier adopted, there were de-

16 I should suggest something like this, which roughly fits the case of sheet L. Wrought-off inner I was lying on the bench with I1^v and I2 its bottom quarters. Quarter 1 from I1^v was taken to fill up outer K. If at the same time, or immediately after locking up outer K, the compositior had put his bench in order to make space for the forme of outer I, or simply to do something about this isolated quarter, it would have been natural to dispose of it by transferring it to an available type-page on the stone. For one reason or another, as suggested above, a quarter had been placed about K3^v. Placing the quarter of I2 about K4 completed the imposition of the lengthwise half of the skeleton. If, subsequently, rinsed outer I had been placed on the bench below the remaining two quarters of inner I, its bottom quarters 1 and 2^v (XI, IX) would have been most readily available when the final imposition of inner K was resumed. The same result is obtained, of course, if the rinsed formes are placed above on the bench but turned so that $1^v, 2 or 1, 2^v are uppermost.

If in connexion with sheet L, and possibly sheets E, G, and I, this explanation seems plausible, then we may trace to some extent the rate of actual composition in relation to the presswork. If the compositor imposed pages on the stone from the lowest forme on his bench (or the uppermost), D1–2^v, for instance, must have been set and imposed before inner C (first printed) has been wrought-off; otherwise, inner C would have been employed. Correspondingly, I1–3^v had been set and I2^v–3^v imposed before inner H was taken off the press. Inner H was rinsed, but the remaining type-pages of I were not imposed until outer H had been wrought-off, rinsed, and placed below or above inner H on the bench; hence when imposition of sheet I was completed, outer H was the skeleton chosen. The same explanation may be given for the imposition of sheet G from outer F.

lays in continuous presswork after the printing of sheets D, E, G, I, and K, that is five delays occuring after the first, second, fourth, sixth, and seventh of the eight sheets supposed to be affected by the altered proofing-printing procedure. This means that when the new process was started with D, there were only two sheets (E and G) after which there was no delay in presswork. On this new evidence brought to light by the examination of the headlines, Okes had hit upon a system which he managed to make a most inefficient one for reasons difficult to ascertain.[17]

Is it possible to explain such apparent delays in presswork as no delays? I have already suggested that an occasional delay could be understood if the completion of the presswork on an edition-sheet coincided with the end of the working day for the pressman. Our somewhat hazy and ambiguous knowledge of Elizabethan speed of presswork does not suggest that with a play quarto like *Lear* an edition-sheet of much more than 900 copies could be printed and perfected in a day. We might expect a play by Shakespeare in its first and looked-for edition to be printed with the maximum number of copies, that is, an edition-sheet of about 1,250, an impossibility to machine completely in one day. Even if we accept the possibility, however, that *Lear* was printed in a smaller edition, one where a sheet could be printed and perfected in a day, or close to it, there is no pattern to the delays in Dr. Greg's system which will fit either a small or a large edition-sheet. The possibility that the delays were caused by the compositor falling behind the press has already been shown to be unlikely.[18]

The situation is admittedly obscure, and it is possible that these five delays in eight sheets, or six in nine, had a reasonable explanation, but all things being equal we should prefer a theory for printing which had fewer delays or which explained them as occurring in some fairly regular sequence. The system for proofing and printing which I have suggested entails only three delays in ten sheets, not five in eight, these three occurring after sheets D, F, and H, that is, after the third, fifth, and seventh sheets. I suggest that this regular sequence after every other sheet once printing was in full swing has some significance. The most accurate conjecture of

17 Dr. Greg seems to imply that inner C was last through the press since he conjectures that the discovery of its errors caused the start with sheet D of a system of proofing different from that previously utilized. If inner C is last off the press, there is a further delay before any forme of D can be printed, thus making six delays in the printing of nine sheets. I have analysed the running titles of a number of Elizabethan plays but have failed to discover an example of any other quarto which suffered so much delay between the printing of its sheets as must have occurred if *Lear* were printed in this manner.

18 Some useful information might be gained by a spelling analysis to discover definitely whether one or two compositors were engaged with *Lear* even though the odds would seem to be very strongly against two.

the speed of Elizabethan printing that I know[19] estimates that the average one-press shop could expect to turn out about 900 printed and perfected sheets each day set from a manuscript as difficult as *Lear*, that is, between two-thirds and four-fifths of a maximum edition-sheet. Therefore, if Okes printed about two-thirds of his edition-sheet each day, we should find him printing about two-thirds of sheet C one day, one-third of sheet C and one-third of sheet D the next day, and the remaining two-thirds of sheet D the next day. Thus presswork would conclude on such a schedule regularly at the end of a day after the printing of sheets D, F, and H, and this is what seems to be indicated by the headlines if the book were printed as I suggest. Obviously there was not complete regularity as shown by the absence of a delay after K, but some irregularity would conform to our normal expectation.[20] Even if an attempt to equate the speed of presswork with the evidence of delay furnished by the headlines is unacceptable, the system I propose was much more efficient in *Lear* than that favoured by Dr. Greg.

We may now turn to the consideration of two problems: the reason for the introduction of the abnormal third skeleton; and the question whether a system of proofing, or of non-proofing, with which the book was started was altered at some point to the system adopted for the later sheets. My position is that the system of proofing for the complete book was that which was normally employed in Elizabethan printing with two skeletons and that the third skeleton had absolutely nothing to do with the basic method or with any alteration of the method of proofing the sheets.

Before starting to print sheet B, Okes would have needed to decide whether he would employ a formal system of proofing or whether he would depend upon the informal scanning of a sheet from time to time with corrections made as seemed necessary. I do not think it possible to decide positively one way or another by which of these methods sheet B was printed and whether it is invariant because it was not proofed, or—like sheets I and L—is invariant in the twelve known copies although variants existed in one forme of lost copies. If correction were prompt,

19 C. J. K. Hinman, op. cit. Dr. Hinman's article presents a condensation of material found in his as yet unpublished dissertation on the text of *Othello* deposited in the Alderman Library of the University of Virginia. It is especially valuable since it equates the internal evidence of headlines with what external evidence of speeds we possess.

20 One could arbitrarily create a delay after K to complete the regular sequence, but the manner of imposition would be less natural. It is possible to contrive a system by which inner L would be first through the press after a delay which afforded time for inner K to be rinsed and its two convenient quarters on the bench used to complete the imposition of L3^v and L4. Yet if so, the quarters from outer K in outer L present considerable difficulty.

relatively few uncorrected copies would have been printed: the uncorrected state of outer E exists in only one copy and the original state of inner C in only one. It would be interesting to know what Okes originally planned, but in fact the point is irrelevant for the method of printing the book.

The question of the order of the formes of sheet C on the press is a crucial one. Dr. Greg seems to infer that outer C was first on the press and printed the entire white paper; and it was not until the successive errors were discovered while inner C was perfecting that the system of proofing he envisages was set up to start with sheet D. There are various strong arguments against the possibility that outer C began the printing and inner C concluded it. If inner C were last off the press, no forme of sheet D could be completely imposed until inner C had been rinsed and stripped, in spite of the fact that the skeleton of outer C should have been available. A sixth uneconomical and inexplicable delay would thus be added to the list. Moreover, if outer C were first, the fact that it is imposed with a third new skeleton must be explained in some natural manner. Since a third skeleton is abnormal, since the first forme of sheet B through the press should have been available, and since by Dr. Greg's theory Okes was still printing the book according to his initially conceived plan (which would have utilized two skeletons only), the imposition of outer C seems utterly irrational if it were first through the press. If, on the other hand, inner C were first through the press and the detection of its errors led to a decision to alter the system of proofing, we must necessarily suppose that outer C was not later printed unproofed. The natural time for proofing it would have been while the press was idle for the correction of inner C. If so, sheet C would have been proofed according to the system I have proposed for the whole book, and it is difficult to see why Okes would have abandoned it with sheet D for a revolutionary system which turns out to have been much less efficient. These various difficulties must be satisfactorily accounted for if Dr. Greg's hypothesis is to stand.

On the other hand, either of two explanations can reasonably account for sheet C according to a system of normal printing. If we suppose that inner C started the machining of the white paper and that its proof was returned much more rapidly than the compositor had expected (only the omission of a speech-heading was rectified in the first correction), it could very well have occurred that he had failed to rinse and strip the inner forme of B (last through the press) to impose the skeleton about outer C now demanded for proofing. The rinsing of a forme described by Moxon before re-imposition can be undertaken does not sound like a very short process, and I conjecture that the compositor decided it was quicker to make up a new skeleton about the outer C pages for quick delivery to the press than to rinse, and in addition strip it to outer C. Inner C in its first corrected state was then returned to the press and resumed printing. If the proof for outer C was now read in conjunction with a re-reading of inner C to secure connected sense,[21] the proof-reader could have noted the misplaced comma in inner C which garbled the text, and returned this second proof with the proof of outer C. At this time the press would be stopped briefly to correct the comma (the forme need not have been removed from the bed), and following the correction would complete printing the white paper before perfecting with proof-corrected and invariant outer C.

The second possible explanation is slightly melodramatic but follows substantially the same sequence. When the proof-reader saw the serious omission of the speech-heading in inner C, he stopped the press before completing his reading in order to have the error corrected. He may have secured such a bad impression of the reliability of the setting of the pages of C that he demanded instantly a proof for outer C as well, and the new skeleton was constructed to save the time in treating unrinsed outer B before it could be re-imposed.

One can readily punch holes in this second explanation, and I much prefer the first which is perfectly consonant with normal proofing and normal printing except possibly for the compositor's failure to rinse outer B before the unexpectedly early demand for proofing outer C. The fact that only two corrections, in all, were made in inner C does not jibe with any special treatment given it, or outer C, or sheet D, to ensure a better system of proofing. I should add to the difficulties of Dr. Greg's hypothesis of a new system of proofing starting with D as a consequence of the errors found in inner C, the contrary fact that the original state of inner C, with only two press corrections necessary, was very tolerably correct by Elizabethan standards.

It seems simple to believe, therefore, that the compositor imposed the first forme of C in the conventional manner for two-skeleton books by taking over the intact skeleton of outer B. The introduction of the third skeleton resulted from an upset in the compositor's normal time schedule. It was introduced for only the one special purpose,[22] but that purpose

21 When not the result of authorial intervention, the second corrected state of variant formes in Elizabethan books may well have resulted from a re-reading of the forme in conjunction with the proofing of the second forme of the sheet [the first time continuous text would be available]. If this is so, the order of the formes through the press which I advocate must have been adopted. Correspondingly, it is possible that the rare variants in 'invariant' formes were caused by a re-reading of an early perfected sheet. I should like to think that this proof for the outer forme of C was made by perfecting a sheet already printed by inner C, but the danger of offset from such immediate perfecting was perhaps too great.

22 I must emphasize again that the introduction of the third skeleton must be specifically explained as resulting from some special circumstance. Any third skeleton used as a systematic part of one-press printing was distinctly abnormal.

having been satisfied it was not discarded but retained as a convenience, perhaps to enable a helper to assist the compositor by partially imposing type-pages before the regular time. Or if the compositor did his own imposing of all type-pages, it gave him considerably more leeway in the time which he could take off from his composing to perform his other duties so that he would not be caught short again as he had been with outer C. There is no connexion between the system of proofing employed and the use of a third skeleton.[23] It seems very likely that *Lear* was proofed and printed according to only one system from start to finish.

A point which is distinctly troublesome in Dr. Greg's proposal is the necessity for the invariant corrected forme, once it is placed on the press for actual printing, to perfect immediately those sheets which had just been printed on white paper by the forme taken off the press for correction. Dr. Greg assumes that the time taken to read the proof and correct the invariant forme, together with the exchange of the formes on the press, would permit the first of the printed sheets to dry so that it could be perfected immediately without danger of serious offset. We have no information on the precise length of time necessary for an Elizabethan sheet to dry before it could be safely perfected, and indeed the interval was probably dependent in part on the composition of different inks. We do know, however, that Moxon advises the use of a tympan cloth instead of paper for perfecting since the cloth could be washed clean from the offsetting. This certainly implies that even in books normally printed, that is with the standard drying time between printing and perfecting, the offset still remained a serious problem.[24] When, in actual practice, we sometimes find

23 Simultaneous imposition, which requires three skeletons, is the heart of Dr. Greg's theory. But if simultaneous imposition was not begun until sheet D, as required by his reconstruction, the introduction of the third skeleton as early as outer C (especially if my arguments are accepted for inner C being first printed instead of outer C) must be explained, as well as the fact that simultaneous imposition without resulting delay in presswork was accomplished with only two sheets for the rest of the book. The fact that the skeletons begin losing their unity with sheet D can have no connexion, moreover, with the adoption of any different method of proofing at that point.

24 According to my understanding, Dr. Greg seems to assume that sheets were dried between printing and perfecting. Moxon very clearly states the contrary. According to Moxon, sheets taken off the press were placed in a pile and kept near the press. This pile was turned when it was time to perfect, and the warehouseman did not take the paper to hang up to dry until the pile had been perfected. We must therefore assume that the sheets of paper stayed sufficiently damp after their first wetting so that they could be perfected without further moistening. In this connexion Dr. Hinman has very pertinently pointed out to me that Moxon advises wetting the paper the night before printing a new sheet; and that if this advice were carried out for further wetting before perfecting, perfecting would be delayed beyond all reason. For a review of the whole question, see R. C. Bald, 'Evidence and Inference in Bibliography',

offsets occurring even after the standard drying time, we may be rather dubious whether perfecting could safely be attempted, sometimes within an hour, in the manner which the hypothesis demands. It is difficult to see why Okes should take the very positive risk of spoiling his sheets by premature perfecting when there was absolutely no reason for him to attempt it.[25] There seems no reason why the invariant corrected forme should not have printed the white paper of the edition-sheet instead of perfecting immediately. The system which I am suggesting allowed the customary period for drying.

Dr. Greg was forced into his assumption of early perfecting by his explanation of the consequential change in the catchword in inner K to suit the changed first line in the second state of outer K.[26] I am not suggesting that sheet K could not have been printed as Dr. Greg describes, since here, as always, his logic is irreproachable. I do suggest, however, that immediate perfecting would create serious difficulty and that the sheet could as easily, and with no particular carefulness, have been printed by the method he rejects. Let us suppose that outer K was the first forme to be placed on the bed of the press (it was necessarily first by my reconstruction) and that printing started with it and continued until its first pull was returned to the compositor by the proof-corrector. Outer K (original state) was then removed for correction, inner K (*ur*-state) was placed on the press and, after some delay perhaps in making ready, a proof or two was pulled. After outer K was corrected by the compositor, it was returned to the press and in its second or corrected state it finished printing the white paper. While it was printing in its corrected state, the proof-reader had corrected the proof of inner K and the compositor had made the necessary alterations in the type. The proof-reader, however, had warned (when he noticed it, perhaps on a re-reading of outer K in connexion with proof of the inner forme) that a consequential change would be necessary in inner K when the corrected sheets of outer K were perfected. Or we may perhaps believe (since catchwords are the peculiar interest of the compositor) that the compositor noticed the necessary change when he looked over the proof. This information could not have been delivered, or perceived,

---

English Institute Annual, 1191 (1942), pp. 178–181. I may add that although some offsetting may have resulted from this practice of piling freshly printed sheets on top of each other to await perfecting, offsetting of this kind is not commonly observed; there is no analogy between such piling and the offsetting from the pressure of the press working on too freshly perfected sheets.

25 Immediate perfecting to get the printed sheets out of the way by hanging them up to dry and thus to avoid some trouble in segregating the proper heaps of paper does not seem a sufficiently urgent reason to risk serious spoilage of the sheets.

26 For a full statement of his position on this most important matter, see *The Variants in the First Quarto of 'King Lear'*, pp. 46–7, 54–5.

until some of the corrected sheets of outer K had been added to the pile of uncorrected sheets. When the warning was given, I conjecture that the pressman distinguished the sheets in which the consequential change would need to be made when perfected either by beginning a new pile of sheets or more probably by sticking a special marker in the pile, or by making a note of the number of tokens he had printed. Perhaps in either case he made a rough estimate of the number of corrected sheets he had printed, and thrust his marker there. Clearly, time was not wasted in examining every sheet to differentiate absolutely the corrected from the uncorrected, and hence no exact division was made.

As a consequence, the problem of stopping the press when the time came to make the consequential change in inner K was considerably simpler than Dr. Greg envisages; indeed, it presented no difficulty at all since the automatic warning to stop for correction came when the separate pile of uncorrected sheets of outer K (which yet contained some corrected sheets) was exhausted; or else, more probably, when the marker was reached which indicated the approximate division of the sheets within the single heap. In either case, some copies of the corrected state of outer K could have been carelessly perfected by the uncorrected state of inner K, as seen in the Gorhambury copy. This process I have sketched entails no such severe difficulties as making consequential changes from sheet to sheet or an exact consequential change without error from forme to forme such as Dr. Greg believes Okes was incapable of performing. The procedure was a perfectly simple one and even then was carelessly accomplished.

Whether Okes was such a careless printer that he would not put himself even to the small trouble necessary to make the correction in the manner I have suggested may perhaps be a matter of opinion, but I think it rather dangerous to base one's fundamental premiss on the belief that he would not and that only the informal method Dr. Greg envisages *could* be adopted. The elaborate stop-press corrections which have made *Lear* a classic example seem to me to indicate that Okes was doing his conscientious best to produce the best text he could from his miserable manuscript, a copy so difficult to decipher that even the proof-reader at his comparative leisure could not always determine the manuscript reading. *Lear* is perhaps not by ordinary standards a carefully printed book, but I submit that the evidence shows it was not a wilfully careless one; and the care Okes took within economic reason to see that at least one forme of each sheet in all its copies (and the other forme in as many copies as possible) was as correct as a proof-reader could make it is not to my mind inconsistent with a desire to see that an altered first word in outer K received its correct catchword in inner K, especially since the change could be made so simply.

It is time to sum up. Dr. Greg's and my theories are both admittedly incapable of proof; both are based on sets of assumptions, and the choice between them must rest on that which better, to use Dr. Greg's acute phrase, 'explain[s] the peculiarities as the necessary outcome of some normal method of working'.[27] Dr. Greg's assumptions are clearly consonant with the particular evidence on which he bases them. In my opinion, however, the new evidence furnished by an analysis of the headlines should raise the question whether several essential modifications in his assumptions are not necessary.[28] Hence we differ in the following: (1) Dr. Greg's method of proofing and printing began conjecturally with sheet D, mine at the start with sheet B but under no circumstances later than C; (2) we disagree about the precise method of proofing, which involves the important and fundamental issue of the order of the formes through the press, including the correcting of inner K.

The new evidence provided by the headlines as they show the probable order of the formes through the press, the progress of imposition, and the breaks in continuous presswork, in my opinion reveals the following difficulties inherent in Dr. Greg's method. (1) It does not explain why, if three skeletons were constructed to secure simultaneous imposition of formes for proofing, the third skeleton was instituted as early as outer C; indeed it does not take account of the difficulties met with if outer C, as required, was first printed. (2) It constructs an elaborate process requiring three skeletons to save time by simultaneous imposition of two formes, but the evidence of the headlines shows that any time saved was squandered in excess by delays in presswork between all but two sheets consequent upon the simultaneous imposition. These delays were of a nature which negated the usefulness of the third forme; hence *Lear* could have been printed for all but two sheets with equal speed using the conventional two skeletons. (3) It arbitrarily requires perfecting within an hour or two, and perhaps less, of some sheets where the ink must have been

27 I must apologize if this conclusion, and indeed the whole article, seems rather argumentative. When one is dealing with facts, the facts may speak for themselves; but when, as here, one is dealing only with probabilities and trying to demonstrate that one set of assumptions is more normal and thus more in accordance with the evidence than another, it is difficult always to avoid the tone of persuasion.

28 I gladly follow Dr. Greg in a number of his original assumptions: (1) Variation is essentially confined to one forme of each variant sheet as a result of a settled system of proofing and printing. (2) The invariant formes of variant sheets, and almost certainly the invariant sheets I and L [I should add sheets B and C], represent in all probability corrected states. (3) Some unknown method of proofing was adopted to correct the more obvious literals so that the 'uncorrected' states of variant formes had already undergone a partial proofing. [Dr. Greg leans to some method of taking rough proofs by hand; I favour the compositor's reading over his type.] (4) The second state of inner K resulted only from an attempt made to aline it with the second state of outer K, and hence inner K was already proof-corrected in its first state.

extremely wet and the danger of offsetting severe; at the very least the
nuisance of a quickly fouled tympan sheet or a change from sheet to cloth
would have been unnecessarily endured. The natural action of the printer
ought by every argument to have been to save this perfecting until the
last.[29] (4) It is based, in the last analysis, on the hypothesis used to explain sheet K; and Dr. Greg's explanation of sheet K is in turn based on
the debatable premiss that Okes would not have troubled to change a
catchword except by semi-accident; the necessity for immediate perfecting
mentioned above is born of the explanation for the consequential change
in the catchword as a purely informal operation. (5) It does not represent
a normal modification of standard Elizabethan proofing as it must have
been handled with one-skeleton books and as it would most normally
develop from this to two-skeleton printing. It is a revolutionary theory
involving a process demonstrably not elsewhere employed in Elizabethan
times, at least as a fairly common practice, and almost certainly not employed, in necessarily modified form, as the normal method for the common two-skeleton printing.[30] Hence we may query whether it was known
at all.

The modifications of Dr. Greg's hypothesis which I have suggested in
this article attempt to explain each one of these doubtful points as according with a more ordinary way of working.

29 In my opinion this immediate perfecting is the weakest link in the chain of Dr.
Greg's original assumptions; yet without it his hypothesis fails for sheet K and is
thereby weakened. It is especially serious since Dr. Greg offers no explanation why
Okes felt it incumbent to perfect the uncorrected states by his invariant formes and thus
to take even the slightest chance of spoiling some of his sheets. Moxon is very definite
on the subject. A sheet of paper can be used to back the tympan, he says, when a press
is printing a sheet since then there is no danger of offset. But if paper is used on the
tympan when perfecting, it quickly wears out since it soon becomes smudged and must
be constantly replaced. Hence a cloth, which can be cleaned with lye, is used for
perfecting. This cloth is a nuisance, however, since the wet tympan and paper continually
stretch it. It also must be cleaned from time to time.

    If these difficulties obtain with sheets spaced at a normal maximum between
printing and perfecting, one can imagine how serious they would be for perfecting within
the comparatively brief time that Dr. Greg envisages. If we are to accept it, we should
know the compelling reason why Okes made such difficulties for himself and his pressman. The possible offset of an 'a' which Dr. Greg observed in the Bodleian copy of *Lear*
(see pp. 37–8, 54) does not necessarily prove early perfecting since such offsetting was
possible, as Moxon shows, after the normal interval.

30 The arguments against its modification for two-skeleton work are too lengthy
to rehearse here. The heart of my objection is that the system, as Dr. Johnson sketches it,
cannot be maintained if the compositor falls behind the press in the slightest. The
time necessary to revise a forme is also involved. Dr. Hinman's modification for *Othello*,
mentioned above, is theoretically possible, however, although I do not personally favour
it. I have prepared an article, "Elizabethan Proofing," supplementary to this present
study, on two-skeleton printing and proofing, which will appear in a projected volume
in honour of the late Dr. J. Q. Adams.

1. Proofing was managed by the same method from the start with sheet B to the end with sheet L. The necessary unusual circumstance which must be brought in to explain the construction of a third skeleton for outer C is conjectured. Hence there is no need to believe that only two required press-corrections in inner C forced Okes into setting up a special method for sheet D and later sheets.

2. The method of proofing which I suggest provides for only three breaks in continuous presswork. The regularly spaced intervals for these delays form a momentary pattern which can be explained according to what we know of the speed of Elizabethan presswork. The explanation is perhaps suspiciously neat, but if it is right, there was never any actual delay in continuous presswork throughout the entire book.[31] If it is wrong, then there are at least only half as many delays left to explain as Dr. Greg encounters.

3. According to my reconstruction, sheets were perfected only after the customary interval so that there was no more danger of offset than would exist with any other Elizabethan book.

4. My hypothesis is based fundamentally on the bibliographical evidence provided by the headlines of this quarto which trace the progress and the manner of imposition. It explains the printing of sheet K only after the method of printing previous sheets has been conjectured by the evidence of the headlines, and then decides that there is nothing in sheet K which would tend to upset the evidence of the earlier sheets since a simple Elizabethan method for consequential correction between formes is perfectly consonant with the printing of sheet K according to the effi-

31 At first sight a possible weakness in my hypothesis is the theoretical waste of time with an idle press when the formes are exchanged, since the proofing of the forme on the press would seem to take less time than the correction of the type in the forme just removed from the press. I believe that this loss of time was more apparent than real, although I do not believe that it was closed by printing any sheets while waiting for the corrected forme to be returned. Various operations could be engaged in which would save time later. Every forme needed to be made ready; that is, its register needed to be adjusted, its lines finally justified if they were not sufficiently tight in the locked chase under the pressure of the press, and some type perhaps needed to be underlaid for even impression or else, like spaces, forced down. Only a small part of this work would need to be done over again when the forme was unlocked for correction, and certainly some time would be saved by thus anticipating a necessary duty. Moreover, it is possible that an entirely satisfactory proof could not be pulled until the forme had been thus prepared. Finally, we should expect certain essential operations at the press. We know from Moxon that the press was sometimes stopped to wet the tympan, to clean the stone on which the type rested, and from time to time to adjust the press itself. Such tasks could be undertaken in the interval of correction, which of itself need not have been a very lengthy process. Finally, this interval was forced on the printer of a two-skeleton book (the normal printing method of the seventeenth century) and it is my conviction that Okes was printing *Lear* according to this conventional method except for his time of imposition.

cient manner of the other sheets. In contrast to Dr. Greg, I believe that the Okes who stopped inner C to change a single comma was capable of taking a minimum amount of trouble to alter an incorrect catchword.

5. My reconstruction of the order of the formes through the press based on the evidence of the headlines attempts to show that *Lear* was printed according to a method which, as a hypothetical reconstruction, was in all probability the standard method for printing the standard two-skeleton books in Elizabethan times. In spite of a certain circularity of reasoning, there may be some force in the fact that a theory independently conceived as the most natural modification of one-skeleton proofing for two-skeleton work is seemingly confirmed by the unique evidence of the headlines in *Lear*. At any rate, I attempt to detach the use of the third skeleton from any connexion with the method of proofing and thus to minimize the significance of its theoretical possibilities for simultaneous imposition. The almost unique shifting about of the quarters is traced and explained as a method of releasing for distribution at a normal rate the extra type that would be immured in the third skeleton, possibly with an extra convenience in enabling a helper to speed the compositor's setting of a difficult manuscript by taking over certain of his duties or in permitting the compositor to impose when it was most convenient, not at a fixed time.[32]

In closing I must state that I have tried only to substitute a more conventional hypothesis for certain features of Dr. Greg's, and one which may better fit the evidence of the headlines, the mechanics of perfecting, and the observed practice of other Elizabethan play quartos. Yet it still remains only an hypothesis. Whether my modifications of Dr. Greg's basic theory prove correct or not, this article will have served its purpose

32 If the introduction of the third skeleton had a significance as marking an alteration in the method of proofing, we should expect, by Dr. Greg's theory, that it was the discovery of a single misplaced comma which showed Okes that his previous proofing was insufficient. If so, then we must believe further that it was not the comma alone which caused the change but that Okes thought other errors would appear in the forme on re-reading although in fact no further errors were discovered. Next, we should expect sheet B and outer C to exhibit text in the state approximating the uncorrected states of the later variant formes. I do not pretend to have any special knowledge of the text of *Lear*, and I question whether anyone who has not given to the text the careful study devoted by Dr. Greg is equipped satisfactorily to answer this question. Nevertheless, a reading of both formes of B and of outer C has in my opinion failed to disclose the really egregious errors found in the uncorrected states of some of the variant formes, and so far as I can see the text approximates to the degree of correctness found in the corrected states, including the invariant formes. This is admittedly a difficult matter to prove one way or the other, and I do not lean very much weight on it. I mention it here only since I believe that outer C and probably both formes of sheet B correspond to the invariant formes of later sheets and represent the same method of proofing used for later sheets. I have not perceived in these formes of B and C evidence to force one to the opposite conclusion.

if it suggests that the order of the formes through the press in Elizabethan printing with more than one skeleton is still perhaps a debatable matter, and if it calls to the attention of critical bibliographers how pitifully little we can actually prove about Elizabethan proofing. If we are ever to progress from theories to facts it can be only by laborious collation of press variants carefully equated with the evidence of the headlines which will show whether books were printed with one, two, or more skeletons and what was the probable order of the formes through the press in these different classes of books.

Elizabethan Proofing

CONSIDERING THE IMPORTANCE of the subject for textual criticism, it is rather astonishing that before the appearance in 1940 of Dr. W. W. Greg's now classic monograph on the Pide Bull Lear[1] no attempt had been made to examine the actual mechanical processes by which the Elizabethan printer proofed his sheets as a part of his normal printing operations. Greg's monograph was concerned only with Lear, and hence he made no conjecture whether his hypothesis for Lear could be applied to the proofing and printing of other books. So stimulating were his theories, however, that two investigations have stemmed from his monograph in an attempt to work out his hypothesis for Lear in terms of standard Elizabethan printing.[2]

The importance which Greg's hypothesis for Lear has attained, and the extensions which are being made of it in bibliographical research, may perhaps warrant a somewhat more precise examination of its probability than has hitherto been offered. I have recently undertaken the first half of this problem and have endeavored to show that the evidence of the running-titles casts severe doubt, in my opinion, on the probability that Lear was proofed and printed according to Greg's reconstruction. Necessarily, I undertook the responsibility of reconstructing the printing

---

Printed in *Joseph Quincy Adams Memorial Studies*, edited by J. G. McManaway (1948), 571–586; reprinted by permission of the Folger Shakespeare Library, Washington, D.C.

1 W. W. Greg, *The Variants in the First Quarto of "King Lear": A Bibliographical and Critical Inquiry* (1940), pp. 40–57.

2 In his "New Uses of Headlines as Bibliographical Evidence," *English Institute Annual, 1941* (1942), pp. 207–14, C. J. K. Hinman mentioned briefly certain results he had attained by applying the Greg hypothesis, with one important modification, to the printing of the 1626 *Othello*, and brought forward the possibility that the method used for *Othello* might have been the standard procedure for Elizabethan books printed with two skeleton-formes. Several years later F. R. Johnson in "Press Corrections and Presswork in the Elizabethan Printing Shop," *Papers of the Bibliographical Society of America*, xl (1946), 276–86, attacked the modification which Hinman had made for two-skeleton printing in Greg's theory and argued for what was in effect the precise application of the *Lear* method to printing with two or more skeletons.

of *Lear* according to a somewhat different system which in my belief was more probable to the evidence of the running-titles.[3]

It may be appropriate, therefore, to extend this special investigation into the more general field of normal Elizabethan printing practice to ascertain what are the probabilities for my hypothesis for *Lear* applying there.[4]

I think it must be emphasized that any consideration of methods of Elizabethan proofing can never be made independently of an examination of the running-titles, which reveal whether one, two, or three or more skeletons were used to impose the formes. Upon the number—but, more important, upon the precise method by which the number of formes was employed—depends our knowledge of the presswork which printed the sheets. Obviously, the proofing is almost completely bound up with the method of the presswork, and specifically with the crucial matter of the precise order of the formes laid on the press not only within the sheet but from sheet to sheet. Only when someone has the courage to embark on a

3 "An Examination of the Method of Proof Correction in *Lear*," *The Library*, 5th Ser., ii (1947), 20–44.

4 I must make clear at the start the purposes and limitations of this enquiry. In the first place, it must be understood that this is a matter on which Dr. Greg has not touched, and therefore I am not attempting to place myself in opposition to any views which he has expressed about standard printing. Secondly, I must refer on occasion to opinions in Dr. Johnson's article cited above, since they represent the natural extension of Greg's *Lear* hypothesis to two-skeleton printing (*Lear* was printed with three skeletons), and must be commonly held beliefs. It is necessary to state, however, that although my investigation of *Lear* was written and accepted in 1941, publication was held up by the war, and hence Dr. Johnson was unaware of the facts contained in it when he published his general review and estimate of current theories. He has since most generously written me that he thinks the views expressed in this present paper based on the *Lear* investigation come closer to the facts than others proposed. Finally, although my examination of the difficulties of applying the *Lear* hypothesis precisely to two-skeleton printing is intended to strengthen my own theory, it also serves to clear the ground in part for consideration of Dr. Hinman's reconstruction of the printing of *Othello* as a perfectly plausible alternative. Within the limits of this paper it is impossible for me to deal with this point adequately, and therefore I must omit all reference. I may say that in theory I find several difficulties in its way, but it would be somewhat improper to discuss these at length until Dr. Hinman has finished his researches and published his results. Hence the attempted extension of the Greg hypothesis to two-skeleton printing which I specifically oppose in this paper is limited to the following: (1) forme *I* of a new sheet was placed on the press, a proof or two was pulled, and the forme was immediately removed; (2) forme *II*, which had been 'simultaneously' imposed, was substituted on the press and printed uncorrected states until the proof of forme *I* was returned and the type corrected; (3) at this point corrected forme *I* was substituted on the press, perfected the sheets already printed by forme *II*, and thereupon continued to print the rest of the edition-sheet; (4) as the last operation, forme *II*, now corrected from proof taken from an early pull, was again placed on the press and perfected the remaining sheets.

huge collation job on books printed by selected printers and then equates his findings with the presswork as revealed by the running-titles and the number of compositors employed can we be able to speak definitively of this matter.

Whether or not a method of informal preliminary proofing was (or could be) adopted, a printer was often faced with the necessity for correcting type from printed proofs made from a forme on the press. Minor variations may be expected in the manner in which this correction was managed, but I suggest there were only two general methods for proofing: one for one-skeleton books and one for two-skeleton books.[5] Except where a printer's type supply was limited, we may hesitate to believe that the most elementary method of proofing was forced upon him by his use of only one skeleton to impose both formes of a sheet when if he wished he might readily use two skeletons, which would offer a more efficient method.[6] The very considerable number of books before the Restoration printed with only one skeleton shows that many printers willingly accepted the waste of time involved in proofing enforced by one-skeleton work. For it was a waste. Variant states in one-skeleton books can be produced by no other method than stopping the press when proof is returned and keeping the press idle while the corrections are made in the type of the forme.

The fact that before 1600 this was a very commonly used method for

5 This is assuming that systematic proofing would be employed. The evidence of variant in relation to invariant formes in two-skeleton books shows clearly that many books were systematically proofed, but we cannot say that *all* books would be treated so. It is my impression that there was more at least semi-systematic than casual proofing. At any rate, if the unsystematic is to be detected and isolated, we must know as precisely as possible how systematic work was managed so that its characteristics can be recognized.

6 Possibly certain books which begin with only one skeleton and later shift to two result from a printer's discovery that more proofing was necessary than he had expected, although a correction of the original estimate of the relation of the time of composition to that of machining may be the better explanation. For this relation, see Hinman, *op. cit.*, pp. 207–214. Another explanation may also be possible. In my article on *Lear*, I advanced the theory that a limited supply of type may sometimes have dictated the use of one rather than two skeletons, since type is available for distribution earlier with one than with two. Hence in certain circumstances, it would not always be possible for a printer to have a free option whether he would use one or two skeletons. For instance, I have noticed that only one skeleton is used for both formes of a sheet respectively in some printing that seems to have been done with two presses printing alternate sheets, a circumstance that seems to be dictated more by limitation of type supply than by the size of the edition-sheet. As another instance, a group of 1661 play quartos I am interested in seem to have been printed on two presses, with two skeletons for each press. Yet peculiar evidence develops that the type supply was insufficient to stand such a strain and that abnormally early distribution had to be undertaken. The relation of the type supply to the number of skeletons and hence to the method of presswork is a subject which will bear investigation.

printing causes me to believe that if we are looking for what can be termed *basic* Elizabethan proofing, we have it here. Two-skeleton printing was an extension of one-skeleton, devised to secure relatively continuous press-work by avoiding the delay between the removal of the wrought-off forme from the press and the start of printing the next forme. For reasons which will become apparent, I feel that this was the major delay which was circumvented and that a certain reduction possible in the time for press-corrections was only a minor consideration. If delay in continuous press-work is avoided in the imposition of formes, we should expect the two-skeleton printer to modify the basic method of proofing in a manner which would be the simplest and most obvious extension of that basic method to the changed circumstances. First, then, the improvement in proofing ought to be a *normal* extension of the one-skeleton method aimed at getting rid of the period of idleness with one-skeleton work; second, it should be so simple and obvious that we should find it almost uniformly adopted.

Now as I have previously pointed out, with one-skeleton printing since there is nothing the press can work on while the forme has been removed for correction, it is forced into idleness. To a printer used to this work the most obvious thing to do when faced with a similar stoppage when he was utilizing two skeletons was to plug the gap by putting his second forme for the sheet on the press at this time and pulling its proofs so that correction in the type could be made at leisure and without inter-rupting presswork further.

Hence we arrive at my hypothesis for the standard printing of two-skeleton books. With one skeleton, correction could not be managed until the press had printed a number of incorrect states of the first forme of a sheet to be machined. When the proof sheet, the first pull, was returned, the press was stopped and the forme removed to be corrected. At this point occurred a delay which the two-skeleton printer was capable of filling, and I suggest that he printed his first forme in the manner sketched up to this precise point and only then substituted his second forme. Thus while forme *I* was being corrected, forme *II* was given a minimum make-ready and a proof or two pulled.[7] Type-correction would normally take

---

7 The necessary make-ready to secure a satisfactory proof would be the knocking up of some and the forcing down of other sorts which had not impressed satisfactorily. I am inclined to believe that this may have been done under any system before a proof was pulled. The rather high proportion of uncorrected states which we sometimes find in variant formes must mean that proofreading was not immediately performed at all times. Indeed, perhaps a possible explanation for some of our invariant sheets is that the proof was read more promptly than usual and returned before the adjustment of register and the final make-ready had been accomplished. Nevertheless, the normal percentage of uncorrected states is higher than we should expect, I think, and ought to have been reduced if the proof had been pulled before make-ready, especially if the adjustment of

no extraordinary amount of time, and I suspect that by the time forme *II* was got in shape for proofing, or had had further necessary work done on it which would save time later, corrected forme *I* had been returned to the press. It is unlikely that any sheets were actually printed by forme *II* at this time. When corrected forme *I* was ready, forme *II* was removed from the press to be replaced by forme *I* which completed printing its heap of white-paper. The process is exactly like that for a one-skeleton book except that the interval of correction of the forme first on the press had been profitably utilized in a manner impossible with one skeleton. The printer had saved stopping the press during the printing of forme *II* and had probably performed some useful make-ready and registration which would save him time later. He had done all this within the standard pattern of one-skeleton printing with which he was familiar, most simply and efficiently adapting it to two-skeleton work.

If proofing were done by this system, the apparent results would approximate those achieved by an application of Greg's hypothesis, in that one forme of each sheet would be variant and one invariant. It seems incumbent, therefore, to examine both possibilities in some detail, after pointing out that it is dangerous to equate Greg's theory, which is suitable only for a three-skeleton book and which was offered only for *Lear*, precisely with the circumstances of simultaneous imposition in a two-skeleton book. In actual fact the circumstances are profoundly different.

Greg's reconstruction of *Lear* ingeniously provides in theory for no delay in presswork from beginning to end of a succession of proofed edition-sheets except for the brief pause necessary to switch the formes on the press. This continuous presswork with truly simultaneous imposition of formes is the very heart of Greg's hypothesis, and therefore it is most important for us to note that it is possible only in a book like *Lear* printed with three skeletons.

In the first place, simultaneous imposition of two formes of a sheet about to be printed can mean only that before presswork on sheet Y is completed, both formes of sheet Z are imposed and locked up with their

---

register and the final make-ready had been performed during the proofreading. This matter is of especial pertinence for one-skeleton books and for the first forme to start printing with two-skeleton work. There may even be grounds for believing that at least on occasion the proof for correction was not pulled until all this preparation of the forme had been completed and printing started. I may well be wrong, but I do not recall seeing an extant proof sheet which exhibited the condition of the type and of the margins which we should expect from a forme which had undergone no treatment whatever from the pressman. [In 1973 in an interesting article "Eight Quarto Proof Sheets of 1594 Set by Formes," *The Library*, 5th ser., 28 (1973), 1–13, D. F. McKenzie illustrated various such sheets; but there are reasons, I think, to consider that this book had special problems in proofreading and that special measures were accordingly taken. Other sheets suggest that these are atypical.]

skeletons so that either one indifferently can be placed without delay on the press to begin printing, or proofing, sheet Z the moment sheet Y is perfected. This is what Greg believes occurred in *Lear*; and although I think I have shown three sheets in *Lear* which were not handled in this manner, I am sure that for most of the sheets he is perfectly correct in conjecturing truly simultaneous imposition of both formes before the pressman demanded the first forme for a new sheet. When two skeletons are used, however, such a state of affairs is impossible. One forme of sheet Z can be imposed at any time after forme *I* (first off the press) of sheet Y has completed impression. But the second forme of sheet Z cannot be imposed until forme *II* (last off the press) of Y is washed, rinsed, and its skeleton stripped and imposed about the remaining forme of Z. The only conditions under which this process would approximate Greg's hypothesis for *Lear* are as follows: forme *I* of sheet Y is rinsed (or only washed) and left unstripped on the stone until forme *II* of Y has been rinsed; both are then simultaneously stripped and imposed about both formes of Z; one of these formes, which one would be indifferent, is placed on the press for proofing and the other for printing.[8]

This circumstance might occasionally be found when presswork on a sheet had ended with the close of a working day, but as a settled procedure it could never be acceptable, and no one, of course, could contemplate such a strict meaning of *simultaneous* for two-skeleton books. Rather, *simultaneous imposition* would imply that forme *I* of sheet Z is ready for *proofing* on the press immediately after forme *II* of sheet Y is removed, but that the actual *printing* of sheet Z does not begin until forme *II* from sheet Y is imposed in Z and, following the proofs from forme *I*, begins the actual printing. Both formes of sheet Z, therefore, are imposed in their skeletons at the moment the real printing begins. This is not actually simultaneous in theory or in results, and its divergences from the theoretical treatment of the imposition of the formes in Greg's hypothesis have two far-reaching consequences which make me doubt whether this theory can be considered to be essentially similar to Greg's.[9]

8 This is perhaps taking too scrupulous a view. Let us say, perhaps, that forme *I* of Y is imposed about forme *I* of Z but is not locked up. Before the press has occasion to call for any forme of Z, forme *II* of Y has been rinsed and its skeleton imposed about the remaining forme of Z but not locked up. Then when the press called for a forme, the choice was indifferently made which forme would be locked and delivered.

9 The crux of the matter is the amount of time taken to impose the second forme of Z from the last forme of Y off the press. Granted that only under irregular and somewhat uncommon circumstances can the true simultaneous imposition of both formes be managed with two-skeleton printing; yet if the delay in imposing the second forme for Z is so slight as not to interrupt continuous presswork (in that it is available sufficiently early after the proofing of forme *I* of Z so that the press is not unnecessarily idle), then of course the effect of simultaneous imposition has been secured—although

The first divergence is, briefly, that under normal circumstances in Greg's system it is indifferent whether the inner or the outer forme is first placed on the press for proofing, since both are imposed before the last forme of the previous sheet is removed from the press. Unsystematic variation in the order of the formes on the press from sheet to sheet is a theoretical characteristic of true simultaneous imposition and is found in *Lear*. On the other hand, in a two-skeleton book there is observable a generally systematic tendency to put formes through the press in a specific order, which means that the skeleton of the inner forme of Y is normally transferred to the type-pages of inner Z, and so forth.[10] I think this uniformity is caused by the very reverse of simultaneous imposition.

The second divergence is of material interest. 'Simultaneously imposed' two-skeleton books necessarily produce a delay in presswork since the physical act of pulling a proof must take less time than the washing, rinsing, and re-imposition of forme *II* of the previous sheet. Whether this delay is more apparent than real is, for the present argument, beside the point. The heart of Greg's true system, to repeat, is the fact that there should be no delays in presswork except those occasioned by the simple exchange of the formes on the press to substitute the printing for the proofing forme. Yet delays in presswork appear when Greg's system is applied to two-skeleton books, since the wait between the pulling of the proof of forme *I* and the imposition of forme *II* was not contemplated in Greg's reconstruction of *Lear*. If continuous presswork is one of the keystones of Greg's hypothesis, any derived hypothesis for two-skeleton books which interrupts actual presswork differs so essentially as to have automatic doubt thrown upon it. That the necessary delay might theoretically be filled by other activities is immaterial when one considers that these

---

it is dangerous to give it that label. Precisely this point is, I think, debatable. It has been implied that the washing, rinsing, and stripping of a wrought-off forme, followed by the re-imposition of its skeleton about the new type-pages on the stone, is a relatively brief procedure which would not alter the effect of simultaneous imposition if we posit certain activities about the press to fill the interval. I shall return to this subject later; but it is pertinent to state here that the account Moxon gives of the whole process of rinsing and imposition seems to me to require a considerable time, and Moxon speaks of the necessity to take considerable pains in the operation. If my explanation for the introduction of the third skeleton in *Lear* is correct, it was constructed for one specific occasion when the compositor found it quicker to build a whole new skeleton than to rinse and then to re-impose from an available wrought-off forme. This does not suggest that the process of treating a wrought-off forme before its skeleton could be laid about the waiting type-pages was so brief that simultaneous imposition in effect could be secured. But Moxon's instructions are perhaps the best evidence.

10 Casual variations between inner and outer formes of sheets are not unusual and can readily be explained, but consistent and systematic variation is much more uncommon than a general uniformity in the transference of skeletons to identical forms in successive sheets.

filling-in activities have no place in Greg's reconstruction and hence are not required by him to cover other operations.

Yet regardless of the place these activities were assigned in the chain of continuous printing, some servicing of the press was necessary. At least between the machining of sheets the heap of perfected sheets had to be removed (but Moxon does not assign this as a pressman's duty), the new heap of paper set out, a clean tympan-sheet adjusted to take the place of the cloth used for perfecting, the ink supply renewed on occasion, and special inking made of the fresh type in the new forme.

Since these activities have not been minutely considered, we may profitably enquire whether any previously overlooked evidence is available which will suggest that they might or might not overlap the compositor's rinsing and imposition of his second forme. Here, I believe, we may introduce a speculation based on the evidence of running-titles. The first wrought-off forme of a sheet would be lifted from the press, washed by the pressman, and handed over to the compositor who might rinse it at that time or later just before imposition. But normally at this point the type-pages for the next sheet would not have been set through the penultimate page (4^r of a quarto); hence this washed forme would lie on the distributing bench until it could be rinsed, stripped, and transferred to a full complement of type-pages in a forme on the stone.[11] If all eight type-pages of a quarto were lying arranged on the stone when this rinsed forme was stripped, it would be a matter of comparative indifference whether it was imposed about the inner or the outer forme of the new sheet;[12] and if this circumstance continued with successive sheets we should have consistent and unsystematic variation in the formes chosen to impose.[13] That we have, in general, fairly systematic imposition of inner

11 I think it can be proved that the type-pages of a forme in a normally printed book were complete before they were imposed. There is every evidence that distribution was delayed until the skeleton of a forme had been removed to impose another. In *Lear* and in some 1661 quartos I am investigating where it was necessary to release type before setting had progressed to the point where complete imposition could be made, partial imposition at an earlier stage in the composition of the new sheet produced unique treatment of the individual quarters of the skeleton used for imposition.

12 Although it cannot be completely ignored in our evaluation of evidence, the early tradition that the inner forme must precede the outer through the press seems to have partly decayed by 1600 except when circumstances necessitated. *Lear* and various other books show that when the choice was indifferent, the selection seems also to have been indifferent.

13 Except in special circumstances detailed below, a switch in the order of the skeletons chosen to impose the formes in a two-skeleton book must always be evidence of a change in the order of the formes through the press. If, for example, we know that the inner forme of Z was imposed from the outer forme of Y which was last off the press, inner Z must have been imposed last and outer Z first if continuous presswork was observed. The only conditions under which inner Z could instead be first delivered to

forme from inner and outer from outer in two-skeleton books is, I suggest, some evidence for a belief that the usual practice was to impose the inner forme from the rinsed forme when signature 4^r (*i.e.*, the seventh type-page of a quarto) was completed and before signature 4^r was composed.

But this general systematic succession of formes is not invariable. Some of the impositions where the succession of the formes is broken may be explained quite naturally as resulting from the start of the process at the very end or the beginning of a printing day when both wrought-off formes would be lying on the bench together after the press had finished ma-chining an edition-sheet. Nevertheless, this explanation will not cover all of the various examples of occasional switching in the skeletons used to impose the formes of successive sheets within a book where a regular pattern of uniformity has been largely established. Thus when we find the skeleton of the outer forme last off the press being used to impose the inner forme of the next sheet, we must sometimes either conjecture an inexplicable delay in presswork or else come to the more rational con-clusion that all eight type-pages were in such cases lying ready on the stone when the first rinsed forme was stripped for the first imposition of the new sheet, and that the compositor therefore indifferently chose to impose the new outer forme with the skeleton of the wrought-off inner.

If we accept the conjecture that *as a general rule* the systematic im-position of skeletons about similar formes indicates imposition from the rinsed forme when the seventh quarto type-page has been composed, then it follows that in those examples not to be explained by overnight breaks in printing, a shift in the imposition of a skeleton about a different forme indicates that the rinsed forme was not stripped for imposition until the eighth type-page was lying on the stone. I think it possible to draw certain inferences from this hypothesis. Obviously, if the compositor waits until he has completed setting the whole gathering before imposing one of its formes, he is under no pressure to deliver a forme to the press at the first possible moment. The fact that as a general rule the reverse is true would seem to indicate that usually presswork and speed of composition were so relatively and economically balanced that the compositor felt the necessity to have an imposed forme ready for the press as early as possible.[14] If this

---

the press are as follows: (1) Presswork on sheet Y concluded at the end of a day, and that night or early next morning the forme of outer Y was rinsed and re-imposed about inner Z before the start of presswork on Z. Even here normal imposition of inner Z from inner Y would have been delayed, but this is possible under the circumstances. (2) The compositor was so far behind the press that he had not rinsed inner Y and had not finished setting inner Z before outer Y was washed and turned over to him. When Sig. Z4^r was set, he had no rinsed forme with which to begin immediate im-position, and so indifferently chose outer Y to rinse and impose.

14 Dr. Hinman's studies, referred to above, of the relation between the number of

is so, and it is what we should ordinarily expect, we should recognize that composing speed, being dependent upon difficulties in the manuscript, extra long lines of text, and certainly accidental pieing from time to time, is more variable than presswork. Hence we must believe that in normal printing various occasions arose when the compositor fell behind the press instead of maintaining a somewhat precarious balance. If he had been consistently ahead of the press, he would have set his eighth type-page, on some occasions at least, before he imposed the first forme, and we should have more books exhibiting general variation in the order of formes. It follows that if he were behind his usual relation to presswork there would be times when the eighth type-page would not be composed at the moment the press was ready for the already imposed first forme of the new sheet. Here the pulling of a proof and the activities about the press would need to cover the setting of 4^v in addition to the treatment and imposition of the newly wrought-off forme. If the compositor were slightly more behind and had completed 4^r but had not imposed the inner forme by the time the press was calling for a forme, then the activities about the press might cover the necessary imposition of the first forme, but certainly not this first imposition, the composition of 4^v, the rinsing of the washed wrought-off forme just released by the press and the imposition of its skeleton about the new outer forme. Presswork would be seriously delayed after the proof of the first forme was pulled and before the press could receive the imposed second forme from which printing was to start. One should not underestimate the time that would be taken in treating a forme, spreading

---

skeletons and the size of the edition-sheet as vitally tied in with the speed of composing versus presswork, bolster the argument that in general the compositor worked under some pressure. We cannot ignore the possibility that some compositors from habit always imposed inner from inner forme even though the outer had been completely set and was lying on the stone. Nevertheless, we have the evidence of those books exhibiting unsystematic and consistent variation that not all compositors were so habituated. One interesting imposition in *Lear*, that of sheet E, may perhaps be best explained as imposition made of E when the first type-page of F was also on the stone, thus indicating that imposition was not made at any automatic point regardless of the time available before the press would require the forme. Here, according to my reconstruction, outer E was first through the press. We cannot ignore, also, the fact that inner forme imposed from inner by no means proves that there was not time to set 4^v before the press actually called for the inner forme. The inference I am arguing for is simply this. Certain books show that the compositor had no fixed choice for imposing one forme rather than another when both were available. Others show a decided preference for regularity but occasional variation. Still others show complete regularity. These last are uninformative, but those with occasional irregularity can be taken logically as indicating that the compositor had no fixed habit but was imposing his inner forme first because the press would soon be requiring it and he had not yet completed setting his outer forme. This shows, what we should expect, that in general there was a close balance between composition and speed of presswork. The rarer completely irregular books show that the compositor was keeping ahead of the press at an ideal rate.

and rinsing the lines of type, and finally picking up the skeleton piece by piece and re-imposing it in its precise place about the new type-pages.

These delays would be largely of no consequence with the system of printing and proofing which I advocate, since the press prints copies of the uncorrected forme first placed on it before the second-imposed forme is substituted for proofing. But with any such rigid system of proofing as has been suggested, *where with every sheet the eighth type-page had to be composed by the time the last forme of the previous sheet was removed from the press,* the delays that inevitably develop in setting would be fatal to efficiency.* It also seems to me to follow that no system which was so delicately balanced that the printer counted on invariably stretching the activities about the press to cover the various delays which would normally develop before the second forme could be delivered is a practical one. Usually only the single act of rinsing and re-imposing a forme is en-visaged; I believe this was a longer process than it is taken to be; but, more important, on numerous occasions this requirement would have to be supplemented by various other time-consuming operations before the all-important second forme could be delivered. The activities about the press which may be listed as performed in the interval between the first and second formes need not have been invariable, and even in aggregate with the two to three men about the press and perhaps other helpers in a shop, they should have taken relatively little time: indeed, they might have been performed only during the necessary make-ready and the washing of the wrought-off forme. Hence I am led to distrust any hypothesis which isolates these press activities and uses them as a normal practice com-pletely to cover the variable interval in the compositor's duties. Under ordinary circumstances one should expect that the compositor was charged with having a forme ready on demand for the press on the basis that presswork attempted to be continuous in the handling of the type. This expectation seems to me to be buttressed by the usual evidence of running-titles[15] which reveals, in comparison, relatively fewer occasions when the

* Like all bibliographical scholars I have given careful attention to D. F. McKenzie's brilliantly argumentative article "Printers of the Mind," *Studies in Bibliography*, 22 (1969), 1–75, but I find I cannot accept his attempted disintegration of relatively ef-ficient and economical printing practices in a small London competitive commercial printing-house in the early years of the 17th and the later years of the 16th centuries from the special evidence of the late-Restoration Cambridge University Press printing practices operating on a non-commercial and non-hurried basis without pressure for completion applied by a commercial publisher. Unless one is to scrap analytical bibliog-raphy altogether (as Dr. McKenzie comes perilously close to recommending) it may seem sounder to base one's reconstructions on the hypothesis of attempted efficiency, as in Moxon, instead of deliberate inefficiency.

15 The principles for using running-titles are partly treated in my "Notes on Running-Titles as Bibliographical Evidence," *Library*, 4th Ser., xix (1938), 315–38, supplemented by "The Headline in Early Books," *English Institute Annual, 1941*

compositor had sufficient leisure to set 4^v of a quarto before finding it necessary to impose the inner forme.

For these reasons, and especially because it seems difficult to believe that the required rigid schedule could possibly be maintained, I am inclined to doubt completely whether an Elizabethan printer would devise or would engage himself to a proofing system which was utterly inelastic, and which on various occasions would lose him money by a seriously idle press. As Dr. Johnson writes: "printing-house process was undoubtedly variable on many points, capable within certain limits of being altered to suit special circumstances. To this one must add the corollary that all parts of the printing process are closely interlinked, so that a change which might seem a desirable means of avoiding delay at one stage of the process would be rejected if it would simultaneously introduce confusion and possible delay at a later stage and thus sacrifice everything that had been gained." [16] These are wise words, and consistent with them I advocate the probability that a printer would devise a method of proofing which was capable of elastic adjustment within a regular process,[17] not a system which could not be consistently maintained when the inevitable bottlenecks developed, and which required a compositor to be consistently farther ahead of the press than the available evidence suggests he usually stayed.

However, in the last analysis I think that any system for two-skeleton work which assumes that the printer pulled a proof of his first forme and then immediately began to print his second must stand or fall with Greg's hypothesis for *Lear* which puts the formes through the press in this order. In my investigation of *Lear* I endeavored to show that the consequential alteration of the catchword in sheet K could have been handled readily with the 'normal' order of the formes through the press, and I echoed Dr. J. G. McManaway's review of Greg's monograph in querying the practicability of the immediate perfecting of early sheets required by his hypothesis, especially in the light of the fact that a tympan sheet, not a specially substituted perfecting cloth, would almost necessarily have been used.[18] My analysis of the running-titles seemed to indicate beyond all

(1942), pp. 185–205. C. J. K. Hinman's "New Uses for Headlines as Bibliographical Evidence" in the same *Annual*, pp. 207–228, ingeniously carries forward certain principles.

16 *Papers Bib. Soc. Am., op. cit.* p. 280.

17 As part of a general elasticity, a printer might well have preferred a system which could dispose of the necessity to proof a forme found not to require it. Any system which envisages rigidly systematic proofing and puts both formes on a press one after another, the first for proofing and the second to begin the printing, is less elastic than one which modifies standard one-skeleton printing and offers a choice whether to stop the press for proofing or to run off the edition-sheet without it.

18 This immediate perfecting of the first printed sheets of forme *II* when proof-corrected forme *I* is returned to the press has always seemed to me a prime difficulty. The

question that *Lear* could not have been imposed and printed with the order of the formes through the press which Greg conjectured without an inexplicable series of delays at the press which would have sacrificed more than the time which might have been gained by the process of simultaneous imposition. Moreover, if the book were printed according to his reconstruction, it was precisely the fact that the new formes were simultaneously imposed in most cases from formes just off the press, although earlier wrought-off and presumably rinsed formes were available, which causes a series of delays the like of which I have seen in no other Elizabethan book.[19] Finally, I attempted to show that the running-titles form a pattern which precisely fits the proofing method I have advocated here on theoretical grounds as the one most likely to be adopted as a modification of one-skeleton printing. If my analysis of the evidence wins any acceptance, then Greg's hypothesis becomes a theoretically logical method but one which on the evidence of the running-titles was not used with *Lear* or with any other quarto I know.[20]

I have made so much of *Lear* in this discussion because in this play we

---

only possible reason would be slightly easier handling of the sheets by getting them immediately out of the way and on the drying rack. Yet I cannot believe the removal of the sheets was sufficiently urgent to risk considerable spoilage. A quite speculative point may be mentioned in connection with the possibility of immediate perfecting. In some books one or more leaves are blank in some copies but in others contain letterpress either in the form of supplements to the text, variant title-pages, or possibly material to be used as a cancellans. When this letterpress is not the result of re-running the sheets at a later date, it must be laid to insertion by press-alteration, with the printer failing to re-run his already printed sheets to impress the additional material in all copies. Certainly on some occasions we may reasonably conjecture that the printer did not re-run his sheets because he did not want to take the time required for this operation and was content to have the new material present only in some, not in all, copies. I am not sure, however, that we can be satisfied with this as an invariable explanation, and I should query whether he *could* re-run these sheets even if he wished. The case would be analogous to immediate perfecting, except here the special frisket would receive an offset (no cloth would be possible). I think we may well speculate whether the offset problem does not account for some of the books with this peculiarity, and if so then there may be additional reason to doubt immediate perfecting.

19 Specifically, from sheet C through L there were only two sheets out of the nine that could have been printed as he conjectures without a delay in continuous presswork which the simultaneous proofing utilizing three skeletons was theoretically set up to prevent.

20 Putting the question of *Lear* aside, I have found in the examination of the running-titles of a number of quartos, both Elizabethan and Restoration, no example where the use of more than two skeletons with one press can be equated with the proofing method of simultaneous imposition. Hence I believe Dr. Hinman was correct in calling Greg's hypothesis revolutionary printing in relation to normal procedure, for the vast majority of books could not have employed it. To me, it is an argument of some weight that though in certain respects it is the most efficient system that can be devised, it was not at least customarily employed. Writers have been too prone to accept three-skeleton printing with one press as a fairly normal process. My experience has been quite the contrary, and I venture to say that when three-skeleton Elizabethan quartos are properly

have an example where the introduction of unique evidence gives us a pattern of running-titles by which we can actually test the probable method of proofing and printing in an Elizabethan book. If my interpretation of the running-titles proves correct, it is possible from them to evolve a hypothesis which seems to coincide precisely with the evidence of the running-titles in two-skeleton printing. Hence until I find myself in the unfortunate position of being clearly corrected, I should like to maintain that probability and the available evidence indicate the average two-skeleton Elizabethan book was printed and proofed as follows:

1) A forme of a fresh sheet was made ready, placed on the press, and machining started. The first pull was sent to the proofreader, and printing continued until the corrected proof was returned.

2) The forme was then removed from the press and corrected.

3) In the interval of this correction the second forme of the sheet (which had been imposed while the first forme was printing) was substituted on the press, and after a minimum make-ready a proof was pulled. If there was still time, possibly further necessary treatment was given it, such as adjustment of register.

4) The first forme, now corrected, was returned to the press and finished machining the white-paper.

5) During this interval the second forme was corrected from its marked proof and was therefore immediately available to perfect the complete edition-sheet, usually in an invariant state.

I may point out that this reconstruction has no effect on the really important consequences for textual criticism of Greg's investigations. In two-skeleton work the 'invariant' forme of a variant sheet is to be taken as proof-corrected.*

---

investigated most of them will prove to be the result of printing with two presses. On the evidence of *Lear*, the use of three skeletons put a severe strain on the supply of type: the compositor of *Lear* got around this difficulty by a most unusual method of imposition which I have not seen paralleled before a group of books in 1661 printed on two presses with four skeletons. It cannot be too much emphasized that (although more may well exist) no one has yet brought forward another book printed like *Lear*. To accept its three skeletons as an example of normal printing, therefore, is a most dangerous proceeding.

* Two additional points may be mentioned which I have treated in other places. In my opinion the usual Elizabethan commercial book was proofread only on the press, although I take it that generally the compositor read over his type-pages for literals before sending them to the press and corrected the type in this manner. Hasty resetting such as is found in Dekker's *Roaring Girl* and *Sun's Darling* may give us some idea of what unread type-pages could be like. Second, in some cases the 'invariant' forme is found press-corrected, although this is a comparatively rare occurrence. That these press-variants are almost invariably fewer in number and often different in kind from those in the 'variant' forme of the same sheet indicates quite clearly that when this situation occurs it marks not the first round of proof-correction on the press but instead a second resulting from a further reading.

Running-Title Evidence for Determining Half-Sheet Imposition

BIBLIOGRAPHERS GENERALLY have assumed that preliminaries or cancellanda of a book would be printed economically as part of the final text gathering (or vice versa) when space permitted. Under ordinary circumstances this may surely be taken as a reasonable hypothesis, but—it should be noticed—only when the two sections are of an unequal number of leaves. In a duodecimo collating π^4 A-N^{12} O^8, as in all the later duodecimos of Sandys's translation of Ovid's *Metamorphoses* except for the 1690 edition, gathering π^4 would surely be printed as the cut-off of the sheet with gathering O. Correspondingly, such formulas as 4^0, A^4 (—A4) B-G^4 H^4 I1 [=A4?]) for Dryden's *Wild Gallant* (1684), and A1 [= O4?] B-N^4 O^4 (—O4) for the anonymous *Feign'd Astrologer* (1668) probably represent the actual facts of printing. Often the physical evidence of a wrap-around in an unrebound copy, or else aberrant binding, will demonstrate the fact for single leaves. Thus, interestingly, the precise formula for Pordage's *Herod and Mariamne* (1673) as A^4 (—A1) B-H^4 I^4 K1 [=A1] is proved by the aberrant Library of Congress copy of the 1674 re-issue in which the prologue leaf A4 is found bound at the end and conjugate with the epilogue leaf K1, the two obviously having been printed as A1.4 but the binder in this copy transferring the outer fold in error instead of only the initial leaf.

However, such printing was not invariable, and there are some dangers in assuming it unless positive evidence is found. For instance, if one hunts long enough, one will find the blank initial leaf, as in the Harvard copy, of Behn's *Forc'd Marriage* (1671), which demonstrates that the actual formula for the book is 4^0, A^4 B-L^4 M^4 N1, with sig. A1 blank and genuine and therefore not used to print sig. N1. Correspondingly, in the 1615 folio of Sandys's *Relation of a Journey*, the final blank in the last gathering 2D^6 is sometimes preserved to indicate that the single-leaf dedication A1 was not printed there as one might otherwise have expected. Nevertheless, when careful search in a large number of copies fails to turn up such blanks, the natural inference in certain conditions is that the blanks never

Printed in [*Studies in Bibliography*,] *Papers of the Bibliographical Society of the University of Virginia*, 1 (1948–49), 199–202.

existed for the simple reason that they were used to print other leaves in the book.[1]

The cases mentioned above have concerned the major probability that two sections of a book—one major and one minor—would ordinarily be printed together for economy on one sheet. It is also generally assumed that when a preliminary and the final text gathering each consists of only half a sheet, the two would be printed together. For example, in a quarto collating A^2 B-L^4 M^2, the usual assumption is that A(i) and M(o) would be imposed together for printing as one forme, and—after being perfected by A(o) and M(i) imposed together as another forme—the two halves of the sheet would be cut apart to form a single copy of each gathering. In my opinion this is a dubious assumption, and I suspect that as often as not each was separately imposed and printed by half-sheet imposition, the four type-pages of A in one forme and the four of M in another. The evidence of watermarks has frequently been taken as bearing on this question: if in such a book A^2, for instance, contained a watermark and M^2 none, the case was considered demonstrated that the two were printed together. This watermark evidence is frequently untrustworthy in any single copy, although my experience suggests that with multiple copies beyond the range of chance it is to be respected.

It is my purpose in this note to suggest a form of truly bibliographical evidence which can be utilized with confidence under certain conditions to determine precisely whether two half-sheets were printed together or separately. (This question is not altogether one of idle curiosity: textual considerations may enter in such a connection.) Since evidence is drawn from the running-titles, one must have a book in which running-titles are present on at least one page each of the outer and inner formes of the half-sheet text gathering under examination.

Given this common condition, the evidence is very simple. If the running-titles from only *one* forme used to print a preceding full sheet of the text are found in *both* formes of the text half-sheet, then this half-sheet was printed by itself by single half-sheet imposition. (The order of the titles is important, as will be seen: for a readily determined exception to this generalization, see footnote 2 below.) To demonstrate this fact, all one needs to do is mentally to transfer the quarters (as in a quarto) from a skeleton-forme and impose them in the same relative positions about the four type-pages imposed for half-sheet printing. For instance, if the skeleton of inner L is being transferred to half-sheet M, the running-title

---

1. Even after a prolonged search, such printing can remain only inferential, however, unless an aberrant copy discloses the actual fact of imposition and printing. For instance, in attempting to establish the true formula for the first gathering of Sandys's 1632 folio *Ovid*, I examined or had reported over 25 copies before a unique copy turned up containing the initial blank leaf.

of $L1^v$ should go to $M1^v$, $L2$ to $M1$, $L4$ to $M2$, and $L3^v$ to $M2^v$. If, in such a book, A (without running-titles) and M were imposed together, by twin half-sheet imposition, inner with outer in one forme and outer with inner in another, the running-titles from certain of the quarters of inner L would be found in the same order as above (depending on the position in the (AM) sheet of the two halves): $L1^v$ to $M1^v$ and $L4$ to $M2$, or the corresponding quarters of the other half of the skeleton. But, when the skeleton of the outer forme of L was transferred to the outer (AM) forme, $L4^v$ would then go probably to $M2^v$ and $L1$ to $M1$, or the corresponding quarters. Thus running-titles from both inner and outer L would necessarily be found in half-sheet M in a manner impossible if M had been printed by half-sheet imposition and the full sheet cut apart to make two copies of the same gathering.[2]

As a practical demonstration, we may take the second edition of Caryll's *Sir Salomon*, which appeared in 1691 with the collation 4^0, A^2 B-I^4 K^2. Here the skeleton of inner H was used to impose the four type-pages of K^2, and hence one may prove that K^2 was printed alone by half-sheet imposition. In this case the forme of H(i) was turned on the bench before re-imposition (a fairly frequent occurrence of no significance), so that the running-title of H4 appears on K1, that of $H3^v$ on $K1^v$, and that of H2 on K2 ($K2^v$ has no title). A more conventional case is the anonymous *Knavery in All Trades* (1664), with the collation 4^0, *A*^{2} *B-E*^{4} F^2. When we find the running-title of $E1^v$ going to $F1^v$, E2 to F1, $E3^v$ to $F2^v$, and E4 to F2, we can demonstrate beyond the shadow of a doubt that—as with *Sir Salomon*—the final half-sheet was printed by itself and not imposed together with the preliminary half-sheet to the book.

Why one method would be adopted instead of another is rather puzzling. In books like the Sandys *Relation of a Journey* and the Behn *Forc'd Marriage* where blanks were not utilized to print a necessary single leaf, we may perhaps conjecture that in each case there was a delay between the printing of the final text and the composition of the preliminaries, so that the printer decided to go ahead without waiting to determine whether the material could be imposed together. However, such a hypothesis will not hold with the second edition of *Sir Salomon*, printed twenty years after the first. So far as I can see, there is no difference in efficiency in presswork

---

2 A complication would ensue if by twin half-sheet imposition A^2 and M^2 were imposed inner with outer, and then the same skeleton were used to impose the opposite formes of each half-sheet for perfecting. But this could easily be detected and the fact demonstrated by the appearance of the identical running-title of $M1^v$ on $M2^v$ and of M2 on M1 by a turned forme, an impossibility if the four type-pages of M had been imposed together in one forme. (The possibility is too remote to consider that the running-titles originally removed from the skeleton in the half used to print the inner forme of A would be substituted for those already present for M in the skeleton of inner (AM) when the outer forme was imposed for perfecting.)

in printing A and M together by twin half-sheet imposition or else separately by single half-sheet imposition (except possibly for more offset of wet ink on the tympan cloth in the latter case), and my observation in the later seventeenth-century quartos has been that, if anything, the separate half-sheet imposition method was perhaps more common. For this reason, bibliographers need to make a running-title analysis whenever conditions permit before assuming that two half-sheets of text and preliminaries were in fact printed together on one sheet and then cut apart.

Bibliographical Evidence from the
Printer's Measure

TYPOGRAPHICAL MEASUREMENTS have always been of important service in bibliography, as instance the basic uses for identification to which incunabulists put the measurement of twenty lines of type. The present study is not concerned, however, with measurements of type for the purposes of identifying fonts held by printers, but instead with certain inferences which the investigator of the presswork of sixteenth- and seventeenth-century books may draw on occasion from identifying the length of the printer's stick, or measure—sometimes, but not always, in conjunction with alterations in the overall type-page opening in the skeleton-formes of a particular book. This study is confined almost exclusively to Restoration play quartos, but only because I have been working closely with these for several years and have been able to keep records of measurements in some hundreds of books. Except for the final section devoted to the identification of compositors setting in relay, there is perhaps nothing very new in the evidence advanced; but since no formal study has, I think, been made of this kind of evidence, it is perhaps useful to bring together in one place a maximum of information even though some part of it is familiar to most analytical bibliographers.

In his stick, or measure, the compositor set the type from his cases, and from this stick he transferred as convenient a series of composed lines to his page-galley. In setting a mixture of verse and prose, he might use two measures, one short and one long, the longer being the full width of his type-page. Which measure was used to set any given line may have considerable textual significance, as Mr. George Williams has shown in his "A Note on *King Lear*, III.ii.1-3."[1]

Printed in *Studies in Bibliography*, 2 (1949–50), 153–167.

1 [In 1973 D. F. McKenzie brilliantly solved the problem of the two 'measures' in Q1 *King Lear* by showing that Okes's compositor used only the long measure but since he was short on pica quads he lined his stick ('indented' in Moxon's word) with longer quads and justified his verse within the space; see " 'Indenting the Stick' in the First Quarto of *King Lear* (1608)," *Papers of the Bibliographical Society of America*, 67 (1973), 125–130. I take it that William's argument is not affected by the different technique; see his note in *Studies in Bibliography*, 2 (1949–1950), 175–182.] In these same lines further bibliographical evidence, which did not concern his argument,

In early times this compositor's stick was made in various fixed lengths, but at some indeterminate period before Moxon's treatise the adjustable stick came into use. It is generally believed that with the adjustable stick, at any rate, and probably with standard widths of the fixed stick, the compositor owned his own measure. Whether this is an absolute fact is not essential for the present argument, but it may be remarked that close examination of a number of Restoration play quartos does not disclose the interchange of measures between compositors during the course of setting books where variant measures may be identified. Whether fixed or adjustable, sticks were likely to vary among themselves by as much as two millimeters even when intended to be used in setting the same width of type-page. This is understandable when the difficulties are taken into account either of two compositors adjusting their sticks identically or of the artisan carving two wooden fixed sticks to give an absolutely precise opening for each.

This small variation in the long measure was of little consequence in the printing. It was too small to be seen by the eye, and it did not prevent type-pages composed in two such variable sticks from being imposed in the same skeleton-formes: the wedges seem easily to have taken up the difference and provided equal pressure within any portion of the forme. There would be a limit of tolerance, of course. My observation has been that up to about two millimeters difference may be taken as normal, although I have seen measures varying up to three millimeters used in setting type for the same formes: when more widely variant measures are found, one will usually discover that different skeleton-formes contain the type-pages of such unequal width.

Measuring to detect these variant sticks is not always easy. The bibliographer must take account of the fact that different letters were cast on different parts of the body of the type and that he must choose roughly similar letters at the beginning and end of successively measured lines if he is not to be thrown off by non-significant variation of as much as a millimeter. This is important, for often he must work with variance between two compositor's sticks of as little as a single millimeter. Moreover, the measurement of no one line on a page can be trusted to identify accurately the stick used for that page owing to the fact that compositors

---

may be adduced from the measure. Much of the discussion as to the nature of the copy behind this passage in the quarto, found in G. I. Duthie, *Shakespeare's* KING LEAR: *A Critical Edition* (1949), pp. 96–99 quoting Hubler and Greg, is vitiated by the fact that the compositor could not have begun to set the opening lines as prose and decided to line it as verse only in the fourth line: since the first three lines are clearly justified in the short [indented], or verse measure, never used in this play for prose, the natural inference is that he began to set them as verse and the mislineation must be accounted for by other means.

seem occasionally to have justified a line by a final thin space. Catchwords alone are the least trustworthy of all, and should not be employed except in cases of necessity: my observation has been that justifying by means of a thin space after the catchword was a fairly common operation. Finally, owing to the variable tightness with which the quarters of the forme could be locked up by the wedges, some normal differential, usually of about a millimeter, is often encountered between type-pages set in the same stick. These are severe difficulties, and for some pages are often serious enough to make measurement untrustworthy when variation between sticks is slight and the compositors did not set according to a reasonably fixed pattern.

The most elementary and easily discerned cases which can be determined by measurement occur when (a) a book is divided in half between two compositors and each simultaneously sets his portion; (b) printing of a book is so materially interrupted that when work is resumed a different measure is inadvertently employed. When running-titles are present, the basic fact of division is ordinarily demonstrable without requiring the evidence of measurement except as a corroboration. A book in which one complete portion is printed with a certain set or sets of running-titles and another portion with a completely different set or sets has manifestly been printed in different skeleton-formes. However, these books are useful for demonstrating the validity of the evidence provided by the printer's measure since the two portions are not always set with a different number of lines per page or with a different font. Moreover, the measure alone can sometimes decide whether (a) or (b) above obtained with a given book.

A typical example is John Crowne's *Calisto* (1675), in which simultaneous two-section printing is demonstrated by the faulty casting-off of copy which resulted in the second press beginning with sheet H although subsequently the first press concluded its section with sheet F. This simultaneous setting and printing is also indicated by the running-titles, which are in lower-case in sheets B-F but in full capitals in sheets H-L. Although the font remains the same, the measurement of the type-page in the first section is 36 lines, 169(182) x 113, 94R, and of the second section 38 lines, 179(190) x 109 mm.

Running-titles are not always present, however, to indicate such a division, and in these cases the type-page measurement may be the only available evidence. Thus in Abraham Bailey's *The Spightful Sister* (1667), which is without running-titles, one observes that the text in sheets B-E is set with a printer's measure of 113 mm., but from sig. F1 to the end of the book on sig. I4ᵛ the measure jumps to 130 mm.

A question often arises whether a book has been simultaneously set in two sections, or whether the break between two portions, as indicated by the type measurement, is only a sign of an interruption in the *seriatim* printing, or else of another compositor taking over not necessarily after a delay. In some cases the same sets of running-titles, and thus the same skeleton-formes, continue regularly throughout a book although at one point there is a shift in the measure which indicates composition by a different workman. A typical book is Peter Bellon's *The Mock-Duellist* (1675), which is printed with two skeleton-formes per sheet, these same two skeletons being maintained throughout; yet sheets B-F are set with a 120 mm. measure and sheets G-I with a measure of 121 mm. In such a book the inference is probable that with sheet G another compositor, who intended to set his stick to the same measure, took over the work. In general, one is likely to conjecture that any interruption of the printing sufficient to cause a single compositor to adjust his stick again after working on some other book would most likely have been sufficient to cause the skeleton-formes to be broken up—but in many books only the conjecture is possible.

However, there is a kind of evidence which can be used decisively in two-section books without running-titles or in books where a change in running-titles and thus in skeleton-formes indicates the possibility either of simultaneous two-section printing or else of a marked interruption in the printing. In a first edition, especially, the normal hypothesis is that separate preliminaries were printed as the final operation. For certain first editions reasonable demonstration of this fact can be made, as when an errata list is present in the preliminaries, or when the text begins on A1 or else on B1 but with preliminaries occupying more than one gathering. In some two-section books the evidence is singularly neat. Thus in *Calisto*, mentioned above, the three-sheet preliminaries signed A⁴ a-b⁴ were set in the 109 mm. measure used to print sheets H-L but not B-F, and thus one can safely infer what the signing would lead one to expect, that these sheets were machined after the last sheet of the text had been wrought off, in this case by the second press.

There is still an ambiguity in such books, however, for this pattern could also result when there had been an interruption, or when without interruption a second workman or press had been substituted.[2] When, on the other hand, in a two-section book one finds that the compositor setting the first section also set the preliminaries, somewhat less question can arise, for unless the preliminaries were set and printed first, this allocation of composition could result only when a book was simultaneously printed. In Thomas Southerne's *Oroonoko* (1696), for instance, the text begins on B and the preliminaries are confined to sheet A. On sig. E1 we

2 For example, in Bellon's *Mock-Duellist*, mentioned above, the preliminaries were set by the second workman, who was conjectured to have substituted for the first towards the end of the book but without interrupting printing.

find the measure changing from the 111 mm. of sheets B-D to the 113 mm. measure of sheets E-M. Here the case at first sight is not certain, since the markedly unequal division of the book seems to militate against simultaneous setting in two sections; and lacking other evidence one might be led to suspect that the appearance of the 111 mm. measure in sheet A should be accounted for by the view that the preliminaries were printed first, even though the book is a first edition. Yet other evidence suggests simultaneous printing.[3]

On the other hand, when a book seems to have been broken rather neatly in half between two compositors, and the compositor of the first section set the separate preliminaries, the evidence is all in favor of simultaneous printing. This is the case with *The Spightful Sister*, where the text division is B-E and F-I, or four sheets to each compositor, with half-sheet A set by the first. Another example is Rochester's *Valentinian* (1685), divided B-G and H-M, the three sheets of the preliminaries also being set by the compositor of the B-G section.

Some rather odd books offer the most positive evidence. Occasionally in two-section simultaneous printing one press would assist the other in cleaning up the job. A first-rate example is John Crowne's *The Married Beau* (1694) in which the text division is B-F, the type-page measuring 46 lines, 187(198) x 108 mm.; and G-K, the type-page being 47 lines, 190(201) x 115 mm. Gathering F consists of three leaves, the fourth having been excised. The preliminaries require the four-leaf sheet signed A plus an unsigned disjunct fifth leaf. When we find sheet A set with the 115 mm. measure used for G-K, but the disjunct preliminary leaf set with the 108 mm. measure used in B-F, and when we also find that the pagination of the book skips from 38 on F3^v to 41 on G1, the case is clear. The book was simultaneously printed in two parts, with the second press printing sheet A but the first press machining the odd preliminary leaf as F4, its text copy not being sufficiently extensive to fill the four leaves of final sheet F.

Another and more complicated example is found in Thomas Southerne's *The Disappointment* (1684) in which the original assignment to two presses had been text sheets B-E and F-I. Gathering E is composed of three leaves, the first two conjugate and set in the measure used for sheets

---

3 Watermark evidence may be useful in two section printing. In *Oroonoko* a different watermark appears in sheets A-D from that in E-M. This watermark division might also develop if there had been an interruption between D and E, but when, as here, no indication of such a work stoppage is found, the evidence rather supports the hypothesis that two presses simultaneously printing different parts of the book had different lots of paper laid out for them, or else two different printing-houses were engaged in the work, always a possibility.

F-I; but sig. E3, disjunct, is set in the different measure used for B-D and also for preliminary sheet A, this last having its fourth leaf excised. The highly irregular gathering E has been mistaken for a cancellans, but a rather complex chain of bibliographical evidence can be constructed to show that the first press was delayed in its printing between sheets C and D, and though gathering E had originally been assigned to it (the second section clearly having started printing with F), to finish the book expeditiously the second press swung over after printing sheet I and the two presses joined to print E. The second press machined E1.2 by half-sheet imposition while the first press was printing sig. E3 in the A4 position of the preliminaries.[4]

Evidence as to the measure becomes more difficult when the preliminaries consist only of a disjunct title-leaf or a half-sheet with preliminary text set in a short measure. However, records I have kept of several hundred books show that in most cases the title-page was set in the same stick used for the text (or for the rest of the preliminaries), and thus that its measure will ordinarily be the same. When, in order to give room for large display type, the title seems to have been set directly in page galley and with an abnormally wide measure, often one will find, as in Dryden's *The Indian Emperour* (1681), that the imprint has been composed in the printer's text stick and therefore can be compared with the measure in other parts of the book. In other cases when the whole title and imprint seem to have been set in a longer stick than that used elsewhere in the book, preliminaries like dedications, forewords, dramatis personae, and so on will usually conform in measure to one or other section of the text. If, on the contrary, as in John Bancroft's *Henry the Second* (1693), the separate preliminaries and title are set in a different measure from the text, we may suppose—according to their nature—either that they were set last after some delay or, as with the second edition of Dryden's *The Spanish Fryar* (1686), that setting of the book began with the preliminaries but a larger measure was employed to squeeze rather extensive material into one sheet. In reverse, we find Dryden's *The Rival Ladies* (1693), the title, preliminaries, and first two pages of text (B2-2ᵛ) set in a 117 mm. measure, but on B3 the measure shifting to the 126 mm. used thereafter.

Sometimes rather interesting facts about the printing may be deduced from the study of the printer's stick. The first edition of Thomas Shadwell's *The Squire of Alsatia* (1688) shows a printer beginning with the typographical plan of a page measuring 38 lines, 176(189) x 110, 93.6R, and setting sigs. B1-C1ᵛ according to this layout. Then, since the play is

---

4 This interesting book is analyzed in detail in my "The Supposed Cancel in Southerne's *The Disappointment Reconsidered*," *The Library*, 5th ser., V (1950), 140–149.

a long one, he apparently felt the need to expand his page to save paper and presswork, and set C2-4^v as 39 lines, 180(194) x 115 mm.[5] Presumably he then found the page too crowded, since with sig. D1 he kept the longer measure but settled on 38 lines and the original vertical type-page opening of 176(189) mm.

The anonymous play *The Triumphs of Virtue* (1697) is unfortunately without the running-titles which might assist in solving its printing, but the facts of its typography may supply some bases for conjecture. The book is a quarto signed A-H^4 and paged 1–4 5 7 6 8–40 33–55 56 [=64]. The pagination numerals in the headlines are in smaller type in sheets E-H than in A-D. The type-page in A-D measures 44 lines, 182(193) x 108, 82.6R; that in sheet E, 44 lines, 178(188) x 113, 80.8R; that in F-H, 47 lines, 192(202) x 118, 80.1R. The pagination suggests that the book was originally planned to be split between two presses in sections A-E and F-H, and that the second press beginning with sig. F1 paged it 33 on the assumption that pagination would start with page 1 on sig. B1, whereas in fact it begins on sig. A3 with page 5. Although one might be tempted to conjecture that the smaller font was adopted by the first compositor in order to compress into the single sheet E rather more copy than had been allowed for in the casting-off, the change in the measure and also in the whole type-page opening (thus presumably in the skeleton-formes) militates against this view. Since the size of the pagination figures in the headlines associates sheet E, instead, with imposition by the compositor of the second section, one might apply the same theory to him, but again the measurements do not encourage this attempt. One fact is clear, at any rate: although sheet E had originally been assigned to the first press, actually the second compositor imposed it, the machining taking place after the conclusion of the F-H section (as indicated by the pagination). One may possibly speculate that the completely different typography of sheet E, showing the construction of a new skeleton-forme, may have resulted from the confusion of the pagination between the two sections, so that when the first compositor came to page 40 (D4^v) he believed he had joined the two sections of the book, since sheet F of press two began with page 41. Only very much later, when the sheets were actually collated—perhaps even for binding—was it discovered that a sheet of text had, in truth, not been set, and thus sheet E may have been composed and printed at a considerably later time to complete the book, certainly at a time after the original skeleton-formes had been broken up.

Important as it is for a study of the presswork to identify the compositors of two or more contiguous sections of a book, one of the more striking

5 This alteration in the type-page opening would require adjustment of the furniture in three of the quarters in both the formes. Just possibly another compositor cut in here.

examples of the usefulness of the printer's measure occurs when this evidence assists in identifying the compositor and also the place of printing for cancels and other separate material originally imposed elsewhere in one forme. Under most circumstances the evidence of the measure alone is not decisive, but certainly a study of cancels shows that the odds are against any material added to a book at a later date than the original printing being set in an identical type-page opening, but more especially in precisely the same measure.[6] Thus the fact that the measure of cancellans leaf G1 in Dryden's *The Indian Emperour* (1667) is that for the rest of the book assists in the belief that it was printed as leaf K4, missing in the seven recorded American copies. Just so, the measure makes it a certainty (evidence of running-titles here assisting) that disjunct sig. E3 of Southerne's *The Disappointment* was printed by the first press as leaf A4 and excised from the preliminaries to be bound in its proper position. Similarly, although in this case the fact can be proved by an aberrant copy, there would have been strong reason to conjecture that the 1681 cancel title-leaf for Crowne's *The Misery of Civil War* (1680), which transformed it into the reissue *Henry the Sixth: The Second Part*, was printed as leaf K4 of *Henry the Sixth: The First Part* (1681) since the cancel title was set to the 114 mm. measure used in that book. For these reasons Dr. Philip Williams in his "The 'Second Issue' of *Troilus and Cressida*, 1609," earlier (*SB*, 2 [1949], 25–33), found the fact that the cancel fold in the quarto was printed in the same measure as the text very comforting to buttress the evidence of the running-titles that this same fold, and not a part of some other book, was the material which was undoubtedly printed in the same formes with half-sheet M.

We come, finally, to an unexplored and difficult use of the measure as bibliographical evidence. As Dr. Charlton Hinman first demonstrated,[7] his results later being confirmed by Dr. Philip Williams,[8] spelling tests can be applied with some certainty to distinguish the work of different compositors setting a book *seriatim* in relay. In this connection, the printer's measure can usefully be employed on some fortunate occasions as powerful corroborative evidence, and it may even become primary evidence when on disputed pages the spelling tests are ambiguous or when, as in the later seventeenth centry, the growing uniformity of spelling may

6 However, these odds occasionally come up. For example, the reset cancellans title for the Bentley-Chapman reissue of the Knight-Saunders 1687 edition of Davenant's adaptation of *Macbeth* is set in the same measure as the original title although it could not have been printed as a part of the original sheets. This is most uncharacteristic for a separately machined reset cancellans leaf.

7 "Principles Governing the Use of Variant Spellings as Evidence of Alternate Setting by Two Compositors," *The Library*, 4th ser., XXI (1940), 78–94.

8 "The Compositor of the 'Pied Bull' *Lear*," *Papers of the Bibliographical Society, University of Virginia*, I (1948–49), 61–68.

make spelling tests of doubtful value. The prime difficulty of the evidence of the measure lies in the fact that when the two sticks were not in perfect adjustment, the variation between them is sometimes no more than one millimeter, although less difficulty is encountered when the variation is two millimeters or the seeming maximum three millimeters.[9] Moreover, uneven shrinkage in the paper may cause apparent variation to upset one's calculations, as well as uneven pressure from the wedges.

In *The Two Maids of More-clack*[10] Dr. Williams found that the usual pattern was for compositor *B* to set \$1-2ᵛ of each sheet, and compositor *A* \$3-4ᵛ. Measurements disclose that compositor *B* used a measure of 88–89 mm. whereas compositor *A* used a measure of 90–91 mm. From sheet C on, these measures coincide precisely with the identification of the two compositors by spelling tests save in the two instances, sigs. H3 and H4ᵛ, where Dr. Williams felt the trend of the spelling evidence enforced breaking the pattern and assigning H3 and H4ᵛ to compositor *B*, although they would normally have constituted part of *A*'s assignment. Since in both these pages the 90–91 mm. measure indicates that *A* actually set these pages and that the regular pattern was maintained in this sheet, the evidence of the printer's stick proves a useful counterweight as a check on spelling tests in cases of doubt. Although the check of measure against spelling as an identification is invariable in sheets C-I except for these two pages, there is some difficulty in sheets A and B;[11] nevertheless, the consistency with which the evidence of the measure operates in the other seven and a half sheets in the book demonstrates that it can be highly effective.

Some results accrue when the evidence of the measure is applied to

---

9 As indicated above, these tolerances were sufficient to go undetected, and typepages set in such slightly varying measures could readily be imposed in the same skeleton-formes, the wedges taking up the slack and making no adjustment of the furniture necessary.

10 Tudor Facsimile Texts (London, 1913).

11 Dr. Williams divides sheet A irregularly, assigning A1ᵛ-2 and A3ᵛ-4ᵛ to compositor *A*, and the remaining A1 and A2ᵛ-3 to compositor *B*. This might look suspiciously like casting-off copy and setting by formes (if A4ᵛ could be transferred to *B*), but the 90–91 mm. measure found in all eight type-pages would indicate that compositor *A* set this sheet entire; and on close examination Dr. Williams's spelling criteria are seen to be somewhat indefinite for the pages assigned to *B*. Real trouble occurs in sheet B, however, which Dr. Williams divides between the two compositors in the regular manner found in subsequent sheets. Yet with the exception of sig. B3 where the measure is perhaps doubtful and could be that of compositor *A*, the measure of B3-4ᵛ is certainly 88–89 mm. and therefore associated with compositor *B*, who had definitely set B1-2ᵛ in this same measure, the spelling tests agreeing for these earlier pages. I do not pretend to be able to explain this aberration, since in the disputed pages the spelling very strongly suggests compositor *A*. I hesitate to conjecture that in this one instance (as possibly in the preceding sheet if the spelling tests there are really precise) the stick passed from hand to hand, but perhaps it did.

Restoration play quartos where spelling tests would be doubtful. Crowne's *The Country Wit* (1693) is a difficult book because it is hard to decide whether certain variations of a millimeter in one compositor's measure are non-significant, or whether they represent the stick of a third compositor. If we take the more difficult but probable view that three compositors were associated with this book, we find that compositor *I* with a measure of 120–121 mm. set both formes of sheet A (which contains text as well as prelims) and then dropped out for two sheets. Compositor *II*, with a measure of 122 mm., then took over and set both formes of sheet B. The third compositor *III*, with a measure of 123 mm. seems to have set C1-2, and thereupon *II* and *III* alternate, *II* apparently setting C2^v-3^v, *III* C4, and *II* C4^v. Compositor *I* returns to set both formes of sheet D, followed by *II* setting both formes of sheet E. Compositor *III*, enters with F1-2 and F4-4^v, *II* interposing with F2^v-3. Compositor *I* set G1-3^v and perhaps the rest of G although *II* seems to have composed G4 and just possibly G4^v. Gathering H, very curiously (since this is a second edition), is only a single leaf and is set by *III*. Perhaps there was confusion in imposition even though the pagination is continuous: it may be significant that with the re-entrance of compositor *I* on G1 the two skeletons which had printed each sheet of the book exchange their formes in sheet G, this arrangement carrying over to sheet I. At any rate, compositor *II* set I1-2^v and *III* concluded the book with I3-4^v. I cannot guarantee the absolute accuracy of every page of this assignment since the tolerances are sometimes very fine between compositors *II* and *III*; but this is what I make of the Harvard copy, and I am inclined to believe that a pattern develops which is accurate in the main and which is not inconsonant with a reasonably exact identification of compositors. In the Harvard copy the paper of sheets D and G, set by compositor *I*, seems to differ from that in the rest of the book.

From several other plays Thomas D'Urfey's *A Fond Husband* (1677) may be selected. Here a fairly regular pattern is established of about four to five type-pages apiece between two compositors in relay using measures of 112 mm. and 113 mm. respectively. This play is especially interesting because, although it is a first edition and thus set from manuscript, the evidence of the measure seems to indicate that for the first two text sheets (possibly to get formes as quickly as possible at the start to the waiting press or presses) the compositors cast off copy and set by formes. Thus the 112 mm. measure set the outer formes of sheets B and C, and the 113 mm. measure the inner formes. Thereupon they begin to alternate by sheets, the 113 mm. measure beginning by composing most of sheet D, both formes.

The evidential value of the measure is not invariable, for there are numerous books almost certainly set by two compositors whose sticks were so nearly equalized that measurement cannot distinguish them. Negatively, therefore, the evidence must always be equated with that of the presswork as shown by running-titles, or as Allan Stevenson has demonstrated,[12] by watermarks, before an invariant measure may be taken as indicating the presence of only one compositor, spelling tests not having been applied.[13] When, however, positive evidence is available that two measures were used in the composition of a book, the analytical bibliographer may find the information thus gained to be of considerable value in any number of unsuspected ways to which his ingenuity may lead him.[14]

12 "New Uses of Watermarks as Bibliographical Evidence," *Papers of the Bibliographical Society, University of Virginia*, 1 (1948–49), 151–182. Printing by two presses must necessarily require the services of two compositors.

13 The determination of the precise spelling criteria which may be used as distinguishing features of the work of two compositors and then the application of these tests to any given book is an extremely onerous task which may on occasion be lightened by at least a tentative assignment of pages between compositors on the evidence of their measures.

14 Since a study of the characteristics of the compositors of a book is necessary before a textual critic can emend with any certainty, the working bibliographer owes it to the critic to analyze a book with the maximum precision in preparing it for criticism. Every available technique should be exploited, therefore, and among these it is possible that in certain cases the extension of the ways in which this evidence of the printer's measure may be employed and the results interpreted will prove of considerable value.

Motteux's "Love's a Jest" (1696): A Running-Title and Presswork Problem

Peter Motteux's play *Love's a Jest* (1696), Woodward & Mc-Manaway no. 847, is a quarto collating A^4 a^2 B-L^4. Extreme haste in production must have been necessary, for the text seems to have been divided into a number of sections for simultaneous working: either the font of the running-titles or the measure of the compositor's stick changes with bewildering frequency. The longest section is only three sheets, C-E, and in this stretch, in sheet D, appear variant running-titles which can be broken down by analysis to reveal an interesting fact about the printing.

Sheet D may contain any one of four different combinations of running-titles in their skeletons. The following arrangement is partly arbitrary and, except for copy 1, does not necessarily imply priority of printing:

Copy 1: This state is the only normal one: it comprises the first sheets to be completed, and demonstrates the original order of transfer of the skeleton-formes from sheet C to sheet D and thence to sheet E. Both the inner and outer formes of sheet C, as evidenced by the running-titles; were transferred regularly to the corresponding quarters of sheet D and similarly to E. Thus, in the outer forme, the C1 running-title is found on D1 and E1, etc.; and in the inner forme, the C1^v running-title on D1^v and E1^v, and so for the other quarters. Five copies observed: DFo, MH, PU, TxU (copy 2), Bodleian.

Copy 2: In this state the four running-titles of inner D were taken over normally from inner C, as in copy 1, so that C1^v-D1^v, etc.; but a completely new skeleton has been constructed for outer D, containing four running-titles different in setting from those in either forme of sheets C and E. It is probable but not certain that printing was concluded on this state before the completion of the state represented by copies 3 and 4. Seven copies observed: MWiW-C, TxU (copies 1, 3), Bodleian (three copies), National Library Scotland.

Copy 3: As with states 2 and 4, this state was completed only after a delay following the machining of the state represented by copy 1. The exact time-of-printing relationship of copy 3 to copies 2 and 4 is not cer-

Printed in *Papers of the Bibliographical Society of America*, 48 (1954), 268-273; reprinted by permission of the Council of the Bibliographical Society of America.

tain, perhaps, but there would be some reason to assign completion of this state of the sheet as prior to the completion of printing the sheet in state 4. In this state 3, the outer forme of C is regularly transferred to the outer forme of D, as in copy 1, and indeed this outer forme is of the same impression in both copies. However, the skeleton of inner D differs, for it is here the same skeleton (containing the same four running-titles) as the outer forme, perfecting the sheet after the skeleton has been turned in the process of transfer. Thus, for purposes of identification, the running-titles of outer D are in the identical positions as found in the outer formes of C and E; but in inner D the running-titles of outer D are found in the following relationship, $D1^v$-$D4^v$, $D2$-$D3$, $D3^v$-$D2^v$, $D4$-$D1$. Four copies observed: DFo, MiU, TxU (copies 5, 6).

Copy 4: This state contains in outer D the same new skeleton described under copy 2. However, its inner D skeleton is of the same impression as that in copy 3; that is, for identification, $C4^v$-$D1^v$, $C3$-$D2$, $C2^v$-$D3^v$, $C1$-$D4$. Seven copies observed: CSmH, NjP, NNC, TxU (copy 4), Bodleian, British Museum, Worcester College Oxford.

If we assign roman numbers to identify the skeleton-formes, and indicate the turned skeleton II as II^t, the four states of sheet D may be graphed as follows. The skeletons of sheets C and E are, of course, invariant.

Copy 1	C(i)I	C(o)II	D(i)I	D(o)II	E(i)I	E(o)II
Copy 2			D(i)I	D(o)III		
Copy 3			D(i)II^t	D(o)II		
Copy 4			D(i)II^t	D(o)III		

There would appear to be only one bibliographical explanation for this very odd evidence, unique in my experience. It will be remembered that printing was rushed on this book, and that sheet E was the last of the separate sequence of sheets C, D, and E, the other sections comprising either two sheets or only one. If therefore, the various presses were working roughly simultaneously, sheet E would be completed later than any other sheet and there would be a delay in binding up the earliest copies for sale until E was available. I suggest that this delay was foreseen while sheet D was being machined, that D was deliberately underprinted, sheet E therefore being sent to press earlier than was otherwise possible, and that printing on sheet D was completed only after sheet E outer forme had been worked off and the inner forme was in process of machining.[1]

---

1 The association of skeleton III with the re-imposition of D(o) is shown by disturbances in the type between D(o) II and D(o) III. In the latter, on sig. D1, line 9, an exclamation mark after "Whip" found in D(o)II has dropped out, as has a space in the last lines on the page, causing "Town we" to run together.

Binding, therefore, could be started with the earliest impressed perfected copies of D and E, and could be completed when the final impression of D became available. In the reconstruction below, it is necessary to posit the use of two presses for both impressions of sheet D and for the normal impression of sheet E. Whether a second press was introduced only with the start of sheet D, or whether two had also been used for sheet C, is not quite demonstrable, but the details of the evidence suggest that the plan to speed the completion of some copies of sheet D before the normal time was conceived only after printing on the sheet had been started with two presses; and hence it may seem more probable that two presses also machined sheet C. For this reason I adopt two-press printing for all three sheets as my working hypothesis. It is also a part of this hypothesis, as suggested by the evidence for the number of copies observed in their various states, that sheet C was printed by each press starting with a pile of white paper and printing this, each thereupon continuing without pause by perfecting the white paper printed by the other press, and that sheet D was started according to the same method. Finally, the evidence suggests that outer D (and therefore presumably outer C) started printing its white paper an hour or two before the other press began to print white paper with inner D. On the basis of these assumptions from the evidence, the following hypothetical reconstruction of the course of events might be made, although in the end it must be rejected.

Press Y, using skeleton II, began to print its white paper with D(o) and had completed approximately two-thirds of its pile when printing was stopped. Skeleton II was stripped and imposed about outer E, the type-pages of outer D were tied up, and press Y printed outer E, carrying through to the end without interruption. A few hours after press Y had begun to print outer D, press Z started its pile of white paper (each pile being one-half the edition-sheet, of course) printing inner D with skeleton I. Press Z had printed about one half, or slightly more, of the white paper with D(i)I, when press Y ceased operations temporarily on D(o)II and turned to machining E(o)II. At this point, press Z stopped printing white paper and began to perfect the pile of Y's white paper of D(o)II. About one-half of this pile was perfected, enough to furnish sufficient copies for the initial binding-up, when press Z also pulled off working this sheet in order to begin E(i)I.

At this point, while sheet E was printing on both presses, the following piles of paper were extant for sheet D. Press Y: pile Q representing the remainder of the white paper printed by Y with D(o)II which had not been perfected by press Z before Z left off work on sheet D to proceed to sheet E. There was also a small pile, R, of completely unimpressed paper representing that portion of Y's half of the edition-sheet left unprinted when Y transferred its efforts to sheet E. Next to press Z were the follow-

ing: pile S, roughly a half of press Z's original lot of paper, printed with
D(i)I but not perfected. This represents Z's original impression of white
paper before it turned to perfecting with D(i)I a number of Y's D(o)II
sheets. Also, there was pile T consisting of the remainder of the paper
laid out for press Z but left completely unimpressed because of Z's early
transfer to working sheet E. Presumably hanging on the battens and drying was pile P, a number of sheets of Y's original impression of D(o)II,
perfected by Z with D(i)I before it left sheet D for E. These copies of D
comprise the earliest state as found in copies 1.

When press Y finished printing E(o)II, it returned to polish off sheet
D. Which forme it chose from the tied-up D type-pages can be only a
matter of speculation. If the skeleton II previously associated with Y were
retained, then E(o)II was laid on the distributing bench turned end for
end (a not infrequent event in hand-printing), and the compositor chose
to strip it for imposition about the D(i) type-pages, although press Y
had previously printed D(o). If so, using D(i)II^t, press Y would very
likely have perfected pile Q (the white paper remaining from Y's initial
impression with D[o]II), this lot comprising copies in state 3. It could
then have continued to print with D(i)II^t the small pile R of previously
unimpressed paper assigned Y, following by printing with D(i)II^t the
larger pile T, which was the unimpressed lot of paper left by press Z. It
may be that sometime during this process, a third press, X, which had
finished with another section of the book, swung over to assist with sheet
D, and that a new skeleton III was constructed for its use. On the other
hand, it is just as possible that when press Z finished machining E(i)I, it
returned to sheet D. The use of a newly made-up skeleton III would
then need to be explained as an attempt to save delay in press time by imposing D(o) with a new skeleton to obviate an idle press Z while its
forme E(i)I was being rinsed and stripped. The compositor who had
rinsed and stripped E(o)II and imposed it about inner D as D(i)II^t
could well have performed this service after making his first imposition.

Such a hypothetical reconstruction, however, contains two irregularities. (1) It provides for a speed-up of printing when press Z shifted back
from sheet E to sheet D, but accepts the delay when, earlier, press Y had
returned to complete its share of sheet D, since Y would have been idle
while E(o)II was rinsed, stripped, and imposed about inner D as D(i)II^t.
(2) It accepts a not impossible yet still a rather odd shift in the formes
when for no useful reason that can be determined press Y chooses the D(i)
type-pages instead of the D(o) pages which it had previously printed.
Finally, if a third press intervened, it is odd that a new skeleton-forme
was constructed for it and that we do not find in use one of the skeletons
previously employed by that press elsewhere in the book, even though

the font of type in the running-titles might have differed from that originally used for sheet D.

The preferred reconstruction, therefore, which provides not only for complete regularity but also for greatest efficiency, is the following. When the two presses were working on sheets C and underprinted D, as well as on E, each had used only one skeleton, presumably because press speed was ahead of compositorial speed and no time would be saved by the two-skeleton method of printing. But when each press returned to complete work on sheet D, this factor no longer obtained, of course. Hence I conjecture that when press Y finished E(o)II, the compositor had somewhat earlier reimposed standing D(o), with the new skeleton III in order to prevent delay in the presswork. The order of impression with this D(o) III cannot be precisely determined. Further completed copies would have been secured most quickly if press Y first perfected pile S, which contained press Z's white paper printed with D(i)I. This would have produced copies of state 2. Next, presumably, Y would proceed to print with D(o)III pile T, press Z's untouched remaining paper, and conclude with pile R, its own previously unprinted lot of paper.

Press Z was occupied with E(i)I for a certain time after press Y had returned to sheet D. By the time that Z had finished work on E, the compositor had been able to rinse Y's E(o)II and to impose it (turned) about the standing type-pages of D(i), thus forestalling any delay in presswork for press Z and utilizing the only available made-up skeleton. The order of impression for press Z is not demonstrable, but it would have been most efficient in terms of maximum drying time for Y's printing if Z had first perfected pile Q, the remainder of Y's original impression, this producing copies in state 3. Presumably, Z then continued by perfecting with D(i)II^t pile T, only shortly before printed by Y with D(o)III, this producing copies of state 4; and printing was concluded with more copies of state 4 by the perfecting with D(i)II^t of pile R, printed by Y with D(o)III.

From the case-history of this book and its analysis, several points of bibliographical interest may be mentioned. (1) Running-titles may provide for seventeenth-century books the same evidence for deliberate underprinting to speed the publication of early copies that press-figures may offer in the eighteenth century.[2] (2) Running-titles showing a two-skeleton pattern for successive sheets do not necessarily indicate efficient one-press printing but may conceal two presses each employing the one-skeleton method. If sheet D had not been underprinted, but instead all

2 See W. B. Todd on press figures as evidence for underprinting in *Studies in Bibliography*, III (1951), 190, and IV (1952), 47; *The Library*, 5th ser., VI (1951), 103–4; PAPERS, XLVI (1952), 55–56.

copies had been machined in the normal state I, the presence of two presses could not have been determined. (3) The detection of interesting printing evidence such as this must usually depend upon the comparison of copies in a number of libraries against a control copy or film. So far as I know, all four states are found in only one library, that is, among the six copies at the University of Texas, although three of the states are present in the five Bodleian holdings.

Textual Criticism
and
Editing

Current Theories of Copy-Text, with

an Illustration from Dryden

THE CHOICE of the best copy-text is often the most serious problem in an old-spelling critical edition of a text printed in the sixteenth through the eighteenth centuries. The uncritical use of the last edition within an author's lifetime is now, or should be, thoroughly discredited, although it is still occasionally found.[1] Recognition of the corruption inherent in reprints and of the necessity to inquire closely into the authority of any old text chosen as the basis for a critical edition has very properly shifted the emphasis back to that printed text closest to the author's manuscript, that is, to the first authoritative edition. When there is only one edition set from manuscript and when all subsequent editions are mere reprints,[2] the first is now the logical and automatic choice. Difficulty arises, however, when authority is present in more than one edition. Thus a later edition may be set from an independent manuscript,[3] or, more commonly perhaps, from a revised copy of an earlier printed text marked by the author.[4]

Printed in *Modern Philology*, 48 (1950), 12–20; © 1950 by the University of Chicago; reprinted with permission.

1 In theory, such an edition was the last which could have undergone authorial revision. Yet the choice of such a final edition was essentially uncritical, in that the editor usually made no attempt to discover if, indeed, alterations were present which could have come from a revising author. In thus declining the responsibility of determining whether or not there was any basis for his choice of copy-text, such an editor invariably saddled himself with a corrupt and unauthoritative reprint. Montague Summers' edition of Dryden's plays is an example.

2 An authoritative edition is one derived from an author's manuscript directly or through intervening transcription. A later edition derived from this primary edition may, somewhat loosely, also be called 'authoritative' when it contains revisions emanating in some manner from the author. However, in this latter case the authority is mixed, since all variants cannot be presumed to be authorial. Properly speaking, only the ascertained revisions are authoritative and not the entire text. A reprint may be taken as any edition derived from an earlier, usually with the sense that no authorial revision is present. Its readings, therefore, even when obvious corrections, have no 'authority.'

3 This special case is not considered here, since the choice and subsequent treatment of the copy-text usually has no bibliographical basis and lies in the province of pure textual criticism.

4 For the purposes of this study I exclude all the intermediate possibilities, such as

In this latter case the most common editorial practice has been to choose the latest authoritatively revised edition as the copy-text. This popular principle of editing has not gone unchallenged, however, and it is noteworthy that the objection has come from editors who have originally been trained as analytical bibliographers. Thus the conservative McKerrow, reversing his earlier views, laid it down as his rule for the Oxford *Shakespeare* that, under ordinary circumstances, he would select as his copy-text the edition closest to the author's manuscript and would thereupon incorporate in this basic text the corrections from any revised edition.[5] More recently, W. W. Greg has re-examined the question in some detail[6] and has materially clarified the problem by his strict differentiation of the *substantives*, or actual wording of a text, from the *accidentals*, or formal presentation of a text in such matters as spelling, punctuation, word-division, and capitalization. In basic form his argument is that an editor should not confuse the authority of substantives with that obtaining for accidentals. Clearly, the accidentals of a text set from manuscript are more authoritative than those of a later edition, even one containing authoritative substantive revisions. Just as clearly, true revisions are more authoritative than are the original readings for which they substitute. Thus when a critical editor encounters a revised edition, under most circumstances he should choose for the texture, or accidentals, of his old-spelling text the earliest edition set from an authoritative manuscript, and into this he should insert those substantive or other alterations from the revised edition which his editorial judgment passes as authoritative.[7]

---

recourse to a manuscript to fill up missing pages of a printed edition used as copy or to incorporate major units of additional material.

5 R. B. McKerrow, *Prolegomena for the Oxford Shakespeare* (1939), pp. 17–18. Special cases, of course, prevent the application of the rule. For instance, no one but a madman would attempt in an old-spelling text to choose the first quarto of *King Lear* and thereupon to substitute all the Folio revisions. The primary reason here is, obviously, that the quarto was not set from a manuscript which had any transcriptional link with the author's manuscript. As a secondary reason, the activities of 'Scribe E,' who prepared a copy of the quarto for the Folio printer, were apparently so extensive that it would be very difficult to disentangle his alterations from those of the Folio compositors, although the attempt would be worth while if the quarto had not been set from a memorial reconstruction.

6 "The Rationale of Copy-Text," in *Studies in Bibliography*, III (1950), 19–36. This paper was originally delivered, *in absentia*, at the English Institute on September 7, 1949.

7 The major difference between McKerrow's and Greg's views lies in the proposed treatment of the revisions. McKerrow's conservatism led him to the position that, once it had been determined that a later edition was authoritatively revised, *all* the substantive alterations (except for obvious misprints and errors) must be incorporated. On the contrary, Greg points out that normal compositor's substantive variants can be expected as readily in a revised edition as in a reprint and that these are by no means always so

It is as yet too early to estimate the effect that Greg's logical argument will have on editorial practice.* Nevertheless, one may speculate about the objections which may be brought forward to the practical application of his propositions. One set will certainly come from editors uneasily conscious of their new obligation to distinguish between readings which are authoritative and unauthoritative, since each variant in a revised edition must, in Greg's opinion, be considered on its own merits.[8] The answer to this is clear. If an editor is not simply reprinting some single authority for the text but is engaging himself to a critical edition, which is supposed to present the best detailed text of an author in a form as close to his intentions as can be managed, then editorial responsibility cannot be disengaged from the duty to judge the validity of altered readings in a revised edition. Automatically to accept all the plausible readings in a revision is an unsound bibliographical principle.

A second objection may be anticipated: that Greg's proposals will result in an amalgamated, or bastardized, text—in effect, the conflation of two or more editions. In so far as it concerns purity in text, this objection has no basis, once the distinction is grasped between a critical edition and a reprint of some single authority.[9] Moreover, the fact that old-spelling texts are in question has no bearing on any difference in principle.[10] Under the circumstances of most revised editions, an amalgamated old-spelling text according to Greg's procedures will actually produce the nearest approach to the author's intentions. A revised edition is usually typeset from a copy of some previous edition suitably marked up by the author, although in some cases the author may, instead, submit a separate list of

---

recognizable as are simple misprints or errors. It is, therefore, an editor's responsibility to select only those variant readings which he estimates are true revisions, while rejecting those which he believes to be unauthoritative.

* Twenty-five years after this statement, Greg's position has been substantially accepted in the United States and in England although not on the Continent.

8 Since Greg's purpose in his paper was primarily to lay down general principles with major illustrations, all parts were not minutely developed, as in an extensive monograph. In particular, there is perhaps room for a textual critic to enlarge by means of a greater number of typical workaday examples that section of the paper devoted to the distinction of authority or nonauthority in variant readings from a revised edition.

9 Under many circumstances a critical edition cannot help being eclectic; but eclecticism ceases to be a word of fear when suitable safeguards are erected to prevent the unprincipled selection of readings according to personal taste and without consideration of authority or bibliographical probability, which was too often a characteristic of eighteenth- and nineteenth-century editing.

10 It would seem to reflect a basic misunderstanding of the rationale of the old-spelling text to accept the usual amalgamated reading edition of *Hamlet* in modernized form but to reject it in a rationally contrived old-spelling version. Greg's remarks on old spelling may very profitably be consulted in *The Editorial Problem in Shakespeare* (1942), pp. liii–lv, but especially in his "Rationale of Copy-Text."

alterations which are to be made in the new edition. Let us suppose that
the author's annotated copy used for a revision had been preserved. Certainly, no editor would print his critical text from the actual revised edition which was set from this marked copy. Without question he would
feel obliged to choose the earlier (especially if it were the first edition)
and to substitute the author's corrections in the same way that errata lists
are incorporated. Thus, when Greg's theory is applied to revisions, it is
seen that the preservation of the accidentals of the first edition but the
insertion of authoritative substantive alterations from the revised text
does, in fact, reproduce as nearly as possible the critical text as it would
be made up from a preserved printer's copy for the revision.[11]

In this line of reasoning, however, there is a possible hitch, and it is
here, we may expect, that the strongest resistance will collect. For example, an editor may feel prepared to take the responsibility for deciding
between variant substantive readings but at the same time recognize what
seems to be the practical impossibility of assigning the variant accidentals
in the revised edition to author or compositor. He may then be strongly
inclined to argue that, although admittedly the general texture of a revised derived edition is one step further removed from that of the author's
manuscript, yet in accepting the later texture he is at least not discarding
whatever alterations in spelling, punctuation, and capitalization the author
may have made.[12]

This general position has recently been stated, although not with ideal
clarity, in Mr. A. Davenport's justification for basing his old-spelling text
of Joseph Hall's first six books of *Virgidemiarum* on the revised 1598
rather than on the original 1597 edition:

> The choice of copy-text was clearly between 1597 and 1598. From the facts
> stated above it is evident that the bulk of 1597 is one stage closer to Hall's
> manuscript than 1602 or the bulk of 1598. On the other hand, the authori-
> tative readings of 1598 must obviously be adopted, and whether the minor
> variants in 1598 are compositor's errors or genuine corrections it is usually

11 The respect given by nonbibliographical editors to the accidentals of a derived
edition, even though revised, seems to be based on the theory that the author in every
respect has approved of this revised edition, whereas, in fact, all he has done is to give
general approval to the copy from which the revision was set. Unless he reads the proof
himself, the author thereupon has no control over what will be produced from this
copy by the printing process. Moreover, at least in the sixteenth and seventeenth centuries, it is unrealistic to believe that a proofreading author ever set himself to restore
the texture of the original by altering the usual accidentals of the second compositor
unless they were in positive error.

12 One might idly speculate on the unconscious influence on textual criticism of
Anglo-American jurisprudence with its initial presumption of innocence. Bibliographers are more inclined to apply to a revised text the theory of certain Continental codes,
according to which the accused is required to demonstrate his own innocence.

impossible to decide. The choice therefore was between printing 1597 and correcting from 1598, or printing 1598 although its authority where it differs from 1597 on minor details, is doubtful. It has seemed wiser to take 1598 as the copy-text, and make no alterations in it without due warning, rather than to produce an amalgam of two editions. But since the authority, on minor details, of 1597 is at least as high as that of 1598 it has seemed necessary to record in the textual notes all variants, however trivial, which could suggest the slightest difference of sense, emphasis or intonation.[13]

This is an example of what Greg calls "the tyranny of the copy-text" as it influences abnegation of editorial responsibility. The plausibility of its general position will not, I think, bear strict examination.[14] Although his wording is not very specific, Davenport seems to be referring to various minor substantive variants in which a choice appears to be indifferent, as well as to certain classes of accidentals (even including capitalization) which might govern emphasis or intonation. In both of these the specific and limited authority which applies to the recognizable substantive revisions (which were not especially extensive) is allowed to affect the question of the general authority of the texture of the two editions. This is, I think, an anomaly; for Greg's arguments in favor of the separation of the two matters are especially convincing and are buttressed by McKerrow's equally thoughtful consideration. As for the indifferent substantives, it is one of Greg's three criteria for determining the authority of variants that when a choice seems indifferent, the odds are in favor of the specific authority of the original reading. If this is indeed correct, then a text constructed on Davenport's criteria will probably contain more corruptions than authentic revisions among these indifferent readings,[15] and, in addition, the general texture will be almost completely unauthoritative.[16]

13 *The Collected Poems of Joseph Hall*, ed. A. Davenport (1949), pp. lxiv–lxv.

14 Nn. 10, 11, and 12 above, as also various remarks in the text, have already touched on certain weaknesses of this theory of copy-text.

15 Greg takes exception to the implicit but fallacious assumption in much textual discussion that some mechanical principle can be evolved which will construct an absolutely perfect and correct text. He very pertinently remarks that the procedure which he advocates will not lead to consistently correct results; but in the hands of a competent editor the results, if less uniform, will, on the whole, be preferable to those achieved through following any mechanical rule. We must, I think, consider which method is likely to retain more authoritative readings than it rejects and also whether, in retaining the maximum possible number, such unauthoritative alteration is elsewhere permitted to enter as to make the over-all text less pure.

16 It is interesting to observe that, in the nine brief satires comprising the first book of *Virgidemiarum*, the editor is forced to return to 1597 a round dozen times to correct, chiefly in the accidentals, the forms in 1598. Yet, on the evidence provided in the collation, if 1597 had been chosen as the copy-text, at the maximum only six alterations (four substantives and two accidentals) would have been drawn by an editor from 1598, and

It is desirable, however, to narrow the case more closely by setting aside the difficulties in the choice between substantive variants in order to concentrate on the question of the accidentals. Editorial judgment, at least in theory, can select from substantives according to some less rough-and-ready principle than the presumed overriding general authority of a revised text, an authority which will frequently not hold up when specifically applied. On the other hand, implicit in most opposition to the Mc-Kerrow-Greg procedure is a sense of helplessness about the possibility of utilizing critical principles to determine an author's revisions of the accidentals. That there is, indeed, greater difficulty in this connection, and sometimes an insuperable one, is not of sufficient importance to justify the adoption of a general system still further removed than the original from whatever characteristics of the author's manuscript have been preserved.[17] Under almost any conditions the successive modernizations, misinterpretations, and rationalizations derived from new typesettings introduce in an early text a score of unauthoritative variants for each legitimate one which might have been introduced by an author. An editor, therefore, is only playing the correct odds when, as a general proposition, he retains the texture of the original edition. Otherwise, in order to preserve a single accidentals variant which *may* have been the author's, he is introducing a very considerable number of other alterations which under no circumstances could possibly have been authorial. This is throwing out the baby with the bath with a vengeance, to destroy, say, nineteen accidentals which *may* be the author's in order to preserve some one unspecified accidental which *may* be a revision.[18]

Investigation of a most arduous and lengthy nature may be applied in

---

of these only three would be positively required. One may well inquire whether more of an amalgamation has not resulted than would have occurred had the text been edited according to Greg's criteria.

17 There is no space here to discuss with proper thoroughness the real interest residing in the accidentals of a critical old-spelling edition. All bibliographical experience indicates that, in general, a compositor imposes a great deal of his own system on a manuscript text but is, to some extent, influenced by his copy. Thus, although no printed early text can be taken as an over-all faithful representation, it is at best of some authority and at worst it is one which is characteristic of the time in which the work is written and therefore usually consonant with the author's style. A later setting, although following printed copy more closely than for manuscript, imposes still further compositorial alteration, most of which cannot stem from authorial markings and, as McKerrow has pointed out, is in effect always a modernization. If one moves away from basic authority, the true purpose of old-spelling editions is vitiated and only "quaintness" remains. For example, one might as well modernize the text as to accept the accidentals of the 1701 Folio or of any of the 1696 quartos of Dryden's *Indian Emperour*, first printed in 1667.

18 After working carefully through his detailed collations, I feel that this is about the proportion which one finds in Davenport's edition of Hall, referred to above.

specific cases to assist in the decision,[19] but in the usual text the matter is not, perhaps, of sufficient importance to warrant the considerable effort involved. In such circumstances, Greg's procedure will undoubtedly yield a superior text both for accidentals and for substantives than can be assured by other less scientific methods.

As a matter of fact, to what extent an early author revising an edition would concern himself with altering accidentals which were not distinctly in error has been insufficiently investigated, in part because of the paucity of materials. The usual examples, such as what we know of Ben Jonson's proof corrections in his Folio, are too specialized for wider application.[20] The care which the average author might devote to improving the accidentals is perhaps not a matter for generalization, since authors could well vary widely in their practice. However, general bibliographical experience founded on a close comparison of texts seems to foster the belief that usually, so long as accidentals were not positively wrong or misleading, the author concentrated on substantive revision and was content, as a general rule, to accept the accidentals which normal printing practice had imposed on his work.[21]

The lack of very much material to test authorial practice in a revised edition, at least in the sixteenth and seventeenth centuries, leads me to present as a kind of case history a brief example in 1668 from John Dryden. The play is *The Indian Emperour*, first published in 1667, with a revised second edition in 1668 and a revised third edition in 1670.[22] My chief concern is with a part of the second edition; but, before we come to this, there is one matter in the first edition worth notice. Collation of six

19 If the text is a most important one, very scrupulous bibliographical investigation may perhaps go a considerable distance toward a separation of compositor's and author's accidentals in a revised edition. A minute study of the characteristics of the compositor or compositors of the revised text, once they have been isolated by bibliographical tests, can be made against the control of other books from the same printing-house and typeset by the same identifiable workmen. Up to the latter part of the seventeenth century the characteristics of different compositors can, in fact, be identified with some accuracy, and when their habitual variants are removed from consideration in the text under examination, a more scientific examination may be made of the residue in an attempt to determine possible authorial revisions.

20 Even after the scrupulous attention which Jonson gave to the proofs of his Folio, Greg is still able to remark a number of cases where an editor, choosing the Folio, must return to the quarto copy to preserve special Jonsonian characteristics modified by the Folio compositors and inconsistently passed over by Jonson in the proofreading.

21 Observation of manuscripts seems to indicate that the punctuation, for example, was often very sketchy indeed, and not of the kind that an author would wish to appear in print as the result of a faithful following of copy. In earlier times, as in the present, most authors seem to count on the printer to correct and fill out their unsystematic practice.

22 J. S. Steck, "Dryden's *Indian Emperour*: The Early Editions and their Relation to the Text," *Studies in Bibliography*, II (1949), 139–45.

of the seven recorded American copies of the 1667 edition discloses six press-variant formes in the nine sheets comprising the text. In four of these formes the correction is far from extensive: four variants appear in one, two in another, and only a single one in the other two. The alterations are almost equally divided between substantives and accidentals, but they are corrections, not revisions, and do not seem to be beyond the capacity of an intelligent proofreader giving a final examination to formes already proofed from sheets pulled on a proofing press. Each of these variant formes is in a different sheet, outer B, D, H, and inner E.[23] Sheet I, however, is abnormally variant in both formes. In the outer forme ten alterations were made, only one of them substantive. Two egregious misprints in the original state lead me to believe that this forme had received no proofreading before being placed on the press and that the unusual number of corrections indicates this fact. The majority are concerned with re-punctuating eight lines on sig. I3r (which seem to have been added to the manuscript at a late date), and the one substantive alteration may actually be unauthoritative if, as seems probable, this is printing-house proofreading.

The case is different, however, when we come to inner forme I, for here almost certainly Dryden himself (and I think for the first and only time in this edition) made the revisions. In the stage direction on sig. I4r, for example, the unusual word 'Zoty' is substituted for 'Balcone,' that is, *balcony*. A marked characteristic of the revised second edition is Dryden's care in substituting 'which' or 'who' for 'that' used as a relative pronoun. On sig. I3^v such a revision is made in 1667 to alter the original lines

> He saw not with my Eyes that could refuse:
> He that could prove so much unkind to thee,

to

> He saw not with my Eyes who could refuse:
> Him that could prove so much unkind to thee. . . .[24]

Finally, a few lines down, a necessary 'and' is added to a stage direction. In these four pages Dryden made four substantive revisions but not a single alteration in any of the accidentals. In the second edition seven lines in these pages were further revised, chiefly by grammatical correction; but, in addition, we note two spelling, nine capitalization, and five punctuation alterations. If an editor, therefore, chose the 1668 edition as his copy-text, in these four pages he would be incorporating sixteen alter-

23 One of the corrected errors in outer H seems to have been caused by imperfectly raised types, and hence there is also a possibility that this forme, as may be conjectured for outer forme I, was not given a careful proofing before printing began.

24 In the 1668 revision the second line finally reads "Him who could. . . ."

ations of the accidentals of the first edition in the belief that they *may* have originated with Dryden, although, on the evidence of the proofreading, Dryden had seemed to express his satisfaction by failing to alter any when given the opportunity in 1667.

But the end is not yet. The third edition, in 1670, was also revised by Dryden from the 1668 copy, although, significantly, no substantive revisions occur after sig. H1^r, where he seems to have dropped the project. There is considerable doubt, then, that he ever went over this inner I forme to revise it for 1670. However, in the revised third edition for these four pages we have added to the sixteen 1668 variants three alterations in word division, eleven in capitalization, and one in punctuation, or a total of fifteen extra variants, none of which, in all probability, is authoritative. Interestingly enough, one of the capitalizations and the punctuation restore original forms in 1667 altered in 1668, though passed then by Dryden. As a consequence, if an editor of this play chose the 1670 edition as his copy-text on the theory that it was the last revised, he would reprint in these four pages a minimum of fifteen variants from the accidentals of 1668, none of which is likely to have been marked by Dryden; and if we take the more probable view that the 1668 variants are in the same class, this editor would reproduce a total of twenty-nine unauthoritative alterations in the readings of the 1667 first edition, which would be his proper copy-text if for various reasons he decided to reject the 1665 scribal transcript of the text in an early state. Under these conditions one might well query whether any rationale exists for an old-spelling text based on the revised editions.

With this background we may now come to an even more interesting, though perhaps less clear-cut, case. Collation of six copies of the 1668 edition reveals that only one forme was press-altered, and, significantly, this was inner forme B, or, as can be demonstrated, the first forme of the text through the press. Seven stop-press alterations were made in this forme, of which one is a substantive revision, three are substantive corrections, and three are concerned with punctuation. The revision shows that the proofreading was authoritative, for it alters relative 'that' to 'which,' a grammatical nicety already started in the author-corrected forme of inner I in 1667 and continued, in combination with other revisions, throughout the 1668 edition.

When we examine the uncorrected state of this forme in 1668, however, we find that it is not wholly a normal reprint of 1667. A speech-heading omitted in 1667 has been inserted, another corrected, and two substantive corrections performed. The first could have occurred to an alert proofreader, since it set right an obvious misprint, but the other would have been recognized only by the author, who in all probability was also responsible for the speech-heading changes. We find, then, this situation. Certain alterations have been made prior to the setting of the original state of the forme, but others, including a grammatical correction which is to be a characteristic of the edition as a whole, have been held over until printing was started. I conjecture that Dryden had sent an errata list covering the correction of various real errors he had observed in the 1667 text and had planned on reading proofs to make whatever other revision seemed necessary. However, it would appear that when he read the proof for the first two formes of sheet B he discovered that a more thorough revision for 'correctness' of diction and style was necessary than he had envisaged and that this—as the evidence of the rewriting in the whole play indicates—involved more alterations than could be conveniently made in proof. Since in the invariant outer forme of B in 1668 we find a number of substantive revisions, including the correction of a relative 'that', it seems a plausible conjecture that Dryden completed reading proof on Sheet B by revising the proof for the outer forme (not yet printed) and then marked up the 1667 copy for the rest of the play.

If this reconstruction of the events is roughly accurate, then we have another instance of a control for separating author's and compositor's variants in a revision. The control is perhaps less exact than for inner forme I of the 1667 edition, for the substantive corrections already present in the original state of inner B of 1668 demonstrate some sort of revision before printing. But if this revision, as seems to be indicated, was the result of an errata list for errors, we could reasonably expect that it was confined to substantives, as was inner I of 1667.

The three proof corrections in the accidentals affect the punctuation. In the first, the original state read

> Each downfal of a flood the Mountains pour,
> From their rich bowels, rolls a silver shower.

Dryden removed the comma after 'pour' in proof to secure a run-on line slightly affecting the sense.[25]

> Which gather'd all the breath the winds could blow.
> And at their roots grew floating Palaces,
> Whose out-blow'd[26] bellies cut the yielding Seas.

25 In 1667 no comma had appeared after 'bowels', but the 1668 comma may not derive from a Dryden marking; for, if he had inserted it in copy, he presumably would have removed the comma after 'pour' at the same time. On the other hand, the debated medial comma is present in the 1665 scribal transcript.

26 'out-blow'd is a misprint for 1667 'out-bow'd', the correct reading being restored in 1670. This is only one of several occasions when Dryden as proofreader or reviser overlooked serious errors on the same page with his corrections.

Dryden changed the period after 'blow' to a colon to secure continuity, although the sentence then was increased to six lines.

> Then judge my future service by my past.
> What I shall be by what I was, you know,
> That love took deepest root which first did grow.

The light comma after 'know' was altered to a colon, perhaps to indicate a stronger pause so that the demonstrative pronoun 'That' would not be mistaken for a relative.

Of these three examples, two seem to be concerned with clarifying the meaning to some slight extent. Since they accompany substantive revision, they are clearly authoritative and should ideally be present in any old-spelling edition. However, if collation had not revealed them and an editor had chosen 1668 as his copy-text for just this contingency, what of an apparently unauthoritative nature would also have been taken over in this forme? In the uncorrected state of inner B, and therefore presumably to be isolated as compositor's variants are two variant spellings, two variant word-divisions, three variant capitalizations, and three punctuation alterations. Since with a 1667 copy-text none of the three authoritative punctuational variants would have called for emendation unless their special status as proof-corrections had been determined by a careful collation of 1668 copies, the choice of the 1668 copy-text produces ten unauthoritative alterations to secure three authoritative.

But for this play the further revised 1670 third edition would need to be chosen if popular procedure is to be followed. In the four pages of the inner forme of B the revised 1670 text makes four substantive alterations, one a correction of a 1668 misreading and another a further revision of a line partly touched up in 1668. There is no way to demonstrate that, at the time he marked the copy of 1668 for these, Dryden did not also make various alterations in the accidentals, even though he had passed these once in 1668. Yet it is impossible to believe that all these variants in 1670 have an authoritative source; for, in addition to following the 1668 alterations, the 1670 edition makes three changes in word division, twenty-three in capitalization, and eight in punctuation, at least one of these last being a manifest error. The 1670 edition as copy-text, therefore, would depart from 1667 in a total of forty-four accidentals, of which only three can be demonstrated as authoritative. Similar rough studies which I have made of the corrections in standing type versus variants in reset pages in Dekker's *Magnificent Entertainment* and *Honest Whore,* in the first few years of the seventeenth century, produce the same conclusions.

These two specific cases in which evidence is available to act as a control for judging the relative contributions of revising author and resetting compositor serve, in my opinion, to discredit the rationale behind the choice of the latest revised edition as copy-text on the grounds that thus one secures every possible authorial correction or revision in the accidentals. It seems clear that by this procedure in old texts one departs from the author more frequently than one follows him. When only printed texts are available, the odds for retaining the closest possible approximation to the author's own accidentals are predominantly in favor of the first edition set from an authoritative manuscript. If an editor chooses this as his basis, as Greg advises under most conditions, and thereupon incorporates in the texture those substantive revisions which in his judgment are authoritative, together with such conservative alteration of accidentals as seems necessary to avoid misreadings or more than momentary ambiguity, he may miss some few refinements; but he will in the long run produce a text which, more accurately than by any other method, comes as close as possible to the author's original and revised intentions.

Old-Spelling Editions of Dramatic Texts

THE RATIONALE of a critical old-spelling edition of an Elizabethan play—or of any text for that matter—is not to be summed up under any single heading. But if we isolate the one unique reason for its existence, surely we must say: The critical old-spelling edition seeks to establish the text and thereby to become a definitive edition.

Let us break this statement down to its various parts.

A critical edition. This has three senses. An edition may be called critical if it is a critic's edition, that is, if it is designed to satisfy the standards for accuracy and completeness that a critic should require of any text on which he proposes to base his investigations. In the second sense, an edition is critical if its text has been edited on critical principles. I take it that the proper application of the critical editorial process is to produce a text that recovers the author's final intentions more faithfully than any preserved transmitted document. Third, in a subordinate sense, the edition (as distinct from the text) may be called critical if it endeavors in its introduction, apparatus, and commentary to provide a critic with all necessary information about the text and the circumstances of its composition and transmission.

The critic addressed is not necessarily of the 'total values' school, one whose insensitivity to the details of a text often makes him impatient with the standards and methods of textual criticism.[1] Rather, the edition is designed for the whole republic of serious readers, ranging from the student anxious to evaluate the literary merit of the play, through every shade of endeavor from the investigator of dramatic technique to the metrist, and even including the philologist concerned with Elizabethan idiom and

Read before the English Drama Section of the Modern Language Association of America, at the University of Wisconsin, September 10, 1957; reprinted by permission from *Studies in Honor of T. W. Baldwin*, edited by D. C. Allen (Urbana: University of Illinois Press, 1958), pp. 9–15; reprinted with permission of the University of Illinois Press.

1 As the critic I once heard argue in a public discussion that it made no difference whether in *Hamlet* Shakespeare wrote *sallied* or *solid flesh*, since the "total values" of the play were not in the least affected by the choice of reading.

orthographic habits. In short, anyone dealing with the work as a literary, ideological, or linguistic document, and therefore anyone who is concerned to read the text in its most carefully established form.

An established text. Much confusion inheres to this phrase. There are two levels at which a text becomes established. At the first level the editor seeks the document containing the text in its most authoritative preserved form; that is, by collation of readings, aided by any other internal or external evidence, he establishes from among the various documents in which the text may be preserved that one that has the most immediate transcriptional link to the author's holograph manuscript. This is a substantive text. If all later texts derive from this without reference to fresh authority, the editor has established the sole authoritative documentary form of the text. Except for whatever evidence is available within this document, no other known authority for the text can exist.

Of course, the case is not always so simple. More than one text may claim authority. A second document may have been inscribed from an independent manuscript, or the text may be partly derived from the initial substantive authority but altered by consultation of some other authoritative document now lost. It is clear in these complex cases occurring within the Elizabethan drama that, in plays where multiple substantive authority exists, even though one text may be much inferior to that in the main substantive document, no one document can be established as representing in every detail the text in its most authoritative known form.

However, we cannot deny that it is usually possible to discover which one or more documents contain the text in any state of authority. The question then arises—if we take the simplest case, in which only a single authoritative document exists, and we can demonstrate that fact, why have we not established the text if we reprint it exactly as found in that document? The first objection, though more than a quibble, is not so peremptory as to dispose of the question. It is legitimate to ask, however, which form of the text and in what concrete example of the document? Are we to accept *any* example without regard for its mixture of uncorrected and corrected states of the type? Shall we accept the uncorrected states exclusively, or the corrected states exclusively even in cases in which the editor admits that the proofreader sophisticated the text? [2] Some

2 See the Malone Society Reprint of Chettle's *Hoffman.* I don't know what a conservative reprint editor would do if most of the press-corrected formes were unauthoritative, but one or more exhibited authoritative alteration. I think it demonstrable, for instance, that Dekker himself corrected one forme of *The Magnificent Entertainment.* Grounds exist for believing that the second stage of the proof correction of one forme of Dekker's *Match Me in London* was ordered by the proofreader referring back to copy so that the alterations are authoritative; and I believe that Dekker himself corrected proof for the first stage of press-alteration of another forme in this play, but not the second stage of the same forme. For various problems connected with the reprinting of

editorial discretion is inevitable; and even here it is obvious that we must move away from the strict reprint concept.

More important, however, is the objection that the establishment of the most authoritative documentary form (ordinarily the first edition) does not in any sense provide the critic with a text that is, in Greg's words, "so far as the available evidence permits, in the form in which we may suppose that it would have stood in a fair copy made by the author himself, of the work as he finally intended it."[3] Until the errors of the printing process, at the very least, are weeded out, it is certainly anomalous to speak of establishing a text. Thus we must distinguish between establishing the documentary form, and establishing the text itself. A photographic or type facsimile, or a diplomatic reprint, of the document remains, therefore, a specialist's tool that presents the text only in its raw and inevitably corrupt state. To invite the literary critic to make his own decisions about the nature and extent of these errors as he reads for quite other purposes is not to furnish him with anything that can be called a critic's edition. And in complex cases, when multiple authority is present, the reprint theory would require a literary critic to face a parallel text of three editions of *Hamlet* from which it would be his privilege to select what he fancied were Shakespeare's intentions.

To establish the text the editor must himself treat it critically. That is, he must attempt to recover what the author actually wrote—in his final intentions—as closely as bibliographical techniques, linguistic analysis, and critical intelligence can guide him. In complex cases he must separate the authority of the substantives (the author's final words) from the authority of the accidentals (the texture of spelling, punctuation, capitalization) that clothe these substantives;[4] and by any necessary ecletic selection contrive that form of the text that in all its details most closely corresponds to what would have been the authorial intentions in print;[5] in other words, present the words of an author in their most authoritative recoverable form. Only an edition made up by the most advanced methods of textual criticism is properly a critical edition, of sufficient trustworthiness for general critical use.

Old Spelling. Such an edition must be in old spelling. If the words of an author are to be presented in their most authoritative recovered form, the

---

the most authoritative readings in a press-variant text, see my "The Problem of the Variant Forme in a Facsimile Edition," *The Library*, 5th Series, VII (1952), 262–72.

3 W. W. Greg, *The Editorial Problem in Shakespeare*, 2nd ed. (Oxford, 1951), p. x.

4 See W. W. Greg, "The Rationale of Copy-Text," *Studies in Bibliography*, III (1950), 19–36.

5 See "Current Theories of Copy-Text, with an Illustration from Dryden," *MP*, XLVIII (1950), 12–20.

form cannot be distinguished from the word. Since the Elizabethan forms of words are an essential part of Elizabethan English, any interference with these forms places the critical reader at an arbitrary remove from the author's characteristics so far as these may be determined, and certainly from the linguistic characteristics of the period. It matters nothing that at the present stage of our knowledge we cannot often be sure what are authorial and what compositorial characteristics in the orthography of dramatic texts. Generalizations are difficult because different compositors certainly treated their copy in very different ways. Yet this is beside the point. As Greg remarks: "For the critic modernization has no attraction in itself. So long as there is any chance of an edition preserving some trace, however faint, of the author's individuality, the critic will wish to follow it: and even when there is none, he will still prefer an orthography that has a period resemblance with the author's to one that reflects the linguistic habits of a later date."[6]

No system of modernization can be contrived that does not do violence to the Elizabethan English of a play.[7] The only consistent form of modernization is the complete and absolute normalizing of all Elizabethan variant forms that do not reflect different meanings. This sounds easier than it is. On the other hand, the school of partial modernizers, as represented by the New Arden and the New Yale editors, save something, but not enough to make their efforts worthwhile. And in the process of attempting to distinguish words in which variant spelling reflects authentic forms (Arden) or different pronunciations (Yale), the editors involve themselves in such logical (and linguistic) contradictions as in fact to do more damage by their commissions than the total modernizers by their omissions. For there is no partially modernizing edition extant that does not retain as significant variation what is actually a mishmash of compositorial misprints, orthographical variants demonstrably *not* reflecting pronunciation differences in the text in question and demonstrable compositorial usages mixed with inferential authorial characteristics, while all the time concealing by modernization about as much true evidence as has been inconsistently emphasized (along with the false) by special treatment.[8] In such a matter it is better to be ignorant than to be misled.

6 Greg, *Editorial Problem*, pp. li–lii.

7 *Ibid.*, p. li: "To print *banquet* for *banket*, *fathom* for *fadom*, *lantern* for *lanthorn*, *murder* for *murther*, *mushroom* for *mushrump*, *orphan* for *orphant*, *perfect* for *parfit*, *portcullis* for *perculace*, *tattered* for *tottered*, *vile* for *vild*, *wreck* for *wrack*, and so on, and so on, is sheer perversion."

8 See Alice Walker, "Compositor Determination and Other Problems in Shakesperian Texts," *Studies in Bibliography*, VII (1955), 4: "Among textual critics, though wiser heads have never supposed that the spelling of printed books was the author's (the Old Cambridge editors, for instance, rejected the idea of an old spelling Shakespeare on this account), there is even yet a great deal of muddled thinking. Spellings of one

By its nature, no modernized text of an Elizabethan play can be trustworthy enough to satisfy the requirements of a serious critic.

A definitive edition is only a comparative term, since we must always believe that from time to time the accumulation of scholarship will enable an editor to improve on the work of his predecessors. But in its own day an edition may be called definitive if—on the positive side—by stretching the limits of contemporary scholarship it has recovered what appears to be the most authoritative form of the dramatist's text. This recovery must always extend beyond the form of the text in any single authoritative document, and only in this extended sense may the text be called truly established and therefore definitive. Thus no facsimile or conservative reprint of an authoritative document can qualify as a definitive edition, except as an edition of that document. Since the printed document represents a transmitted form of the author's holograph, the critical editor's attempt to go in back of the document to recover as much as he can of the purity of its source must always transcend the value of the conservative editor's labors.

On the negative side, a definitive critical edition—though admitting editorial correction, emendation, and even the conflation of authorities—should not unnecessarily interpose the editor between the original and the reader. Unnecessary interposition may be regarded as (1) any interference with the author's final intentions so far as these may be ascertained; (2) any interference with the transmitting agent's intentions when these do

---

writer are compared with those of another on the evidence of printed texts of different dates from different printing houses [f.n.1: H. T. Price, for instance, in *English Institute Essays 1947* (1948), 143–58] and the vagaries of compositors are erratically introduced into modernised texts of Shakespeare [f.n.2: I have remarked on this in a recent review of the New Arden *Titus Andronicus*. It is the general policy of the new series 'to preserve all older forms that are more than variant spellings'—a policy which has not, I suspect, been seen in relation to its logical linguistic conclusions. When Muir, for instance, in the New Arden *Lear*, followed the Folio's 'murther', what was he reproducing—the compositor's spelling or a scribal alteration of the Q1 spelling on the authority of the *Lear* prompt-book? If it was the prompt-book spelling, was it Shakespeare's? Further, if consonant variants, like 'murther' and 'vild', are preserved, why not the vowel variants in 'show' and 'shew', 'blood' and 'bloud'? Why not the common 'alablastar' or 'abhominable' and (contrariwise), in early texts, 'clime' for 'climb' or 'limmes' for 'limbs'? Muir went so far as to reproduce Compositor B's arbitrary distinctions between — 'd and — ed of weak preterites and past participles in prose. But what will happen in the New Arden *As You Like It* where there are two compositors favouring different conventions? Modern English is one thing; the habits of the compositors of Shakesperian texts are quite another, and the arbitrary preservation of a selection of the latter has no linguistic principles behind it.]" See also Greg's review of the New Arden *Titus Andronicus* in *MLR*, XLIX (1954), 362, and Arthur Brown's comments in "Editorial Problems in Shakespeare: Semi-Popular Editions," *Studies in Bibliography*, VIII (1956), 19.

not appear to differ significantly from what we may suppose to represent the author's intentions; and (3) any interference with the general linguistic habits of the period contemporary with the documentary form of the copy-text when these do not appear to differ from (1) or (2) above.

Under these conditions, the modernized text (though sometimes qualifying as critically edited) must be rejected as nondefinitive, since it unquestionably interferes (no matter what its form) with the linguistic and orthographic habits of author, of compositor, and of the period.

The critical old-spelling edition seeks to establish the text and thereby to become a definitive edition. This is its rationale.

It would appear, therefore, that a need exists for a class of text aimed at an audience somewhere in between the bibliographer and the school child, or the drugstore trade. I suggest that this need may be filled by properly constructed critical old-spelling editions. At the upper level these editions should be qualified to serve as a trustworthy basis for advanced critical inquiry; at the lower level they should not be beyond the ability of a literate undergraduate to handle.

Let us not be too solemn about this critical old-spelling edition. It should be a reading text first, and a reference text only secondarily. And the editor should make every effort to appeal to the maximum group of users so long as this catholicity is not achieved at the expense of critically dangerous modifications. Briefly, these old-spelling editions can and should be made more attractive to the general user, first by removing all but the most immediately pertinent of the apparatus to appendices in the rear, thus freeing the text page from all information that is only of reference value and so of no immediate concern to the reader.[9]

Second, at the risk of offending some conservatives, I strongly advocate that an old-spelling editor should modernize the *u:v* and *i:j* conventions, just as he now customarily normalizes the old long *s* in the interests of the present-day reader. The period of the Elizabethan drama is not itself consistent in this usage;[10] and we shall do ourselves a good turn by removing what is probably the most serious bar to the use of old-spelling texts by general readers.

It is a shameful thing that we are bringing up a generation of undergraduates who are scarcely conscious that the language of the past differed in its forms from that of the present, that Shakespeare did not write in logically punctuated Johnsonian periods, and that the speech of characters in Elizabethan plays was not almost entirely a series of exclamations start-

9 See the treatment of the apparatus advocated in the prefatory remarks to *Dramatic Works of Thomas Dekker*, Vol. I (Cambridge, Eng., 1953).

10 For two excellent examples, both from the year 1604, see the practices of the different compositors within each first edition of Dekker's *Magnificent Entertainment* and *The Honest Whore*, Part I.

ing with "Good Morrow!" Yet it is our fault, and not the undergraduates'. If we deliberately alienate them by associating an old-spelling text with specialized scholarship over their heads, instead of offering it as the normal means of reading the literature of an earlier period—and a means that can be materially eased by a few typographical reforms—we alone, and our pedantry, are to blame. The methods by which we can contrive that textual good money should drive out the bad are so obvious and so sane as to reflect seriously on our competence as teachers and as scholars if we reject this offered good and do not shape the editing of texts to our purposes instead of to the purposes of the publishers of textbooks and the laziness or timidity, but often only the inexperience, of our academic textbook editors.

Textual Criticism and

the Literary Critic

THE RELATION of bibliographical and textual investigation to literary criticism is a thorny subject, not from the point of view of bibliography but from the point of view of literary criticism. In contrast to the general uniformity among textual critics about ends and means, literary critics—as we might expect—hold diverse opinions about the operation of their discipline. At one extreme are those higher critics whose chief concern is for the 'total' or 'essential' values of literature, and whose contemplation of an author's work is correspondingly lofty. At the other extreme are critics whose analysis of a work is so detailed that scarcely a word of the text, no matter how ordinary, can escape a searching interpretive inquiry.

In so far as the application of large philosophical and aesthetic concepts to broad problems may dull a critic's awareness of the significance of small details, it is easy for a bibliographer to understand that not all critics may be expected to share his concern for the exactness of representation given to the physical form of the work to be handled. On the other hand, what sometimes seems to be a critic's almost perverse disregard for specific accuracy may offer the bibliographer a nasty shock. Several years ago, in a paper before the English Institute held annually at the invitation of Columbia University, I hoped to stir up some questions and discussion by remarking *inter alia* that I felt I could prove on physical evidence not subject to opinion that in *Hamlet* Shakespeare wrote 'sallied flesh', and not 'solid flesh'.[1] I confess I was taken aback when the first commentator rose to give it as his opinion that really there ought to be some law to keep bibliographers—who otherwise seemed normal intelligent persons capable of better things—from wasting their lives poking around in such minutiae. Whether Shakespeare wrote 'sallied' (that is, 'sullied') flesh, or 'solid' flesh, was of no importance at all. He personally had read 'solid' all his

Delivered on January 20, 1958, as the first of the Sandars Lectures in Bibliography entitled "Textual and Literary Criticism," at Cambridge University. Reprinted from *Textual and Literary Criticism* (Cambridge University Press, 1959), pp. 1–34, 151–167; reprinted by permission of the Syndics, Cambridge University Press.

1 This argument later appeared as 'Hamlet's "Sullied" or "Solid" Flesh: A Bibliographical Case-History', *Shakespeare Survey*, IX (1956), 44–48.

life, found it quite satisfactory, and saw no reason for changing. Whether it was technically right or wrong did not affect the argument that the Folio phrase had got itself generally accepted. People were used to it. Moreover, the 'essential values' of *Hamlet* the play were not at all affected by retaining the conventional reading here.

Whether this is quite that passion for truth one looks for in a professing critic, I leave aside. I am not really concerned to satirise the 'total values' school and its frequent insensitivity to the actual values of the material on which it chooses to operate; or to invoke laughter at the inadvertencies of the anti-historical 'new critics'. As always, when one is working with a difference in degree, not in kind, the point at which one feels a need to defend the bridge is shifting and uncertain. How many conventional readings in the text of *Hamlet*—one, two, five, ten, twenty, fifty, a hundred, two hundred?—must be proved unsound before the 'total values' of the play *are* affected and the literary critic should begin to grow uneasy about the evidence on which he is formulating his hypothesis for the whole? Because the traditional Old Cambridge text of Shakespeare's *Richard III* was based on the bad first quarto instead of the revised good Folio print, current editions can advertise that they contain more than a thousand variants from the conventional text. How many values are affected here?

However, the real danger comes when such a critic—who seems to believe that texts are discovered under cabbage plants (or in bulrushes) —when such a critic tackles a subject in which some knowledge of textual processes is required. For example, in what I understand is—in my country at least—an admired essay on *Lycidas*, John Crowe Ransom argued that Milton, for artistic purposes, deliberately roughed up an originally smooth version of the poem. Characteristically, Ransom made no attempt to examine the transmission of the text from manuscript to print in order to see if there were any physical evidence for his theory. If he had, not only would he have found no support, of course, but evidence to the contrary.[2] How far can we trust the ideas and methods of critics who think so little of analysing the nature of the texts with which they work?

Even scholarly investigators on a less rarefied plane encounter trouble when they ignore textual facts. The identification of Shakespeare's symbolic imagery in play after play has become a popular indoor sport at learned meetings; the study was largely begun by Caroline Spurgeon though she may not be held accountable for the excesses of her imitators. Does it make any difference that some of the images she uses as evidence

2 'A Poem Nearly Anonymous', first printed in the *American Review* in 1933, and reprinted in *The World's Body* (1938). See Martin C. Battestin, 'John Crowe Ransom and *Lycidas*: A Reappraisal', *College English*, XVII (1956), 223–8, for a critical analysis of Ransom's position.

for her thesis are editorial emendations and not necessarily Shakespeare's
words—and that she did not attempt to assess the purity of the evidence
she was collecting by using an edition that would show her what was
editorial and what not?[3] Does it make any difference that the linguist
Kökeritz has sometimes used derived instead of primary texts and thus
muddied the waters of his evidence;[4] or that when he utilised primary

[3] Kathleen Tillotson, reviewing Professor Spurgeon's *Shakespeare's Imagery and
What It Tells Us*, wrote: 'Before appraising the results one should consider the ways
in which the methods can be no more than approximate; for the margin of error, or
variation, may be wide enough to lessen the scientific value which seems, at times, to be
claimed for the results, though it need not lessen their value as accumulated impressions. The ultimate source of all data is the text. But what text? Professor Spurgeon has
used Gollancz's *Larger Temple Shakespeare*, which generally gives the text of the Cambridge edition. It is a conservative text, but it has, for instance, about sixty emendations in *Antony and Cleopatra*, and many of these affect the images. In *"lackeying* the
varying tide," and *"an autumn* 'twas That grew the more by reaping," the effective
image-words are Theobald's; they may have been Shakespeare's words, but we cannot
know, and so long as any case can be made for the Folio readings "lacking" and "An-
thony," conclusions about "motiveless subservience" and "the perennial seasons" must
be accepted cautiously. Again, in I *Henry IV* "the plumed estridges that *wing* the
wind" are Rowe's, and the context would imply that Shakespeare's "interest in the
flight of birds" is not here in question. It would have been safer, perhaps, to follow the
original texts or to omit or qualify images based on doubtful readings' (*Review of
English Studies*, XII (1936), 458–459.
[4] Helge Kökeritz, *Shakespeare's Pronunciation* (1953). It is distressing to find in
this book so little care for textual accuracy that all quotations are taken from the Folio
without regard for the different forms of the primary Quarto texts in cases when the
Folio is derived and unauthoritative. We have, thus, the anomaly that when forms are
quoted from the good Quartos (the only true authoritative texts for most of the plays
printed before the Folio), the special notation (Q) is affixed. Irregularities result from
this practice, of course. For instance, if we are concerned with the forms that appear in
the print nearest the manuscript and therefore *may* be Shakespearean, we may object to
the listing under *syncopation* (p. 376) of *mockry M.N.D.* 2. 1. III from F instead of
Q *mockery*. Here F has no authority, and the fact that the F compositor elided the *e* is
not quite the point that Kökeritz had in mind when on p. 28 he remarked on the
omission of a syncopated vowel: 'The poet himself rather than the typesetter is to
blame for this carelessness. . . .' Obviously a linguist who makes statements like this
when innocent of information provided by compositor analysis is likely to be wrong
about the agencies that produce the forms he is treating. For another instance, see the
listing (p. 379) of *bach'ler M.N.D.* 2. 2. 59 from F instead of Q *batcheler*.
    Doubtless there is as much significance in these variant forms as there is to his
careful distinction (p. 376) between the spellings *watrie M.N.D.* 3. 1. 203 and *watry*
1. 1. 210, 2. 1. 162, when in fact all three are *watry* in authoritative Q and the *watrie*
form is merely an unauthoritative F variant. Quotation of derived texts from the Folio
thus results in constant distortion of spelling, elision, and so on; and the harm is not
confined merely to forms in the quoted text that are not immediately under scrutiny.
Moreover, the habit of quoting from F leads to the reproduction of various unauthoritative F substantive errors for Q's substantive purity, as when (p. 116) he follows corrupt F *or* in *R.J.* 2. 4. 102 for correct Q2 *for*; or (p. 146) F's corrupt *to* in *R.J.* 1. 4. 20

texts for an analysis of Shakespeare's linguistic forms he totally ignored the whole body of bibliographical evidence dealing with facts about variance in different compositors' spelling habits, and, in spite of marked differences in date of printing and in printing-houses, persisted in treating each print of a play, ignoring its origin, as if it were a literally exact tran-

----

for correct Q2 *so*; or (p. 147) F's *the* in *R.J.* 3. 2. 126 for Q2 *that*; or (p. 155) corrupt F *into* *M.N.D.* 2. 1. 191 for Q1 *vnto*.

The corrupt texts from which he often draws his quotations may affect the weight of the evidence supporting a linguistic argument. A typical case comes on p. 85 where Kökeritz is suggesting a pun on *woe-woo* and quotes F 'These times of *wo*, affoord no times to *wooe*' from *R.J.* 3. 4. 8. Then after remarking that "The Q2 spellings are *woe* and *woo* respectively', he adds, 'This line should be compared with 3. 5. 120 where Juliet says:

> "Ere he that should be Husband comes to *woe*,"

whose last word is spelled *wooe* in Q2.' But it must be obvious, surely, that the spellings in the derived F text of *Romeo and Juliet* cannot be utilised to show Shakespeare's intentions, which can only be determined by analysing the primary evidence of Q2 which was set from a manuscript commonly thought to be autograph. Hence the fact that F at 3. 5. 120 spells *woo* as *woe* is no evidence at all for a Shakesperean homonymic pun at 3. 4. 8 when at 3. 5. 120 Q2's spelling is *wooe*. Another instance comes on p. 83 when the pun Kökeritz is examining in *R.J.* 2. 4. 66–70 is materially aided by the sophisticated F text that he utilises, 'when the single sole of it is worne, the jeast may remaine after the wearing, sole-singular', although the correct (but unmentioned) Shakespearean reading as found in Q2 is 'soly singular'. On p. 155, in relation to a pun in *M.N.D.* 2. 1. 192, the substantive Q1 reading (never mentioned) 'wodde, within this wood' is certainly more significant linguistically than the quoted unauthoritative F '*wood* within this *wood*' which has been sophisticated by a compositor.

Kökeritz's use of bad-quarto (memorially transmitted and corrupt) texts for the ostensible purpose of making points about Shakespeare's own practice is, of course, quite illogical, as when (p. 104) he resorts to Q1 *Hamlet* 4. 3. 20 f., 'At supper, not where he is *eating*, but where he is *eaten*.' He then indicates that he believes Q1 to be a primary text, from which Q2 and F derive (and not a corrupt memorial report of the basic Q2-F text) when he adds, 'Perhaps the ambiguity of the pronunciation [ẹ:tn] was the reason for changing *eating* into *eat(e)s* in Q2 and F'. If in 1953 linguists operate on the theory, discredited since the publication in 1941 of G. I. Duthie's *'Bad' Quarto of Hamlet*, that Q2 and F represent later texts than Q1, so that Shakespeare could have changed Q1 *is eating* to Q2-F *eats*, they are creating a merry world indeed. Similarly, the propriety of including under the heading 'An Index of Shakespeare's Rhymes' various jingles found only in the bad quartos is very doubtful. Care for the transmission of a text cannot be of no concern to linguistic inquiry.

IF *Hamlet* 4. 3. 20 above had been in an area in which Q1 can be demonstrated to have contaminated Q2, and IF Q2 is in fact physically in some manner the basic copytext for F, then it could be argued that Q1 represents the true Shakespearean reading, corrupted in the printing of Q2 and thence passed on in error to F. But in Act IV there seems to be no such contamination as is found in Act I. This first-act contamination (not known to Kökeritz) affects the argument on p. 193 (see also p. 305), 'But the spellings *bettles* Q2 and *beckles* (Q) for *beetles* *Hamlet* 1. 4. 71 can hardly mean anything else than the short vowel [ẹ]'. Actually, this series means anything but the short

script of a Shakespearean autograph?[5] Yet this false line of reasoning is basic to his arguments from statistical evidence that such and such forms are Shakespearean spellings. Does it make any difference that even the great *Oxford English Dictionary* has occasionally failed to reproduce an Elizabethan form of a word when it has been ironed out by emendation or modernisation?[6]

We should be seriously disturbed by the lack of contact between literary critics and textual critics. Every practising critic, for the humility of his soul, ought to study the transmission of some appropriate text. If he did, he would raise such an outcry that we should no longer be reading most of the great English and American classics in texts that are inexcusably corrupt. We should no longer complacently accept the sleazy editing that

---

vowel. In Q1 *beckles*, on the evidence, is an actor's faulty recollection (provided it is not a compositorial error), and there is every reason to suppose with Dover Wilson and Alice Walker that Q2 *bettles* owes its odd form to contamination from Q1. Hence no phonological assumptions that have any likelihood of being valid can be made in this case, and an imperfect notion of textual relationships has vitiated the linguistic conclusion.

Like Spurgeon, Kökeritz is on dangerous ground in taking his evidence for certain statements from the unauthoritative corrections of derived texts. Very likely F *checkring* is correct for *R.J.* 2. 3. 2, but is it advisable to use this compositorial emendation for Q2 *checking* as a valid example of authorial vowel syncopation (p. 381)?

5 Kökeritz's lack of information about bibliographical investigations leads him into such statements as (p. 22): 'The many phonetic spellings of one kind or another in the early Quartos and the First Folio need not, of course, reflect his [Shakespeare's] own usage, *though most of them undoubtedly do so* [my italics]. Even a copyist may have adhered pretty closely to Shakespeare's own spelling—at any rate, *not a single spelling can, even conjecturally, be attributed to such an intermediary*' (my italics). This rash statement ignores F. P. Wilson's study of the scribe Ralph Crane, whose characteristics can be detected in the Folio text of *The Merry Wives of Windsor*. It is directly controverted by the investigations of Dr Philip Williams into the Folio's variant spellings in such plays as 1 *Henry VI* and *King John*. These show variant spellings in the work of the same compositor within each play, and they differ according to the *literary* divisions of the plays and must therefore be representative of the work of two different inscribers.

No bibliographer or working textual critic of Renaissance literature would subscribe without serious reservations to the optimism, based on insufficient or outdated evidence, that marks p. 23: 'These studies by Simpson, Darbishire, and Byrne prove Wyld (pp. 112 f.) to have been correct in laying down as his working hypothesis that the printers were "unlikely to introduce, of themselves, any considerable novelties in spelling"; that they were conservative and conventional; that they would be more likely to eliminate the "incorrect" spellings of the author's manuscript than introduce these themselves; and that consequently we are justified in regarding the outstanding linguistic features in printed literature of the period as really reflecting the individualities of the authors and not of the printers.'

6 Such as its failure to record the three examples in Shakespeare and the one in Dekker of the word *sally* meaning *sully*, although willing to record some other forms on a single suspect example.

even today too often marks the presentation of works of literature to the student and to the general public.[7]

There is every reason to deplore the common ignorance of textual conditions and of editing standards that puts the critic quite at the mercy of the editor. For example, in 1901 A. H. Thorndike thought that a splendid formula to distinguish the collaborated work of Fletcher from that of Massinger was the frequent use of the contraction *'em* in Fletcher as against the invariable use of the full form *them* in Massinger.[8] The only trouble was, as he discovered too late, that he had used Gifford's edition of Massinger from which to quarry his evidence; and in this edition Gifford had silently expanded Massinger's *'em* forms to *them*. His edition was untrustworthy, and a man who was at the time an inexperienced scholar— though later a great one—suffered from his misplaced confidence in an improperly edited text.

Fifty years later it is still a current oddity that many a literary critic has investigated the past ownership and mechanical condition of his second-hand automobile, or the pedigree and training of his dog, more

---

7 A fascinating study of corruption in modern reading texts will be found in R. C. Bald, 'Editorial Problems—A Preliminary Survey', *Studies in Bibliography*, III (1950), 3–17. See also Gordon N. Ray, 'The Importance of Original Editions', *Nineteenth-Century English Books: Some Problems in Bibliography* (1952), pp. 8–12.

A typical case of reprints ignoring authorially corrected editions and returning to less authoritative texts is given by Stanley Godman in 'Lewis Carroll's Final Corrections to "Alice" ', *Times Literary Supplement*, 2 May 1958, p. 248. For the 1897 editions of *Alice* and *Through the Looking-Glass* Carroll minutely revised the text. Mr Godman writes: 'The collation of the author's corrections with the editions of 1897 which I have made shows that, with two exceptions—one of them a regrettable oversight, the other owing perhaps to an understandable disagreement on the printer's part—his copious and sometimes finicking instructions were observed as scrupulously as they were made. A study of a representative selection of the editions that have appeared after his death shows, however, that the author's final intentions, as represented by the corrections in Mrs Stretton's copies and the 1897 editions based on them, have rarely been respected in their entirety. For example, the edition in Macmillian's "Sixpenny Series (1898) and the Macmillan "Miniature" edition (1907) complied with only about a half of the amendments for the 1897 editions. Notable editions such as the Everyman (1929) and the Puffin (1946) ignore them altogether, the latter even reverting to the pre-1886 editions which contained only the first four lines of '"Tis the voice of the lobster" which was expanded in the edition of 1886 and the People's Edition of 1887.' It is clear from this and other evidence that the copy-texts for modern cheap reprints are likely to be most negligently selected. For various examples of corruptions, see Bruce Harkness, 'Bibliography and the Novelistic Fallacy' in *Studies in Bibliography*, XII (1959), 59–73.

8 *The Influence of Beaumont and Fletcher on Shakespeare* (1901), pp. 24 ff., noticed by Cyrus Hoy, 'The Shares of Fletcher and his Collaborators in the Beaumont and Fletcher Canon (I)', *Studies in Bibliography*, VIII (1956), 131, a thorough survey of the problem using just such linguistic evidence but with some care for the texts from which the evidence is drawn.

thoroughly than he has looked into the qualifications of the text on which his critical theories rest. One may search the history of scholarship in vain to find parallel examples—in relation to the *zeitgeist*—of cultural *naïveté* and professional negligence. Moreover, the danger is not confined to early texts. A critic of *Richard III*, say, who reaches up to his bookshelf and does not care whether he pulls down the Old Cambridge or the New Cambridge volume is no more simple-minded than one who reads Melville or Whitman in texts altered for an English audience, or who—in America—reads most of the Victorians in nineteenth-century American editions,[9] or even T. S. Eliot or Yeats in corrupt American editions instead of the more authentic and often the revised English texts.

9 Carl J. Weber, 'American Editions of English Authors', *Nineteenth-Century English Books: Some Problems in Bibliography* (1952), pp. 31 ff. surveys the state of the text in early American editions of Wordsworth, Thackeray, Fitzgerald, Hardy, and Housman. Typical findings are as follows. In the 1802 James Humphreys edition of Wordsworth published in Philadelphia, the sixteen lines of 'Lines Written when Sailing in a Boat at Evening' have been wrongly inserted as the opening lines of 'Lines written near Richmond, upon the Thames', with a composite title of the publishers' invention, 'Lines written near Richmond, upon the Thames, at Evening'. Although Thackeray was most concerned about his illustrations for *Pendennis*, the contemporary authorised American edition by Harper omitted both the frontispiece and the twenty-two full-page steel engravings. Later, a pirated Lovell edition in New York included fifteen of these but omitted all the smaller wood engravings. 'Some one in the Harper office in New York struck out an entire page in one chapter of Hardy's *Return of the Native*, solely to make the book fit the format planned for the American edition; and after Hardy had revised the text of this novel for the definitive London edition of 1912, the American reader was still being offered the debased New York product twenty-five years later. Most of the pirates stole their own texts from just such debased, even though "authorized", editions as the one here referred to, and the likelihood that any librarian or scholar or collector would, in buying an American copy, get the author's approved text was very small, as long as the lack of international copyright permitted the continuance of the chaotic conditions here described. . . . Not until 1928 could any American librarian be *sure* that if he bought a copy of *Tess* from the American publisher, he would get the text as approved by the novelist himself.' Hardy's *Woodlanders* by 1926 had been printed in at least thirty American editions, all retaining the wording of the original London serialisation in *Macmillan's Magazine*. But even before the first book publication in England, Hardy had found the magazine text unsatisfactory and had revised it, and he made additional revisions for the second edition. In 1895, in preparation for the Uniform Edition of his writings, he once more revised the text, and finally—for the fourth time—for the 1912 London edition. Yet not until 1928 did an American edition appear (save in the reissued sheets of the expensive set of his entire works) with the text in its definitive state, or in a state representing *any* of the previous revisions. These early unrevised texts are still, of course, prominent on library shelves in the United States. After various other examples, the inevitable conclusion is drawn: 'The student of nineteenth-century English literature has only one safe rule to follow: if he is working with an American edition of his author, nothing can be taken for granted. . . . The wise man . . . will *know* his American edition before he goes far with it. He will trust it as he would a rattlesnake. He will neither quote from it, nor rely on conclusions drawn from it, until he has compared it, word for word, with the present

Professor R. C. Bald has remarked on the curious fact that as late as 1948 and 1949 respectively, G. B. Harrison and O. J. Campbell, two active and distinguished Shakespearean scholars, put out editions of Shakespeare that were close reproductions of the Old Cambridge, or Globe, text of almost a hundred years before. He adds, 'It is not as if there had been no advances in textual study of Shakespeare during the present century, nor are these two editors ignorant of the work of Pollard, McKerrow, Greg, and Dover Wilson; but is there any other branch of study in which a teacher would be satisfied to present students, as these books do, with the results achieved by scholarship up to, but not beyond, the year 1864?' [10]

If the public, or students and their professors, will not demand good texts, publishers will not offer the means for textual scholars to provide them. Indeed, I have heard it said that Harrison chose to use the Globe text only after his publisher had polled a number of teachers and found the familiar Globe was their preference. I am far from asserting that there is a vast backlog of excellent editions of texts waiting to find a publisher. I am aware that editions of early literature are not considered to be best sellers; and especially if they are in old spelling they may find some serious difficulty in getting into print. I am aware that for too long editing has been esteemed the proper province for the amateur, the pedant, or the dullard who could not even write a biography; and that for too long editing has often deserved its lowly reputation. Moreover, I am conscious

---

English edition, or has assured himself that the English author saw and approved of what his American publisher put into print for him. This has, unfortunately, *not* been the practice of all American critics, scholars, bibliographers, and others who have worked with the books of English authors. They have thus opened the door to unsound judgments, to inaccurate quotations, to misleading conclusions, and to the perpetuation of faulty texts.'

That the practice is not confined merely to nineteenth-century texts may be seen in an example kindly furnished me by Mr Frederick Woods, who is proposing a bibliography of Sir Winston Churchill. Galleys of *The Second World War* were made up from the typescript, but successive stages of revision were given to the galleys, so heavy as to amount to actual rewriting in proof. At a certain stage in the process the American publisher is reputed to have grown tired of waiting for further textual revisions and revised maps and to have sent the book to press. On the contrary, the English publisher waited for the further corrections and several months after the appearance of the first American edition published a different and certainly more authoritative text in the first English edition.

This is an extreme example, of course, but in many minor ways texts may differ between the two countries. I recall my own sense of shock on finding that Heinemann had religiously substituted 'petrol' for 'gas' or 'gasoline', even in the speech of the American characters where it was singularly inappropriate, when in 1952 my wife's novel *The Sign of Jonah* was reprinted in England. Bruce Harkness, 'Bibliography and the Novelistic Fallacy', *Studies in Bibliography*, XII (1959), should be consulted for further examples of misleading prose-fiction texts.

10 'Editorial Problems', *Studies in Bibliography*, III (1950), 5.

that even today the newer editorial methods are only dimly understood by various would-be practitioners. At least, the manuscripts that publishers occasionally send me for an opinion indicate a troubled awareness of the word 'bibliography' though little understanding of its method.

Yet even if we could posit for the future none but ideal editions, I expect there would still remain a considerable isolation of textual bibliographers from their ultimate consumers, the literary critics. This is a pity. I waste no tears on the wounded egos of the bibliographers; the damage is on the other side. I could wish that general critics knew more, and knowing more would care more, about the purity of the texts they use.

In some small part present-day editorial concern with what seem to be relatively minor matters of accurate decision may alienate the critic, such as the one who became impatient at anybody wasting very much time finding out whether Shakespeare wrote *sallied* or *solid*. In this particular case I fancy the choice is important on grounds of meaning, for the word *sullied* supports my contention that Hamlet feels his natural, or inherited, honour has been soiled by the taint of his mother's dishonourable blood. But the weight that may be put on this word is perhaps unusual. For instance, not much is changed whether Hamlet's father's bones were *interred* as in Q2, or *inurned* as in the Folio. Yet I hold it to be an occupation eminently worth while, warranting any number of hours, to determine whether Shakespeare wrote one, or the other, or both. The decision, if clear-cut, might be crucial in the accumulation of evidence whether on the whole the Folio variants from the quarto *Hamlet* are corruptions, corrections, or revisions. If this is a problem no editor has fairly faced, neither should a literary critic be indifferent to the question. Depending upon what can be proved, some hundreds of readings will be affected if an editor decides that Shakespeare revised the text after its second-quarto form; for in that case there could be an argument for choosing the Folio variants in all but the most obvious cases of sophistication. Or he might decide that in only a few cases, where the second quarto compositors have corrupted the text, should the Folio readings take precedence over the generally authoritative second quarto.

True, certain 'values' will not be materially affected one way or the other. Hamlet will not be revealed as a woman, or as the villain; he will still be melancholy and at odds with the life about him. Denmark will still be a prison. Yet what modern author would view with equanimity an edition of one of his plays that substituted several hundred words scattered here and there from the corruptions of typists, compositors, and proof-readers? Not to mention editors. The critic who is so airy about the relation of textual accuracy to 'essential values' would be more touched if an essay of his own were involved in the general corruption.

Nevertheless, I should not wish to rest the case on such a special problem as *Hamlet*. I do not myself think it pedantry to make a fetish of accuracy in scholarship, or in criticism. Only a practising textual critic and bibliographer knows the remorseless corrupting influence that eats away at a text during the course of its transmission. The most important concern of the textual bibliographer is to guard the purity of the important basic documents of our literature and culture. This is a matter of principle on which there can be no compromise. One can no more permit 'just a little corruption' to pass unheeded in the transmission of our literary heritage than 'just a little sin' was possible in Eden.

As a principle, if we respect our authors we should have a passionate concern to see that their words are recovered and currently transmitted in as close a form to their intentions as we can contrive. It should matter to us, as it should matter to all critics, that if one wants to read F. Scott Fitzgerald's *This Side of Paradise* with several of the author's final revisions, one must go to the fourth or later impressions made from plates altered on his instructions, though one must then guard against a proofreader's error inserted when the plates were unauthoritatively further corrected for the seventh impression.[11]

It should matter to us that in modern reprints of *Tristram Shandy*, to quote an investigator: "Errors in punctuation amount on many pages to 15 to 20 to the page. . . . Modern reprints have frequently set in lower case words which Sterne required to be set in small capitals. Alterations in spelling have not been confined to modernizations; . . . errors destroying Sterne's sense and meaning have been perpetuated, like *area* for *aera*, *clause* for *cause*, *port* for *post*, *timber* for *tinder*, *catching* for *catechising*,

---

11 Matthew Bruccoli, 'A Collation of F. Scott Fitzgerald's *This Side of Paradise*', *Studies in Bibliography*, IX (1957), 263–5. A total of thirty-one changes were made in the original plates between 1920 and 1954: 'corrections of misspelled references to books and authors (10); corrections of misspellings of names and places (5); other corrections in spelling and usage (6); corrections of errors involving careless proofreading (3); corrections of miscellaneous errors (3); and revisions of non-errors (4)'. Although the literary critic will be most concerned with the final category, the others are of some account, as Edmund Wilson noticed, when he wrote: 'It is not only full of bogus ideas and faked literary references but it is full of English words misused with the most reckless abandon.' Some but not all of these original faults were concealed by the correction of the plates.

The analysis of a modern author's linguistic habits by studying the changes made in different printings of his books is still a rare pursuit, but interesting results may follow. The correction of faulty grammar in the second printing of Sherwood Anderson's novel *Winesburg, Ohio* as a result of a caustic newspaper review is interesting in its own right; and in addition it established for collectors the order of the first two printings, which—on evidence that collectors usually get bilked by—had been confused. See William L. Phillips, 'The First Printing of Sherwood Anderson's *Winesburg, Ohio*', *Studies in Bibliography*, IV (1951), 211–13.

and *caravans* for *caverns*.' Many of these errors apparently originated in some popular nineteenth-century reprint, and have been repeated ever since.[12]

I agree with Professor Bald that just critical appraisal is not possible until a text has been established. It should matter to us whether the thirteenth of John Donne's *Holy Sonnets* ends triumphantly,

> so I say to thee,
> To wicked spirits are horrid shapes assign'd,
> This beauteous forme *assures* a pitious minde

as in Grierson's alteration on manuscript authority, or flatly, as in the printed texts,

> This beauteous forme *assumes* a pitious minde.

It should matter to us that the very bases for establishing the texts of such important Shakespeare plays as *2 Henry IV*, and *Hamlet*, are still undecided.[13] Until we have the physical facts upon which the establishment of these texts may proceed, no one can quote from such plays with any assurance that he is repeating what Shakespeare intended to write. In the present day it may surprise the complacent to learn that the text of Mr T. S. Eliot's *Murder in the Cathedral*, in respect to his final intentions, is very much in doubt.

I do not say with the classical scholar John Burnet, 'By common consent the constitution of an author's text is the highest aim that a scholar can set before himself'. But I do assert that the establishing of the texts of our literary and historical monuments, and the preservation of their purity through successive processes of transmission, is a task for a scholar of depth, not an employment for the spare hours of a dilettante or the drudgery of a pedant. On the one hand, some textual investigation and recovery calls for creative and imaginative efforts within the discipline of hard fact that compare very favourably indeed, in my opinion, with the broad intellectual powers that often characterised the nineteenth-century literary critic in England, powers that one would like to see still displayed today, on both sides of the Atlantic. On the other hand, bibliography is the only sure foundation on which to rear the necessary wide acquaintance with the whole complex of the past, the intimate knowledge of its thought, the feeling for its idiom, and above all the knowledge of its language for which no amount of enthusiastic dilettante sensibility can

12 *Times Literary Supplement*, 20 May 1949, p. 329; quoted by Bald, *op. cit.* III, 4.

13 In each case the exact nature of the Folio printer's copy is still in dispute. Until this is demonstrated once and for all, the authority of some of the Folio variants (or concurrences) cannot be determined.

adequately compensate, despite the invaluable aid of the *Oxford English Dictionary*.

If we may concede that even the most widely ranging criticism must occasionally descend to exact readings and their interpretation, we must then agree that the critic whose general ideas are in any way related to specific evidence—that is, to the precise details of an author's text—should be most sensitive to the accuracy of that which generates his critical theories.

It is bad enough to have critics disagreeing about whether a great poet's revisions are successful, as—for example—about the altered final lines of Yeats's 'Cuchulain's Fight with the Sea'.[14] One critic maintains that 'The second [ending] is fine too, but has not the same sense of water flowing on and on that is heard in the [first]'. But another writes the exact contrary; for him, the new ending 'transformed a mediocre poem into a work of quite extraordinary power'. Point blank oppositions like these are deplorable, of course. It is worse, however, when a critic is apparently not even conscious that changes of import have taken place. For if we attempt to resolve the above impasse by reference to a third opinion, this one remarks quite blandly, 'The changes do not concern the contents— apart from one small detail: the name Finmole has disappeared'. Obviously we have here a member of the 'total values' school of night, for the revision deleted seven lines and re-did forty-two of the remaining eighty-six, in the process changing the original ending,

> In three days' time, Cuchulain with a moan
> Stood up, and came to the long sands alone:
> For four days warred he with the bitter tide;
> And the waves flowed above him, and he died.

to

> Cuchulain stirred,
> Stared on the horses of the sea, and heard
> The cars of battle and his own name cried;
> And fought with the invulnerable tide.

We may pass from this example of other-worldliness to the point of real importance: what a literary critic should know about the causes for unsatisfactory or corrupt texts and the processes by which textual critics recover and guard the purity of an author's words. The biblio-textual critic finds that his problems are likely to sort themselves into three major, though not mutually exclusive, categories.

14 This illustration is drawn from an article by the Yeats Variorum editor, Russell K. Alspach, 'Some Textual Problems in Yeats', *Studies in Bibliography*, IX (1957), 51–67, which contains many more significant examples.

First, when an author's manuscript is preserved, close analysis of the physical characteristics of this manuscript as they bear on the process of composition may yield information of real critical value. Moreover, the preservation of an author's manuscript by no means sets up such an absolute authority as to obviate editorial investigation. If the manuscript is not the exact one used by the printer, a problem in transmission may develop; for revision, or corruption, can enter in the transcripts represented by a secondary manuscript sent to the printer and in the printer's typesetting and proof-reading, with authorial revision always a possibility in the proofs. When, years after publication, we are now able to study the proof sheets of William Faulkner's *Sanctuary* and to learn how a comparatively weak novel was turned into a strong and exciting one by extraordinary revision in proof,[15] we gain a fuller understanding of the structural grasp of a notable artist; and this vital information is secured by observing the pre-publication history of the text between its original and final proof sheets. Yet even if we determine that the translation of author's manuscript into print was normally accomplished, the textual critic cannot be indifferent to the subsequent transmission of the text through various printings and editions.

Secondly, when an author's manuscript has not been preserved, as is the general rule in literature of the past, an attempt must be made to discover as many as possible of its characteristics in order to estimate the relation of the hypothetically reconstructed manuscript to the earliest preserved printed example.

Thirdly, the transmission of a text must be followed with particular scrupulousness in order to sift its variants and assign them to unauthorised changes resulting from the printing process, or to true authorial revisions. This transmission may be separated into two parts: first, the stages from manuscript, through various proofs and trials, to actual publication of the first edition in an approved form; and, second, the transmission of the text through various impressions, or printings, as well as through various typesettings, or editions, from the first edition to the present.

In our first category, of manuscripts, I should emphasise that—no matter what the layman may think—an author's manuscript is not always self-

---

15 Linton Massey, 'Notes on the Unrevised Galleys of Faulkner's *Sanctuary*', *Studies in Bibliography*, VIII (1956), 195–208. The structure of the novel was completely altered, and the original hero demoted to a quite minor role. In Mr Massey's words, 'Faulkner altered the entire focus and meaning of the book; he clarified the obscure passages where ambiguity was not an asset; he amplified those portions requiring emendation; he gave the novel a climax; and he freed it from its bonds of previous servitude to an earlier book'.

sufficient or self-explicatory. For example, the earliest preserved autograph manuscript of Walt Whitman's 'Passage to India', at the New York Public Library, yields some very interesting results to pure bibliographical treatment of it just as a material object.[16] Several early leaves are composed of strips of paper pasted together. By observing the contours of the edges, where they were cut apart, one may reconstruct large portions of the original leaves and thus show what is rearrangement of the earliest level of inscription and what is revision and amplification. Later on, a complete change of paper accompanies the insertion of an extensive independent poem, 'Oh Soul Thou Pleasest Me'. Then, when 'Passage to India' continues, the use of substantially the same paper as in the inserted poem instead of the original paper of the earlier part demonstrates that the whole original conclusion (whatever it was) has been revised and copied out fair to take account of the new material that had not at first been contemplated. Earlier, a slight variance in the original paper had accompanied the use of slips of pasted-on proof sheets interspersed with autograph lines. By a somewhat complicated line of reasoning it is possible to show that these proof insertions from two other independent poems were made after the original inscription of the first form of the whole manuscript, but that the addition of the complete poem 'Oh Soul Thou Pleasest Me' was a later operation still, with the consequential revision of the ending, and that this last addition came close to the final stages of the working-over that Whitman gave to the completed manuscript. In some lines one may even distinguish precisely which textual revisions in the added poem were made before the insertion, and which afterwards.

Armed with this information, all of it secured from physical evidence alone, a critic can apply the results to a new understanding of the nature of the poem by his ability to trace the stages of its growth. And in my opinion the critic who neglected this first avenue of approach to understanding would be very foolish indeed. For instance, it is more than a side-issue, in my opinion, that most of the transcendental lines in the poem appear in the late-added 'Oh Soul Thou Pleasest Me'. Any possible imbalance between this section and the earlier original material can thus be

16 A study of this manuscript will be found in Bowers, 'The Earliest Manuscript of Whitman's "Passage to India" and its Notebook', *Bulletin of the New York Library*, LXI (1957), 319–52, which forms a preface to the account of the later Harvard manuscript and its proofs in 'The Manuscript of Whitman's "Passage to India" ', *Modern Philology*, LI (1953), 102–17. Reference may also be made to the critical value of the evidence for stages of composition and revision in two other Whitman manuscripts, 'The Manuscript of Walt Whitman's "A Carol of Harvest, for 1867" ', *Modern Philology*, LII (1954), 29–51; and 'The Manuscripts of Whitman's "Songs of the Redwood Tree" ', *Papers of the Bibliographical Society of America*, L (1956), 53–85.

accounted for not as a failure in Whitman's compositional inspiration and architectonic vision but as a recasting of preceding lines not perfect enough to lead adequately to the concentration of idea in the insertion.

This is an author's holograph manuscript; yet without what may be called bibliographical analysis most of these facts would not be uncovered or their significance put together into the correct interlocking sequence of reconstruction. If a critic studied this manuscript from photostats, for instance, he would be quite unconscious of most of what I have been elaborating. Author's manuscripts, therefore, are not always the final word unless one can call the author up from the grave to testify about the significance of the physical features. Bibliographers, or their equivalent, are still on occasion needed to make a factual examination and to draw the necessary conclusions before the literary critic can step in.

A critic who becomes impatient at the bibliographer's concern to establish the exact form of a text in all its possible pre-publication states of variance is throwing away, almost wilfully, one of the best possible ways of understanding an author by following him step by step at work. For example, suppose we took the easy attitude—very well, we have the author's earliest manuscript and the first printed edition that presumably contains all the revisions he made. What more do we want? I should say that we lose the opportunity to study the shaping development of idea as represented by stylistic and substantive revision, the manner in which one revision may have given rise to another or to a modification of the initial concept. As in Whitman's 'Passage to India', when one analyses very closely the numerous revisions in the New York Public Library manuscript, especially in their relation to the successive stages of growth in the poem marked by the addition of initially independent material, one learns a great deal about the way Whitman's artistic mind worked. Then if we continue the process, as we should, we may compare the changes made between the final form of the New York Public Library manuscript and the fair copy of it represented by the Harvard manuscript, which was the last holograph before print. But before it was put into type this Harvard manuscript was very considerably revised at different times, in its turn, and a lost early stage of proof—in which a number of changes were made—intervenes between the preserved proof sheets and the final form of the manuscript. Then between this known proof and the printed edition a further twenty-seven alterations appear, including the omission of two whole lines. By a close study of this development of the text up to its first publication we cannot fail to gain an insight into just what Whitman was striving for in the relation of idea to its expression.[17] Most of this evidence

17 The complexities of this process, and its importance for understanding the operation of an author's mind as he shapes his work, contrast with what I must regard as the narrowness of such a passage as this, quoted by R. C. Bald from Wellek and

would be lost if no more than a simple collation were made of the variants between the earliest or latest form of the New York Public Library manuscript and the printed edition of 1870–1.

Robert Beare, who has made a trial study of the text of T. S. Eliot, came to some interesting conclusions in this matter.[18] After surveying the elimination of punctuation and the deletion of words and phrases to achieve concentration between the pencil holograph and two separate typescripts of 'Marina', preserved in the Bodleian Library, and noting that as late as the very proof copies circulated in advance to reviewers there appeared a line that was deleted only in the actual published state, he concludes, 'The study of the stages of a poem or play which precede publication are of interest and significance for the genesis of the poem rather than as a check of its final published form'. In other words, so many changes can take

---

Warren: 'If we examine drafts, rejections, exclusions, and cuts, we conclude them not, finally, necessary to an understanding of the finished work or to a judgment upon it. Their interest is that of any alternative, i.e., they may set into relief the qualities of the final text. But the same end may very well be achieved by devising for ourselves alternatives, whether or not they have actually passed through the author's mind' (*Theory of Literature*, p. 86). The quotation comes as a footnote to Professor Bald's own position: 'No one, I fancy, will dispute the fact that one of the functions of a definitive edition is to illuminate as much as possible the origin and development of the work edited. Every student of the Romantic Period, for instance, knows something of the fascinating struggle for artistic perfection revealed by Keats's manuscripts, or of the information about the development of Wordsworth's thought and art furnished by the new Oxford edition.'

But editorial duty aside, if we take such a test case as David Hayman's 'From *Finnegans Wake:* A Sentence in Progress', *PMLA*, LXXIII (1958), 136–54, a fascinating analysis of the growth in meaning of a single sentence, it is difficult to hold that only the finished result is of critical interest for the explication of a work or of any of its parts. Most great works contain some mystery, some levels of allusiveness that may easily be overlooked or even misunderstood, although, as with Joyce, the evidence for their growth will clarify and explain. The school of criticism represented by Messrs Wellek and Warren is confident that the single perspicuous critic, face to face with the work in isolation, requires no aids to understanding, such as early drafts fixing the stages of growth. This may well be true if the critic (as they seem to do) searches the drafts only for rejected or imperfect variants which serve to highlight the superior values of the finished product. If one takes it that the end result is perfect, of course the critic can himself contrive alternatives that will serve to show the superiority of the final form. But if the critic is like Dr Hayman, for example, and is endeavoring to demonstrate on the evidence of early drafts what the meaning of the end result must be, he is concerned with a method of criticism quite different from that pursued by Wellek and Warren, and one with far different ideals. That unaided critical speculation about meaning in the New Critical manner of explication must always fail in its full objective is adroitly argued by W. Y. Tindall in 'The Criticism of Fiction', *The Texas Quarterly*, I (1958), 101–11, especially on p. 109.

18 Information in this chapter about Eliot's text comes, unless otherwise stated, from Robert L. Beare, 'Notes on the Text of T. S. Eliot: Variants from Russell Square', *Studies in Bibliography*, IX (1957), 21–49, which is packed with interesting examples.

place between holograph manuscript and first edition that we should study these changes through various transcripts and proofs not for the simple mechanical purpose of checking the accuracy of the printed text (for which the manuscript may or may not be trustworthy in all respects) but instead as an independent act of critical inquiry into the author's mind and art.

And a little later, after a survey of the variants in 'The Waste Land', Beare writes:

> There are many incidental gains through approaching an author's work by studying the development of texts of his work. There is the added insight into recurrent phrasing and themes in the poems and plays, and a stricter sense of their chronology and possible relationships. In Eliot's poetry there is also room to discuss under variants the alterations in phrasing which borrowings from other authors have undergone. Again, unless we have the sense of the actual chronology of the works, we cannot discuss influences in their proper perspectives, such as the possible influence of Joyce on 'The Waste Land' through the serialization of *Ulysses*.

If anyone inquires what all this has to do with the independent life of the poem as we have it in the form that the author wanted to present to the world, I think we can answer that we are likely to know an adult better if we have followed him through all the stages of his childhood. Though a poem, like a man, may stand rejoicing in finished maturity, we must surely understand it with superior intimacy if we have watched its growth and seen its perfection in the very act of shaping. There is such a thing as love, I should urge, in our response to a perfect poem. The current games of intellectual chess, of subjectively drawn tensions, ambiguities, and *discordia concors*, too often overlook or overlay that simple act of love, which the textual critic may help us toward in his concern for the childhood and adolescence, awkward or charming, of the living seed of a writer.

We may turn to the second category in which biblio-textual problems cluster: the attempt to recover as many as possible of the characteristics of an author's lost manuscript from the evidence of the earliest printed edition related to the manuscript. Here we come to a very broad area of textual bibliography which is devoted, often in a highly technical manner, to estimating the effect of scribal transcript or of compositorial typesetting on the author's lost original. Textual critics of biblical, classical, and medieval manuscripts have developed to a relatively high point the art of recovering details of the lost original and of reconstructing a synthetic text that is superior to any single preserved form. In later periods, the more strictly bibliographical investigation of the effect of the printing process on an author's text is in its early stages, and its results are at present only provisional. I shall have something to say on this point when in my third lecture I come to textual studies of Shakespeare; my remarks now must be taken as being in their turn quite provisional.

Ordinarily it is true that the nearer one comes to modern times, the more difficulty one has in penetrating the veil of print and recovering the characteristics of the lost manuscript. The uniformity of compositorial usage, added to the strong-minded styling given a typescript by the publisher's reader before setting, at the present day has a marked tendency to impose standard characteristics of syntax, punctuation, spelling, and sometimes of phrasing, on an author's individuality of expression. Yet we must not over-estimate these forces, powerful as they are in smoothing out individualities found in an author's manuscript. Louis N. Feipel, whose hobby was proof-reading printed books, supplied Harcourt, Brace with a list of about a hundred inconsistencies and errors in the first printing of Sinclair Lewis's novel *Babbit*. To which Lewis commented in awe, 'This man Feipel is a wonder—to catch all these after rather unusually careful proofreading not only by myself and my wife but also by two or three professionals'. Even so, Lewis showed himself uncertain of the meaning of *B* in *B.P.O.E.* since he twice gave it in error as *Brotherly* and only once correctly as *Benevolent* (*B.P.O.E.* is the abbreviation for an American fraternal society, The Benevolent and Protective Order of Elks). And Lewis's spelling of *Oddfellows* and *Redmen* (two similar orders) as one word instead of two is not quite the way in which these organisations choose to denominate themselves. The mordant satirist of American 'joiners' and their groups did not, on the evidence, always have a keen eye for such details in the objects of his laughter.[19]

The various misspellings and inaccuracies that crept into the references to proper names in Fitzgerald's *This Side of Paradise,* and were only partly rooted out by successive alterations of the plates, provide some evidence of his carelessness, vagueness, and even ignorance. Indeed, it is clear that when one collates the text of successive impressions of modern books, the various alterations that may be detected in the plates are often indications of original aberrancies repeated direct from the authors' manuscripts. It is amusing at the very least to know that despite his considerable display of erudition, James Branch Cabell—another American novelist—had frequently to correct his Latin in second impressions, and sometimes his French. Cabell, like Fitzgerald and Lewis, also took such occasions to make textual revisions in the plates, as well as corrections.[20]

19 Matthew J. Bruccoli, 'Textual Variants in Sinclair Lewis's *Babbitt*', *Studies in Bibliography*, XI (1958), 263–8.
20 A number of examples exposed by the Hinman Collating Machine will be found in Matthew J. Bruccoli, *Notes on the Cabell Collections at the University of Virginia*

I am sorry that my best modern illustration of the application of bibliography to recover the features of a manuscript appears to be hypothetical. At least, no one else present on the occasion agrees with my memory that I was shown a second edition of a modern English poet. In this second edition were four to six lines in an altered version that seemed patently inferior to the version in the first edition. The problem was—did this author revise for the worse, or could a bibliographical explanation be evolved? I suggested that an explanation was indeed possible. The book had been printed in England and therefore almost certainly had been set in Monotype. Monotype is set by punching a paper-tape roll that is subsequently run through a caster that automatically sets the type. If a second impression is much delayed, and the book has not been plated, the type can be distributed in the interval, since for a second printing [before the days of offset] all one need do is run the tape through the caster again to secure an exact duplicate of the first-impression typesetting. Of course, the publisher must carefully repeat all the stages of corrected proofs, or conflate them into one; for *all* proof changes made in the first typesetting must be repeated by hand in the second. If, as was possible, the revision of the lines in question had been made at a late stage and there had been a slip-up in preserving or conflating these proofs, the situation would be brought about that the first printing had given us the revised lines but the second printing the original lines before revision. The last would have been first here with a vengeance. The illustration is so neat that it is a pity it is very likely not true. Observe, of course, that the explanation would not fit if the book had been printed in America where Linotype is ordinarily used for commercial printing: under these conditions a second printing could be made only from standing type or from plates; and there would be no possible way in which the types of the original reading could reappear, as in Monotype.

As a sidenote on the importance of knowing the process of printing, and its effect on the transmission of texts, we may observe that the excision of a line from Eliot's *The Rock* in the Harcourt, Brace printing is not an instance of authorial initiative but instead the result of a bad splice made in the negative for the American photo-offset edition.

Sometimes quite mechanical evidence can be brilliantly used to recover facts about a lost manuscript. Professor Donald Bond observed that the folio first-edition issues of the *Spectator* papers kept headlines, rules, and advertisements in standing type, but that a curious alternation existed between the complete sets of such standing material. When he further associated each set of standing types with certain spelling peculiarities, he

---

(James Branch Cabell: A Bibliography, Part II; University of Virginia Press, 1957).
See especially the entry for *Jurgen.*

was able to demonstrate that two printers, Buckley and Tonson, alternated in producing the *Spectator* papers in order to allow enough time for sufficient quantities to be printed without duplicate composition. He thereupon observed that of the papers readily attributable to Addison the vast majority were printed by Tonson; and of the papers attributable to Steele the vast majority were printed by Buckley; and he further observed that this assignment was invariable after a certain point. Not only could unidentified work of these two men be assigned to the correct authorship on this evidence; but the work of contributors who were closely associated either with Addison or with Steele could also be allocated to Tonson or to Buckley on the same basis. Hence ranges of lost manuscript could be identified on merely mechanical printing evidence.[21]

In an earlier period Dr Cyrus Hoy observed that compositors were generally faithful enough to small details of contractions, so the collaborated work of Beaumont, Fletcher, Massinger, Shirley, Rowley, and Field can be identified by small linguistic patterns peculiar to each author, like the use of *'em* for *them,* of *i'th* for *in the,* or of *o'th* for *of the,* and so on. This identification, moreover, could sometimes be carried to such a state of refinement that Dr Hoy could offer evidence as to the exact status of the manuscript for some plays, whether the holograph of different authors, or a fair copy by one author of his own and his collaborator's scenes, or a scribal transcript of both.[22] In a recent article another scholar, Dr Frederick Waller, has shown from physical evidence the possibility that Fletcher touched up in various specific places several of the scenes customarily assigned to Shakespeare in *The Two Noble Kinsmen.*[23]

Characteristics of the printed texts have for some time revealed excellent reason for assigning the manuscripts of some Elizabethan plays to the scribe Ralph Crane; whereas other evidence relating to the punctuation of stage-directions in some plays has suggested that the printer's manuscript was a transcript by Edward Knight, book-keeper for the King's Men.

Indeed, my own experience with *The Virgin Martyr*, a play printed in 1622, indicates that despite some difficulties the manuscript behind the first edition was very likely not a scribal copy but instead the assembled autograph papers of the two authors, Massinger and Dekker. For this play the separate spelling habits of the two authors come through the type-

21 Donald F. Bond, 'The First Printing of the *Spectator*', *Modern Philology*, XLVII (1950), 164–77.

22 'The Shares of Fletcher and his Collaborators in the Beaumont and Fletcher Canon', *Studies in Bibliography*, VIII (1956), 129–46 (see especially pp. 137–42); *S.B.*, IX (1957), 143–62 (see especially pp. 144–5); *S.B.*, XI (1958), 85–106, and later volumes.

23 'Printer's Copy for *The Two Noble Kinsmen*', *Studies in Bibliography*, XI (1958), 61–84.

setting by a single compositor with sufficient clarity to make this hypothesis plausible, and join with certain linguistic traits to settle the authorship of the scenes in this collaboration on better evidence than stylistic impressions. In fact, the evidence is such that it is possible to conjecture that in at least one scene, and perhaps two, of the fourth act, Dekker copied over original Massinger composition in the course of amplifying and revising the scene.[24]

The significance of such studies as I have mentioned, and the means by which the evidence is brought together and analysed, I propose to discuss more fully in the third lecture on Shakespearean textual criticism.

In the third category, the transmission of a text may pose serious problems for a literary critic, all the more serious in that he is ordinarily quite unaware that such problems exist. In more spacious days it was customary for dilettante editors, unacquainted with the rigours of textual criticism, to reprint the last edition of a text issued in the author's lifetime. The reason alleged was that this edition—in ordinary circumstances—would be the last that an author might have revised. It rarely occurred to such editors that they were under an obligation to show whether or not the author had in truth revised the edition chosen. The possibility was taken as sufficient warrant. As a result, without any determination of authority, all the accumulated corruptions from successive reprintings were carefully reproduced by editors as if, tacitly, they were authorial variants—no attempt being made to sort out and to analyse the relation of the different editions to each other and, on the evidence, to determine whether at any point fresh authority had intervened. For example, when in 1868 Henry Morley came to re-edit the *Spectator* papers, he estimated that some three thousand textual corruptions had accumulated in the last standard edition.

The transmission of texts, and what happens in this transmission, is a subject of particular fascination, worth a discourse in itself instead of the very few examples I can devote to it. Although the last-edition-in-the-author's-lifetime formula no longer holds the estimation formerly accorded it, a reaction that exalts the first edition at the expense of all others can be dangerous too. Only when the transmission of a text has been carefully studied, and each edition after the first established firmly as a mere reprint without authority, can an editor rely wholly on the first edition, after due regard for its misprints. Otherwise, whenever revision is established in any later edition, editorial procedures of some delicacy may be involved, and the bibliographical facts become paramount as the basis for general as well as specific decision.

The new edition of Goldsmith by Professor Friedman, and the new edition of the *Spectator* papers by Professor Bond, provide badly needed models for the editing of eighteenth-century texts, a field that has usually

24 *The Dramatic Works of Thomas Dekker*, vol. III (1958).

been one of the disgraces of scholarship.* [To these models, one hopes, may be added the Wesleyan-Clarendon edition of *Tom Jones* (1974).]

Shortly after the *Spectator* first-edition folio had been completed, an edition in octavo was announced, and a cheaper edition in duodecimo was printed, in great part simultaneously with the octavo. Collation establishes just about every possible form of revision and transmission. In some cases (when there was alteration) the folio papers were revised for the octavo, but in others not for the octavo but for the duodecimo. In some cases the duodecimo follows uncorrected folio sheets, in others corrected folio sheets, in some the octavo sheets, in others octavo sheets annotated with revisions. After careful study of the transmission an editor will in each case choose the folio as copy-text, following Greg's classic advice to select as one's basis the printed edition that was set up directly from manuscript; but when variants in readings appear he will choose some from the folio, some from the octavo, and others from the duodecimo, this choice depending not—as customarily—on mere intuition but instead quite rigorously on what the evidence of transmission has shown to be the particular pages of a particular edition set from the most authoritative revised copy.[25]

From the nineteenth century I select as an interesting case the text of Shelley's *Posthumous Poems*. These were first printed in 1824 by Mrs Shelley, who edited them again, revised, in the collection of 1839. Modern editors have contented themselves with reprinting the presumed authoritative text of 1839 without inquiring into the history of its transmission; and in so doing they have perpetuated a number of errors by their negligence. Briefly, the story is this. In copies sold very late in 1824 an important errata leaf containing twenty-four corrections was bound in; but this leaf is so rare as to have escaped general knowledge. The 1824 poems were promptly pirated, and piracies were made of the piracies, most of which had not used the errata-leaf corrections. When Mrs Shelley came to re-edit the poems for the 1839 collection, by bad luck she did not choose as printer's copy the 1824 edition, but instead took one of the piracies of a piracy, though—by good fortune this time—the text (even if sometimes corrupt) had printed most but not all of the errata-leaf variants. Mrs Shelley, of course, had quite forgotten about the errata leaf by 1839. Although she made a fresh comparison of the print with the manuscripts in her possession, as one would expect she missed three of the late but important errata-leaf corrections and allowed various of the piracy's accumu-

---

*As examples, see the reviews of the edition of Samuel Johnson's *Works* in *Journal of English and Germanic Philology*, 58 (1959), 132–137; and in *Modern Philology*, 61 (1964), 298–309.

25 Donald F. Bond, 'The Text of the *Spectator*', *Studies in Bibliography*, V (1952), 109–28.

lated corruptions to stand; and these, as a consequence, appeared in her 1839 text, to be copied by all subsequent editors as authoritative readings. This is true *naïveté*, which a study of the transmission would long since have exposed if any editor had troubled to make the inquiry, before Dr Charles Taylor's Yale dissertation worked out the problem.[26]

There should be no complacency about our modern texts. The plates of a book may be altered without notice in any impression, yet the latest printing from altered plates is not necessarily the most correct. For example, Sinclair Lewis's novel *Babbitt* had two sets of plates made in 1922 from the original typesetting after proof-correction. The first set of plates printed the first to the fourth impressions. In the first impression we have two readings corrected in a rare example of modern stop-press alteration of plates. Six more readings were changed in the plates for the second impression, and thirteen more in the fourth. However, after 1942 all printings were made from the second set of plates; but these had not been carefully kept up-to-date with the alterations made in the first plates and hence all printings from 1942 to the present day revert in fourteen out of twenty-one cases to original first-impression errors that had been corrected either in the second or the fourth impressions. A critic who uses any other printing of *Babbitt* than the fourth may quote a passage that in some detail does not correspond to certain of Lewis's revised intentions.[27]

In *Babbitt* the consequences may not be very serious, except in principle. But one never knows when an error in modern texts will rise to plague a critic who is not aware of the transmission of the text he is using. A good example of utter confusion is illustrated by Delmore Schwartz, writing about Yeats's poem 'Among School Children'. Schwartz was aware that the reading 'Soldier Aristotle' was new in the 1933 American edition of the *Collected Poems* instead of the older reading 'Solider Aristotle'; but he felt helpless to determine whether it was or was not a misprint. Hence he circled about the subject gingerly, interpreting the fifth stanza in two ways depending upon whether one reads 'Soldier' or 'Solider' Aristotle. He is not very happy about his results, since 'Soldier' imports the wars of Alexander rather unbecomingly into a poem about school-children, but what else can he do he does not know.

His comments are instructive. 'The whole problem of the meaning or meanings of any poem is raised by this example', he writes, '. . . but in one form or another much of Yeats's verse raises the same questions for any

26 *The Early Collected Editions of Shelley's Poems: A Study in the History and Transmission of the Printed Text.* The pertinent details are excerpted in Dr Taylor's 'The Errata Leaf to Shelley's *Posthumous Poems* and some Surprising Relationships between the Earliest Collected Editions', *PMLA*, LXX (1955), 408–16.

27 Matthew J. Bruccoli, 'Textual Variants in Sinclair Lewis's *Babbitt*', *Studies in Bibliography*, XI (1958), 263–8.

reader, namely, what are the limits which define legitimate interpretation? Are there any limits?'

The answer he finds puzzling. Quite rightly he rejects the Empsonian attitude that the more simultaneous interpretations one can give to a poem the better. He also rejects, though more reluctantly, the thesis that an interpretation is valid if it is consistent with the whole context of the poem taken as a literal statement. Again, because he cannot reconcile the divergent meanings of 'Soldier Aristotle' and 'Solider Aristotle', he feels this criterion will not operate. Thereupon he gives up the quest, and goes over completely to something like mysticism:

> Whatever the answer to the whole problem of interpretation or this partic-ular instance of it may be [he writes], this problem and all the problems . . . should add up to a definition of ignorance. Yet this defined ignorance assumes, knows, and depends upon an inexhaustible substance like Life itself. Only ad-miration of this substance could bring one to a concern with its problems and mysteries. It is with this admiration, with a conviction of the greatness of this poetry, that our author will begin and end. All will begin and end with ad-miration and love of the greatness of this poetry.[28]

I submit that we may feel admiration and love for the greatness of poetry without having a critic ask us to admire and love a misprint that he has failed to recognise as an error. This peroration seems to me to be high-faluting nonsense. Humility before a great work of art is a proper attitude. But to exalt ignorance of the principles of textual criticism into admiration of the protoplasmic mysteries of Life (with a capital L) is more than we should be willing to stomach.

One could carry on indefinitely with such examples. Mr Beare quotes Eliot's lines from *Ash Wednesday*:

> And the light shone in darkness and
> Against the Wor[l]d the unstilled world whirled
> About the centre of the silent Word.

He comments: 'The "l" which found its way into "Word" has persisted through every subsequent printing of the *Collected Poems*, every selection from it, including the new *Selected Poems* of a year or so ago, [it is] in every foreign translation, and I remember seeing these lines used once somewhere as an example of the difficulty of interpreting Eliot's poetry.'

Even when authors cultivate ambiguity of expression, critics should be particularly careful to view the text with some caution before giving the

28 'An Unwritten Book' in *The Permanence of Yeats*, ed. James Hall and Martin Steinmann (1950), pp. 327–8, reprinted from *The Southern Review*, VII (1942), 488–90.

devil more than his due. On page 29 of the first English printing of *The Cocktail Party* occurs a misprint in the earlier copies from the press, though corrected part way through the run. The unidentified guest, in the corrected version, replies to Edward's statement that he wants to see Lavinia again:

> You shall see her again—here.

This is sufficiently portentous, but the earlier printed line reads, in error,

> You shall see here again—here.

We may look forward with apprehension, perhaps, to reading some day a metaphysical discourse on Eliot's view of time and the nature of reality, as expressed in the pregnant line, 'You shall see here again—here'.

Criticism of modern literature as if it were written by seventeenth-century 'metaphysicals' has produced various admirable treatises, but sometimes the approval of *discordia concors* is carried to the lengths of extravagant praise for the *discordia* of a printer's error without the *concors* of the poet's intention. Such an instance is found in F. O. Matthiessen's discussion of a phrase of Herman Melville's in *White-Jacket*. Melville is describing his fall into the sea from the yard-arm of the U.S. frigate *Neversink*. In the Constable Standard Edition of Melville's *Works* we read the following description of his feelings as he floats under water in an almost trance-like state:

> I wondered whether I was yet dead or still dying. But of a sudden some fashionless form brushed my side—some inert, soiled fish of the sea; the thrill of being alive again tingled in my nerves, and the strong shunning of death shocked me through.

Commenting on these lines Matthiessen writes:

> But then this second trance is shattered by a twist of imagery of the sort that was to become peculiarly Melville's. He is startled back into the sense of being alive by grazing an inert form; hardly anyone but Melville could have created the shudder that results from calling this frightening vagueness some 'soiled fish of the sea.' The *discordia concors,* the unexpected linking of the medium of cleanliness with filth, could only have sprung from an imagination that had apprehended the terrors of the deep, of the immaterial deep as well as the physical.

The only difficulty with this critical *frisson* about Melville's imagination, and undemonstrable generalisations such as 'nobody but Melville could have created the shudder', and so on, is the cruel fact that an unimaginative typesetter inadvertently created it, not Melville; for what Melville wrote, as is demonstrated in both the English and American first editions, was *coiled* fish of the sea.[29] It is disheartening to find the enthusiasm of critics so easily betrayed; just as it is disheartening to find sensible critics defending with their heart's blood a Yeats misspelling or misprint in the *disdain-distain* controversy from 'Byzantium' that enlivened the pages of *The Times Literary Supplement* in 1950.[30] Although I deplore the national allusion, I have some sympathy with the disgust of the correspondent Mr John Christopherson who midway in the discussion (*T.L.S.* 1950, p. 581) declared roundly that Yeats was a notoriously bad speller, and this was the sole explanation for the error *distain*; and continued, in criticism of earlier letters on the subject, 'Such barren discussion and dissection as is at present being carried on in America and elsewhere is no doubt what

29 See John W. Nichol, 'Melville's "Soiled" Fish of the Sea', *American Literature*, XXI (1949), 338–9. Dr Nichol comments, 'It is interesting to note that the change in this case does not invalidate the general critical position arrived at by Matthiessen; it merely weakens his specific example. However, such a textual slip could, in the proper context, have promulgated an entirely false conception.'

30 The discussion was initiated by the following communication from R. A. Auty (*T.L.S.* 11 August 1950, p. 50): 'I find my efforts to read modern poetry made very difficult by never being certain what a poet wrote. Sometimes this may not matter very much, but in a poem like "Byzantium" every word is supposed to count. I had become used to

> A starlit or a moonlit dome disdains
> All that man is

when I came upon "distains" in Miss Gwendolyn Murphy's *The Modern Poet*. She informed me that she nearly always took the text for her anthology from the first printing, and that "distains" appeared in the original Irish edition, and that "disdains" crept into Macmillian's first printing and has persisted ever since. She thinks, and I agree, that "distains" is so much the better that it surely must be right.

'On asking Messrs Macmillan about the matter I am told that the suggestion has been made to them before. "We consulted Mrs Yeats about it. As she did not reply we took it that no alteration in the present text was necessary. We do not possess a copy of the first printing of this poem, and can only say that the author saw it several times in proof in various forms, and that he did not alter "disdains".

'This does not make me feel any more hopeful. If literature lessons, examinations and criticism are based on what a poet did not write then the whole thing becomes more of a dishonest game than they already are.'

Thereupon the reading was inconclusively debated, and other errors in Yeats's text noticed by Gwendolyn Murphy, Richard Murphy, Maurice Craig, Peter Ure, Dennis Silk, John Christopherson, Vernon Watkins, and Bonamy Dobrée on 25 August, p. 533; 1 September, p. 549; 8 September, p. 565; 15 September, p. 581; 22 September, p. 597; 3 November, p. 693, respectively.

In this general connection one may cite a recent article that attempts to analyse why critics generally prefer the corrupt reading of a metaphor to the author's true reading: see Walker Percy, 'Metaphor as Mistake', *The Sewanee Review*, LXVI (1958), 79–99.

Yeats himself had in mind when he spoke of pedants "coughing in ink" '.
I do not myself object to word-mongering so violently as Mr. Christopherson, nor do I recognise it as so palpably characteristic of my country's
critical habits as he chooses to believe; nevertheless, I am sure we should
agree that it is indeed somewhat indicative of the over-subtlety of our
times, even of our international times, to find the complexities of a misprint so eloquently preferred to the relative simplicity of the author's own
phrase.

In the matter of finding preferential literary excellences in misprints
Professor Empson is a frequent offender by reason of his careless use of
imperfect texts, complicated by a more than ordinary inaccuracy of quotation from these texts. I can only mention in passing his gaffe in *Seven
Types of Ambiguity* in which he argues most persuasively for an added
eeriness in Eliot's 'Whispers of Immortality' caused by the slight doubt
about the syntax in the tenth, eleventh, and twelfth lines (a doubt materially aided by his punctuating of the twelfth line in a way not found in
any Eliot text). In fact, on the ambiguity of the syntax he ultimately
comes to the position that 'This I take to be the point of the poem, and it
is conveyed by the contradictory ways of taking the grammar'.

Well, when a critic arrives at conclusions about the point of a poem
that are reached through the interpretation of printer's errors in the text,
we may see how readily white may be made black, and black white, and
we may be forgiven if we treat his opinions in general with some reserve.
The truth is that Empson studied Eliot, and spun his finely drawn theories
about Eliot's literary art, not from the relatively pure first or second
editions, but from either the third or the fourth edition. By bad luck a
printer's common transpositional error in the third edition exchanged the
terminal punctuation of lines 10 and 11, making the end of the sentence
come at line 10 instead of line 11, and wrongly beginning a new sentence
with the final infinitive phrase of the correct old sentence; and the mistake
was not caught up until the sixth edition. On the evidence of the periodical
text of the poem, followed by its first two book editions, and the correction
of the sixth edition, it was the faulty printer—and not the poet—who
introduced the syntactical ambiguity that Empson so greatly admired and
felt was the point of the whole poem. I should dearly like to know whether
Eliot blushed, or laughed, when he read Empson on this poem and its
non-existent point.

Nevertheless, this example illustrates a real problem; and Empson
might well have felt aggrieved at the original slip on Eliot's part when he
passed the punctuation error, for some revisions in this poem indicate
that the poet had overlooked these verses when making some changes for
the third edition.

I conclude with an anecdote that has its pertinence.

Some years ago a visiting lecturer was to speak on Eliot at the University of Virginia, and for the occasion a little complimentary programme was printed, containing the text of 'Gerontion'. Our then curator of rare books consulted the 1936 Harcourt, Brace *Collected Poems*, which was conveniently at hand, and, being a man of conscience, also looked at a few earlier editions to check the text. When he began turning up variants, he then amused himself by constructing an eclectic text. Subsequently, the late Peters Rushton showed this text to Mr Eliot at a luncheon and pointed out a few of the differences, but unfortunately not all the twenty-one variants that had developed between 1919 and 1936. Eliot checked some in confirmation, and altered two. Presumably he thereupon approved of the text in the form he really wanted it; but if so, he passed over one obvious misprint in the programme lines, and approved a text that in all its details conforms to no printed edition. In a few cases he approved an earlier reading which had been changed in a revised edition; in others, he approved the revision.[31]

The moral as I see it, here and in the Empson case, is this. If a literary critic is going to do much with fine points of text, even though he escape 'barren discussion and dissection', he would be very well advised (lacking a truly scholarly edition of his author) to make some independent investigation into the transmission and what it shows before he bases, in print, an assertion about 'the whole point of a poem' on small matters of ambiguous punctuation, syntax, or even—as with 'Soldier Aristotle' or 'Against this World'—individual words. A revised edition of a modern author (as of an earlier one) is no guarantee that errors in transmission from preceding editions will not be perpetuated in the printer's copy; and the author's approval of the real revisions in an edition cannot be made to cover every exact detail. Revision will very likely exist side by side with corruptions resulting from the new typesetting or passed on from earlier editions.

The literary critic must become sophisticated, and leave his childish faith in the absoluteness of the printed word. Before he expatiates upon subtle ambiguities and two-way syntax he had better check his facts, that is to say his text. This problem of the text of a modern author is in some respects more acute than with older writers.[32] Problems in transmission are

31 William H. Marshall, 'The Text of T. S. Eliot's "Gerontion" ', *Studies in Bibliography*, IV (1951), 213–17.

32 I am indebted to Professor Oscar Maurer in the University of Texas for the following illustrative note: 'The two editions of James Joyce's *Ulysses* commonly read in America are the Random House edition, published in 1934 soon after the decision (December 1933) by Judge Woolsey which made its publication legal in the United States, and the Modern Library edition, which was from the same plates in the same year. The Modern Library "Giant" has been reprinted several times: later printings, after Joyce's death, include a notice of copyright by Nora Joyce (1942, 1946).

no less prevalent, and revising authors like James,[33] Yeats, and Eliot may baffle the critic about the form of the text to be preferred, as with *Murder in the Cathedral.* The latest author-revised edition of a modern writer is, I should say, often less trustworthy than a scholarly edition of an older

'All the copies I have seen have a misprint on p. 76 which has the effect of defeating the author's purpose. Line 5 of the letter received by Leopold Bloom from his unknown correspondent Martha Clifford should read, "I do not like that other world" (a deliberate error on Joyce's part). The American editions correct this to, "that other word"—an alteration which makes meaningless two later passages in the novel. When Bloom replies to the letter (p. 275) he meditates, "Other world she wrote." Again on the beach after the Gerty MacDowell scene (p. 375) the phrase recurs, 'What is the meaning of that other world."

'A comparison with the Paris editions (Shakespeare and Co., 1922, etc.) will show that Joyce originally wrote "world". The significance of the slip in Bloom's later thoughts about it, and its suggestiveness in the work of a verbally sensitive writer (who was also interested in the psychological meaning of errors in speech—e.g. Bloom's "wife's admirers" for "wife's advisers", p. 307) show the importance of a valid text, especially in widely circulated editions like the Modern Library *Ulysses.*'

James F. Spoerri, 'The Odyssey Press Edition of James Joyce's *Ulysses*', *Papers of the Bibliography Society of America*, L (1956), 195–8, contributes a list of other misprints in the course of transmission.

33 'Henry James Reprints', *Times Literary Supplement*, 5 February 1949, p. 96. Notice is taken that James extensively revised his works for the definitive New York edition of 1907–9, and for some time thereafter all reprints—protected by copyright—were based on this revision. In 1941 republishing became possible for anyone willing to pay the statutory royalty fee; but it was not until after the war that Rupert Hart-Davis reprinted the earlier versions of the text and John Lehmann the revised forms. Commenting on Hart-Davis's defence of his position, the *T.L.S.* writer remarks: 'If this is arguable of the stories of the middle years, comparatively lightly revised after a comparatively short interval, then *a fortiori* to read the stories that made James's name in 1875–80—*Roderick Hudson, The American, Daisy Miller, Four Meetings, Madame de Mauves, The Portrait of a Lady*—to read these in texts that he sophisticated after thirty years is to make a mockery of "development" and to deaden the impact of a fresh mind upon a receptive generation.'

He then points out that in *The Great Tradition*, F. R. Leavis 'suggests that there is danger in centring critical attention upon James's development, the danger of overlooking "the striking measure of achievement that marks even the opening phase of his career"—that marks, for example, James's "first attempt at a novel, *Roderick Hudson* (1874)"'. Dr. Leavis sees the strong influence of Dickens on *Roderick Hudson*, and quotes as an example the passage describing the visit of Mr Leavenworth to Hudson's studio in Rome. The only difficulty is that the text of the quoted passage supposedly illustrating James's manner in 1874 comes from the greatly revised edition of 1907; and when the corresponding text from the first book edition in 1876 is placed beside it, one can see that Dickens's influence came in the 1907 revision and was not present, as Leavis believed, in the original writing. The *T.L.S.* writer was justified, therefore, in his wintry summation: 'When after having quoted this [the 1907 text of *Roderick Hudson*], Mr Leavis "jumps forward a dozen years" to seek the influence of Dickens in *The Bostonians* (1886), he is really jumping backward a score. So much for the danger of paying too much attention to development'—and, one may add, too little attention to text.

author. Paradoxically, a critic quoting from an uncomplicated Shake-spearean text is more likely to be closer to his author's full intentions, so far as these can be ascertained, than he is in quoting Yeats—unless he is very careful indeed about his editions.

In the one case, whether he appreciates it or not, he can rely on a certain amount of enlightened textual criticism to have provided him with a trustworthy text. For most modern authors, however, he is—unfortunately —on his own; and the eclipse in which he often wanders may find a suit-able commentary in the lines that Empson darkened instead of illuminated by finding eeriness and ambiguity in their syntax:

> Donne, I suppose, was such another
> Who found no substitute for sense
> To seize and clutch and penetrate.

The kind of *sense* that Mr Eliot is imputing here to John Donne differs from the kind I have been advocating in this lecture, however, for I should like to prefix to my kind the simple adjective—*common.*

The Folio Othello: Compositor E

1. Printer's Copy: Problems in the Transmission of Texts

AMONG the various serious problems of Shakespearian texts, none is
more baffling than the group of plays printed in a version altered in
the Folio from the form in which they had appeared in quarto. These
plays divide into two main categories. In the first come those like *The
Merry Wives of Windsor*, *Henry V*, and *King Lear* that were first pub-
lishd in what are technically known as 'bad quartos'. These texts seem to
have no transcriptional links with any Shakespeare autograph manuscripts;
instead, they appear to be the product of memorial reconstruction, the
exact (and probably variable) nature of which is still in some doubt.
Without much question such plays in their bad-quarto versions represent
the maimed and deformed texts mentioned in the Preface to the Folio, and
it was clearly of considerable importance to the Folio 'editors' that these
texts should be offered in an authoritative corrected version.

In the second group come *Troilus and Cressida*, *2 Henry IV*, *Othello*,
and *Hamlet* that had been issued in quartos printed from manuscripts that
appear to have had a transcriptional link with the Shakespeare autograph,
or to have been an autograph itself of some stage of the text. To this extent
such quartos are authoritative for their texts. But it must have seemed to
the Folio editors that the company owned manuscripts of a superior version. Copyright troubles may just possibly have enforced the use of a
different text for *Troilus and Cressida* as Sir Walter Greg suggested, although the matter is not demonstrable;[1] but for the rest there is no hint of
external difficulty. It is possible that a conscientious literary purpose was
behind the Folio printing of these texts revised by comparison with manu-

---

* The sixth James R. Lyell Lecture in Bibliography, delivered at Oxford University
in Trinity Term, 1959; printed in *Bibliography and Textual Criticism* (1964), pp.
158–201 as "The Copy for the Folio *Othello*"; reprinted with permission of the Clarendon Press.

1 *The Shakespeare Folio* (1955), pp. 445–9 and references. Greg's arguments are
very persuasive, but the need to assign different reasons for *Troilus* from those obtaining for *Othello*, *Hamlet*, and *2 Henry IV*, for instance, may give one pause. It may be,
after all, that the delay in printing *Troilus* and coming to an agreement about its copyright merely gave the opportunity for an alteration of the printer's copy that had not
originally been contemplated.

scripts different in their tradition from those that had served as copy for the quartos.[2]

For each play the central critical problem is to reach some conclusions about the nature of the manuscript behind the Folio text and of its relation to the manuscript from which the quarto had been printed. Strict bibliographical method does not touch upon this problem except as the establishment of the exact physical forms in print, and the recovery of what can be learned about the physical characteristics of the printer's copy, may provide some evidence to assist or to limit critical conjecture.[3] Nevertheless, although the literary relationship of the quarto and Folio texts is essentially a critical problem, the question of the physical relationship of the two prints lies within the province of bibliography. Although a corrected text from a bad quarto like *The Merry Wives of Windsor* appears to have been printed in the Folio directly from a manuscript, the printer's copy for other plays, like *King Lear* from a 'bad' quarto and *Troilus and Cressida* from a 'good' quarto, has been established as a quarto interlined or annotated marginally, and doubtless by inserted slips, with altered readings drawn from comparison of the print against some manuscript.

The general bibliographical problem is, first, to demonstrate whether or not the Folio text derived from an annotated quarto; and, second (if such a transmission can be established and if there is more than one prior quarto) to decide which quarto edition was employed and whether it was the copy throughout, or whether leaves from some other quarto might have been used to supplement the basic edition employed for annotation.

The correction of a printed edition to bring it into general conformity

2 This statement implies that the theatrical company, or the Folio editors, supplied the printer with the 'corrected' copy. But we have no right to assume such a process, at least as the norm. It may be that the editors sent a manuscript to the printer, who himself had the quarto brought into general conformity with the manuscript in order to provide his compositors with printed copy, as is tempting to conjecture happened with certain bad-quarto texts. However, in favour of the assumption that some of the annotated quartos of this second good group originated in the playhouse is this: in at least two of these texts the Folio version seems to be more theatrical in its form than the Quarto and may represent the text of the prompt-book, which the company would be unwilling to send to the printer. On the whole, a critic can speculate more reasonably with good texts than with bad that the company could have provided the annotated printed copy for Jaggard.

3 To take an extreme case, unless the bibliographer could provide evidence that they all could not be compositorial, the source of the prissy expansions of the colloquialisms made in the Folio 2 *Henry IV* text might remain in doubt. But when, from our knowledge of the typesetters involved, we can offer this evidence, the critic is free to choose between the hypothesis (*a*) that they were present in the manuscript copy used by the annotator, or (*b*) that they were made on the initiative of the annotator. If the copy for the Folio were assumed to be a manuscript and not an annotated quarto, for 'annotator' merely substitute 'scribe'.

with a manuscript was a recognized Elizabethan method of providing a printer with copy, as may be seen in the revised second quarto of Beaumont and Fletcher's *Philaster* and *Maid's Tragedy*, each set from an exemplar of the first quarto corrected by reference to a superior manuscript. That even extraordinarily heavy revision could be handled in this manner is illustrated by Ben Jonson's own use of the quarto of *Every Man in his Humour* in preparing the much-altered Folio version. Quite naturally, the question has arisen whether the annotation of a printed quarto was a device by the theatrical company to keep an irreplaceable manuscript from the dangers of the printer's shop. If a company had sold a revised text to a stationer, it has been argued, the theatrical owners might find that the correction of an already existing printed exemplar by comparison with their manuscript was a quicker and cheaper way of providing copy for the printer than the commissioning of a whole new scribal transcript, such as—on the evidence—was made by Ralph Crane for *The Tempest, The Two Gentlemen of Verona, The Merry Wives of Windsor, Measure for Measure,* and *The Winter's Tale.*

On the other hand, at least some of the manuscripts used for the comparison do not show any clear signs that they were prompt-books. If, then, a non-theatrical manuscript such as an author's 'foul papers', or some approximation of them, were used for the collation of the print, two oddities appear that cast doubt on the preparation of the printer's copy in the theatre. It is unusual to find that a theatrical scribe had not collated from a prompt-book, which would be the most legible copy and the one that the company would regard as having the greatest authority.[4] Also, if another manuscript were in the company's possession, it is odd that this was not sent to the printer to serve as his copy, and be done with it. Any objection would seem unrealistic that the company would be concerned to provide the printer with the most desirable kind of copy from the printer's own point of view, and that they would go to the trouble and expense of puzzling over foul papers, say, to make up an annotated quarto for the sole purpose of saving the printer the labour of setting from a difficult manuscript.[5] These considerations have led various critics to believe that at least some annotated quartos were made up in the printer's own shop from the manuscript the company had furnished him as copy. In other words, the printer himself felt that it was easier and more eco-

---

4 We must not confuse modern textual sensibility with Elizabethan. There is every indication that a theatrical company regarded its prompt-copies as the last word in authority, and indeed—for Elizabethan theatrical purposes—they were, though not for modern textual criticism.

5 We may recall such manifestly foul manuscripts as that behind Q2 *Hamlet* given to the printer instead of clean scribal transcripts.

nomical to send even heavily corrected printed copy to his compositors than to have them set direct from manuscript.

The complexion of the case is quite altered if this theory is right, and it would seem that in some part it certainly is right. The Folio *Richard III*, and even Q2 *Romeo and Juliet*, may be too conjectural to serve as an example, but a certain illustration is Roberts's consultation (though not annotation) of printed Q1 to assist in the typesetting of Act I of Q2 Hamlet. Inevitably, so long as the annotation was supposed to have been made in the theatre, critics could hypothesize some contamination from the theatrical agent's memory of the play (especially if he were the book-keeper) to explain why sometimes manifestly inferior readings appear to have been transferred from a generally superior manuscript. But if the alteration were done in the printer's shop, this avenue of critical escape is closed, and editor (and critic) must presumably deal with a much more naïve transcript in the manuscript portions of the text. It may be that in some circumstances the theatre would make up such a revised quarto from its prompt-book, but that in others the printer would independently take advantage of an earlier edition to ease his labours when the theatre had sent him its spare manuscript.[6] By and large the distinction is a critical problem not susceptible of bibliographical solution even though it is of interest to the textual bibliographer concerned to estimate what corruption in the print came direct from copy and what from the compositor.

However, it is the bibliographer's proper function to confine himself to the relationship that can be established, or conjectured to exist, between physical documents. Thus the bibliographer can claim to settle the question whether an annotated quarto or a manuscript was the printer's

6 For the usefulness of printed copy in connexion with setting from manuscript, see 'The Textual Relation of Q2 to Q1 *Hamlet*', *Studies in Bibliography*, viii (1956), 39–66. In some respects Roberts's consultation of Q1 to assist in deciphering the text of a difficult manuscript suggests what should be the modern critical point of view about the effect on the text of the conflation in the printer's shop of two textual sources. That is, so long as one could believe in the annotation of Q1 to serve as printer's copy for Act I of Q2, one could theorize that the annotation was performed in the theatre by an agent of the company. Such an origin could open the door to further theorizing about the effect on the text of a comparison made by someone familiar with the play and thus tempted at times to rely on his own memory, instead of the manuscript, to correct the print. But if the annotation were confined to the printer's shop (or if consultation on the order of Roberts's can be established), then the case is altered. The comparison may not be exact but it will be naïve, and there will be small chance that the scribe will write in what he thinks should be the correct text instead of what he thinks he sees in the manuscript. Variation will be inadvertent, therefore, and sophistication largely nonexistent. The critical treatment of the text will be correspondingly affected. [On the other hand, there is always the horrid example of the sophisticating scribe of the B-Text *Dr. Faustus*, but this appears to represent a very special case.]

copy; and if a corrected print of some earlier edition, whether this printer's copy was homogeneous or consisted—for convenience—of leaves from more than one exemplar, perhaps by chance of two editions.[7]

In determining the genetic relationship of texts, criticism relies almost exclusively on the study of variant substantive readings according to the principle that identity of reading implies identity of origin. Under most conditions found in a series of reprints[8] (I am speaking now only of printed books), the normal progress of corruption[9] in successive type-settings offers quite enough evidence from which to determine the derivation and order, even in moderately complex circumstances of mixed copy.[10]

On the contrary, when some correcting agent interferes with the text— like the collator charged with bringing a print into conformity with a manuscript of different textual tradition—substantive readings may prove to be unsatisfactory evidence. The normal reprint transmission of variants is disrupted by the annotator's correction of error and by the alteration or revision of seemingly satisfactory readings. This smoothing-out of the evidence on which textual criticism normally operates may occur in two different circumstances, each with its separate problems.

In the first, the original text has been reprinted at least once before the revision. In such a situation, if no interference had appeared with the normal course of reprint transmission, one's decision about the copy-text would rely on such evidence as whether the later editions had copied some of the unique variants of an earlier printing. The principle is firm that when error can be traced to some link in the process of transmission, and the error is repeated in a subsequent edition, this later text must derive (at least ultimately) from the intermediate edition.

---

7 I do not mean that two different copies of the same edition could ordinarily be distinguished. The reference is to leaves from two different editions such as Dr. Cairn-cross has guessed made up the copy for the Folio *King Lear*.

8 The major condition in which simple readings are likely to fail as demonstrable evidence comes if one must distinguish the original from an immediately derived reprint when external evidence about their chronological order is wanting or is ambiguous. The falsely dated Pavier Quartos tripped up the Old Cambridge editors. A modern example is the evidence for the true first edition of Dryden's *Wild Gallant*.

9 Correction is less frequently of use, for any edition can usually make the same correction independently, and thus the appearance of the identical correction is not necessarily proof of a genetic relationship. On the other hand, miscorrection may be fruitful evidence of relationship, especially if the basic miscorrection is further altered and rationalized in the text under consideration.

10 Examples are Sir Walter Greg's demonstration that Q5 of *Richard III* was set from a mixture of Q3 and Q4 leaves, *The Library*, 4th ser., xvii (1936–7), 88–97; and James Steck's that Q8 (1694) of Dryden's *Indian Emperour* derives from a mixture of Q6 and Q7 according to the two compositors. *Studies in Bibliography*, ii (1949–50), 139–152.

Thus if a variant appears first in Edition B and is repeated in Edition C, the inference follows that C derives immediately from B and not from A. One proviso is that the variant is not of the sort that could be supposed to arise independently in both B and C, each using A as its copy. Almost any individual reading is susceptible of such an explanation, and usually there is no way of truly demonstrating the contrary.[11] Indeed, so variable are some forms in any text that a certain number of fortuitous independent agreements are to be expected. Whether C follows A but not B in such a reading as *these* versus *those*, in *gentleman* versus *gentlemen*, in *speaks* versus *speaketh*, is of no account as evidence in any individual case. Some words are constantly shifting back and forth in reprints; other changes of no significance may result from the similarity of compositors' linguistic habits. Obviously if C is dated in 1659, B in 1641, and A in 1599, many forms of C would agree with those of B even if A were indubitably its source.[12] Sometimes quite astonishing random hits may be scored, as in the independent concurrence of the Folio *Richard III* with Q1–2 in the error *hop'st* instead of Q3–6 corrected *holp'st* (IV. iv. 45), or the independent agreement of F and the later Q7 at I. i. 168 in *smoothing word* for Q1–6 *soothing word*.[13]

What gives one caution in assessing as positive evidence any such individual shared aberrance is the thought that whatever forces operated on one compositor to produce the variant might on occasion also affect another compositor in a similar manner. The independent memorial contamination of one phrase by another may be explained readily, and experience with reprints shows how easily some words like *the* and *thy* exchange with considerable frequency. That the immediate cause of the shared error cannot always be determined indicates only that the stimuli are often obscure that produced similar reactions in the operation of two men's minds.

Another proviso is that the critic should not take seriously an agreement of any two editions in the correction of error when independence of action may easily be conjectured. Thus concurrence of F and Q3 *Richard III* in *balme* instead of in Q5–6 *blame* (I. ii. 13) can scarcely be used as

11 Once in a while bibliographical evidence can encourage or discourage a particular view, as in the variant *tidings-news* in *Richard III* (see *Bibliography and Textual Criticism* (1964), pp. 152–154).

12 As another example, the general concurrence of F with the accidentals of Q2 *King Lear* as against Q1 does not necessarily demonstrate Folio derivation from Q2. Instead, we must consider that Compositor B set Q2 and was reprinting himself in part of the Folio text. When he was not typesetting, the apprentice Compositor E was operating, and his habits were in many respects similar to those of B.

13 See also such common errors as F and the later Q2 *Othello* in *over* for *overt* at I. iii. 107; F and Q8 *Richard III* in *he* for *to* at I. i. 100; Q4 and F *Romeo and Juliet* in *else in* for *else is* at II. vi. 23.

evidence, since *balme* is manifestly correct. F might have followed Q3 copy in *balme*, but it might as readily have corrected *blame* if Q6 had been the source.[14]

In such circumstances a textual critic learns to weigh the significance of his evidence. One agreement in simple error may mean nothing, but fifty agreements (excluding modernizations) ought to be decisive, providing, of course, there are not thirty or forty on the other side. With selected though unslanted evidence, a point should be reached at which our common-sense view of probability rebels at being asked to accept any more coincidence as the result of mere chance. How much resistance a critic can put up before capitulating is very much an individual matter. Sir Walter Greg accepted Mr. Walton's case for the Q3 copy of F *Richard III* as self-evident; but Professor Alexander differed: 'This simplification [he writes] depends, however, on a notion of what Mr. Walton calls "indifferent variants" that runs counter to the principle that identity of reading implies identity of origin. The only exceptions to the principle must be accidental coincidences, and Mr. Walton asks us to accept more readings in Q6 as the "more or less unwitting discovery of the right reading" by the compositor of that reprint than our sense of probability can readily admit.'[15]

In most cases of straight reprints, fortunately, the evidence is overwhelming, on the positive side, since the divergences of some intermediate edition from its source are almost certain to be followed, in the main, by its successors. The case is altered when (in the second category) the late edition under examination derives from the original edition or some other early print that is not an immediate predecessor. Here the force of the evidence turns from the positive to the negative. The agreement of the edition with any individual positive divergence is no longer in question except as an accidental factor to be sifted out.[16] Instead, the failure of the

---

14 That Q6 followed Q5 and failed to correct the error *blame* is no argument that F would have reproduced the reading if Q6 had been the copy. (It is a special case that in *Richard III* the annotator might also have corrected the error if Q6 had been the copy.)

15 *Review of English Studies,* N.S., ix (1958), 69–70.

16 That is, if B is set from A, C from B, and D from C, there are only three basic situations:

	A	B	C	D
(1)	is	was	was	was
(2)	is	was	is	is
(3)	is	is	was	was

In the first, whether D was set from B or from C is not to be determined. In the second, C (and therefore D) has reverted to the original reading, probably on the basis of sense; but whether D was set from A or from C is in question, or indeed whether D was set

late edition to follow in general the unique divergences of any one of its ancestors is taken as grounds for ruling out such an ancestral edition as copy. Thus chiefly on negative evidence that variants are *not* repeated as one would anticipate, the critic can reduce the competitors to two editions only, and then revert to positive evidence to decide between these two final alternatives.[17]

When only two touching editions are in question, it is probably true that in some situations the derivation of the second from the first instead of from a manuscript may be almost impossible to demonstrate from verbal readings alone. The only proof, indeed, rests in positive evidence for the transmission of error from one to the other. Here a distinction must be made, for literary error may go back to a common source and may therefore have nothing to do with any case for the direct derivation of one print from the other.[18] For example, *pious bonds* shared at I. iii. 130 by

---

from B but its compositor independently made the same corrections as did the C compositor. Only in the third series is it clear that the two touching editions are related.

If both C and D were independently set from B, we should have:

	A	B	C	D
(1)	is	was	was	was
(2)	is	is	was	is
(3)	is	was	were	was

Here no one can know in the first whether D was set from B or from C. In the second, D might be set from A or from B. Only in the uncommon situation represented by the third can one show that D derived from B. The difference between the rareness of no. 3 in this series when the related editions are not touching, and the commonness of no. 3 in the first series when the editions are touching, is the indication of the ease with which positive evidence can be found, or the considerable difficulty, according to the conditions. In the latter circumstance, most of the evidence must be negative and cumulative.

17 Once intermediate editions are eliminated by negative evidence, the two remaining possibilities can be treated as if they were a touching series. What can correspond to C (although it may be H) must derive from A (which might be D) or from B (which might be F). If C derives from B, then the only significant series will be:

A	B	C
is	was	was
(is	was	were ?)

H(C) will be set from F(B), without regard for the fact that E and G could also read *was*, provided that negative evidence has eliminated E and G. If C derives from A, the only significant series will be:

A	B	C
is	was	is
(is	was	be ?)

H(C) will be set from D(A), even though E, G read *is*.

18 As in the common error drawn from the prompt-book by unrelated Q1 and F *Merry Wives of Windsor* in 'minutes rest' for 'minim's rest' (or minim-rest)—although the original has been defended.

Q2 and F *Hamlet* has been variously argued as the correct reading, as evidence that F was set from the Q2 error, and as a common error independently deriving from an ambiguously written original. It follows that the more mechanical the error and the less likely to have a literary origin, the more critics are inclined to give it superior weight. Thus Sir Walter Greg brilliantly demonstrated the dependence of F *King Lear* on Q's different states of press-variants, and press-variants alone would have been sufficient to indicate the correct order of the two 1669 editions of Dryden's *Wild Gallant*. The strongest evidence that some 160 lines begining Act III of *Richard III* are unquestionably printed in F from Q3 is the appearance in F of the mechanical repetition unique to Q3 of *as as* in the line at III. i. 123:

> I would that I might thanke you as as you call me.

No opportunity can exist in a case like this to argue for common origin of error in some other document instead of immediate derivation; nor could one conjecture that Q3 and F independently fell at this precise spot into the identical dittography, nor that the repetition was the right reading that Q3 and F had independently stumbled on—all these being the excuses ordinarily avouched for such identity of readings.

This reading also illustrates another method that may be used by textual critics to show derivation. This is the alteration of a reading that in a case of divergence could reasonably have come only from one and not from the other exemplar. In the illustration above, the Folio's Compositor A obviously was troubled by the repetition, but he preferred to retain it, though adding commas, rather than to take a chance on correction by dropping a superfluous *as*; and so the Folio reads:

> I would that I might thanke you as, as, you call me.

That the simple mechanical stutter of Q3 is being rationalized is an inevitable conclusion. One would scarcely like to argue that the F compositor independently made the same dittographical error as the Q3 workman, and then in a lost stage of proof-correction the proof-reader inserted the commas as somehow adding to the sense.[19]

Correspondingly, at III. v. 66 Q6 misprinted Q1-5 *cause* as *ease*, a reading that makes nonsense. The compositor of Q7 thought that he recognized the common foul-case confusion of *c* and *e*, and quite naturally he 'corrected' *ease* to *case*, thus establishing that Q7 was set from Q6. None the

---

19 Or, that the proof-reader marked a comma to be added after *you*, and an *as* to be excised, and Compositor A misunderstood him and added commas after each *as*.

less, how difficult it is to deal even with such mechanical errors when they have some possible literary basis (as *as as* did not) may be shown by Mr. Walton's surely desperate argument that the Folio reading *case* did not originate in a similar independent rationalization of Q6 *ease* but instead was the F compositor's alternative and acceptable doublet form of the *cause* found in his Q3 copy.

When meaning is concerned, an argument can often be evolved that would defend either side. The more mechanical the evidence, or the more clearly the final reading must have developed from one of the two variants but most improbably from the other,[20] the less subject to exception is the evidence. Yet even at its most mechanical, some very odd fortuitous hits may occur to warn a critic against over-rash assumptions on too narrowly based evidence. For instance, the misprint *witchraft* for *witchcraft*, though readily explicable, is so far from inevitable that one might venture very long odds indeed against its coincidence in the same spot in two unrelated reprints; yet it is shared quite independently by Q4 and F2 *Hamlet* at I. V. 43, and so is *misheathed* independently by Q5 and F *Romeo and Juliet* at V. iii. 204, in error for *missheath'd*.

The problem of demonstrating whether a Folio Shakespeare text was set from a manuscript or from an annotated quarto when verbal readings constitute the only evidence is immensely complicated by the smoothing-out results of the annotation. When, as in *Othello*, only one quarto was printed before the Folio, or when, as in *Hamlet*, the first 'good' edition of Q2 and not a later one must have been the copy if a revised print were used, the errors in the printed copy are fewer, and the transfer of any manifest verbal error from Quarto to Folio is materially decreased through the correction of faulty printed readings by the collation with the manuscript. Hence only from scribal carelessness could any substantive error originated in the printing of the Quarto be carried over to the Folio to prove that the Q print must have been the basic copy. (Moreover, the manifest verbal errors of the Q compositor that would most clearly fall in this category are the very ones apt to call themselves most prominently to the collator's attention.) Those that elude his vigilance and are inadvertently passed are likely to be plausible enough to be argued for as no errors at all,[21] or else (since they are often close in their respec-

---

20 As in the *cause-ease-case* sequence for F as against *cause-cause-case*. This latter is one of the readings that Professor Alexander believes violate our sense of probability when an argument is derived that Q3 was nevertheless the copy throughout. See above, footnote 15.

21 The determination of error is certainly a serious problem, and there is little doubt that a number of wrong readings could slip by the annotator's attention, as we know from *Richard III* when F reproduces a variant that exists in Q2–6 but not in Q1. How-

tive forms) [22] as error independently derived from a common original.

Against this line of defence there is no crushing rebuttal except the sheer weight of the quantitative evidence. But in the nature of the case, the quantity of transmitted verbal error about which there can be little difference of opinion has always been materially reduced by the normal operations of the annotator. In fact, in modern times every Shakespeare Folio text for which critics have suggested annotated-quarto copy has been in dispute whenever the first edition of a 'good' quarto is the only one that could have been corrected. *Troilus and Cressida, Othello, Hamlet*, and *2 Henry IV* are texts in which substantive readings alone have failed to settle the question authoritatively.

When in such examples as *Troilus and Cressida* the decision in favour of printed copy has received universal assent, the crucial evidence came not from the verbal readings but from the forms of the accidentals— specifically, in *Troilus and Cressida*, the variable lengths of speech-prefixes and the variable practice of setting names in italic or in roman, wherein the Folio repeated the Quarto's irregularities so faithfully as to go far beyond any possible suggestion of mere chance or of independent derivation from a common source. [23] These were details that the particular annotator of the copy for the Folio did not bother with, and fortunately the Folio compositors were on strange ground with classical names and so followed copy more conservatively than they did when reprinting English history plays, in which their fixed habits almost entirely removed such evidence as abounds in *Troilus and Cressida*.

Mechanical details from the printing process settled the problem of *Troilus and Cressida*. In a similar manner, mechanical details had long before settled that the Folio text of *King Lear* derived from printed copy. Here the transmission of forms that were press-variants served to isolate in quite mechanical fashion certain readings in the Folio that demonstrably originated with the compositor or the proof-reader of the First

---

ever, when the only check is critical suspicion, demonstration that the passed-on reading is corrupt is very difficult. For instance, were it not for the Q1 reading *vast*, it is likely that *dead wast and middle of the night* shared by Q2 and F *Hamlet* (I. ii. 198) would never have been questioned.

22 Like *pith* (Q2) or *pitch* (F) *of merit* in *Hamlet*, I. iii. 22. It is a critical axiom that closeness of form like this marks error in one element, not revision.

23 In this illustration one need not depend upon the mere quantity of evidence. These shared features of Q and F *Troilus and Cressida* are so mechanical in the nature of their variation (i.e., so dependent upon the printing process for their origin) as to make any argument absurd that independent derivation from a manuscript could have created them in an identical manner. [See Philip Williams, 'Shakespeare's *Troilus and Cressida*: The Relationship of Quarto and Folio', *Studies in Bibliography*, III (1950–51), 131–143.]

Quarto and could not have derived in the Folio from manuscript copy.[24]

On the evidence, if the remaining problems in this category are to be solved in a manner permitting general acceptance, the mechanical or bibliographical method that succeeded in *Troilus and Cressida* and *King Lear* is the only hope, for the normal textual-critical reliance on substantive readings has manifestly failed under the abnormal conditions fostered by annotated copy. At present, *Hamlet* and *2 Henry IV* appear to be very seriously snarled in controversy, whereas the proponents of manuscript copy for F *Othello* are silent under Sir Walter Greg's approval of Dr. Walker's annotated-quarto hypothesis. Yet Dr. Walker's case (though correct) is not nearly so copious or rigorous in its evidence as to make for an acceptable demonstration, and the application of another range of mechanical evidence is needed to supplement its narrow base.

11. *The Example of* Richard III

The peculiar problem of these plays is the identification of features of the Folio text reproducing features in the Quarto that must have resulted from the printing process. If the annotator slipped and failed to alter a corrupt Quarto reading, no way exists for us to know that this reading in the Folio (if indeed recognizable as corrupt) was produced in the Quarto by the printing process when the situation is one in which the shared reading can be defended on literary grounds or else assigned as error in a common source.

On the other hand, when as in *Richard III* the Folio printer's copy must have been some quarto later than the first edition, enough unauthoritative variants that crept into the text in its transmission did in fact escape the annotator so that we may identify at least some of the characteristics deriving from the printing process that were transmitted. As a consequence, since 1885 there has been no doubt that the Folio text as a whole was based on a corrected quarto, and the only modern controversy has concerned the identification of this quarto either as Q3 of 1602, which contributed two extensive unannotated passages in Acts III and V, or as Q6 of 1622, or perhaps as both according to some exigency of annotation if a scissors-and-paste job were done.

Again it may be said that substantive readings have failed to settle the complex matter, for the heavy blanket of correction has destroyed in large measure the readings from which exact conclusions may be drawn. By the process of elimination from negative evidence one can de-

24 W. W. Greg, *The Variants in the First Quarto of* 'King Lear' (1940).

cide with tolerable certainty that (among the extant editions) the basic
quarto must have been Q3 or Q6; but the evidence of the readings has
been thought to be so conflicting between the two as to lead only to a
sterile controversy that has tended to bring textual discussion as a whole
into some disrepute. In 1885 P. A. Daniel found 8 readings peculiar to
Q6 and the Folio, to which he added 3 instances (only 2 of which were
legitimate) of conjectural emendation in the Folio of errors peculiar to
Q6. In 1955 J. K. Walton put forward Q3 as the sole candidate. Analysis
of his arguments shows that he can offer only 2 true cases of verbal readings uniquely shared by Q3 and the Folio,[25] although he conceals this disheartening shortage by sandwiching them in a longer list of 22 'readings
peculiar to Q3 and F—peculiar to Q3 and F, that is, when we ignore
quartos coming after Q3'. Since all but these two are shared by Q6 as
well, the 20 superfluous readings common to Q3 and Q6 scarcely serve
as evidence to govern a decision between the two quartos.

One can place 2 readings pointing to Q3 against 11 or 12 favouring
Q6. This is precious little evidence on which to decide the case, and one's
confidence is not increased by the minor nature of some of the shared Q6
and F verbals. Two concern the use of a natural singular instead of an
equally natural plural, a variation the compositors frequently fell into
from memorial error. Common idiom or the possibility of independent
memorial contamination from the context cast some doubt on a few others,
so that if one disregards the cumulative weight of insignificant agreements,
no more than three or four readings remain common to Q6 and F that on
any individual basis might perhaps offer valid evidence.

That in truth this cumulative evidence can be ignored is Mr. Walton's
proposition. Independent analysis confirms in some part the principle behind his position (although not necessarily his application). Actually,
it is only the unique readings shared by the Folio with one or other quarto
that can have any textual significance. This uniqueness need not be narrowly interpreted, however, in any absolute sense: once all quartos except
Q3 and Q6 have been eliminated, any reading is unique for the purposes
of decision between Q3 and Q6 (no matter how shared with other quartos) so long as it is not shared by the two surviving competitors. Yet despite the most liberal interpretation placed on the question of uniqueness,
it is inevitable that any terminal edition is likely to agree uniquely with
its chronological predecessors more often than with an earlier edition,

25 These are Q3–4, F agreement in *no manner person* versus Q1–2, 5–6 *manner of
person* (III. v. 108), and Q3, F *I bury* [Q3 *burie*] versus Q1–2 *I buried* and Q4–6 *Ile
burie*. A third concurrence is not noted: this is Q3, F *it is* versus Q1–2, 4–6 *is it* (IV. ii.
82). However, since *it is* appears to be correct, one could argue for Q6 copy *is it* altered
by the annotator to *it is*, and the effect of the Q3, F concurrence vanishes.

even though the earlier edition is the copy and the immediate predecessor is not.[26]

Any reading that is not so obviously wrong or eccentric or in need of modernization as to be independently corrected will in normal course be passed on from the edition in which it originates to all descendants in the same line.[27] The Third Quarto of *Richard III* has about 42 substantive readings diverging from Q1–2 that are accepted by the Folio. However, 39 of these 42 were passed on through Q4–5 to Q6 as well. Thus the only verbal readings that can be used as evidence in favour of Q3 are Q3 variants from Q1–2 that in turn were varied further by Q6* but appear in the Folio in their Q3 form. These conditions are so stringent as to remove almost all possibility that agreement of substantive readings alone could ever prove that Q3 served as copy for the Folio.

Correspondingly, evidence that is not necessarily significant, although it may seem so, will usually accumulate in the chronological predecessor of a terminal edition even though one does not derive from the other. In this text 1 reading that originated in Q4 and 2 in Q5 may be added to the 12 originating in Q6 to make a total of 15 that are uniquely shared by Q6 and the Folio against Q3. Mr. Walton has very properly pointed out the odds that these are fortuitous. For example, if we make a comparison we find that 17 unique readings are shared by the 1623 Folio with Q7 of 1629, and 9 different unique readings with Q8 of 1634, both quartos that could not possibly have served as copy for F. Moreover, there is no credible evidence that F in any way influenced these two quartos. Not all of these readings are of equal strength, but there are enough that are pertinent to give one pause. Mr. Walton takes these statistics as automatically disproving the significance of the set of 12 (actually 15) that Q6 shares uniquely with F. Of course, they do nothing of the kind, for the Q6 readings could still be legitimate evidence; and Mr. Walton gives us no idea of what we should expect in the way of agreement if Q6 had indeed been the copy.

However, the evidence from Q7 and Q8 does have its value in enforcing caution before the Q6 list is accepted as valid. With only a few exceptions these readings from Q6 may be fortuitous, or they may be significant. The point is, we do not know. Hence the dispute about *Richard III* shows the

26 Of course, the 'predecessor' must derive genetically from the 'early edition' in question so that it shares readings with this early edition.

27 That is, the fortuitous agreement in unique readings between a terminal edition and its immediate chronological predecessor (though not its copy) will ordinarily outnumber the unique agreements with an early edition that was the copy, provided the conditions stated above in footnote 26 are met.

* Variation in Q4–6 or in Q5–6 would be equally acceptable in this case.

inadequacy of conventional methods to solve the problem of Folio copy-text when an annotated quarto is a possibility. Because in *Richard III* the transmission of the text through a series of prints allows identifiable corruption to be transmitted to the Folio, the difficulty is not present (as it is with *Hamlet* and *2 Henry IV*) in deciding whether the F copy was a manuscript or annotated-quarto printed copy. But the almost insuperable problem remains of determining which of the two ultimate quarto candidates was the actual printer's copy. The unique readings originating in any intermediate quarto like Q3 are almost all passed on to its successors so that the odds are almost prohibitive against more than one or two remaining unique between it and the Folio to act as evidence.

Correspondingly, the usual forces of correction and corruption will inevitably produce a group of shared readings between any terminal edition and the one chronologically just before it, as may be seen in the coincidences between *Richard III* F and Q7. Examples of this process may make us wary of accepting readings as significant evidence when they are not so incontrovertible in their nature or so extraordinary in their profusion as to enforce belief. Most of the readings shared in *Richard III* by the Folio and Q6 do not qualify under these rigorous requirements, although several are not easy to explain away. Nor, it may be said, do the readings of Q3 qualify either.

Yet it is difficult to know how a critic is to judge what is an acceptable quantity or quality of evidence. Something will depend upon his estimate of the annotator's care. For instance, if Q3 were the copy for F *Richard III*, the corrector discarded 97 of its original divergences from Q2 and returned these to the Q1 readings, which were presumably those of the manuscript. If Q6 had been the copy, the corrector would have returned 110 of its original divergences to the Q1 forms. These figures are so close as to be useless. If we properly add to the 97 Q3 variants the 46 Q2 divergences from Q1 accepted by Q3 but returned by F to the Q1 forms, we have a total of 143 readings in which Q3 differed from Q1, and F agreed with Q1. But it seems meaningless to discover that by the time the accumulated textual corruption was passed on to Q6, the corrector would have rejected a total of 287 Q6 readings in favour of the Q1 verbals. Whether more of this large number should have slipped through into the Folio in their Q6 form than the noticed 15 is a matter of opinion that is not demonstrable one way or the other.

Mr. Walton takes it as significant that some 22 (actually about 42) readings that in Q3 differed from Q1 (though shared by Q6) were accepted by the Folio, versus only 12 (actually 15) originating in Q6. But by this line of argument Q2 would qualify for serious consideration, since of its 74 divergences from Q1 the Folio corrector would have passed 28 while rejecting 46 if it had been the copy. That the annotator—if Q6 had been the copy—would have rejected 110 of the variants originating in Q6 while accepting only 15 seems at first sight disproportionate, especially in view of the small number of divergences in Q4 and Q5 that proved acceptable. Nevertheless, it would seem that in this text the big push to 'correctness', or normality, was made in Q2 and Q3, and after this stage the additional variants, especially those in Q6, were evident corruptions of a nature to call themselves most obviously to the annotator's attention.

III. *Compositorial Spellings as Bibliographical Evidence*

Whatever line of inquiry we take, we are forced back to the original position that in either of the two categories of annotated quartos the traditional evidence of substantive readings has not solved, and often cannot solve, the special problems involved in the positive identification of quarto copy with enough force to receive general acceptance. And if this is so, the verbal readings are even more useless to settle difficult questions that have been raised whether pages from one or from more than one edition were brought together to form the printer's copy.

Under these circumstances it is proper to inquire whether bibliographical methods cannot be applied to the general problem in the hope of securing evidence that will be supplementary and perhaps even decisive. The two major problems that have been solved by the demonstration of printed copy—*King Lear* and *Troilus and Cressida*—each succumbed to different kinds of bibliographical evidence; in the one instance the forms of press-corrections, and in the other the forms of speech-prefixes and the variable use of italic in the setting of names. Neither of these methods is very useful in the other plays, and hence—pending the discovery of some other technique—it would seem that the remaining problems must be attacked by a study of the transmission of the accidental readings, that is, the details of spelling, capitalization, punctuation, and word division in which the substantives are clothed. These will be combined, of course, with whatever other evidence from the mechanical printing process that suggests itself as significant.

In preparing annotated quartos, the annotator's concern to bring the wording of the print into conformity with the manuscript wipes out most of the evidence one customarily secures from the transmission of substantive variants in normal reprints. We may not suppose that in all instances the corrector was indifferent to the accidentals of the printed copy, and in fact it can be shown that in some categories he might indeed alter them to accord with the manuscript form. But many—if not the majority—of the divergences in the accidentals in control reprint texts appear to have been untouched, and it is from these that the hoped-for evidence must derive, since they alone can be conjectured to have escaped the corrective process.

The use of spelling tests to separate and to identify compositors is now well established, and a handful of studies have appeared separating the work of various compositors in Elizabethan play quartos. These spelling tests identify compositors by the positive evidence of their habitual or characteristic trend towards imposing their own spellings on the copy being set. That is, the evidence consists exclusively of the compositors' divergences from copy. On the contrary, the technique of establishing the nature of the copy from which a compositor set rests on examples of the compositor's agreement with his copy; that is, on the evidence of the occasions in which his copy influenced the compositor either to forsake his habitual characteristics or else to choose the copy form a remarkable number of times when his own practice was largely indifferent.

Irregularity in the copy being tested is usually a desideratum. For instance, if the assumed copy agrees with the compositor's known spelling habits for a word, nothing is proved when he sets the word according to his habitual spelling. Moreover, unless irregularity is present, the concurrence of spelling in indifferent forms cannot be detected. As an example, a text might spell *feel* consistently as *feele*, but if a compositor used this edition and set a number of *feel* forms, as well as *feele,* the concurrences in *feele* would be meaningless as evidence for derivation whenever the compositor's practice was ordinarily indifferent and therefore without detectable preference.

Most attempts to establish the influence of one or other form of copy on a given edition have been unsystematic and partial. Both faults have been forced on the undertakers by the difficulty that no complete spelling and other accidental analysis exists for any Elizabethan compositor other than a few of the most conspicuous ways in which he diverged from copy. This situation has been brought about, of course, by the inquiry into compositorial spellings chiefly from the point of view of departures from copy, evidence from which compositors could be identified and separated. Words in which these compositors were likely to be influenced by copy have been so valueless for the purpose of identification (except as a contrast to a marked characteristic of another compositor being compared) as to escape notice.

Thus those critics who have tried to use the evidence of the accidentals have had a tendency to ignore the compositor altogether and have unsystematically chosen various examples of what they regarded as copy eccentricities repeated in the Folio text, arguing for these as evidence of the direct connexion of the two texts. No proof is usually advanced that these were indeed eccentricities in the original, and that the corresponding form in the Folio text was not possible or customary for the compositor to use, or could not have derived ultimately from a common original. Hence because this is partial and subjective selection of evidence without a basis in ascertained fact, no case has been or could have been advanced that has touched the borders of proof; and the abuse of the method has served only to arouse scepticism about the validity of accidentals as evidence.

The other method, of attempting to explain divergences from habitual spellings as due to the influence of copy, is more easily approached because of some information that has accumulated about Compositors A and B in the Folio. But, again, this information has concentrated on discovering their mutually opposed habitual spellings rather than those in which they were subject to the influence of copy. And in addition test words and the degree of fidelity to be expected with them are not wholly trustworthy, because the evidence for B was compiled before he was distinguished from E [and D], the evidence for A does not as yet distinguish him from C, who had been partly included in pre-Hinman analyses, [and F].

Pending a more satisfactory statistical study of A and of B, it has seemed possible to illustrate and in some sort to test the technique for the investigation of mechanical evidence by a provisional study of Compositor E, the workman whom Dr. Hinman has identified as an apprentice.[28] This workman set from printed copy almost all of the Folio *Titus Andronicus,* and *Romeo and Juliet.* He also set the first 3 pages of the original *Troilus and Cressida,* 13½ pages of the Folio *King Lear,* 6 of *Othello,* and 4 of *Hamlet.*

Several factors favour such a study. First, an inexperienced and therefore cautious compositor might be supposed to feel the influence of copy more strongly than a thoroughly routined workman, and it should be of some interest to see if this deduction is valid as applied to E. Second, E set two plays, and three pages of another, from printed copy that as a whole had not been corrected, and these should provide adequate information about the influence of copy on his setting of accidentals. To these may be added a third incentive. Compositor E set some pages in *King Lear, Othello,* and *Hamlet,* all plays that in one textual respect or another are in dispute; and it may be that fresh evidence can assist in our taking a firmer view about the nature of their copy. Finally the total amount of Folio text set by E is not so large that an attempt may not be made to study his work in relation to copy without an electronic computer or old-spelling concordance.[29] Undoubtedly, some of his indifferent characteristics that cu-

28 'The Prentice Hand in the Tragedies of the Shakespeare First Folio', *Studies in Bibliography,* ix (1957), 3–20.

29 The emphasis here is on *study.* No definitive account of E and his relation to copy can be made without laborious hand-indexing of every word he set, or the computer sorting of the same evidence from the text on tapes. What follows, therefore, is at best a

mulatively would be of the highest value to know will not be apparent without mechanical computation. Nevertheless, even though the hoped-for results may be only provisional, if they are at all positive they should be of interest as an exercise in method, and they may produce some useful hints towards the solution of a problem or two.

IV. *Compositor E and the Folio* Othello

Compositor E was first identified by Dr. Hinman on evidence that was completely mechanical. While A and B were setting *Coriolanus, Julius Caesar,* and *Macbeth,* one or other of their type-cases was being used at the same time by someone else to set intercalary formes of *Titus* and of *Romeo,* plays before and after the texts with which A and B were concerned. Dr. Hinman ingeniously suggested that this stranger E was an apprentice who was trusted only with printed copy and who worked, at first, while A and B were setting from manuscripts. Compositor E would take over the type-cases from either one when he was absent from the Folio and presumably busy about some other job in the shop involving a different fount of type. This new workman began setting with *Titus Andronicus* (from Q3 of 1611) and followed with *Romeo and Juliet* (from Q3 of 1609). The sheets were more carefully proof-corrected than were those set by the other Folio compositors, and indeed the need for such a review is shown by the considerable number of mechanical errors, such as mis-spacings and transpositions and also loosened types indicating improper justification. After completing *Romeo and Juliet* he started *Troilus and Cressida* from an unannotated copy of the quarto. But when work on this was halted after three pages, he may be said to have graduated. When A departed from the Folio towards the end of *Macbeth,* and C also, towards the end of *Hamlet,* E worked in regular conjunction with B through the last pages of *Hamlet* and all through *King Lear;* and he set the first six pages of *Othello* (I. i. to I. iii. 391), starting in the same formes as his last two pages of *Lear* in gathering ss, until B came in to set the outer forme of the outermost sheet of ss. Thereafter B took over and set the remainder of the Folio unaided until A returned at the very end to speed *Troilus and Cressida* and complete the volume.

---

trial investigation from selected, not from bulk, evidence. Evidence from the texts of *Hamlet* and *King Lear* has been excluded since the copy for the Folio is still in some measure in dispute, and only the parts of *Titus, Romeo,* and *Troilus* have been used as controls. [The hoped-for completion in 1975–76 of the Howard-Hill computer old-spelling Shakespeare concordances will materially assist any further compositorial study of E and the other workmen.]

Compositor E, I am pleased to be able to suggest, was very likely John Leason, son of John Leason of Husley in Hampshire. He was bound to William Jaggard on 4 November 1622,[30] a few months before Dr. Hinman estimates work was started on *Titus.* The identification seems plausible since it is indeed clear that E was not an expert typesetter, and the apprentice bound immediately before Leason was Laurence Yardsley as far back as 1614. The date at which Leason was made free is not recorded.

Compositor E was not allowed to set the first page of *Titus* or of *Romeo,* presumably because the balance and spacing of the head-title and ornament might have caused him trouble. He did set the first page of the original *Troilus and Cressida,* but not of *King Lear,* and he was allowed to start with the first page of *Othello.* It may be that some mislineation at the beginning of *Othello* was caused by the trouble he experienced in adjusting text about the ornamental initial letter that headed I. i.

Dr. Alice Walker's argument for the use of the Quarto as copy for the Folio *Othello* catches at several pieces of evidence that are susceptible of other explanation and finally comes to rest on a combination of orthographical similarity and common error. Given the verbal divergences in the two texts that demonstrate a tendency to verbal substitution in the Quarto, 'it is very remarkable to find that [Q] agrees with the Folio in readings such as "This present warres", "Toth' very moment" (I. iii. 133), "morties", "lushious", "my currant runnes", and so on. It is, in fact, only possible to reconcile the evidence of the verbal variants between the printed texts with their close orthographical connexion, common errors, and common typographical features by supposing that the Folio text was printed (with correction and amplification) from a copy of the Qurto.'[31]

Since the orthographical evidence adduced is confined to a handful of examples without reference to established compositorial characteristics,[32] I propose to bring to bear on the problem some spelling evidence gathered from a study of Compositor E's habits, and therefore confined to the first six pages of the Folio text (I. i. 1 to I. iii. 391), to suggest that Dr. Walker is indeed correct in her general assumption. My purpose here is not to demonstrate the nature of the copy beyond all question—a task too lengthy and complex for oral presentation—but to illustrate some of the possibilities of a different method of investigation from the conventional use of verbals or of undifferentiated spelling 'hits'.

---

30 D. F. McKenzie, 'A List of Printers' Apprentices, 1605–1640,' *Studies in Bibliography,* xiii (1960), 125.

31 'The 1622 Quarto and the First Folio Texts of *Othello*', *Shakespeare Survey,* 5 (1952), 23.

32 See Appendix below.

As with Compositors A and B in the Folio, the three best words with which to test Compositor E are *do, go,* and *here.* Fortunately, he was much more willing to accept copy spellings of these than were A and B, and though he had a preference for the short forms *do* and *go,* and the long form *heere,* we find in the control texts that he set numerous examples of *doe, goe,* and *here* when the copy encouraged them. However, he would very seldom indeed set one of his non-preferential forms against a copy that had his favourite spelling, and then ordinarily in prose when he was perhaps justifying his line.*

That E could be influenced by his copy is well illustrated by his treatment of the word *here.* The characteristics of the *Titus* and *Romeo* quartos vary widely in respect to this word. The *Titus* Q3 compositor set a vast majority of the long form *heere,* whereas the *Romeo* Q3 compositor set a vast majority of the short forme *here.* In each play E's characteristics are correspondingly affected. In *Titus* Q3 appear 65 *heere* spellings that E followed,[33] 11 *here* forms changed to *heere* by E, 1 anomalous *heere* changed to *here,* and 3 *here* spellings reproduced in the Folio. But in the Folio *Romeo* 60 short forms are repeated from Q3 and only 9 short forms are changed to long. In *Troilus* 3 *heere* spellings are followed, 4 *here* forms are changed to *heere,* 1 *heere* to *here* (an anomaly in a prose passage), and 3 short *here* spellings are reproduced.

The pattern in E's six pages of *Othello* follows that in *Romeo* where the conditions were roughly the same, and is not inconsistent with the evidence of *Troilus.* Of 15 occurrences in *Othello* the Folio follows the unusual long form twice, changes *here* to *heere* 3 times, and reproduces Q's short *here* 10 times. By itself the treatment of this word does not show that the Quarto was the copy for the Folio, but it strongly indicates that, whatever the printer's copy, it must have corresponded very closely to the characteristics of the Quarto in respect to the spelling of this word. On E's record in the control texts, the Folio copy must have had a majority spelling of *here.* That the copy's preferential form might have been *heere* is a hypothesis that cannot be entertained.

* This study unfortunately did not take account of a refinement introduced by later investigators of compositorial spellings by which the only primary evidence accepted is that from the 'short' lines of verse that do not extend to the right margin and may be taken, in general, to have been justified by spaces instead of by alteration of the forms of spellings. These should be distinguished in the statistics from lines of verse that extend to the full length of the measure and thus could have been susceptible to justification by tinkering with spellings. By common consent, because of the justification problem, spellings in prose are often disregarded in any statistical study.

33 Although the statistics in this chapter have been independently checked, data of this sort secured by inspection and not by computer may vary slightly in absolute accuracy.

From *Titus* through *Romeo* and on to *Troilus* we see Compositor E hardening in his preference for the short forms of *do*. In *Titus* 25 short *do* forms are followed, 22 *doe* spellings are shortened to *do,* but 39 long *doe* spellings are reproduced. In *Romeo* 44 short Q forms are followed, 19 long forms are changed to short, and only 13 long forms are followed, with one anomalous change of short to long, in verse. In *Troilus* 10 short forms are followed, and the only 3 long forms are shortened. There is one anomalous change of short to long, but in a prose passage.

The statistics for *Othello* do not suggest that the printer's copy was very mixed in its characteristics but instead that it ran strongly to the long *doe* form. In the Quarto 34 of the 35 examples are spelled *doe,* which the Folio sets as *do* in 30 cases, agreeing with Q *doe* in 4 occurrences and with Q *do* in its single appearance. The figure of 4 repeats is about what we should expect to slip through Compositor E at this stage of his experience when setting from copy that ran strongly against his preferential short form. Thus whatever the copy was for Folio *Othello* it would seem to have resembled the Quarto fairly closely in its spelling of this word.

Compositor E's treatment of *go* is not so rigorous as what he does with *do*. In *Titus* the invariable Q *goe* is changed to *go* only 6 times and is followed on 32 occasions. In *Romeo* 16 long forms are followed, 3 long forms are shortened, and 51 short forms are reproduced. In the three pages of *Troilus,* E follows *go* twice, *goe* twice, and alters one *goe* to *go*.

By the time *Othello* was set, E was opting more firmly for the short form, with the result that of the 12 occurrences of the word in his stint he set 10 as *go* and only 2 as *goe*. In this group the 2 short Q spellings are short in F, but 8 of the Q *goe* spellings appear as *go* in F and in only 2 of the Q *goe* forms is there agreement.

At the least, one can say that, in view of the evidence, if Folio *Othello* were set from a manuscript, the manuscript must have been very close indeed to the Quarto practice in the mixed characteristics of these three words, with a predominance—as in the Quarto—of the forms *here, doe,* and *goe.*

But the evidence can be viewed more narrowly. Not much, if any, significance attaches to the fact that the one time Q *Othello* set *do* and the two times it set *go*, the Folio agrees, although if a manuscript had been the copy, and the long forms were in these places, chance might have led E to follow the non-preferential spelling. But with *here* we have a different situation. There are only 5 *heere* spellings in the Folio *Othello* set by E as against 10 *here* forms, and it would seem to be more significant that the only 2 times that the Quarto printed the long form *heere*, it also appears in the Folio. That is, 2 of the 5 preferential *heere* spellings in the Folio would have come from the Quarto. The 2-to-1 setting of *here* in F does not produce a *here* in the only two places where Q spelled *heere*.

This agreement is not beyond chance, of course, but if we combine the odds against this happening for *here* with the added odds for the *goe* agreement twice out of the 10 long forms in the Quarto, we may find it logically significant that in no case in these three words in *Othello* (and Q is mixed in its characteristics for all three) does a non-preferential E spelling in the Folio appear when there was a preferential spelling in the Quarto. This result corresponds to the evidence from the control texts that never more than once in any single text does E set a non-preferential form against a preferential. Whether this unusual result in *Othello* might have been achieved if the Folio had been set from an independent manuscript, the characteristics of which must certainly have differed in some respects from the Quarto print, may remain a matter of opinion. But, at least, the evidence should persuade us to entertain a working hypothesis that the Quarto was the copy for the Folio, since there is nothing in the evidence contrary to that hypothesis and some positive indications that favour it.

Yet if we continue to test the possibility that a manuscript was the copy, nevertheless, we find that this hypothetical copy and the Quarto would seem to have agreed in another respect, in spelling *answer* at least a few times without a final *-e*. In *Titus* the 3 times the word appears it is spelled *answere* in Q and F (*aunswere* in Q at II. iii. 298), and in *Romeo and Juliet* both texts agree 8 times in *answere* although once F changes Q *answere* to *answer* and once the unique Q *answer* to *answere*. In *Troilus* E follows copy twice in *answere* and once in repeating *answer*. In the 5 times the word appears in *Othello*, the Q spelling is invariably *answer*, which F follows twice while altering the remaining 3 times to *answere*. The short form, uncharacteristic of E, would seem to have been produced by his following copy.

Ordinarily Compositor E follows copy in setting *heauen* with a lower-case *h* or a capital *H*, although he has a general tendency to capitalize when a change is made. Never in *Titus* and *Romeo* does he reduce a capital *Heauen* to lower case. This being so, the evidence in Folio *Othello* is of considerable interest. Of the 7 occurrences of the word, 1 comes in an added Folio passage (set from manuscript) where it is capitalized. Folio and Quarto agree once on the capital, and twice the Folio raises Q lower-case to capitals. Interestingly, the only 3 times that *heauen* appears in E's stint in F *Othello,* it reproduces Q's use of lower case. Whether or not it is chance that the single Q capitalization is also capitalized in F, the fact is apparent—given E's characteristics—that the F copy must have read *heauen* a majority of the times (Q is 5 to 1 for *heauen*), else the 3 lower-case spellings would not have appeared in F. (In *Titus* 19 cases of *heauen*, which is invariable, are reproduced in F; in *Romeo* 26 lower case are followed, 1 capital is followed, and 1 lower case in raised to a capital.)

A sprinkling of other spelling or accidentals evidence is not worth mentioning at present because of a lack of full information, such as the QF agreement in *inioynted* whereas E ordinarily alters such prefixes to *en-*. However, E normally seems to follow copy in *honor–honour* although he may have some slight preference for the *-our* form. For instance, in *Titus* he follows *honour* 10 times, *honor* once, and alters one *honor* to *honour;* in *Romeo* he follows *honour* 4 times, and raises the single *honor* to *honour*. There may be significance, then, to the *Othello* QF agreement in the only two appearances of the singular, once as *honor* and once as *honour*, although plural *honors* is altered in F to *honours* in its one occurrence. Such words can be multiplied, but they are too scattered and unsystematic according to our present information to offer convincing evidence in themselves.

Typographical evidence is not very weighty, although it is consistent with the emerging picture of F as derived from Q. For instance, in *Othello* E rejects the Q italicizing of names of countries and of nationalities, such as *Cyprus* and *Turk*. It may be, therefore, that the F italics in *Ottamites* and *Ottoman* that correspond to Q's and go contrary to E's usual practice resulted from E's unfamiliarity with the words, just as he followed Q in italicizing *Anthropophagie* although reducing Q's italics in *Canibals* to roman. The splitting of pentameter lines in F that may follow Q is of no significance: E very seldom turns under or over a long line and almost invariably prefers to set such as two independent lines, breaking at the caesura. Thus a line so long that Q would break it would automatically be broken by E regardless of its form in his copy.

Some minor information of this sort bearing on the accidentals[34] can be skipped in favour of three concluding pieces of evidence.

The common readings like *lushious* and the name *Luccicos*, noticed by Dr. Walker, could come from a common source as she recognizes. But the false emendation of an error is customarily taken as excellent proof of direct genetic relationship, and thus—while far from conclusive in itself —may be utilized, in view of the accumulation of evidence retailed above, as a strong corroboration once a working hypothesis has been established from spelling evidence in favour of the Quarto having served as annotated copy for the Folio. At I. iii. 230, as Dr. Walker points out, Othello's phrase

34 As, for instance, the treatment of round brackets. In *Titus* and *Romeo* E adds 6 pairs of round brackets while dropping only 1. In his short stint in *Troilus* he increases this tendency by adding 3, as many as in the whole of either full control play. In *Othello* he freely adds 31, retains the 2 present in the Q, and drops none. Chance might dictate, thus, that F could agree with the two Q pairs, regardless of the nature of the copy, but the evidence, still, is not inconsistent with the view that F was set from Q.

the flinty and steel couch of war is misprinted in Q as *Cooch* and in F is falsely corrected to *Coach*. This is so little the sort of error one could assign to a common original that the conclusion seems natural that the Q error was overlooked by the annotator and badly rationalized by E, or (perhaps more probable) that E misread the annotator's correction of *u* as *a*. In either case, the Quarto must have been the physical printer's copy.

The remaining two are much more speculative, and they could hardly be mentioned at all as evidence except after the establishment of a working hypothesis. Neither has been noticed previously.

Othello I. iii. 106 in the Quarto reads

Du. To youth this is no proofe,

whereas the Folio omits the speech-prefix in error and alters to read

To vouch this, is no proofe,

It is tempting to speculate that the annotator in correcting the error *youth* to *vouch* in some manner seemed to E to have deleted the speech-prefix. The fact that the prefix is wrongly omitted at the very point where the start of the line is emended in the Folio could well be significant.

When the conflicting reports about the Turkish fleet are being brought to the Venetian council, a messenger arrives. In the Quarto at I. iii. 12 his speech-prefix is *One within*, and a line of text is followed by the stage-direction *Enter a Messenger*, who thereupon has two speeches, each headed by the prefix *Sailor* spelled with an *i*. In the Folio the corresponding forms are *Saylor within* and *Enter Saylor*, with a *y*. However, the first Folio prefix is *Officer* (substituting for Q *Sailor*) and then, for the first time (line 14) F sets the prefix *Sailor* but with an anomalous *i*. Given the two settings of *Saylor* with *y* in a passage of written alteration when the Quarto read respectively *One* and *Messenger*, the conjecture is attractive that the speech-prefix with an *i* at line 14 resulted from E following the Quarto's form *Sailor* the one time he would have been setting this word from print. In the circumstances it is unfortunate that the word does not occur in any of the control texts set by E and thus no proof is available whether *saylor* or *sailor* was his preferential form, or whether he was inclined to follow copy without preference.

It would seem, then, that Dr. Walker was admirably right to challenge received opinion and to assert that the Folio *Othello* was set from an amplified and altered copy of the print of Q1. The application attempted here of a provisional and certainly incomplete analysis of Compositor E[35]

35 The full case must, of course, await an analysis of Compositor B in relation to

has, I hope, confirmed the somewhat sketchy evidence heretofore available by the introduction of another range of evidence based on ascertained compositorial characteristics[36] of the kind that would most likely escape the hand of the annotator.[37]

Indeed, it appears in all problems of these annotated play quartos that substantive readings alone have failed to settle vexed questions of copy in any manner that has secured general approval of the results on evidence that appears to demonstrate the case. The hand of the annotator has so frequently destroyed or concealed evidence from the verbals of the text that significant coincidences generally available in simple reprints dwindle in marked-up copy into inconclusive similarities. Most substantive errors that can be trusted to be errors are ordinarily subject to the counter-hypothesis of independent transmission from a common original.[38] Thus the only evidence in ordinary circumstances that is not susceptible of significant change by this annotation and that is copious enough to be of use in tackling difficult problems of mixed copy is the evidence from the transmission of the accidentals.

Nevertheless, it is idle to attempt to apply concurrences in these accidentals except on the basis of a thoroughgoing compositorial analysis. Concurrence can be meaningless if the Folio and Quarto compositors' characteristics or usual spellings are the same. That the Folio *Othello* follows the Quarto in the divided *my selfe* but the run-together *himselfe* is of no consequence when one knows that the identical distinction is habitual with Compositor E. That the Folio religiously agrees with the

---

the Quarto. At the present moment, however, although we have some information about B's divergences from copy of the sort that usefully distinguishes him from Compositor A, we do not have a full-scale study of how he followed copy. D. F. McKenzie's 'Compositor B's Role in *The Merchant of Venice*, Q2 (1619)', *Studies in Bibliography*, xii (1959), 75–89, makes an excellent start on the problem [although his assignment of B as the sole compositor of the Pavier quartos has recently been attacked and is perhaps not entirely valid. A larger-scale study by Sidney W. Reid, "Some Spellings of Compositor B in the Shakespeare First Folio," is forthcoming in *Studies in Bibliography*, 29 (1976)].

36 The emphasis here is on *ascertained* evidence about an identified compositor drawn from control texts and applied to the problem at hand.

37 An annotator can, it is clear, occasionally concern himself with relatively common words, as evidenced by *Othello* Q *darlings* but F *Deareling* at I. ii. 68, a change not otherwise observed in E's work. If *2 Henry IV* were indeed set from annotated printed copy, the extensive alteration of remarkably small points would constitute a very special case.

38 Moreover, such evidence is not frequent enough to settle difficult questions of mixed copy such as has been asserted exists in F *King Lear* by A. S. Cairncross, 'The Quarto and the Folio Text of *King Lear*', *Review of English Studies*, N.S., vi (1955), 252–8.

Quarto in the full form of all *-lesse* and *-nesse* endings is meaningless when we know that by the time he came to *Othello* Compositor E never set anything else, regardless of his copy. Concurrence can also be meaningless if the spelling agreement derives from the habitual practice of the Folio workman regardless of the mixed habits of the Quarto compositor. Thus any attempt to argue for Quarto copy in a Folio text set by Compositor B is doomed to failure if the Quarto has irregularly set *do* or *doe*, and the 'hits' in the short form are taken as significant. Compositor B was so confirmed in his preference for the spelling *do* that this regularity (or his rare lapses) give us no hint in this respect about the nature of the underlying copy from which he was setting.

Random 'hits' that cannot be confirmed as significant are highly misleading used as evidence. Possibly F *Off-capt* and Q *Oft capt* (I. i. 10) constitute evidence in their agreement in the *-t* ending, but no means exist to demonstrate the conjecture when this is the only use of the preterite in Shakespeare, according to the Concordance. Moreover, analogy often does not work in establishing spelling characteristics. For instance, one compositor of Q2 *Romeo and Juliet* is an inveterate *-ie* speller but he consistently spells *Lady* and *body*.[39] Thus it is not enough in any case to argue from the assumed evidence of similar words: the exact words, and only these exact words, can constitute evidence, or else such forms as influence spelling without regard for the word itself. It may be (I do not know) that this compositor in Q2 *Romeo and Juliet* would set all words with *-ie* endings except for the combination *-dy*. Certainly such inexplicable distinctions may be observed in many Elizabethan compositors. In *Othello* Compositor E set at least 19 words in *-ly* and only 3 in *-lie*, but 21 in *-tie* versus 7 in *-ty*. Obviously, until one analyses the preceding consonant(s) nothing can be said about any habits he may have had in ending words with *-ie* or *-y*, and any attempt at a statistical study of the undifferentiated evidence would offer a most misleading picture.[40]

39 George Walton Williams, 'The Printing of *Romeo and Juliet* (1599)', *Studies in Bibliography*, ix (1957), 111. Dr. Williams privately informs me that *lady* appears at least 34 times and *ladie* not at all save for *Ladie-bird* reproducing Q1 *Ladie bird* in a reprinted passage. *Body* occurs 7 times and *bodie* not at all. For *ready* and *already* the compositor is indifferent: *ready* appears 3 times and *readie* twice; *already* appears twice and *alreadie* once. For all other nouns and adjectives he is a *-die* speller, as in *bandie* (1), *bloudie* (5), *studie* (1), *unwieldie* (1), and *tardie* (1).

40 In fact, the one serious piece of evidence in *Othello* against Q as copy-text for F concerns E's treatment of the *-y* endings. In *Titus* and in *Romeo* he has a tendency to follow copy, but any change will definitely be in the direction of shortening *-ie* to *-y*. The large number of words in *Othello* in which *-y* would have been lengthened to *-ie* if Q were the copy certainly runs contrary to the practice observed in the control texts. It is likely, however, that this treatment of *-y* and *-ie* according to the preceding con-

What seem to be somewhat odd individual spellings that agree in two texts may turn out not to be so odd after all, or else susceptible of explanation as deriving from a common source. An eager critic might, just for example, seize on *Gardiners* in both Q and F *Othello* (I. iii. 324), only to find that *Hamlet* Q2 *Gardners* (V. i. 34) is changed by E (if Q2 were the copy) to Folio *Gardiners*. Whether *Epithites* in QF *Othello* is a significant agreement is not to be determined, since *epithet* is not found elsewhere in E's work. Whether Q *syen* and F *Seyen* (I. iii. 337) for *scion* is evidence for Q copy or for common derivation from an eccentric manuscript spelling is surely not demonstrable in the lack of evidence from controls.

Just as insufficient to bear the weight of any hypothesis is the quotation of passages of generally similar accidentals. We may compare a random passage from *King Lear* to see what this sort of impressionistic or merely statistical evidence could reveal about the problem of Q1 or Q2 copy. Here is I. i. 248–60 in the Folio, with all accidentals italicized that differ between Q1 and Q2 where F agrees with one or the other:

> *Bur.* I am *sorry* then you haue so lost a Father,
> That you must *loose* a husband.
>
> *Cor.* Peace be with *Burgundie,*
> Since that respect and Fortunes are his loue,
> I shall not be his wife.
>
> *Fra.* Fairest *Cordelia,* that art most rich being poore,
> Most choise forsaken, and most lou'd *despis'd,*
> Thee and thy vertues *here* I *seize* vpon,
> Be it lawful I take vp *what's* cast *away.*
> Gods, Gods! 'Tis strange, that from their *cold'st* neglect
> My Loue should kindle to enflam'd respect.
> Thy *dowrelesse* Daughter *King,* throwne to my chance,
> Is Queene of vs, of ours, and our faire France:

---

sonant was a developing characteristic with E, and one that might be traced in E's share of *Hamlet* and *King Lear* (which intervene between the control texts and *Othello*). Certainly such an alteration of characteristics may be observed in another word in *Hamlet* and *King Lear* with the result that evidence in *Othello* at first sight contrary to the Q copy-text hypothesis may be shown to be neutral after all. The example is the exclamation *O* or *Oh,* which in *Titus* and in *Romeo* is irregularly spelled but the copy form invariably followed by E. Yet in *Othello,* wherein the Q is invariably O, the Folio prints *O* only once but *Oh* 7 times. Nevertheless, despite the evidence of *Titus* and of *Romeo,* in *King Lear,* regardless of the quarto serving as copy, E develops a tendency to alter *O* to *Oh* and the same process may be observed in *Hamlet* if we assume that Q2 was the copy. The *Oh* spellings in F *Othello* contrary to Quarto *O* would seem to have no significance, therefore.

The respective readings are:

F	Q1	Q2
sorry	sory	*sorry*
loose	*loose*	lose
Burgundie	*Burgundie*	Burgundy
Cordelia,	~ ^	*Cordelia,*
despis'd	despisd	*despis'd*
here	*here*	heere
seize	ceaze	*seize*
what's	whats	*what's*
away.	~ ,	*away.*
cold'st	couldst	*cold'st*
enflam'd	inflam'd	*enflam'd*
dowrelesse	dowreles	*dowrelesse*
King,	~ ^	*King,*

Of 13 differences in the accidentals, F agrees with Q2 10 times and with Q1 only 3 times. Yet this raw statistical concurrence cannot take account of the number of times that the agreement of Q2 and F can have no significance since E's customary practice is being reflected in F, not necessarily the influence of Q2 copy. With these cases out of the way, the evidence becomes almost wholly neutral except for the powerful effect of the concurrence of F and Q1 in Compositor E's non-preferential *here* versus Q2's *heere*. After all that we know of E's treatment of this word in the control texts, to suppose that E has gone against Q2 copy and set non-preferential *here* in this passage is much more difficult than to explain away the largely insignificant agreements of F with Q2. Thus unanalyzed statistical evidence must always be viewed with reserve. It may mean much, or nothing.

Wanting such strict bibliographical evidence as can be drawn most happily from the typographical irregularities of *Troilus and Cressida*, the only other trustworthy method (when substantive evidence fails) is to assemble some quantity of examples in which the Folio compositor broke with his own ascertained preferential habits in order to follow the Quarto spellings or significantly agreed with these when his own practice was largely indifferent. Individually most of these small pieces of evidence may seem to be of little consequence; yet when they have been properly analysed from control texts and when they point in the same direction, their cumulative agreement exerts a powerful leverage. But obviously this evidence cannot qualify for serious consideration unless one knows one's compositor and has some information about the amount of variation that can be expected under specified control conditions that approximate those under examination.

Finally, when the case is not just one of deciding which of two printed editions was the copy (as in the *Richard III* problem) but instead is one of deciding between a lost manuscript and an annotated copy of a known quarto (as in *Othello*), a further leverage can be exerted by another form of evidence, one that may be described as qualitative.

Quantitative evidence may be defined as the normal estimated percentage that an identified compositor will set a non-preferential form when his copy is invariable or nearly invariable in printing the non-preferential spelling. For instance, in Q *Othello* appear 34 spellings *doe* and 1 *do*. The argument in favour of Q copy for F concerns E's strong attachment to the short *do* spelling that leads him to alter Q *doe* to *do* 30 times. The case for the Q copy does not rest on the fact that none of the 4 E settings of *doe* occurs at the point where Q sets its solitary *do* (for the odds are against such qualitative coincidence). Instead, we may argue quantitatively that the four times that E is persuaded by his copy to forsake his strong preference for *do* coincide with the proposition that the copy had as a characteristic a major if not invariable preference for *doe*. It is unlikely that E would have set so many examples of *doe* if the copy had been relatively mixed. This argument is based purely on the quantity of non-preferential forms that appear, without regard for their position in relation to the corresponding readings of the conjectured copy. This quantitative analysis is the only one that can be used when the copy being tested is very strongly in favour of a particular spelling form that disagrees with the preference of the compositor of the reprint. Of the two orders of evidence, the quantitative is the less valuable because it is grounded wholly on inference and is very general in its application. However, the accumulation of such evidence is not to be ignored.

On the other hand, qualitative evidence is used when the critic can show not only that the compositor of the disputed text under the influence of copy sets accidental forms variant from his usual practice, but also that these variants from his usual preference seldom if ever appear except when the corresponding non-preferential form is present in a copy that has reasonably mixed characteristics in respect to the variant being analysed. In *Othello* the treatment of *here* is a partial example in that significance can be given to the fact that, frequent as were the appearances of the uncharacteristic *here* spelling in the Folio (3 to 1, in fact), none occurred in contradiction to the 2 examples in the Quarto of E's preferential *heere*. Another example concerns the Folio treatment of *heauen* and *Heauen*, where we may take it as significant that in the 6 occurrences of the word, none of the 3 Folio lower-case forms appeared in the single place that the Quarto set the more characteristic capitalized *Heauen*. Again, once E's general preference for *honour* is established, the fact would seem to be evidential that the single time we find *honor* in F it coincides with one of the two *honor* spellings in Q, and not with the one time that Q spells *honour*.

In *Othello* the qualitative argument needs to be a little fine-spun because of the small amount of material available for analysis in the six pages set by Compositor E. But better illustrations appear in the control texts. If one were analysing *Titus* Q3 as the copy for F, one would direct attention to the qualitative evidence that 3 of the 4 non-preferential *here* forms found in the Folio agree with 3 of the 14 occurrences of the short form in Q3 and only 1 of the 4 clashes with any of the 65 long *heere* forms in the Quarto. In the Folio none of the 39 uncharacteristic *doe* spellings reproduced in *Titus* agrees with any of the 25 *do* spellings in the Quarto. In *Romeo and Juliet* only 1 of the 14 long *doe* spellings appears as setting any of the 44 short forms present in Q3, and none of the 16 long *goe* spellings appears as a substitute for any of the 51 Q3 short forms. The odds from such examples can be calculated to demonstrate the validity of this kind of qualitative evidence. That quantitative evidence is also valid can be demonstrated by the example of the effect of copy on Compositor E in respect to *do, go,* and *here.* When the copy, like *Romeo,* is in strong general agreement with his preferential spellings, he is led to alter a larger number of non-preferential forms than when, as in *Titus,* the copy runs strongly against his own habits and he is correspondingly affected.

The distinction between quantitative and qualitative evidence and the evaluation of their respective weight has not been commonly made by textual critics; but such a differentiation is very useful indeed, especially when dealing, as in *Othello,* with a comparatively small amount of text where in any given instance chance might be thought to explain the evidence as satisfactorily as design. That is, that Compositor E set *Titus Andronicus* from Q3, and *Romeo and Juliet* from Q3, can be demonstrated from substantive readings (since each case is an uncomplicated reprint), but if necessary the demonstration could also have been made by copious evidence from the accidentals, both by quantitative and by qualitative analysis. Whereas a critic might not be willing to accept the spelling evidence of any one word as conclusive, the pyramiding of the force of the qualitative evidence is very rapid indeed, and might be thought conclusive from the evidence even of two well-established balanced words.

In *Othello* where the evidence in E's stint must perforce be more delicate that in *Titus* or *Romeo,* the full force of the qualitative can be understood when it is not confused with the less precise quantitative evidence. Only by this separation can the leverage exerted by full qualitative concurrence within a series be appreciated as forming a cumulative broad unit so consistent in its coincidences with the special mixed features of the Q copy

that chance must finally be ruled out as an operative force. Once the
necessary compositor studies have been made, the rigorous application of
this evidence, in place of the conventional impressionistic studies (or the
unanalysed raw statistical studies), may hopefully lead to a final determination of disputed printed versus manuscript copy in the Folio.

Beyond that, with still further refinements made possible by the use of
large electronic computers, it is not inconceivable that we may progress
to an attempt to determine with superior precision to the present the more
or less exact nature of certain manuscript printer's copy behind the authoritative quartos as well as the plays first printed in the Folio. Indeed, that
some demonstrable features of Shakespeare's holographs may eventually
be recovered from the prints is not entirely a dream.

APPENDIX

Dr. Walker isolates three nonce words in QF (*moraller, probal, exsufflicate*),
of which two appear in identical spellings in both texts. She admits, rightly, 'It
might be argued that their unfamiliarity encouraged copyists and compositors
to preserve them as they found them, but this explanation will not account for
the identical spelling of more common words which could be spelt in a number
of ways.' She then selects *morties* (i.e., mortise), 'though half a dozen spellings
were possible'; *lushious* 'as against "luscious" in the Folio text of *A Midsummer
Night's Dream* is again common to the printed texts'; so too is *Pyoners* 'as
against "Pioners" in the Folio text of *Henry V* and all three texts of *Hamlet*'.
This evidence does not get us very far. In fact, *luscious* appears only twice in
Shakespeare. That Compositor E spells it *lushious* (as does Q) cannot therefore be utilized to show the nature of his copy, since *luscious* in the *Dream*
was set by a different compositor. Correspondingly, *Pioners* in *Henry V* and
in *Hamlet* was set by Compositor A; thus whether in setting *Pyoners* Compositor B was following Q's copy or using his natural spelling cannot be determined. Only in B's *morties* can any sort of comparison be made: for what
it is worth, in *Hamlet* B once set Q2 *morteist* (if Q2 were the copy) as *mor-
tiz'd*. Yet this single occurrence cannot establish whether or not he might
have had other spellings, one of which was *morties* as in *Othello*. Dr. Walker
then quotes *Othello*, IV. ii. 57–64, and comments: 'The Folio reads "garnerd",
"dries", "heere" and emends "thy" to "thou". We have, of course, to reckon
with the fact that the *Othello* printed texts are contemporaries. The compositors of Okes (the Quarto printer) and Jaggard have certain spelling conventions in common, and "heart", "beare", "fountaine", "keepe", "Ces-
terne", "complexion", "looke", "grim" and "hell" are normal Folio spellings;
but others are what may be described as Folio variables: "currant", "runnes",
"foule", "Toades" and "young" might well have been otherwise spelt without
infringing such rules as existed in Jaggard's printing-house.' But only a
moment's reflection is necessary to recognize that whether or not these words
might have been spelled in a variety of ways by the four other Folio com-

positors, no evidence is being adduced that the identified Compositor B is or is not following copy in this passage. Only if it were shown (as it is not) that B was significantly influenced by his copy to go against his usual habits here and in some number of other passages could we admit an argument of this general nature. (The attempt below to put E's established characteristics up against the Quarto represents quite another order of evidence.) In Dr. Walker's *Textual Problems of the First Folio* (1953), p. 153, *pudled* is added as an anomaly passed on from Q to F. It is true that Compositor B, setting from manuscript in *The Comedy of Errors*, spells it *puddled*; but again one swallow does not make a summer and we have no means of knowing whether his spelling of this word was indifferent or whether he was following copy in either text. As for *timerous*, also put forward, E nowhere else sets this word, and hence whether this is his typical spelling cannot be determined. (Arguments in spelling tests from analogy are always dangerous, and so it may or may not be significant that in *Romeo*, II. i. 31, E follows copy in setting the spelling *Humerous*.) Finally, in pp. 153–156 it is noticed that the spelling of weak verbs with *-t* or *-'d* in preterite and past participle is significantly similar in the two texts. The Quarto and Folio both agree in *-t* spellings on 24 occasions, in *-'d* spellings on 25 occasions, and differ on 23 occasions when Q has *-t* but F has *-'d* or *-ed*. Once more the evidence adduced from other plays about variable practice is not associated with identified compositors, and therefore is suspect, despite Sir Walter Greg's singling-out of this as the clinching evidence for the association of the two texts (*The Shakespeare First Folio* (1955), p. 363) although the other spelling evidence adduced seemed to him to be weak. When the spellings associated with Compositor E are surveyed, the evidence of his section proves to have little if any primary value. In his stint Q has 7 *-t* endings, 4 of which are duplicated in F. However, one of these, *capt*, does not appear elsewhere in Shakespeare. The second, *stufft*, comes twice in E's setting of *Romeo and Juliet* where E is following his copy and hence we have no means of knowing whether he did or did not prefer this spelling. The third and fourth are *past* (for *pass'd*), which comes under the same stricture, for E follows his copy *past* twice in *Titus* and once in *Romeo*. Hence E's personal characteristics for these words cannot be determined, and in these circumstances no conjecture about the influence of copy on his forms in *Othello* is permissible. In the remaining three cases he spelled Q *-t* (*blest, blusht, wisht*) with *-'d* and he once set *profest* from manuscript. Since E often followed copy in *-t* but also had some tendency to change to *-'d*, it is not necessarily significant that in none of the few remaining possibilities does he set Q *-'d* as *-ed* or as *-t*. As Greg indicated, in the *Othello* argument the random notice of unusual spellings as evidence for the genetic relationship of two texts is not sound practice, at least when such evidence is adduced as primary and not as merely supplementary to a case already well on the way to being established by other means.

Established Texts and Definitive Editions

NOTHING BUT CONFUSION can result from the popular assumption that only one form of an established text can ever exist, and hence that a definitive edition of a single form of a literary work is invariably possible.

In some major part the confusion stems from the application of concepts suitable for manuscript textual criticism to the usually quite disparate problems of texts preserved in printed books. For example, in an English Renaissance printed text the bifurcation of authority between the words themseleves and their transient forms ('substantives' and 'accidentals' in Sir Walter Greg's convenient terminology[1]) is unknown in classical-manuscript textual theory, for the distance between the classical holograph and the inscription of the preserved examples makes it impossible, usually, for any of the accidentals to derive from the holograph with enough fidelity for any question of authority to inhere in their forms. Thus it is customary to modernize these accidents of a classical text, and it follows that the establishment of such a text does not include the variant forms of its accidentals.

On the contrary, a printed text usually stands in such close relationship to its holograph[2] that one of its editions will derive without intermediary from the manuscript archetype, and on some occasions this manuscript may even be the ultimate holograph. The sometimes demonstrable assumption follows that various of the print's accidentals have been transmitted faithfully from the author's original and therefore that they may have a significant authority, even though this authority will be less than that held by the substantives. Little doubt ordinarily arises that the first

Printed in *Philological Quarterly*, 41 (1962), 1–17. This volume of *PQ* was entitled *Studies in English Drama, Presented to Baldwin Maxwell*, edited by C. B. Woods and C. A. Zimansky; reprinted with permission of the Department of Publications, The University of Iowa.

1 For his statement of this principle, see "The Rationale of Copy-Text," *Studies in Bibliography*, III (1950–51), 19 ff.

2 I use 'archetype' not as the first, or original inscription of the text, but instead as that lost manuscript, whatever its assumed nature, from which all surviving documents may be presumed to trace their descent.

printed transcript of a text has been preserved, whereas few manuscripts can claim to derive without lost intermediaries from the holograph or its archetype. And if there is reason to believe that a holograph manuscript served as printer's copy, a closely knit sequence results along which authority is transmitted in some detail. The loosely woven texture of manuscript transmission with its unknown gaps between preserved specimens, and the frequent collateral relationship of these specimens, can at best pass along only verbal authority.

The various methods for establishing a manuscript text depend, in general, upon the collation of all known copies, the systematic separation of their texts into allied divisions, and the construction of a family tree that will reveal the primary sources of authority. When, as usual, two or more divisions radiate from the archetype in collateral relationship to each other, no one among the texts that head these divisions can automatically be assigned superior authority to any other on the ground that it is in a closer position to the archetype. Thus all texts at the head of radiating collateral series have some authority, and the problem of establishing the text—once the family tree is drawn—devolves upon linguistic analysis, palaeographical reasoning, and literary criticism applied to the various primary documents, all of technically equal authority as a whole.

Authority at the head of radiating collateral branches is very seldom found in printed texts; and thus the rationale appropriate for establishing manuscript texts has little validity in a strictly bibliographical situation where direct derivation is almost invariably one's postulate. When documents are not in collateral but in direct (derived) relationship, verbal variation can result from only two causes: (1) corruption inherent in the process of transmission, together with some unauthoritative correction of obvious errors; or (2) in addition to the above, the entrance of fresh authority as by authorial intervention or by conflation with an independent manuscript,[3] in either case as part of a reprint of the basic text.

The determination whether variants between any two editions result from corruption or from the entrance of fresh authority is largely a critical

---

3 Strictly speaking, few such 'independent' manuscripts would be found utilized in this connection, for 'independence' ought to mean independently derived in radiation from the archetype and thus in a different family from the manuscript used as printer's copy. But in ordinary bibliographical work it is customary to speak loosely of an 'independent' manuscript only as one that differs from another in respects that go beyond normal transmissional variation, no matter whether it be in collateral or in genetic relationship. Thus if we may assume that the Folio *Hamlet* printer's copy was Q2 collated with a manuscript from a series of altered theatrical transcriptions, we should ordinarily call it 'independent' because it was not the same manuscript (or a close transcript of it) used as printer's copy for Q2 but instead one that had been modified, even though it must have been derived from the manuscript behind Q2 if this is taken to have been holograph foul papers.

problem, although bibliographical considerations exercise an important check on critical findings in so far as bibliographical experience may assist in establishing normal limits for corruption.[4] But once the clearcut determination of the source of the variation has been made, the bibliographical critic proceeds to establish the text according to principles very different from those used in manuscript criticism where one must assume that all primary collateral texts are relatively equal in authority.

If in a printed book no new authority has entered within a series of derived editions, no variant in a derived text can possibly have authority, even though it may correct an error in the primary, authoritative edition. If the author revises a derived text, as Dryden revised for the second and third editions of *The Indian Emperour* in 1668 and 1670, the verbal variants must be assumed to be authoritative except for those suspected to represent transmissional corruption. Thus as a whole the variant words in the first edition, in such a case, cannot be assumed to be theoretically as authoritative as the altered words of the revised third edition. It follows that a critic may not pick and choose between the first and third-edition variants, according to criteria suitable for the establishment of a classical-manuscript text whereby one may select variants between two collateral manuscripts of technically equal authority.

Even the very few difficult Elizabethan texts like Shakespeare's *Hamlet* and *Othello* are no longer subjected to the treatment appropriate for manuscript texts, as they were in the eighteenth and early nineteenth centuries. Instead, these have come under the influence of the bibliographical rationale even though the complexity of their situation calls for more eclectic treatment than is proper for the relatively simple situation found in *The Indian Emperour.* In contrast to the usual situation among collateral texts where variation is normally postulated as caused by corruption on one part from the relative purity of the archetype, some elements or revision (in fact or in effect) are found in all these Elizabethan texts, and thus the task is not alone one of choosing between correct and corrupt readings but also of choosing between two truly authoritative variants. When this latter choice is involved, the eclecticism appropriate for collateral manu-

---

4 This 'experience' may operate in two ways (1) General experience with the transmission of texts at a given period may usefully suggest the kinds of variants to be expected from normal corruption, and their rough extent. (2) Precise identification and testing of the agents of transmission may establish, much more accurately, the norms to be expected under the given conditions. Thus we may know that some fresh authority has entered the text of the Folio *Othello* as against the Quarto (1) because the variation is more extensive in quantity, and qualitatively quite different, from that normally predictable in simple reprinting; and (2) because a study of Compositor E, who set Act I in the Folio, shows that in certain control reprint texts like *Titus* and *Romeo and Juliet* he did not produce of his own accord variation in quantity or quality approaching that found in Folio *Othello* in his typesetting.

script texts is inappropriate in an essentially bibliographical situation where other methods more suitable for the peculiar problem must be devised.

The bibliographical establishment of texts differs, therefore, in two important respects from the rationale for the establishment of most manuscript texts. First, authority resides in some part in the accidentals of a text as well as in its substantives, and it is even possible that the most authoritative edition in respect to the accidentals may not be the same as the most authoritative edition in respect to the substantives. Second, the verbals, or substantives, of a printed text (as well as its accidents) are not established by critical selection made from a corpus of variants accumulated by collation of all available copies, with especial relation to the variants in the manuscripts that head each major radiating family.

In most situations textual bibliography, with reference to critical reasoning, can determine that only the readings in a single edition have any authority and that the variants in all other editions are unauthoritative. In other situations when two or more editions possess some authority, the physical derivation of one edition from the other can usually be demonstrated. In such a situation the readings of one or other edition will have pre-eminent authority because of the superiority of their source in a manner theoretically impossible for collateral manuscripts radiating from a single archetype.[5]

That the establishment of printed texts depends on a different rationale from that of manuscripts was perceived in some part by the mid-nineteenth century although the bibliographical method did not become fully operative, perhaps, until after the first world war. Yet the implications of the older thinking still linger on, especially in the concept that in all cases a single established text can be contrived. In what follows I attempt a summary explanation of the theories of the newer bibliography, as I see them, as applied to the problems of establishing printed texts and thence to questions of definitive editions and what may be expected of them.

The classical theory of establishment of a text envisaged the recovery of the most authoritative verbals from a number of partially corrupt documents in so logical a manner that (barring the discovery of new primary documents) the task would never need re-doing since the results would in the main be universally acceptable. Thereupon, the establisher attacked all remaining cruces, or anomalies, by what was known as the method of

5 This whole discussion has been greatly simplified in order to point up the difference in basic rationales, and thus the frequent complexities of manuscript criticism have been ignored. For example, although in theory manuscript texts heading collateral branches are technically equal in authority, an editor is not likely to find that this is so in practice. But the essential point remains that an edition of a book subsequent to the first is not often set up directly from a new manuscript serving as printer's copy.

higher criticism; i.e., the deployment of palaeographical, linguistic, and critical reasoning to bear on emendation. When human ingenuity and learning seemed to have exhausted the correction of the text, and general consent was secured as to the results, the text could be declared to be finally established. That is, although future critics might here and there improve isolated verbals by emendation or by substituting a rejected documentary reading (or the discovery of subsidiary manuscripts might suggest the solution to a few difficulties), the major framework of the text had been recovered and 'established' as that of the archetype in the vast majority of its readings by the exhaustion of all available or pertinent evidence. A definitive edition could then be prepared that presented this established eclectic text together with the major evidence for its formation to serve as proof that correct conclusions had been drawn.

In this procedure are present two major divisions: the exhaustion of the documentary evidence, followed by critical emendation.

The exhaustive establishment of the most authoritative form of the readings present in the various documentary forms of the text requires three steps. First, the collection of the full range of textual variation which, in a sense, establishes the facts about the different detailed forms of the text in all preserved documents that might have some claim to authority. Second, the establishment by means of a family tree of the only truly authoritative documents, a process that immediately narrows the significance of textual variation to those forms present in a limited number of manuscripts.

The third step may vary according to the circumstances and to the textual method favored by the critic. On the one hand, he may be required to select some single documentary form of the text as superior to all others as a whole and to establish the text on its evidence, admitting substitute readings from other authoritative documents only when manifest corruption is present in the 'best' manuscript. On the other, he may treat all authoritative manuscripts as substantially equal in authority, and on the basis of his critical judgment select readings eclectically from any of these documents according as they appear to him to represent the correct variant and the others to be errors. In either case, the text at the conclusion of this stage is 'established' in its final documentary form in so far as all readings are drawn from some preserved physical example. Whether little discretion is allowed the textual critic, as with Lachmann, or maximum discretion, as with Housman, whether systematic or higher criticism has gone into the selection of the readings in the established text, all readings have some documentary authority.

In the final polish of the second phase, all remaining errors are corrected by critical emendation applied to the established documentary form of the text. Since no such emendation can have any documentary authority, in one sense emended readings depend utterly on their apparent inevitability, and the resulting common consent, to secure an authority of their own on different grounds from documentary authority. This inevitability will not be granted unless (a) textual corruption is accepted as present in all variant documentary forms; (b) the emendation seems not only suitable and manifestly superior to all others suggested but also so satisfying as to prevent further curiosity in the matter; and (c) preferably, as part of the satisfaction, an explanation can be made of the process by which the conjecturally recovered pure reading came to exist in the corrupt documentary form(s).

Given the numerous ways in which textual corruption evolves during the process of transmission, it may be a moot question whether in many decisions there is any essential difference between an editorial choice from among variant documentary readings and the act of independent editorial emendation. Certainly the same powers of critical, linguistic, and palaeographical reasoning lie behind results secured from correct selection as behind independent recovery. Thus the second major stage should be considered as much a part of the final establishment of a text as is the intermediate process of the establishment of its most authoritative documentary readings.

In the simplest bibliographical circumstance only one early document that could contain textual authority is preserved; i.e., a book is known only in its first edition and there is no evidence to lead one to suppose that other contemporary editions were ever printed. Thomas Dekker's *Match Me in London* (1631) may be taken as an example. If in such a situation the press's multiplication of copies from a single typesetting were in fact of no significance, the situation would be the same as if only one manuscript copy of a text had been preserved. No opportunity to establish the text from multiple documents could exist, since the single document must represent the only extant authority, one that is automatically established by its singularity.[6] That the authority of the document and of the details of its readings are simultaneously established through necessity means that the corrective emendation of the text is isolated from the process of documentary establishment.

However, uniqueness of documentary authority in this narrow sense is

6 This statement needs qualification when, as frequently in early prints, the inking of the impression is so poor that it may be no single copy can establish the authentic details of the text. Dekker's *If This Be Not a Good Play* (1612) needed collation of almost a dozen copies before every mark of punctuation could be firmly identified. The types of the commas and periods are so worn in the quarto of Marlowe's *Massacre at Paris* that examination of all recorded copies may be insufficient to distinguish these two marks accurately in every place of doubt. Under such conditions the evidence from multiple copies is required in order to establish the exact details of the typesetting that made the impression.

not a usual characteristic of Elizabethan hand-printed books.[7] The custom of proofreading while early sheets were printing, and then of stopping the press to make corrections in the type (perhaps several times during a run), leads to variant readings within the same edition-typesetting. For example, a comparison of twenty-six copies of *Match Me in London* has disclosed 199 variant readings made in press, and there is reason to suppose that more exist as yet unseen.

These variants, impossible in a unique manuscript, offer a difficult problem in authority. The original readings, we know, were set by the compositor, that workman who was in immediate relation to the archetypal printer's copy. The corrected readings, we know, were ordered either by the author or by the printing-house proofreader. Any demonstrable authorial variant must be accepted, whether correction or revision.[8] Moreover, if the proofreader could be shown to have read proof back against the copy, many of his alterations would be more authoritative than the readings of the compositor's original typesetting that had presumably altered the copy; and it could be argued that a text established in its most authoritative form must necessarily substitute the corrected proof-alterations for the assumed compositorial errors.

On the other hand, bibliographical investigations suggest that the number of early authors regularly attending the press was severely limited. Moreover, it is clear that the usual Elizabethan proofreader did not consult copy regularly, if at all. Since he usually relied on his own judgment for his alterations, he could sometimes misunderstand the meaning and corrupt the text by his 'corrections,' as happened in Chettle's *Hoffman* and Dekker's *Match Me*. Even at best, his alterations (however advisable, or even necessary) could not in any sense be authoritative when made without reference to copy; and hence his ministrations generally interfered with the only authority we have—the compositor's typesetting from manuscript.

A finally established text might adopt some of the proofreader's own alterations, but these would be substituted for original readings not because they possessed archetypal authority (as would variant readings selected from collateral manuscripts) but because they had been put on the same basis as editorial emendation. That is, the acceptance of unauthoritative proofreader's variants must ordinarily belong in the second

---

7 It can exist in the unusual circumstances whereby an edition of a book is preserved in a unique copy, as is Q1 of *Titus Andronicus*, or when collation fails to discover any press-correction, as in the eleven completely similar copies of Dekker, Ford, and Rowley, *Witch of Edmonton* (1658).

8 An author may correct an error made by the compositor, or he may revise a correct and originally authoritative reading. In the latter circumstance, both readings would be authoritative and correct, but the revision would carry the superior authority of the author's later intentions.

division of the establishment of the text (its correction), not in the first. It is true that they constitute documentary evidence, but critical and bibliographical investigation have disclosed their lack of authority and hence they have no status except as unauthoritative alterations that are technically the same as editorial emendation in the second phase. They cannot represent primary documentary authority. Indeed, it would be dangerous, perhaps, even to award them a secondary authority merely because they are a part of the total documentary evidence were it not that some critics might feel a doubt on occasion about the question of their origin and thus of their authority or non-authority.

If it is improper to include unauthoritative press-corrections in the establishment of the documentary form of the text, they should not be included in the finally established form if they would not ordinarily be made as editorial emendation. The argument here rests on the narrow question of true authority and how it is transmitted. One might object that the final form given to the text in the printing shop constituted the highest authority as representing the corrected state that the printer intended to offer to the public. But this is to attribute to 'the printer' a control over the product of his press that is, in this instance, vested in the proofreader, with his variable practice. Moreover, it suggests that the printer's authority is higher than the author's. We no longer believe in such hypotheses as that a distinctive house-style was imposed upon a manuscript as a matter of policy by an Elizabethan printer; but we do know that a compositor was sure to overlay some of his own personal characteristics upon a text, and the proofreader some of his own too.

Even when we have no certain means of knowing the archetypal manuscript form of a reading, we recognize that the odds favor that form found in the state of the text that lies nearest to the manuscript. If the duty of a textual critic is to recover from the print as many characteristics as he can of the lost manuscript that served as copy, he must take as his primary authority the earliest state of the typesetting, and he must think of proofreaders' alterations as having, generally, no more authority than the variants that would be deliberately introduced by the compositor of a reprint edition.[9]

Bibliographical logic suggests, therefore, that the object of the collation of multiple copies of a single edition is not to discover all known press-corrections in order to adopt them. On the contrary, the collation should

9 However, in some circumstances an editor may find it more convenient, or consistent, to adopt most of the proofreader's variants in accidentals if he can argue that in so doing he is preserving an even texture with the similar forms of the accidentals as they largely appear elsewhere in the document. Occasionally this may be a valid argument in a particular text in so far as it concerns the practical process of editing for reading purposes.

be undertaken in order to discover the original readings underneath the usually sophisticated press-altered typesetting and thus to establish the exact details of the original typesetting and complete the first phase of the total establishment.

The simplicity of the unique and therefore automatically single edition is not in the least altered when all subsequent editions are derived reprints containing no fresh authority. 'Authority' here, as always, is to be strictly interpreted as direct authorial correction or revision, or else the conflation of a printed text with some authoritative manuscript. Of course, a critic must collate all editions in a range wherein authority might exist in order to reconstruct their familial relationship. But if they are straight reprints (or editorially altered reprints), they will all derive ultimately from the single authoritative edition. Hence the critic cannot treat their variant readings as he can collateral manuscript variants, for no variant in a reprint can possibly have any authority. When all editions derive from it, the first edition is isolated as the sole documentary authority and we have essentially the same situation as if only the first edition had been published as our sole witness.

The editor of a definitive edition would correct this substantive text by emendation (either his own or drawn from various other unauthoritative sources) and he would note the details of his departures in these respects from the established documentary form of the original typesetting. As evidence for his reconstruction of the original documentary form, the editor would provide the complete list of press-variants, identified by the copies collated; and as evidence for his isolation of the one authoritative edition he would print a historical list of the substantive and other significant variants in the later editions collated.

It is a truism too often neglected by editors that the reader of a definitive critical edition should (a) be able to reconstruct from the data the significant details of the copy-text; (b) be in possession of the whole number of facts from which the editor constructed his text. Under (a) appear the records of all departures from the copy-text (both of substantives and accidents) except for those listed categories that have been made silently. Obviously, no so-called 'significant' departure should come under the heading of silent alterations. Space does not permit a full discussion of this matter. It is clear, however, that the first question is: significant to whom? Here a firm distinction must be made between the requirements of a critical reader and those of a bibliographer, and it must be recognized that most of the needs of the latter can be satisfied only by the original, or by an excellent photographic facsimile. The bibliographical analysis of the text should have been made by the editor, who in his introduction has reported the evidence and his findings. Hence there is no need to record in a critical edition such points of purely bibliographical interest as wrong-font letters, and so on. For an attempt at the separation of the significant from the non-significant in Elizabethan dramatic texts, one may consult the Textual Introduction in Vol. I of *Dramatic Works of Thomas Dekker.*

Under (b), the retailing in a definitive edition of the facts available to the editor from which he constructed his text, one may place the records of press-variants in their formes, a historical collation of substantive variants in early editions, and possibly a collation of significant substantive variants in the texts of previous editors. In each of these categories an editorial choice has been involved, and the proof of one's editorial integrity is the recording in a usable form of the data bearing on the matter. Thus only when press-variants are listed in their formes, and with a notation of the copies in which they appear, can a critical reader have the evidence to assess the editor's judgment about their authority or non-authority, and the facts on which to judge the editor's selection in his text. The historical collation of variants in early editions serves as the record of the evidence on which the editor's choice of copy-text was based, and his estimate of the authority or non-authority of editions other than the copy-text. This list has a secondary usefulness in that it also preserves the record of textual corruption for the informative interest this has to textual critics, and it may serve as the basis for the identification of the copy used by other editors. The recording of substantive variants from preceding editors is a more vexed question. Certainly an editor must collate these editions in order to have a conspectus of the emendation proposed for the text and to give due credit when he adopts any of these emendations. Moreover, by listing the rejected emendations an editor can provide his reader with the total body of opinion from which he himself worked, and a reader may be able to judge whether or not the editor's emendation practice has invariably been well-founded. On the other hand, a full collation of editorial variants would contain a vast number of errors, faulty readings from an improper choice of copy-text, modernizations of early grammar, and so on. Little reason seems to exist for the recording of this sad record of editorial corruption (except to point with tacit pride to one's own probity). Thus if an editor will take the responsibility for deciding between the emendations of earlier editors (which he can list) and their errors of commission and omission (which he should not list), a powerful argument exists for the value of such a collation. But this is a far cry from the non-selective variorum principle, which should have no place in a critical definitive text and its apparatus.

The establishment of a text becomes more complex when an author selects some printed edition as the basis for his revision, and turns over to the printer this printed text embellished with autograph deletions, additions, and substitutions. In these circumstances the original edition set throughout from manuscript retains all the authority that accrues from its closeness to the archetype. The author's revisions, in so far as these can be isolated from other variants, also have authority, one that must usually supersede his original intentions.[10]

As a part of the first phase of the establishment, the documentary forms both of the original and of the revised edition must be ascertained independently. Then by a combined bibliographical and critical inquiry these two established texts are compared in order to isolate the author's revisions from the unauthoritative variants normally concomitant with a reprint typesetting.

In this process there are both similarities and dissimilarities with the choice of readings from collateral manuscripts. The most marked difference is that the critic is not chiefly concerned with discovering which are the authoritative (pure) and which the unauthoritative (corrupt) forms of all variants, but, instead, he focuses his inquiry on ascertaining which are the authoritative revisions of the initially authoritative pure readings (and, of course, which are the corrections of initial error). The question of corruption versus authority enters only in respect to the probability that a small number of substantive variants in the revised edition will be transmissional corruptions of satisfactory original readings that were left untouched by the revising author.[11]

In so far as the initial presumption must hold that all substantive variants in each edition have authority, the method for distinguishing the original pure reading from the corrupt form in the revised text has some resemblance to the final stage of the documentary establishment of manuscript texts. But the similarity is more apparent than real. Once the fact

10 Space does not permit examination of the exceptions to this principle. For example, if it could be shown that the revisions were made in order to adjust the work to a lower grade of reader, the work would be brought into the two-text category where the most authoritative documentary form of each would need to be established. It would then be up to the editor of a definitive edition to print a corrected version of each in parallel, or to choose the superior literary form of the text and to record variants from it. Nevertheless, such an exception would not justify the editor of a definitive edition in selecting on his own literary preference the earlier text when the author had revised the later without prejudice. That is, some of the alterations of the final authorized edition of *Leaves of Grass* may seem to a literary critic to be inferior in merit to the readings of earlier editions. But when only a single definitive reading text is being constructed (and not independent definitive editions of the two or more forms of the text), an editor must choose Whitman's final intentions.

11 Of course, some corruption may also enter in the transmission of the author's revisions, but the detection of these is part of the emending stage, not of the documentary establishment. From the strict point of view, a corrupted revision has more authority than the originally authoritative reading that was revised. The logic of this position should be obvious: the reading that is closest to the autograph revision must be that in the later edition, even though it is a corruption. If the original had more authority, a critic would be forced to prefer it instead of emending the corrupt revision in order to recover the author's revised intention.

of revision has been established, and the physical derivation of one text from another ascertained, a presumptive superior authority that is difficult to secure in most collateral-manuscript situations can be given to the readings in the revised edition as a whole. Moreover, the fact of derivation, and the preservation of the relevant documents with no gaps caused by lost intermediaries, means that a bibliographical analysis of variants is possible that could scarcely occur in manuscript study where the exact copy used by a scribe can seldom be preserved or recovered. In these special circumstances, eclecticism is strictly limited and is under the rule of bibliographical probability.

In such a situation we have, then, the following established documentary texts: (1) the authoritative original edition as a whole, and (2) the authoritative revised edition as a whole. The textual critic will ordinarily proceed for each text to the second phase of establishment, the correction by emendation of each text in its respective authoritative form.

Here the matter rests, with two established texts, unless a definitive edition is called for. At this point an editoral decision must be made about the form of this edition. If the revisions are not so numerous or far-reaching as to constitute a major recasting of the work, the editor may decide that the text as presented for reading should reproduce the author's revised intentions, the original readings being listed for the reader's information in footnotes or in an appendix. If this is the decision (as ordinarily it should be), the problem of divided authority between the substantives and the accidentals immediately arises.

Throughout the sixteenth and seventeenth centuries, and to a slightly lesser extent in the eighteenth, the compositor was accustomed to superimpose a number of his own characteristics on the accidents of his copy, with the result that the separation of authorial forms from compositorial is no casual matter. The usual experience of textual critics suggests that in the sixteenth and seventeenth centuries, at least, many an author accepted with indifference the accidents of a print and would make slight effort to improve them except in cases of egregious error. Thus the variant accidentals of a revised edition are likely to differ little in their kind from the unauthoritative alterations that are quite normal in simple reprints.

Moreover, in these same centuries enough evidence may be found to suggest that even when an author, like Dryden in *The Indian Emperour*, had some concern with the presentation of his spelling and punctuation in print, and made an effort to revise it, together with his substantive revision, the general overlay of the characteristics of the compositor of the revised edition makes it impossible to do more than guess at a few of his accidentals revisions. Indeed, statistical evidence can be gathered from the textual history of *The Indian Emperour* to indicate that if one reprinted the accidents of the revised edition, one would be reproducing many more of the compositor's unauthoritative variants than of Dryden's possible revisions.[12]

In the eighteenth century some examples have shown us that the greater faithfulness of compositors to copy that accompanied the regularization of spelling, and so on, enables a critic, occasionally, to identify the majority of the revised accidents of an author. In such a situation, it is obvious that the authority of identifiable accidentals as well as substantives is superior in the revision to that in the original version and thus that the definitive edition may be based on the established documentary form of the revised text in both its parts.[13]

However, in earlier times when the compositor exercised a more powerful influence on the accidents of a text, in ordinary course one must acknowledge the superior authority of the revised substantives but the superior authority of the original accidentals since these are necessarily in closest relationship to the manuscript forms, whatever they were.[14] Thus a definitive critical edition[15] would ordinarily incorporate the authoritative substantives of the revised edition with the authoritative texture of the accidentals of the original printing.[16] Properly accomplished, the resulting text would be the closest obtainable approximation of the revised printer's copy (assuming the original edition served as the basis for the revision) or of an author's fair copy of his revised intentions. As such it could be called the established form of the most authoritative eclectic text.

At some point the quantity and quality of an author's revisions may make quite impracticable the conflation of two different editions in respect to the substantives and accidentals. The Quarto and Folio texts of Ben Jonson's *Every Man in his Humour* are an early example; *The Prelude* of Wordsworth, *Leaves of Grass*, of Whitman, and Henry James's *Roderick Hudson* are later ones. In any such occurrence, the principle already suggested holds with added force that original and revision are

12 See "Current Theories of Copy-Text, with an Illustration from Dryden," *Modern Philology*, XLVIII (1950), 12–20.

13 See Arthur Friedman, "The Problem of Indifferent Readings in the Eighteenth Century, with a Solution from *The Deserted Village*," *Studies in Bibliography*, XIII (1960), 143–147. [This is, however, a special situation; in general in many eighteenth-century texts, the accidentals of a revised edition have little or no authority compared to that of the primary document.]

14 This distinction is made easier, of course, when an author chose for the printer's copy of a revision not the original edition but some later reprint, as in *Tom Jones*. Here the variant accidents from the forms of the original editions can have no authority, and therefore they do not gain authority from being transmitted to the revised edition through the indifferent choice of copy.

15 For some consideration of the meaning of this term, see my *Textual and Literary Criticism* (Cambridge University Press, 1959), Lecture IV, particularly p. 119 ff.

16 See references above in footnotes 1 and 12.

two separate entities, that the documentary and final form of each text can be established but that no conflation is practicable (as it is in Dryden's *Indian Emperour* or in Dekker's *1 Honest Whore*) to conjoin the special authoritative features of the respective editions. In this situation definitive editions can be made up of each established text separately, as has been done with the first and last editions of *Leaves of Grass*. Or, as with Wordsworth's *Prelude*, the early and the revised forms may be printed together as parallel-texts.

Although the ideal of this present discourse has been the critical edition, since I believe that this is the most highly developed form that a definitive text can take, we must not overlook the requirements for definitive editions of established texts in photographic and type-facsimile form (like the Shakespeare Quarto Facsimiles and the Malone Society Reprints) or various diplomatic reprints of some particular authority. The establishment of the text of any single authority has been considered above, and I have examined elsewhere some of the problems of reproducing such essentially reprint texts in definitive editions suitable for their kind.[17]

Difficulties and anomalies are sure to arise, but troubles in dealing with special cases should not obscure the general validity of principles that apply with ease to the vast majority of problems. The Elizabethan drama, and particularly Shakespeare, has a small number of peculiar texts in which the difficulty stems chiefly, one may suspect, from the anomalies of the theatrical transmission in manuscript before printing as against the usual literary transmission of other genres or else of dramatic texts under firmer authorial control.

These Shakespeare texts divide roughly into two categories: (1) that in which the text appears first in a corrupt version that is subsequently corrected; (2) that in which the text appears in two authoritative versions.

Representative of the first is *The Merry Wives of Windsor*, *Richard III*, and *King Lear*. These are now generally believed to be so-called 'badquarto' texts; i.e., memorial reconstructions of a good text without transcriptional link to a holograph of the original. In *The Merry Wives* no sufficient evidence has ever been advanced to lead us to suppose that the Folio has any bibliographical relation to the Quarto print. But in *Richard III* and *King Lear* we know that the Quarto was annotated by reference to a good manuscript in an attempt to bring the print into general conformity so that it could substitute for the manuscript as the copy for typesetting a corrected edition.

In each text the exact relation between the manuscript text that was

17 See my "The Problem of the Variant Forme in a Facsimile Edition," *The Library*, 5th ser., VII (1952), 262–272.

memorially reconstructed and the manuscript collated to make up the printer's copy is obscure. Nonetheless, it is clear, whatever the history of the lost manuscript(s), that the superior print stands in relation to the inferior as a correction of a greatly corrupt minor authority, and not as a revision of an originally pure text. This being so, each text can be established on its own merits in documentary form. Then, in the final stage of the establishment—the correction of the superior text—the critic can survey the variants between the two in order to investigate whether the superior text needs emendation in any individual readings by substitution of verbals from the bad quarto. To some limited degree all such texts have admitted a few readings from the inferior text as corrections of errors in the superior. But the choice if usually a straight one between error and correction.[18] The text of any definitive edition would, of course, be that of the corrected superior edition. It should be noticed that except when the later compositor was setting from manuscript annotations, the accidents of neither edition have any authority, since the bad-quarto edition had no transcriptional link with the holograph.

On the other hand, such plays as *Troilus and Cressida, Hamlet,* and *Othello* exist in two authoritative textual versions, Quarto and Folio. For *Troilus* there is some reason to believe that the two versions represent original and authorial revision, perhaps in reverse order; but the situation for *Othello* and *Hamlet* is complicated by what seems to be evidence of theatrical alterations, some of doubtful authority, perhaps mingled with some authorial revision. In these plays the only truly established text, in any pure sense, must be the documentary corrected state of each as a separate entity. (Incidentally, the correction of either text does not preclude the substitution of readings from the other, provided that the readings affected are corruptions that resulted from the transmission of the printer's copy into print. But the eclectic choice of

18 In some circumstances it might be argued that the Bad Quarto contained a later stage of the text than the manuscript that served as printer's copy for the good edition and thus that there could be a choice between a revision and the original. However, such a hypothetical situation can have no bearing on the choice of readings, for demonstration is usually impossible that a corrupt text contains a revised variant. Thus to all practical purposes the choice is invariably between the preservation of the original true reading in the bad text as against a corrupt reading in the good text. For instance, if in *Romeo and Juliet* a traditional editor (somewhat inexplicably, perhaps) prefers "a rose by any other name" from the bad Q1 to "a rose by any other word" from the good Q2, he can justify his choice from Q1 only if he takes it that "word" in Q2 is a compositorial memorial error for manuscript (and Q1) "name". The established derivation of Q2 chiefly from an authoritative manuscript permits no other assumption than corruption, for it would be idle to try to argue that "word" was Shakespeare's original reading, which he altered in the acting manuscript to "name", whence the Q1 reporter recalled it.

superior readings under any other conditions would destroy the logic of the establishment of each text as the closest reconstruction possible of its separate printer's copy.)

In such a complex situation where the authority of any satisfactory pair of variants is much in doubt—whether representing sophisticated corruption and pure reading, or pure reading and revision—the establishment of an eclectic text on any sound terms other than tradition is very difficult. The author's final intentions, which in simpler problems act as a sufficient guide, are here greatly obscured by the unknown theatrical history of the underlying manuscripts. It is very likely that some of these modern traditionally established texts made up from critically superior readings represent, actually, a curious mélange of literary and theatrical intentions. All that can be said is that the current tendency seems to be in the direction of formulating a more unified text than in the past by emphasizing a single rather than a freely mixed textual tradition.

In this process of feeling one's way towards a new establishment, the critical intelligence is guided by the criteria evolved from the hypothetical reconstruction of the history of the two lost manuscripts. Although such an inquiry is not the concern of bibliography, the critical method is in some considerable part aided by the bibliographical limits placed on conjecture according as the two prints can be shown to be in roughly collateral relationship (each set from a different manuscript) or in partly derived (the Folio set from an annotated Quarto). In this endeavor the principle of separate authority for substantives and for accidentals also holds, according as the printer's copy for one or other edition appears to be in the closer relation to a holograph. When the Folio can be shown to have been set from an annotated Quarto, as with *Troilus* or *Othello*, the Quarto accidentals alone are authoritative but the Quarto substantives for the most part must yield to the revised substantives of the Folio whenever these can be shown to have authority.

The Text of Johnson

T HE SECOND VOLUME of the Yale edition of Johnson's works contains *The Idler* edited by W. J. Bate and John M. Bullitt of Harvard, and *The Adventurer* edited by L. F. Powell of Oxford with the help of Professor Bate in the commentary.[1]

It is unfortunate that this division of labor has resulted in a number of anomalies that have not been ironed out by the general editorial supervision. Chief among these irregularities are the quite divergent views of the editors in respect to the theory of copy-text.

The Adventurer was published serially in folio between 1752 and 1754, consecutively signed and paged with the intent to gather the sheets later into a collection. This binding-up of the original printing of the papers, with general title-pages and preliminaries, was issued in two volumes dated 1753 and 1754, respectively. In 1754, a second edition was published in four duodecimo volumes, the text containing some authoritative revisions and corrections by Johnson. No later edition appears to have authority.

Dr. Powell has very properly followed the textual theories of his compatriot Sir Walter Greg in the classic essay "The Rationale of Copy-Text." This important statement distinguishes the authority of the 'accidentals,' or the forms that words take in their spelling, capitalization, and division, together with the punctuation that relates them to one another, from the authority of the 'substantives,' or the words themselves of a text. Under ordinary circumstances in printed books the accidentals can be authoritative only in an edition immediately derived from a manuscript, and therefore the closest to the author's practice so far as can be ascertained from the preserved documents. Later reprintings only accumulate the styling of other compositors that places the accidentals system at a farther remove from its ultimate source of authority.

A review-article printed in *Modern Philology*, 61 (1964), 298–309; © 1964 by the University of Chicago; reprinted with permission.

1 *The Idler and the Adventurer.* By Samuel Johnson. Edited by W. J. Bate, John M. Bullitt, and L. F. Powell ("Yale Edition of the Works of Samuel Johnson," Vol. II.) New Haven, Conn.: Yale University Press, 1963. Pp. xxviii + 516.

On the other hand, an author may correct and revise his substantives in later editions so that the verbal readings of such a revised edition are more authoritative than those in the earliest edition set from manuscript. Usually a critic can distinguish most of these revised substantives on literary grounds; but if the author paid any attention to a revision or correction of his accidentals in preparing a new edition, the results are ordinarily indistinguishable from normal compositorial variants in the accidentals expected in any early reprint. Under these circumstances, Greg suggested, an editor produces a critical old-spelling text that combines the maximum authority in both its parts if he uses as copy-text the edition set from manuscript, and therefore reproduces its generally more authoritative accidentals, but substitutes for any of the verbal readings of the copy-text the more authoritative words of a revised edition insofar as he identifies these as actual revisions and corrections.

In *The Adventurer* Dr. Powell follows this sound textual theory generally accepted since its enunciation in 1951. His copy-text is the first edition of 1753–54, but he incorporates such variant readings from the revised second edition of 1754 as he believes to represent Johnson's own substantive alterations.

On the contrary, the Harvard editors of *The Idler* follow the old-fashioned textual theory that chooses the revised edition as such for copy-text in both its parts. *The Idler* was first printed in the newspaper the *Universal Chronicle* between 1758 and 1760. In 1761, the papers were collected and reprinted in a revised edition (format unstated, but duodecimo), and a third edition (format unstated, but duodecimo) appeared in 1767, each in two volumes. According to Bate and Bullitt (pp. xxiii–xxiv), Johnson also oversaw the 1767 edition, although they allow 'few changes' beyond the correction of misprints and the introduction of new errors. Yet since the major revision was made in 1761, they ignore the claims of the theoretically final revised edition of 1767, select the 1761 second edition as their copy-text, and reprint it in all its details except for assumed errors that they correct from the first or third editions.

The editors' account of the textual transmission is so vague that the reasons for their choice of copy-text are not clear. Nowhere is there any discussion whether the 1761 edition was set from a fresh manuscript (which might have justified its choice as copy-text) or from annotated pages of the *Universal Chronicle*, as actually happened. If the latter seemed so self-evident as not to require comment, then the case is by no means so cogent for the authority of the third edition of 1767, since the editors do not trouble to establish what was used for copy and content themselves with the casual footnote that the 1767 printer "probably" based his text on 1761 without consulting the *Universal Chronicle*.[2]

2 This interpretation of their position may do an injustice to the editors, whose footnote reads, "The printer probably did not consult the *Universal Chronicle* but based

According to the outmoded textual theory adopted, favoring the superior over-all authority of a revised edition, they should have chosen the 1767 edition as copy-text; but it is fortunate that they did not. Indeed, no evidence is produced that 1767 was actually corrected by Johnson, nor do the readings enforce any such conclusion. No new revised reading whatever appears in the 1767 text, and when its readings differ from 1761 they are usually in error or (in a handful of cases) revert to the *Universal Chronicle* readings; these latter few are so trivial or obvious, generally, as not to demonstrate Johnson's correction of the edition.[3] But no discussion of these variant readings of 1767 is found in the textual introduction. Thus the 1761 edition is selected on the curious ground that "however cursory the proofreading may have been, [1761] is likely to be closer to the text customarily approved by an author in a first edition." This statement presupposes that Johnson read proof on 1761, but no evidence is adduced to support the view. (The only mention is the footnote [p. xxiii], "The collected edition was published in October 1761 but may have been printed off some months earlier; Johnson was in London so far as is known throughout the summer.") The choice of copy-text thus rests on the unsupported hypothesis that Johnson may have read proof[4] and on the odd implicit assumption that in reading proof he would have altered any house-style accidentals that did not agree with his own system; and hence that he had 'approved' of the 1761 edition in accidentals as well as in substantives. These presuppositions will not convince anyone who has read Greg.

In *The Idler* verbals the results of this choice of the 1761 as copy-text should be equal in authority to the 1758–60; but a manifestly inferior authority for the accidentals has been reprinted. When critical old-spelling texts are concerned, as here, the two textual theories followed by Bate-Bullitt and by Powell differ as the night from the day; and it is singularly unfortunate that no general control was exercised over the

---

his text entirely on 1761." However, the construction is so loose that one cannot be sure that the intention is to make a positive statement that 1761 served as the copy for 1767 but a question might exist whether the *Universal Chronicle* was consulted in the preparation of the copy. The 1767 is, in fact, a line-for-line and page-for-page reprint of the 1761 edition.

3 The chief agreements of *Chronicle* and 1767 against 1761 that might be adduced in arguing for correction by Johnson (or for consultation of *U.C.*) are the appearance of 'the' twice in balanced constructions (omitted in 1761) in page 62, note b, and page 74, note f. and the form 'conveniencies' as against 1761 'conveniences' in page 93, note b. The editors are not entirely consistent. They accept the first two from 1767 but reject the third.

4 He may also have read proof in 1767, if possibility is to be taken as the equivalent of probability. The editors are uncertain about 1767; but though there is no more evidence that he read proof in 1761, the possibility that he did so has dictated their choice of copy-text.

editors in order to secure uniform textual procedure, even within the same volume, for what purports to be a definitive edition of this author.

Textual difficulty within the Yale edition goes deeper, however, than this serious conflict. It is bad enough that *The Idler* is generally authoritative in its substantives but less authoritative in its accidentals, whereas *The Adventurer* employs a different method of editing that should produce maximum authority in both respects. In addition, certain textual rules that appear to have been imposed by the editorial board on both sets of editors effectively preclude general authority in the accidentals even in Powell's section, and make a mishmash out of any theory of what constitutes an established text.

The general editors of the Yale Johnson, in other words, while paying lip service to the principle of a critical old-spelling scholarly edition, have effectively sabotaged a number of the virtues of this form by requiring partial modernization. The Yale text preserves the spelling, hyphenation, and punctuation of whatever edition is chosen as copy-text but reduces all capitals to lower case in the process of modernizing capitalization, possessives,[5] and typography. (Dr. Powell, however, retains capitals "when they have special significance.") No one would wish to retain such features of the original typography as the use of heading capitals to paragraphs, for instance, but the Yale modernization of typography interferes with certain features that are not purely formal, and in the process substitutes conventions that are not characteristic of the period, such as the silent use of double quotation marks about quoted words or phrases in roman which these copy-texts, as usual for the time, put in italics without quote marks. Italicized names of countries and of nationalities are silently put in roman, in an uncharacteristic manner. These are arbitrary distinctions that make for a halfhearted compromise between a popular reading edition and a trustworthy scholarly text, and the result is the usual one attending on compromises in that this edition is not thoroughly satisfactory for either purpose. A popular reader will surely be thrown off stride in his pleasure in the text by the constant and distracting barrage of superior numbers and letters that enforce his attention to footnotes both textual and commentary. And he must still grapple with a punctuation and spelling system that is at least slightly unfamiliar (as unfamiliar as italicized quotations). A scholarly reader cannot take this Yale text to reproduce its copy with an exactitude that

---

5 No clear statement is made as to what is meant by the modernizing of possessives. If the silent regularization of apostrophes in the singular is in question, one can only approve of this sensible procedure. But are plural possessives to be given apostrophes, quite against the usage of the time? This would be a dangerous modernization, and it may be worth noticing that Powell rejects this practice at 349.11 despite the comprehensive editorial statement.

he can trust, because he has no way of knowing whether he is or is not accepting in ignorance any of the extensive editorial silent departures from the copy-text features, some of which end by being interpretative.

Clearly, the decision should have been either to modernize throughout, or to offer a definitive, trustworthy, and scholarly old-spelling text. As it is, the mythical popular reader might well have been able to cope with eighteenth-century capitalization practice if he had any business reading these very eighteenth-century essays; whereas the scholar is short-changed, and no definitive edition of Johnson is yet available to him for trustworthy reference. *The Idler* is not a definitive text because of its faulty textual theory. *The Adventurer* is not a definitive text, though better than *The Idler*, because of its arbitrarily imposed partial modernizations. The specific audience at which this edition is aimed is open to query.

Even the futile attempt to make the edition more attractive to the popular reader is not and cannot be consistent. If we take the second of Johnson's *Adventurer* papers, No. 39, we see that the original capital in 'Sleep' is allowed to stand in the third line on page 345, presumably as a personification. The remaining seven times the capitals in 'Sleep' are silently reduced to lower case, although in some of these as much argument could be advanced in favor of personification as in line 3. Again, on page 345, the capitalized 'Night' is allowed to stand, although the element of personification is far from apparent, and in line 5 of page 346 'Luxury' is capitalized. Yet in the final line of the essay the capital in 'Virtue' at least as much a personification as 'Night' or 'Luxury,' is silently reduced, with some inconsistency.

In *The Idler* the modernizing rules require the editors to change silently to roman the customary italics of *Idler* except when the paper, and not the person, is denoted. Inevitably, their practice is open to the charge of inconsistency because even their retained italics may be questioned, so much has Johnson identified character with paper. In 4.15 'who can be more idle than the reader of the *Idler?*' can we be positive that the paper and not the character is intended? In what way does the intention here differ from such other instances in which roman is silently substituted for italic as 'If those who depend on the Idler for intelligence and entertainment' (5.22)? If we allow italics at 9.10, 'for five letters in the year sent to the *Idler*,' then why did the editors substitute roman at 6.1, 'let him that writes to the Idler remember'?

These examples illustrate the concealed dangers of such basically useless and always inconsistent modernization as is attempted in the Yale editorial practice. It is obvious that by what can often seem only capricious choice the editors of this volume are subtly steering the reader into certain interpretations of meaning, whether of degrees of personification in Johnson's intention, or an assumed distinction between person and paper, without the reader having the opportunity to recognize what is happening to him because the evidence is concealed. In paperback modernizations this danger is accepted as a normal risk; but it has no place in an edition that must necessarily pre-empt the field in addressing a scholarly audience, to whom the fine shades of authorial intention are of rather more significance and who have no desire to be misled by concealed editorial interpretation.

Indeed, if we consider what gain has been secured by opening this Pandora's box of partial modernization, the answer may seem hard to come by. For instance, in *The Adventurer* No. 39, the gain to the hypothetical popular reader in retaining three capitals and silently reducing only nine is not overwhelming in a paper of approximately 1,700–1,900 words. Capitalization is more extensive in *The Idler,* though seldom so common as in No. 1. Yet in Nos. 3, 4, and 5 the reader would have had to encounter only 37, 25, and 33 capitals, respectively, that have been silently reduced for his benefit. Incidentally, not all of these reduced capitals are what are known as 'emphasis capitals'; some of them are partly syntactical, as when they begin a new independent clause after a colon or semicolon used instead of a period, and these may be of more than casual interest.[6]

Other forms of modernization, of doubtful value, lead to anomalies that would make a scholarly critic quite despair of recovering the system of the original documents for these texts. For instance, the silent alteration of italicized quotations to roman within double quotation marks not only is offensive in the texture at this time but also introduces the problem of the relation of these editorially added quotation marks to the accompanying punctuation. The Harvard editors follow the American system, in which no distinction is made between syntactical and actually quoted punctuation marks except for the exclamation and the query. Thus in their text all commas and periods are set within quotes and (following the American typographical practice) all colons and semicolons at the end of a quote are placed outside the quotation marks.

On the other hand, Powell, who, as an Englishman would normally have used the logical English system of distinguishing syntactical from quoted punctuation by its position, seems to have tried to adopt the American system. But not understanding its illogical peculiarities, he ordinarily places *all* punctuation inside the quotation marks and thus goes contrary to the practice both of the United States and of England in respect to his treatment within quotation marks of colons and semicolons (cf. 341.20, 341.24, 351.9 versus the usage in *The Idler* as in 96.5 or 130.20). How-

---

6 The regrettable decision to reduce the typical eighteenth-century 'emphasis capitals' has also carried over to the structural or syntactical capitals that sometimes mark the major divisions of a Johnsonian sentence after semicolons or colons and has thus destroyed a useful signpost to ready comprehension and made the going more difficult for the reader.

ever, as one might anticipate, either he was not consistent or the American compositor could not resist altering copy so that at such a place in his part as 343.17 a semicolon, correctly but inconsistently, stands outside the quotation mark.

The general editors do not seem to have anticipated this problem when they formulated their instructions.[7] Nor do they seem to have been aware of another problem in editing texts: the font of punctuation to be used following an italic word in roman context when the punctuation is entirely syntactical and bears no relation to the italics of the preceding word. The uninstructed Yale printer seems to have followed the popular and (in learned works) unscholarly practice of italicizing this punctuation contrary to all textual logic.

In all-italic passages it would be mere pedantry, surely, to follow in a critical text the eighteenth-century roman commas; but it is not necessarily pedantry for an editor to take the trouble by marking copy to preserve certain traditions that are worth clinging to in scholarly writing and to insist on making logical distinctions between the use of roman and italic punctuation in his edited text. For example, on some occasions the unthinking use of italic violates meaning in a significant manner. When in *Idler* No. 1 at 4.15 Johnson inquires, 'who can be more idle than the reader of the *Idler?*' the editorial use of the italic query violates the usage that would be found if '*Idler*' here had been put into roman within quotation marks; that is, 'who can be more idle than the reader of the "Idler"?' After all, the question mark applies to the sentence as a whole, and not to the word '*Idler*', and hence should share in the typographical logic of the sentence, not as an incorrect modification of the final word as logically indicated by an italic query.

One may expect editors to differ in their view of various texts; and perhaps no two scholars would ever edit a given text critically in an identical manner. But there are other inconsistencies between the editors of this volume that should have been settled by the intervention of the central board. For example, in the footnotes that detail emendation to the copy-text or variant readings of editions other than the copy-text, normal editorial practice does not reproduce terminal punctuation unless it is also in

---

7 Nor did they anticipate another difficulty that results from their policy of altering the use of italic. For instance, not all italic words are quotations. From at least the sixteenth century in English printing it was customary to indicate technical words, or imported words not yet acclimated, by italic. Such a usage appears in *The Adventurer* section, 366.9–10, in the sentence, 'There is, I think, an antient law in Scotland, by which *leasing-making* was capitally punished.' At least, this is the way it appears in the original, but the Yale edition has 'by which Leasing-making was...' A student of the language, who trusted the Yale edition to be accurate enough for him to consult about contemporary usage, would be seriously misled here in his estimate of the status of this word in 1753.

question as a variant in its own right. Powell, correctly, follows this custom, although he is not entirely consistent.[8] On the other hand, the Harvard editors regularly provide in the collation notes the punctuation associated with any words that are listed, even though the punctuation has nothing to do with the variation under scrutiny.

Thus (as only one illustration from many) in the first *Adventurer* paper, No. 34 (p. 341, n. h), the text reads, 'to make merriment supply the place of demonstration;[h] nor was I' and the footnote properly records the emendation, as 'h. 2 demonstration *I* conviction', without indicating that a semicolon common to both variants follows. On the contrary, the Harvard editors regularly (and superfluously) list in their apparatus such accompanying punctuation as on page 17 in *The Idler* No. 5. Here the text reads 'to languish in distress;[h] two hundred thousand ladies', and the footnote recording the *U.C.* variant is given as, 'h. vexation;', complete with redundant semicolon.

A more serious inconsistency between the editors is the amount of information provided in the collational footnotes. These textual footnotes agree with the outmoded variorum practice of mixing together without discrimination the important records of emendation of the copy-text with the less important historical material noticing the variant readings of other collated editions. In remarking on the principle to be used in listing rejected readings from editions other than the copy-text, the Harvard editors state, "We have noted only the variants that are uncommon or in any way ambiguous." Powell contents himself with the statement, "All important variants in the two editions are recorded in the textual notes."

Of the two, Powell keeps his contract in a sensible manner and interprets 'important' as meaning, in the main, substantive. Hence his textual notes concentrate, very properly, on recording departures from his copy-text, whether substantive or accidental, and the source of the emendation. In the second range, his notice of variant readings is confined to the substantives of the second revised edition that for one reason or another have not been accepted. Rejected accidental variants in the second edition are not listed.

On the contrary, the Harvard editors clutter their textual footnotes with dozens of variant readings from the first or third editions (the latter of very doubtful authority) that in no possible sense could come under their criterion of "uncommon or in any way ambiguous." Although the text is in prose, and syllabic value given to the weak preterite is not in question, they regularly list variant elided forms from other editions, as in accepted copy-text 'endeavoured' but *U.C.* 'endeavour'd' (p. 12, n. j), or copy-text 'bewildered' but *U.C.* 'bewildred' (p. 145, n. f), or copy-text 'teaz'd' but

---

8 As in p. 458, n. f, where such punctuation appears.

U.C. and 1767 'teazed' (p. 98, n. g), or copy-text 'remembring' but 1767 'remembering' (p. 85, n. d). Since even the most scrupulous linguist would deny that a difference in pronunciation or in anything else of significance existed between variants such as these, the propriety of listing such compositorial small change as if it were meaningful is obscure. They are not uncommon, and they certainly are not ambiguous.

Powell does not worry about variant spellings in editions other than the copy-text, but the Harvard editors have curious ideas of what constitute uncommon or (in any way) ambiguous spelling variants worth recording. Thus the footnotes carefully pass on to the reader the useless information that the 1761 copy-text 'merely' is spelled 'meerly' in *U.C.* (p. 13, n. b), copy-text 'langour' is spelled 'languor' in 1767 (p. 31, n. i), copy-text 'born' is spelled 'borne' in 1767 (p. 86, n. a), copy-text 'sate' is spelled 'sat' in 1767 (p. 102, n. b; p. 105, n. j) but 'sate' is rejected for 'sat' in the same essay (p. 104, n. e.), copy-text 'withold' is spelled 'withhold' in 1767 (p. 110, n. f.), copy-text 'burden' is spelled 'burthen' in 1767 (p. 110, n. g), copy-text 'bachelors' is spelled 'batchelors' in 1767 (p. 111, n. n), copy-text 'gardiner's' is spelled 'gardener's' in 1767 (p. 116, n. a), copy-text 'sollicit' is spelled 'solicite' in *U.C.* (p. 122, n. c), copy-text 'tailors' is spelled 'taylors' in *U.C.* (p. 128, n. c), copy-text 'lightning' is spelled 'lightening' in *U.C.* (p. 129, n. b), copy-text 'Shakespear's' is spelled 'Shakespeare's' in 1767 (p. 156, n. a), or that copy-text 'economy' and 'economist' are spelled 'oeconomy' and 'oeconomist' in *U.C.* (p. 165, n. a; p. 179, n. f).

These are relatively ordinary spelling variants of no significance whatever, and certainly none qualifies for recording under the criteria of "uncommon or in any way ambiguous." Moreover, as is inevitable when editors engage themselves to such trivia, they cannot be consistent. If there is any principle other than simple variation warranting the footnotes of such minor spelling forms as gardiner-gardener, bachelor-batchelor, tailors-taylors, or lightning-lightening, then it was editorial neglect not to inform the reader that copy-text 'authours' was spelled 'authors' in *U.C.* (3.7), or that copy-text 'lyricks', 'heroicks', critick' (twice), 'antient' (twice), 'publick', 'philosophick', and 'critick' were spelled in 1767 respectively as 'lyrics', 'heroics', 'critic', 'ancient', 'public', 'philosophic', and 'critic' (7.20, 7.21, 12.5 and 12.14, 13.3 and 14.15, 17.5, 17.10, 17.26) and so on. No rationale for the selection of the superfluous information chiefly about modernized spellings in these historical collation notes can be detected.

The Harvard editors, moreover, besides imputing a false importance to the commonplaces of spelling variation, are unnecessarily eager to emend their old-spelling text by substituting modern spellings for quite acceptable older forms. Once a copy-text is chosen, logic dictates that its spellings be emended only when they are manifestly impossible by the standards of the time and therefore clearly are real errors. But (to offer only a selection) there seems to be no reason why the editors should have rejected copy-text 'secresy' in favor of 1767 'secrecy' (p. 9, n. h), or substituted 'unwieldy' from 1767 for copy-text 'unweildy' (p. 89, n. d), or 'discoloured' from 1767 for copy-text 'discouloured' (p. 108, n. f).

Powell's footnote on page 338 might well have been taken to heart by his American colleagues: "It is, of course, obvious that the spelling in the folio [his copy-text] tended to be the house style, so that one cannot safely argue as to the evidence of Johnson's preference in his 29 essays. But since the same difficulty applies to the second edition, the spelling of the folio is as authoritative as any." (Greg would have said *more* authoritative than any.)

The case is especially serious when the identical (and acceptable) reading in all three editions of *The Idler* is rejected in favor of a modernized form, as in editorial 'alleys' substituted for 'allies' in all editions (p. 41, n. a), editorial 'plums' for 'plumbs' in the three editions (p. 49, n. b), or editorial 'sole' (twice) for 'soal' in the three editions (p. 102, n. a; p. 104, n. d). These rejected spellings are not errors. The latter two are especially worthy of note because the theory of copy-text ill-advisedly adopted by the Harvard editors forces them to accept what they must regard as 1761 Johnsonian revisions in essays that were not written by Johnson. If there is any sanctity in an author's text, it should extend to the scholarly rejection of alterations made in it by another, unauthorized hand; but the acceptance of the 1761 edition as copy-text means that in this Yale edition substantive variants that cannot be the authors' are incorporated in the purportedly definitive text in *Idler* Nos. 9, 15, 33, 54, 67, 76, 82, and 98. Even if one might speculate (and there is no evidence on which to do so) that Johnson theoretically could have consulted the original authors before making these changes, the hypothesis cannot hold for Nos. 9 and 54, where he himself was unaware of the authorship.

In this sophistication of another writer's text permitted here, No. 15 containing the alteration of 'plumbs' to editorial 'plums' and No. 33 containing the repeated change from 'soal' to editorial 'sole' only increase the tampering; and indeed in No. 33 in the Yale text the editors have been willing to accept the 1761 'conveniences' for *U.C.* 'conveniencies,' 1761 'sat' for *U.C.* 'sate' (despite the appearance earlier in the essay both in *U.C.* and in 1761 of 'sate' and also a later appearance), 1767 "'Tis' for *U.C.* 'This is', and 1761 "'Tis is', and 1761 'ingenious' for *U.C.* 'ingenuous'. In No. 9 the editors accept the Johnsonian 1761 'favourable' for the original author's *U.C.* 'favourite', 1761 'give' for *U.C.* 'compose', 1761 'find' for *U.C.* 'find the plague of', 'that' for 'your', 'cannot' for 'can't' (twice), 'that is' for 'that's', 'has' for 'has yet', 'protected' for 'appeared to favour', 'those' for 'some', and 'him' for 'my correspondent'. The original author might not be disposed to thank them, nor should scholars who ought to be more concerned with reading the style of the anonymous author than the way that Johnson thought he ought to have written.

As a marked contrast to their practice with accidentals, the Harvard editors are conservative in admitting verbal emendation from other editions into their 1761 copy-text. In their treatment of substantives they are certainly right on balance, since 1761 is manifestly a revised edition. Whether a largely indifferent reading in a revised edition is in fact an authorial alteration or a compositorial corruption is not always possible to demonstrate, and editors must be granted some leeway in their judgment of such matters without undue carping from observers. Most of the emendations are clearly required, as in the addition of 'this' from 1767 (p. 189, n. 1), or the addition of 'the' from *U.C.* and 1767 (p. 62, n. b; p. 74, n. f). But the necessity to reject *U.C.* and 1761 'any' for 1767 'an' is obscure at page 106, note a, especially given the suspect authority of 1767.

Indeed, the editors' rejection of 1767's sophistication 'for some time' of 1761's error 'for time' (*U.C.*'s correct 'for a time') exhibited good editorial acumen and ought to have shaken their confidence in the hypothesis that Johnson actually corrected this late text.[9] Moreover, if 1767 is suspect (as it must be), the acceptance of the isolated reading 'an' for 'any' (p. 106) is the more questionable, and especially illogical is the considerable editorial reliance on 1767's more modern spellings to 'correct' the spellings of 1761 that were not truly errors.

Confusingly, a strange edition of *The Idler* not mentioned in the textual introduction occasionally makes an appearance in the collational notes to record some variant reading it possesses. This is the 1825 (Oxford) edition of no possible authority; and why its manifestly erroneous variant reading should be noticed on page 155, note e, for example, is not clear.

A collation of the Yale *Idler* text against the 1761 edition for the first five essays discloses exact concurrence and scrupulous accuracy except for

9 However, the reasons for their rejection remain obscure, since they cite the series in n. 6, p. xxiv, and remark, " 'for a time' in the *Universal Chronicle* reads 'for time' in 1761, and is then corrected in 1767 (by Johnson or the printer) to 'for some time.' " But if the 1767 reading were indeed a 'corrected' one (Bate and Bullitt use this word with some looseness, often meaning no more than 'altered'), and especially if it were corrected by Johnson, it should have been adopted in the text. That it was not adopted, but the *U.C.* reading substituted, ought to indicate that the editors regarded the 1767 reading as compositorial. But their footnote does not suggest that they had come to any firm conclusions, despite the necessity to justify the choice of readings in the text before adoption.

the unfortunate dropping, without record, of the assignment to *Anacreon-tea* of the Greek epigraph heading No. 5.[10] Although no statement is made in the textual introduction to the effect, the identification of the works from which the epigraphs are taken is editorial, and some silent alteration is made, such as 'Iliad' for 'Homer' in the epigraph to No. 4. Again without warning, the forms of the headings do not agree with those in the copy-text. In Latin epigraphs, and also in the text, both editors silently alter the Latin digraphs *æ* and *œ* to *ae* and *oe*.

In his emendation of the copy-text of *The Adventurer* Powell is more conservative than Bate and Bullitt in admitting modernized spellings from other sources, but he is less conservative in his tinkering with the punctuation and in his choice of substantives. Any editor who engages himself to a critical edition, and therefore to an eclectic text, must risk the gains from knowledgeable alteration of the copy-text against the losses possible from unnecessary or ill-advised changes. On balance, Powell is a shrewd editor, but in some respects his practice may be queried. He is apparently unwilling to take the responsibility for any alteration not supported by some document, without regard for its authority. Thus in a non-critical and inconsistent manner he carefully reprints in his text errors in the Latin on page 357, note c, page 361, note a, page 421, note d, and page 446, note a, and provides the correct form only in a footnote. On page 459, note h, he feels impelled to reach up to an edition of 1766 for his authority to add a comma, even though this late edition is not described or even mentioned in his textual introduction.

In certain of his attempts to normalize punctuation beyond the real need of the sense or the practice of the time, he undoubtedly chooses some sophisticated readings that in no manner can be thought of as correcting errors in the copy-text. Certainly it is unnecessary to emend the first edition from the second merely to insert a comma to set off a brief inverted phrase, as in footnote e on page 358: 'In a long series of action,[e] some will languish with fatigue', the more especially since he emends in the opposite direction on page 446, note b, by removing such a comma from his copy-text, in 'Of some images and sentiments[b] the mind of man may be said to be enamour'd.' Nor is the enclosing of 'however' in commas from the second edition really required on page 367, note b. Given eighteenth-century indifference to distinguishing restrictive from non-restrictive relative clauses by means of punctuation, the addition of a comma on page 377, note e, is simple modernization of a peculiarly unnecessary kind: 'The

10 The assignment is made in the commentary footnote, but no critic could know from the evidence that the original had printed an ascription. The reader is nowhere warned of this procedure, and its purpose is obscure. No. 6 also drops the assignment into the text, but in this case the commentary footnote indicates its presence in *U.C.* and all later editions.

nicety of these minute allusions I shall exemplify by another instance,[e] which I take this occasion to mention, because, as I am told, . . .' Eighteenth-century usage did not object to a comma between subject and verb, but Powell modernizes his copy-text by removing such a comma in page 457, note e: 'yet there is no reason for believing, that the dogmatical legions of the present race[e] were ever equalled in number by any former period.'[11]

Editorial tinkering with acceptable copy-text usage could be justified only by the conviction that in altering the first-edition copy-text by reference to the usage of the second edition, the editor was following authentic Johnsonian revisions. However, no discussion of the second-edition authority in such respects takes place in the textual introduction, where we are informed only that "some numbers are fairly heavily revised . . . but others show only minor changes of punctuation, not necessarily authorial." (The punctuation examples cited above are not drawn from any essay that Powell believes was heavily revised.)

Yet a respect for the authority of the revised second edition in minute detail is indicated, very curiously, in one emendation, in No. 58 (p. 372, n. b). Here for obscure reasons Powell normalizes the copy-spelling 'bigottry' to the modernized second-edition form 'bigotry'. But since the colon of the first edition that followed this word is replaced by a semicolon in the second edition, he feels impelled to accept the semicolon punctuation along with the spelling despite the fact that the colon division of a lengthy sentence is a marked and constant characteristic of the copy-text. Hence this substitution is mere sophistication, and the rationale for the change suggests a certain naïveté of editorial attitude about authorial alteration in a revised edition, or else an undue rigidity of mind about the editorial process.

Occasional exception may be taken to Powell's treatment of the substantives. Any editor faced with a considerably revised later edition must give more than ordinary authority to variant readings in the revision, even when they may seem to be relatively indifferent. Yet the more indifferent the reading, the harder it sometimes is to account for the original error and the easier to assume compositorial sophistication, conscious or inadvertent, in the later text. Any editor must be allowed considerable freedom in assessing such textual situations, and hence one need only query in passing whether, for instance, the singular 'colour' from the second edition is really a correction (or revision) of the plural in the copy-text in page

---

11 The Harvard editors in the *Idler* also make such a sophisticating emendation in n. f, p. 21, where a comma present in *U.C.* and 1761 is removed on the dubious authority of 1767: 'But common rules are made only for common life, and some deviation from general policy[f] may be allowed in favour of a lady, that rode a thousand miles in a thousand hours.'

384, note a. In page 486, note d, the rejection of copy-text 'fashions' for second-edition 'fashion' can perhaps be justified, but the case for then preferring copy-text 'decoration' for second-edition 'decorations' in note e is less clear.

Such emendations may well be a matter of opinion, and allowable; but there can scarcely be a question that the copy-text has been improperly sophisticated by modernization when the editor in page 409, notes g and h, accepts the plural 'pounds' from the second edition as a correction or revision of copy-text idiomatic 'pound' in such phrases as 'twenty thousand pound'.

One sometimes wishes that textual notes discussing the choice of readings were permitted in this Yale edition. For instance, it would be interesting to hear the editor give his reasons, complete with cited passages of both usages from his text, for his rejection of the second-edition 'or' as a correction or revision of copy-text 'and' in page 459, note i: 'A man uneducated and unlettered may sometimes start a useful thought.' Johnson's *Dictionary* defines *illiterate* as *unlettered*. Thus if a man were unlettered he would be sure to be uneducated and the phrase with 'and' has little meaning. On the other hand, by Johnson's definition an *uneducated* man is not necessarily illiterate. In this sense the distinction indicated by 'or' is a rising and meaningful one. Yet against this argument might be balanced the Hooker quotation in the *Dictionary* under *unlettered* that could be taken as justifying the use of the co-ordinate 'and'.

Textual notes have the advantage that they give the reader an insight into the editor's reasons for various of his choices; thus they help to soften some of the arbitrary nature of unadorned emendation, and they may still an occasional dark suspicion that choice has not always been sufficiently reasoned. For instance, Dr. Powell's justification for the rejection of the second-edition excision of first-edition 'the persuit of' would be interesting to follow in the sentence on page 339, note b: 'Opulence and splendor are enabled to dispel the cloud of adversity, to dry up the tears of the widow and orphan, and to increase[a] the felicity of all around them: their example will animate the persuit of[b] virtue, and retard[c] the progress of vice.' We may notice that this No. 34 is one of the three essays singled out by the editor as heavily revised in the second edition, and that in notes a and c immediately adjacent second-edition revised readings are accepted. Should we match the possibility of compositorial eyeskip against the possibility that in this sentence Johnson was willing to sacrifice formal balance for a more positive statement about virtue? An editor's discussion would be illuminating.

Similarly, one may wonder why the second-edition omission of 'always' was editorially rejected in favor of the copy-text in page 481, note b: 'In order to the right conduct of our lives, we must always[b] remember, that we are not born to please ourselves.' This is the first sentence in a paragraph that contains an undoubted second-edition revision in the next sentence but one. Is there more cause to suspect second-edition compositorial eyeskip than to credit Johnson with an attempt at superior epigrammatic phrasing? Powell is extraordinarily reluctant to accept second-edition excisions of words as authentic revisions, but his reasons are not always apparent.

On the other hand, whenever the second edition breaks into two sentences by the substitution of a period a long Johnsonian copy-text sentence that had been joined in its two parts by a colon or semicolon, Dr. Powell unhesitatingly accepts the second-edition form as presumably an authoritative revision. Some study of Johnson's practice in writing such sentences would be very useful to enable a reader to estimate the evidence behind the editorial assumption that this change is not compositorial. A reader of the Yale edition will, of course, not be aware that the second half of such a sentence might begin with a capital anyway in the copy-text.

In connection with the important matter of the kind and extent of Johnson's revisions in the second edition, it is not evident that Powell made a control study of the variants in the numerous *Adventurer* essays not by Johnson in order to discover whether other authors had similarly revised their texts; and if they had not, then what was the fidelity with which the second edition followed unrevised copy. The absence of such an analysis is something of a blot on the editorial investigation of the transmission of *The Adventurer* text and the specific authority of some of the second-edition variants in Johnson's part.

The accuracy of Dr. Powell's text is not up to the high standard set by his American colleagues Bate and Bullitt. Collation of the first five essays discloses only one without an error of some kind. The following list for the remaining four represents what must be either positive errors or unrecorded editorial alterations: "339.12 Yale *embittered* copy *imbittered* 342.2 Yale *siege*; copy *seige*: 350.7 Yale *frumentumque* copy *frum entumque* 350.13 *soporis,* copy no comma 354.29–30 Yale *extravagance* copy *extravagace* 362.16–17 Yale *consolations,* copy no comma 366.9–10 Yale *Leasing-making* copy *leasing-making.* This last example also illustrates a violation of the editorial rules that italic phrases in the copy-text will silently be put in roman and enclosed by double quotation marks. In the copy-text *leasing-making* is in italic, but no quotes are found in the edited text; and if the silent editorial substitution of a capital is an attempt to replace quotation marks, then the accuracy of all capitals in the *Adventurer* text must be suspect.

Editorial policy has not taken into account, in either work, the ambiguity of possible hyphenated compounds broken between lines in the modern print. As example, no way exists for a student of eighteenth-century usage to recover from this edition the exact form of the copy-text (whether hyphenated or unhyphenated) of Yale "dinner-time" (28.7–8). In these essays, because of the sparseness of compound hyphenation in the copy-texts the chance of misreading is not frequent, although it is present. On the other hand, a more dangerous because concealed source of confusion can appear when a possible compound is hyphenated at the line-end in the copy-text and the editor has marked the preferred form for the printer, or, as perhaps more commonly, has left the solution of the unseen difficulty to the modern printer. Here notes are a necessity in a definitive text to alert the reader to the fact that what really corresponds to an editorial emendation has been made. For instance, on page 17 (Yale) 'fire-works' is the divided reading in the 1761 copy-text and 'lap-dogs' (ll.2, 31). The editors print 'fireworks' and 'lapdogs', which may well be the preferred forms according to the *U.C.* text, or the characteristics of 1761, or the ascertained Johnsonian practice. Nevertheless, the reader has no means of knowing from this edition that an editorial decision (which may or may not always be justified, depending upon the amount of care taken to check such readings elsewhere for confirmation) has been silently made.

It is a serious fault in this edition that neither editor identifies the exact exemplar, and its provenience, that he used as the basis for his text, and thus a critic is helpless to check points of variance to know whether they are authentic or else are editorial oversights. Moreover, although Powell records a few readings that come from press-correction in one of the sheets of *The Adventurer* and is thereby able to establish the source of the apparent second-edition variation as from the uncorrected state, he does not list the provenience of the copies in their respective states nor does he indicate in any way the extent of the collation of copies of the first edition that he undertook in order to discover press-variants that might have textual significance. The Harvard editors give no indication that they troubled to consult more than one copy of the 1761 copy-text (or of the *Universal Chronicle*) as an aid to establishing the true and complete documentary form of *The Idler* text.

The critical introduction to *The Idler* is a crisp and workmanlike job detailing briefly the essential facts that a reader would like to know about the characteristics of the essays, their history and their publication. Powell's introduction is a reprint of an article he published in 1927 in *Review of English Studies*, with some additions and revisions. It is chiefly concerned with questions of authorship.

The commentary for both sets of essays is calculated somewhat more for purposes of reference than for immediate enjoyment or illumination. For instance, quite properly footnote 5 on page 346 quotes the passage from Ramazzini's *De morbis artificum* (in an English translation) to illustrate Johnson's casual reference in the text. In contrast, when the text remarks that the lady in *Clelia* thought it highly desirable to live without sleep, we are referred to the page number of the French 1654–61 edition of Scudéry's *Clélie* and are offered only the information that Johnson apparently read the work in the English translation of John Davies and George Havers (date not provided). The circumstances of the lady's remark, which might have been entertaining if not illustrative of Johnson's point, will remain hidden except for those who have access to a large library.

However, the pressure on writers of commentary to be concise (in part for financial reasons, in part to expedite publication, and in part because of the occasional loquacious abuse of the process) is a feature of present-day publisher's policy, and the depth as well as breadth of a commentary is very much a matter of taste. Most readers will find the Yale commentary sufficiently detailed and adjusted to the text.[12]

The Yale policy of interrupting the reader's attention by making him wade through a thicket of footnote signs in the text itself to point him without delay to the commentary at the foot of the page does not make for agreeable reading of the essays themselves. But, though supererogatory, it is at least more useful than the quite indefensible practice of signs in the text, according to a different system, that constantly urge the reader to break off the thought and drop his eyes to learn nothing more than that such-and-such a variant (and rejected) reading was present in an edition other than the copy-text. A record of editorial emendation, and a historical collation of substantive variants in the editions chosen for collation, is a prime necessity in any scholarly edition; but it may surely be more modestly and inconspicuously exposed to the reader, so long as it is available for the specialists who wish to make a particular study of the text, its formation and transmission.

The Yale Johnson in future volumes would be materially improved not only by some reassessment of its present editorial theory and practice, but also by the removal from the text of all superior signs that point to foot-of-the-page notation, these being replaced by prefixed line numbers to the commentary items that readers can count off for themselves if necessary.

12 Just in passing, however, one may select two from many examples, and comment that in *Idler* No. 6 not all readers may be so sporting as to know what and where New-Market is without commentary enlightenment. In n. 2, p. 352, the commentary writer has missed a little joke derived from the horsemanship meaning of 'carreer'. Benedict had made a similar one in *Much Ado About Nothing*.

Old Wine in New Bottles
Problems of Machine Printing

BIBLIOGRAPHICAL CRITICS are apt to distinguish sharply between the eras of hand and of machine printing and their problems. At the extremes a true distinction does indeed present itself in the technical difficulties faced by an analytical bibliographer applying his craft to solve problems of text. The crudities of hand composition from a fount of limited size and of hand machining of sheets on a wooden press leave a trail of evidence that is quite obscured by linotype or monotype keyboard composition and by printing from rolls of paper on huge mechanical presses, or from very large formes and sheets.

Whereas in an Elizabethan book some individual pieces of type can be identified by their imperfections and thus traced in groups through the typesetting, the distribution, the setting in other formes, and so on through the book, the uniformity of modern type-metal and the appearance of any sort only once in the composition removes at a stroke all of the kind of mechanical evidence that in early books enables us to determine a number of most valuable facts. As Professor Charlton Hinman has shown us in

Read on November 4, 1966, before the Second Annual Conference on Editorial Problems held at the University of Toronto; printed in *Editing Nineteenth-Century Texts*, edited by J. M. Robson (Toronto: University of Toronto Press, 1967), pp. 9–36; reprinted with permission of the University of Toronto Press. In the discussion that followed on this paper various participants in the Conference demonstrated that here and there considerably more has been discovered in isolated cases about printing problems than I had allowed. However, the general point remains valid, I think, that we do not know enough to know how common or conventional were the pieces of evidence that are adduced; moreover, nowhere is a continuum of our present knowledge available with the mutual support that would accrue from a systematic survey. Indeed, even the traditional nineteenth-century printers' manuals have not been edited, with notes explaining the exact nature of the procedures that are too often allusively described in them, and how from bibliographical evidence within books the described processes may be detected and identified. As one small instance, the brief mention in the present paper of the two methods for bridging the settings of simultaneously working compositors analysed from the manuscripts of Hawthorne's *House of the Seven Gables* and *Blithedale Romance* could never be recovered with equal precision from the accounts of the treatment of takes either in MacKellar's *American Printer* or De Vinne's *Modern Methods of Book Composition*.

his monumental analysis of the Shakespeare First Folio, and as Professor Robert Turner has confirmed in several studies of Elizabethan dramatic quartos, the identification of individual types can demonstrate whether a book were set by formes or seriatim. The association of a set of type-cases with a compositor, as suggested by identified types, can also serve powerfully to back up spelling tests that may in themselves be less than demonstrable.

The identification of types is also at the base of the analysis of early printing procedures from the subsequent evidence of the progression of running-titles in their formes through the sheets during successive impositions.

In the late seventeenth century the bibliographer's ability to identify running-titles begins to decrease, and as the eighteenth century progresses this evidence becomes practically extinct. Outside of the difficulty in identifying types from the increasingly uniform founts, bibliographers are faced with such a multiplicity of presses that could be brought to bear in printing a book that the pattern of running-titles would be almost impossible to interpret even if the sets could be identified with confidence. But, increasingly, we are learning the extent of what we do not know. And we do not know whether it was usual in eighteenth-century printing, or when it may have become usual, for running-titles to be set with the pages, not transferred from forme to forme as part of the furniture, as was the earlier procedure. This matter is almost completely a mystery.

The increasing uniformity of compositorial spelling habits as the eighteenth century progresses begins to deny to the textual bibliographer the evidence of variant spellings as a means of identifying the different workmen who typeset a given book. Nevertheless, exceptions do occur. Something can be done, at least in broad outline, with a few spellings and certain variable punctuation habits in Fielding's *Tom Jones*. And indeed, as late as Hawthorne's *Fanshawe*, printed in Boston in 1828, spelling evidence plus variant treatment of punctuation conventions identified five compositors and the stints they set with fairly sharp demarcation.

New printing methods call forth new bibliographical techniques for dealing with the changed problems, as may be indicated by Professor Todd's investigation of eighteenth-century press figures that McKerrow thought of little account. Likewise, plated books were at first taken to be a completely closed bibliographical secret. The return in printing to what is actually a modified block-book system, without seeming opportunity for variation, appeared at first sight to close the door to bibliographical analysis. But, in fact, the use of plates in printing has opened the way to new investigations of printing practice. Thus, the discovery that in reprinting, plates might be imposed in variable relation to each other, a relationship that sometimes can be detected by measuring the gutter margins, has made it clear that not all reprintings from plates need be unidentifiable. Yet the art of dealing with plates has gone much farther. By comparing multiple copies of plated books on the Hinman Collating Machine, the evidence of progressive type-batter can be utilized to suggest an order of printing; and when the batter is of the kind that occurs during the storage of plates, the opportunity exists to identify unremarked separate printings.

In addition to type-batter, the repairs of plates may present evidence. Plates wear out unequally, or become damaged. Plates may contain errors that need correction. When holes have been cut in plates and types soldered in as repairs, the Hinman Machine detects this evidence instantly whether or not there are actual changes, and the bibliographer can begin to sort out printings and to observe the progress of textual variation within a set of plates. Some very sophisticated bibliographical and textual evidence has been derived from the study of plated books by these techniques, as for example the sorting-out of four previously undifferentiated and otherwise unidentifiable printings in 1851 of Hawthorne's *House of the Seven Gables*, or the assignment of a fifth printing to 1852 though its title-page is dated 1851. Or Professor Bruccoli's even more important distinction of five Boston printings in 1860 of *The Marble Faun*. As an even more refined example, Professor Tanselle, who is associated with the project for a new edition of Melville, is accumulating data to determine what can be used as evidence for plate alteration even before the first printing; that is, whether inequalities of inking or alignment can show that first-printing plates were altered in any respect from the typesetting that produced them even before they were sent to press.

The changing methods of book manufacture marked by ever increasing uniformity are not the only factors that baffle bibliographical analysis or else demand the invention and application of new bibliographical techniques. Vitally affecting textual and bibliographical critics of modern books is the increased role played by the publisher as a middleman between the author's manuscript and the finished product of the book. That is, historians of Elizabethan books customarily speak of the printer but seldom of the publisher as in any way affecting the transition from manuscript to printed sheets. This identification has been carried to such extremes, indeed, that careless writers often impute to the printer what must have been the publisher's unique functions of securing manuscripts, deciding on the size of editions, and even dictating the form and often the content of title-pages. In fact, this identification is valid only when the printer was his own publisher, or vice versa. The Elizabethan job printer who manufactured books exclusively for others has long since become the norm. This extreme separation of publishing and printing responsibilities has opened up a vast no-man's land where historical studies have by no means filled in the topography. For instance, when did it become customary, as now, for a publisher to style an author's manuscript instead of leaving the responsibility to the printer? Hawthorne's manuscripts in the United States in the early 1850s and in England in the early 1860s show no sign of editorial intervention. [Stephen Crane's typescript of *Active Service* in 1897 was not styled by Heinemann. In 1907 and in 1909 William James took his book copy directly to the Riverside Press instead of sending it to his publisher.] At about what date do preserved printer's-copy manuscripts begin customarily to be marked in this manner for the press?

The question has a bearing, of course, on the use of the common phrase "house style." Rightly or wrongly, most writers on text have grown so accustomed to using these words as tacitly applying to the printer of nine-teenth-century books that it came as something of a shock to me, recently, to find that a reviewer of the Hawthorne edition had assumed that we were, instead, referring to the publisher's house-style and was worried about the evidence we had for such an application.

When did it become customary for a printer (or publisher) to return an author's manuscript with proof? This question became of some real import in the analysis of the printing and proofing of Hawthorne's *Marble Faun* in late 1859, in England; and the evidence is by no means clear whether or not the copy was indeed returned to him. On the other hand, do the curious folds still present in the manuscript leaves of *The House of the Seven Gables* and *The Blithedale Romance* signify that the copy was returned with the daily sheet of proof by Ticknor and Fields, or the printer, in the United States in 1851 and 1852? No reference tells us, nor do historians know. Indeed we have no means of knowing whether Ticknor or Fields read proof before or after it was sent to Hawthorne, or whether he dealt directly and exclusively with the printer in the matter of the entire proofreading. That a publisher's reader had *some* concern with the text, however, even though at a later date, can be demonstrated by some interesting changes made in the second edition of *The Scarlet Letter*, as will be remarked.

A rather extraordinary case demonstrating how little we know of the history of printing, to say nothing of the relation of printer and publisher and author, came to light in the edition of Hawthorne's *Seven Gables* and *Blithedale Romance*. *The House of the Seven Gables* was printed in 1851 by Metcalf and Company, and *The Blithedale Romance* in 1852 by Thurston, Torry and Company. Yet the names of several of the composi-tors marked on the manuscripts are the same, and it seems manifest that both manuscripts were set in the same printing-house. From this anomaly emerged what, I think, was a new historical fact in printing, that at this date, in Boston at least, the so-called printer was quite literally the printer in that he machined the sheets and nothing else. The type was set by the firm that was named as the stereotyper, the one that made the plates. This is information of crucial importance for the textual critic, of course, for the identification of the printer in the sense of the shop in which the type was set is the first step towards assumptions about accuracy, styling, and so on. Printing historians, so far as I am aware, have not noticed this separation of functions, when it began, when it ended, and how it came about. Until they do, no statement about the printer on a title can be taken at its face value, necessarily.

It is difficult to tackle the editorial problems of almost any complex nineteenth-century book without coming upon new and unsuspected evidence about printing methods. For example, the assignment of the exact compositorial stints—and thus an estimate about the faithfulness to copy of the various workmen—could not be made for Hawthorne's *House of the Seven Gables* and *Blithedale Romance* until the markings in the manuscript printer's copy were correctly interpreted.

When a manuscript is set simultaneously by a group of compositors, the copy is divided into 'takes,' or sets of manuscript leaves, assigned to each workman. In the Hobart and Robbins shop in 1852, with *The Blithedale Romance* manuscript, when a compositor in a group had, towards the end of his take, either paged his galleys himself or had a maker-up mark his copy as the pages were determined, he could decide to continue to set type from the remaining text on the last manuscript leaf of his take, and to keep on until he had completed the unset material above the compositor's signature on the first leaf of the succeeding take. Or, on the contrary, he could turn over his final leaf, and its remaining text below the marked page ending, to the next compositor. The latter would then know where his first page could begin and would set from the lower part of this leaf and continue from the top of the first leaf of his own take until he came to the paragraph opening where, according to his signature, he had earlier started to set. He could then page, or turn his galleys over to a maker-up for paging, and when he came to the final leaf of his take he could treat the next compositor, in turn, according to the material on his final leaf.

This is the simple interpretation of the markings on the leaves of the *Blithedale* manuscript, which at the foot of some printed page—the last leaf of a take, usually—will exhibit a pencil bracket, the next page number, and the name of the compositor who was to begin that page. The assignment of the compositorial stints, hence, required little interpretation since ordinarily on completion of the final page, the last leaf of a take was handed over to the next workman, who would then set type until he had reached the type already composed from the first paragraph on the initial leaf of his own signed take. And so on, through the group of simultaneously composing workmen in staggered order. The stints of the workmen, as a result, would generally correspond with the beginning or end of a page, and a new page immediately succeeding would mark the start of a different compositorial stint.

On the other hand, the manuscript of *The House of the Seven Gables,* set a year earlier in the same shop and in part by some of the same workmen, reveals a quite different system of markings that needed to be interpreted from scratch in order to demarcate the compositorial stints. That is, as in *Blithedale,* the first leaf of a take had the compositor's signature in the first paragraph opening (since that alone could provide the first full line of type he could be confident of setting when he began his take). But the brackets with signatures and page numbers on the last leaf of the preceding take were missing, ordinarily, and thus the system for bridging the takes must have differed.

The interpretation finally arrived at of this evidence was that for *Seven Gables*—quite contrary to the *Blithedale* practice—each compositor automatically continued typesetting over onto the first leaf of the next one's take until he came to the end of the paragraph above where the compositor of this take had begun his typesetting, as indicated by his signature in the paragraph indention. The number of type-lines would then be entered in the foreman's book so that credit could be given each compositor for the linage set.

The use of these two systems had never before this investigation been distinguished, nor has their rationale, which may depend in part on the distinction between short takes (as in *Seven Gables*) and long takes (as in *Blithedale Romance*), been determined. The difference between the systems is of singular importance for the textual bibliographer, however, for in the one the compositor's stints are defined by the page units whereas in the other the work of a new compositor will ordinarily begin at the start of a paragraph within a page of type. The distinction may prove to be important in bibliographical analysis. For instance, the assignment of compositorial stints in *Fanshawe* was made by the investigators on the hypothesis that the page was the unit, whereas some anomalies that developed in the application of this hypothesis, particularly among the short takes at the end, may have resulted from the transfer of copy within the page, instead, according to the then unsuspected method of *Seven Gables.* Moreover, as a consequence, the significance of the transition from relatively long takes in the first two-thirds or so of *Fanshawe* to relatively short takes at the end, doubtless marking a transition from seriatim to simultaneous composition, was not fully understood in the Textual Introduction to the Centenary Edition of *Fanshawe.*

In Elizabethan times an author was ordinarily expected to attend the press daily if he wanted the opportunity to proofread and correct his book. Time, tide, and printers waited for no man, and machining of the sheets would begin at convenience, with the first pulls laid aside for whichever functionary in the printing-house was to serve as proofreader. When proofs were marked and returned, the press was stopped, the alterations made, and printing resumed. Proofs might be read and corrected in this manner in several stages. If the author wished to substitute at any stage for the printing-house reader, that was his privilege if he chose to be present at an appropriate time. Otherwise, he would never see proofs.

Some commercial printing by the late Restoration seems to show signs that an author might have proofs pulled for him to be read at leisure. Certainly this was the established procedure long before Henry Fielding had his *Joseph Andrews* printed in mid-eighteenth century. But what about revises? Hawthorne's correspondence with his publishers in mid-nineteenth century never mentions these second opportunities to correct or alter one's work. In *The Marble Faun* at least one reading appears, in the Preface, that was almost certainly a revise from the original reading of the first proof-sheet. But did Hawthorne make this change in a physical revise sent him as a matter of course, or did he order it by special message after re-reading a spare copy of the proofs that he had retained after the first and only round of actual reading? No historian appears to tell us with anything like precision what is the history of authorial proofreading, let alone of the vital question of automatic revises.

Hawthorne's proofs were sent him both in the United States and in England in what we would call page-proof form but with the pages already imposed and proofed in a folded sheet such as would later form a gathering in the printed book. English publishers of the present day prefer to send out the first proofs in just this manner, but American commercial printers, especially of novels, now send proof in galleys. When did this latter custom begin? The answer is of considerable importance, for a revising author can add or subtract freely in galleys whereas cavalier re-writing is so extremely expensive in page-proofs as to be almost prohibitive, and therefore rare. Although Hawthorne in the United States received only page-proofs from Hobart and Robbins in Cambridge, I have seen galley proofs for a Mark Twain book, as I think I recall. The historians do not tell us whether the difference in method was an individual case or a change in procedure at a later date.

Not too many years ago an American novelist would receive galleys first, and then revises in the form of page-proofs though not imposed in sheets. In the present day he is sent only galley proof and in normal circumstances sees no revises. When did this change occur, and how uniform was it, or is it? A textual critic of the future, and certainly even of the present, would like to know.

These are samples of the wide gaps in our knowledge that have resulted from a changed relationship of publisher and also of author to the finished product of the book that began with the submission of manuscript. Moreover, publishers, and printers, have often made little effort to keep their records, or to make them available to investigators. Thus although a bibliographer of modern books might expect to have a mass of external evidence about the numbers of printings and their dates as well as the size of the impressions, bills for plate changes, and so on, in fact it is a rare scholar who can speak with as much authority about these details in a book of the present day as about their equivalents in the Elizabethan age.

Authors themselves have contributed to the difficulties that face textual criticism and bibliographical investigation. A trained textual critic can sometimes make important assumptions about the accuracy of a text—leading occasionally to necessary emendation of readings—by correlating the known difficulties and ambiguities of an author's handwriting with what seem to be textual errors. But the author who types his own work offers fewer opportunities for reconstruction. On the other hand, when authors turn over their own handwritten or typed copy to professional typists, the opportunities for undetected error multiply. Particularly, these days, many authors send draft copy to their agents, who assign it to typists, and the author never proofreads the resulting script until it is set in type. His own copy will not be preserved unless he specifically requests it, and thus he has no ready means but his memory to know whether he wrote some questionable phrase or not when he has not annotated his carbon copy (if he made one) as fully as his revised typescript.

Yet these differences called for in the techniques of bibliographical examination, and the results that can be anticipated according as one deals with old or new printing and publishing conditions, should not obscure the general experience of editors that principles behind the applications of bibliographical techniques remain largely the same, that the same laws of evidence hold good, and thus that the continued search for physical evidence to be applied to textual problems will yield results, according to the circumstances, whether one is working in the sixteenth or in the twentieth century. The editor of Stephen Crane, as of Shakespeare, finds the same problems of copy-text and of the transmission of text affecting his editorial decisions. The same bibliographical rules of evidence that distinguish authorial revision from compositorial sophistication apply to Hawthorne's *Marble Faun* as to Thomas Dekker's *First Part of the Honest Whore*. Various techniques of bibliographical expertise will differ in their applicability, but editorial logic remains constant in its relation to bibliographical evidence. And the best training for the textual editor of nineteenth- and twentieth-century books is still a broad experience in the sixteenth, seventeenth, and eighteenth centuries. It is this constant factor within the physical changes that attend book manufacture and publication that I want to illustrate by a few selected examples.

It is a hard fact, but a true one, that the easiest texts for an editor to deal with are those about which he knows the least, in the sense that the minimum evidence has been preserved concerning the translation of the text from manuscript to print. In the nineteenth century a typical text is that of Hawthorne's *Scarlet Letter* of 1850. Here the manuscript was destroyed and the first edition thus becomes the major authority. When one inquires whether any physical evidence about the printing of this text assists in the search for ultimate authority, what are perhaps a surprising number of pieces of bibliographical fact can be gathered together for survey.

This first edition was printed from type-metal, not from plates. In preparing the Centenary edition it was therefore of the first importance to collate a number of copies on the Hinman Machine to see if variation had occurred during the course of printing. The eight copies machine-collated disclosed no attempt to correct or revise the text during the course of printing, such as one customarily encounters in sixteenth- and seventeenth-century books. I should venture to say that the usefulness of multiple collation in order to discover authorial or printing-house corrections made during the printing of the sheets vanishes in the early eighteenth century when the major shift in proofing procedures seems to have been completed. That is, what slight evidence we have* suggests that in the late seventeenth century many commercial books began to be proofed, in something close to final form, whether authorially or professionally, before the formes were laid on the press for machining, and that this process was the normal one within a few decades. The very valuable insight that Elizabethan books can provide between the readings of the original typesetting and those that resulted from the casual ministrations of the printing-house proofreader is barred to the editor of most nineteenth-century texts.

On the other hand, this comparison of copies by machine collation is still a necessity, although for reasons other than those that obtain with earlier books. For instance, although attempts to correct or revise the text while sheets are in press must be rare indeed, the plates of the text can degenerate from the form represented by its original typesetting, or the relative purity of the original typesetting cannot be established without the facts gleaned from collation. In *The Scarlet Letter*, for example, lines 9–11 on page 321 were reset during the course of printing, no doubt to repair some accident to the type. In this place no textual variant was created, but whenever resetting of any variety is encountered the opportunity for error exists, whether in type or in plates. In the fourth printing

---

*For instance, in all of *Tom Jones* only one or two stop-press variants have been observed by the collation of four copies, and these seem to have been made by a pressman casually looking over sheets as they came off the press.

of the first American edition of *The Marble Faun*, the plate for page 98 of the second volume seems to have been damaged since the whole page was reset and a new plate made. Five textual errors occur in the resetting of this one page. In *The Scarlet Letter* the collation disclosed the previously unknown fact that the two pages of text that comprise the last gathering of the first edition were set in duplicate for easier machining. The evidence in this case had no textual significance because the duplicate setting was identical in every respect; but in somewhat the same situation in duplicate plates made from a single setting in *The House of the Seven Gables* a comma appears in one plate but not in the other, and an editor must decide whether to include or omit it. The answer, of course, is based on what must have been the order of the two sets of plates made from the type-page, which in turn is based on the physical process by which plates are made.

The degeneration of a text during its first printing from type-metal may be illustrated by the five variants that were revealed in the eight *Scarlet Letter* collated copies. Two of these were trivial in the extreme in that they represented only the shifting of loose type that produced variant spacing. The other three variants also resulted from loosened type in which one or two letters dropped out. The errors are so obvious, however, that no editor could be misled. One rather interesting variant remains, in which we know that an exclamation point completing a speech dropped out before the quotation mark, early in the printing since it is present in only one of the copies examined. Trifling as this variant is, it had its editorial significance in that the second edition, set from a copy without the point, substituted a comma, which has appeared in every version of the text up to the Centenary edition. By good luck, the correct exclamation point was present in a single copy among the eight collated for this edition.

The only other bibliographical fact discovered about the first edition was that its octavo gatherings had been imposed both formes together in one sixteen-page forme and printed by the work-and-turn method.

Two other editions of *The Scarlet Letter* were printed in 1850 and these, of course, had to be examined scrupulously to see if any authorial intervention had occurred in the transmission of the text. Bibliographical examination turned up a considerable amount of previously unknown material about the second edition, also printed from type-metal. Both preliminary quires a and b were set in duplicate, the only difference between them being the absence of a comma from the first edition in one page; but since the third edition was set from a copy with the comma missing, this punctuation became lost to the textual tradition.

Of major import, however, was the discovery of a fact not previously known, that standing type from the first edition started to appear irregularly in gatherings 14 and 15, and beginning with gathering 16 and continuing to the end the second edition was printed entirely from standing type of the first. In the 96 pages of standing type eight variants appear, of which three are in spelling, four are in punctuation, and one in word-division. Obviously an editor had to attempt to discover whether these were authorial changes, since a decision would then affect at least some of the 62 variants that appeared in the 226 pages of reset type. Fortunately, at least two of the eight variants moved away from first-edition Hawthorne forms that could be established as characteristic from his manuscripts, and thus it was possible to decide that a publisher's reader but not the author had ordered the eight changes in the standing type, no doubt by marking a copy of the printed first edition throughout. This point settled, logic required an editor to reject automatically all variants in the reset pages as non-authorial, a decision that might not have been so easy were it not for the decisive evidence of the changes made in standing type, which could be identified as non-compositorial. The third edition offered no problems in deciding that it was a straight reprint of the second, without any authority.

In the careful bibliographical examination of *The Scarlet Letter* problem, the results were not directly illuminating in the sense that they led to no new substantive readings (although in fact one new substantive emendation was made independently by editorial decision), no unsuspected revelation of authorial intervention in later editions. This fact disappointed one reviewer, a mid-Western library-school Dean, who declared roundly:

At the end of this long journey through the bibliographic under-brush, one might hope to find evidence of textual alterations that would throw significant light on the maturation of Hawthorne's philosophy, the development of his characters, or the course of the plot. But no such happy discovery rewards the investigator. Textual variants are limited to . . . typographical trivia . . . and so on and on through some forty pages of introduction and seven appendices dealing with such topics as variants in the first and second editions, editorial emendations in the copy-text, word division, and special collation lists. All of these add up to the conclusion that there were in the first edition very few substantive departures from the text of the lost manuscript of the novel, that publishing-house style accounts for many of the variants and that most of the corrections in proof were not made by Hawthorne but by another hand, or hands, associated either with the publisher or the printer. . . . [One] cannot suppress the wish that [the] heavy bibliographic artillery had bagged quarry more worthy of the ammunition. . . . Doubtless . . . one should be grateful for the labor of those bibliographic drones who spend countless hours in a tireless search for printers' errors, no matter how fortuitous or trivial; but let us not confuse it with scholarship, not even when done with a Hinman Collator or, for that matter, a bright and shining IBM 7090.

I take it there is little need to enter an extended defence against confusion of this variety. False hopes among the ignorant may often be raised by the claims of textual bibliography—although I do not think, in passing, that to expect bibliographical examination of a simple text like *The Scarlet Letter* to shed significant light on the maturation of Hawthorne's philosophy, the development of his characters, and the course of the plot is to betray a certain naïveté of attitude. Analysis of Hawthorne's manuscripts in one or two cases can perform these wonders, especially in respect to the plot and characters of *The Marble Faun*; but Hawthorne was not a re-writer of what he had in print.

I take the time with this long and rather foolish quotation, which in fact I have materially condensed, to exemplify the non-scholarly resistance that the bibliographical method may encounter in its normal operations. The history of *The Scarlet Letter* text following its first edition was one of constantly increasing corruption. The results of the bibliographical examination demonstrated that the original edition was the only authority and that changes made in the second edition, although sometimes inviting, had no relation to Hawthorne's wishes. The first edition thus established as copy-text was shown to be variant but only in insignificant ways, so that an editor was faced as his ultimate authority with the typesetting of this first edition and nothing else. On this point, the whole editorial method converged. To an amateur, evidence that is negative is useless and disappointing. Unless one can find something by bibliography that will change the author's text, one becomes a bibliographic drone. To a scholar, however—and here I think we may separate ourselves from this reviewer—the negative evidence of the examination of *The Scarlet Letter* that constantly narrowed the authority of the text back to the first edition and only the first edition was as valuable for the accuracy of the editorial job at hand as more exciting evidence would have been that broadened the spread of authoritative texts by the discovery of authorial intervention during the printing or in some later form than the first edition.

An editor's job is to recover from the extant documents the purest final form of the authorial text in every minute detail. It was too bad that Hawthorne did not revise his texts in print. But when it was established that he did not (and it was a new fact that was thus established), the rigour of the examination and the analysis of the evidence then in a most helpful manner prevented an editor from making an ass of himself by dealing with variants in the second edition, especially in the reset pages, on a subjective critical basis that might readily have led him to accept some of these compositorial or editorial changes as Hawthorne's own. Negative evidence, therefore, in no uncertain fashion delimited textual authority and established the exact materials proper for an editor to utilize from among the various extant documents. This was a singularly valuable gift that bibliographical analysis offered to textual criticism, and its true though unassuming usefulness should not go uncelebrated despite its frequent misinterpretation by incompetent critics.

In *The Scarlet Letter* the extrapolation of evidence from sections of the book printed from standing type in the second edition to sections printed from reset type, in an endeavour to establish by this evidence the nature of the alterations in the reset portion, was a form of textual criticism based on bibliography, in that the physical facts of standing versus reset type were used as the basis for inferences about the nature of the changes in each section according to the physical circumstances of the print.

Yet the problem was elementary in *The Scarlet Letter* compared to cases where two or more authorities can exist for a text. At one extreme, an editor of Shakespeare faced with a play first printed in the Folio can rely on his own analysis of the variants in the Second, Third, and Fourth Folios, and on the experience of editors of other plays with the variants in these editions, to come to the conclusion that he has only a single authority for his text and must do what he can by emendation, or refusal to emend, to reconstruct the purest text from the only extant authoritative document. This was *The Scarlet Letter* situation.

On the other hand, certain Shakespeare texts, like *King Lear, Othello, Hamlet, Troilus and Cressida, Richard III, Romeo and Juliet, The Merry Wives of Windsor,* and *2 Henry IV,* exist in texts of different traditions and of multiple authority. Immediately, two central problems arise. First, what is the physical relationship of these two forms of the text; and second what is the history of the text behind each and thus the nature of its authority? It is well established that the first edition of *Hamlet* is a memorially reconstructed text, as are the first editions of *King Lear, Romeo and Juliet, The Merry Wives,* and *Richard III,* although perhaps in varying measure. These texts are, then, less reliable than texts like *Othello* or *Troilus* that have some transcriptional link with the original Shakespearean manuscript although with differing authority.

The physical relationship between two variable texts is singularly important to establish since much textual logic depends upon it. For example, if Polonius is to call Hamlet's vows to Ophelia "pious bauds" instead of the "pious bonds" found both in the Second Quarto and in the Folio, the emendation is easier if we suppose that an annotated copy of Q2 was behind the Folio text than if we attempt to explain this as a common error in two independent manuscripts.

The problem of Stephen Crane's *Maggie* in some respects resembles that facing an editor of Shakespeare's *2 Henry IV.* The Folio *2 Henry IV*

offers a text that has been remarkably cleaned up from its Quarto colloquialisms and made much more of a literary text. It is bad enough for
an editor to have to conjecture what could have been the agent and
authority for this change; it is worse that the case is not wholly demonstrable either for an annotated quarto or an independent manuscript as
the Folio copy-text. Thus an editor does not have the basic physical information at hand from which the assessment of the nature of the Folio
variants as authorial, editorial, or compositorial must stem.

Stephen Crane published *Maggie* in 1893 under a pseudonym, and
after the success of *The Red Badge of Courage* was encouraged by his
publisher to revise the raw tale of vice and squalour for a more general
audience. The second edition, published in 1896, is a curious mixture of
Crane's stylistic revision and rewriting for purely literary purposes, of
his own alteration of objectionable words and phrases under the general
instructions of his publisher, of some alterations that are very likely the
publisher's additional 'improvements' or censorship, and no doubt of
some undetected compositorial variation as well.

The editorial problem can be approached in various ways, and in
some respects a parallel-text edition would be ideal. But if an eclectic
text is attempted, a critical edition, I suggest, should reject all alterations
dictated by censorship while accepting all alterations that are literary in
origin. I see nothing bibliographical in this series of decisions, which are
of the utmost critical difficulty, but I do see some foundation given to
the attempt to separate not only the two traditions but also any compositorial interference by the establishment of the fact that Crane made his
changes in a copy of the 1893 *Maggie* and not by writing out a new
version. If we could positively demonstrate even this simple fact for *2
Henry IV,* we should be much farther advanced in our knowledge of
the transmission, and thus in part of the origin, of Folio changes.

The need to establish the exact facts of the transmission of a text are
particularly acute when a manuscript is preserved. Any variations in the
first edition from the manuscript must be either compositors' errors not
detected in the proofreading or else authorial proof-changes. The one
kind is to be rejected, the other to be accepted as the author's final intentions. This is a clearcut case in respect to the Hawthorne texts of *The
House of the Seven Gables, The Blithedale Romance,* and *The Marble
Faun,* where printers' markings demonstrate that the preserved manuscripts were the actual printer's copy. But the textual problem of Crane's
Red Badge of Courage is very considerably complicated by a lost intermediate typescript, made by a professional typist, that intervened between the preserved manuscript and the typesetting. Some changes
difficult to assign to Crane, the publisher, or the compositors originated

in this intermediate transcript and flowed into the final text undetected, mixed with various authoritative revisions that Crane is known to have made in the typescript.

Even under the ideal circumstances of the Hawthorne romance texts, however, the decision about readings is not an easy one. I recall vividly that when I first started to edit *The House of the Seven Gables* I gave it up about a third of the way through the collation, since I could not understand the nature of the variants between manuscript and first edition. I then turned to *The Blithedale Romance,* which fortunately seemed to offer much less difficulty, and was able to cut my teeth on that. Only later, when once more engaged with *Seven Gables,* did I discover the reason for my difficulty.

In *The Blithedale Romance* various differences between the manuscript and print could be assigned quite plausibly as compositorial misreadings, since a comparison with the manuscript word often showed how the compositor had misconstrued its letters. Other variants were so widely separated in their wording as to remove either compositorial misreading or memorial error or sophistication as a cause, leaving only the hypothesis that these must be Hawthorne's own proof-alterations. In between was a group of neutral changes to which no definite agent could be assigned with any initial confidence. In this group, as in the others, the bibliographical analysis by compositors of all variants proved to be helpful: it established the proportion of alteration in each man's work (since the stints were marked on the manuscript), and his proportion of clearcut error; finally all such evidence was applied to an analysis of the neutral variants. This scientific approach, factually based, could not neglect an editor's critical opinion, but criticism was definitely limited by the evidence first secured by bibliographical analysis. The result led to an acceptance as Hawthorne's proof-alterations of roughly two-thirds of the variants between manuscript and print.

It then developed that the difficulty with *Seven Gables* lay in the fact that the same methods established, on the contrary, about two-thirds of the variants as printer's errors to be rejected, as against only one-third authorial proof changes. The proportion was so high as to be puzzling and indeed inexplicable on my first encounter with the text. But physical circumstances did seem to have resulted in this wide disparity. *Seven Gables* proof, sent a sheet a day, was corrected on the counter of the Lenox County post office and mailed back by return, after a walk of several miles through the mud that Hawthorne detested. Clearly, there was a reason for carelessness here in comparison with the *Blithedale* proof, corrected under more agreeable and leisurely circumstances near Boston.

The Marble Faun illustrates how refined methods of bibliographical analysis can, when the right conditions obtain, result in a marked increase of editorial certainty. Superficially the conditions are the same as in the two preceding romances with preserved manuscripts. That is, we have the exact printer's copy and the first edition each as an authority. We have the compositors' stints marked off, and analysis shows the same highly varying degree of competence in the London workmen as had appeared in the compositors within the Hobart and Robbins shop in America. The proportion of error is very considerable indeed, due in some part to the difficulty these compositors had with Hawthorne's hand and in some part, perhaps, to the freedom they felt they should take with his American style and idiom. Thus the problem is particularly acute to separate Hawthorne's proof-corrections from the large amount of compositorial variation that he overlooked in proof and did not alter.

Here a purely bibliographical situation develops that is of peculiar interest to any editor of nineteenth-century books. *The Marble Faun* was printed in England before Hawthorne left to resume his residence in the United States after his term as consul at Liverpool. Ticknor and Fields, his Boston publishers, had made arrangements to have the English printed copy sent to them in sheets from which they could set the American edition. Owing to some mixup about arrangements, copy was delayed in the sending and a serious question arose whether Hawthorne would lose his American copyright if the Boston edition could not be produced quickly enough. Thus some correspondence developed that gives us the dates when the copy for the English first and third volumes was sent across the Atlantic, with the date for the second volume still indeterminate.

We now come to the fascinating bibliographical situation about the textual relationship of these two editions. Some fifty-two recognizably significant substantive variants exist between the first English edition in three volumes and the first Boston edition in two volumes. These are distributed with considerable unevenness. For example, in the whole area of the Boston edition where the first volume of the English served as printer's copy, the Boston text was so carefully printed that in no case did it depart from its source to create a substantive error and the five verbal differences that appear are all necessary corrections of obvious English errors. These pages, then, offer a sample that is large enough to be significant for estimating what should be expected in the remaining two-thirds of the text, even though no compositorial analysis of the Boston edition is possible.

As compared with this record of five variants from Vol. I of the English copy, when Vol. II was set in Boston twenty-seven variants appear between the two editions, and twenty in Vol. III. Moreover, in only a very few cases do these variants agree with those in Vol. I as correction of the errors in the English copy.

When we examine the variants in the Vol. II copy, we see a further odd fact. The text of this second English volume begins with preliminary quire 19 and ends with sheet 37. Only six variants appear in the seven text sheets 20–26, but a total of twenty-one occur in the eight sheets 30–37: that is, six variants in the first seven sheets versus twenty-one in the last eight sheets. Moreover, the nature of the variants seems to change from misprints or memorial errors to clearcut substantive alteration of a distinctive kind.

The same anomaly is found in Vol. III of the English copy. In the first nine sheets, 38–46, there are only two variants, one a correction of an error and the other an obvious mistake. But beginning with sheet 47 and continuing through the next eight gatherings to the final sheet 55 of the English edition, the number, the concentration, and also occasionally the nature alter almost as markedly as in Vol. II. That is, in the first nine sheets two variants occur, but eighteen appear in the remaining nine sheets.

It is the nature of bibliography to deal with printing units, in this case with the sheets. If variation occurs within a pattern that can be distinguished by the sheets treated as units, then a mechanical explanation in the printing process must be sought.

Here the only hypothesis that will interpret the statistics in a reasonable manner is that Vol. I was sent to Boston in sheets that had been revised after Hawthorne's proof-corrections; indeed the copy was almost certainly the printed sheets themselves as later issued in England. Thus no differences appear that cannot be imputed to the Boston correction of errors in the copy. The low percentage of variation in the first seven sheets of Vol. II (six variants) and in the first nine of Vol. III (two variants) also argues for essentially the same conditions. In the latter half both of Vol. II and Vol. III, however, the ratio of variation increases markedly, and the nature changes. The inference follows that in each case the package sent to Boston was a mixed one containing already printed sheets or their final proof form, and also proof-sheets that had not yet been marked with Hawthorne's corrections or revisions. The critical analysis of the variants agrees with this bibliographical hypothesis: those variants from the English text in the later sheets of Boston Vols. II and III that agree with the manuscript represent the original readings of the English proofsheets that were subsequently corrected or revised by Hawthorne to the form of the readings in the English first edition.

It follows that where we have the controls of the reconstructed original English proof-sheets (and they represent about a third of the romance), editorial decision may be governed almost exclusively by bibliographical logic. Whenever in the conjectured proof-sheets the manuscript and the English edition agree and Boston differs, the Boston variant must represent either an original English typesetting error corrected later in proof but perpetuated in its early form in Boston, or else a Boston error made from correct English copy save for the rare cases when Boston might correct a joint manuscript and English printed error. Whenever the manuscript and Boston agree against the English print, the English edition's reading must, of course, be established as a Hawthorne proof-correction, save in the rare cases when the English is a misprint and Boston independently corrects it and thus returns to the reading of the manuscript. Finally, whenever the English and Boston editions agree against the manuscript, the reading must be either an original error in the London sheets perpetuated in Boston, or else a natural London correction of a faulty manuscript reading.

To summarize, whenever the manuscript and London agree against Boston, the odds favour acceptance of the English reading as a Hawthorne proof-correction that returned the error in the proof to the correct reading as represented in the manuscript. These London readings should be accepted. Whenever the manuscript and Boston agree against London, the odds favour the London reading as an authorial proof-revision that must be accepted. Whenever the London and Boston editions agree against the manuscript, the odds favour the acceptance of the manuscript as the authentic reading.

This series of syllogisms clarifies completely the editorial problems in the seventeen sheets printed in Boston from the English proofs. The conclusion thus reached is a blessing, as any editor can testify, because it removes all personal, subjective judgment from the choice of readings among the three extant authorities. Almost as important, it reconstructs the proof-sheets that Hawthorne marked, and so provides a body of fact about the nature of his proofreading of this book and also about the correctness of the various compositorial stints in the proofs. In these control sheets, therefore, statistics about the compositors' rate and kind of variation are fully trustworthy. Finally, all this valuable information can be extrapolated to serve as a guide to editorial decision about readings in the two-thirds of the book printed in Boston from the English sheets in their extant printed form.

A non-bibliographical editor would flounder in this complex textual situation, the nature of which he could not recognize, and whose very existence he would not suspect. His critical taste would inevitably be wrong in a number of choices, as I can testify from the preliminary choices I made between the manuscript and the printed London readings before the significance of the Boston evidence penetrated my skull. As a result, I think the final text of *The Marble Faun* will represent the most scientifically edited and accurate text to date of a nineteenth-century

American author. If it warns editors to investigate carefully the value of
evidence in editions printed both in England and in America when related
to hypotheses about the nature of printer's copy it will have served its purpose.

Other rich goodies are contained in the bibliographical analysis of this
text, but I should like to reserve a few surprises for the edition itself. I
can mention, however, that some variant readings made by plate-changes
in the third Boston printing appear to go back to a supplementary marked
proof sent from England at a later time, and thus may help to reconstruct
that proof-sheet. Moreover, a study of the variant foliation of the manuscript demonstrates one area where a single chapter has been revised to
form two chapters, and somewhat later another chapter has been inserted,
all this during Hawthorne's inscription of the romance in its present fair-
copy form from a lost original. These changes made during the last stage
of preparation of the manuscript do seem to reflect a development by
Hawthorne of the relations of Miriam to the Model and thus have a direct
bearing on the plot leading to the crime on which the romance turns.

It would be easy for critics to seize on this interesting evidence from
the manuscript about the plot and characters and to dismiss as bibliographical dronism the whole painful reconstruction of the lost proof-sheets
that in turn served as the basis for the establishment of the text, of what
one reads, on an evidential basis and in a form far superior to the corrupt
first edition or even to the manuscript. They would be mistaken to do so,
however, for the text is the foundation stone of all literary criticism, and
only when it is established in definitive form can the critic proceed about
his evaluative business with any confidence.

The nineteenth century, and the early twentieth, remains the period
where critics have been least interested in textual concerns, however. Not
only the complacency with which critics quote from corrupt texts in any
sort of reprint edition, whether English or American, is shocking. It is
even more shocking to find so little critical attention paid to the transmission of an author's text from manuscript to periodical to first edition
and then to collected edition. A revising author shows us what he is trying
to achieve and thus points the way not only to a more refined analysis of
his style but also to a more precise, because evidential, evaluation of his
literary intentions in general as well as in specifics. Most critics simply are
not interested in such studies—the worse for them.

This being so, it is perhaps inevitable that they have not yet learned
to demand pure texts that are as close to the author's intentions as the
most painstaking and informed bibliographical investigations can contrive.
The emphasis should be on the *not yet,* however. Sometime in the future
the textual sophistication that marks the Elizabethan scholar will extend

itself into nineteenth-century precincts, and recognition will come that the study of texts is the most intimate and exact study of an author. And that no other study has any demonstrable validity until study of the text is completed.

Datta. Dayadhvam. Damyata.
Shantih shantih shantih

Practical Texts and
Definitive Editions

EDITORS HAVE EXISTED from the time that scholars first began to order the texts of the classics that had been inherited in manuscripts of divers traditions. The eighteenth century added Shakespeare to these classics as worthy the attention of critics and scholars, and the nineteenth century saw a massive effort to make available the major English authors from among Shakespeare's fellows both in the dramatic and the nondramatic mode. The main characteristic of almost all of this effort was that it dealt with what was considered to be the literature of the past in the sense that its style and language were not natural to those of the audience to whom the editions were addressed. Shakespeare's genius was universally recognized, but Pope felt his diction and idiom were out-of-date and, indeed, sometimes barbarous. No nineteenth-century reader of Dyce's editions of Elizabethan dramatists or Grosart's reprints of Renaissance prose writers could feel that he was engaged with a sensibility that was near-contemporary. The distance that separated authors from their new public is clearly indicated by the constant modernization of the old texts to make them readable. Finally, the obscure textual transmission of much of the older literature, its printing on a hand press, and its frequent textual corruption owing to the circumstances of transmission and of printing, combined with its linguistic uncertainties to pose special problems of editing.

The traditional activity in examining the texts of the literature of the past is still with us and is beginning the process of a technical change ushered in by the computer. However, a new and growing editorial effort is now being made with literature that, if not contemporary, is at least near enough to our time to be read less as the historical product of another age than as a part of our more or less immediate cultural heritage, with no

Read on February 16, 1968, at the invitation of the Ohio State University Center for Textual Studies and the Department of English on the occasion of the publication of *The Marble Faun* in the Centenary Edition of the Works of Nathaniel Hawthorne. "Practical Texts and Definitive Editions" was originally published in *Two Lectures on Editing: Shakespeare and Hawthorne,* by Charlton Hinman and Fredson Bowers, published in 1969 by the Ohio State University Press; reprinted by permission.

very marked sense of separation. I am referring to nineteenth-century authors, both English and American, but specifically to a group of American writers like Hawthorne, Howells, James, Twain, and Stephen Crane, most of them writers whose works are currently in process of re-editing under grants from the National Endowment for the Humanities dispensed through the Modern Language Association's Center for Editions of American Authors.[1] It is in this area that the most rapid developments in modern scholarship are taking place as principles and techniques developed to deal with editorial problems of the older literature are tested on new material that had superficially appeared to present fewer difficulties in textual transmission, printing, or in language, and hence in the editorial reconstruction of a pure and accurate text.

We may properly call this the field of modern editing. It is worthy of note that only in comparatively recent years has it been recognized that appearances have indeed been deceiving and that the complexity of modern editorial problems is often equal to that in the older literature.[2] Hence it is now slowly becoming accepted, although not without reservations by

1 I do not ignore the valuable work being done on the text of more strictly contemporary writers like Faulkner and Fitzgerald, but I take it that the problems met with in them are in the main an extension of the problems of standard nineteenth-century authors like Dickens, Whitman, Poe, Hawthorne, Crane. The editing of earlier literature also has a surprising amount in common with that of nineteenth-century authors, but in general a linguistic barrier exists that makes 'old-spelling' texts a technical phrase and that creates problems, with corresponding changes in methods and principles, that are confined to works of earlier times. As only one prcatical example, it is feasible and useful to do a considerable amount of regularizing emendation in nineteenth-century texts in matters of spelling, word-division, capitalization, and occasionally even in punctuation. But from the days of McKerrow the regularizing of old-spelling texts from the sixteenth and seventeenth centuries in such respects has been recognized as a practical impossibility.

2 A dissenter is Mr. Edmund Wilson, who sturdily denies the necessity to edit the texts of American authors. He is willing to allow the term 'editing' to be applied to Elizabethan texts but insists that all that is required for the American classics is 'checking.' See *The Fruits of MLA* (A New York Review Book, 1968), p. 17. In Mr. Wilson's view of the CEAA projects there is no balm in Gilead. In dealing with the Centenary *The Marble Faun* he makes the peculiar assertion that the fact that the names of some characters were changed during the course of inscribing the manuscript 'is of no interest whatever.' He continues, "Nor is it of any interest to be told that Hawthorne's wife corrected certain inaccuracies in the Roman descriptions and otherwise made occasional suggestions, which Hawthorne did not always accept." These statements of what is and what is not of 'interest' may be so highly personal as to be of limited interest themselves, save that they suppress the really significant fact about Sophia's alterations in the manuscript, which is that various that were accepted bowdlerized the text and have never been removed. That Miriam as she develops in *The Marble Faun* might earlier have been conceived as a minor German princess has some bearing, perhaps, on the eventual form of the story; and it is a pity that Mr. Wilson suppresses the evidence of what an analytical examination of the manuscript revealed

older-fashioned critics, that modern texts, even those of the twentieth century, cannot simply be reprinted but must be edited in traditional form with the refined techniques that were previously associated only with the literature of the more distant past. One may remark now, with some confidence perhaps, that it is as 'respectable' to edit Hawthorne, say, as to deal with Marston, or Chapman, or Middleton, or Shirley.

Present-day editions take two major forms. The first is the scholarly definitive edition (the form of which is now tolerably well established);[3]

---

about the addition of two chapters, each of which definitely affected the plot concerning the murdered man.

Hawthorne would often smudge out the wet ink of words in the course of inscription and substitute others, although most of the trials can be read under a strong glass. The Centenary apparatus takes a number of pages to list every alteration made in the writing-out of the manuscript, and the records distinguish those with smudges from those without, which were made at the stage of final review and hence have a different order of critical interest. Mr. Wilson seems to believe that, here as well, all of the varied evidence about Hawthorne's care as a stylist has 'no interest,' for he suppresses the reason for the recording of the variants as a mere matter of listing 'the places where these smudges occur'; thus since he never reveals the circumstances in which the smudges are recorded, he leaves the reader with the impression that pages of the apparatus have been devoted to no more than listing of the appearance of smudges in the manuscript. If true, such an apparatus would indeed merit Mr. Wilson's strictures; but it is not true. He then concludes, "It seems to me that this whole procedure meets an insurmountable obstacle when no corrected proofs survive that show the revisions of the author." This is indeed a *non sequitur* in a discussion of the author's manuscript revisions, which outnumber his proof alterations by several hundreds to one, and are of superior critical interest. More important, the statement reveals that Mr. Wilson, despite the serious charges he levels of triviality, had not himself troubled to read very far into the Textual Introduction of the Centenary Edition he was supposedly reviewing: if he had done so, he would have found there the recovery by bibliographical evidence of the authorial proof-revisions for about one-third of the book. I am on friendly terms with Mr. Wilson and can testify from my own acquaintance with his works (not from hearsay) that his hallmark as a critic has always been his scrupulous pursuit of fact before he committed his opinions to print. In *The Fruits of the MLA* the singular disregard for factual accuracy throughout presents a sobering spectacle to his admirers—and I am one—for it is unworthy of such a notable figure as America's first critic.

3 See, for example, "Established Texts and Definitive Editions," *Philological Quarterly*, XLI (1962), 1–17; "Textual Criticism," *The Aims and Methods of Scholarship in the Modern Languages and Literatures*, ed. James Thorpe (New York: Modern Language Association of America, 1953, [revised 1970]), pp. 23–42; "Hawthorne's Text," *Hawthorne Centenary Essays*, ed. Roy Harvey Pearce (Columbus, Ohio: Ohio State University Press, 1964), pp. 401–425; "Some Principles for Scholarly Editions of Nineteenth-Century American Authors," *Studies in Bibliography*, XVII (1964), 223–228. The "Editorial Principles" contained in the first four volumes of the Centenary Hawthorne may also be consulted [as well as "A Note on the Editorial Method" in each volume of *The Works of William James* (Cambridge, Mass.: Harvard University Press, 1975–).]

the second is the commercially inspired product that I call a 'practical' edition. The best modern practical editions present to a broad audience as sound a text (usually modernized and at a minimum price) as is consistent with information that may be procurable through normal scholarly channels and thus without more special research than is economically feasible. On the contrary, a definitive edition attempts (quite simply) to present an established text that, with luck,[4] will never need to be done again in its particular manner, and in all its detail, in the foreseeable future.[5]

The definitive edition is a unique creation of scholarship in which, ideally, the profit motive does not enter, at least as a governing consideration affecting principle and method. Indeed, by any reasonable rate of pay, no publisher could afford to subsidize the production of a definitive edition if the editors (even those aided by National Humanities Foundation grants) did not choose to substitute scholarly reputation for hard cash as the reward for their labors. (Recipients of these grants, incidentally, relinquish all rights to the royalties accruing from their editions.) On the other hand, the practical text is ordinarily a commercial proposition, in which the initiative lies with a publisher, and a major inducement to the scholar is the day-dream of an endless flow of annual royalties to make glad his latter days.

4 'With luck' means not only that the editor has been fortunate in his comprehensiveness, his accuracy, his textual analysis, and his application of all these to the matter at hand. It also means, in quite practical terms, no subsequent discovery of new substantive forms of the text unknown to him, like the revelation of a lost holograph manuscript, or the like. It is, of course, an eminently practical matter—to which no commercial editor could hope to engage himself—to reduce the possibility of future surprise to a minimum by a thorough search for all surviving examples of textual documents. For example, the Virginia edition of Stephen Crane delayed publication of three volumes of short stories and sketches until forty American newspapers could be searched over a period of seven years for variant forms of his work, as well as a series of English magazines and newspapers. The discoveries so far made beyond all previous bibliographical information have been numerous and sometimes of crucial textual importance.

5 An important element in the definitive edition is the complete textual history that it records. A future editor may, for instance, disagree with a Centenary Hawthorne emendation (or refusal to emend) in *The Scarlet Letter*, but he will never need to collate the first, second, and third editions for variant substantive readings and a decision about their authority. That task has been fully and accurately performed in the definitive Ohio State edition down to the last plate change made during Hawthorne's lifetime in the third edition text. In short, all the preparatory editorial work is over with and is properly listed in the edition. Nothing bearing on the authority of the Centenary text that any future editor could possibly wish to know about has been omitted. A future editor of Stephen Crane's *Maggie* may disagree with the Virginia editor's view of the eclectic revised text that Crane would have preferred to see published in 1896; but he need only refer to the Historical Collation in the volume to have spread before him every difference in wording between 1893 and 1896.

Until comparatively recent times most practical editions were a disgrace, and the majority still are. That is, having committed himself to a hack job, some scholar contents himself with writing a general introduction and sends this off to the publisher with a note about the text of some edition that can be reprinted without charge. Hawthorne's *Scarlet Letter* may serve as a convenient example. The Modern Library Giant (1937) and the competing Hendricks House popular edition (1949) were printed independently from the 1883 Houghton Mifflin Riverside text, the most corrupt of all editions available at the time. No text note is present in the Modern Library Giant, but the Hendricks House edition asserts that it "reprints the text of the earliest corrected edition of *The Scarlet Letter* issued as the third edition, in 1851" (p. 423). This is wrong on three counts. First, it was the second printing of the third edition that was issued in 1851, the first printing having taken place in September, 1850. Second, although some minor printer's errors in the first edition were automatically corrected in the second and third editions, serious substantive corruption also occurred, especially in the third edition; and for neither of these two reprint editions did Hawthorne perform any supervision whatever. If this peculiar definition of a 'corrected' edition is to be employed, moreover, the second would be 'the earliest,' but in fact to label the third edition as in any sense 'corrected' is to imply that Hawthorne was responsible for the variants and thus to mislead the reader about the value and authority of its text. Third, collation establishes that even this misleading statement is literally false, for it is not the third edition that the publisher has reprinted but instead the 1884 state (Centenary VI^d) of the 1883 Riverside plates which had been typeset from the 1879 state (Centenary IV^b) of the 1875 Little Classics edition plates which in turn had utilized the 1871 state (Centenary IIIe) of the 1850 third-edition plates as its copy.

The Holt, Rinehart and Winston edition (1947) also reprinted the 1883 Riverside text, as did the Viking Portable (1955), although the new Portable will use the established Centenary text. The Signet edition of 1959 went back to the third edition as its copy, perhaps misled by the erroneous Hendricks House statement about the authority of this derived text.

Most of these practical texts had stated on the title-page that their foreword or introduction was by Professor X or Y, but at least one erroneously reported that it had been 'edited' by Professor Z, a statement that might give an innocent reader something of a misconception, for, contrary to the ordinarily established meaning of the word, the editorial process in the observed example consisted only of writing the critical introduction. No investigation whatever was made of the text, nor was even a single reading altered in the late and bad reprint edition that had been chosen for convenience as printer's copy.[6]

As a marked contrast, when the new Riverside Edition of *The Scarlet Letter* was issued in 1960 and a reputable practical text was produced according to the high standards for editorial care that mark this unusual series, an editorial assistant collated the first and second editions of 1850 and correctly reported that the second-edition variants did not seem to be authorial. For the first time in its editorial history, therefore, *The Scarlet Letter* was reprinted from the most accurate available source, the first edition. Moreover, this first edition was scrutinized for errors, a small amount of emendation was attempted, and the editorial changes were recorded for the information of the reader. Since 1960 the textual situation has improved. The Dell edition, if collation can be trusted, reprints the new Riverside text since it appears to follow it both in weal and woe, that is both in its conscious emendations and in its unconscious errors. The Dolphin Books edition (1960) asserts that it is an exact reprint of the first edition. Other popular editions have utilized the Centenary text by lease arrangement.

The Scarlet Letter text presents few editorial problems once the choice of copy-text has been decided, and thus the investigation that marked the new Riverside edition was well within the commercial limits of practicality (meaning that the editor could afford to pay for it from his royalties), and the resulting text—though not infallible—was certainly worth the money, and still is, even though it must yield in ultimate refinement and accuracy to the Centenary Edition (1962) and its leased reprints, a text that was edited to be definitive in all its parts though at a prohibitive cost for a purely commercial venture.

In more complex textual situations, however, the distance widens between the quality of a definitive edition and one of a practical and commercial nature, since the costs rise beyond all possibility of recoupment when a practical text of any real value is to be produced from difficult materials. For example—if I may be autobiographical—I was once approached about my interest in doing a sound text of *Tom Jones* that would satisfy the very real concern this publisher felt to make his practical editions valuable contributions to informed use. This novel had not previously been edited by modern techniques, and the single article that had been published on the text in *The Library* suggested a complex and difficult

---

6 The flood of paperbacks has also seriously misled the buying public about the authority of texts produced by offset from completely out-of-date editions (like the Mermaid series of plays), often with no date of the original text present to serve as even a partial warning that scholarship a hundred or more years old is being passed off as if it were current.

situation involving the identification of mixed copy and of authorial revisions extending over at least four editions,* all of which (with the
addition of the fifth for certainty) would need to be collated word for
word (and then re-collated a second and third time as a check) to secure
the facts before an editor could even begin the process of evaluating the
variants as author's revisions or as unauthoritative printer's changes.

I am used to collating multiple copies of Elizabethan plays, and indeed
find the drudgery useful as a means of closely acquainting myself with the
minutiae of a text before attacking it as an editor, but *Tom Jones* is a
novel epic in its proportions as well as in its intentions. Since the publishers
were not prepared to pay for this collation, it occurred to me that the
modest scholarly acclaim that might accompany a practical trade-edition
text did not incline me to the sacrifice of a thousand or more hours of my
time (at the going rate) before the text could be prepared and final proofs
passed. On the other hand, if I were to pay for the fifteen separate collations and re-collations of the five editions, plus the several more such
collations involved in checking the proofs for accuracy, and attempt to
recoup the very considerable expense from the modest royalty that the
publisher was prepared to assign, I calculated that my heirs might begin
to enjoy the fruits of my industry about the year 2050. With such crass
considerations weighing heavily in my thinking, I felt impelled to decline
the tender. Indeed, how a practical text of any lasting value can be formulated in such a situation I cannot think.[7]

---

* As it turned out, only the fourth was revised.

7 The problem is indeed acute. The publisher who feels he must repay himself for
the expenses of an edition within a few years does not want to tie up capital in necessary editorial costs, much as he may want a good text that involves such costs—especially
when he must sell his edition at a competitive price with other practical texts more
cheaply put together on a simple reprint basis and not freshly edited from the ground
up. Thus the whole burden of expense is placed on the editor—the publisher dis-
claiming all responsibility for editorial costs except to offer an advance against royalties—and this editor, after all, expects to profit from his commercial venture. That as
many fairly respectable texts get published under this system as are in fact produced
is something of a miracle, although indeed it is largely a testimony to the scholarly
integrity of those who engage themselves to such undertakings in a serious manner,
plus a perhaps naïve hope among the younger that some professional kudos will result that will be of indirect financial benefit. Otherwise, with more experienced and
more cynical scholars the impasse between costs and results discourages most editors
from atttempting anything but the minimum that will satisfy an undiscriminating
public. Some publishers allege that the buyers of cheap editions are bemused by the
editor's name on the title-page and are indifferent to the actual quality of the text, or
unable to distinguish between good and bad texts and so always seek the less expensive.
This may be so. On the other hand, recent reports indicate that publishers are becoming much concerned to secure the emblem of the MLA Center for Editions of
American Authors on their reprints and are now willing to pay the costs of leasing
these definitive texts, with the accompanying warranty of soundness. This change in

If the plain fact is, as I suggest, that few of any scholarly note would engage themselves to a practical text, instead of a definitive one, except for money and whatever modest increment of reputation inheres to such a project, then the hope of scholarly reward that may attach to such editing must be that the practical text has indeed been made good enough so that it offers a significant contribution to student welfare.

Under these terms we are witnessing the publication of a fair number of such practical editions chiefly for the schools and colleges, like the new Riverside or Norton Critical texts, or the Regents series of play texts from the University of Nebraska or the Curtain series from the University of Chicago or the Revels series from Methuen in England, that are useful and, unlike the old Mermaid series of outdated texts offset and offered as if new, can represent a certain small contribution to scholarship in the absence of established texts for these literary works. But let us not because of our good will for these needed ventures, confuse them with the real thing, like the Clarendon edition of the *Spectator Papers*, or the Clarendon *Works* of Goldsmith, the Wesleyan-Clarendon Fielding, the Southern Illinois Dewey, or the Centenary Hawthorne. In methodology and in results these and these only define what is meant by the ultimate establishment of the text, from which the best practical editions thereafter should derive by a lease arrangement such as is an obligatory built-in feature of the emblem award by the Center for Editions of American Authors. An editor who thinks that he is really establishing a text when working on a practical basis is deluding himself and his readers.

To some extent I have put the cart before the horse in talking about the end-results of these texts without first analyzing the conditions under which, respectively, they operate. But I hope that the familiar recital of a few of these conditions will gain from such a preview. Because the case is really a simple one. A text can scarcely be established for a definitive edition until all the relevant bibliographical as well as critical evidence has been identified and then exhausted in its implications. For example, the excellent practical new Riverside *Scarlet Letter* compared only the first two editions of 1850 for authorial changes. This procedure was certainly better than reprinting the bad old 1883 Lathrop Riverside text, but a number of risks were involved. If the possibility existed that Hawthorne would take the opportunity of a fresh typesetting to correct or revise his text, then it is incomprehensible why the third edition, also in 1850, was not collated along with the second, for just as much reason obtains for analyzing its text as for the second. Moreover, at any time before his

---

attitude suggests that the ultimate academic consumer is growing sophisticated and is requiring good texts for his money. The emphasis has shifted within the past few years, evidently. It is a heartening development.

death Hawthorne might have chosen to correct or revise the text by plate-alteration in one of the numerous printings made from the third-edition plates. No attempt was made to ascertain whether or not such changes occurred. As a result, whether the first edition of *The Scarlet Letter* in fact represented the author's final intentions was not fully investigated.

The Centenary editors collated not only the first printing of this third edition back against the first two editions but also the further five reprintings of the third edition in 1851 and 1852, and so on all through the printings made during Hawthorne's lifetime. That the results were negative and disclosed only the accumulation of error does not automatically prove the labor to have been in vain, for the case might well have been otherwise. Moreover, the facts have now been determined and no other editor need investigate the matter again. We do not need any longer to speculate—we now *know* by physical demonstration that Hawthorne never concerned himself with the text of *The Scarlet Letter* after he passed the proofs for the first edition. Thus no reading except in the first edition can have any authority. This we now *know.*

More to the point, the new Riverside collator of the first two editions missed the crucial fact that in the second edition ninety-six of the three hundred and twenty-two type-pages were reprinted from the standing type of the first edition. Hence the decision that the second edition lacked authority was made impressionistically, by ordinary critical review of substantive readings. But when the Centenary editors came upon this bibliographical fact, they were thereby enabled for the first time to distinguish the changes made in the standing type (all of which must have been intentional) from the changes made in the reset pages (some of which must have been inadvertent compositorial errors). On the basis of this informed analysis of physical evidence—and the standing type contained the essential control evidence from spellings and word-division that Hawthorne had not ordered the changes—a decision was made that I think may fairly be called scientific and demonstrable that all the second-edition variants originated with a publisher's reader (though in the reset pages in part with the compositors) and thus that they must be completely ignored when they are not obvious corrections. Original scholarly investigation of this scope and intensity, and I may say delicacy, can scarcely by expected of a non-bibliographical practical editor, whose methods must be rougher and readier and his results, therefore, the less trustworthy.[8]

8 In the course of what can be regarded only as a tendentious review of the Centenary *House of the Seven Gables*, the reviewer, exercised over what he mistakenly felt was a slight to the new Riverside editor in the Centenary Textual Introduction (see note 9 below), wrote, "This treatment of a scholar of high repute [noted in the preceding sentence as "of higher stature and more deeply committed than any of the scholars involved in the Ohio State project"] suggests, I trust incorrectly, that the

Let us face the fact that many reputable scholars who are lured into preparing an edition of a text do not have the specialized bibliographical training for the job, especially when they attempt more than the minimum. An example comes to hand in the practical new Riverside text of Hawthorne's *House of the Seven Gables*,[9] a particularly difficult and complex text though less so than *The Marble Faun*.

Ohio State editors have assumed sole authority over the texts of Hawthorne," *American Literary Scholarship an Annual 1965*, ed. James Woodress (Durham, N.C.: Duke University Press, 1967), p. 24. The reviewer has not been mistaken. For the reasons given in the present paper about the inevitable differences between a definitive edition and a practical one, the Centenary editors have indeed "assumed authority" over the Hawthorne texts with the blessing of the MLA Center for Editions of American Authors, and the assistance of its funding to the generous funding given the edition by the Ohio State University. Unless a team of reputable critical and bibliographical scholars is prepared to challenge the Centenary project with comparable funding and expertise, the Centenary editions of Hawthorne are likely to remain the "sole authority" for the text on the simple ground that no one else acting in a private capacity could possibly perform the enormous and expensive research that lies in the back of the technical 'establishment' of the Hawthorne texts by the Centenary editors. This is a fact, as impersonal as the weather. It will no doubt apply, as well, for the other CEAA-sponsored editions.

9 The reviewer mentioned in the preceding footnote objected to an impersonal and carefully neutral note appended to the Centenary Textual Introduction in page proof that remarked on the prior publication of the new Riverside edition, based on the manuscript, but commenting that differences existed between the two texts that were of considerable extent. This statement is quite literally true, and was so intended. It seemed at the time, and still seems to me, an impertinence to discuss the merits and demerits of a competing edition in the pages of another, as the reviewer thought should have been done. Tastes may differ, of course, as to what is suitable, but my own taste does not incline toward controversy, particularly within a severely factual bibliographical and textual introduction to a purportedly definitive edition. On the other hand, the Centenary editors did in fact at the time prepare an analysis of the differences between their own text and the new Riverside and found it to their benefit in a few readings even though they chose to reassert the propriety of their own choices or emendations in the hundreds of other variants that do indeed exist between the two texts both in respect to substantives and to accidentals. Although any analytical distinction seemed out of place in the edition itself, a paper like the present may offer briefly some account of the two texts. In doing so I am responding, in effect, to the invitation of the reviewer since without the stimulation of his confusion of the true issues it is unlikely that this paper would ever have been written. If the net result is to place the Centenary *Seven Gables* above the new Riverside in accuracy, in the useful application of bibliographical techniques to problems of text, and in the general consistency and superiority of textual principles, the intent is by no means to imply that the new Riverside editor was in any way deficient according to the natural standards for a practical edition. Indeed, it is appropriate to say here that the results that he singlehandedly achieved within the time he could allot to the project and the limited area of research thus enforced, without the benefits of co-operative cross-checking by expensive teamwork, were quite remarkable and praiseworthy. That his

Instead of contenting himself with reprinting the first edition, the new
Riverside editor very properly recognized the peculiar authority of the
printer's-copy manuscript and decided to base his text on that in conjunction with the first edition. To this end he compared the manuscript
with two arbitrarily chosen copies of the first edition (the relationship of
which he confused, however, when he did not recognize duplicate plates
within the same impression, and took a variant created in their manufacture as evidence for two distinct printings of the edition). He did not
and could not have been expected to identify and collate the five actual
printings dated 1851 from the first-edition plates in order to ascertain
whether changes had been made in these plates (as they were in *The
Marble Faun* early printings), a routine performed by the Centenary editors who also added the collation of all other printings during Hawthorne's
lifetime in order to establish the unauthoritative nature of the subsequent
plate-changes.

But having correctly chosen the manuscript as his copy-text, the editor
then had no bibliographical methodology to attack the vexed problem of
the first-edition variants. He remarked that more than one compositor had
set the first edition and thus, "Since their names are in the margins [of
the manuscript] beside the parts they did, it would be possible, if anyone
wanted to, to decide which one of them was the best interpreter of Hawthorne and which the worst" (p. xxxiii), without recognizing that this very
question lay at the heart of the textual-critical problem of the first-edition
variants. Such a compositorial analysis ultimately provided the Centenary
editors with the necessary physical and critical evidence that could be
utilized to distinguish Hawthorne's final intentions as manifested by his
proof-revision from the numerous printer's corruptions that remained in
the print.

But it was less easy than alleged to determine the exact lines set by
each compositor, and indeed a new hypothesis about the marking of
printer's manuscripts for cast-off copy and simultaneous typesetting had
to be formulated before the system employed in *Seven Gables* (which
differed from that in *The Blithedale Romance*) fell neatly into place and

---

labors consciously paralleled those of the editors of an avowedly definitive edition
with resources beyond the capacity of any single research-scholar may be thought to
be unfortunate since the critical introduction of the new Riverside text (in which
there is no competition with the severely historical Centenary introduction) could
as well have been prefixed to a leased reprint of the Centenary text, with superior benefits all around for the purchaser of this practical paperback edition. To repeat, the intent of the brief analysis that follows is not controversial or in the least personal.
Instead, it is aimed at suggesting the nature and extent of the differences between a
definitive edition and a superior practical text in order to clarify what may be expected
of each in respect to its reproduction of the author's intentions within a complex textual
situation.

each workman's stints could be identified exactly and with confidence. Only when the variants between the manuscript and the first edition were categorized by compositors could the editors then proceed to analyze the kinds of changes made, to isolate those of sophistication and memorial failure from simple misreading of handwriting, and to prepare a chart that ordered the eight compositors according to their degree of variation and of error. From this vantage the troublesome neutral variants could be assessed systematically, compositor by compositor, and a decision made about their authority on physical evidence, not on mere impressionism. Finally, the editors established that first-edition variants in the ratio of two to one had to be rejected as printer's errors as against almost precisely the opposite ratio in *The Blithedale Romance* set the next year in the same shop and partly by several of the same compositors. Since he did not envisage the necessity for this bibliographical analysis of each substantive variant, compositor by compositor, the new Riverside editor could judge among the differences only *en bloc* and by criteria based on personal taste: as a result, he accepted and printed in his text as what Hawthorne wrote about fifty percent of the compositors' mistakes, which is a rather high proportion of editorial error. The moot problem of the authorial proofreading and its true identification he did not really tackle at all.

Since the differences between this practical text and the Centenary definitive edition have been queried, perhaps some statistics will help to illustrate the facts. The Riverside editor listed thirty-one intentional word variants between manuscript and first edition and twenty-four further variants in which, in his opinion, the compositors corrected what were Hawthorne's mental lapses in writing out the manuscript. These latter range from simple dittographic slips like manuscript *that a a murder*, through spelling slips like the twice-repeated *shokeeper* for *shopkeeper*, to readings like manuscript *barn-door fowl* but first-edition *barn-yard fowl*.

Let us look at this list of manuscript lapses as a satisfactory and accurate representation of the facts. In the first place twenty more such lapses exist than the twenty-four that are recorded in the list.[10] In the second place, the reported twenty-four lapses include three readings as manuscript errors that are perefectly correct. Thus the editor apparently did not bother to consult the *O.E.D.* to discover that *barn-door fowl* is a quite acceptable phrase and that no reason existed to label it an error and to adopt the first-edition compositorial sophistication of *barn-yard fowl*.[11] Correspondingly,

10 These appear as Centenary 24.23, 35.31, 43.1, 45.14, 48.34, 58.21, 81.1, 152.24, 178.26, 181.2–3, 181.8, 182.26, 186.1, 213.4, 242.16, 243.3, 282.1, 285.26, 299.19, 318.15.

11 On this reading the *American Literary Scholarship* reviewer rationalizes, "[The editor] accepts the printer's emendation of Hawthorne's 'barn-door fowl' to 'barn-yard fowl,' while Centenary comments that the OED sanctions 'barn door' in references

when both manuscript and first edition agree in the phrase *series of calamity* the editor mistook the syntax and 'corrected' it, as he supposed, to *series of calamities*, presumably without knowledge of the similar phrase *series of enjoyment* in *The Scarlet Letter*.[12] For no particular reason, he assumed that Hawthorne's innocent personification capital *Eve* for *evening* was an error. A fourth assumed error, the position of the apostrophe in *Maules* reflects a too literal interpretation of the casual position authors are prone to adopt in their handwriting about the exact placement of the punctuation, although their intention is perfectly clear, and can scarcely be called a manuscript lapse. Adjusting for these mistakes, we find that the editor reported in his list only twenty of the forty actual manuscript slips, for a ratio of fifty percent accuracy in the notation of these data.

The new Riverside list of the thirty-one verbal variants between manuscript and first edition, with the editor's choices between the two authorities, is seriously incomplete although purporting to be definitive. Actually there are thirty-five more of such differences that were overlooked and thus not recorded in what was perhaps the most important record of editorial procedure in the volume. Of these unnoted thirty-five, fifteen[13] represent readings in which the editor chose the manuscript over the first edition, and twenty[14] in which also without record he chose word differences of the first edition instead of the manuscript readings. Here, then, over fifty percent error also exists in the listing of important data for the use of the critic.

A necessarily quick and by no means necessarily accurate collation reveals that at least nine editorial substantive errors are introduced into the new Riverside text that are, of course, unrecorded. These vary from such cases of misreading the manuscript as the transcription of manuscript

---

as late as Sir Walter Scott. [The editor] reasons that 'barn-door' is simply a mental slip of Hawthorne's among quite a number of others in the manuscript and in his proofreading. In this instance the problem of idiom is too difficult to permit of any certainty, but posterity has sided with the printer and [the editor]. 'Barn-door fowl' would immediately strike a twentieth-century reader as a false note." The reviewer does not explain how 'barn-door' could be a slip for 'barn-yard' when it is a respectable old-fashioned idiom of the sort that Hawthorne loved; nor does he explain the pertinence of the reaction of a naïve twentieth-century ear to the realities of what Hawthorne wrote in 1851. That reprint editions, wholly unedited, have chosen to follow the first edition's corrupt 'barn-yard' because nobody before the new Riverside editor was aware that the manuscript read 'barn-door' scarcely provides useful evidence for the weight of the judgment of 'posterity' on the authority of the reading.

12 See the Centenary textual note to 240.21 and *The Scarlet Letter* 19.10.

13 In the Centenary reference system these are recorded at 31.33, 32.4, 52.4, 62.26, 79.19, 81.17, 106.26, 129.14, (a first-edition misprint), 137.23, 192.24, 254.5, 255.31, 287.31, 304.11, 306.35.

14 These are Centenary 37.30, 44.7, 45.33, 64.10, 65.8, 69.6, 88.20, 103.23, 106.31, 127.32, 151.26, 169.31, 170.9, 171.2, 179.19, 185.5, 209.15, 266.17, 280.26, 299.22.

tested as *tasted* (C 98.20), of manuscript *humanity* as *humility* (C 264.24), through the passing of what is no doubt a typo[15] like *scramp* for *scamp* (C 290.27), to such silent sophistications of the text not encouraged even by first-edition variance as *drop* for *droop* (C 107.22) or the silent tinkering with acceptable old-fashioned Hawthorne grammar as reading *a one* for *an one* (C 104.2). Especially indicative of a lack of linguistic background is the silent sophistication at C 152.21 of the perfectly acceptable eighteenth-century phrase *whispered her* found in both manuscript and first edition (and a favorite idiom in Dryden's stage directions) to the modernized *whispered to her.* If a lexicographer were to use a computer concordance made from this practical text he would be misled time after time about Hawthorne's true usage and idiom, since the language is usually modernized when a choice exists, often silently. The editor, however, did not emend or note the manuscript and first-edition concurrence in the nonce form *horticulturalist* (C 24.16–17), blessed by no dictionary.

The treatment of Hawthorne's perfectly acceptable and characteristic spellings (largely derived from the eighteenth century) is erratic in the

15 For the differences possible in the quality of the proofreading between a practical and a definitive text, I am indebted to the following remarks in a letter from Professor James Meriwether: "I have concluded, on the basis of working on half a dozen books for two publishers, that the real barrier between a definitive text and a commercial publisher lies in the area of proofreading. Even if the commercial publisher means, and agrees, to proper proofreading procedures and precautions, the odds are against their being carried out. Everyone involved in the process—publishers, editors, publisher's proofreaders, printers, printer's proofreaders—is, quite naturally and properly, used to saving money by saving time. No matter how many claims are made that proof is being read *against copy*, it isn't—not carefully, not entirely. No matter how many claims are made that no changes will be made in corrected proofs, there is great danger that someone will do a little more styling and editing. The result is apt to be a text which contains a minimum of obvious typos—but a lot of minor changes, especially in accidentals, from the original text. A scholar might well prepare a definitive text for a commercial publisher. In extraordinary circumstances he might be permitted sufficient time for the multiple readings of galley proof necessary to find and correct all errors. Under even more extraordinary circumstances he might have page proof long enough to make sure that all errors had been corrected, and that all re-set lines contained no new errors. But even if he were allowed revises of page proof until no errors remained, the chances are good that lines would be re-set after he had approved the proof, and that he would not know the lines had been re-set. Only if the editor could machine a set of the approved page proof against a set of the sheets of the book could he be sure that all was well. This is asking too much of a commercial publisher —not only would his whole staff have to be re-educated, but he would have to be convinced that the effort to bring out such a text was worth jeopardizing his relationship with a printer—and the printer would have to know in advance how much trouble and time this text would take, so he could make a realistic estimate on the book. Otherwise, confronted by an unexpectedly expensive printing operation, who could blame him for cutting corners?"

extreme, and most of these are silently reduced to the house-style of the first edition even though in a text that bases its accidentals on the manuscript. For a few of the numerous examples, one may compare the choice of first-edition modernized house-styling instead of Hawthorne's acceptable *scull* (C 33.26, 59.18), *canvass* (57.15, 139.19, 273.21, 297.8), *developement* (122.34, 141.32, 215.14), *handfull* (C 164.21, 276.21), *aukward* (C 79.14, 124.22), *ancles* (C 255.7), and so on and so on. The editor usually forsakes the characteristic use of *z* in such words as *merchandize* for the first-edition *s* (35.29, 48.31, 201.20, 257.20), although misreading of the manuscript probably occasioned these pointless variants. He is erratic in sometimes following manuscript *farther* as against first-edition *further* but other times first-edition *further* against the characteristic *farther* (C 123.28, 178.22, 229.10) of the manuscript.

No principle save a preference for a modernization from the first edition not characteristic of Hawthorne's own usage seems to govern this arbitrary treatment of the manuscript's authoritative accidentals.[16] On the other hand, the Centenary editors had logically thought-out and tested principles for dealing with these accidentals, and every departure from the manuscript was scrupulously recorded. In contrast, the arbitrary and unrecorded changes of the practical edition away from the manuscript copy-text and its practice in spelling, word-division, capitalization, and punctuation run into the hundreds.[17]

16 After scrupulously editing the four Hawthorne romances, three of them from manuscript, the Centenary editors can confidently assure the reviewer from *American Literary Scholarship* that he is mistaken in his undocumented assertion (p. 23) that Hawthorne "was interested in his words, not in punctuation, capitalization, nor even very vitally in spelling." But the reviewer, like the editor, seems to approve of the unnecessary modernization of authentic forms of the accidentals though in an edition based on the manuscript as copy-text. He writes, for instance [p. 25], "The passages I have examined show no important discrepancies [between the two editions] and no discernible differences of tendency, unless it be a very slight preponderance of literalness in the Centenary's adoption of the styling [,)], an impossible usage today." The pertinence of present-day punctuation usage to the question of the faithful Centenary reproduction of an almost invariable Hawthorne punctuation characteristic quite acceptable in his own time is not wholly clear. What is a fact is that the new Riverside editor modernized his text from the manuscript by reference to the first edition without any warning to the reader so that his edition does not reproduce the perfectly acceptable manuscript characteristics in some hundreds of readings. On the other hand, certain of these agreements with the first edition accidentals instead of the manuscript are manifestly the result of inadvertence in failing to bring into accurate conformity with the manuscript the marked copy of photographs of the first edition presumably sent to the printer. This is a danger which the Centenary editors and their team of checkers can feelingly remark.

17 This Centenary concern for absolute accuracy in presenting the eighteenth-century-derived characteristics of Hawthorne's style obscured by silent modernization even in the new Riverside text merits better than the reviewer's sneer (p. 26) that the

Further statistics may be of interest. Both the Centenary and the new Riverside texts agree in choosing the manuscript readings twenty-five times in verbal differences where the first edition varies, two of which consist of obvious first-edition misprints.[18] Both editions agree in nine cases in choosing the first-edition variant reading over the manuscript, when obvious manuscript lapses are not involved.[19] The Centenary and the Riverside texts disagree in twenty-five word differences[20] in which the new Riverside chooses the first-edition variant but the Centenary authenticates the original manuscript reading. In five cases[21] the Centenary selects as Hawthorne's proofreading changes the first-edition variants where the practical text denies this hypothesis and treats the variants from manuscript as first-edition compositorial errors. To sum up, the two texts—if we disregard their agreement when one or other authority is a manuscript lapse or a first-edition misprint—agree in their choice of thirty-three word variants and disagree in forty-one.[22] In hundreds of cases they disagree about the readings of the manuscript in respect to its

---

Centenary's "concern with Hawthorne as an important and a unique American writer was small; he was merely a corpus of important texts upon which scholars could exercise their virtuosity." It seems to us that our concern for Hawthorne as a unique writer is manifested by our scrupulous attempt to get his text right, at whatever cost. If dedicated accuracy to the recovery of an author's most minute intentions, and the bibliographical discoveries that make such a process possible, are to be dismissed as mere editorial virtuosity—as if bibliographical expertise existed in a vacuum—then the reviewer's final sentence (p. 27) is an example of heroic insensibility: "Literary studies have always given adequate prestige and emolument to editorial labors; there is no present need at all for campaign for greater recognition of their value." Whatever truth may reside in this ambivalent statement as applied to practical texts, the reviewer's preceding remarks about textual matters suggest an insufficient scholarly acquaintance with the principles and standards of definitive editions, as well (to descend to the mundane) as a bland ignorance about the contractual relationship of the editors to the Center for Editions of American Authors by which not one penny of the profits from the original editions or the leasing of the texts to the most remote future returns to the editors.

18 Centenary 31.33, 32.4, 52.4, 62.6, 64.25, 79.19, 81.17, 84.1, 89.34, 106.26, 127.11, 127.14, 129.14, 137.23, 149.25, 171.22, 192.24, 224.8, 254.5, 255.31, 275.3, 304.11, 306.35, 307.12, 308.27.

19 Centenary 7.24, 24.31, 102.23, 169.31, 186.24, 214.27–28, 266.17, 299.22, 310.26.

20 Centenary 37.30, 44.7, 45.33, 64.10, 65.8, 69.6, 88.20, 90.27, 103.23, 106.31, 113.4, 127.32, 170.9, 171.2, 174.34, 179.19, 185.5, 209.15, 214.14, 228.12, 228.18, 280.26, 303.20, 307.11.

21 Centenary 80.32, 234.3, 276.8, 287.31, 309.2.

22 They disagree further, of course, in the nine known cases of new Riverside substantive misreadings of the manuscript that differ from the first edition as well, and in the one Centenary misreading of the manuscript (*indefinable* for *undefinable* at 300.8) which the search revealed and for which we apologize. The error will be corrected in the next printing.

accidentals, or at least as to what—on the evidence—Hawthorne would have wished printed if he had not felt obliged to accept house-styling.

Whether as the dean of a mid-Western library school disdainfully remarked about the care taken to make the Centenary *Scarlet Letter* text definitive, that this was the product of "bibliographical drones" searching tirelessly for "printers" errors, no matter how fortuitous or trivial,[23] we may leave to the scholarly judgment of posterity, which is, instead, likely to see in the Centenary *Scarlet Letter* the first truly bibliographical and definitive critical editing of a printed American-literature text. As a contrast, a different reviewer, who had some understanding of the value of textual scholarship, after comparing this Centenary text was horrified to see within the space of sixteen lines in the Modern Library Giant four textual corruptions of which two (he felt) were of critical significance.[24]

What is of 'critical significance' is, of course, subject to varying interpretation. The new Riverside editor made his own definition when he wrote: ". . . considering the variants in *words* [between MS and first edition], Hawthorne's 'jewels,' I discovered not one single 'soiled fish,' that is, not one corruption of a sort that would be likely to mislead an intelligent critic into elaborating a false interpretation of the novel's meaning. There is a sense in which it would be perfectly true to say that not one of the thousands of changes the printers made in Hawthorne's manuscript—from hyphens to words—makes any important *critical* difference, when 'critical' is understood as having to do with interpretation and evaluation of the novel" (p. xxvi). This is only a more cautious statement of a simplistic position the library-school dean reviewer had boldly carried to its logical and inevitably extravagant conclusion when he earlier denied any particular virtue to the Centenary *Scarlet Letter* text because it did not reveal in its record of textual alterations any variants "that would throw significant light on the maturation of Hawthorne's philosophy, the development of his characters, or the course of the plot."

It is really a comic philosophy of criticism to demand that each definitive text should produce some significant reversal of all literary evaluation of a work as a whole else it is not worth the doing, or is not to be distinguished in scholarly value from a practical text that both creates and perpetuates verbal error. I cannot find it in my heart, for instance, to reprove the twentieth-century attempt to refine *Hamlet* from the errors of the early documents, and the accretions of eighteenth-century emendation, because the resulting new texts still offer us the same old melancholy

23 *American Notes and Queries*, I (June, 1963), 159–60.

24 "The Critic, the Editor, and the Organization Scholar," *Mad River Review*, I (1964–65), 74–77.

Prince of Denmark and not a woman in disguise. This is a matter to which I shall revert in my conclusion.

Addressing both students and established scholars as I do here, I am concerned to appeal to enlightened self-interest, to the position that critical readers of whatever persuasion must understand something of the standards that cause definitive editions to be unique in their kind. When they do so, they may the better appreciate—and value—the peculiar virtues that make worth while and justify the enormous labor and money spent on the refinements of editorial procedures that go to form these unique established texts. Only then can they use the current commercial texts as they should be used, and with something other than scholarly naïveté comprehend the practical standards of excellence that conscientious scholars in such series of paperbacks as the new Riverside have attempted to maintain. In fact, only when one can understand the methodology of a definitive edition can one know enough to distinguish the proper value of these new practical texts, and their standards appropriate for their kind, from the shoddy that hacks produce in such numbers for the marketplace. However, even the best of the practical editions cannot replace the established text of a definitive edition as the final court of all appeal. If the final court, then why not the day-to-day companion of the critic either in the original form or—after initial investigation—in a convenient paperback reprinted in a carefully controlled version from the leased established text?

If I were to place one virtue of the established text above all others, I should emphasize its accuracy. Accuracy is a virtue that is neither humble nor to be despised. A comprehensive accuracy to the facts, without regard for the cost of such a luxury, is a characteristic of definitive editions, difficult to achieve under the conditions governing the production of even the most ambitious of practical texts. Accuracy of identification and special expertise in the interpretation of the technical evidence dredged up by bibliographical research is also a characteristic, and one that is not widespread although it is so intimately associated that it cannot be divorced from the critical choice of readings that forms the establishment of an accurate text.

Accuracy resides in a definitive edition at three levels.

First, the definitive edition establishes with absolute accuracy the exact documentary forms of all authoritative early texts of the work being edited. That is, if a manuscript is the basic text, the editor transcribes it exactly. When a printed text, as usual, then follows, the definitive editor by collation of multiple copies determines (*a*) any variants that occurred during the printing of the text itself, and (*b*) any variants that occurred in previously unknown as well as known printings after the first as part of the transmission. He cannot be content with his own hoped-for but inevitably faulty accuracy. Every step of transcription and collation is checked by a team and errors are weeded out. As a result, *humanity* is not mistranscribed as *humility* and *tested* does not become *tasted* as in the practical text of *Seven Gables*, nor is *Hillard* confused with *Hilliard* as in the practical text of *The Scarlet Letter*.

However, as the second step, accuracy is not confined to simple fidelity of transcription and of reproduction. Accuracy to facts demands that a trustworthy record should be printed of all variant forms of the text during the author's lifetime and such a reasonable period thereafter as to cover the possibility of the posthumous publication of authorial corrections and revisions. By collation all concealed variant forms of the text are identified, like the superficially identical five printings of *Seven Gables* dated 1851, and the presence or absence of variants is determined once and for all; just as, once and for all, the third edition of *The Scarlet Letter* was collated and its changes evaluated, and thereupon its different printings through Hawthorne's lifetime were compared in order to *demonstrate* whether or not authorial changes had been made in the plates. Positive or negative as the results may be, the critic now knows precisely where he stands when in a definitive edition all these processes are gone through and the complete and accurate results printed in list form as the concrete evidence on which the establishment of the text has rested. If the critic chooses to disagree with the judgment of the editor in the next important step of the treatment of the text, he has all the evidence available in the form of accurate lists. He is not put in the position of a reader of the practical text of *Seven Gables* in which a list of thirty word differences is provided wherein the editor has made a choice between manuscript and first-edition variant reading, although an accurate list would have comprised seventy-eight such readings. The definitive edition of *Seven Gables*, moreover, by listing every one of its variants in punctuation, capitalization, word-division, and spelling from the manuscript copy-text does not conceal from the reader, as did the numerous silent changes made in the practical text, the spelling system derived from the eighteenth century that Hawthorne favored.

The third step in the accurate establishment of the text consists of the combination of authorities into a critical version that will reflect the author's final intentions insofar as these can be recovered by systematic, principled selection from among the variants of different authoritative forms of the text, supplemented by editorial emendation. Accuracy to the author's intentions is on a much higher and more critical level than in previous stages because here flower the peculiar skills that distinguish modern editors from the traditional harmless drudges.

When more than one authoritative version of a text is in existence, analytical bibliography takes over the tracing of the transmission of the text in all its details. The chief function of analytical bibliography is to guide and to set the limits within which the critical judgment must operate in the final selection of readings. The editorial ideal is to work within a closed field in which these choices are dictated more by bibliographical than by critical, which is to say by merely tasteful, criteria. The prime example comes in Hawthorne's *Marble Faun*, which I think is a classic case. Whenever a manuscript is in existence, as is the printer's copy for the *Faun* (set in England under the title of *Transformation*) and we have the first edition that was printed from this manuscript, the ultimate editorial problem is to choose between the variants, which is to say to identify in the first edition what were the author's corrections and revisions that would have been found in the proof-sheets and to adopt them, while at the same time identifying and rejecting the compositors' errors and sophistications that had crept into the typesetting and had not been recognized and weeded out in the proof. How variable the proportion of these may be in different decisions, may be illustrated by the fact that in the established text of *The Blithedale Romance* two-thirds of the verbal differences in the first edition were accepted as authorial proof-alterations, and only one-third rejected as printing corruption, whereas in *Seven Gables* the editors felt impelled by the evidence to accept only one-third of the first-edition variants as proof-revisions and to reject two-thirds as compositorial sophistication and corruption.

In *The Marble Faun* the number of differences between manuscript and print were more numerous than with the other two romances and posed a correspondingly difficult problem. Fortunately, analytical bibliography solved the problem completely for almost one-third of the whole text. Briefly, what happened is this. The interpretation of a curious pattern of variation by sheets between the first edition printed in London from the manuscript and the first Boston edition printed from the English led to the recognition that the latter half of both the second and third English volumes had been sent to Boston in proofsheets uncorrected by the author, whereas the rest of the Boston edition was typeset from corrected final proof or from the printed sheets themselves. Thus the editors could apply the following criteria for selection in the area represented by approximately one-third of the text which was sent to Boston as uncorrected proof. When the manuscript and the London edition agreed against Boston, the Boston variant must be an American printer's error. When the two printed editions agreed against the manuscript, the reading was a compositorial error in London and the manuscript variant must be chosen. When the manuscript and the Boston edition agreed against the London reading, the London version must be accepted as an authorial change made in a later state of the proof.

No critical judgment, therefore, was necessary to decide with absolute accuracy between the readings of three different forms of the text in a third of the book. Moreover, the area where this evidence was present was large enough to furnish a reliable control over three important matters that could then be extrapolated as principles for dealing with the variants in the remaining two-thirds of the text. First, the average amount of Hawthorne's proofreading could be estimated so that a calculation could be made about the probable number of variants in this larger area to be expected as authorial changes in proof; second, the kind of changes could be analyzed in the light of the relatively consistent kind of alterations made in the control section. Third, in the control section where compositorial error was completely identified, the accuracy to the copy of the various compositors could be ascertained both quantitatively and qualitatively, and the results of this study could then be applied to the pages set by the various compositors in the non-control section as further evidence to guide as well as to limit the critical choice of variants between the two authorities. As a result of the application of advanced bibliographical techniques to the editing of *The Marble Faun*, an astonishing amount of demonstrable evidence was uncovered and put to use in what may fairly be said to be a scientific manner to solve one of the most difficult problems in the editing of texts—the identification of authorial proofreading.

Without the advantage of the control sheets found in *The Marble Faun* it was yet possible in *Seven Gables* to apply the techniques of compositorial analysis to the problem of identifying authentic proof-alterations and discarding compositorial variants. The editor of the new Riverside text had dismissed the idea of working with such evidence: ". . . it would be possible, if anyone wanted to, to decide which of them [the compositors] was the *best* interpreter of Hawthorne and which the worst." Seemingly it did not occur to him that any editor would need to have this information as a practical guide to the choice of variants within each compositor's pages. At least, any scientific and bibliographical editor of a definitive edition would be required to secure this information, although not (on the evidence) the more easygoing editor of a practical text of lower standards. It was the application of just such an analysis that resulted in such a marked difference in opinion between the Centenary editors and the Riverside editor about what variant readings in the first edition were Hawthorne's proof-corrections and what not. The Centenary editors decided that five-sevenths were not. If they were right, and they must be so in the majority of choices, then the practical-text editor operating on non-scientific evidence made about as many wrong decisions as he did right ones (judging as many as thirty-three to be proof-corrections as against thirty as not).

I must pass over too quickly a most interesting example of the application of bibliographical techniques to textual criticism that occurs in the text of the last of Stephen Crane's *Whilomville Stories*, "A Little Pilgrim." The manuscripts of eleven of the thirteen stories have been preserved, although a lost intermediate typescript must have served as the actual printer's copy for the first appearance of these stories in print, in *Harper's Magazine* between August, 1899, and August, 1900. The nature of this typescript, as well as the amount of Crane's proofreading, and hence the authority of the differences between manuscript and magazine, constitute a serious editorial problem. Editors of these stories have always reprinted the book version published in 1900 by Harper's about the time the last story appeared (posthumously) in the magazine. This is a derived text for the first twelve stories, a mere reprint of the magazine version with a few corruptions of its own. A more enlightened editor, like Robert Stallman in an edition he has prepared, used the magazine form as his copytext; this is better, but it ignores the authority of the manuscripts and assumes that every difference between manuscript and magazine resulted from Crane's proofreading, a proposition that cannot be defended.

The final story "A Little Pilgrim" furnishes just the sort of control the bibliographical editor wants in his investigation of the text. To make a long tale short, and to omit all the interesting evidence (provided *in extenso* in the Virginia edition), it develops that the book collection required copy for the thirteenth story before it had been set up in the magazine, although all of the preceding twelve had been available either in magazine clippings, or else from corrected proofs that Crane had returned for stories that had not yet appeared. For an obscure reason, though perhaps from mere haste, the lost typescript was cast off according to the book pages it would occupy, and the first half was given to a magazine compositor but the second half to a book compositor. Each set independently from typescript until the end of the divided copy and then transferred to the proofsheets of the other to set the opposite half. The book was rushed into production with no more than editorial proofreading, but the magazine proofs were sent to England where they were revised by Crane before he died; and so the magazine printed the most authoritative form of the substantives, in general.

We then have the following textual situation. When all three authorities of manuscript, magazine, and book agree, we know we have absolutely authoritative text (which is true for the vast majority of the readings); and we further know (a useful piece of information for extrapolation) that the lost typescript must have been the same as the manuscript. When the manuscript and the book agree but the magazine differs, we are positively in on an authentic Crane proof revision made in the late state of the type from which the magazine was finally printed, at least in that first half of the story in which the book was set up from the proofs of the magazine setting. (Some small uncertainty could hold in the other half whether the variant might not be a magazine-setting corruption of the book proof not caught by the author.) Here also we know, incidentally, that the typescript must not have differed from the manuscript in the original reading. However, when the book and magazine agree against the manuscript, we have either a printer's error not recognized by Crane or else a change from the manuscript in the lost typescript from which the copy was directly set. Such variants in the typescript could be authoritative or unauthoritative, of course. Finally, when manuscript and magazine agree against the book, we must have a case of a printer's error in the early magazine proof from which the first part of the story in the book was typeset but one that was later caught and changed back to the original manuscript form by Crane when he read the magazine proof; or else we are seeing an error in the book made in setting from the original magazine proof. (Several such variants occur, and they are of some importance.)

Thus in both halves of the story the Crane proof alterations can be isolated with considerable confidence and automatically adopted as the truly authoritative final intentions of the author. In the remaining combinations we have some evidence to estimate the amount of printer's error and also the amount and kind of change in the typescript together with its authority. For example, it can be demonstrated on such evidence that the change from manuscript *Dutch Reformed Church to Big Progressive Church* of the book and magazine took place in the typescript. In turn, this evidence that Crane was already concerned with the religious satire in the typescript is most useful when later in the story some satirical phrases are omitted in the magazine though present in manuscript and in the book version. It seems more likely, on this evidence, that they were critical changes made by Crane to curb certain excesses of tone rather than editorial censorship in a final stage of proof.

No non-bibliographical editor or critic of these *Whilomville Stories* ever noticed the odd facts about the textual transmission of this story which, when analyzed, make for almost absolute accuracy in getting every word of this story exactly right as Crane finally wanted it. The analysis also may be used to improve the accuracy of the editing of the preceding twelve stories because of the evidence this final story furnishes about the nature and extent of Crane's proofreading and the nature and extent of the alterations made from the manuscript in the lost typescript.

These are a few case histories from among the many more that can be offered to illustrate the peculiar kind of accuracy in ascertaining and then in reproducing the author's final intentions about his text that is a closed book to the practical editor but a normal technique for the careful and bibliographically informed editor of a definitive edition. When we return to the ultimate usefulness to the critic of the extraordinary efforts toward accuracy made in the establishing of a text as against the useful product of a non-definitive editor, I think we can agree that it is too much to expect that the differences between the two methods will produce texts of novels, say, that affect plot or character to the extent that the over-all evaluation of criticism will be altered, *insofar as these parts of the novel are concerned.*[25] On the other hand, fiction consists of more than plot and character, independent of the exact words an author wrote. When a recent critic discusses Crane's "A Little Pilgrim" and makes certain assumptions about Crane's literary methods on the sole basis of the book text and selects as evidence for his thesis the original passages that Crane was later to revise in proof for the magazine version, the critical conclusions are distorted when the reader is not informed that what the critic had to say was applicable to the early concept of the story but less so to the final.[26]

This is an obvious example but there are many more. The new Riverside editor remarked that in the *Seven Gables* variants between manuscript and first edition he had found no "soiled fish" error "of a sort that would be likely to mislead an intelligent critic into elaborating a false interpretation of the novel's meaning." He is here referring to a well-known incident in which the late Professor Matthiessen exclaimed in ecstasy about the metaphysical implications of the phrase "soiled fish of the sea" in Melville's *White Jacket,* unaware that he was taking as authorial what was in fact a printer's error in a derived English edition for the authentic "coiled fish of the sea."

But I fancy that the editor mistakes the case. First Matthiessen did not hinge his whole concept of the novel on his interpretation of this phrase, and, second, the phrase leaps to mind not because of any intrinsic quality in the error but only because an important critic chose to single it out for special attention, and proved to be wrong. We cannot prophesy what

25 However, some cases do occur. For an especially pertinent example, see T. C. Duncan Eaves and Ben D. Kimpel, "Richardson's Revisions of *Pamela*," *Studies in Bibliography,* XX (1967), 61–68.

26 See "Whilomville as Judah: Crane's 'A Little Pilgrimage'," *Renascence,* XIX (1967), 184–89. Other Crane criticism has also suffered from the lack of a reliable text. For example, Robert Stallman comments on Crane's having sent a copy of "The Revenge of the *Adolphus*" to Commander J. C. Colwell, naval attaché in London, but states that his advice to modify the beating to quarters to agree with the practice on the class of cruiser to which Crane's *Marblehead* belonged was ignored (*Stephen Crane: A Biography* [New York, 1968], p. 452). On the contrary, Crane adopted it in the version of the story published in the *Strand Magazine* in December, 1899, but seemingly was too late to make the changes in the *Collier's Weekly* version of October 28, 1899, the text that, unfortunately, was used for the reprint in the book *Wounds in the Rain* (1900). The Virginia text of *Wounds in the Rain* reproduces not only this but other important revisions found only in the Strand publication.

a hair-triggered critic of refined sensibilities might not make out of the mistaken Riverside choice of the first-edition *Seven Gables* reading, "It was the final throe of what called itself old gentility" instead of the correct manuscript words "final term" (C 37.30), so badly written as readily to accommodate themselves to the compositor's misreading of what he thought he saw in the manuscript. May not an article in the future be written (using this practical text) on Hawthorne's view of the violence that accompanied the change from the old gentility to the new middle class in New England on the basis of the misreading *throe*? Who knows? Really, it has amazing possibilities when one contemplates what an ingenious mind could make of it in treating Hawthorne's attitude to Hepzibah and Clifford.

Quite seriously, however, I am prepared to argue that it is extremely important to the interpretation of Hamlet's state of mind and of his actions in two particular scenes of the play whether he thought that his flesh was *solid* as in the Folio, or *sallied* (i.e., *sullied*) as in the Quartos. Or, in the symbolism of Hawthorne's *Marble Faun*, whether Donatello is or is not consciously aware when he shudders that he has pressed Miriam's hand over his heart.[27]

On the other hand, such examples constitute *ad hominem* arguments that could be suggested as of too rare occurrence to be serious in the average text. I would agree if we were to adopt the elementary criteria that plot and character, without regard for the exact words that give them being, constitute the only critical values of major significance in fiction or in drama. But the critics who are so careless about the accuracy of words neglect the cumulative effect of an author's style upon the literary subject. If we are content again and again with a mere approximation of what an author wrote—an author who on the evidence of manuscript changes during composition and alterations in proof values his exact words more than do the critics—then we are missing one of the most exquisite pleasures of reading and of literary delight as well as of accurate evaluation. If we are not permitted to savor Hawthorne's use of the old-fashioned phrase *barn-door fowl*, because a practical editor does not trouble to consult a dictionary before he labels it an error, we are losing something. If words keep coming across wrong, as whether Phoebe had *enjoyed* (C 174.34–35) or *employed* (Riverside) a little time in reading her Bible, or, more important for exact meaning, whether Hepzibah's distrust of Judge Pyncheon was *unreasoning* (C 228.18) or *unreasonable* (Riverside), or whether the old gentility's passage was in its final *throe* or *term* (C 37.30), the cumulative effect is to wear away the fine edge of

27 Centenary 198.4 emends the manuscript slip "un-|tentionally" (MS 220.31) to "unintentionally," which is the clear intent. *Transformation* 83.13 (and all following editions) reads, in error, "intentionally."

style and to blunt our refined consciousness of a civilized medium to the dulled apathy of a reader of advertisement language.

There is a further consideration. If scholarship consists in getting things right, in being accurate, whether dealing with materials or with ideas deriving from these materials, how can we trust the standards of critics who in wilful ignorance care so little about the exactness of the texts whose contents they are evaluating for our benefit that they pick up any edition that comes to hand, with no regard for its editorial authority and exactness of representation of the author's wishes. This representation (for informed criticism) must extend down to the very last minute detail of sentence cadence the author heard in his mind as transmitted by the precise punctuation he placed in his manuscripts as a guide, whether conscious or unconscious, to something more than overt meaning. We cannot have the author's true voice obscured for critic or for reader by, for instance, the plea that compositors' house style is justified 'in a good many instances' in setting right Hawthorne's allegedly inconsistent and often wrong punctuation when in *Seven Gables* at the most fewer than twenty adjustments in punctuation are advisable or required, various of these, indeed, being purely formal.[28]

This guilt-by-association argument is tellingly employed by a *Times Literary Supplement* reviewer (January 18, 1968, p. 69) in reply to a critic's protest against being chided for using a bad text of *Joseph Andrews* in his book about Fielding. The author challenged the reviewer to name a case in which his avoidance of the definitive edition of this novel corrupted his argument in any way. (This, of course, is the Russian roulette line of thinking.) The reviewer properly took a higher ground: "The first point raised in Mr. Irwin's letter," he writes, "is that of the desirability of using the best texts available. Although he agrees, he declares that 'a failure to do so can be justifiable and need not be damaging.' And he says that it is my job as reviewer to discover whether his avoidance of the Wesleyan *Joseph Andrews* 'corrupts' his argument. On the principle that a man is innocent until proven guilty I dare say that this declaration has some force, but Mr. Irwin's employment of various unreliable and unscholarly texts (specified in my review) makes one wonder whether his criticism is actually addressed to what his authors actually wrote. That is to say, there is a matter of confidence here that has nothing to do with

28 These necessary punctuation emendations in *Seven Gables* disregard the obvious lapses such as failure to close a quotation with the proper mark or a sentence with a period, and the number given here does not take account also of the regularization in the Centenary edition of the use of hyphens in word-division. The facts here about the faulty punctuation give the lie to the standard undocumented remarks about Hawthorne's carelessness in this respect. The Centenary editors can state categorically from their study of the manuscripts of three lengthy romances that he was particularly careful in the details of his punctuation except occasionally in purely formal matters.

corruption of argument, though the employment of dubious texts necessarily leads to dubious arguments."

This matter of confidence is a singularly important factor in scholarship, since a man who is careless and unthinking in one matter may well prove to be careless and unthinking in others. If a critic wishes to be heard with respect he should care enough about his author to read him and to quote him in a form that is as absolutely accurate and authoritative as the most advanced methods of textual criticism can make it. It is not merely that, like Matthiessen and Empson and Delmore Schwartz, various critics have been caught out because they wrote fancifully about some specific bad reading in a corrupt edition.[29] Not merely the lack of confidence that is generated about their real knowledge of the authors they are considering if they can impute meanings to a writer that involve words he never wrote. In my view, their insensitivity to an author's style when they care so little about him as to read him habitually in a corrupt text is even more shaking in what must be its final results.[30]

29 See "Textual Criticism and the Literary Critic" in my *Textual and Literary Criticism* (Cambridge: Cambridge University Press, 1959; paperback 1966), pp. 1–34.

30 Critics grow lethargic about textual accuracy when they confine themselves to fiction where, with such exceptions as Donatello's reaction already mentioned in the error in *The Marble Faun* perpetuated since the first edition and only to be revealed in the manuscript, imprecise words do not affect the outcome of the plot, and so on. But the case is altered when one deals with philosophic or expository writers. One may profitably compare the transmission of the exact opposite of what Henry Adams wished to say in the error of *to* for *or* exposed in the *Education* in the following footnote from J. C. Levenson, "Henry Adams and the Art of Politics," *Southern Review*, IV, N.S. (January, 1968), 58: "On p. 496 of the Houghton Mifflin, Modern Library, and Sentry editions, the second complete sentence should be corrected to read: 'If any analogy whatever existed between the human mind, on the one side, and the laws of motion, on the other, the mind had already entered a field of attraction so violent that it must immediately pass beyond, into new equilibrium, like the Comet of Newton, *or* suffer dissipation altogether, like meteoroids in the earth's atmosphere.' (My emphasis.) The private printing of 1905, which Adams himself supervised, is authority for the correction. By changing *or* to *to*, the public editions have made Adams seem deliberately to use bad astronomy for morbid and obscurantist purposes."

Mr. Edmund Wilson, who is much influenced in his judgment of the value of a text by its lightness and convenience, admits to reading *The Marble Faun* on an airplane trip to Rome "in an English pocket edition from Bohn's Popular Library, 'reprinted from the first published, with such alterations from the American edition as appear to have resulted from the author's own revision' " (*The Fruits of the MLA*, p. 18). He quotes this description in approval of the editions he likes to read. On the other hand, the Centenary Edition demonstrates that not a single reading in the American edition resulted from the author's own revision, and indeed that the American variant readings are either printer's corruptions or else *unrevised* Hawthorne readings from an early state of the English proofs. Mr. Wilson's case for the convenience of pocket editions for light reading on an airplane can scarcely be contested, and one hopes that the reprint rights to *The Marble Faun* will soon be leased by some paper-

One can only wonder after the exhibitions of indifference and lethargy that one encounters about the proper bases for scholarship, whether critical or historical, what the next generation of graduate students, and thus of critics, trained in such a wilful lack of concern for scholarly truth, will make of the words of an author of the past trying with his heart's blood to speak through the obscuring mists of time—to our deaf ears.

---

back publisher to assist the traveling public. The scholarly world, however, does not share Mr. Wilson's dislike of the full records contained in definitive editions like the Centenary Hawthorne that have been designed to serve the requirements of editors of leased popular texts, of literary critics concerned to study Hawthorne's style in full detail, literary critics interested in what can be discerned of the development and rounding of his ideas (as well as his plotting and characterization) as he wrote, literary historians of Hawthorne, bibliographical students of nineteenth-century printing practices, and even lexicographers and linguists who must have accurate evidence about the development of the language and will someday be using computer concordances made from the Centenary texts and apparatus appendices. Mr. Wilson's unfortunate foray into the world of technical scholarship so alien to his sensibilities rests on too narrow a base. In their day the Bohn's Popular Library volumes had their uses; but they have never before been recommended to scholars as exemplary texts.

The Facsimile of
Whitman's Blue Book

THE MASSIVE EFFORT toward the building of a 'New Bible' represented by the third or 1860 edition of *Leaves of Grass* by no means exhausted Whitman's creative energies. The Civil War soon led to the planning of *Drum Taps*, which was being sporadically readied for the press as early as May 1863. But before leaving Brooklyn for Virginia at the end of 1862 he had begun the preparation of the fourth edition of *Leaves* by marking up his copy of the third, in blue wrappers, unsewn, now known as the Blue Book. Having left it behind in Brooklyn, he resumed the revisory process in November 1863, simultaneous with his major application to *Drum Taps*, the two in a sense influencing each other. Printer's copy for *Drum Taps* was completed in January 1865, publication following in May. By this time the bulk of the work was also done on the Blue Book although smaller revisions followed until the publication in 1867 of the fourth *Leaves*.

The Civil War helps to explain the increasingly national fervor of the *Leaves* alterations. *Drum Taps* drained off most of the new poems he had written, and only six were put aside for the new *Leaves*, but Whitman also removed a net of thirty-four from the 1860 list. In addition to the insertion of patriotic references, the revision sometimes amplified but most frequently was aimed at reducing, tightening, and paring the earlier exuberant flow of language and of idea. For reasons of his own, perhaps to reduce the personal note, the cluster arrangement of 1860 was largely broken up and rearranged.

The Blue Book itself may not have been the printer's copy for the 1867 *Leaves* (at least Dr. Golden presents no evidence pro or con), and a number of changes appear in 1867 not present in the marked-up 1860

A review printed in the *Journal of English and Germanic Philology*, 68 (1969), 316–319; reprinted by permission of the Board of Editors of the *Journal of English and Germanic Philology*.
Walt Whitman's Blue Book: The 1860–61 *Leaves of Grass* containing his manuscript additions and revisions. Facsimile of the unique copy in the Oscar Lion Collection of The New York Public Library. Textual analysis by Arthur Golden. Two volumes. New York: The New York Public Library, 1968. $30.

copy, additions and substitutions as well as the restoration of cuts marked in the copy. However, this Blue Book, preserved in the Oscar Lion Collection at the New York Public Library, is a singularly important document, for it reflects with almost total exactitude the literary impulses that formed the 1867 version of *Leaves* and demonstrates the cumulative process by which they were born and shaped. More for critical than for textual purposes, therefore, it deserves the publication now accorded it.

In two handsome boxed volumes Arthur Golden has issued a photographic facsimile accompanied by a critical introduction and several hundred pages of 'textual analysis.' The facsimile volume was prepared by the Meriden Gravure Company using a 300-line screen offset lithography process. Thus the shadings of the original are substantially reproduced, with accurate contrast between pencil and ink and even the actual colors of the occasional red and blue pencil markings. The book has been so contrived as to imitate the original in all detail, even to the inclusion of the revisory paste-over slips placed so that they fall over the appropriate text. As a practical substitute for the original, therefore, this facsimile is astonishingly faithful and completely successful. Nevertheless, a fault exists that will vary in different copies. Some of the insert slips in the review copy were so liberally treated with glue in the margin that they have stuck down down farther on the text page than intended, and as a result some of the text is obscured in the left margin and cannot be looked at except by damaging the paper of the facsimile. If this review copy had been purchased, it would have been returnable for a substitute in which the slips had been inserted with greater care by the binder.

In a suitably brief introduction Dr. Golden recounts the story of the formation of the third edition which was to become the Blue Book, and then provides a perhaps unduly brief account of the preparation of the copy for the fourth edition. In the former not all of the statements are accurate since Dr. Golden in this part has engaged in no new research but has instead relied on older authorities without bringing them up to date. For example, in an added footnote 4a on page xxii that discusses the preserved manuscripts of the 1860 poems his count relies exclusively on the Barrett Collection manuscripts published in 1955, and he is evidently not aware of the additional eleven in the Henry E. Huntington Library that were subsequently listed in the *Huntington Library Quarterly*, XIX (1955), 89–90. In the latter, one misses any over-all survey of the alterations in the Blue Book according to the medium, whether ink, lead pencil, or blue or red pencil. The discussion of the nature of the revisions, hence, is made without reference to their media and what might have been told about their order from the physical evidence, an order that might or might not have proved significant in any analysis of the kind of revision to which Whitman engaged himself. It may be that ink and pencil are so intermixed as to defy generalization in the volume as a whole, but even that statement is wanting so that a reader has no means of knowing whether such an investigation was undertaken. In the case of the 1860 manuscripts such an analysis proved fruitful, and some results might have been obtained here. In short, although a general critical statement is essayed about the revisions and their nature, no specific analysis based on the physical evidence is attempted. If generalization about the volume were impossible, at least some indication of the order of the correcting agents for each poem, and no doubt for certain groups of poems, should have been possible as a help in orienting the reader.

In the body of the second volume, which systematically reprints these revisions page by page from the Blue Book, some orientation is, indeed, necessary for the reader. Dr. Golden has chosen to rely in considerable measure on the much criticized use of diacritical marks within a transcription as a means of indicating additions, excisions, cancellations and restorations, and so on. Although not wholly unscathed, he has in some part succeeded in escaping the difficulties of this pseudo-scholarly method so justly castigated by Lewis Mumford in a *New York Review* consideration of Emerson's Journals.

That is, two major but opposed methods exist for recreating for a reader the facts about revisions in a document. The method adopted by the editors of the Emerson Journals reprints the original inscription of the text in clear form and by a series of symbols identifies internally the various revisions. The result is that the final version of the revised text, in which a critic is most interested, is never transcribed as a unit and cannot be read as such since it appears only as the final element of a maze of symbol-categorized readings. Whatever its dubious value as a scientific instrument providing the evidence for an often painful reconstruction of the details of a document, the resulting text is useless for any other purpose and is completely unreadable in complex circumstances. An example of this method applied to a relatively simple situation would provide a chronological account of the revision of the eighth line of "Proto-Leaf" on page 5 of the Blue Book as follows:

Far from the clank of crowds, my extasy [my extasy] ⟨through extasies⟩
    [through] ⟨my⟩ [my extasies] ⟨intervals⟩ passing, rapt and happy,[1]

Using other of Dr. Golden's symbols in which a superior ᶜ stands for can-

---

[1] This utilizes Dr. Golden's symbols by which square brackets indicate deletion and pointed brackets indicate addition. The transcript of 'my extasy' in clear text follows the usual custom, but Dr. Golden would have omitted it since according to his system the following '[my extasy]' would sufficiently have suggested that the phrase was in the original inscription.

cellation, one might reduce the transcript but at the expense of its chronological narrative:

Far from the clank of crowds, my extasy [my extasy] ⟨through extasies⟩ᵉ ⟨my⟩ᵉ
⟨intervals⟩ passing, rapt and happy,

The opposing method prints only the final form of the text and then by a series of descriptive footnotes informs the reader in a shorthand manner of the stages of the revision. For example, the final form of the eighth line was:

Far from the clank of crowds, intervals passing, rapt and happy,

To this a footnote would be appended:

8 intervals] *original* 'my extasy' *deleted in pencil and* 'through extasies' *interlined,* 'through' *then being deleted and* 'my' *interlined, followed by the erasure of interlined* 'extasies', *a guideline then being drawn to indicate the return of original* 'extasy'; *finally interlined* 'my' *was deleted and* 'intervals' *interlined with a caret, original* 'my extasy' *standing in its partially deleted state.*

Dr. Golden recognized the advantage he possessed in that his descriptions are intended to be followed with the facsimile open before the reader, and thus their main purpose is simply to clarify the stages of revision, not to reconstruct the text from scratch. With this end in view he made a compromise between the two procedures. Quite properly from the point of view of the reader, he first prints the line in its final form, followed by any differences in the 1867 print. Then by a numbered series of diacritically marked transcripts, starting with the original inscription, he traces the stages of revision. His version of the eighth line is as follows:

8 Far from the clank of crowds, intervals passing, rapt and happy, (RR: т';') ²
    1   Far from the clank of crowds, my extasy, my extasy, rapt and happy,
    2   ... crowds, [my extasy] ⟨through extasies⟩ passing, ...
    3   ... crowds, [through] ⟨my⟩ extasies passing, ...
    4   ... crowds, [my] extasies passing, ...
    5   ... crowds, [extasies] ⟨intervals⟩ passing, ...
Erasures obscure what appear to be a word(s)? and a guideline following
    'happy,'

Since Dr. Golden can let the facsimile do a great deal of the work for him, the number of arbitrary signs that he needs is considerably reduced

2 RR means that the revision was retained in 1867; the rest signifies that the terminal punctuation was changed to a semicolon in 1867.

from those required in the Emerson Journals or in the reconstruction of the manuscript of Melville's *Billy Budd*; moreover, the ordering of the different stages of revision each into its own line is definitely a clarifying and simplifying process encouraged by the presence of the facsimile and the consequent function of the transcription more as a commentary than as a replacement for the reproduced document. Whether the space required is worth the results (a matter that does affect the cost of the book, of course) in contrast to the purely descriptive method is an open question; and indeed the editor is sometimes forced by the inadequacy of formulaic means to resort to description, as in the note that ends the example above of the eighth line of "Proto-Leaf," or in the note to line 14: "The 'f' and 'r' of 'far' were mended, respectively over the 'w' and the tail of the 'd' of rejected 'wild'. A slip appears to form the crossbar of a letter following the mended 'r'." A much lengthier note for a knotty question on line 12 of page 6 requires fifteen lines of type. The formulaic method fails, as well, on page 235, lines 4–5, and a fourteen-line note is needed to supplement the attempted transcripts.

On the other hand, although it does sometimes seem to be a long way round Robin Hood's barn, the sometimes wasteful combination of formula and explanatory note does usually serve to transmit the facts of the manuscript alterations and a reader can get accustomed fairly quickly to translating such entries as this for line 3 of "Proto-Leaf":

3   After roaming many lands—lover of populous pavements, (RR: T';')
   1   After roaming various for many years, lover of populous pavements,
       through
   2   ... for many ⟨a⟩¹ year[s,]¹⟨—⟩¹ lover ...
  'through' was inserted as an alternate to 'for'.
       through
   3   ... for many [a]¹ year⟨s⟩¹—lover ...
The sequence of WW's next pencil revisions, in which he again toyed with 'various', 'through', and 'for' as replacements for the same words, which he had rejected, is uncertain. He replaced 'years' with 'lands', adding 'tallying all,' which he cancelled, to the end of the line.

Here the true complexity of the changes, partly concealed by the breakdown of the formulaic transcription and the recourse to a note that disclaims the ability to order the subsequent revisions in pencil, enforces a somewhat longer description if one were to translate all this into the simpler system:

      After roaming many lands—lover of populous pavements,

3 many lands] *original* 'various for many years,' *was altered to* 'many a year' *by the interlineation of* 'a' *and the deletion of final* 's' *and its comma, followed by the interlineation*

of a dash, all in ink. Then, in ink, 'through' was interlined as an alternate above undeleted
'for', interlined 'a' was deleted, and 'year' was restored to 'years'. In pencil a series of re-
visions was later undertaken, the order of which seems to be as follows: 'various for' was
deleted and a caret inserted to authenticate interlined ink 'through' which was in turn
deleted and followed by interlined 'for'. Then 'lands' was interlined above deleted 'years'
and 'through' interlined before previously deleted 'through' only to be deleted in turn.
Finally, 'various' was interlined before this pencil 'through' and deleted. At some point,
'tallying all,' was added in pencil at the end of the line but deleted.

With or without the facsimile as a point of reference, it may prove to
be something of a matter of taste whether Dr. Golden's reliance on the
transcriptional method broken up into stages, with explanatory notes
when the method fails, is the happiest, most economical, or most accurate
means of solving the numerous problems that faced him. One can say,
however, that in general it works, with perhaps a single exception. That
is, the formulaic transcript is incapable of distinguishing between a
change made *currente calamo* and one made at a later time as part of a
revision. For instance, in the transcript of the second stage of line 8 above,

> . . . crowds, [my extasy] ⟨through extasies⟩ passing,

the reader can never tell whether, as it was, 'through extasies' was interlined at a later time above deleted 'my extasy' or whether Whitman wrote
'my extasy' and then before continuing deleted it and followed it with
'through extasies' before inscribing 'passing'. In the circumstances of this
edition, perhaps the point is a trivial one; but if a reader were to try to
grapple with the textual part of this edition without the facsimile open
before him, he would be deprived of a considerable amount of necessary
information.

It is not a trivial point, however, to query here and there the completeness of Dr. Golden's over-all account of certain complex revisions. Given
the evidence of the facsimile, the order provided in my descriptive account
of the pencil revisions in line 3 above is almost inevitable, and little doubt
can obtain about this order save for the addition and deletion of "tallying
all,'. (A question might arise about the stage at which 'various' was interlined, but its position in relation to the rest makes evident the order I
have assigned.) Under these circumstances, the note Dr. Golden appended (quoted above at the end of his entry for this line) is not so helpful as it would have been if he had applied rigorous critical and textual
logic to the physical evidence. This same failure to penetrate the reasons
for the alterations as a guide to their order (supplementing the physical
evidence) is also present in the note to his entry for line 8 quoted above,
which is positively misleading. Here the purpose of the guideline, never

mentioned, was to restore the original reading 'extasy', and since this point was not understood only uncertainty and confusion could follow.

Examples like these constitute flaws in the execution, but fortunately they are rare. If criticism of Walt Whitman is to get back to first principles and to study his developing concept over the years both of style and content in *Leaves of Grass*, this present edition will stand as a key document. The New York Public Library has been a public benefactor to make available this one of its treasures in a form that will prove of maximum value to the student and at a price that, all things considered, is relatively moderate considering the value of the facsimile itself and of Dr. Golden's careful labors.

[Addendum: The present writer has contrived a new system for transcribing manuscript variants that reverses the usual process and transcribes the final form of the manuscript text, all the antecedent forms being described within square brackets. In order to clarify what words in the text are being revised by the bracketed description without quoting them again, an asterisk is placed before the first word affected by the description within the brackets; thus it should be taken that all words following the asterisk up to the start of the bracketed description are a part of the text treated within the brackets. A brief example illustrates the working of the system. The text originally was written 'with something anarchistic about him if', but in the course of revision 'almost' was interlined above deleted 'something' and 'in his informality' was added, interlined with a caret. This text could be transcribed with footnotes detailing the alterations, or else in the following manner: with *almost [*above del.* 'something'] anarchistic about him *in his informality. [*interl. w. caret*]. Various complex applications may be observed in the transcripts contained in *Pragmatism*, in the ACLS edition of *The Works of William James*, ed. Bowers, (Harvard University Press 1975–), but more particularly in *The Meaning of Truth* and in *A Pluralistic Universe*. The system is explained in detail in "Transcription of Manuscripts: The Record of Variants," *Studies in Bibliography*, 29 (1976).]

Multiple Authority: New Problems and

Concepts of Copy-Text

THE ATTEMPT to determine what the author wrote defines textual criticism. Ultimately the attempt involves a word-by-word analysis to test authority in so far as the evidence permits. But before any verbal analysis can be undertaken, a number of larger issues must be settled which concern the specific as well as the general authority of all preserved documents. Although it is quite true that any literary document is no more than the sum total of its words, including the texture of the accidentals in which these words are clothed, yet the whole is indeed greater than the sum of its parts. Thus it is idle to try to determine specific verbal authority until the general authority of the documents in which the text has been transmitted is determined. And, as Sir Walter Greg has shown us, the general authority of these documents may differ as between the words themselves and their accidentals, that is, the spelling, capitalization, division, contraction, and occasional italicization in which these words are embodied, as well as the punctuation that surrounds them as specific direction to their interrelationship and meaning.

For its day McKerrow's *Prolegomena for the Oxford Shakespeare* was a most valuable document that had an important and lasting influence on textual theory and practice; and indeed it is a work that can still be mined with profit for its clarity of thinking and the value of its insights that have been allowed to recede too far from our memory. A close reading, even today, is a salutary experience; the impact in 1939, as I can testify, was memorable. In the matter of copy-text, however, *Prolegomena* betrays at once a vagueness of general concept combined with a too narrow application, a fault that I impute directly to McKerrow's not having progressed far enough into the actual editing of the more complex plays at the time that he published his theoretical approach. In the simple definition of copy-text—a word that McKerrow invented for his edition of Thomas Nashe in 1904—he has not been outmoded. This singularly useful term means simply the early text that an editor uses in each particu-

Read in abbreviated form before the Bibliographical Society in London on April 18, 1972; printed in *The Library*, 5th ser., 27 (1972), 81–115; reprinted with permission of the Council of the Bibliographical Society.

lar case as the basis of his own (p. 12, fn.). Inexperienced editors today impair the usefulness of this term by applying it to the physical printer's copy that *any* edition utilizes as its basis, as in the mis-statement 'the copy-text for the second edition of *Tom Jones* was the first', but in this they know not what they do and I am not moved to urge their forgiveness.[1]

The basic confusion in McKerrow's application of *copy-text* to concrete examples, and thus as a formula in textual theory, lay in his almost total identification of the term with what he called the 'most authoritative' edition. In the simplest cases he was on sound ground. Faced with a situation in which only one authoritative edition printed from manuscript exists, and all other editions derive from it as mere reprints, McKerrow correctly rejected the 'last-edition-in-the-author's-lifetime' fallacy and unhesitatingly selected as copy-text the single primary edition as that 'one [which is] as near as possible to what the author wrote'. Even if a later edition had been casually corrected by an author, his view of the correct copy-text was not changed.[2] This is still unexceptionable theory. On the other hand, since he did not find (or at least did not mention) the prob-

---

1 A recent formal attack on the McKerrow definition is that of Paul Baender, 'The Meaning of Copy-Text', *SB*, xxii (1969), 311–18, which has been most properly answered by G. T. Tanselle, 'The Meaning of Copy-Text: A Further Note', *SB*, xxiii (1970), 191–6. I think nothing more need be said on the subject except to emphasize that it is a worse misuse to confuse *copy-text* with an editor's arbitrary choice of printer's copy as distinct from the early text that an editor uses as the basis for his own. For example, in the preparation of printer's copy for Stephen Crane's romance *The O'Ruddy* it proved slightly more convenient to bring photographs of the first edition into conformity with the copy-text manuscript than to order a typescript of the manuscript. However, my copy-text did not become the first edition because of this technical procedure; it remained the manuscript, on whose readings I continued to base my own modern text. The confusion that would be created by the loose and imprecise use of the term as anything but the text that was the true basis for one's edition is sufficiently obvious here.

2 'Even if, however, we were to assure ourselves on what seemed quite satisfactory evidence that certain corrections found in a later edition of a play were of Shakesperian authority, it would not by any means follow that that edition should be used as the copy-text of a reprint. It would undoubtedly be necessary to incorporate these corrections in our text, but unless we could show that the edition in question (or the copy from which it had been printed) had been gone over and corrected throughout by Shakespeare, a thing in the highest degree unlikely, it seems evident that, allowing for the usual degeneration customary in reprinted texts, this later edition will (except for the corrections) deviate more widely than the earliest print from the author's original manuscript. This deviation is likely to be mainly apparent in spelling and punctuation, neither of which would matter if the text were to be used as the basis for a modern-spelling edition, as both would be normalized, but which matter greatly in the case of an edition of the type of the present one. We may indeed, I think, take it as certain that in all ordinary circumstances the nearest approach to our ideal of an author's fair copy of his work in its final state will be produced by using the earliest "good" print as copy-text and inserting into it, from the first edition which contains them, such corrections as appear to us to be derived from the author' (pp. 17–18).

lem in Shakespeare, his view about the selection of copy-text from two or more independent editions (except 'Bad Quartos') was conventionally stated and too simplistic to be an accurate guide to textual theory and editorial practice. For example, if it were ever determined beyond all question that the Folio *Hamlet* was actually set from manuscript and not (as seems more probable) from an annotated example of the Second Quarto, the advice is certainly dubious 'that an editor must select the text which appeals most to his critical judgement, and this, in turn, will as a rule be the one which appears to be the most careful copy of its original and the most free from obvious errors'.[3]

This theory for the selection of a copy-text from among competing independent authorities—what we may call radial texts—illustrates the serious flaw that Sir Walter Greg was later to isolate. That is, McKerrow seems to have thought of the copy-text as invariably to be identified as the most authoritative text as a whole, this being defined as 'that one of the early texts which, on a consideration of their genetic relationship, appears likely to have deviated to the smallest extent in all respects of wording, spelling, and punctuation from the author's manuscript' (pp. 7–8). This is to think of authority in an impossibly comprehensive manner for many texts. [It is certainly appropriate for a single edition set from manuscript with a later dependent series of reprints. It is also applicable, at least in theory, to radiating texts in which the preserved examples are at unequal distances from the lost archetype as seems to be the situation with Beaumont, Fletcher, and Massinger's *Beggars Bush*, where investigations point towards the preserved scribal presentation manuscript as having been transcribed from a promptbook that in turn had been transcribed from the identical manuscript that was subsequently used as printer's copy for the 1647 Folio.* In the editing of this play for the third volume of the Cambridge Beaumont and Fletcher not only theory but also convenience dictated the choice of the Folio as copy-text; nevertheless, by the time the two incompetent Folio compositors had got through imposing their habits and care-

---

3 'Obviously, if a work has been transmitted to us in several manuscripts or printed editions, none of which appears to have been copied or printed from another, and all of which may have originated during the lifetime of the author, it will, in the absence of any external evidence as to the relationship of the texts, be the duty of an editor to select for the basis of a new edition that text which in his judgement is most representative of the author and most nearly in accord with what, in view of his other works, we should have expected from him at the date to which the work in question is assigned. In the majority of cases this will mean simply that the editor must select the text which appeals most to his critical judgement, and this, in its turn, will as a rule be the one which appears to be the most careful copy of its original and the most free from obvious errors' (pp. 13–14).

* The evidence for this problem is worked out in "*Beggars Bush*: A Reconstructed Prompt-Book and Its Copy," *Studies in Bibliography*, 27 (1974), 113–136.

lessnesses on the accidentals, it was an open question whether in fact the Folio accidentals were any closer to the lost holograph than the farther removed scribal presentation copy of earlier date.][4] Indeed, no holograph material by Beaumont or by Fletcher being preserved, little trustworthy evidence is available to serve as a norm by which to compare the faithfulness of the two texts to these authors' general characteristics.[5] [Moreover, compositorial corruption is so prominent in the Folio text affecting the substantives as well that it would be dangerous to prefer them automatically in all cases of doubt when the manuscript differs simply because of the presumed authority of the Folio's nearer genetic relationship to the authorial papers.]

Indeed, McKerrow's theory is too narrow to apply with any justice to the problems of the Quarto and Folio texts of *Othello* or of *Troilus and Cressida*, to say nothing of *Hamlet*. It seems to be established that the scribal manuscript of Dryden's *Indian Emperour* is more faithful as a whole to the spelling and punctuation of the lost holograph from which it was copied than is the printed edition set from a lost revised manuscript,[6]

4 Although written in connection with medieval manuscripts, Professor A. A. Hill's dictum is theoretically sound for such a case as *Beggars Bush*: 'Distributional studies are powerless to deal with differences unless there are at least three surviving manuscripts, since in the two-text situation no variant has a better chance of having been in the original than another' ('Some Postulates for Distributional Study of Texts', *SB*, iii (1950–1), 69). Whether the practice in this particular example would be bound by the theory is another matter, for a study of the habits of the scribe (who also transcribed the manuscript of *Aglaura*) and of the two compositors who set the play in the 1647 Folio might be expected to lead to some conclusions about their respective alterations of copy. Narrowly viewed, the printer's-copy manuscript of Hawthorne's *Blithedale Romance* and the derived first edition give us a two-text situation in respect to the substantive variants which may be either printer's corruptions or Hawthorne's proof-corrections. But a study of the incidence as well as the kinds of error made by each of the book's compositors yields results of real value in determining the authority of most of these variants. Technically they are of equal authority, but, practically, bibliographical supplemented by critical analysis separates them with reasonable certainty. Direct derivation whether linear or radial may make all the difference when enough material is available to suggest which of two variants is authoritative. In Stephen Crane's stories printed in two magazines from a typescript and its carbon an editor is by no means so helpless as if they had been medieval manuscripts. But these are practical considerations stemming from special circumstances.

5 Conjectural evidence drawn from what appear to be authorial characteristics in other printed texts may be of some occasional use, however, as in the well-known Fletcherian *ye*.

6 The editors of this play in the University of California edition of Dryden deny the superior faithfulness of the accidentals in the manuscript and assert the authority of the forms in the first edition (see also Vinton Dearing, 'The Use of a Computer in Analyzing Dryden's Spelling', *Literary Data Processing Conference Proceedings* [IBM, Armonk, N.Y., 1964], pp. 200–10). However, the statistics on which they base their findings have been shown to be seriously faulty by Philip Harth reviewing *John Dryden:*

although this latter text is more faithful in certain other respects of the accidentals and undoubtedly represents with greater fidelity Dryden's second thoughts for the words. McKerrow wrote, indeed, 'If we had external evidence[7] that a particular text of any work had been revised throughout by its author, such a text should undoubtedly be made the basis of a modern edition', that is, should be made the copy-text. But if on this basis the first edition of *The Indian Emperour* were selected, although it would qualify for its wording, violence would be done to the requirement that the copy-text should be the one that 'appears to be the most careful copy of its original' and that 'appears likely to have deviated to the smallest extent in all respects of . . . spelling and punctuation from the author's manuscript.'[8]

When the situation is complex, therefore, McKerrow's concept that a copy-text can exhibit unified, or comprehensive, authority necessarily breaks down, and since the whole inclination of his argument was to place a premium on the authority of the words in the selection of copy-text, as in a more than casually revised derived edition which he was prepared to accept over an unrevised primary edition, he does indeed lay himself open to charges of inconsistency and even of contradiction.

The essential weakness of McKerrow's position that led in various

---

Four Tragedies, ed. L. A. Beaurline and F. Bowers (1967), in *Modern Philology*, lxvii (1970), 379–82, and the views of the present writer in 'The 1665 Manuscript of Dryden's *Indian Emperour*', *Studies in Philology*, xlviii (1950), 738–60, appear to be vindicated, to his relief.

7 In McKerrow's '"Prolegomena" Reconsidered', *RES*, xvii (1941), 145, W. W. Greg observed that in this quotation 'the question of "external evidence" . . . is anyhow rather irrelevant'.

8 After noting the predominance of Dryden's spellings in the manuscript (except for three specific classes of spellings in the quarto in which the compositor reproduced Dryden's forms but the scribe archaized them), Professor Harth comments on the California editors' choice of the quarto as copy-text: 'Yet it is scarcely reasonable to sacrifice a great number of Dryden's own probable spellings for the sake of purifying the text of these anomalies, while at the same time accepting in their stead the far greater number of modern spellings which the compositor of the 1667 quarto presumably substituted for Dryden's archaisms. If Dearing was convinced that certain spelling groups in the manuscript were the responsibility of the scribe rather than of the author, the proper procedure was not to reject the Trinity College manuscript as his copy-text, but to make use of the editorial discretion recommended by Greg. "I see no reason," he wrote in "The Rationale of Copy-Text," "why [the editor] should not alter misleading or eccentric spellings which he is satisfied emanate from the scribe or compositor and not from the author".' I think it only fair to say that what is sauce for the goose applies to the gander. The manuscript *is* the better choice of copy-text but if I were ever to re-edit the play I should be much tempted to take to myself Harth's advice to Dearing and to emend the manuscript more freely from the quarto in at least two classes of spellings that appear to represent Dryden's own practice as reproduced in the print, despite the burden thereby placed on the apparatus.

cases to 'the tyranny of the copy-text', was rectified at one stroke by the genius of Sir Walter Greg in 'The Rationale of Copy-Text', ten years later.[9] With his usual instinct for the jugular, Greg perceived the difficulty of applying the 'most authoritative text' hypothesis—the text being treated as an indivisible whole—when an author or some agent working from an authoritative source had altered an extant edition in order to make up printer's copy for a new and revised text. To solve the problem Greg split apart the authority of the words, or substantives, from the authority of the accidentals, or the texture of spelling, punctuation, division, capitalization, that clothed them. When only one primary edition is extant, it will command authority in both respects. But when for convenience an author takes a copy of, say, the first or primary edition and annotates it with corrections and revisions, the vast majority of these annotations will ordinarily affect the wording alone, not the accidentals. These latter will be transmitted from the primary text to the revised edition with little or no authority as in an ordinary reprint, which in effect the revised edition remains—for the accidentals.

Thus a double authority must be recognized. The accidentals of the revised edition, having been shaped by another round of printing-house styling, are at one further remove from their original extant authority. On the other hand, the substantives, or words, having been corrected and revised, are on the whole more authoritative than those of the earlier edition. Greg argued logically that this split authority required different treatment in each of its two parts. The choice of copy-text must be dictated by the authority of the accidentals, not by the authority of the substantives. Thus the copy-text must be that document on the family tree that is closest to the ultimate authority of the lost manuscript, since only this document preserves the accidentals in their purest extant form from the author's own manuscript, having undergone the absolute minimum of printing-house or scribal interference. The text of this document is then altered as necessary by the substitution of those verbal readings from the revised or altered edition that the editor believes to represent authoritative changes from the copy-text readings. The result is an eclectic text that combines the edition containing the most authoritative accidentals with the edition containing the most authoritative substantives. Since these procedures are calculated to weed out the majority of the unauthoritative printing-house changes, of whatever nature, that are inevitable in any reprint while yet retaining the author's verbal intentions in their final revised form, the resulting critical text will necessarily preserve more of authority in both its parts than the revised edition itself.

What in effect this procedure does in straightforward cases is to recon-

9 *SB*, iii (1950–1), 19–36, reprinted in *W. W. Greg: Collected Papers*, ed. J. C. Maxwell, Clarendon Press, 1966, pp. 374–91.

struct the document that was actually made up to be the printer's copy for the revised edition. For instance, it is now established that the Folio text of *Othello* was set from a copy of the First Quarto that had been revised by collation against some independent manuscript, the variant substantive readings being marked in the margin or interlined as convenient.[10] An eclectic text of *Othello* edited according to Greg's principles would choose the more authoritative accidentals of the Quarto since these derive from a manuscript and those of the Folio derive from the Quarto. But in so far as the editor accepted the Folio substantive variants, the reproduction of these in the texture formed by the Quarto's accidentals merely represents what would be a critical reprint of the actual marked Quarto printer's copy had it been preserved. This is the ideal, and in my experience it has proved its application as the most workable editorial principle yet contrived to produce a critical text that is authoritative in the maximum of its details whether the author be Shakespeare, Dryden, Fielding, Nathaniel Hawthorne, or Stephen Crane. The principle is sound without regard for the literary period. That Greg was an Elizabethan scholar and had no special knowledge of textual problems in the Victorian period does not alter the essential fact that his theory is adaptable under extremely varied conditions.[11]

10 See Alice Walker, 'The 1602 Quarto and the First Folio of *Othello*', *Shakespeare Survey*, 5 (1952), 16–24, and *Textual Problems of the First Folio*, Cambridge University Press, 1953, pp. 153–6; also, F. Bowers, *Bibliography and Textual Criticism*, Clarendon Press, 1964, pp. 182–97, for another range of evidence.

11 This flat statement is made with knowledge of the various exceptions that prove the rule. Among these exceptions, however, I cannot place the position taken by Donald Pizer, who in an attack on the Greg theory of copy-text, and specifically on the eclectic text that results when two or more editions are authoritative, holds: 'This aspect of copy-text editing is textually sound but it bears little relationship to one of the principal characteristics of modern American literature and to one of the principal interests of the modern American critic. For most American writers an editor has available many more authorial revisions between printed appearances than he has for most Renaissance authors. To the modern critic, each such revision constitutes a distinctive work with its own aesthetic individuality and character. In the instance of a short story, say, which exists in three distinctive, authorially-sanctioned printed versions, to coalesce these versions into an eclectic text and its apparatus is to blur the nature of each version despite the accuracy of the method and the availability in the apparatus of all the evidence needed to reconstruct each version. It is the rare reader who can recreate the imaginative "feel" of a literary work out of textual notes. Thus, the suspicion inherent in the theory of copy-text and the resultant drive toward a "pure" eclectic text often undermines one of the major reasons for editing a literary work—to make it available to literary criticism. It may seem absurd to suggest that an editor publish three versions of a story, but such a practice is probably less absurd than that of creating, in an eclectic text which may incorporate changes made by the author over many years, a text which never existed and which has little or no critical interest' ('On the Editing of Modern American Texts', *Bulletin of the New York Public Library*, 75 (March, 1971), 149–50). English readers may be interested in the thoroughgoing answers to

Minor and logical adjustments are easily made. Fielding annotated the third edition of *Tom Jones*—except for one patch in the Man of the Hill episode that returns to the first edition—to provide the printer's copy for the revised fourth. Since the third edition had been set from the first, its accidentals are at one remove from the extant basic authority, and the fourth, of course, is at two removes. The choice of the first-edition accidentals but the majority of the fourth-edition verbals reconstructs not the actual annotated third edition, which would be impure in its accidentals, but instead what the fourth edition copy would have been like if it had been a marked example of the more authoritative first. The physical document thus reconstructed never existed, but that is of no account whatever. If the publisher had not wanted the fourth edition to be a paginal reprint of the third, he might well have given Fielding a copy of the first to serve as the basis for the revision. That the third was used instead is an historical accident and it would be to the highest degree pedantic to insist on a literal reconstruction of the annotated third instead of the ideal copy of an annotated first.[12] The justice of this view may be illustrated by the exam-

---

this and other points by Norman Grabo in 'Pizer vs Copy-Text', *NYPLB*, 75 (April, 1971), 171–3, and by Hershel Parker, 'In Defense of "Copy-Text Editing"', *NYPLB*, 75 (October, 1971), 337–44. Little more need be said except that the theory of every literary critic his own collator is an eccentric one, and such critics are usually not equipped to determine how much 'feel' in a version is due to the author and how much to the printing-house and editorial styling. When for special reasons a critic wishes to read a particular version of a literary work for its 'feel', the xerox process is readily available. If, instead, he wants the facts, he must go to the edited text that establishes the author's full intentions with all the evidence bearing on the growth of the literary work in question as in the example of Stephen Crane's 'Revenge of the *Adolphus*' discussed later in this paper.

Of course, it would be ridiculous to attempt an eclectic text of Henry James's *Roderick Hudson*, which must be read either in its pure first edition or its essentially altered New York Edition form. But when standard editions that can establish a text in only one version are practicable, I should myself query the usefulness either for general or for specialized critical reading of the 'feel' of a passing experimental phase in Dicken's presentation of *Oliver Twist* such as we find marmoreally preserved in the third-edition copy-text reprinted in the recent Clarendon Press edition. It would seem that a more generally useful text would have been one based on the uneccentric earliest form but including all the substantive revisions up to the end of Dickens's concern with the novel.

12 This view of revision in the fourth edition differs from that originally advanced by Aurélien Digeon in *Le Texte des Romans de Fielding*, Paris, 1923, pp. 70–7, and followed by G. E. Jensen, 'Proposals for a Definitive Edition of Fielding's *Tom Jones*', *The Library*, 4th ser., xviii (1937), 314–30. Both critics assumed that the third-edition revision of the Man of the Hill's narrative required the minor variants in the rest of this text to have originated with Fielding. The bibliographical facts isolating this single block of revision to one first-edition gathering in the third edition's copy, the marked differences between the stylistic revisions in this sheet and the third-edition variants

ple of Fielding's *Joseph Andrews.* The second, third, and fourth editions are derived reprints, each one of its immediate predecessor, but each revised substantively by Fielding. By the time one reaches the revised fourth edition, for which the printer's copy was the revised third, the question of what printer's copy is being reconstructed in a modern critical text has very little importance in comparison to the basic Greg procedure that inserts in the authoritative accidentals of the first edition those newly revised readings from the fourth, added to those of the second and the third that have passed critical scrutiny, the whole purified of compositorial corruption and as close to a finally revised authorial fair copy as the preserved documents permit.[13]

The theory works also under certain modern conditions that could scarcely be envisaged in Elizabethan times. When the manuscript is preserved, the normal authority of the first edition is shifted back to this more exact representation of the author's intentions, with particular reference to the accidentals, so that the manuscript, not the derived first edition, becomes the only proper copy-text. No more desirable textual situation could exist, of course. The problem then arises as to the details of this first edition printed from the manuscript or from some transcript or even revision of it. When the preserved manuscript itself served as the printer's copy, as in Nathaniel Hawthorne's *House of the Seven Gables,* or *Blithedale Romance,* or *Marble Faun,* the flexibility and essential rightness of Greg's position can be further demonstrated. An editor of any one of these texts finds some hundred or so substantive variants in each first edition embedded in three to four thousand accidentals differences, the

---

in the rest of the novel, and a critical survey of these other differences effectively demonstrate the contrary. Moreover, the thorough revision of the fourth edition cannot be dismissed as printer's variation, for in the nature of its stylistic alterations it exactly parallels the authoritative revisions made in successive editions of *Joseph Andrews.* A full discussion of this matter will be found in the Wesleyan Edition volumes of *Tom Jones* (1974).

13 The question of the alterations an author might make in the accidentals when revising for substantives is illustrated by the case-history of the revised second edition of Dryden's *Indian Emperour,* 1668, followed by the again-revised third edition in 1670. Here proof-corrections in the second-edition sheet B show that Dryden did not trouble to alter the majority of the compositor's own accidentals variants from the first-edition copy although he tinkered with a few. If an editor to secure these few had reprinted the second-edition text because of its substantive revision, he would have given factitious authority to several times the number of compositorial accidentals readings than actual authorial changes. The accidentals of the third edition, based on the second, depart even farther from authority in this text sheet. For the details and the conclusions to be drawn from them, see Bowers, 'Current Theories of Copy-Text, with an Illustration from Dryden', *Modern Philology,* xlviii (1950), 12–20. These conclusions are supported in the nineteenth century by the examples from Nathaniel Hawthorne cited below.

results of the printer's styling of Hawthorne's manuscript. A certain number of the substantive variants represent Hawthorne's proof-alterations in galleys now lost, but these are mixed in with more printer's corruptions than one likes to contemplate that Hawthorne failed to notice in the proofs. By various bibliographical and critical tools an editor can hope to distinguish these two categories of authority and error with some reasonable accuracy.[14] But no tools exist for a similar distinction between the several thousand printer's variants and the relatively few accidentals changes that Hawthorne may have made in the proof. The logical extension to this relationship of manuscript and first edition of the McKerrow doctrine of indivisible authority would require an editor to reprint the first edition *in toto*, substantives and accidentals alike, since it is clear that the Hawthorne proof-revisions make the substantives generally more authoritative in the first edition.[15] But the same can scarcely be said for

14 Comparison with the manuscripts sometimes suggests simple misreading as in the printer's constant difficulty with distinguishing Hawthorne's *could* and *would*. But for indifferent variants an analysis of the substantive departures, compositor by compositor, will usually reveal habits of corrupting copy that can usefully be applied, plus different incidences of error, so that by qualitative and quantitative analysis the more trustworthy workmen can be distinguished from the less, and the editor can be given some bibliographical guides to aid his critical judgement. For an example, see the compositorial analysis of variants in the Centenary Edition of *The House of the Seven Gables*, Ohio State University Press, 1965, pp. xlviii–lviii; *The Blithedale Romance* 1964, pp. xxxiii–xliv; and *The Marble Faun*, 1968, pp. lxxii–cxxi. In addition, the setting of the English edition of *The House of the Seven Gables* from different stages of American proof-sheets, but particularly the textually important setting of the American edition of *The Marble Faun* in part from uncorrected English proof-sheets, establishes with complete accuracy the authorial or non-authorial nature of a number of variants.

15 Actually, this inference may not be quite fair to McKerrow, but his discussion of the subject (pp. 17–18) quoted above in footnote 2 is not so clear as it might be. I interpret the distinction he is drawing as that between occasional corrections drawn by some agent from a Shakespearian source (as may or may not have occurred in the Folio *Merchant of Venice*) and the author himself going through an edition and correcting it. In the former he would retain the first edition as copy-text, but in the latter (if I read him right) the revised edition. I assume that an author's proof-corrections—not all of which can be isolated wih full confidence—might qualify by analogy in the second category. As Greg remarked, McKerrow never distinguished satisfactorily between the kind and amount of correction that he would permit in a revision while still retaining the primary edition as his copy-text and the cases envisaged in 'If we had exernal evidence that a particular text of any work had been revised throughout *by its author*, such a text should undoubtedly be made the basis of a modern edition' (p. 14). No question can be raised, however, that by these criteria McKerrow would have felt impelled to take as copy-text the fourth edition of *Tom Jones* since it was certainly corrected and revised throughout by the author, and possibly even the fourth edition of *Joseph Andrews*, a disastrous conclusion. The point about an author's proof-corrections is worth inquiry, for some textual critics reject

the accidentals, for no one in his wildest dreams could suggest that Hawthorne altered several thousand of these in proof, most of them contrary to his habits in the entire body of his preserved manuscripts. To reprint the first-edition forms of Hawthorne's accidentals is wilfully to reject his known and continued preferences, completely native to his style, in favour of those of a contemporary printer's shop.

I suggest that the situation between a first edition typeset from known manuscript, or a document relatively close to it, and then corrected and revised in proof before printing, is logically identical with that between a first edition and a revised later edition. No argument for McKerrow's integrity of the text or Hawthorne's assumed correction of some accidentals could possibly justify the choice of a Hawthorne first edition as copy-text when a manuscript is available. Greg's separation of the authority of substantives from that of accidentals permits us to retain the full ultimate authority of the punctuation, spellings, word-division, and capitalization of the manuscript while yet including in the substantives the later intentions represented by Hawthorne's revisions made in proof. Similarly, no argument can justify the adoption of the printing-house texture of accidentals in a revised edition merely to secure formal coincidence with authoritatively revised substantives in the same edition.

Nor is the problem essentially different—although it may grow more complex—when lost intermediaries exist between the earliest form of the text in manuscript or typescript and the first edition. The principles treating a revised edition in relation to the first primary extant text apply with the same cogency to tracing a series of pre-printing alterations up to the earliest printed edition. Some questions are being raised, for Victorian and later literature, about the virtues of manuscript copy-text as against the allegedly superior authority (evidently in McKerrow's terms) of the first edition or even of a derived revised edition.[16] I must say that it seems to me anomalous for Elizabethan scholars to pursue the most rigorously

---

a modern manuscript in favour of the first edition for reasons that appear to agree closely with McKerrow's ultimately vague position.

16 Two examples are J. M. Robson, 'Principles and Methods in the Collected Edition of John Stuart Mill', *Editing Nineteenth Century Texts*, ed. J. M. Robson, University of Toronto Press, 1967, pp. 96–122; and Simon Nowell-Smith, 'Editing Dickens: For which reader? From which text?', *TLS*, 4 June 1970, p. 615, which called forth a brief reply from G. D. Hargreaves on 11 June, 1970, p. 638. Mr. Nowell-Smith's remarks about copy-text are largely vitiated by his failure to observe Greg's distinction that the copy-text selection is dictated by the accidentals and not by the substantives; thus his interesting observations about the difficulties among choices of substantive variants apply only to the editorial process and have little relation to copy-text, except possibly a tyrannous one. For some other remarks on this subject, especially in relation to the selection of a revised edition as copy-text, see my review of the Clarendon Press *Oliver Twist* in *Nineteenth-century Fiction*, xxiii (1968), 226–39.

selective methods for recovering a text that is as close as possible to the lost manuscript only to have editors of nineteenth-century books in effect continue the fallacy of comprehensive authority in a copy-text first or revised edition by their rejection of the authority of manuscript accidentals on the unsupported grounds of authorial 'approval' of what the printing house has made of the manuscript style.[17] Critics who neglect Greg's principles of divided authority and elevate the printed text above the manuscript lay themselves open to the charge of insufficient sensitivity to the virtues of an author's accidentals as an integral part of his expression when compared with the bland uniformity, and conformity, of printing-house styling.

I speak with some fervour on this subject. To read Stephen Crane's romance *The O'Ruddy* with the spare punctuation of its manuscript, which gives a rapid pace to the style, as against the lumbering effect of the posthumous first-edition's heavy punctuation, is a new and to me an invigorating experience. On the other hand, if an author carefully calculates his rhythms and punctuates his periods, like Hawthorne, it is enlightening to read him with the parenthetical effects he heard in his own ear while writing out his manuscript. I have always been impressed by the late Professor William Charvat's testimony in a letter to me, expressing the astonishment he felt in reading Hawthorne's texts edited from the manuscripts, and the way in which this first acquaintance with the special characteristics of Hawthorne's manuscripts—although he was a distinguished Hawthorne scholar—had quite altered his view of Hawthorne's style. The complex parentheses and balances of meaning revealed by Hawthorne's habitually heavy punctuation he could appreciate for the first time, he wrote, once the text had been altered back to the original form from the lighter printing-house styling that had obscured these intentional relationships.

Indeed, I am bold to think that there are signs in McKerrow's writings that he would have embraced Greg's theory of copy-text if he had lived to see it formulated. The strong note of conservatism that is so constantly struck in *Prolegomena* stems by his own admission from his concern at our ignorance of many of the vital details behind Elizabethan texts and their transmission. Within this general area of ignorance he would certainly have lumped the question of the alteration that might have taken place in the accidentals of a revised edition. Before Greg the only answer

17 I do not know what clauses hold in English publishers' contracts, but I do know that in the standard American contract for novels and non-academic books in general an author binds himself to accept the publisher's styling of his work. He would bankrupt himself quickly if in proof he attempted to restore his own accidentals characteristics. Restyled manuscripts in commercial publishing are not customarily submitted for an author's approval before typesetting.

was a conservative one, partly based on despair. If the authority of a revised edition is known in one respect but unknown in another, the presumption of the known—McKerrow implied—must be taken as governing the treatment of the unknown. This is the doctrine that Greg so successfully attacked by offering an alternative that had not previously been envisaged except in a narrow sense. Greg's concept of the eclectic text limited by bibliographically generated principles has proved to be the great contribution of this century to textual criticism. McKerrow's conservatism was a reaction against the unprincipled impressionism of nineteenth-century editing which had given a bad name to eclecticism. The most important result of Greg's theory of copy-text and of the methodology that flows from it is that it made eclecticism respectable when governed by scholarly principles that can be defined and can be applied to a number of different situations in a manner to meet with general approval.

It is proper to examine some situations to which the theory cannot be adapted. Greg himself indicated one. For the sweeping rewriting of the Folio version of *Every Man in his Humour* Jonson marked up a printed Quarto so thoroughly that it is almost impossible to disentangle what was compositorial in the Folio from what was Jonson. Under these circumstances an editor has no choice but to accept the accidentals of the minute revision as more authoritative on the whole than those of the first edition and thus to take the Folio as copy-text. Some exceptions there are, of course, as in the instances when the Jonsonian apostrophus in the Quarto was by error not transferred to the Folio; but these remain exceptions. Under the circumstances, of course, it is infinitely simpler to record the relatively few emendations to the Folio copy-text drawn from the Quarto than to reverse the process with almost unreadable apparatus attempting to record the necessary alterations from the Folio if the Quarto had been chosen as the copy-text. In more recent times the careful revisions that Walt Whitman gave to minute details of the accidentals in combination with important and constant changes in the wording and internal arrangement of *Leaves of Grass* make it logical to take each successively revised edition as the latest authority in all respects up to the so-called 'deathbed edition', even though this last will need some correction of transmissional corruptions from earlier texts. It is worth remark that these Whitman changes are not hypothetical but demonstrable, for in some cases the copy for the revision has been preserved with all its detailed markings. Yeats is another poet whose constant reworking of his poems produces an end so distant textually from his beginnings that Greg's distinction of the two authorities may have little bearing on the problems of the different editions except when corruptions in unrevised editions used as copy get perpetuated, in which case they can be isolated and removed. Although the matter has not been rigorously studied under controlled conditions, it may well be that given Henry James's habitual carefulness, and the thorough rewriting of certain early works, an editor need look no earlier than the New York Edition for his copy-texts of some of these revised versions. Perhaps the case may be different for other works only casually altered in this Edition. Textual critics have attacked only isolated problems in James, never the text as a whole, which we take on faith. A test or two that has been made of T. S. Eliot's works suggest that in some cases it might be dangerous to accept his last revised edition as copy-text.[18]

Something of a parallel to the case of Jonson's *Every Man in his Humour* may occur in modern times, also, when the only preserved manuscript is an early draft so much altered in the lost rewritten form that stands behind the print as to prove an impossible copy-text. An example is Stephen Crane's little sketch 'A Detail' first published in 1896, for which the original draft varies greatly from the published texts. Another is a typescript made up posthumously from the original draft manuscript (now lost) of a sketch published in considerably rewritten form in 1892 as 'The Octopush'. All shades and differences will appear in situations like these, of course. In the end the decision is perhaps basically a practical one. When rewriting has so altered the original syntax and wording as to make the manuscript punctuation largely untransferrable to the revision, it should be obvious to an editor that the problem of listing as emendations to the manuscript copy-text all the accepted variants from the revised text in the accidentals as well as in the substantives would create an apparatus so massive as to defeat its purpose of supplying a reader with the means of reconstructing both forms of the text. As on practical grounds one chooses the Folio *Every Man in his Humour* as copy-text but emends from the Quarto, so in such extreme cases as Crane's 'Detail' and 'Octopush' it is only common sense to shift the copy-text to the thoroughly rewritten version, giving the reader the draft form in its original version as a separate text. Nevertheless, whenever the two versions are sufficiently parallel for the superior authority of the accidentals of the early manuscript to be applicable to the revised text, an editor of Crane, like an editor of Jonson, would be advised not to print the reworked printed text verbatim but instead to emend it from the superior earlier authority. In such a procedure the apparatus recording the emendations would not be excessive and a critical text of maximum authority would be obtained that in all possible respects purifies the later print from the corruptions of the transmissional process in so far as the preserved documents permit.

It is necessary to point out that the above examples do not alter the

18 See, as an instance, W. H. Marshall, 'The Text of T. S. Eliot's "Gerontion" ', *SB*, iv (1951–2), 213–17, but particularly R. L. Beare, 'Notes on the Text of T. S. Eliot: Variants from Russell Square', *SB*, ix (1957), 21–49.

propriety of Greg's theory since it is on practical grounds alone that the shift is made in the choice of copy-text. The actual critical text that results still retains maximum authority in its two divisions so long as the editor, whether of Jonson or of Crane, accepts the authority of the accidentals of his revised but derived-edition copy-text only when (*a*) the accidentals of the primary genetic authority have no application to the revised substantives, or (*b*) specific reason exists to believe that in any individual crux where the substantives are roughly parallel and the accidentals differ, the revision of the substantives has extended as well to the accidentals. This is a very different case from accepting the accidentals of the revised edition en bloc and discarding the authority of these accidentals in the earliest form of the text, which would be as improper in the case of Jonson or of Crane as it would be in the case of the Folio *Othello* or of the fourth edition of *Tom Jones* or of *Joseph Andrews*.

The distinction seems to me to be this. For *Othello* or *Tom Jones* the earliest extant document is chosen as copy-text and its accidentals are given supreme authority as a whole, for the working hypothesis that the evidence provides is that in the one case the scribe and in the other the author did not significantly alter the accidentals in the process of annotating a copy of this edition with substantive revisions. Thus if an editor feels that the accidentals of his copy-text are faulty in some reading, for *Othello* he would go to the First Folio to see if a satisfactory substitute were present, and if not he would search through the Second, Third, and Fourth Folios. If he found a satisfactory emendation in the First Folio, he would most properly regard it as a correction of the Quarto (not as a revision that could be said to have any authority) simply because the Folio accidentals derive from those of the Quarto. In *Tom Jones* an editor wishing to correct some first-edition accidental's form would normally go to the earliest genetically related edition, the unauthoritative second, and be content with that regardless of the reading of the revised fourth edition unless he had reason to suspect that the still further variant fourth edition reflected an actual Fielding annotation. That is, the purely derived and unrevised second and third editions would be as acceptable sources of correction as the revised fourth in all cases where the reading was the same, or even where the fourth-edition reading differed unless the fourth-edition variant appeared to reflect some peculiarly Fieldingesque characteristic that might be authoritative.

The principle as it develops is this: by Greg's theory, in the search for authority the substantives of a revised edition are sifted on a critical basis in comparison with those of the first-edition copy-text; but the accidentals of the first edition are not treated on this critical basis as against the accidentals of the revision and instead are merely corrected as necessary from the most convenient source. Since correction alone is in question, not revision, the authority of the source from which the correction is drawn is of little or no importance. This principle is a sound one when an extant edition has been marked up to serve as printer's copy for a revised text and thus there is a direct and contiguous relationship between the two documents. Indeed, how little a text revised in these circumstances is likely to produce new authority in the accidentals can be demonstrated when the marked-up edition used as printer's copy was not the first edition. It is a fact that the accidentals of the fourth edition of *Tom Jones*, set from an annotated copy of the unauthoritative third, are considerably closer to those of the third than to the basic authority of the same accidentals in the first. The steady compositorial departure from the authority of the earliest accidentals in inverse relationship to the rising authority of the substantives can be traced in *Joseph Andrews* in the revised second edition set from a marked-up first, the revised third set from a marked-up second, and finally the revised fourth set from a marked-up third.

On the other hand, in the case of *Every Man in his Humour*, or of Crane's 'Detail', the substantive revision is so thoroughgoing as to generate with it a new set of accidentals. But it must be emphasized that the authority given these, as manifested by the choice of the revision as copy-text, extends only to the accidentals that are an integral part of the substantive revision and have no counterparts in the earlier text. These integrated accidentals must be accepted as the earliest extant authority on the same basis that one normally accepts the accidentals of a first edition deriving from a lost manuscript. However, whenever the two texts are parallel enough for a comparison of the accidentals to be pertinent, variants in the revised edition might or might not have had an origin in Jonson's annotations or in the lost rewritten manuscript that was the printer's copy for the printed text of Crane's 'Detail'. Under these circumstances an editor has the option of almost automatically selecting the forms of accidentals of the earliest source by applying Greg's principles to suitable conditions within the two texts; or else—if he feels competent to judge—he can make some essay at treating the accidentals of the revised edition on the same critical basis as its substantives. That is, he may test each pertinent variant in the light of what he knows about the author's characteristics and accept or reject the forms of the revised edition according as he has reason to believe that they were also revised or else have varied merely because of compositorial styling. What he must not do, I suggest, is to succumb to the tyranny of the copy-text in the McKerrow manner and accept the superiority of the revised edition throughout in situations when, in fact, the odds favour the authority of the primary text. Finally, if he treats these situations critically and is as prepared to contrive an eclectic text in the case of a revised-edition copy-text as he is in the case of a primary-edition copy-text, in an ideal state he would arrive at comparable results without regard for the choice of copy-text.[19] The edited text would not differ in the least, but only its apparatus. Thus I return to my original suggestion that the choice of copy-text for revised editions should actually be motivated by practical convenience, not by ideological considerations.

If the results are to be comparable, however, an editor must resist the strong pull that the copy-text always exerts on him to let well enough alone and to perform a minimum of critical changes, especially in respect to the accidentals. Any lassitude of this kind will produce a modern text that in both its parts is of unequal authority. Hence in addition to questions of the apparatus and the convenience of the reader's use of its documentation,[20] the choice of the copy-text is almost bound to have an

19 Emphasis of course needs to be put on *ideal state*. In practice not every variant, especially in the accidentals, is readily adjudicable and hence the copy-text can in the long run exert a considerable influence in cases of honest doubt. The main point is that when by force of necessity an editor adopts a revised derived edition as copy-text, he must remain sceptical of all differences of accidentals in the revision and as a general rule adopt an active preference for the accidentals of the primary edition. Like a hanging judge, he should view the parallel but variant accidentals of the revision as guilty until proved innocent, and actively welcome the opportunity to emend from the primary edition whenever the opportunity offers. That this is the very reverse of the stance towards emendation of the accidentals when the copy-text is the primary edition needs emphasis, for the two editorial attitudes must not be confused.

20 I assume that the apparatus to accompany the establishing of a text will consist of two main parts: (1) A list of all alterations both substantive and accidental (barring the agreed-upon silent alterations of typographical features) that the editor had made in the copy-text; (2) An Historical Collation or record of all substantive variation from the readings of the modern edited text within the range of the collated documents. By comparing the List of Emendations with the readings of the modern text a reader can reconstruct the copy-text in both respects of accidentals and substantives; by comparing the Historical Collation the reader can observe the total evidence for substantive variation in collated editions and can assess the editorial decisions to accept or reject these variant readings. The Historical Collation will not differ in the number of its substantive items according to the choice of copy-text, but the List of Emendations is vitally affected. It seems obvious that a reader's convenience is best served if in the Emendations he can view the revision in the light of the changes made in the primary copy, this being of especial moment when the primary copy or one of its derivatives has been used as the basis for the revision, and also of moment when as in *Joseph Andrews* there is a series of revised editions. On the other hand, if the copy-text is the revised edition, the movement is reversed and what become isolated for notice in the Emendations are only the rejected readings of the revision which the editor felt to be corruptions requiring emendation from the primary copy. The nature of the revision is quite obscured and a reader must turn to the Historical Collation to reconstruct the substantive readings of the primary edition and the extent of their revision. This is a less useful system than to bring all accepted revised substantives together where they belong in the Emendations, the relatively few rejected readings being listed in the Historical Collation. For the accidentals, however, the reader's situation is much worse, for he can never learn from the list what were the accidentals of the primary edition that were altered in the revised but only the relatively few revised-edition errors that

effect on the editor that can be for good or for ill. In practical terms, therefore, the selection of the copy-text according to Greg's principles remains important, for only in an ideal world *will* the results be indifferent; and an editor will find it a sounder guide to his judgement to be forced to trace the course of the revision, and to justify his alteration of the copy-text in terms of what the author may be presumed to have marked in the printer's copy, than to be faced with a *fait accompli* and to confine himself to a search for presumed corruption in it. For these reasons, an editor is well advised to heed Greg's advice and to choose a revised derived edition as his copy-text only in cases of the sternest necessity when to select an earlier document would pile up lists of emendations of staggering proportions.

These seem to me to be the chief problems of copy-text wherein Greg's rationale furnishes the solutions. We may turn now to a group of textual situations to which Greg's rationale does not apply, or may apply only in part according to special circumstances. These have not been discussed in connection with questions of copy-text, at least for printed books, and thus they are in need of explication. The practical problems of Shakespeare's text are almost exclusively associated with printed editions in derived or linear ralationship to each other. A great deal of speculation has been devoted to the pre-printing history of the lost manuscripts behind the extant Shakespeare prints, such as the question of the two manuscripts of *Hamlet* or of *Othello* and their respective authority according to their assumed transmissional history. For the so-called Bad Quartos like those of *Richard III*, *Romeo and Juliet*, or *King Lear* quite revolutionary results have been achieved by this reconstruction of pre-printing transmission, and even for the good texts, like the Second Quarto and Folio *Hamlet* or *Troilus and Cressida*, an editor is scarcely equipped to begin his task unless he has a working hypothesis that will cover the respective authority of the two substantive, or generally authoritative manuscript traditions that were put into print. On the other hand, many problems of editing such plays come to centre on the crucial fact that in the good texts—with the possible exceptions of *2 Henry IV*—the genetic relationship is one of physical derivation in linear form. That is, the Folio-altered texts of plays

---

have been emended. It is usually impracticable to record in the Historical Collation all rejected accidentals as well as substantives. Thus the amount of useful information provided by the apparatus is materially reduced when the copy-text is the revised edition; moreover, the material is necessarily presented in an uncritical manner since it does not trace the forward course of the authoritative revision and as a consequence forces the reader to accept on the faith of the copy-text the alterations, particularly in the accidentals, without specification. In my opinion this is a faulty editorial procedure, to be avoided except as a last resort.

like *Othello* and *Troilus and Cressida* derive directly from the Quartos in one sense because a Quarto was marked up for printer's copy to bring it into general conformity with a manuscript in a different textual tradition from that behind the Quarto. The physical derivation can be an important fact in evaluating common error, as in the *good kissing carrion* or the *pious bonds* cruxes in *Hamlet.* If an error in a revised Folio edition derives to it from a mistake in its Quarto copy, the case is very different indeed from common error being reproduced in two texts that physically stem from different manuscripts, as in the *minutes rest* crux in *The Merry Wives of Windsor* that must have been a mistake in the prompt-book.

If one approaches the matter more narrowly, Greg's rationale of copy-text is seen to rest on the assumption of a linear relationship between primary and revised text: one can scarcely prove the accidentals—which dictate the choice of copy-text—to be largely unauthoritative in the revised reprint if their primary form had not been visible in the immediate printer's copy for the revision. Thus both McKerrow's and Greg's views were conditioned by the generally derived nature of Shakespearian texts and neither took account of the problems that arise when one cannot select a copy-text as the extant edition in the closest genetic relationship to the lost manuscript. This situation will most commonly occur when two extant texts are not gentically related to each other in a linear or derived manner but instead stem immediately from two independent lost documents and thus radiate in some manner from the lost archetypal manuscript.[21]

It is true, of course, that problems of radiation are rare indeed in the Elizabethan drama and thus did not appear to be of moment either to McKerrow or to Greg. One can scarcely criticize them on this account. But the closer one approaches modern times and the invention of the type-writer, the more pressing become the editorial difficulties in dealing with radiating texts and the more essential it is to determine to what extent

---

21 That the different manuscripts behind the two texts of *Hamlet, Othello,* and *Troilus and Cressida* must themselves have radiated in their pre-printing history so that their transmitted substantive variants are to be accounted for by this radial relationship has nothing to do, of course, with the genealogical relationship of the two printed texts in their accidentals, since one was printed from a marked-up copy of the other. So far as questions of copy-text go, there is no essential difference between such texts and the revised fourth edition of *Tom Jones* set from an authorially altered copy of the third edition. The problem of the authority of the substantive variants in the revised edition of *Tom Jones* is, of course, much simpler, since it was Fielding himself who marked them for the printer. Because of their scribal origin, and their derivation from a manuscript whose general as well as specific authority must be scrutinized, the variants in Shakespeare's revised plays offer a truly vexing problem. But this matter has no pertinence to the rationale of copy-text.

the Greg rationale of copy-text will apply or what modifications or even new principles must be substituted.[22]

The basic problem is this. Greg's rationale in its application boils down to the simple proposition that the authority of variant substantives is determined critically in revised or altered editions but that the authority of the accidentals is governed purely by their relative genetic closeness to the lost manuscript. So long as the relationship of texts is linear, Greg's principles work with efficiency and with justice no matter what the literary period. But when two or more substantive texts radiate from a lost original, either they are demonstrably equidistant in their transmission from that original or at conjecturally established unequal distances. And for some texts it is not always possible to demonstrate whether they are linearly or radially related.[23] Thus Greg's genetic test for the authority of accidentals either breaks down completely when texts radiate or else requires considerable modification. The question is, what to put in its place. Some of the answers will evolve, I hope, from the following illustrations taken from Stephen Crane's writings.

In October 1895 Crane's short story 'A Grey Sleeve' was syndicated in a number of American newspapers, each of which printed the text from the common typesetting of pulled proofs distributed by the Bacheller syndicate. It is obvious that in an absolute sense any one of the eight observed newspaper versions is as authoritative as any other, for all are at

---

22 Problems of radiation are commonplace in classical or medieval manuscript texts, but because of linguistic difficulties and the gaps between extant copies the question of copy-text seldom arises in terms of the accidentals. Analogies with these conditions do not appear to be pertinent to the present discussion.

23 I shall not discuss these fortunately rare cases since as sports they have nothing to do with the establishment of principles for dealing with texts. A convenient example occurs, however, in three of Stephen Crane's Mexican fables—'The Voice of the Mountain', 'How the Donkey Lifted the Hills', and 'The Victory of the Moon'. So far as can be determined, these appeared in only a single newspaper, the *Nebraska State Journal* in May, June, and July of 1895, and some months later in Bacheller's *Pocket Magazine*. The works are brief and the texts so close in newspaper and magazine versions that in the absence of printing errors in the newspaper transmitted to the magazine (which also might have come from common printed copy like syndicated proofs) one cannot determine from the internal evidence whether newspaper and magazine radiate from the manuscript directly; whether they radiate from typescript and carbon made from the manuscript, possibly with a lost master syndicate proof intervening between the typescript (or manuscript) and the newspaper; or whether the magazine was set in derived relationship from a clipping of the newspaper. However, proofs for other of Crane's syndicated Mexican sketches of the period are in existence that show that Bacheller at the time was using the *State Journal* as his printer; the inference is that the *Pocket Magazine* was set from such a proof (in effect, a clipping), but the whole case is conjectural. Since no internal evidence goes against this linear derivation, an editor may well adopt it as a working hypothesis, taking the *State Journal* as his copy-text.

identical distances from the same copy. McKerrow and Greg rightly insist that within the pattern of derived or linear texts the only true authority is a formal or genealogical one. By that criterion, however, we
have here eight genealogically equal authorities. We see, I think, that the
copy-text cannot be determined genetically, in Greg's terms, as that document with the most authoritative accidentals. Of course, since so much of
Crane's holograph material has been preserved, an editor may have a
reasonably precise idea about certain of Crane's specific spellings and
punctuation habits so that he has critical tests to assist in selecting what
for the purposes of the modern edition will prove to be the most convenient copy-text. In fact, this is all he has: he cannot confirm his critical
conclusions by arranging the documents at relative distances on a family
tree. The major difference, then, in the treatment of the authority of revised but genetically derived texts and of radiating documents is that
critical tests (guided by bibliographical probabilities) must be substituted
for the test of genealogical relationship.

Greg had always insisted on the necessity for this exercise of critical
judgement in dealing with the substantives of revised editions; but with
radiation this same critical judgement must be extended to all accidentals.
The incidence of variation among these being so much higher than among
substantives, and the means of distinguishing authority varying so markedly in the two cases, a serious editorial problem results. An editor can
make some shift to apply literary criteria to substantive variants, even relatively indifferent ones, and have some reasonable hope of a generally
successful conclusion. I for one am prepared to believe that the best
modern edited texts of *Othello* represent Shakespeare's intentions better
than either the Quarto or the Folio individually. On the other hand, critical
tests suitable for the meaning and idiomatic usage of words are markedly
more difficult to apply to questions of accidentals, especially when such
profuse variation occurs as in the eight authoritative versions of 'A Grey
Sleeve'.

In this particular situation a form of bibliography can provide some
basic evidence. Although the compositors of the eight newspapers frequently altered the accidentals of their copy to accord with their own
habits or understandings, the odds favour the hypothesis that if a strong
majority in any given case set the same form, the weak minority is likely
to be unauthoritative. Certainly, when one of eight newspapers varies
uniquely in the form of an accidental, we may conjecture with confidence
—as we should do with a substantive—that this single witness is in error
in transmitting its copy. Using this statistical approach as a general guide,
an editor can whittle away by degrees, but only up to a point and always
with the recognition of two possible sources of error to affect his conclusions. That is, since compositorial style tends to conventionality, a

majority of compositors faced with an unconventional accidental may sometimes opt for normality, leaving the true authorial reading preserved only by the dogged or indifferent few.

Thus statistics need to be interpreted in the light of the editor's special knowledge of his author's accidentals characteristics, for the minority reading may sometimes need to be adopted on critical grounds. It follows that quantitative evidence is not always enough and that qualitative evidence, the real nature of the variant, needs to be considered. This real nature is frequently less obvious for the accidentals than for the substantives.[24] Moreover, it is subject to differences according to the date of the document with which an editor is dealing. In 1894 Crane was as likely as not to put a comma between two adjectives in series before a noun. In 1898 such a comma would be rare indeed, as shown by the manuscripts.

One further caveat should be mentioned. McKerrow is undoubtedly right as a general proposition in urging that an editor's ideal is the reconstruction of what would be an authorial fair copy in so far as the preserved documents permit. Specifically, this ideal must always be tempered by a realistic acknowledgement of what the preserved documents do in fact permit. As I have remarked, when in linear derived texts Greg proposes that an editor insert the authoritative substantives of a revised edition into the texture of the accidentals of the primary edition, what an editor actually comes out with is as close a replica as he can manage of the actual marked-up printer's copy of a first edition that has been authorially revised or else scribally altered from some other authoritative document. He must recognize that in no sense has he the opportunity to reproduce the author's manuscript from documentary evidence except to the extent that the manuscript details may have been transferred to the first edition. He cannot go in back of this first edition except to correct error, whether in substantives or in accidentals, on a conjectural basis.[25] McKerrow can-

24 For example, Crane's grammar was occasionally uncertain. If the possessive use of *it's* for *its* were to appear in one of ten witnesses, I should myself conclude that this one compositor had failed to correct an authorial reading that had been recognized as a fault by the other nine workmen. If a singular verb were hitched to a collective plural subject in, say, two witnesses, I should conclude that eight compositors had sophisticated the reading. If one witness read *sort of a* and the rest *sort of*, my conclusion would be the same because I have seen many examples of compositorial alteration of this idiom commonly found in Crane's manuscripts. However, if five witnesses punctuate a compound sentence with a comma before the *and* and three do not, an editor could be permitted to feel that the three were following the usual Crane practice and the other five were regularizing the punctuation; but he could hold this conviction with much less certainty than with the substantives I have cited.

25 This statement needs modification only as an editor is prepared to regularize variant accidentals to a single form known to be the author's. For instance, one com-

not be faulted in his rigorously logical view of what constitutes documentary authority. It follows that an editor of a work that exists only in a primary edition and a series of derived reprints can do no more than offer a text of this primary edition conjecturally purified of error. That can be his only realizable ideal, for no other source is available to lead him back to the readings of the document that was the printer's copy for this primary edition.

Correspondingly, an editor of *Tom Jones* can accept the substantive revisions of the fourth edition, set from the third, and by this action he can embody Fielding's further intentions;[26] but for the rest when these cannot be presumed to correct the first edition by restoring the manuscript reading corrupted in the first, he has no documentary evidence available—despite his multiple texts—to pursue the matter farther back than the readings of the first edition, save by conjecture.[27]

---

positor of Marlowe's *Edward II* spells the interjection *Ah* with some frequency as *A*, whereas the conventional *Ah* is the invariable spelling of his fellow. If the manuscript fragment of *The Massacre at Paris* is in Marlowe's hand, as there is every reason to believe, we know that Marlowe spelled *Ah*—at least in that preserved part of the manuscript. It is indeed probable that *A* is a compositorial spelling imposed on a manuscript copy that read *Ah*; hence an editor who felt it worth while to attempt to regularize spelling in an Elizabethan play could justify emendation of *A* to *Ah* on that ground. But he could be sure of his case only if he were prepared to show the probability that the manuscript copy for the First Quarto were holograph. Otherwise it would be as easy to speculate that *A* was a scribal characteristic in the copy which only one compositor consistently regularized to *Ah*.

26 Except in one area of the Man of the Hill where Fielding had revised a single sheet of what became the third edition, but the fourth edition rejects this revision by returning to the first-edition sheet (not even corrected by the errata list) as copy. This constitutes a pretty puzzle, for it can be demonstrated bibliographically that the substitution of a first-edition sheet here must have been on Fielding's instructions. However, an editor can identify critically the reason for Fielding's instructions—which was to remove a rewritten passage that he had inserted in the third edition in order to return to the saner original version of the first edition. In this case the baby was thrown out with the bath, for by substituting the whole first-edition sheet (perhaps by a misunderstanding of the instructions) the printer of the fourth edition also removed various purely stylistic revisions in this sheet of the third that Fielding could scarcely have wished to cancel in favour of the original. An editor is advised to treat this situation eclectically by observing Fielding's later intentions in the one to restore the original block passage but in the other by retaining the inadvertently omitted stylistic revisions.

27 Of course, Fielding's errata list attached to the first edition provides the opportunity to restore readings corrupted in the text, as well as to carry on, in a manner of speaking, Fielding's proof-correction, which appear to have been numerous. But Fielding did not catch all errors. As one example, probably by compositorial error in one group of pages in Volume I, Bridget Allworthy is *Mrs. Bridget* whereas before and

It has not been generally remarked that the case is altered for radiating texts. In Crane's 'A Grey Sleeve' other witnesses are present that have an authority, if it can be determined, for indicating what were the readings in the lost printer's-proof from which each newspaper was independently set. The copy-text, therefore, is not the single primary document behind which an editor cannot penetrate except by conjecture. Instead, it is only one of eight equal witnesses, of no greater presumptive authority than the other seven. This holds as true for the accidentals as for the substantives.

Two related principles now follow. In such a situation as 'A Grey Sleeve' with its eight radiating texts, all equidistant from the lost printer's-proofs, an editor can in fact penetrate one step in back of the extant documents and from their multiple evidence he can reconstruct in considerable detail the lost printer's-copy, which will be of superior authority to any single preserved document. At whatever distance they may stand from the ultimate authority of Crane's holograph, these syndicated proofs are yet genetically more authoritative, in Greg's sense, than is any one of the eight newspaper texts. And they can be reconstructed, given enough witnesses, with one hundred per cent fidelity to the substantives and a percentage well within the nineties for the accidentals. So far as I am aware, editors have not contemplated this principle, or if so they have not implemented it. Every multiple text in Crane, for instance, and there are many of them, has always been edited as if the single example chosen as copy-text blocked all access to antecedent authority, as indeed it would were it a linear primary authority and not a member of a group with radiating multiple authority.

This is the first principle. Related to it, though subsidiary, is the question of immediate concern in this present discourse—the matter of copy-text. In my experience with these multiple documents, no single one is likely to be invariably superior to any other in every respect of accidentals or substantives, although certain ones may be less heavily styled and there-

afterwards she is *Miss Bridget*, which seems to have been Fielding's intention. An editor should emend *Mrs.* but he cannot avouch authority for the correction in any McKerrow sense of the word. Since the errata list does not cover Volume VI, an editor's corrections need to be bolder in this volume. For instance, whether the amateur highwayman whom Jones relieves of want, married to Mrs. Miller's niece, was named *Anderson, Enderson,* or *Henderson* needs to be straightened out. The three preserved cancellanda leaves in the Rothschild copy now in the Trinity College Library, Cambridge, enable an editor to restore two accidentals back to the forms set from manuscript. One may be grateful for such small favours, which can be assisted by a judicious amount of regularizing of spellings varied by compositors but established in the few leaves of Fielding's preserved holograph of an early poem.

fore generally more trustworthy witnesses.[28] However, since all these documents are of equal theoretical authority, no firm principle like that of genetic relationship can differentiate them. In principle, then, the choice of copy-text is often indifferent except in certain two-text situations where qualitative evidence may be ambiguous without the support of quantitative evidence. These special cases are more likely to occur when the only two extant documents radiate not from the author's manuscript without intermediary but from some lost transcript of it when the problem of incalculable styling then arises.

The choice, therefore, is theoretically indifferent because the only function of copy-text in such a situation is to serve as the physical basis not for a purified reprint in the shape of a modern edition but instead for a reconstruction of the immediate lost printer's-copy, in which process all the preserved documents will participate. Although it is perhaps hypothetically true that a modern text edited by such a method might be said to accept as its copy-text this reconstructed proof, nevertheless the problem of what form an apparatus would take for such a non-extant copy-text is acute, and it is a matter of economy to select some one of the documents that as a whole conforms most closely to the reconstructed proof in respect to its accidentals and to use it as the copy-text or basis for the emendation that will embody the reconstruction. Since, in fact, an editor in this situation selects his copy-text only after he has reconstructed the lost, common printer's-copy, it is largely a question of convenience which document he uses. That one requiring the least amount of apparatus to record the necessary alterations (it is hard to call them emendations) is the most economical in printing costs and certainly the most convenient for a reader's use of apparatus.[29]

28 This is a not unexpected conclusion, but it can be supported by the half a dozen or so examples where the actual printer's proof for a newspaper-syndicated Crane piece is preserved, so that an editor can amuse himself by reconstructing this document from the multiple witnesses and then seeing how accurately his bibliographical and critical methods have brought him to the truth. The validity of this textual principle for recovering a lost document is not theoretical, therefore.

29 Paradoxically, the copy-text most faithful to the reconstructed printer's-copy conceals more information in its list of emendations by recording fewer of the multiple variants than would be the case for a copy-text less faithful. How far this concealment of the evidence on which the work was edited can be rectified by including among the substantive variants of the Historical Collation the accidentals variants rejected from the other witnesses is a procedure sometimes practicable on a limited basis. I suggest that an editor should be consistent and not merely present those rejected accidentals that he himself considers to be 'significant' (almost a dirty word in textual criticism). Instead, he can start by omitting at least the unique variants—since these will have little or no claim to authority—and then progress up the scale so far as

It is quite literally true that the modern text edited from this number of witnesses should be exactly the same no matter which document was used as the physical copy-text. Even when the eight witnesses split four and four, there is usually nothing in any copy-text that would lead an editor to decide in favour of one rather than the other side. It must be admitted that as the number of witnesses decreases the importance of selecting a copy-text on qualitative grounds may well increase. When relatively few documents are available, the value of majority evidence declines and an editor will be thrown back more and more on his own judgement in cases of conflicting evidence. It may well be in such a situation that the over-all opinion he has formed of the general fidelity of the accidentals of his copy-text can materially influence his judgement in cases of honest doubt. Yet an editor should to the best of his ability exhaust his qualitative evidence (in combination with the quantitative) before throwing back on the copy-text the responsibility for the authority of a reading. Over-all fidelity may be difficult to apply to specifics. For instance, a compositor may appear to be following a Crane manuscript when he generally omits the punctuation between the clauses of a compound sentence but he may have his own ideas that he imposes on the setting-off of an inverted phrase or clause, or the punctuation of a series of three with two commas instead of one.

When an editor is involved in this problem of multiple authority, it is important that he should recognize precisely what document it is that he is reconstructing, for McKerrow's ideal of coming as close as possible to an authorial fair copy—though true—needs to be severely qualified by his further caution that the success of the process is limited by the evidence of the preserved documents. In Crane's short story 'A Grey Sleeve' the evidence of these documents enables an editor to recover not anything like an authorial fair copy but instead the intermediate stage between manuscript and extant newspaper texts in the form of the lost syndicated proofs. Since these are at least one stage removed from the holograph manuscript, an editor must always consider that they represent what a printer made out of his copy, which will certainly not be an exact transcript of the manuscript but instead a printing-house styled version. The eight newspaper texts enable an editor to balance the statistical distribution of the variants against his private knowledge that certain ones will represent Crane's own accidentals characteristics (assuming that these had been faithfully transmitted to the proofs) and, according to his judgement, to arrive at something close to the precise accidentals (as well as substantives) of the syndicated proof-sheets, with documentary authority

---

seems practicable to the point where the presentation of the total evidence would be of legitimate concern to a critic.

behind every decision. However, it is not his concern whether in their recovered form these proofs agree or disagree with Crane's habits of punctuation, spelling, and so on; and indeed when the bibliographical evidence of the distributional variants indicates clearly that the proof has departed from Crane's own habits, it is not an editor's business to print what he may be morally certain the manuscript reading would have been when the evidence indicates strongly that the recovered proof read otherwise.[30] The law of the specific authority being recovered, and the docu-

30 This statement may seem harsh but it is not in basic disagreement with Mc-Kerrow's principle that the aim of an editor should be to recover a text that will approximate an authorial fair copy *in so far as the documentary evidence permits*. This last is the key phrase, for the documentary evidence may permit very little of such a recovery. The substantive Folio text of *Julius Cæsar* was set chiefly by Compositor B from a manuscript that was very likely a scribal fair copy of Shakespeare's own papers, although it is just possible that in parts of three scenes Shakespeare's own revision of the original text may have served as the copy. An editor of *Julius Cæsar* attempts by conjecture to set right B's (or the scribe's) substantive mistakes and he may repunctuate here and there to clarify the sense or to rectify B's frequent transpositional errors. If he chooses he may cautiously tinker with a spelling or two like *tapor* for *taper* or adjust to normality a very few aberrant spellings that seem to have been produced by justifying a tight line in the full measure. That the result approximates a Shakespearian fair copy any closer than is permitted by a typesetting by Compositor B from a scribal transcript of Shakespeare's papers, the whole corrected of its more obvious errors by editorial conjecture, is not an illusion that McKerrow would have held. The documentary evidence permits no nearer approach. However, by choosing F1 as the copy-text instead of, say F4, an editor does indeed reprint a text that in its accidentals as well as its substantives is closer to a Shakespearian fair copy (even though filtered through scribe and compositor) than would be the case for a text based on F4. It is doubtful that McKerrow meant any more than that. Similarly, an editor of any one of Crane's fugitive newspaper sketches which exist in only a single text in the *New York Tribune* or the *New York Press* is bound by the rules of copy-text to reprint his source faithfully save for necessary correction of error. The most he can do (and not all critics would allow this) is in cases of internal variation of accidentals to normalize according to that form of the copy-text variation that comes closest to Crane's usual practice at this date (see the next footnote). But if the copy-text is invariant for a form of spelling or punctuation that is not characteristic of Crane, in a single-text situation an editor is not permitted to alter it on his own responsibility—lacking all other documentary authority for this particular text—to a form that he knows must have been in Crane's manuscript that was the printer's copy. Nor if a primary text has an unauthoritative reprint is an editor permitted—except in case of error in the copy-text—to emend from the reprint when this latter has fortuitously stumbled into characteristics that must have been those of the lost manuscript. Such a procedure would create a synthetic text with a vengeance, completely lacking in the necessary control of documentary authority. The situation is no different when recovery is in question from multiple documents that derive immediately not from a manuscript but from intermediate syndicated printer's proofs as in 'A Grey Sleeve'. From the extant newspapers a recovery cannot be made of the manuscript itself (as in examples given below) but only of these proofs. These proofs in their recovered form, then, correspond to a *New York Press*

mentary evidence that applies to the treatment of any text, must prevail.[31]

The point is worth emphasis because an editor of multiple documents is not always in the happy position of working with the number of texts that can assure him of something very close to exact recovery of the immediate underlying authority, as in 'A Grey Sleeve'. An example is Crane's little sketch 'A Yellow Under-sized Dog' which has been observed syndicated in only three newspapers in August 1896, set from lost proofs supplied by the McClure syndicate. The substantive variants present no serious problem in adjudication, for a unique reading is almost certain to be wrong when the other two authorities do not appear to print an obvious sophistication of an error or rough spot preserved with fidelity in the third text. The case is by no means so open and shut with the accidentals. In this story when two newspapers agree against the third in a

---

single-text of a *Sullivan County Sketch*: in 'A Grey Sleeve' an editor comes as close as he can to the manuscript by the recovery of the proofs and the reprinting of this form of the text; in 'Killing his Bear' he reprints the newspaper text as the closest form to the lost manuscript. In neither case can he arbitrarily insert Crane's characteristics in the accidentals without documentary authority. Documentary authority is to be taken in a narrow sense when multiple witnesses are present. That is, if the quantitative evidence in 'A Grey Sleeve' indicates that a minority reading, though characteristic of Crane, is fortuitously so, an editor has no business to go against the clear evidence of his documents to select that reading on the sole basis of his belief that this would have been the manuscript reading even though the proof must have read otherwise. His business is to reprint the recovered proofs, which is all that logical interpretation of his documentary evidence permits. In doing this he will at least be coming closer to what would have been a fair copy by Crane than he would by reprinting any single newspaper text.

31 This statement is always to be qualified by the amount of regularization an editor of a nineteenth-century text may feel competent to perform when the recovered text is inconsistent within itself. As a matter of real emendation, that is, without documentary authority except for analogy within the document's range of variation, an editor may choose to bring those clear-cut variants to be attributed to the compositor into line with the other forms in the text itself that agree with the author's known practice. On the other hand, how far an editor can go in the matter of regularization when the document itself is uniform in its contradiction to the author's practice involves questions too complex for present discussion. In my view any such emendation should be severely limited since it involves a step beyond what the evidence of the document(s) permits and could lead to any number of abuses: only by some strain could emendation of this nature be put in the category of the correction of error. However, it is perhaps a harmless exercise to emend British spellings to the author's own American forms (or vice versa), carefully recording these in the List of Emendations. One is on firm ground here, except when—as in the manuscript of Hawthorne's *Marble Faun*—an American author planning on English publication attempted to spell in a manner foreign to his usual practice. Fortunately such cases are rare, although in the last year of his life Crane himself sporadically and inconsistently—at least in the manuscript of *The O'Ruddy*—might adopt here and there an English spelling under the influence of his residence in this country.

reading of an accidental that is taken to be characteristic of Crane, an editor may happily accept the majority evidence. But here the same two newspapers occasionally punctuate a compound sentence with a comma before 'and' in a manner largely foreign to Crane, and it is an open question whether these two compositors independently styled alike or whether on the contrary they were following with greater fidelity than the third the proof-sheets' styling of the manuscript. In such a case a conservative editor may choose to follow the majority evidence no matter where it leads him, or if he chooses to take the responsibility I should argue he could convince himself that the actual proofs without the commas were represented in this detail as in the third newspaper. I mention this specific case only because it leads to the next form of pure radiation when only two documents are preserved.

Here the chips are really down in the matter of the copy-text and its treatment. Because both documents are of equal authority I suggest that it would be a clear case of abnegation of editorial responsibility and of tyranny of the copy-text if an editor treated the document he chose as copy-text in the conventional manner as if it had more inherent authority than the other. Multiple authority inevitably creates an eclectic text and the copy-text cannot be treated with the respect accorded a primary, single document heading a linear series of derivations; that is, not if the editor is in fact making an attempt to recover from the extant documents the authorial readings of maximum fidelity both for substantives and accidentals. On some occasions the choice of copy-text may be more meaningful than in others, as is true for Crane's Spanish-American War story 'The Price of the Harness' which he wrote in Havana in October 1898 and sent in manuscript to his New York agent Paul Reynolds. It would seem that Reynolds had a typescript and carbon made, one copy of which he sold to the *Cosmopolitan* in the United States and the other, as suggested by Crane, to *Blackwood's* in Britain, which had arranged earlier for the first refusal. Both were printed with some haste in December. Although both versions are of equal authority by their immediate radiation from the same typescript without any opportunity for authorial changes in proof, it is clear that the *Cosmopolitan* text is closer in its American accidentals to the typescript and is thus almost automatically preferable as copy-text, although a number of readings must be introduced into its texture from *Blackwood's*, including seemingly more authoritative accidentals.

More difficult is Crane's Civil War story 'An Indiana Campaign' syndicated by Bacheller in six observed newspaper versions in May 1896 and published in his *Pocket Magazine* in September. Internal evidence suggests that the Bacheller syndicated proof-sheets and the magazine radiate from a typescript and its carbon, although radiation from the manuscript itself is not an impossibility. Here we have seven radiating authorities, then, but the case is not a simple one as in 'The Price of the Harness' or 'The Bride Comes to Yellow Sky', for a different genealogical relationship can be established between the two branches. That is, each of the six newspapers was set from a copy of the common proofs so that any individual newspaper text is at two removes in the transmission from the typescript, whereas the *Pocket Magazine* is at one. Any newspaper is still a substantive text, of course, but the genetic relationship of each line to authority is unequal and hence the *Pocket Magazine*—one step nearer the lost typescript—is a superior copy-text on principle. Nevertheless, one can succeed so well in recovering the readings of the accidentals of the common syndicated proofs from the six witnesses that this reconstructed text can be placed almost on a par with the magazine as at only one remove from the typescript despite the two removes at which each of its six components stands.

But some areas of doubt still remain in the accidentals, and in this uncertainty the *Pocket Magazine* provides the technically sounder copy-text because, for better or for worse, we know precisely what these readings are. There is no room here for tyranny, of course, but for a considerable flexibility. It is only in the areas of doubt that this recovery from the newspapers is at all inferior in authority to the magazine. Where both lines agree there can be every confidence that the lost typescript has been restored, so that the synthesis of the newspapers becomes a powerful force in confirming the magazine readings. Where there is significant disagreement among the newspapers, often the agreement of the magazine with the majority or even the minority may serve to give the reading the best authority that the documents can furnish. When there is clear disagreement between a confirmed reading in the newspapers and the magazine, one has arrived at a situation where either the proof or the magazine compositor has strayed in fidelity to the typescript and one is back at the problem of two radiating texts to which only qualitative evidence can offer a conjectural answer. Even so, in these cases of clear disagreement when there is no doubt what the proof read, the superior genetic relationship of the magazine has no bearing at all on which line is in error. The only real virtue of the selection of the magazine as copy-text (outside of its convenience) is its possible genealogical authority when the divergent reading of the proof is in some doubt. Yet in some cases this may be balanced by the editor's decision that on the whole what can be recovered of the proof is qualitatively superior to the magazine, in which case he has the option of exercising the courage of his convictions, for the magazine can scarcely be perfect. Perhaps it is only when he has no convictions (and should have none) that the weak excuse of the magazine's partial genetic authority can salve his conscience for following the copy-text simply because it is the copy-text. We live in a naughty, not an ideal world, and in almost every radiating situation, especially with two texts, the true authority cannot always be arrived at for every accidental on qualitative evidence that an editor can regard as sufficiently trustworthy. It is in these situations, and these situations only, that in default of a better principle an editor can justify playing the odds by following his copy-text automatically. In these fine points there may be in textual criticism no better justification than Old Bill's classic advice in a case of dilemma—'Well, if you knows of a better 'ole, go to it.'[32]

32 Radiating documents can have even more complex histories especially when international publication is involved or some quirk of syndication affects the copy. Crane's 'Reluctant Voyagers' is a case in point. Although originally drafted perhaps as early as 1893–4, as a short holograph fragment suggests, it seems to have been put aside and brought out again in the spring of 1899 when Crane sent it to his London agent Pinker, probably in the form of a typescript. Pinker sold this typescript to the Northern Newspaper Syndicate, known as Tillotson's, which had it set up in proof form. A copy of this English proof is preserved among the pieces that Cora Crane sent to Reynolds in New York after Crane's death for the proposed American edition of *Last Words*. Tillotson's sold the American rights to an individual, D. T. Pierce, and the sketch appeared in four observed newspapers in February 1900. Later, it was printed in the English *Last Words* (1902) for which Cora Crane had provided the copy. So far as is known, Tillotson's did not syndicate the piece in England although it may well have appeared in the provincial press: the Tillotson records have been destroyed. So much for the external evidence. Internal evidence suggests that the Tillotson's proof was set up from the typescript Pinker had sold to them and *Last Words* from a carbon of this typescript but without a scattering of revisions that Crane had made in the Pinker typescript. Thus the proof and *Last Words* radiate at equal distances from the lost typescript. The copy for the four American newspapers exhibits some curious features that suggest that Tillotson's sent some proofs and also the original edited typescript to Pierce. Three of the newspapers radiate from the proofs, but the *New York Press* text shows every sign of setting from the typescript, perhaps when Pierce ran out of proofs. As a consequence, three of the newspapers are derived reprints of no independent authority, but the *Press* joins the preserved copy of the proof and *Last Words* as radiating from the typescript. In this case of tripartite equal authority, the American styling of the *Press* makes it the most convenient copy-text but the recovery of the lost typescript from the additional evidence of the other two documents requires free alteration of the *Press* copy-text. In substantives the main problem rests in the unrevised state of the chronologically latest *Last Words*. This text proves to be of value not only in isolating the Crane revisions present in the other two documents but also in suggesting a few purer substantive readings sophisticated by editorial change made direct in the typescript by Tillotson's. This example illustrates authorial revision, as well as editorial tinkering, in one branch of a radiating series, a possibility that an editor must always take into account although, presumably being confined to the substantives, the choice of copy-text made on the basis of the accidentals is not thereby affected.

Reversed substantive authority going against the genetic relationship is illustrated in a certain number of manuscript reports that Crane sent from Cuba to the *New York Journal*. The evidence of the texts suggests that the *Journal* customarily put these reports on the wire to the *Chicago Tribune* and the *Philadelphia Press* using Crane's

Although only two extant documents radiate from a lost authority, something substantial can be done by informed selection of accidentals— no matter which document is chosen as copy-text—to recover the antecedent document from which each text independently derived. The more the number of witnesses contracts, the greater is the reliance on what may be called qualitative evidence; that is, the selection from variants in the two documents of the readings that appear to be more characteristic of the author's practice. The nature of the lost text being reconstituted is of some importance, of course, whether manuscript or typescript. If it is a typescript and its carbon, the common readings will represent only its authority, which will not necessarily always be in the style of the author; thus the eclectic selection of authorial characteristics in a qualitative manner in cases like 'The Price of the Harness' and 'An Indiana Campaign' assumed that in such cruxes the typescript had followed the manuscript. This may in part be an optimistic assumption, but in any event the odds favour the recovery of basic authority by this method better than could be attained by rigorously following the derived authority of only one document as copy-text. The greater the number of preserved radiating witnesses, the more quantitative evidence can assist and even correct the qualitative in distinguishing the actual readings of a lost intermediate document in cases where it may have diverged from the primary manuscript, as well, of course, as distinguishing the readings where it is plausible to believe that the intermediary in fact agreed with the manuscript. The editorial process is a complex one, but it is worth the effort in view of the greatly superior results that accrue in recovering what the author wrote, in all respects, in comparison to what could be obtained by a blindfold reliance on the authority of a single copy-text to the neglect of the equal authority of one or more other documents.

---

original manuscript before editing. The copy-desk would then go over the manuscript and alter it before it was set by the *Journal's* printers. Since the *Journal* text was set direct from the manuscript, its accidentals are one step closer to authority than those in the other newspapers where the telegraph operator has intervened. However, for the substantives the texts of these other newspapers, despite occasional corruption in transmission, may sometimes be purer than the copy-text *Journal* since when they agree against the *Journal* it is clear that they represent the reading of the manuscript.

In another interesting case Cora Crane made a typescript from the now lost manuscript of Crane's 'Great Boer Trek', one copy of which was sold to the *Cosmopolitan* magazine. The mate she retained and when after Crane's death she was sent a clipping of the *Cosmopolitan* she collated this typescript with the magazine text and entered in it the more prominent of what seem to be the alterations the magazine editor had made in the copy he printed. The copy-text of the typescript is genetically one step nearer to the manuscript than the *Cosmopolitan* but its substantives need to be purified from the unauthoritative annotations that stem from the magazine and do not represent Crane revisions in the copy sent out for sale.

In the examples I have given of the manner in which a critic can recover the text of a lost document from extant copies that radiate from it, the document has been an intermediary between the manuscript and the published texts like a syndicated printer's proof or a typescript and its carbon. Since with simple radiation from only one document (a typescript and its carbon counting as a single unit) we can always go back one step towards authority from the preserved versions, it follows that if the manuscript itself were the source from which two or more documents radiate, then the ultimate authority of the manuscript can be reconstructed. Obviously such cases are much rarer but they do occur. The evidence appears in Crane's story 'The Snake'. Crane sold the manuscript to Bacheller, who used it as the immediate copy for the proofs that were sent out to newspapers for publication in June 1896, and perhaps at the same time and place it was also set from the identical manuscript for publication in the *Pocket Magazine* for August. This we know, because the printer's-copy manuscript is preserved. The evidence is tricky, of course, when the lost manuscript is not preserved. We may suspect that a very short vignette called 'A Detail', for which we have only a draft manuscript that cannot represent the final holograph, parallels 'The Snake', for Bacheller syndicated it to the newspapers in August 1896 and printed it in the *Pocket Magazine* in November. There is not enough text for evidence to develop, but an editor can feel reasonably certain that when he recovers the printer's proof from the four observed newspapers and then conflates this text with the *Pocket Magazine* copy-text he will have substantially recovered the authority of the lost rewritten manuscript of 'A Detail'.

There are situations, however, in which the lost manuscript can be recovered from printed texts even when these were set from lost intermediaries. The principle involved is that one can always go one step in back of any two radiating texts whether these are both extant or both reconstructed, or one of each. A partial example occurs in Crane's Spanish-American War naval story 'The revenge of the *Adolphus*' which has a complex and amusing history. This story was published in the United States in October 1899 in *Collier's Weekly* and in December in England in the *Strand Magazine*. The printer's copy for these must have been a typescript and its carbon. However, after the copy had been sent off to America Crane sought the advice of the American Naval Attaché in London on his use of naval terms. The letter is preserved in which the attaché made a number of corrections not only in Crane's misuse of terminology but also in the conduct of several incidents of the plot which went against naval procedure and etiquette. Crane made most of these revisions in the copy for the *Strand* but he did not trouble to transmit notes of them to *Collier's* or to record them in his manuscript. Later, when he came to prepare copy for the collection *Wounds in the Rain* he found that he had in his possession only the original uncorrected manuscript. From this he had a fresh typescript prepared but he had mislaid the attaché's letter and had only a hazy memory of most of the comments. However, in this final version of the story he inserted what he remembered, often in a different form, of course; he inadvertently omitted quite a few of the previous revisions; and with a handful of stylistic changes, and a typescript error or two uncorrected, he sent the copy off to the book publisher in the United States.

But there is more to the history. The book publisher found that Crane's typescript was incomplete as received, and despairing of getting any satisfaction from Crane he ordered his printer to complete the story from a copy of the *Strand* that he was eventually able to locate in New York. This has a crucial effect on the story's conclusion, which differs in the American *Collier's Weekly* text from that in the *Strand* and, automatically, in the book. Which is Crane's intention? In every other place concurrence of the *Strand* and the book—both radiating from the manuscript through two independent typescripts—put against unique variation in *Collier's* establishes the authority of the readings.[33] But when the book derives from the *Strand* towards the end, its independent authority ceases and we have merely the evidence of simple radiation from the same typescript between the *Strand* and *Collier's*. To solve the two-text problem one notices that the *Strand* has a large illustration on its final page, and that the ending fits perfectly into this page with the Finis on an extra line at the foot. It becomes obvious that the longer *Collier's* ending (even though most critics would dislike it) is the only authoritative one since the English magazine editor must have cut the text in order to fit it into the last page without ordering the already manufactured illustration reduced in size or else running the story some half dozen lines over on to the next page. The book follows the *Strand's* truncated ending because it was not set from manuscript at this place. Although for various reasons connected with its superior accidentals the final form in the book is the most convenient copy-text, its version badly needs editing because it contains an ending that Crane did not write and its substantive text throughout is only an imperfect version of the *Strand's* earlier and more authoritative revision of the original text as found in *Collier's*. In its substantive readings, indeed, the book offers the least satisfactory text of the three, even though—in its accidentals—it is the best copy-text.

The recovery of the lost manuscript is what concerns us, however. Between the *Strand* and the *Collier's* texts the editor can make some shift to

33 Similarly, the agreement of *Collier's* and *Wounds in the Rain* against the *Strand* is authoritative, because of their independent transmission. Agreement of the *Strand* and *Collier's* against the book merely establishes the reading of the common typescript behind the two magazines.

recover a fair amount of the exact details of the typescript that underlies them both. In so far as the book version, set from an independent typescript, stands for its lost copy, it represents another line of the text radiating with the first typescript from the manuscript. By comparing the admittedly incomplete authority of the book, up to the point where it derives from the *Strand*, with the authority of the partly recovered typescript behind the two magazines, an editor can reduce the problem essentially to two typescripts radiating from the manuscript. Then since one can always progress one step farther back from two radiating documents, he can be relatively assured of manuscript authority in each respect of accidentals, as well as substantives, in which there is uniform agreement. When the agreement fails, then he can attempt a conjecture from his knowledge of Crane's style whether either reading is likely to represent manuscript authority. With the basic substantives and accidentals thus in some considerable part established, the editor can attack the separate problem of the substantive variation and can contrive a version that will with relatively few exceptions represent what Crane would have written in a revised fair copy with the attaché's letter before him, and his final stylistic revisions in mind as found in the book.

What makes the recovery of the manuscript less than satisfactory is the single book version as one arm of the radiating family tree since this book text cannot reproduce its typescript so faithfully as the recovery of the text of the first typescript from the magazines can be said to reproduce that copy.

My last illustration corrects this partial deficiency by offering four texts which radiate in pairs from two independent typescripts and thus provide the situation for a truly textbook recovery of the manuscript in something close to satisfactory detail, one incomparably superior to the evidence of any single witness. This situation is found in Crane's story 'The Wise Men', but the example I choose is Crane's more important story of the Battle of Velestino in the Greco-Turkish War, 'Death and the Child'.

'Death and the Child' was first published in two parts in the English magazine *Black and White* on the 5th and 12th of March 1898 and a fortnight later in the United States in *Harper's Weekly*. Within the same year it became part of the collection of tales *The Open Boat* published by Heinemann in England in one form, and by Doubleday, McClure in the United States in another form and in a different typesetting and arrangement. The evidence of the readings leaves no doubt that the *Black and White* and the Heinemann *Open Boat* texts in England radiate from a typescript and its carbon stemming from the manuscript. Correspondingly, the American line of *Harper's Weekly* and the Doubleday, McClure *Open Boat* radiate from a different typescript and carbon, made up independently at a different time from the manuscript. Although the substantive readings have little or nothing to do with the choice of copy-text, some indication of the editorial problem may be of interest. Given this family tree an editor can discard immediately any unique substantive variant once he has assured himself—as is the case here—that no version was proof-corrected by the author. Hence thirteen unique verbal differences from all the rest in the Heinemann *Open Boat*, eight from *Black and White*, five in *Harper's Weekly*, and an amazing number of twenty-one in the American *Open Boat*, or a total of forty-seven substantive variants in the four authorities, can be removed from any serious consideration. Once this is done, and the ground cleared in a manner impossible unless the editor has first established the family tree of these four texts, only ten substantive readings occur in which the two members of the English line agree against the two members of the American line. Clearly these are alterations of the manuscript that derive from one or other of the two different typescripts. With this history an editor can be comforted that he is not dealing with the matter of relative authority as in the readings of a primary edition and the readings of a revision;[34] instead, as between these ten readings in each case one must be wrong and the other right—a much simpler problem and one that critical judgement one hopes may be able to solve correctly in at least the majority of the variants. The reduction of fifty-seven substantive variants to ten isolated examples is a testimony to the powers of bibliographical analysis in paving the way for the ultimate critical inquiry.

The question of copy-text rests on the accidentals, however, and here the critic is faced with a much more difficult situation. It is to be anticipated that in some respects each of the two textual lines will agree within itself when both compositors followed the typescript copy in the same manner but that considerable disagreement can also be expected because of differences in house styling even within the same country. The rough statistics bear out this expectation. For example, in punctuation alone the

34 By *relative authority* I mean not those cases in which a revised edition may be said to correct the earlier edition's reading but instead to revise it; that is, both readings have the authority of the writer's full intention. The earlier was what he intended to write at the time: later, he decided to express himself in a different manner. When the revision may seem relatively indifferent, the problem of compositorial sophistication always arises, especially when the process of revision continues on a diminishing scale in later editions, as in the second, third, and fourth editions of Fielding's *Joseph Andrews*. Here at least the revising was always performed by annotation of the immediately preceding edition. But in cases such as the *Spectator* and the Preface to Johnson's *Dictionary* the editorial problem of relative authority may grow acute when the author revised a later edition after also revising the second, but used a copy of the first so that he neglected to take into account his second-edition alterations. See for examples, Donald F. Bond, 'The Text of the *Spectator*', *SB*, v (1952), 109–28, and W. R. Keast, 'The Preface to *A Dictionary of the English Language*: Johnson's revision and the establishment of the text', *ibid.*, pp. 129–46.

English line agrees in its two members against the two of the American line about fifty times. On the other hand, *Black and White* has at least fifty-two punctuation variants that are unique to it against the other three, the Heinemann edition has forty-one, *Harper's Weekly* is low with twenty-nine, and the Doubleday *Open Boat* high with eighty-three. Somewhat over 200 punctuation variants, therefore, are found in only one authority where the other three agree, as against about fifty in which the two lines disagree. On the other hand, to indicate how chance may operate in the matter of compositorial styling, the two magazines *Black and White* and *Harper's Weekly*, in different lines, agree with each other in punctuation variants against the two books some eighteen times, and *Black and White* and the American book agree against *Harper's* and the Heinemann book also some eighteen times. In essence even though statistics do not by any means always provide an acceptable answer, it is true that in punctuation alone some 285 variants in the four authorities can be reduced to little more than fifty on which qualitative analysis can then operate. The other problems in accidentals other than punctuation can be similarly reduced.

After performing the crucial textual analysis that led to the establishment of the genetic relationships or family tree of the four authorities, what an editor does is to recover to the extent of the evidence the details of the lost typescript behind *Black and White* and the Heinemann *Open Boat* and then the details of the lost typescript behind *Harper's* and the American *Open Boat* collection. The basis for such a recovery is of course the concurrences both of accidentals as well as substantives within the two members of each branch of the family tree. When the English magazine and book disagree, or the American magazine and book, the variant is compared with the two authorities of the opposite line, and in all 200 cases when they concur with one or other variant the unique reading is discarded and the variant within the branch that agrees with the yoked readings of the other branch is added to the authority of the reconstructed typescript. In this manner the recovery of each typescript is built up in its details on what may be called a bibliographical basis. Two areas of decision then remain. In the first, an accidental in one line is variant, and one member of each line agrees with a member of the other in the variant. That is, a semicolon might appear in *Black and White* and in the Doubleday *Open Boat* versus a comma in the Heinemann *Open Boat* and *Harper's Weekly*. Analysis of the approximately thirty-six punctuation variants of this nature suggests that the variation is due to compositorial styling and very little if at all to variation in the two basic typescripts. This being so, qualitative analysis is greatly aided, for it is possible to learn something about the habits of the compositors who set these four authorities and to notice the specific ways in which they are likely to diverge from copy, with especial reference to their unique variants. These cases, then, can mostly be decided on a conjectural basis but with fair certainty, and the recovered reading of each line can be added to the general concurrences. In this manner more of the details of each typescript can be built up until we reach the accidental variants in which the two lines agree against each other, as in the fifty punctuation variants in this category. Since these isolated variants are now not to be attributed to the printing process except as they may be presumed to stem from fidelity to copy by each of the four compositors, they may be taken to represent the variant readings of each typescript. Bibliographical analysis having reached this point can go no farther, and it is up to the editor exercising his critical judgement to choose among these variants (without regard for his copy-text) whichever pairs he thinks were actually the manuscript readings. In this case, of course, the reading of the typescript that appears to coincide most closely with Crane's usual practices is more likely to reproduce the manuscript than the other.

It should be clear that the process of reconstructing each typescript is dependent upon three factors: first, the agreement of its two radiating members with each other; second, the agreement of one of its members with both of the authorities in the opposite line (these two being factual); and third the conjectural placement of cross-variation between the two lines in one or the other branch as more faithfully representing its typescript. Only this minority cross-variation (usually to be settled without too much difficulty) prevents the perfect and demonstrable reconstruction of the antecedent documents—the typescripts—on the one hand behind the *Black and White* and Heinemann collection, and on the other hand behind the *Harper's* and the Doubleday, McClure collection.[35] Once these two documents are in existence in their recovered forms, they in turn can be compared with each other and the continued reconstruction progress one step farther back, which brings us to the manuscript itself. All common details between the two typescripts may be taken as characteristic of the manuscript; these are in the majority. Only the minority group of

35 It is, of course, the opportunity to utilize the evidence of one branch to decide problems in the other that permits this almost physically exact reconstruction of the respective typescripts. If the story had never been published in the United States, for instance, then when *Black and White* and Heinemann disagree only qualitative evidence could conjecturally decide between the variants. But in 'Death and the Child' and (although to a lesser degree) in 'The Revenge of the *Adolphus*', disagreement in one line can be checked against the evidence of the other. In the majority of cases one element in the disagreement will prove to be unique and therefore an unauthoritative compositorial variant. Only in the one or two cases of complete or quadripartite disagreement, and in the cross-variation between lines, need conjecture supplement fact in order to complete the detailed reconstruction.

disagreements (a small portion of the total) needs the application of critical judgement, working through qualitative evidence, to complete the process by informed conjecture.

What will be printed in the modern edition is the recovered manuscript, only in small part conjectural. Of course this text will be completely eclectic, drawn in varying degrees from each of the four documents according to their specific authority in each isolated detail in question. The end product cannot help being more faithful to the author's intentions both for accidentals and for substantives than are any of the four witnesses. It should also be clear that this edited text is constructed without the least regard paid to questions of copy-text: no single document could properly serve as the starting-point for the operational recovery of the manuscript. In a manner unknown for texts in linear relationships and therefore essentially derived, the analysis of radiation removes the copy-text as the foundation of the edited text at the beginning of the editorial process and places it as the final and indifferent choice when the apparatus which is to hang on the copy-text comes to be made up.[36]

The choice of copy-text, then, is not integral to the editing of radiating documents except in some small part when they are at different removes from the manuscript. The modern text that results is not based on a specific copy-text in the form of an extant document except as a convenience for the apparatus. Instead, the true text is formulated from the reconstructed document that is one step farther back in the chain of transmission from the earliest extant document on that chain. This recovered text may be some intermediate document when as in 'A Grey Sleeve' and 'The Bride Comes to Yellow Sky' the radiation is not from the manu-

36 Greg's statement that the adoption of a copy-text is only a convenience—sometimes quoted out of context—is of quite a different order from the point made here. His words are, 'Since the adoption of a copy-text is a matter of convenience rather than of principle—being imposed on us either by linguistic circumstances or our own philological ignorance—it follows that there is no reason for treating it as sacrosanct, even apart from the question of substantive variation' (*SB*, iii. 29–30). What Greg meant here by *principle* was not the editorial principle he was enunciating in his rationale but instead the 'reliance on one particular authority [which] results from the desire for an objective theory of text-construction and a distrust, often no doubt justified, of the operation of individual judgement' (p. 28); in short, the 'undue deference to the copy-text' that results in considerable part from the application of Lachmann's methods. Hence the copy-text could be called a *convenience* because it must not be taken as 'some arbitrary canon', a course that will 'produce, not editions of their author's works at all, but only editions of particular authorities for those works, a course that may be perfectly legitimate in itself, but was not the one they were professedly pursuing'. The *convenience* of the copy-text results, then, only because in Elizabethan works we do not know enough about the language and its forms to reconstruct the author's manuscript from the documentary evidence.

script itself. On the other hand, when the extant texts stem from two lost documents that themselves radiate from the original manuscript,[37] to the extent that these lost intermediate texts can be reconstructed the ultimate common original behind them can be recovered, imperfectly in 'The Revenge of the *Adolphus*' but with something close to exactness in 'Death and the Child' and 'The Wise Men'. As a consequence, the linear genetic relationship of texts does not decide the copy-text as in extant editions derived one from another; on the contrary, the choice of copy-text has no connection with the methodology of editing and of authority. The choice is indifferent and is governed chiefly by which copy-text will produce the most compact and convenient apparatus from which the reader can reconstruct the details of the radiating documents.

Sir Walter Greg is as sound as a—let us say, Swiss franc—in his rationale of copy-text and its importance as the crucial element in the editing of extant texts in a derived relationship and especially for texts in which a later derived edition has been revised, like *Tom Jones*. He is also completely authoritative for texts in which radiation has produced revision or alteration in the lost pre-printing stage but a revised printer's copy has been manufactured by altering an extant document to accord with the other authority, as in *Othello* or *Troilus and Cressida* where a derived relationship can be established between the primary and the altered extant editions. Moreover, no matter what the conditions, Greg's revolutionary insistence on the separate treatment of the respective and quite distinct authority of the substantives and the accidentals in a text is always completely valid save in such special circumstances as are represented by

37 An interesting footnote on one of the many differences in drawing family trees between modern and classical or medieval manuscript texts is provided in A. A. Hill's logical dictum ('Some postulates for distributional studies of texts', *SB*, iii [1950–1], 90) that it is inadmissible to draw a manuscript tree in the form

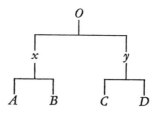

since such a tree should be reduced to a two-text situation in which it will always be assumed that either *x* or *y* is identical with *O*. Yet because of the bibliographical probability that documents will be in contiguous or immediate relationship, precisely this tree as rejected for manuscript studies is the one that must be drawn for Crane's 'Death and the Child' and also for his story 'The Wise Men'. Moreover, in these stories from the four extant documents *A–D* both *x* and *y* can be recovered, and also from them the major part of the text of *O* with a minimum of conjecture, even for accidentals.

Every Man in his Humour, or Walt Whitman, and perhaps some of Henry James.

My concern here has been to suggest that in modern times, and especially after the invention of the typewriter, many texts will radiate with no derived relationship between their extant forms. To these changed conditions when identified—which is the business of the textual critic—it is inappropriate to attempt to apply Greg's linear-derived rationale.[38] Such a procedure would establish a real tyranny of the copy-text and would destroy the practicability of recovering the accidentals as well as the substantives of the lost ancestor document at one and sometimes even at two removes from the extant texts, a concept and a methodology that I make bold to claim is one of the original contributions (although as yet largely unutilized) of modern textual criticism.[39]

38 This is true without qualification when the radiation is immediate and equidistant. When the radiation is not equidistant, as in the two branches of 'An Indiana Campaign' (one of which stems directly from the typescript and the other through intermediate proof-sheets set from the typescript), then genetic considerations may influence the choice of copy-text, as Greg would advise, but not the treatment of the copy-text accidentals that the linear rationale demands.

39 That is, of textual criticism devoted not to classical and medieval (or Renaissance) radiating texts but to documents susceptible of bibliographical analysis. The theory of radiation is, of course, no news to manuscript scholars of the past. But the conditions I have outlined for the textual treatment of modern authors have about as many points of difference as of similarity with conventional manuscript investigation. From these I should select two of particular pertinence, both intimately related to the fact that in bibliographical investigation, one may, usually with perfect propriety, assume immediate relationship between two documents. When in manuscript studies gaps that may include a large number of lost documents occur, two important consequences follow. First, no attempt can be made to recover the accidentals of any common lost ancestor, for the distance is usually too great for evidence to operate. Thus the basic reasons for the scholarly insistence on 'old-spelling' texts of more modern authors that are at the heart of McKerrow's and Greg's editorial theories are impossible to implement except on a purely artificial basis. To arrive as close as the extant documents permit at what would have been an authorial fair copy is an ideal fruitless to contemplate on any evidence that can properly be called authoritative. Second, the unknown distances between documents, and the conditions of manufacture, give rise to problems of contamination of authority in the substantives that are unknown, ordinarily, in printed texts except in cases like *Hamlet* or *Othello* where the conditions are so different as scarcely to be worth mentioning as a possible parallel. In considerable part because of this special problem of contamination, the techniques of the recovery of unauthoritative ancestral substantives vary so considerably as to constitute two quite separate disciplines.

Remarks on Eclectic Texts

AS WITH SO MANY commonly used but little analyzed concepts, one must grope for a definition of eclecticism in editing among popular commonplaces and general scholarly usage—not always in a technical or an informed sense—instead of appealing to a logically shaped thesis agreed upon by textual critics. Popularly, an eclectic text may be any text in which readings different from those of the document serving as the basis for the edition have selectively been admitted from other sources as substitutes for originals that, conjecturally, have been transmitted in error. This is a lengthy way of saying that any text admitting emendation of error is necessarily eclectic in the purest sense, for the principle of choice has been invoked. If we were to rest here, however, we should not be much forwarder. On the one hand we should have photographic or type facsimiles of documents, and we should also admit to this group diplomatic reprints,[1] in which no choice is given the editor to substitute readings from other documents or from editorial tradition. His function is

* An abridged form of this paper was read at a Conference on Editorial Problems at the Villa Serbelloni Study and Conference Center, Bellagio, Italy, 20–25 September 1973. Reprinted from *PROOF: The Yearbook of American Bibliographical and Textual Studies*, edited by Joseph Katz, 4 (1974), 13–58, by permission of Joseph Katz, Copyright © 1974 by Joseph Katz.

1 A diplomatic reprint may be defined as an exact transcript of a document but the text run on without consideration for the original line and page endings, whereas a type facsimile is a line-for-line and page-for-page reproduction of the original. No strict rules for such diplomatic reprints have been laid down, in fact, except for the requirement of absolute fidelity to the transcription of the substantives and accidentals of the document without anything that could properly be called emendation of the text itself as distinguished from some few of its formal typographical details. Offhand, it seems to me that a diplomatic reprint of a printed text may normalize the typography by ignoring, for example, the reproduction of display and ornamental capitals, variant spacing, and such irregularities as wrong-font types, whereas these must be reproduced in a type facsimile. The diplomatic text, of course, will not reproduce running-titles and paginal numbering or signature and catchword notation in the original, also required in a type facsimile. However, both forms of reproduction should be as responsible as a photographic facsimile for providing records of press-variation during the course of printing, for which see footnote 2 below.

to make available to scholars in completely trustworthy form the exact details of the text of a particular document, errors and all, to serve as a substitute in one's own study for the manuscript or book that may be preserved in some distant or inaccessible library. Such reprint and facsimile[2] editions are scholarly tools but they have little or no appeal to the usual literary critic, historian, or general reader, who ordinarily will want to work with a closer approximation of what the author intended, at least verbally, than such exact reprints furnish—paradoxical as such a statement may sound, for what can be more authoritative than authority? If we hold to McKerrow's necessarily strict and narrow definition of authority, the answer is necessarily, 'nothing'. McKerrow rightly points out that authority can reside only in authoritative documents, that is, in texts that descend in some direct line from the author and do not, as a whole,[3] derive from other texts without the infusion of independent au-

2 The emphasis should be on the trustworthiness of the form, which in turn is as much the product of the facsimile process as of the editor. Fine-screen offset, which has now displaced collotype for all practical scholarly purposes, is not susceptible of retouching that will alter negatives of the photographed document. On the other hand, the cheaper lithographic process that produced the inaccurate Pretorius facsimiles of Shakespeare quartos was peculiarly liable to retouching that altered the text, and a general suspicion has attached itself to the similarly produced Methuen Shakespeare Folios because of a few identified examples of manipulation. An editor, of course, in collotype or fine-screen offset may substitute leaves without warning from another copy to procure more sightly examples (as in the Lee Folio facsimile) and thus create bibliographical monstrosities because of clashing results among textual states of press-variation. Even when editors of lithographic reproductions are themselves guiltless but are negligent in supervision, serious faults may occur. The facsimile of the Yale First Folio was consistently retouched by a series of ignorant underlings, it would seem. For the extraordinary details of this modern venture, see my review in *Modern Philology*, 53 (1955), 50–57. Consistent principles for the treatment of press-variant formes must also be expected in a photographic facsimile, as well as in a type facsimile and diplomatic reprint. On this point one may consult 'The Problem of the Variant Forme in Facsimile Editions,' *The Library*, 5th ser., 7 (1952), 262–272, although C. J. K. Hinman's procedures in his Norton facsimile of the Shakespeare First Folio (1968) call for serious consideration as dealing successfully with the problems found in that document, less acute than may be encountered elsewhere.

3 'As a whole' is inserted here to take account of the common authorial practice of annotating an already printed edition to form the printer's copy for a revision instead of furnishing the printer with the manuscript from which the annotation was being drawn. Such a revised text is, of course, of mixed authority since part of it is derived and part of it is authoritative, consisting of the author's alterations—at least as reflected in the manuscript being used for the purpose. Thus mixed texts are susceptible of considerable variety. A scribe may copy a holograph manuscript and the author then look it over with greater or lesser care to make what corrections and revisions occur to him. This situation is also created when an author's copy is given to a professional typist. Marked copies of any non-holographic derived form, in short, having passed through another hand in a vital part of the transmission from holograph (or author's

Textual Criticism and Editing

thorial alteration whether directly or through some intermediary. If this is so—and I think textual critics are unwise if they write of authority in any other terms—it follows, as McKerrow points out, that even obvious errors are authoritative and their corrections, no matter how judicious, are without authority according to the definition.[4]

The tribe of editors has grown up to fulfill the requirements of the majority of scholarly purchasers of texts for general purposes, those who find more useful to their needs a text soundly corrected by editorial expertise than one of pure documentary authority with all its errors. Depending upon the nature and extent of the apparatus, it may not be a misnomer to state on the title page that the scholar who has supervised the production of a photographic or type facsimile has 'edited' it, but the strict view of an editor is one who edits, that is, one who does his best to restore the purity of the author's text from the imperfection of the preserved transmissional documents even when these may include the author's holograph.[5] In the simplest cases this restriction of meaning may require no more than enlightened emendation of established errors in the original. In the most complex, when more than one authoritative document is preserved, editing may involve highly sophisticated critical and bibliographical choices among the various authorities not only to weed out error in the basic document chosen to represent the text, in the main, but also to ensure that the latest—if possible the final—readings representing the author's most comprehensive intentions have been introduced.

---

own typescript, its equivalent) are only rarely exact reproductions of the original. Moreover, the corrections and revisions an author may make in such a document are not likely to restore in every detail the exactness of the original from the styling of the transcriber, or even all of his significant verbal departures from copy. When a non-authorial hand annotates the document by reference to some source of authority, the situation is exacerbated. Indeed, unless the author furnished the document on which annotation is to be based, it is possible that inferior readings may enter the text under the guise of revision. That is, the scribe may take as his authority what is actually a document early in the history of the text and therefore in a state that the author had rejected. Hence a non-authorial intermediary in the revision of a text is always subject to suspicion not alone on questions of his accuracy but also because the authority of the documents used may be in doubt.

4 R. B. McKerrow, *Prolegomena to the Oxford Shakespeare* (Clarendon Press, 1939), p. 12.

5 The more useful meanings of 'edit' are often obscured in these days of commercial scholarship by the misapplication of the term on titlepages of paperback reprints, stated to be 'Edited by Professor X.' It is rare that this 'editing' consists in more than the writing of a popular introduction and the furnishing the printer with some previous edition out of copyright, without investigation of its readings and usually with no alterations. Most readers of these paperbacks do not understand the distinction and believe the text has a value that it does not possess.

The aim of a critical edition, remarks McKerrow, is to reconstruct as nearly as is possible from the preserved documents what would have been an author's careful fair copy of his work.[6] One must comment that this ideal edition envisages a careful fair copy of the latest and most comprehensive form and in any case is a theoretical concept although a generally useful one even in cases where an author has revised proof after submitting a careful fair copy to the printer. In most examples the deficiencies of the preserved documents (especially if printed) will prevent a reconstruction as minute as the recovery of every detail of the accidentals of an author's lost holograph; nevertheless, a fully worth-while result may usually be obtained for the substantives and enough progress made with the accidentals to justify the effort.[7] For instance, when Henry Fielding's publisher gave him a copy of the third edition of *Tom Jones* to annotate as printer's copy for the revised fourth edition, the decision to choose the third edition was made on practical grounds, for the fourth was to be a general paginal reprint of the third, which in its turn had been a typographically condensed version in four volumes of the six volumes of the first and second editions. It was fortunate that the third was a reprint of the first, not of the second, edition, but even so it had created fresh errors of its own which Fielding failed to correct so that these unauthoritative variants became inextricably mixed in the fourth edition with Fielding's own revisions. Not quite inextricably, of course, when the work is properly edited, for these errors can be isolated and removed by a scholar who can exercise more care than did Fielding in surveying the text. Moreover, since Fielding did not read proof on the fourth edition, apparently, new mistakes by the compositors were added to the existing underlay of error. It follows that the first step in the process of clarifying the text is for the editor to reconstruct as best he can the annotated copy of the third edition as it left Fieleding's hands for the printer. But he may not stop there, for he must then do what the author did not do, which is to remove the third-edition errors that Fielding had perpetuated by passing them over without knowing that these were indeed printer's variants from his original manuscript as it had been represented by the first edition.

For substantives, therefore, an editor in effect creates a text that would have resulted if Fielding had annotated a copy of the purer first instead of the more corrupt third edition. If he then follows Sir Walter Greg's

6 *Prolegomena,* p. 6.

7 *Substantives* are the words of a text as meaningful units. The *accidents* of a text— or its *accidentals*—are the spellings, capitalizations, punctuation, word-division, contractions, and emphases in which these substantives are clothed. Of course, on occasion an accidental can have a vital effect on the transmission of meaning, even changing white to black, in which case it is convenient to distinguish it as a semi-substantive.

principles of copy-text,[8] as he should for this book, he will reject all the accidentals in the fourth edition that in his opinion vary from the first because of the printer,[9] and thus he will end by substituting the revised fourth-edition variant substantives for those of the first but incorporating them in the texture of the spelling, punctuation, capitalization, word division, contraction, and emphasis of the most authoritative document for these, the first edition set directly from holograph. Behind this edition he cannot go in respect to these accidentals, but experience suggests that they will retain a number of personal characteristics of the author that are worn away by the successive restylings of later editions. Finally, the editor must attack the problem of printer's errors in the first edition passed on to the third and unaltered in the fourth; having emended these and conservatively clarified the first-edition accidental texture when faulty according to its own standards, he can offer an ideal text of Fielding's last recorded intentions. This will not be an exact reconstruction of what a careful fair-copy holograph would have been like (for the original holograph is lost that would have furnished the basis for such a detailed recovery), but instead the closest reconstitution that the preserved documents permit of what would have been its major features, generally comprehensive for the substantives and at least approximate for the accidentals. When the intermediate step of reconstructing the annotated third edition has progressed to the final transfer of the identified revisions to make up a hypothetical reconstruction of the similar annotation of a first edition, the modern critical edition enters the realm of the ideal and leaves the evidential world of the material in which such a document never existed. But since McKerrow's definition of a critical edition is itself an ideal and even in the simplest cases of single-text authority requires that process of reconstruction furnished by emendation, the difference is one only of degree and not of kind. If one swallows the gnat, one might as well swallow the camel.

It is obvious that a critical text of *Tom Jones* is at a far remove from any text that a type or photographic facsimile could present. If one reproduced the first edition, not alone its compositorial errors would be embalmed but also all of Fielding's desired later revisions would be omitted. If one reproduced the fourth edition, the reader would un-

---

8 'The Rationale of Copy-Text,' *Studies in Bibliography*, 3 (1950–51), 19–36, reprinted in W. W. Greg, *Collected Papers*, ed. J. C. Maxwell (1966), pp. 374–391. This classic and definitive statement for early texts is resurveyed, principally for its pertinence to modern conditions, in 'Multiple Authority: New Problems and Concepts of Copy-Text,' *The Library*, 5 ser., 27 (1972), 81–115.

9 Less, of course, all necessary corrections made either in the terminal second or in the derived third edition, regardless of their source when they are of a nature as to be made in normal course and independently in any careful scholarly edition of the work.

wittingly accept scores of plausible third-edition corruptions as part of the authorial intention,[10] as well as fresh compositorial errors, and in addition a texture of accidentals at three removes from those of the holograph. Also, a part of the Man of the Hill episode that by an accident was unrevised would be presented in the midst of a revised edition.[11] A reprint edition, or a facsimile, of the first edition, then, would give a reasonably but not fully accurate picture of Fielding's original intentions (provided the errata list variants were substituted in the first five volumes for the original misprints or rejected readings) but would be silent on his more sophisticated stylistic and artistic second thoughts. A reprint of the only fully revised edition, the fourth, would provide these final intentions (except for the Man of the Hill) but so intermixed with an accumulation of transmissional error as to be an untrustworthy witness for critical study. Some critics—especially among the amateur explorers of the jungles of textual criticism of American literature, but also in England—would adopt the aesthetic attitude that each of the two editions is an artistic entity in itself that must be preserved without the intermingling of eclectic editing that joins the best features of both.[12] *Tom Jones* is a long novel. One may grant that there could be a pleasure in reading both versions separately for whatever flavor and general impressions an aesthetic critic might absorb on an overall basis for each text. (Precious little, in fact.) But *Tom Jones* is not *Roderick Hudson* or *The Portrait of a Lady* and the revisions of its fourth edition have quite other purposes than the thorough reworking of concept and texture that Henry James performed on his early work for the New York Edition. There is no argument that some of these James novels require parallel texts or separate editions; but neither a text of the first nor of the fourth edition of *Tom Jones* (without

10 That these errors would have been approved by Fielding since he passed them (although in ignorance) is a textual concept sometimes advanced in other connections but one that logically dwells in cloud-cuckoo-land. The case is quite different from Pound's conscious and expressed preference (whether or not perverse) in one of the *Cantos* for a printer's error over what he had written and his incorporation in later editions of this originally unauthoritative variant now given authority.

11 The complex history of *Tom Jones,* and its implications, will be found in the Wesleyan Edition of Fielding, edited by F. Bowers with Critical Introduction and Commentary by Martin C. Battestin (1974).

12 This extreme view about works of American literature is adopted by Donald Pizer in 'On the Editing of Modern American Texts,' *Bulletin of the New York Public Library,* 75 (March, 1971), 149–150. For answers to this rejection of eclectic texts as scholarly tools, see Norman Grabo, 'Pizer on Copy-Text,' *NYPLB,* 75 (April, 1971), 171–173; Hershel Parker, 'In Defense of Copy-Text Editing,' *NYPLB,* 75 (October, 1971); and Bowers, 'Multiple Authority,' *op. cit.,* pp. 86–87, fn. 11. See also footnote 28 below. For other anti-eclectic arguments, see Pizer in *Fifteen American Authors before 1900,* ed. R. A. Rees and E. N. Harbert (1971), p. 100, and *MP,* 68 (1970), 212–214.

a table of variants that for the accidentals would be impossible) would be suitable for detailed study of the work as a whole. Thus it is probable that ordinary mortals will continue to prefer McKerrow's concept of an ideal edition that attempts to offer a composite text of *Tom Jones* that is closest to what the author would have secured if the printer had produced an exact corrected reprint of the first edition that incorporated his later revisions. This is not the equivalent in all its details of an authorial fair copy, but it is the farthest reach in the pursuit of this ideal that the preserved documents permit. Literary or other works so different in their forms in different editions as to represent quite distinctive artistic concepts are not here in question,[13] and textual theories based on their unique status merely serve to muddy the waters.

Not all texts by any means require the eclectic treatment suggested here as necessary for *Tom Jones*. The question then arises whether every text to which the McKerrow doctrine of ideal edition can be applied is necessarily eclectic. I suggest that such application creates too broad a criterion to be useful. It is true that viewed with extreme narrowness any text that admits emendation is eclectic in comparison with the rigorously non-emending principle applied to facsimile or diplomatic-reprint texts. But the spectrum of edited texts is too broad in its variety for any one point of view to be valid, even though it can be argued, and I think successfully, that it is proper to apply the McKerrow definition of ideal edition to the most limited textual situation of all, that in which only a single edition (or document) exists, for any editorial alteration of the copy-text here would certainly represent an attempt to restore readings that the editor believed were correct and therefore would have appeared in a careful authorial fair copy.

We may start with the general proposition that an eclectic text should be defined more narrowly than the admission of alteration from some external source. The first step in the process of definition is to look into the varieties of emendation made in single-text works—that is, material that has been found to exist in no more than a single authoritative document. If only one early edition of the text has been published, emendations will necessarily come from the editorial tradition. Those who mistrust eclec-

---

13 Not in question here or elsewhere in the present study is the special problem of modern plays and the manner in which the original text accepted by the producer will be substantially rewritten in a communal manner on the battlefield of rehearsals, so much so indeed that a dramatist may feel impelled to publish his own 'literary' version of the play in competition with that of the final acting script. For a discussion of the problems and some illustrations, see L. A. Beaurline, 'The Glass Menagerie: From Story to Play,' *Modern Drama*, 8 (1965), 142–149; but especially 'The Director, the Script, and Author's Revisions: A Critical Problem,' *Papers in Dramatic Theory and Criticism*, edited by D. M. Knauf (1969), pp. 78–91.

ticism are not ordinarily perturbed by such emendation,[14] but it might be possible to regard as an eclectic operation an editorial choice of variants drawn from other early editions although these are reprints without authority. Here we ought to be clearsighted enough to admit that, *au fond*, no real distinction holds between an editor's own emendations not found in some documentary source and those that are present in early though unauthoritative forms of the text as, for instance, in Shakespeare's Second, Third, and Fourth Folios. The notion that early forms of a text, even though mere reprints, have some vague 'secondary authority' was prevalent in eighteenth-century Shakespearean textual criticism when the derivation of the printed texts one from another was not really understood and had not been established. But authority is authority. Authority can derive only from the author. Since neither Shakespeare himself nor independently derived forms of his papers had anything to do with the Second Folio text of *All's Well That Ends Well*, it makes no basic difference for the value or the rightness of the emendation whether the First Folio error *there was never Virgin goe, till virginitie was first lost* (TLN 133– 134) is corrected to *never Virgin got* by some editor's own estimate of the sense or else by that of the Second Folio compositor's. Since I have a respect for the historical details of the transmission of a text, I should myself always record the Second Folio as the originator of the corrected reading—one, incidentally, which has never been challenged—but in no sense should such a notation be taken to imply that the Second Folio gives the emendation any more weight in the conjectural recovery of the word in Shakespeare's manuscript than, for instance, Theobald's unchallenged *loneliness* for the reading of the first four Folios, *now I see | The mistris of your louelinesse* [i.e., *lovelinesse*], *and find your salt teares head* (TLN 497–499). In either case one must apply McKerrow's strict definition of authority as limited to what an authoritative document reads, whether sense or nonsense. In this light whether the Second Folio or an eighteenth-century editor conjectures that *got* and *loneliness* are the right readings has no bearing whatever on the question of their correctness, for in such a case correctness and demonstrable authority are not synonymous.

If simple substantive emendation of a single-text authority is not to be taken as producing eclecticism except in the very limited sense that the strict reprint pattern has been broken, then of course the correction of faulty accidentals in a similar manner must come under the same head. Most editors of old-spelling editions content themselves with the cor-

14 In fact, it is interesting to contemplate how much eclectic editing of Shakespeare (where it is the normal method) is swallowed without comment by the most rigid adherents of faithful reprints of one authority in American literature and among English scholars in relation to nineteenth-century works. *Hamlet* and *King Lear* are excellent examples of eclectic texts constructed from multiple authority.

rection of what appear to be errors and of serious ambiguities that might puzzle even an informed reader. In some texts, however, another kind of correction is possible. McKerrow once speculated on the possibility of normalizing Shakespearean accidentals not by modernizing but by a system that would bring them into agreement according to their own standard; but he concluded that such a feat was impossible because of our lack of sufficient linguistic or philological knowledge to perform the task. This passage is one of several in the *Prolegomena* that exhibit what may be some basic confusion of idea or else an insufficiently worked-out though defensible notion.

I have long been interested in the problem of the limited normalization possible both in early and in late texts and my sympathies lie in this direction. But in the Elizabethan period the lack of uniformity of spelling found in almost every author makes desperate any attempt, at least in a single-text work, to penetrate the screen of possible scribal transcription and then of the styling of perhaps several compositors working on the same text.[15] Even a project to normalize the accidental characteristics of a single compositor would be defeated by the hard fact that most compositors in the sixteenth and early seventeenth centuries in England had relatively few invariable spellings when options were open, although they used a number of more or less preferential forms, and their punctuation system was on occasion so much affected by the relative quantity of sorts in the typecases as to make the distinction, say, between a semicolon and a colon sometimes as much a matter of mechanical supply as of rhetorical convention. If Compositor B in the First Folio *Julius Caesar* sets an apostrophe in *'tis* with relative consistency but omits perhaps two or three, I see no harm in supplying the few missing ones by recorded emendation, although I would see harm in an old-spelling text if he had had no conviction in the matter or had had even just a general preference for the apostrophe. We have no means, of course, of knowing whether or not the apostrophe in *'tis* was customary in the manuscript of *Julius Caesar* from which Compositor B was setting. Even if we did we should be no wiser about Shakespeare's own practice, for the printer's-copy manuscript was almost certainly a scribal one except, just possibly, for one or

15 Actually, the presence of several compositors offers evidence not otherwise available to penetrate to some degree the characteristics of the underlying copy if one makes the assumption that common characteristics result from common copy, at least when these characteristics are normally variable according to compositors. For example, in Shakespeare's *Measure for Measure* in the First Folio, set by compositors from idiosyncratic copy transcribed by Ralph Crane, each compositor exhibits the frequent use of parentheses and the occasional Jonsonian apostrophus known to be characteristic of Crane. Thus the case is stronger for an underlying Crane manuscript than if only one compositor had set the play, for it would then have to be demonstrated that these were not this particular compositor's own characteristics that he had imposed on the copy.

two hundred lines of holograph in three revised sections. Thus if one added an apostrophe or two to make B consistent, in no sense could one believe in the recovery of the lost holograph, as one does in substituting *got* for *goe* in *All's Well*. Instead, one is merely normalizing a minor feature of the accidentals to make it accord with the usual compositorial pattern. An editor's ability to do anything significant in this direction in a Shakespearean text is at present strictly limited. As for the possibilities of true reconstruction, few early authors have left us sufficient holograph material to serve as a proper basis for selection of their accidental characteristics from the conflicting evidence presented in the prints. McKerrow, however, seems to have been thinking less of an authentic reconstruction of authorial characteristics than of the possibility of adopting a kind of standard Elizabethan that could be applied to any author, somewhat in the manner that editors may normalize Middle English texts. The virtues of such normalization are arguable, and McKerrow never took the subject seriously enough to move beyond his speculative remark. (The edition of Samuel Johnson published by the Yale University Press has drifted unsystematically in this direction with deleterious results, although it is evident that the editors have in fact been concerned with partially modernizing the text and not with standardizing it according to eighteenth-century practices.[16]

On the contrary, once the language and its accidentals have become relatively standardized by the nineteenth century, certain forms of normalization may be contemplated in 'old-spelling'[17] texts when enough manuscripts of the author close to the date are preserved to give an editor confidence that in at least some features (although by no means in all) he can recover the characteristics of an underlying lost holograph. I am not suggesting that an editor rewrite the text in respect to its accidentals as

16 As another example of fruitless attempt at normalizing an Elizabethan text one may take the problem of the capitalization of titles in Q1 of *Richard II*. Here one compositor normally capitalizes such titles as *King, Liege, Sovereign, Duke,* and so on, whereas the second compositor is mixed in his habits and often leaves them uncapitalized. If an old-spelling editor were to amend all non-capitalization in the work of this compositor in order to make him correspond with the other, he would be violating a compositorial characteristic (not firmly established as the result of type shortage) in only one matter while neglecting dozens of others. Nor could the restoration of the characteristics of the underlying copy be adduced as a reason for this isolated attempt, for we have no means of knowing what the manuscript read. It is just as possible that the one compositor imposed capitals on his uncapitalized copy more frequently than the other as that the other compositor reduced from time to time his capitalized copy.

17 One wishes that another phrase could be found to apply to the editions of books from the nineteenth century on that conform in their accidentals to the original copy-texts. Perhaps *copy-text form editions* would do—better certainly than *author-form editions*—although a superior phrase is no doubt suspended in someone else's consciousness. *Unmodernized* may be the best term.

he fancies the author would have written them if a manuscript had been preserved. But some small though significantly useful normalizing of consistent authorial characteristics can be managed in certain circumstances if an editor is prepared to agree to a few key rules to ensure some appeal always to authority in the copy-text, or another authoritative document of the same text, to back up the nature of the alterations, as the recent editions of Nathaniel Hawthorne and of Stephen Crane will illustrate.[18]

I doubt very much that normalizing of this kind produces a true eclectic text even if the emendations—although they restore conjectural departures of a compositor from his copy—can scarcely be said to repair errors in the sense that Theobald's *loneliness* corrects the error *lovelinesse.* Ultimately, the full control of an editor over the accidentals, as in a modernized Shakespeare—or a modernized Hawthorne that imposes present day standards of light punctuation on an author who preferred intricate parenthetical comma constructions—seems to me also to have nothing basic to do with eclecticism. The original has been vastly altered, and choices have been made of what does and what does not need modernizing, but no suggestion can hold that the resulting selection is likely to restore the accidentals that the author himself would have written. On the contrary. Accordingly, in the last analysis the selective process of modernization is as arbitrary as an emendation of whatever kind when it is made in a single-text work. Nothing that is done in this textual situation can have authority; hence I query whether eclecticism is possible under these circumstances. As for normalization of accidentals according to the author's own system, in a single-text situation the authority comes from analogy with preferred characteristics elsewhere within the same

18 References throughout this paper to Stephen Crane's texts are to the *Works,* published by the University Press of Virginia; Hawthorne's texts are cited in the Centenary Edition published by the Ohio State University Press. Briefly, the important rule is that the document itself being edited must be variant so that one form of the variant is recognizably authorial and the other, then, presumably compositorial in origin. It is obvious that spelling and word-division can often be normalized in this manner, but questions of enforcing uniformity on punctuation habits is far trickier owing to the fact that most authors are not themselves invariably consistent, and also their habits may change with the years. Author will differ from author in all these respects. However, some occasional characteristics like Crane's use of a colon to introduce dialogue may prove to be practically invariable in the manuscripts, and in general his punctuation (or rather non-punctuation) of adjectives in a series can be forecast, as well as his lack of a comma before the *and* of the final element in a series. Hyphenated compounds versus unhyphenated are usually a solvable problem. It seems to me improper to normalize a text in respect to these characteristics when they are not present in variant form in the document being edited and hence no evidence can be offered other than opinion that they existed in its copy.

document. Thus no conflation with another authoritative document is taking place, and no eclecticism results. It should be possible, then, to exclude single-authority texts from consideration. They cannot be edited in an eclectic manner because no combination with another authority is possible.

I am not an historian of textual criticism, but my understanding is that in the early days of scholarship the recovery of texts was often an eclectic process. In biblical and in classical scholarship one is often confronted by a large group of manuscripts of uncertain origin, interconnection, and date, manuscripts that can seldom be totally excluded from authority the way in which the Shakespeare Second Folio can be excluded. Even in a bad and generally corrupt manuscript, or even in an almost totally derived one, if contamination—or cross relationship with another line—is suspected as present, the theoretical and sometimes the practical possibility always exists that some one reading may have been transmitted in its purity although corrupted in other documents. For many years, thus, all documents were thought, in essence, to be of substantial authority; and even if some were distinguished as of primary and others of secondary authority, the difference was a vague one and in any isolated crux an editor could pick and choose among variants according to his personal taste with small regard for the often unsolved questions of derivation, date, and evidence of authority. The process was greatly aided, also, by the custom of modernizing the accidentals of the texts, or at least of normalizing them according to some arbitrarily selected document. It was to counteract the lack of principle inherent in this essentially subjective form of editing that, as I understand it, Lachmann became the proponent of the most-authoritative-manuscript hypothesis, from which divergence was to be accepted only with what may be described as extraordinary reluctance. In this manner the most important effort of the editor was diverted to the selection of a text to reprint and away from the treatment of that text after its selection.* Again as I understand it, the classical scholar A. E. Housman so devastatingly criticized the results of a rigid adherence to this principle as markedly to reduce its value as a scholarly panacea. I am not here concerned with biblical, classical, or medieval vernacular manuscript texts to which these theories apply, and so I wish to avoid the editorial quicksands of a form of editorial problem with which I have had

---

* Even at the present day German textual scholarship still clings to the fetish that treatment of a selected text should be held to a minimum, or not permitted at all; see Hans Zeller, "A New Approach to the Critical Constitution of Literary Texts," *Studies in Bibliography*, 28 (1975), 231–264. For a conspectus of the opposite view, see G. T. Tanselle, "Greg's Theory of Copy-Text and the Editing of American Literature," *ibid.*, 167–229.

no practical experience. My point even in raising it is to suggest two particular considerations: (1) The distrust of eclecticism in editing has an
historical basis in the treatment of material that is not really in question
with us since it is not, in general, subject to what can properly be called
bibliographical analysis as are most textual problems from the Renaissance
to the present day that involve the printing process. Thus it is worth
emancipating ourselves from prejudices about eclectic texts inherited from
a past inapplicable to our present concerns, which are devoted to texts
that are printed, or are mixed manuscript and printed, dating roughly
from the sixteenth century to the present. (2) In retrospect it seems clear
that the controversy about this earlier eclectic editing proved to be less
about its principle than about the abuses in its practice which had been
confused with its principle.

The principle was clear enough: it was no more than an attempt to
recover a lost original by reconciling the evidence of multiple authorities.
When joined in old-spelling texts with the important theory governing
copy-texts, this early principle is perfectly operative today in controlled
bibliographical situations. The treatment of multiple authority, I suggest,
is the operative key to all questions of eclectic texts and their formation.
It is proper, then, to examine some standard situations in which multiple
authority evolves. A text may be said to exist in multiple authorities when
more than one document is preserved that derives ultimately from the
author's holograph and not in its entirety—immediately or with lost antecedents—from some other preserved document. In the period with
which we are concerned the standard examples involve two central situations: first, the recovery of the author's intentions from more than one
authoritative document when variants in the different witnesses result
exclusively from the transmissional process and not from authorial revision; second, the recovery of an author's intentions when one or more
of the preserved multiple documents represents a revised or variant text—
that is, some other authorial form of the text than that contained within
a single holograph not thereafter altered by the author in itself or in
some derived (or, earlier, in some antecedent) form.

The examples of the first situation may serve to illustrate those texts
in which the problem centers on the recovery of the author's original intentions only. The limbs of the family tree that can be drawn are likely to
radiate from the X, the lost archetype, in as many independent lines as
there are preserved documents. The simplest illustration may be drawn
from the newspaper syndication of an author's work. Here the customary
process (when it is not sent out in boilerplate) is to typeset X, the author's manuscript or a derived typescript, and to mail proofs pulled from
this master typesetting to subscribing newspapers which in turn use these
identical proofs as copy for their own compositors. When the proofs are

indeed identical,[19] each newspaper is at an equal distance from the same master copy and is thus of precisely equal authority. It follows that the central problem is one of recovering the lost proofs by stripping away the unauthoritative variation in the different newspaper texts and arriving at what general consensus should establish was the form of the common copy, the proofs. Given even relatively few witnesses, something close to one hundred percent accuracy in establishing the substantives is certainly possible. The accidentals are more difficult to recover than the substantives, and the difficulty is increased if enough holographic material to guide the editor to a knowledge of the author's characteristics has not been preserved. Stephen Crane's 'An Impression of the Concert' (1897) about the fleet of the allied powers at Crete during the Greco-Turkish War is an example. Eight newspaper versions are known, all stemming from an identical set of proofs syndicated from New York by the S. S. McClure Co. With only a handful of doubtful accidental readings, it is possible to reconstruct these proofs from the variable evidence of the witnesses with almost absolute and demonstrable accuracy. The result is certainly eclectic in that on sufficient evidence the readings of some authorities are rejected and others accepted and the final result is a composite text that in all its details reproduces no single one of the authorities. However, one may remark that no logical reason exists to favor any one of these eight authorities over the others, for all are at the same transmissional distance from their common source. Obviously some of these newspapers reproduce the basic proof more faithfully than others. Nevertheless, no bibliographically determinable reason can be found for this diversity save for the care or carelessness of a number of unknown compositors, and the fact itself cannot be determined until the collation of variants has been analyzed and a composite text arrived at from its evidence. Hence under usual circumstances the generally determined superior fidelity of one newspaper to its source has no bearing on the editor's reconstruction of the text, for in this process one authority is not ordinarily matched against another on a qualitative basis. In this sense, the final composite text can scarcely be said to be based on any one of the documents except arbitrarily. Given the opportunity to print his reconstructed text of the basic proof, at one nearer remove to holograph than any preserved witness, an editor

19 This is the normal assumption. That a few anomalies in Crane's newspaper syndication may go back to proof somewhat altered between pulls is only a suspicion. One or two cases exist, however, in which the Nebraska *State Journal* set up the master proof, mailed it out, and then printed the article in its own columns from the same typesetting but slightly edited. Of course, this represents a very special situation. In another special situation, the newspaper syndication of Crane's *The Red Badge of Courage* came from identical proofs, but one late reprinter—the San Francisco *Examiner*—somehow got hold of a copy of the more complete book proofs and in part conflated the two versions.

would be singularly narrow minded to select, instead, the most generally correct of the newspapers and to reprint that as it stood, in the name of pedantry.

A more elementary but essentially similar situation occurs—especially in international publication—when an author's typescript may be set in one country from the ribbon copy and in another country from the exact duplicate represented by the carbon copy of the typescript, or in these days from electroprints. The example of Crane's short story 'The Price of the Harness' (1898) may be cited. Crane wrote the manuscript in October 1898, when he was living in Havana immediately after the end of the Spanish-American War. He mailed the manuscript to his agent Paul Reynolds in New York, who had a typescript and a carbon made up. One copy he sold to the *Cosmopolitan* magazine in the United States and the other to *Blackwood's* in England, both of which printed the story in December. This is close to a laboratory case in its purity, for Crane's isolation prevented him from correcting the typescript or reading proof. Variants between the two magazine texts are exclusively transmissional, therefore, with no possibility of authorial revision to disturb an editor's choice. Since each magazine text is of equal authority with the other, the typescript text may be substantially recovered from the common readings supplemented in cases of variation by editorial selection from either document of what critical and philological evidence suggests were the typescript words and their forms. At least for substantives, ordinarily the reading of one or the other magazine will represent the typescript except in cases of double sophistication.[20] From this process emerges an elementary eclectic text that for the author's original intentions is superior to either of the imperfect forms of the magazines.

An example from earlier literature introduces more troublesome prepublication problems and a lost intermediate stage in one branch of the family tree, but the principle is the same as in the illustrations from Crane —that is, essentially direct radiation in two branches from a lost archetype without authorial revision in either branch. The play *Beggars Bush* by Beaumont, Fletcher, and Massinger was first published in the 1647 Beaumont and Fletcher Folio but it also exists in the form of a presentation or favor manuscript. Analysis of the readings reveals the following textual history. The underlying manuscript seems to have been the copy sold by the dramatists to the King's Men. From this lost manuscript the book-keeper of the company (probably Edward Knight) made a prompt-book, now lost, and from this prompt-book was transcribed the preserved

20 Double sophistication may occur in theory even in texts set from an authorial manuscript, for these are not necessarily impeccable. But it usually occurs in an attempt to repair some blunder in a transmitted form of the text being used as copy, like a typescript or a syndicated proof.

Lambarde manuscript, now in the Folger Shakespeare Library. On the other hand, the 1647 Folio was set directly from the original copy, which had been preserved in the theatre. In this case the Folio branch of the family tree derives directly, without intermediary, from X, the fair copy, but the Lambarde manuscript is at two removes from the same document since the lost prompt-book intervenes. Only transmissional error appears in the Folio text except for some censorship cuts in the printing-house and the accidental loss from the manuscript of a song, probably written on a separate sheet of paper, as well as a similarly written part of an amplified scene. On the other hand, the book-holder Knight introduced a few (although a surprisingly few) attempts at reordering the impossible time scheme of the play, and these unauthoritative modifications of the original must be added to the partly inadvert, partly sophisticating corruptions natural to the double copying, although on the whole the manuscript substantives are in better shape than those transmitted through the incompetent Compositor B of this section of the Folio. At least for the accidentals, however, and sometimes for the substantives, the unequal distance from X of the 1647 Folio and the Lambarde manuscript makes for a greater presumption of authority in the Folio; but the two Folio compositors were of unequal carefulness in their typesetting and in their ability to read the handwriting of the manuscript, and the physical deficiencies of the Folio printer's copy after the passage of years created lacunae that must be filled from the manuscript. Thus an editor concerned with recovering the authorial intentions must make eclectic use of both documents and sometimes choose readings from the more distant source both in substantives and in accidentals, since in all its readings the genetically superior Folio is by no means practically superior to the manuscript at one farther remove.[21]

At this point it is legitimate to stop for a moment to enquire how these examples of non-revised texts differ in respect to eclecticism of treatment from the texts of single authority admitting alterations from other early editions that are unauthoritative reprints, as well as from editorial tradition. Both are similar in that the editorial attempt is entirely one of *correction* to recover the lost source (in whatever form that was) from which the documents immediately derive. That is, when by emendation in a single-text situation an editor alters a reading, he is correcting what must be regarded as a transmissional error and therefore conjecturally restoring the pure original. But the document or other source for the correction can have no authority, and the correction is thus basically

21 This textually significant play in its period is printed in *The Dramatic Works in the Beaumont and Fletcher Canon*, ed. Bowers, III (1975). For an account of the investigation and evidence, see '*Beggars Bush*: A Reconstructed Prompt-Book and Its Copy,' *Studies in Bibliography*, 27 (1974), 113–136.

undemonstrable even though universal approval may canonize it.[22] On the other hand, when two or more documents have equal authority, or even a relative authority stemming from their unequal distance from the archetype, multiple witnesses exist to the readings of this common source. In general one variant will be wrong and the other right (in a bibliographical situation when revision has not entered); but only in cases of relative authority is there possible even a presumption of superior rightness in one document over another, and such a presumption is often proved false in any specific application to an individual reading. When in single-text authority an emendation is made, no demonstration is possible that it actually recovers the pure source that has been corrupted. But when multiple authority exists, something close to demonstration *is* possible in ordinary cases that one variant is presumably right and the other wrong. No unauthoritative document can be a witness to the archetypal form of a work, but each independent or partly independent multiple authority can constitute such an authoritative witness since its comparison with similar witnesses serves to reconstruct its own and their immediate common source. In simple radiation no one multiple text is technically more authoritative than another; thus a true merging or conflation of witnesses results from the editorial selection of variants. Indeed, when one document has been selected as the basis for an edition and is being emended or amplified by the others, the process is often only an editorial convenience and not an inherent methodical principle. The selection from among any variation, which is the root of eclectic editing, is made almost exclusively from variants of presumptive authority in one or other of their forms.

Further differences characterizing the two editorial situations have some bearing on eclecticism, also. For instance, the conservative editor of a single-authority text is likely to retain almost any plausible reading in the original from which sense can be made, for no demonstration may be possible that the text reading is wrong or—if wrong—that the most favored emendation is any closer to the original than the assumed error. In *All's Well That Ends Well*, for instance, the well-known crux *I see that men make rope's in such a scarre* | *That wee'l forsake our selves* (TLN 2063–64) is retained by most editors less on the ground that it is correct in some obscure manner than that they despair of recovering what the original read. If double authority had been present (and if the error had not originated in some post-holographic scribal copy from which both

22 'Universal approval' may have its temporal aspects, of course. A reading that is given common consent by one generation may two hundred years later seem in positive error or at the least of doubtful validity. However, one does what one can, and it is scarcely news that all truth is relative. Methuselah should have added editing to his other accomplishments.

documents radiated), an editor finding, say, *take hopes in such a scare* in one of these two texts would be strongly tempted to view it as authoritative in origin and to accept it with little question, even though conscious of the possibility that it was a printer's sophistication. Demonstration that it was sophisticated could not be made, in fact, unless of three independently radiating documents from the same source two read *make rope's* and one *take hopes*.[23] It must also be remarked that by presenting equally authoritative alternatives variation in multiple-authority texts reveals error where it might not be suspected as present in single authorities. For example, if *Hamlet* had come down to us in only one authoritative textual line, any editor would have reprinted without hesitation either the *pitch and moment* phrase as now found in the Second Quarto, or *pith and moment* (TLN 1740) in the Folio, with no suspicion that he was perpetuating error, for each reading is plausible. Moreover, if the Folio *Hamlet*, say, had been wholly derived from the Second Quarto as a mere reprint, it is doubtful that any editor (perhaps after the mid-nineteenth century) would believe he had sufficient grounds to emend Quarto 'pitch' to Folio 'pith'.

Thus the reconstruction of a lost original by the identification and then the eclectic selection of readings among multiple authorities is ordinarily more complete than is possible for single-texts where emendation alone can be the corrective agent, for emendation, strictly, is always unauthoritative. This greater comprehensiveness arises partly in that multiple-text authorities will ordinarily contain the correct reading in one for the corruption in the other[24] in a form not necessarily occurring to an emender, or if so in a form so undemonstrably the correct one as to persuade him that he might as well retain the original as make what could be only sophisticated sense. For example, when Hamlet in the Quarto addresses Gertrude as *cold mother* (TLN 258), a modern editor might be uneasy about the reading but it is not certain that he would risk *good mother* if it were not that this Folio reading has independent authority. Nevertheless, the essential difference, as I see it, still remains this: In texts existing with only single authority, alteration can constitute nothing but emendation.

---

23 Of course, if the radiation were not fully independent, as from one source, but the two documents reading 'make rope's' radiated from one source and the text reading 'take hopes' from another, then 'take hopes' could be re-established as a possible authoritative reading. I may remark that I hold no brief for 'take hopes': I use it only as a convenient example.

24 This is likely to be absolutely true only when both documents radiate from a holograph. Radiation from a transcript derived from the holograph may produce authority and lack of authority, but also two different attempts to patch manifest error. And derivation from two different sources may produce the same situation. However, even under the worst of conditions a general presumption of authority in a variant reading will normally be justified.

To emend one must have some basic text to alter, a text that in this situation is automatically provided by the only available authority. On the contrary, in the purest form of multiple authority—independently radiating texts from the same lost document—it is really improper to think in terms of emendation instead of selection, for no standard exists to emend, not even a copy-text in the classic manner of single authority. All texts being equally authoritative, one cannot be 'emended' by the other. Instead, only a composite text can be constructed by the selection of variants. So far as I can reason, this is a difference that constitutes a distinction in the two textual situations.

That not all multiple-authority texts are so pure, and that some—like *Beggars Bush*—exist with one document farther removed from authority than the other, does not, I take it, alter the principle. If the arm nearer to authority—the Folio text of *Beggars Bush*—is selected as the basic text, it would be only because the principle of copy-text (which operates for accidentals when distances are unequal) dictates the choice, or else simple convenience. The substantives of the more distant document might, in fact, have been more faithfully transmitted than those of the nearer one, all depending upon the standards of fidelity maintained by the respective agents. Even the selection of a copy-text from the nearer document may not always guarantee what are actually the most authoritative accidentals. In Stephen Crane's novel *The Third Violet* (1897) the accidentals of the book form are immediately derived from the professional typescript that was the printer's copy, whereas any one of the newspaper versions derives from the carbon of this typescript only through a lost intermediate syndicate proof. Yet because of the heavy house styling given the book text in comparison with the relatively naive following of copy in the lost proof, an editor familiar with Crane's characteristics will recognize that on an overall basis any one of the newspapers radiating from this proof is likely to be closer in its accidentals to the typescript version of the lost holograph than is the nearer book.[25] But to return to the central thesis—an editor constructs a single-authority text by emending the only standard he has, which is the earliest version. In contrast, an editor confronted with multiple authorities usually has no standard on which he can rely from the start (except presumptively), even in ordinary cases of unequal distance from the archetype in the several branches of the family

25 Ordinarily the substantives of the book form of *The Third Violet* reflect the considerable revision that Crane gave its typescript copy after he had sent off the carbon to the newspapers. However, the choice of the book form from among variant substantives is not an inevitable one. The book has its share of compositorial errors not caught in proof. In addition, mixed in with Crane's own authoritative revision of the typescript is a layer of editorial and compositorial alteration of his more strikingly odd idiom and syntax which an alert editor can detect by comparison with the characteristic forms of the newspapers.

tree. If he finally comes to estimate one document as more reliable than another, it is only after the facts, and his text, have been decided upon by the eclectic process and he has distinguished the relative faithfulness of each document to his ideal composite. Under these circumstances it is a misconception to think in terms of emending one text by another. Even when a copy-text is finally chosen, the document so selected is only a peg on which to hang the apparatus of variation;[26] under no circumstances can this document be taken as the standard, in a single-authority sense, which is to be emended to produce the final text. Copy-texts are chosen for the authority of their accidentals—not for the authority of their substantives.

An author's revision of his work, the two or more stages preserved by multiple authorities, provokes the most serious editorial problems. The manner in which revision may be accomplished takes a number of forms and is seldom pure since it is often mixed with correction, but the two main situations that affect eclectic editorial method may be identified as pre-publication and post-publication.

In post-publication revision two or more documents showing the original and the revised shapes of the text are likely to be in linear relationship. The examples must be few and far between (save for such thorough recasting as took place in the manuscripts of Wordsworth's *Prelude*) in which an author so heavily revises an already published work of any length as to require an entirely new holograph manuscript as an independent act of creation. Ordinarily he annotates and interleaves an earlier printed form, not always the best edition by modern standards of authority, as Fielding worked over a set of the third edition of *Tom Jones* to make up printer's copy for the revised fourth edition. Since the basic copy revised was the third, the fourth edition is in linear relationship to it, for it derives immediately from the third except for the specific authorial revisions. In linear relationships like this, the agent for the fresh authority entering the text may not be the author himself. Instead, a copy of an early printed edition may be brought into general conformity with some example of an authorial manuscript (or a copy thereof at any remove) by a scribe. It seems firmly established, for instance, that when Jaggard found copyright problems had arisen about a simple reprint of the Quarto text of *Troilus and Cressida* for the Folio, he had a quarto annotated by reference to a

26 This view is elaborated in 'Multiple Authority,' *op. cit.,* p. 101 ff. More recently, G. T. Tanselle has put forward an interesting proposal for a form of apparatus to deal with such multiple-authority texts. Here instead of one list of alterations made by the editor in the copy-text and a separate historical collation of rejected readings from the collated authorities, Dr. Tanselle proposes only one amalgamated list without reference to any copy-text but showing the variation of all authorities from the edited text alone. See "Some Principles for Editorial Apparatus," *Studies in Bibliography,* 25 (1972), 41–48. The theory seems logically planned. I have not had the opportunity to test it in practice.

manuscript preserved in the theater that was in a different stage of composition or revision from that underlying the Quarto. The theater's manuscript itself was not set by Jaggard but instead this marked-up printed copy was prepared which his compositors preferred. As a consequence, the nature of the Folio *Troilus and Cressida* is mixed. In some part it derives linearly from the Quarto, which was its physical copy. In some part its variants from the Quarto reflect the annotation from the theater manuscript plus scribal error. In some part, like the fourth edition of *Tom Jones*, a proportion of the variants are unauthoritative because they originated with the later compositors.

Once these unauthoritative variants are identified and removed from the *Tom Jones* text, and once the third-edition departures from first-edition copy are removed from the fourth edition, the fourth-edition substantives may be said to represent Fielding's final intentions save for first-edition errors that he did not notice and correct. On the other hand, when some agent other than the author is the corrector, the situation changes and the authority of the revised edition is materially reduced. The scribe's collation of printed edition with manuscript will almost inevitably be imperfect so that not every authorial variant is transferred to the printer's copy. It seems reasonably evident in *Hamlet* that the repetition in the Folio of the Second Quarto reading *a good kissing carrion* (TLN 1219)—universally corrected to Warburton's *a god kissing carrion*—resulted from the scribe's error in passing over an error, granting the hypothesis that the Folio printer's copy was an annotated Second Quarto. Sins of commission will be found as well, as when a scribe mistakes an author's handwriting or his intention and with his best will either alters a correct reading in the print to a corrupt one, or inadvertently makes a faulty correction that does not reproduce the original in the manuscript. Then there is always the question of the faithful transfer of corruptions from the manuscript being compared if it is a derived one, or even if it happens to be in an earlier state than the manuscript behind the copy being annotated, as has been suggested may be true for *Troilus and Cressida*. Moreover, as happened in *Doctor Faustus*, a scribe may take it upon himself to 'improve' the copy. When an author is not personally involved in the preparation of revised printer's copy, massive corruption can follow an attempt at revision if a document at some remove from the author and thus itself corrupt and sophisticated is used as the correcting agent. The sophistication of the Folio text of Shakespeare's *2 Henry IV* in comparison to the Quarto is so extensive as to lead to queries whether an annotated quarto or a fresh manuscript were the Folio printer's copy; and it is moot how much of the Folio variant text is composed of sophisticating attempts at correction (probably in the manuscript being utilized), how much of purer readings transmitted correctly in the Folio underlying copy, and how much of authorial variants that hypothetically could have been present in this copy. Thus when an agent other than the author is charged with annotating a printed edition to prepare copy for a new edition, a mixture of authority results owing in some part to the non-authority of the agents departures from copy but also to the superimposition in a post-publication stage of readings from a source that originated in the pre-publication stage and may or may not be superior as a whole or in some of its parts to the source of the original printed edition.

When an author is the revising agent as in *Tom Jones* or in *Joseph Andrews*, or as in the philosopher William James's revision of earlier journal articles for book collection, a reprint of the revised form will on the whole be roughly satisfactory for the substantives; and in this respect it may seem to be only a semantic distinction whether in *Tom Jones* an eclectic text is being constructed by merging the selected revised readings from the fourth with the first-edition substantives, or whether the fourth-edition substantives are being corrected (in a non-eclectic manner) by reference to the first edition and to the transmissional history of the substantives in the third edition. Perhaps in such an example a considerable part of the case for eclectic versus non-eclectic editing—at least in the popular sense —could be argued as resting on the question of the copy-text chosen. If *contra* Greg's principles the fourth edition of *Tom Jones* or the Folio edition of *Hamlet* were selected as copy-text, then at first sight it would seem more logical to take it that variants introduced from the first edition and from the Second Quarto are corrections of transmissional error (including a stage of pre-publication transmission for *Hamlet*) than that they create an eclectic composite of two texts. On the other hand, if Greg's theory of copy-text is observed and the selected revised and corrected substantives of the fourth edition and of the Folio are merged with the accidentals of the earlier editions, then even in a popular sense the fact of eclectic editing cannot be avoided. However, that the question of copy-text cannot truly affect the situation should be apparent when it is considered that the choice of copy-text affects accidentals but not substantives and it is the substantives that must be in question. Thus if my definition of eclectic editing as the selection of variants between two or more authoritative texts is valid, the revision of an earlier publication to produce a linear-derived document serving as printer's copy must always represent the merging of authority with authority. The authority of the earliest edition may be strong owing to its immediate relation to a holograph as is true for *Tom Jones* and very likely for the Second Quarto of *Hamlet*, or it may be weak as in the case of Elizabethan bad quartos ranging from *The Merry Wives of Windsor* to *Richard III* and *King Lear*; but even a memorially transmitted text like a bad quarto has *some* relation to authority just as do the mutilated and much altered newspaper versions of *The Red Badge of Courage.* And we know from the example of *King Lear,* as well as *Doctor Faustus,* that not every variant from the source behind the more authoritative later edition is superior in its authority to that of the bad: a memorial transmission may preserve truth and a scribe or a non-holograph manuscript used for revision may import error.

Common as are the examples of post-publication revision, as in nineteenth-century English novelists like Dickens between periodical and book forms and even between successive book editions, a wider variety and often a more serious set of editorial problems is found in pre-publication changes reflected in a revised document. The simplest cases, again, are those that are linear, for the limitation imposed by their transmission controls or at least exposes error more forthrightly than radiating documents. In its most elementary form we may see linear pre-publication authorial revision in Nathaniel Hawthorne's *The Blithedale Romance* (1852) or *The House of the Seven Gables* (1851). The printer's-copy holograph has been preserved for each of these novels as well as the first edition. Missing are the proofsheets that Hawthorne corrected and that account for the actual revision and correction of the original typesetting made from the preserved manuscript. If these proofs were available, especially in their entirety, they would also serve to isolate the printer's departures from copy that Hawthorne overlooked from those that he recognized and corrected. An example of post-publication revision of a substantially similar nature is found in the twelve leaves of cancels that Fielding ordered for the first edition of *Tom Jones* to supplement the extensive errata list. The originals of only four of these leaves have been preserved but in each case they give occasion for an editor to distinguish between the revisions and the corruptions found in the substitute leaves, a process impossible when only the cancellans are present. A more complicated but still linear problem occurs with Stephen Crane's *The Red Badge of Courage.* Here we have preserved the final holograph manuscript (and portions of an antecedent draft) but this manuscript was not the printer's copy. Instead, a lost professional typescript was made from it, which Crane worked over for a few days in New Orleans, making numerous small revisions, before returning it to New York for typesetting. Therefter he read proof on the pages with no great care before the sheets were printed. The authoritative revisions in the book that derived from the annotated copy of the lost typescript are thoroughly mixed with an unauthoritative restyling by the publisher and by the compositors that affected Crane's syntax and occasionally his idiom and grammar. To these may be added the undetected range of printer's errors as well as the overlooked defects of the typescript ranging from the misreading of words to the omission of parts of several passages through a misconstruction of markings in the manuscript. Correspondingly, a major excision of a whole battle scene in the manuscript was restored in the typescript, perhaps from the original manuscript leaves but more likely, perhaps, from a lost secondary source, a discarded earlier typescript made from the manuscript before the manuscript itself had been revised for its present state. Because of the gaps in the documentary transmission in this linear situation an editor must recover the purity of the authorial text while yet doing justice to Crane's intended revisions. This necessary selection of readings from two authorities (manuscript and first edition) in order to reconstruct the substantives of a third (the missing typescript and proofs), and then to purify it, creates an eclectic text if any attempt is to be made to recover the author's final intentions other than as found in the first edition with its numerous and sometimes serious corruptions.[27] There is nothing purist in reprinting this faulty first edition in the name of scholarship instead of making an eclectic attempt to restore Crane's true authority from the preserved documents, including the all-important manuscript.[28]

27 This account for the sake of brevity neglects the influence upon the editing of this work of a radiating authority produced when a considerably abridged and unauthoritatively adjusted version was typeset from the unrevised (or very likely separately and differently revised) carbon of the book typescript and the resulting syndicate proof was reprinted in various newspapers. Distant as these newspaper texts are, and fragmentary, they have a form of authority and in a few places can testify to the state of the typescript before the New Orleans authorial revision as well as the Appleton editorial revisions.

28 Such a position will be unacceptable to those who maintain that multiple-authority texts should be edited only in their discrete single-authority forms without reference to each other for corrections of error or for revisions. In this matter two particular confusions seem to have arisen. In the first, it is evident that a certain kind of critic dislikes eclectic texts because he wants editions in which he can sense the distinctive quality of each form without the hard work of studying the development of the text by the use of the apparatus. (This is to quote Donald Pizer; see above, footnote 12). It is, of course, important for critics to have general impressions of works and to describe these impressions in appropriate terms for their readers to share. It is also important, however, for critics (and their readers) to know the *why* of their impressions, which can be arrived at only by hard work and the analysis of concrete and often minute evidence, a process that requires an exact knowledge of the verbal differences between two texts in full detail. A critic who wants parallel texts for general impressions and sensing distinctive qualities is unlikely to put in the labor necessary to collate these texts thoroughly for himself in order to isolate and then understand the facts that have triggered his impressions, and it is probable that he will remain content with his generalities. These may be valuable but chiefly on a subjective basis, a different matter from moving men's minds by evidence. Thus it is a narrow critical point of view—basically more impressionistic than analytical—to object to the necessity to use the apparatus of a definitive edition in order to reconstruct the history of the text. (Once more, all questions of texts like *Roderick Hudson* and others that cannot be conflated according to Greg's rationale of copy-text are not in question.) So far as I can

Pre-publication radiation of authority is likely to develop more variation, and more editorial difficulty in assessing its nature and extent, than
strictly linear revision. *Beggars Bush*, already described, exhibits just this
pre-publication radiation when the prompt-book was transcribed from
the early copy and then itself became the source for the Lambarde manuscript, whereas the early copy was preserved to become the printer's
copy for the 1647 Folio. In this case, however, the only revision that took
place between the fair copy and the prompt-book was unauthoritative and
thus outside the present discussion. More to the point, if textual theorists
are right the quarto edition of Shakespeare's *Othello* in 1622 was printed
from a manuscript representing an early state of the composition whereas
the copy behind the First Folio was a later authorially revised manuscript.
If this situation had existed in a pure state, in which each manuscript di-

---

determine the intellectual basis for objections to final-intention texts arrived at by
eclectic methods, it appears to be aesthetic. Next, objections seem triggered by an
uneasy suspicion of the alteration of any authority by reference to another, seconded
by little practical knowledge of the sifting of evidence, both bibliographical and critical, that is part of the modern editor's peculiar responsibility. For instance, there is a
general exaggeration of the difficulty of assessing the relation of authorial proof-
correction to compositorial departures from copy as between a printer's-copy manuscript and the text printed from it. In this connection, 'Current Theories of Copy-
Text with an Illustration from Dryden,' *Modern Philology*, 48 (1950), 12–20, may
still be useful. Thirdly, the objectors still do not understand Greg's basic doctrine that
copy-texts are chosen on the authority of the accidentals and not of the substantives, and
thus that the copy-text substantives may be inferior to those of some other authoritative
edition and should be replaced when they can be shown to be errors or readings that
were later revised. Because of this confusion Pizer finds himself in the odd position
of arguing that he would prefer to read the misprint *flashed* in Crane's 'The Monster'
instead of the correct *flushed* since *flushed* comes from the manuscript being used as
copy-text in this part of the text and he wants the copy-text to remain the first edition.
The point of the selected reading is not one of copy-text at all, for that *flashed* is a
typist or compositorial misreading of the manuscript *flushed* is perfectly clear from
parallel passages. Thus *flushed* was printed in the Virginia edition of Crane not because it appeared in the manuscript (which had no copy-text bearing on the case) but
because it was demonstrably the reading that Crane had first written and no evidence
could be brought forward to suggest that he had altered it in proof. Like *pitch* and *pith*
in *Hamlet* this is obviously a case of one reading being right and the other wrong. If
the situation had been reversed, the manuscript could still have remained the copy-text
for this passage because of its authoritative accidentals, but the correct *flushed* would
have been inserted from the first edition for the inadvertent mis-inscription *flashed* of
the manuscript which, after all, was not here the printer's copy. One would wish that
the old Lachmann-Housman debate could have been revived at the present day among
students of American literature with more historical awareness and with less confusion
about the issues involved. [For an acute analysis of prevalent misunderstandings, see
G. T. Tanselle, "Greg's Theory of Copy-Text and the Editing of American Literature,"
SB, 28 (1975), 167–229.]

rectly behind the printed copies was holograph and unworked-over by any other hand than the author's, each text would have equal basic authority and an eclectic choice of readings would have been required in order to remove the compositorial errors of each print and effectively to isolate the authentic revised readings. As it is, the errors behind the Quarto are perhaps no more than the compositor's, at a minimum, providing the manuscript actually were a holograph. But the copy behind the Folio offers more difficulties. It may be scribal, not holograph, and thus it may exhibit sophistication by another hand as well as the normal double layer of error resulting from two transmissions. This murky pre-publication history ensures that neither preserved document is adequate to represent the author's intentions. Moreover, it has been established that although a revised manuscript of some sort lies behind the Folio, the Folio printer's copy was a scribally annotated example of the quarto, brought into general conformity with a manuscript from the theater. The usual errors of omission as well as commission may be expected as a consequence of this additional stage of transmission and its peculiar nature. It is generally believed that the wording of the Folio *Othello* represents a form of the text closer on the whole to Shakespeare's ultimate intentions than the Quarto. But however true this estimate may be on an overall basis, it can scarcely operate as a decisive factor for individual readings, given the farther distance from the holograph source (even a revised one) from which the Folio suffers. A conservatively emended reprint of neither authority would be satisfactory for Shakespearean critics: what is needed is a critical eclectic text that attempts to weed out errors from both preserved documents by reference to the authority of now one and then the other, with the intent to establish the authority of the original text; and then finally completes the task by identifying and retaining the authoritative revisions found in the Folio, once they have been distinguished from error and sophistication, and conflating these with the established original composition.

In the late nineteenth century a case of mixed authority requiring eclectic treatment occurs in Stephen Crane's *The Third Violet* (1897) which has a complex pre-publication history. When a rural typist failed to make a copy that he thought satisfactory for the printer, Crane expressed the manuscript to his New York publisher for a professional typescript to be prepared. The carbon of this typescript became the copy for syndication in a number of newspapers. Before the book was set some months later, Crane worked over the ribbon copy of the typescript and revised it, and as usual the Appleton editor took a hand with eliminating some idiosyncracies of usage and syntax that characterize Crane's writing. Any individual newspaper is at three removes from the holograph—the unrevised typescript carbon, the syndicate proof, and the newspaper setting. However, from the various newspaper witnesses something approximating the syndicate proofs can be recovered for the accidentals as well as an exact reconstitution of the substantives. By comparison with the book a very close reproduction of the original typescript substantives of the original can then be put together, a text that has its historical interest but is scarcely worth reprinting in its entirety for the study of scholars. Critics concerned with other than textual matters will want to use Crane's final intentions as the evidential basis for their conclusions about such matters as Crane's powers of characterization, his ordering of scenes, his humor, sentimentality, language, and whatever else interests them. If they are wise enough to evaluate these matters by studying the early state of the text from the security of the final, the apparatus of variants to a critical text can record for them the precise verbal forms of either. A reprint of the book text would not, of course, provide a scholar with Crane's intentions in their exact form since it would leave untouched the compositorial and editorial sophistications of Crane's style, the original authorial readings for which can be recovered only from the composite reconstruction of the syndicate proof, with due allowance for its share of error and sophistication. Only an eclectic text contrived in this manner can bring to a critical reader what he must have: a reconstruction as close as textual scholarship can manage of Crane's share of the revised typescript that served as printer's copy for the book. This is the ideal, and it includes even the hypothetical (and probably very few) corrections and revisions that Crane may have made in the book proofs, since these alterations cannot be distinguished on the evidence from his alterations of the typescript. The documentary evidence does not permit us to penetrate farther back into the text than this to link it with the antecedent manuscript: the original of any plausible departures from copy by the typist can never be known unless by chance they were altered in the revision of the typescript.

Two final examples of mixed texts requiring eclectic treatment can only be mentioned, since a full account of them may be found elsewhere.[29] In Crane's short story 'The Revenge of the *Adolphus*' a typescript and its carbon were made from the manuscript. The carbon, say, was sold in the United States and published there in a magazine without Crane seeing proof or concerning himself with the text beyond what may be a change or two (not transferred to the ribbon copy) that he made before mailing. The ribbon copy was very considerably revised after criticism of its technical naval details had been given Crane by the United States Naval Attaché stationed in London, and in this form it appeared in an English magazine. Later when Crane was collecting his Spanish-American War stories for the book *Wounds in the Rain* he discovered that he had no

29 See 'Multiple Authority,' *op. cit.*, p. 108 ff.

typescript, nor did he have a copy of the revisions he had made for the English magazine. By returning to the manuscript he seems to have made up a new typescript in which he included some true literary revision as well as what he could remember of the Attaché's technical criticism. This version, accidentally less its final page or two, was sent to the book publisher who set it up only to find that the missing end had to be supplied from a copy of the English magazine that he was able to procure in New York. However, in order to make room for an illustration this magazine had, unfortunately, cut the original ending that may be found only in the American magazine, and so the book of course follows the unauthoritatively reduced conclusion. If anything less than an eclectic text can do justice to this extraordinary textual situation, it would be a miracle.

The second example is less one of revision, since this seems to be very slight in the texts, but instead one in which eclectic editing can succeed in recovering a text that in even small details of accidentals is substantially that of the lost manuscript. This is Crane's short story 'Death and the Child', which radiates from one typescript and its carbon in an English magazine and book collection, and, made from the same manuscript, exists in an independent typescript and carbon radiating in an American magazine and book collection. Briefly, the common features of all four, or even any three, of these printed forms must represent the common consent of the two typescripts and therefore the features of the manuscript.[30] A reprint of any one of these four authorities would provide only an imperfect text for critical study, and its imperfections could scarcely be ameliorated by an apparatus that would enable the reader to reconstruct the features of the other three, since he would still lack the expertise to evaluate these and recover Crane's actual text. The Variorum principle applied to literary, not to textual, study is of very little use and may even be a positive danger to a critic since it puts the business of determining bibliographical and textual authority on inexperienced shoulders. A literary critic would have notable difficulty for example, in knowing what words of *Hamlet* he should be writing about if he had been furnished only the Variorum volume containing a reprint of the First Folio, with all Second Quarto variants, all other early editions, all editors' emendations from 1709 both apt and foolish, everything jumbled together in the collation at the foot of the page.

---

30 The principles governing the reconstruction from radiating witnesses of a lost document so that one can always penetrate one step farther back towards authority than any single preserved document are remarked in 'Multiple Authority,' p. 101 ff. It follows that when, as in 'Death and the Child,' two lost radiating typescripts can be reconstructed, by comparing them one can then reconstruct in turn the document from which they radiated, in this case the holograph manuscript at two removes from any preserved document.

I conclude with a general categorizing of the main kinds of single and of multiple authority, and a brief analysis of the eclectic or non-eclectic editorial treatment appropriate for the different categories.

Single authority exists in its simplest state in an unpublished manuscript representing the only textual authority available. More commonly, it is found in the first edition with or without the printer's copy, and with or without subsequent editions so long as these are simple reprints lacking the intervention in any manner of fresh and independent authority. Stephen Crane's novel *George's Mother* (1896) exists in only one edition, the first, although with a scrap of an early draft for part of a page. Except for the accidentals of the brief draft fragment, the only recovery of antecedent authority that is possible is contained within the printed text itself; hence a faithful reprint, corrected as necessary, is all that an editor can manage save perhaps for the normalizing of some of Crane's accidentals to agree with Crane's known characteristics when there is variance in the text itself. The first edition of Shakespeare's *Measure for Measure* appeared in the First Folio of 1623, which was thereupon reprinted in 1632, 1664, and 1685. In none of the later Folios did authority enter. The pre-publication history that can be recovered for *Measure for Measure* suggests that the manuscript given the printer was a transcript of Shakespeare's 'foul papers' made by the professional scribe Ralph Crane. The recovery of this information assists an editor materially in his conjectual emendation, because he can expect error not only from Compositors B, C, D, and F who worked on the play but also from the scribe's manipulation. Thus he may be emboldened to more and certainly to different kinds of emendation from what may seem appropriate for *All's Well That Ends Well*, also a Folio play, that was almost certainly set directly from Shakespeare's own working papers. However, in either case the appearance of later unauthoritative Folio editions has no bearing on the recovery of antecedent authorial text. The First Folio print is the only authority we have, and a conjecturally emended reprint of this is the best any editor can manage to present Shakespeare's work in a scholarly manner. The only evidence of its immediate antecedent is locked in the witness itself and cannot usually be disengaged to recover the details of the manuscript that Ralph Crane copied, or even Ralph Crane's own transcript except here and there when recognizable idiosyncracies peer through the compositorial overlay.

On some occasions pre-publication forms of a text may be preserved without interfering with the concept of single authority so long as the relationship is linear and the different forms derive one from another without fresh authority entering into the chain of transmission. One curious case is Stephen Crane's short story 'A Little Pilgrim'. The manuscript of this was sold to Harper's and was set for the firm's magazine in such a hurry to get it out before the book, already close to completion,

that one compositor set the magazine text from the first half of the manuscript (cast off for the book) while the book compositor was setting from
the latter half. When each came to the end of his stint he exchanged not
the manuscript copy but instead the proofs pulled from his setting: hence
the book proof became the printer's copy for the latter part of the story
in the magazine, and the magazine proof for the first part of the book.
Since in this mixed manner each witness is one-half original and one-half
derived, an eclectic editor chooses from each the primary and non-re-
print typesetting as his copy-text. Another interesting case comes in Crane's
article 'The Scotch Express.' This was set up in England in 1898 by *Cassell's* magazine from manuscript. Proofs were pulled and immediately
mailed to *McClure's* magazine in the United States, which set up its own
version of the article from this copy. However, between the two witnesses,
one authoritative and one derived, two differences appear beyond normal
compositorial variation. First, *Cassell's* cut some of the article for publication, so that the *McClure's* text for such excisions (derived from the
lost Cassell's proofs before cutting) is the only printed form to preserve
the original text. Secondly, the editor of *Cassell's* proceeded to make what
he regarded as judicious changes in the proofs of Crane's article before
publication so that the *Cassell's* version here and there differs from the
original state of the proofs as reproduced by *McClure's*. This situation
might be thought of as verging on multiple authority, and in a sense it
does; but in a more important sense no new authority ever entered the
printed transmission of the text not present in its original typesetting from
the manuscript, which was not again consulted or made the source of
another typescript. If this manuscript had not, fortunately, been preserved
so that an editor would have been forced to work only with the printed
results, it could be said (lacking the manuscript) that the *Cassell's* copy-
text, the only document set from manuscript, must be *corrected* (not *revised*) from the evidence of the derived reproduction in *McClure's* in order
to restore as nearly as possible the state of its original proofs before
editorial alteration. In point of fact although the manuscript is preserved,
and must become the copy-text, the evidence of *McClure's* settles for an
editor any question he might have had about the authority of the variants
between *Cassell's* and *McClure's* as resulting in *Cassell's* from Crane's
own intervention. The only editorial problem that remains is to assess the
authority of the variants between the early state of the *Cassell's* proof (as
preserved by the *McClure's* text) and the manuscript.

The question of derivation also puts Crane's romance *The O'Ruddy*
(1903) into the single-authority category despite its complicated history.
Crane's part of the novel exists in a holograph manuscript from which a
lost typescript with carbons was made. One carbon went to a magazine,
which began serializing the story, whereas the ribbon copy went to the

London publisher Heinemann where typesetting of the book started. After several installments of the magazine, the book setting had caught up with the magazine text, and thereafter the magazine became a simple reprint of the book proofs, with some added cuts and censorship. If the manuscript had not survived, the textual problem would certainly have involved the double authority of book and magazine set independently, in the early part, from typescript and carbon although reverting to single authority once the book proofs became the magazine copy. But since the typescript was, apparently, never revised except perhaps for one or two insignificant readings of doubtful validity, it is utterly derived from the manuscript and thus unauthoritative; hence a reconstruction of the typescript from the evidence of magazine and book in the early part of the romance, which otherwise would have been of crucial textual importance, has now only an historical significance owing to the preservation of the manuscript, the only possible copy-text especially considering the fact that publication was posthumous.

When only drafts are preserved of a work and the printed version stems from a rewritten but lost later holograph, we enter a gray area between single and multiple authority. In respect of its substantives, no question holds but that the single newspaper version of Crane's Sullivan County sketch 'The Octopush' has ultimate authority since it was set from a now lost manuscript that had thoroughly rewritten and revised the state of the text in an untitled draft generally called 'The Fishermen,' which is known only in the form of a posthumous typescript made by Cora. On the other hand, if we assume that when the two texts are closely parallel Crane's rewritten arrangement would in manuscript have reproduced, on the whole, the accidentals of the draft, these accidentals would be of superior authority in a relatively naive typescript to those of the printed version which has been strongly compositor-styled. But the two texts are by no means always parallel except in scattered patches; hence when the substantives markedly diverge, the printed text's accidentals must join them in general authority in their new and changed form. I would not say that an editor would be wrong to treat this problem as if it did not exist and to reprint 'The Octopush' from the New York *Tribune* (July 10, 1892) as a single-text authority without regard for the shifting authority of the accidentals of the draft manuscript. One hopes, of course, such an editor would then add the text of the typescript draft in an appendix, a sop to the scholar in a definitive edition but of little use in truly attempting to establish the best overall text of 'The Octopush' for reading. Nevertheless, in the parallel portions the textual problem may seem partly to approach that of *Othello*; and an editor may certainly be tempted to try emending the printed accidentals whenever the authority of the draft accidentals could be applied without creating a real mishmash of texture clothing the basically single-text authority of the substantives.

Another inhabitant of this gray area is a book like Hawthorne's *The House of the Seven Gables*, preserved in the printer's-copy holograph manuscript and in the first edition set immediately from this copy. The missing link is the lost corrected proofs. But since these are of the same typesetting as the first edition, it is only the variants between book and manuscript assessable as Hawthorne's revisions in proof, and not as compositorial departures from copy, that can be given any authority. If the proofs had been marked by another hand without reference to the author there could be no question of anything but single authority resident exclusively in the manuscript. However, authorial proof-corrections do insert fresh and independent authority and to that extent they introduce problems of multiple text into what is essentially a single-authority textual situation. But the setting of the derived book text remains the same after proof-correction except for the specific corrections, and thus the proportion of conflation of two stages of authority is so small that no comparison can be made with a situation in which a book has been set up from the lost authorial fair copy of a preserved earlier holograph, where multiple authority would certainly be present. At any rate, the copy-text situation for *The House of the Seven Gables* is perfectly clear, in that the manuscript remains the sole authority for the accidentals, and indeed for the substantives, also, when an editor feels convincing evidence is present that a variant book substantive was not the result of authorial proof-correction. It may be assumed for Hawthorne, and the case is nearly demonstrable, that he concerned himself little if at all with revisions in proof of the forms of the manuscript accidentals; thus all book accidental forms can ordinarily be taken as derived and unauthoritative. With an author like Whitman, who consistently revised accidentals as well as substantives, no such assumption could be made and the choice of copy-text would necessarily shift to the printed edition that had most lately come from his hands, with a minimum of necessary *correction* from earlier editions.

Fortunately such scrupulous revising authors in the proof stage are less common than authors whose main purpose in reading proof is to correct printer's error; but when such authors appear, as in William James's *Meaning of Truth* (1909), the identifiable alterations can be treated on their merits as special exceptions. One cannot build a principle upon them. The ideal copy-text will ordinarily remain any preserved holograph manuscript relatively close to the print that derives from it. This is an application of Greg's principles—devised for Elizabethan conditions—to modern times: generally (although not invariably) they are quite pertinent and will produce the best text.

Obvious exceptions will exist, and obviously an editor cannot apply Greg's principles rigidly unless he knows that they are, in fact, applicable to the material. An example about halfway between Hawthorne and Whitman exists in the book *Pragmatism* (1907) by the American philosopher William James. Some part of the text is known only from the book; some was set from annotated clippings of journal articles; but the last two chapters were set from holograph used as the direct printer's copy and preserved. In addition, James's own copy is known containing seventy-four small variants marked in his hand, only six of which are represented among the nine changes made in the plates between the second and fourth printings. The marked revisions indicate that here and there he was as concerned with eliminating such accidentals as parenthetical commas as he was to correct misprints or mistakes in names and occasionally to touch up his idiom. When one compares the text of the book with the seventh and eighth chapters set from holograph, one sees that James made numerous substantive changes in the galley proofs; and the alteration of a number of the accidentals seems to be attributable to him as well, although it is also clear that a number represent the printer's styling and are unauthoritative. On the whole, the evidence of the last section suggests that the printed text represents his final intentions more faithfully on the whole than the printer's-copy manuscript, which was his first draft but which he heavily revised before sending it to the press. The special circumstances that the holograph printer's copy was not really a finally approved fair transcript but from the start seems to have been intended for further revision in proof, the evidence that perhaps more of the significant accidental differences are due to authorial proof-correction (or to positively necessary compositorial styling) than to unauthoritative house-styling one would wish removed to restore the purity of the manuscript's intention—this situation makes possible a choice of the first edition as copy-text to be corrected by reference back to the manuscript, instead of the manuscript as copy-text to be revised by those book variants thought to be authoritative.

Actually, if the editing were scrupulously performed, the resulting text would in theory be identical since by whichever process it was arrived at it should reproduce only ascertained authority. Two caveats may be mentioned, however. First, despite the best efforts of an editor to seek evidence for his decisions, not all necessary choices have an equally evidential basis and for some no evidence whatever as to their origin is available. In such conditions it is almost inevitable that an editor will find it more convenient to accept the general authority of his copy-text even though that authority may be split between substantives and accidentals and of lesser weight in the category in which the decision lies. Thus on practical grounds it is most unlikely that two identical texts would be produced by the same editor working on the one hand from the manuscript as copy-text and on the other from the first edition. Second, the mundane question arises of the form of the apparatus. If the copy-text is the manuscript, all changes made in the print that are accepted will be recorded among the emendations so that the exact form of the manuscript will be recoverable from the apparatus, but not the exact form of the book text when its accidentals are rejected: its rejected substantives would of course be recorded. On the other hand, if the book is the copy-text, only the corrections of its accidentals from the manuscript would be noted in the emendations list and thus the reader would have no chance whatever of reconstructing from this the form of the authorial manuscript (which may ordinarily be taken as holding more interest for close students of a writer than the form of the readily available printed book) unless the editor were to obligate himself to give in his Historical Collation a list of the rejected manuscript accidentals as well as of the substantives that would automatically be recorded. (Of course, with the manuscript as copy-text an editor could provide a list of the rejected book-text accidentals, but in some cases this listing could get out of hand and the scrupulous recording of non-authority would be ridiculous to perpetuate.) The balance governing an editor's decision about copy-text in examples like *Pragmatism* is so delicate that each case must certainly be judged on its merits. Any rigid following of a principle not really applicable to the special circumstances would be mere pedantry. On the other hand, when an editor violates the sound and usually operative principles enunciated by Sir Walter Greg, it should be treated as an exception and the decision made on that basis, not on the false basis that Greg's principles do not apply to modern texts, or the false hypothesis that since some authors give no evidence that they cared about the form their accidentals took in print, the editor can safely ignore what they wrote in manuscript and happily plump for house-styling as the ideal for an edited definitive text. Moreover, when such exceptions are made, one would always like to hear a reasoned account by the editor of the causes that moved him to depart from a generally sound principle.

Multiple authority, it has been remarked, exists both in linear and in radiating documents or in some combination of the two. This authority may exhibit itself either in simple or in complex relationship among the textual documents. I take simple relationships to consist of linear or of radiating authorities from which the same antecedent document immediately behind each can be reconstructed in whole or in part. Put another way, the preserved documents are immediate witnesses to the source behind them, and this source is identical in cases of radiation. Whenever a work is printed in two or more different typesettings from the same document (whether a typescript and its carbons, or photographic reproductions) simple radiating multiple authority results. As remarked, even the principle of copy-text vanishes except perhaps for the purposes of the apparatus (in cases where Professor Tanselle's proposals are not adopted), and with reference to quantitative and qualitative evidence the editor reconstructs the lost common source so far as the documentary evidence permits. Crane's short story 'Three Miraculous Soldiers' (1896) is known in eight newspaper texts set independently from a common proof. It is clear that when all eight agree, the exact reading of the proof has been recovered. Statistically considerable weight can be placed on a seven-to-one or on a six-to-two agreement. Qualitative evidence—the nature of the variant as compared with Crane's known habits—may begin to enter with a five-to-three and certainly with a four-to-four split, and even when an editor may select a variant supported by a reasonable number of witnesses although it is in the minority, provided he conjectures that some marked characteristic of Crane has been subject to standard restyling by the majority of the compositors. Obviously the use of qualitative evidence is based on the conjecture that in the particular reading the proof reflected faithfully the manuscript copy so that an idiosyncratic feature was transferred to it though rejected by a majority of the compositors who set from the proof.

Experience with trial reconstructions of Crane's newspaper articles against a few examples of surviving proofs confirms the hypothesis that the agreement of more than one compositor in an idiosyncratic accidental will often reflect the actual proof. For example, in an article called 'Nebraska's Bitter Fight for Life', syndicated on 24 February 1895, and known in nine newspapers the tenth—the Nebraska *State Journal* typesetting—having served as the common proof, the misspelling *phenominal* in the proof was followed by one newspaper although corrected in the remaining eight, and the proof's variant spelling *meagrely* was followed in two. The proof was erratic, and often wrong, in reproducing what must have been the manuscript's lack of capitalization in *East* and *West,* but, even so, two or three compositors would usually agree. In no case of substantive variation from the proof did more than one newspaper differ from the other eight and the proof except for one highly ambiguous reported piece of dialogue where several compositors thought they were correcting the original and sophisticated it in the same manner. In the whole article of about 4500 words, the comma punctuation of the proof was rejected by a majority of the newspapers only nine times, and then usually by a five-to-four split.

One must never forget, of course, that in simple multiple authority only the document immediately behind the preserved witnesses can be recovered. Obviously, the syndicate master proof for Crane's newspaper articles and sketches is not the full equivalent of the holograph from which it was set; nevertheless, even though the proof will normally differ

from the manuscript in some respects, except for the conjectural correction
of positive error in the proof an editor cannot go in back of its characteristics to the holograph on any form of documentary evidence.[31] It may be
that in the recovered proof an editor of Crane will find accidental characteristics violating Crane's consistent practice that must have differed in
the holograph. In such a situation, when the recovered document is not
the holograph itself I suggest that an editor should be satisfied with the
progress he has made back toward ultimate authority, and without further
documentary evidence in the work he should not arbitrarily emend what
he finds in the proof to what he believes would have been holograph
characteristics when the evidence of the witnesses does not permit the
assumption. Documentary evidence bearing on this matter may be viewed
in two ways. First, literally, the evidence for the reading under examination.
That is, in all his holographs with the rarest of exceptions Crane introduced
dialogue or reported speech with a colon (or occasionally no punctuation)
and only a handful of times in the whole body of manuscripts with a
comma. If of eight newspaper witnesses to a text every one prints a comma
before a certain speech, the assumption must be that the common copy
read a comma there, without regard for what was the punctuation of the
holograph one step further back. Hence it would be improper, because
without documentary evidence, to emend by a colon even though an editor could, of course, be morally certain that a colon had been inscribed
in the holograph. However, if—secondly—the editor accepts the principle
of selective normalization on documentary evidence, he can conjecturally
emend to a colon here if elsewhere in the document being edited the
colon introducing speech is found. This is a form of documentary evidence,
not for the reading in question but for the document as a whole, indicating
that the compositor(s) were not consistent in following the characteristics
of the holograph when they set introductory commas. Thus since known
idiosyncratic characteristics appear, although not consistently, an editor
may assume that they were present throughout the basic copy but were
erratically transmitted. If he is prepared on this form of evidence to emend

---

31 That is, if the simple-radiating documents are all that are preserved, as is usual
in newspaper syndication. In complex cases something more must be done. Crane's
sketch 'The Snake' (1896) shows that the syndicate proof was set from a holograph
and that this identical manuscript was thereupon employed as printer's copy for an
associated magazine publication in different format. Here the features of the proof can
be recovered from the newspapers, and insofar as this reconstruction is complete one
has a text to compare with that of the magazine, both radiating directly at one remove
from the same manuscript. Thus many of the features of the holograph can be recovered in an eclectic text based on the common readings of reconstructed proof and
printed magazine. Variants can then be analyzed on an informed basis according to
the estimate of their respective authority in each specific case, since technically the
magazine and the reconstructed proof are in general of equal authority.

to a consistent texture such accidentals known to be strongly authorial
that appear in inconsistent form, then discreet normalization (always with
record) may be a useful editorial intervention even though not justified
on the normal basis of the positive evidence for a specific reading.

The fewer the witnesses the more reliance must be placed on qualitative
over quantitative evidence until one arrives at the irreducible split of 'The
Price of the Harness', printed in two magazines in different countries
from a ribbon and carbon copy made from Crane's manuscript. On the
evidence that the American magazine restyled certain of Crane's accidentals
—like his spelling—less than the English compositorial adaptations, an
editor with perfect freedom to use his critical judgment about the authority
of variant substantive readings from either magazine may extend this
freedom and although preferring in general the texture of the American
typesetting yet admit other accidentals from the English for their specific
characteristic features. A reprint of neither witness for this story would be
as satisfactory for substantives or for accidentals as an eclectic text.

Simple linear authority would seem to be classified in the same relationship as simple multiple whenever the same criterion is possible: the recovery of the immediate antecedent of a revised derived document. As
has been illustrated for *Tom Jones*, the fourth edition was revised by
Fielding marking a copy of the third; thus there is no problem in substantially recovering the fourth's antecedent, the annotated example of the
third. More conventionally, when Fielding revised the second edition of
Joseph Andrews by marking a copy of the first, then the third by marking
a copy of the second, and the fourth by marking a copy of the third, the
linear relationship remains simple despite the layers of revision.

Linear relationship becomes complex when the derived revised edition
may be reconstructed but the source of the revisions is not immediately
authorial since it has been transmitted to the printer's copy not by the
author but by a scribal intermediary and thus is at one or more stages of
remove from the holograph, corresponding to the author himself. *Hamlet*
is perhaps the classic case. Here, if the reconstructed textual history is
accurate, we have a copy of the Second Quarto (supposedly set from
Shakespeare's own working manuscript) brought by scribal annotation
into general substantive conformity with a late prompt-book which would
have been a modified scribal transcript either of the working manuscript
or (more likely) of an intermediate copy of that manuscript, or else of
an earlier prompt-book based on such a copy. Here the Second Quarto
stands as the immediate witness to its manuscript copy, but the annotated
example cannot be reconstructed with the precision of *Tom Jones*'s authorial revisions nor can the manuscript that was the basis of the scribal
annotation be perfectly reconstructed even in its substantives from the
Folio variants since at best the annotation was inaccurate and incomplete.

That the perfect authority of the readings in the manuscript that underlies the Folio variants may also be questioned is a part of the problem as well.

With authorial annotation, on the other hand, one can be sure of the author's full intentions at that particular time (attested by the changes he chose to make) even though these may in fact fail completely to correct or revise imperfections in the text that he might alter on a later occasion. When William James annotated a few journal articles to serve as printer's copy for chapters in his book *Pragmatism* (1907), he missed various desirable if not necessary alterations that he subsequently marked in his privately corrected example of the first printing, some few of these then being incorporated into the text by changes in the plates of the second and third printings. These annotations in the journal texts (as demonstrated by some preserved printer's copy) preceded still another layer of revision made before publication when he considerably modified the text in the galley proofs where it had not been marked in the copy; as a result, the first-edition text, by this further revision, does not always conform to the revised printer's copy that had been prepared. A still more complex case occurs when an author makes separate revisions of the same copy. Samuel Johnson in revising the second edition of the Preface to his *Dictionary* annotated a copy of the first; but when he came to revise the text for the fourth he inadvertently chose another copy of the first so that the two layers of revisions do not reflect each other.[32] In more modern times precisely the same situation arises in the works of William James. When he was working just before his death on the posthumously published *Some Problems in Philosophy*, he had a family typescript made from his manuscript, and while in England worked over one copy of this typescript but—without reference to the English revisions—he later revised the other typescript copy in America. Since he died before he could put the two stages of revision together, his mixed intentions are known well enough from these two marked typescripts, but not necessarily his final intentions.

Whatever the completeness of the author's own attempts at revision and correction, therefore, the total evidence at each stage is almost wholly recoverable and is fully authoritative even though some of the final intentions may need critical analysis. On the contrary, no critic can guarantee that the readings of the Folio replacing those of the Second Quarto *Hamlet* are either a complete record of substantive variation in the manuscript behind the Folio annotations or fully authoritative for the changes that were made: the readings may have become corrupted in their transmission

32 W. R. Keast, 'The Preface to *A Dictionary of the English Language*: Johnson's Revision and the Establishment of the Text,' *Studies in Bibliography*, 5 (1952), 129–146; 'Some Emendations in Johnson's Preface to the *Dictionary*,' *R.E.S.*, n.s. 4 (1953), 52–57.

through stages up to the document itself, and authoritative readings that survived transmissional error may have been incorrectly (and incompletely) transmitted by scribal annotation. Even James's careful proofreading passed various errors, and Stephen Crane—a reluctant and careless proofreader—seems to have made only token changes in the proofs for *The Red Badge of Courage* and 'approved' a thoroughly anomalous and often corrupt text. Since Fielding did not himself (apparently) read proof for the fourth edition of *Tom Jones,* a fair number of errors made by the printer in setting from Fielding's revised copy for the edition went unnoticed. It follows that in cases like the Folio *Hamlet* where the author neither prepared the revised copy nor read the resulting proof, departures from authority will be frequent.

In the most clearcut cases a complex relationship is established between radiating documents when the immediate physical antecedent of each form of the text differs (authorial annotations aside) regardless of its origin. If the Folio *Hamlet* had been set from the identical manuscript behind the Second Quarto (whether or not further revised), simple radiation would have resulted. But because the manuscript that provided the source for the scribal annotation of a copy of the Second Quarto (the purpose being to bring that Quarto into such general conformity with the source manuscript that it was considered to be the equivalent of sending that manuscript to the printer) was a later derivative of the working-papers manuscript behind the Quarto, a complex relationship develops, one that would obtain even if this other derived manuscript had itself been the Folio printer's copy. The situation, indeed, is substantially the same in this mixed linear relationship as it would be if in complex radiation the Folio *2 Henry IV* had been set from a scribal copy at least one remove from the working-papers manuscript behind the Quarto edition. In complex radiation, of course, neither antecedent document in the two lines can be recovered as fully as, for example, even 'The Price of the Harness' typescript from its two simple radiating witnesses. In simple radiating documents, of two variant readings one is almost certainly bound to be right and the other wrong except in the special cases of independent sophistication of an error or ambiguity in the copy. On the other hand, in complex radiation the impossibility of reconstructing at least one of the documents that has affected the transmission makes for concealment of error, and a distortion of authority that cannot always be documented. The superior authority of some readings in the Folio *Hamlet* is manifest, and they must be adopted in preference to the authority of the Second Quarto, but these seemingly pure and authoritative words are sometimes embedded in a tissue of scribal and compositorial error. That an editor should follow Greg's precepts and select the Second Quarto as copy-text on the basis of its closeness to the holograph is incontestable. That no

critical text of *Hamlet* has ever been attempted that did not blend together in various proportions the readings of Quarto and of Folio is equally
incontestable. There can scarcely be an argument here about the necessity
for eclecticism.

Finally, we come to a practical consideration that I think cannot be
ignored. The more 'scientific' the editor the more likely he is to brush aside
suggestions that his main job should be to establish not merely a simple
form of a text, such as a manuscript in one particular line but not in
another, or the Folio form of the *Hamlet* text, or the revised edition of
Crane's *Maggie*, or the unedited manuscript form of William James's
A Pluralistic Universe, except as a part of the necessary preparation of
textual documents for the final editing process. Nevertheless, except for
the narrowest investigations, ones usually quite satisfied by facsimiles or
diplomatic reprints plus apparatus (as in the German manner[33]), the
main scholarly demand is for an established critical text embodying the
author's full intentions (not merely one segment of them in an inevitably
imperfect form) insofar as these can be ascertained by an expert who has
had available all documentary sources and has devoted time and study to
their transmissional history and authority. It is then important, I believe,
to put this expertise not exclusively to the determination of the best documentary form of a text to reprint, in the Lachmannian manner, but instead
to the eclectic reconstruction of the author's intentions in as full a sense
as they can be realized from the multiple authorities, as Housman advocated, but with the application of controlled bibliographical as well as
critical reasoning behind the selection of readings such as he could not
have envisaged. With the accompanying apparatus that a definitive edition should offer, a reader who needs to trace the evidence for the eclectic
results can be provided with substantially all of his legitimate needs for
the purpose. There is neither need nor market for two texts of *Tom Jones*,
the first and the fourth editions, when the fourth-edition revisions can be
incorporated in the first-edition accidentals (the third-edition corruptions
having been weeded out) and from the apparatus the reader can isolate
every change in the first-edition substantives and accidentals from whatever source, and every rejected substantive from the second, third, and
fourth editions. If he wants to know what were the rejected unauthoritative
accidentals of the fourth edition, he is making an unreasonable request,
and it would be proper to refer such specialized enquiry to a set of electroprints. It is only the textual scholar who is concerned with the exact forms
of Quarto and Folio *Hamlet, Othello, 2 Henry IV, Troilus and Cressida,*

33 [The clearest presentation of modern German principles of editing and the construction of apparatus will be found in Hans Zeller, "A New Approach to the Critical
Constitution of Literary Texts," *SB*, 28 (1975), 231–264. Despite the title, the principles advocated are substantially those for simple Variorum editions.]

King Lear, and the like, beyond what can be made readily available in collations. That such textual scholars provide the editions should not blind them to the essential fact that the rest of scholarship does not share their specialized interests which in fact require photographic facsimiles, and that the basic demand—by no means entirely a popular one—is for the concentration of textual expertise on producing a single text that reflects as far as the evidence permits what Shakespeare would have liked to see published.

Literary critics, historians, general scholars, students of all kinds—these need as authoritative a reconstruction of a full text as the documents allow, not editions of the separate documents, except when the distance is so great as to make eclectic reconstruction impossible, as with Henry James's *Roderick Hudson* or Wordsworth's *Prelude.* When this aim should constitute the finest flower of textual scholarship, what Galsworthy in another connection calls 'the spire of meaning,' and when our increasing knowledge and expertise can constantly be stimulated to assist the validity of our recovery of an author's true text in its most authoritative form, to distrust the eclectic methodology that in some cases can alone assist in this process of recovery is to thrust one's head with the ostrich under the sand. The difficulty and expense of producing definitive editions these days are so acute that a good edition cannot shortly supersede an imperfect one as a good textbook can drive out a bad. An edition is likely to pre-empt the field for several generations or more. Under these circumstances it ought to be the most authoritative and comprehensive that can be contrived for its time and place in the history of scholarship.

Fredson Bowers

A Checklist of Publications to 1976

Chronology

Checklist

Books

The Dog Owner's Handbook. Boston: Houghton Mifflin Co., 1936. xviii, 274
Reprinted by the Sun Dial Press, New York, 1940

Elizabethan Revenge Tragedy 1587–1642. Princeton: Princeton University Press, 1940. x, 288
Reprinted by Peter Smith, Gloucester, Mass., 1959
Reprinted (paperback) with an added "Postscript" by Princeton University Press, 1966

Principles of Bibliographical Description. Princeton University Press, 1949. xviii, 506
Reprinted by Russell and Russell Co., New York, 1962 etc.

On Editing Shakespeare and the Elizabethan Dramatists. Rosenbach Fellowship in Bibliography Publications. Philadelphia: University of Pennsylvania Library, 1955. x, 132
Reprinted (hardcover and paperback) with added "Postscript" and fourth and fifth lectures "What Shakespeare Wrote" and "Today's Shakespeare Texts, and Tomorrow's." Charlottesville: University Press of Virginia, 1966. xii, 186

Textual and Literary Criticism (The Sandars Lectures in Bibliography 1957–58).
Cambridge: Cambridge University Press, 1959. x, 186
Reprinted (hardcover and paperback), 1966

Bibliography and Textual Criticism (The Lyell Lectures, 1959). Oxford at the Clarendon Press, 1964. xii, 208

HAMLET: An Outline Guide to the Play. New York: Barnes & Noble, Inc. 1965. iv, 124
Adapted by the Staff of Barnes & Noble and published in paperback, 1967, as *William Shakespeare: Hamlet*. 88 p.

Essays in Bibliography, Text, and Editing. Charlottesville: University Press of Virginia for the Bibliographical Society of the University of Virginia, 1975

Pamphlets

A Supplement to the Woodward and McManaway CHECK LIST OF ENGLISH PLAYS *1641–1700*. Charlottesville: Bibliographical Society of the University of Virginia, 1949, 24 p.

George Sandys: A Bibliographical Catalogue of Printed Editions in England to 1700 (with Richard Beale Davis). New York: New York Public Library, 1950. 54 p.

The Bibliographical Way. University of Kansas Publications: Library Series. Lawrence, 1959. 34 p.

Bibliography: Papers Read at a Clark Library Seminar May 7, 1966, by Fredson Bowers and Lyle H. Wright, with an Introduction by Hugh G. Dick. William Andrews Clark Memorial Library, University of California at Los Angeles, 1966. vi, 54. "Bibliography and Restoration Drama," pp. 1–25

Bibliography and Modern Librarianship. Berkeley: School of Librarianship; Los Angeles: School of Library Service, University of California, 1966. iv, 28

Two Lectures on Editing: Shakespeare and Hawthorne. By Charlton Hinman and Fredson Bowers. Columbus: Ohio State University Press, 1969. 70 p. "Practical Texts and Definitive Editions," pp. 21–70

Editions

THE FARY KNIGHT OR OBERON THE SECOND: A Manuscript Play Attributed to Thomas Randolph. University of Virginia Studies, no. 2. Chapel Hill: University of North Carolina Press, 1942. xlii, 88

The Dramatic Works of Thomas Dekker. Cambridge: Cambridge University Press, 1953–1961.
Vol. I (1953), xviii, 470; reprinted 1962, 1970
Vol. II (1955), viii, 592; reprinted 1964
Vol. III (1958), iv, 650; reprinted 1966
Vol. IV (1961), viii, 418; reprinted 1968

Whitman's Manuscripts: LEAVES OF GRASS (1860), A Parallel Text. Chicago: University of Chicago Press, 1955. lxxiv, 264
Reprinted, 1969

William Shakespeare: THE MERRY WIVES OF WINDSOR. The Pelican Shakespeare, general editor Alfred Harbage. Baltimore: Penguin Books, 1963. 132 p.

Reprinted in *William Shakespeare: The Complete Works*, general editor Alfred Harbage. Baltimore: Penguin Books, 1969, pp. 335–364

The Centenary Edition of the Works of Nathaniel Hawthorne. Columbus: Ohio State University Press, 1962–1975

    I.   THE SCARLET LETTER, with an Introduction by William Charvat (1962), lxviii, 290

   II.   THE HOUSE OF SEVEN GABLES, with an Introduction by William Charvat (1965), lxvi, 418

  III.   THE MARBLE FAUN, with an Introduction by Claude M. Simpson (1968), cxxxviii, 612

  IV.   OUR OLD HOME, with an Introduction by Claude M. Simpson (1970), cxvi, 498

   V.   THE BLITHEDALE ROMANCE, with an Introduction by Roy Harvey Pearce (1964), lviii, 502

  VI.   TRUE STORIES FROM HISTORY AND BIOGRAPHY, with an Introduction by Roy Harvey Pearce (1972), x, 370

 VII.   A WONDER BOOK AND TANGLEWOOD TALES, with an Introduction by Roy Harvey Pearce (1972), xii, 464

  IX.   TWICE-TOLD TALES, with an Historical Commentary by J. Donald Crowley (1974), xi, 637

   X.   MOSSES FROM AN OLD MANSE, with an Historical Commentary by J. Donald Crowley (1974), x, 664

  XI.   THE SNOW IMAGE, with an Historical Commentary by J. Donald Crowley (1974), xi, 488

The Dramatic Works in the Beaumont and Fletcher Canon, General Editor, with L. A. Beaurline, I. B. Cauthen, Jr., C. Hoy, R. K. Turner, G. W. Williams. Cambridge: Cambridge University Press, 1966—

Vol. I (1966), xxvi, 670. THE MASQUE OF THE INNER TEMPLE AND GRAY'S INN, pp. 111–144

Vol. II (1970), viii, 696. CUPID'S REVENGE, pp. 315–448

Vol. III (1975). BEGGARS BUSH

John Dryden: Four Tragedies, with L. A. Beaurline. Chicago: University of Chicago Press, 1967. x, 412 (THE INDIAN EMPEROUR, AURENG-ZEBE, ALL FOR LOVE, DON SEBASTIAN)

John Dryden: Four Comedies, with L. A. Beaurline. Chicago: University of Chicago Press, 1967. x, 368 (SECRET LOVE, SIR MARTIN MAR-ALL, AN EVENING'S LOVE, MARRIAGE-A-LA-MODE)

The Works of Stephen Crane. Charlottesville: University Press of Virginia, 1969–1975

    I.   BOWERY TALES, with an Introduction by J. B. Colvert (1969), xcviii, 186

II. THE RED BADGE OF COURAGE, with an Introduction by J. C. Levenson (1975), xcii, 424

III. THE THIRD VIOLET, ACTIVE SERVICE, with an Introduction by J. C. Levenson (1975).

IV. THE O'RUDDY, with an Introduction by J. C. Levenson (1971), lxxiv, 362

V. TALES OF ADVENTURE, with an Introduction by J. C. Levenson (1970), cxcvi, 242

VI. TALES OF WAR, with an Introduction by J. B. Colvert (1970), cxcii, 402

VII. TALES OF WHILOMVILLE, with an Introduction by J. C. Levenson (1969), lx, 278

VIII. TALES, SKETCHES, AND REPORTS, with an Introduction by E. H. Cady (1973), xlii, 1184

IX. REPORTS OF WAR, with an Introduction by J. B. Colvert (1971), xl, 678

X. POEMS AND LITERARY REMAINS, with an Introduction by J. B. Colvert (1975)

The Complete Works of Christopher Marlowe. Cambridge: Cambridge University Press, 1973.

Vol. I, xii, 418 (DIDO, TAMBURLAINE, JEW OF MALTA, MASSACRE AT PARIS)

Vol. II, vi, 542 (EDWARD II, DOCTOR FAUSTUS, FIRST BOOK OF LUCAN, OVID'S ELEGIES, HERO AND LEANDER, MISCELLANEOUS PIECES)

Stephen Crane THE RED BADGE OF COURAGE: A Facsimile Edition of the Manuscript. A Bruccoli Clark Book. Washington, D.C.: NCR / Microcard Editions, 1973. Part i, Introduction and Apparatus, xiv, 124; Part ii, The Manuscript, viii, 264

TOM JONES: THE HISTORY OF A FOUNDLING, by Henry Fielding, with Introduction and Commentary by Martin Battestin. Middletown, Conn.: Wesleyan University Press and Oxford: Clarendon Press, 1974.

The Works of William James. Cambridge, Mass.: Harvard University Press, 1975—, for the American Council of Learned Societies

PRAGMATISM, with an Introduction by H. S. Thayer (1975)

THE MEANING OF TRUTH, with an Introduction by H. S. Thayer (1975)

ESSAYS IN RADICAL EMPIRICISM, with an Introduction by John J. McDermott (1975).

A PLURALISTIC UNIVERSE, with an introduction by Richard J. Bernstein (1976)

ESSAYS IN PHILOSOPHY AND RELIGION, with an Introduction by John J. McDermott (1976)

Articles, Notes, Correspondence

1925

College Slang: A Language All of Its Own, *Literary Digest*, 84 (March 14, 1925), 64–65. [A reprint of an article from the *Brown Daily Herald* by its editor]

1930

An Addition to the Breton Canon, *Modern Language Notes*, 45 (1930), 161–166

1931

Kyd's Pedringano: Sources and Parallels, *Harvard Studies and Notes in Philology and Literature*, 13 (1931), 241–249

1932

The Stabbing of a Portrait in Elizabethan Tragedy, *Modern Language Notes*, 47 (1932), 378–385

1933

The Date and Composition of ALPHONSUS EMPEROR OF GERMANY, *Harvard Studies and Notes in Philology and Literature*, 15 (1933), 165–189

ALPHONSUS EMPEROR OF GERMANY and the UR-HAMLET, *Modern Language Notes*, 48 (1933), 101–108

1934

The Audience and the Revenger of Elizabethan Tragedy, *Studies in Philology*, 32 (1934), 160–175

Notes on Gascoigne's A HUNDRETH SUNDRIE FLOWRES and THE POSIES, *Harvard Studies and Notes in Philology and Literature*, 16 (1934), 13–35

A History of Elizabethan Revengeful Tragedy, *Summary of Theses, Harvard University 1934*, pp. 304–308

1936

Bibliographical Problems in Dekker's MAGNIFICENT ENTERTAINMENT, *The Library*, 4th series, 17 (1936), 333–339

Dekker and Jonson, *Times Literary Supplement*, Sept. 12, 1936, p. 729

1937

The Audience and the Poisoners of Elizabethan Tragedy, *Journal of English and Germanic Philology*, 36 (1937), 491–504

Ben Jonson the Actor, *Studies in Philology*, 34 (1937), 392–406

Ben Jonson, Thomas Randolph, and THE DRINKING ACADEMY, *Notes & Queries*, 183 (1937), 166–168

The Date of REVENGE FOR HONOUR, *Modern Language Notes,* 52 (1937), 192–196

Gascoigne and the Oxford Cipher, *Modern Language Notes,* 52 (1937), 183–186

Henry Howard Earl of Northampton and Duelling in England, *Englische Studien,* 71 (1937), 350–355

THE FAIRY KNIGHT, *Times Literary Supplement,* April 17, 1937, p. 292

Middleton's A FAIR QUARREL and the Duelling Code, *Journal of English and Germanic Philology,* 36 (1937), 40–65

Thomas Dekker: Two Textual Notes, *The Library,* 4th series, 18 (1937), 338–341

Dekker and THE SHOEMAKER'S HOLIDAY, *New York Times,* Dec. 26, 1937, sec. X, p. 3

1938

Notes on Running-Titles as Bibliographical Evidence, *The Library,* 4th series, 19 (1938), 315–338

[Correspondence on] Glapthorne's REVENGE FOR HONOUR, *Review of English Studies,* 14 (1938), 329–330

Problems in Thomas Randolph's DRINKING ACADEMY and Its Manuscript, *Huntington Library Quarterly,* 1 (1938), 189–198

A Note on THE SPANISH TRAGEDY, *Modern Language Notes,* 53 (1938), 590–591

1939

A Possible Randolph Holograph, *The Library,* 4th series, 20 (1939), 192–194

A Sixteenth-Century Plough Monday Play Cast, *Review of English Studies,* 15 (1939), 192–194

An Interpretation of Donne's Tenth Elegy, *Modern Language Notes,* 54 (1939), 280–282

Marriott's Two Editions of Randolph's ARISTIPPUS, *The Library,* 4th series, 20 (1939), 163–166

1941

Thomas Nashe and the Picaresque Novel, *Humanistic Studies in Honor of John Calvin Metcalf, University of Virginia Studies,* 1 (1941), 13–27

1942

Thomas Randolph's 'Salting,' *Modern Philology,* 39 (1942), 275–280

The Headline in Early Books, in *English Institute Annual 1941* (New York: Columbia University Press, 1942), pp. 185–205

1945

Evidences of Revision in THE FAERIE QUEENE, III.i.ii, *Modern Language Notes,* 60 (1945), 114–116

1946

Notes on Standing Type in Elizabethan Printing, *Papers of the Bibliographical Society of America,* 40 (1946), 205–224

Bibliographical Miscellanea, *The Library,* 5th series, 1 (1946), 131–134

1947

Criteria for Classifying Hand-Printed Books as Issues and Variant States, *Papers of the Bibliographical Society of America,* 41 (1947), 271–292. [Reprinted in *A Reader on Descriptive Bibliography,* edited by J. P. Immroth]

An Examination of the Method of Proof Correction in LEAR, *The Library,* 5th series, 2 (1947), 20–44

1948

Correspondence [a reply to P. S. Dunkin's discussion of article in *PBSA* (1947)], *Papers of the Bibliographical Society of America,* 42 (1948), 341–343. [Reprinted in *A Reader on Descriptive Bibliography,* edited by J. P. Immroth]

Running-Title Evidence for Determining Half-Sheet Imposition, [*Studies in Bibliography*] *Papers of the Bibliographical Society of the University of Virginia,* 1 (1948), 199–202

The First Series of Plays Published by Francis Kirkman, *The Library,* 5th series, 2 (1948), 289–291

Two Notes on Running-Titles as Bibliographical Evidence, *Papers of the Bibliographical Society of America,* 42 (1948), 143–148

Certain Basic Problems in Descriptive Bibliography, *Papers of the Bibliographical Society of America,* 42 (1948), 211–228. [Reprinted in *A Reader on Descriptive Bibliography,* edited by J. P. Immroth]

Elizabethan Proofing, in *Joseph Quincy Adams Memorial Studies,* edited by J. G. McManaway, G. E. Dawson, and E. E. Willoughby (Washington, D.C.: Folger Shakespeare Library, 1948), pp. 571–586

Bibliographical Evidence from a Resetting in Caryll's SIR SALOMON 1691, *The Library,* 5th series, 3 (1948), 134–137

[Final section of] R. B. Davis, George Sandys v. William Stansby: The 1632 Edition of Ovid's METAMORPHOSIS, *The Library,* 5th series, 3 (1948), 193–212

1949

Variants in Early Editions of Dryden's Plays, *Harvard Library Bulletin,* 3 (1949), 278–288

The Cancel Leaf in Congreve's DOUBLE DEALER 1694, *Papers of the Bibliographical Society of America*, 43 (1949), 78–82

Thomas d'Urfrey's COMICAL HISTORY OF DON QUIXOTE 1694, *Papers of the Bibliographical Society of America*, 43 (1949), 191–195

Bibliography and the University, *University of Pennsylvania Library Chronicle*, 15 (1949), 37–51

Thomas Dekker, Robert Wilson, and THE SHOEMAKERS' HOLIDAY, *Modern Language Notes*, 44 (1949), 517–519

Printing Evidence in Wynkyn de Worde's Edition of THE LIFE OF JOHAN PICUS by St. Thomas More, *Papers of the Bibliographical Society of America*, 43 (1949), 398–399

Bibliographical Evidence from the Printer's Measure, *Studies in Bibliography*, 2 (1949), 153–167

THE WITS, in *A Bibliography of Francis Kirkman*, edited by Strickland Gibson, Oxford Bibliographical Society Publications, new series, 1, fascicule ii for 1947 (1949), 135–139

1950

A Late Appearance of 'Cornwall' for 'Cornhill,' *Notes & Queries*, 195 (1950), 97–98

Nathaniel Lee: Three Probable Seventeenth-Century Piracies, *Papers of the Bibliographical Society of America*, 44 (1950), 62–66

The Prologue to Nathaniel Lee's MITHRIDATES 1678, *Papers of the Bibliographical Society of America*, 44 (1950), 173–175

The First Edition of Dryden's WILD GALLANT 1669, *The Library*, 5th series, 5 (1950), 51–54

Current Theories of Copy-Text, with an Illustration from Dryden, *Modern Philology*, 48 (1950), 12–20. [Reprinted in *Bibliography and Textual Criticism*, edited by O. M. Brack, Jr., and Warner Barnes (University of Chicago Press, 1969), pp. 59–72.]

A Crux in the Text of Lee's PRINCESS OF CLEVE 1689, II.i, *Harvard Library Bulletin*, 4 (1950), 409–411

The Supposed Cancel in Southerne's THE DISAPPOINTMENT Reconsidered, *The Library*, 5th series, 5 (1950), 140–149

Some Relations of Bibliography to Editorial Problems, *Studies in Bibliography*, 3 (1950), 37–62. [Read before the English Institute at Columbia University, September 9, 1949; reprinted in *A Mirror for Modern Scholars*, edited by L. A. Beaurline (New York: Odyssey Press, 1966), pp. 16–39]

[With Lucy Clark] A Selective Check-List of Bibliographical Scholarship for 1949: Part II, Later Renaissance to the Present, *Studies in Bibliography*, 3 (1950), 295–302

[Articles in] *Collier's Encyclopedia* (New York: Collier, 1950): Thomas Dekker, 6, 349; THE SHOEMAKERS' HOLIDAY, 17, 559; Thomas Nashe, 14, 371; THE UNFORTUNATE TRAVELLER, 19, 18

1951

THE FAERIE QUEENE, Book II: Mordant, Ruddymane, and the Nymph's Well, *English Studies in Honor of James Southall Wilson, University of Virginia Studies*, 5 (1951), 243–251

The First Editions of Sir Robert Stapylton's THE SLIGHTED MAID 1663, and THE STEP-MOTHER 1664, *Papers of the Bibliographical Society of America*, 45 (1951), 143–148

Robert Roberts: A Printer of Shakespeare's Fourth Folio, *Shakespeare Quarterly*, 2 (1951), 143–148

The Revolution in Shakespeare Criticism, *University of Chicago Magazine*, November, 1951, pp. 11–14

The 1665 Manuscript of Dryden's INDIAN EMPEROUR, *Studies in Philology*, 48 (1951), 738–760

The Variant Sheets in John Bank's CYRUS THE GREAT 1696, *Studies in Bibliography*, 4 (1951), 174–183

The Two Issues of d'Urfey's CYNTHIA AND ENDYMION 1697, *Princeton University Library Chronicle*, 13 (1951), 32–34

1952

The Text of Marlowe's FAUSTUS, *Modern Philology*, 49 (1952), 195–204

Essex's Rebellion and Dekker's OLD FORTUNATUS, *Review of English Studies*, new series, 3 (1952), 365–366

Bibliography, Pure Bibliography, and Literary Studies, *Papers of the Bibliographical Society of America*, 46 (1952), 186–208

The Pictures in HAMLET, III.iv: A Possible Contemporary Reference, *Shakespeare Quarterly*, 3 (1952), 280–281

The Pirated Quarto of Dryden's STATE OF INNOCENCE, *Studies in Bibliography*, 5 (1952), 166–169

The Problem of the Variant Forme in a Facsimile Edition, *The Library*, 5th series, 7 (1952), 262–272

1953

A Definitive Text of Shakespeare: Problems and Methods, in *Studies in Shakespeare*, edited by Arnold Matthews (Coral Gables, Fla.: (University of Miami Press, 1953), pp. 11–29

A Note on HAMLET I.v.33 and II.ii.181, *Shakespeare Quarterly*, 4 (1953), 51–56

Dryden as Laureate: The Cancel Leaf in KING ARTHUR, *Times Literary Supplement*, April 10, 1953, p. 244

Purposes of Descriptive Bibliography, with Some Remarks on Methods, *The*

Library, 5th series, 8 (1953), 1–22. [Reprinted in *Readings in Descriptive Bibliography*, ed. John Bush Jones (Kent, Ohio: Kent State University Press, 1974), pp. 12–41]

The Manuscript of Whitman's "Passage to India," *Modern Philology*, 51 (1953), 102–117

Ogilby's Coronation ENTERTAINMENT (1661–1689): Editions and Issues, *Papers of the Bibliographical Society of America*, 47 (1953), 339–355

1954

Shakespeare's Text and the Bibliographical Method, *Studies in Bibliography*, 6 (1954), 71–92

Whitman's Manuscripts for the Original "Calamus" Poems, *Studies in Bibliography*, 6 (1954), 257–265

Scholarship, Research, and the Undergraduate Teacher, *Bulletin of Randolph-Macon College*, 26 (September, 1954), 3–4, 20–23. [The 1954 Randolph-Macon (Ashland, Virginia) Phi Beta Kappa Address]

The Manuscript of Walt Whitman's "A Carol of Harvest, for 1867," *Modern Philology*, 52 (1954), 29–51

Motteux's LOVE'S A JEST (1696): A Running-Title and Presswork Problem, *Papers of the Bibliographical Society of America*, 48 (1954), 268–273

Further Observations on Locke's TWO TREATISES OF GOVERNMENT, *Transactions of the Cambridge Bibliographical Society*, 2 (1954), 63–78

Underprinting in Mary Pix, THE SPANISH WIVES (1696), *The Library*, 5th series, 9 (1954), 248–254

1955

The Printing of HAMLET Q2, *Studies in Bibliography*, 7 (1955), 41–50; additions and corrections in *Studies in Bibliography*, 8 (1956), 267–269

McKerrow's Editorial Principles for Shakespeare Reconsidered, *Shakespeare Quarterly*, 6 (1955), 309–324

Hamlet as Minister and Scourge, *PMLA*, 70 (1955), 740–749. [Read before the Shakespeare Section of the Modern Language Association of America, December 1954: cited in the Seventy-Fifth Anniversary Number of *PMLA* as one of the nine articles in the past seventy-five years "which have really affected the course of scholarship and criticism." Reprinted in *Twentieth Century Interpretations of* HAMLET, edited by David Bevington (Englewood Cliffs, N.J.: Prentice-Hall, 1968), pp. 82–92]

Another Early Edition of Thomas Jevon's DEVIL OF A WIFE, *Papers of the Bibliographical Society of America*, 49 (1955), 253–254

The Yale Folio Facsimile and Scholarship, *Modern Philology*, 53 (1955), 50–57

1956

The Manuscripts of Whitman's "Song of the Redwood-Tree," *Papers of the Bibliographical Society of America,* 50 (1956), 53–85

Hamlet's 'Sullied' or 'Solid' Flesh: A Bibliographical Case-History, *Shakespeare Survey,* 9 (1956), 44–48

The Textual Relation of Q2 to Q1 HAMLET, *Studies in Bibliography,* 8 (1956), 39–66

1957

The Earliest Manuscript of Whitman's "Passage to India" and Its Notebook, *Bulletin of the New York Public Library,* 61 (1957), 319–352

1958

Textual Criticism, *Encyclopaedia Britannica,* 22 (January, 1958), 13–19

Old-Spelling Editions of Dramatic Texts, in *Studies in Honor of T. W. Baldwin,* edited by D. C. Allen (Urbana: University of Illinois, 1958), pp. 9–15. [Read before the English Drama Section of the Modern Language Association of America, University of Wisconsin, September 10, 1957]

1959

The Death of Hamlet, in *Studies in the English Renaissance Drama: In Memory of Karl Julius Holzknecht,* edited by J. W. Bennett, O. Cargill, and V. Hall, Jr. (New York: New York University Press, 1959, pp. 28–42.

The Function of Bibliography, *Library Trends,* 7 (1959), 497–510

Walter Wilson Greg, 9 July 1875–4 March 1959, *The Library,* 5th series, 9 (1959), 171–173

The Copy for the Folio RICHARD III, *Shakespeare Quarterly,* 10 (1959), 541–544

1960

Bibliography, *Encyclopaedia Britannica,* 3 (1960), 539–543

1961

Sir Walter Wilson Greg (1875–1959), in *The American Philosophical Society Year Book 1960* (Philadelphia: American Philosophical Society, 1961), pp. 143–147

The Business of Teaching, *The Graduate Journal,* 4 (1961), 389–405

A Bibliographical History of the Fletcher-Betterton Play, THE PROPHETESS, 1690, *The Library,* 5th series, 16 (1961), 169–175

1962

Established Texts and Definitive Editions, in *Studies in English Drama Presented to Baldwin Maxwell,* edited by C. B. Wood and C. A. Zimansky [*Philological Quarterly,* 41 (1962), 1–17]

The Star Symbol in Henry Vaughan's Poetry, in *Renaissance Papers 1961,*
edited by G. W. Williams (Durham, N.C., 1962), pp. 25–29. [Read before
the Southeastern Renaissance Conference, Durham, N.C., April 22, 1961]
Herbert's Sequential Imagery: "The Temper," *Modern Philology,* 59 (1962),
202–213
Hamlet's Fifth Soliloquy, III.ii.406–417, in *Essays in Shakespeare and Elizabethan Drama in Honor of Hardin Craig,* edited by R. Hosley (Columbia:
University of Missouri Press, 1962), pp. 213–222. [Reprinted in *Ap-
proaches to Shakespeare,* edited by N. Rabkin (New York: McGraw Hill,
1964), pp. 24–50. Originally read as the Annual Phi Beta Kappa Address,
Washington and Lee University, Lexington, Virginia, April 12, 1962]
Classical Antecedents of Elizabethan Drama, *Tennessee Studies in Literature,*
7 (1962), 79–85
What Shakespeare Wrote, *Shakespeare-Jahrbuch,* 98 (1962), 24–50. [The
Annual Phi Beta Kappa Address at Vanderbilt University, Nashville, Tenn.,
December 5, 1962; reprinted as an addition to *On Editing Shakespeare*
(Charlottesville: University Press of Virginia, 1966), pp. 103–136; re-
printed in *Approaches to Shakespeare,* edited by Norman Rabkin (New
York: McGraw-Hill, 1964), pp. 264–289]
William Faulkner, 1897–1962, *University of Virginia Topics,* Summer, 1962,
[p. 2]

1963

Shakespeare's Dramatic Vagueness, *Virginia Quarterly Review,* 39 (1963),
475–484
Textual Criticism, in *The Aims and Methods of Scholarship in the Modern
Languages and Literatures,* edited by J. Thorpe (New York: Modern Language Association of America, 1963), pp. 23–42. [Revised second edition,
1970, pp. 29–54]

1964

Some Principles for Scholarly Editions of American Authors, *Studies in Bibliography,* 17 (1964), 223–228. [Read before the American Literature
Section of the South Atlantic Modern Language Association, November
22, 1962; reprinted in *Bibliography and Textual Criticism,* edited by O. M.
Brack and Warner Barnes (Chicago: University of Chicago Press, 1969),
pp. 194–201; reprinted in *Art and Error: Modern Textual Editing,* edited
by Ronald Gottesman and Scott Bennett (Bloomington: Indiana University Press, 1970), pp. 54–61]
Shakespeare's Art: The Point of View, in *Literary Views: Critical and Historical Essays,* edited by C. Camden, Rice University Semicentennial Publications (Chicago: University of Chicago Press, 1964), pp. 45–58. [Read
in the Semicentennial Series at Rice University, November 16, 1962]

Dramatic Structure and Criticism: Plot in HAMLET, *Shakespeare Quarterly*, 15 (1964), 207–218. [Reprinted in *Shakespeare 400: Essays by American Scholars on the Anniversary of the Poet's Birth*, edited by J. G. McManaway (New York: Holt, Rinehart and Winston, 1964)]

Hawthorne's Text, in *Hawthorne Centenary Essays*, edited by R. H. Pearce (Columbus: Ohio State University Press, 1964), pp. 401–425

The Text of Johnson, *Modern Philology*, 61 (1964), 298–309

The Moment of Final Suspense in HAMLET: 'We Defy Augury,' in *Shakespeare 1564–1964*, edited by E. A. Bloom (Providence: Brown University Press, 1964), pp. 500–555. [Read before the Shakespeare Section of the Modern Language Association, Washington, D.C., December 28, 1962]

1965

Death in Victory, *South Atlantic Bulletin*, 30, no. 2 (March, 1965), 1–7. [Read before the South Atlantic Modern Language Association, Atlanta, Georgia, November 12, 1964]

Doctor of Arts: A New Graduate Degree, *College English*, 27 (November, 1965), 123–128

1966

Today's Shakespeare Texts, and Tomorrow's, *Studies in Bibliography*, 19 (1966), 39–65. [An address delivered in the President's Lecture Series at Wayne State University, March 10, 1964; reprinted as an addition to *On Editing Shakespeare* (Charlottesville: University Press of Virginia, 1966), pp. 137–179]

Hal and Francis in KING HENRY IV, PART I, in *Renaissance Papers 1965*, edited by G. W. Williams (Durham, N.C., 1966), pp. 15–20. [Read before the Southeastern Renaissance Conference, April 2, 1965]

Textual Criticism, in *The Reader's Encyclopedia of Shakespeare*, edited by O. J. Campbell (New York: Thomas Crowell Co., 1966), pp. 864–869

1967

[Correspondence] TROILUS AND CRESSIDA, *Times Literary Supplement*, March 16, 1967, p. 226

Old Wine in New Bottles: Problems of Machine Printing, in *Editing Nineteenth Century Texts*, edited by J. M. Robson (Toronto: University of Toronto Press, 1967), pp. 9–36

Death in Victory: Shakespeare's Tragic Reconciliations, in *Studies in Honor of DeWitt T. Starnes*, edited by T. P. Harrison, A. A. Hill, E. C. Mosser, J. Sledd (Austin: University of Texas Press, 1967), pp. 53–75

1969

Crane's RED BADGE OF COURAGE and Other 'Advance Copies,' *Studies in Bibliography*, 22 (1969), 273–277

Adam, Eve, and the Fall in PARADISE LOST, *PMLA*, 84 (1969), 264–273. [Originally delivered as the Christopher Longest Lecture at the University of Mississippi on November 28, 1967]

Bibliography Revisited, *The Library*, 5th series, 24 (1969), 84–128. [Read before The Bibliographical Society in London on October 17, 1967, during the seventy-fifth anniversary celebration]

1970

Theme and Structure in KING HENRY IV, PART 1, in *The Drama of the Renaissance: Essays for Leicester Bradner*, edited by E. M. Blistein (Providence: Brown University Press, 1970), pp. 42–68

The New Look in Editing, *South Atlantic Bulletin*, 35 (January, 1970), 3–10. [The Presidential Address at the Annual Meeting of the South Atlantic Modern Language Association]

On a Future for Graduate Studies, *AAUP Bulletin*, 56 (1970), 366–370. [An address to the Convocation of the Graduate School of Brown University, June 1, 1970, on the occasion of an award of the degree of Doctor of Letters. Excerpted as "The Dilemma of Graduate Education," *PMLA*, 85 (1970), 118–120]

1971

Clifton Walter Barrett, *Antiquarian Bookman's Weekly*, August 2–9, 1971, pp. 239–242. [An address at the University of Virginia Library at a banquet on June 1, 1971, in honor of Clifton Waller Barrett's seventieth birthday]

Four Faces of Bibliography, *Papers of the Bibliographical Society of Canada*, 10 (1971), 33–45. [Read before the Society on November 5, 1971, in Toronto, Canada]

1972

Was There a Lost Edition of Marlowe's EDWARD II? *Studies in Bibliography*, 25 (1972), 143–148

The Early Editions of Marlowe's OVID'S ELEGIES, *Studies in Bibliography*, 25 (1972), 149–172

Multiple Authority: New Concepts of Copy-Text, *The Library*, 5th series, 27 (1972), 81–115. [Read before The Bibliographical Society in London on April 18, 1972; an early brief version was read on December 29, 1971, before the Bibliographical Evidence Section of the Modern Language Association of America, meeting in Chicago]

Seven More Years? in *Shakespeare 1971: Proceedings of the World Shakespeare Congress, Vancouver, August, 1971*, edited by C. Leech (Toronto: University of Toronto Press, 1972), pp. 50–58. [A position paper read before the Congress]

Notes on Editing THE O'RUDDY: A Posthumously Published Work; Stephen Crane, THE O'RUDDY: Editorial Process; Notes on Editing "Death and the

Child": Four Independent Texts; Notes on Editing "The Revenge of the ADOLPHUS: A Combined, Selective Text, in *The Author's Intention: An Exhibition for the Center for Editions of American Authors* (Columbia, S.C.: for the CEAA, 1972), pp. 10–24, 28–41

1973

Marlowe's DOCTOR FAUSTUS: The 1602 Additions, *Studies in Bibliography*, 26 (1973), 1–18

The Ecology of American Literary Texts, *Scholarly Publishing*, 4 (1973), 133–140

McKerrow Revisited, *Papers of the Bibliographical Society of America*, 67 (1973), 110–124

1974

BEGGARS BUSH: A Reconstructed Prompt-Book and Its Copy, *Studies in Bibliography*, 27 (1974), 113–136

Remarks on Eclectic Texts, *Proof: The Yearbook of American Bibliographical and Textual Studies*, edited by J. Katz, 4 (1974), 13–58. [Read at a Conference on Editorial Problems at the Villa Serbelloni Study and Conference Center, Bellagio, Italy, September 22, 1973]

1975

Linton Reynolds Massey 1900–1974. *Chapter & Verse-3:* A Report to the Associates of the University of Virginia Library. Charlottesville: February 1975, pp. 5–8.

1976

Transcription of Manuscripts: The Record of Variants, *Studies in Bibliography*, 29 (1976)

Reviews

Shakespeare's Influence on the Drama of His Age Studied in Hamlet by D. J. McGinn. *Modern Language Notes*, 54 (1939), 314–315

Repetition in Shakespeare's Plays, by P. V. Kreider; *The Character of Hamlet and Other Essays*, by J. E. Hankins; *The Life and Works of George Turbervile*, by J. E. Hankins; *The Poems of Sir John Davies*, edited by Clare Howard; *Ignatius His Conclave*, edited by C. M. Coffin; *Divine Vengeance: A Study in the Philosophical Backgrounds of the Revenge Motif As It Appears in Shakespeare's Chronicle History Plays*, by Sister M. B. Mroz; *The Elizabethan Sermon, a Survey and a Bibliography*, by A. F. Herr; *Robert Gould, Seventeenth Century Satirist*, by E. H. Sloane. *Modern Language Notes*, 57 (1942), 468–473

Transactions of the Cambridge Bibliographical Society, edited by Bruce Dickins and A. N. L. Munby, I, part I (1949). *Papers of the Bibliographical Society of America,* 44 (1950), 196–198

Shakespeare's Producing Hand, by Richard Flatter. *Modern Philology,* 48 (1950), 64–68

The King's Printers, 1660–1742, by A. F. Johnson. *Philological Quarterly,* 29 (1950), 238

Transactions of the Cambridge Bibliographical Society, edited by Bruce Dickins and A. N. L. Munby, I, part 2 (1950). *Papers of the Bibliographical Society of America,* 45 (1951), 172–175

Shakespeare's KING LEAR, edited by George Ian Duthie. *Modern Language Quarterly,* 12 (1951), 363–364

The Plays and Poems of William Cartwright, edited by G. Blakemore Evans. *Modern Philology,* 50 (1953), 60–64

Jonson's MASQUE OF THE GYPSIES: *An Attempt at Reconstruction,* edited by W. W. Greg. *Review of English Studies,* new series, 4 (1953), 172–177

KING LEAR (New Arden Edition), edited by Kenneth Muir. *Shakespeare Quarterly,* 4 (1953), 471–477

The Composition of Shakespeare's Plays: Authorship, Chronology, by Albert Feuillerat. *Modern Philology,* 51 (1953), 132–135

An Evening with William Shakespeare, direction and narration by Margaret Webster. *Shakespeare Quarterly,* 5 (1954), 330–331

The Works of Nathaniel Lee, edited by T. B. Stroup and A. L. Cooke, 2 vols. *Philological Quarterly,* 35 (1956), 310–314

New Readings in Shakespeare, by C. J. Sisson, 2 vols. *Modern Language Quarterly,* 18 (1957), 156–157

Shakespeare, HENRY V, 1606; LOVE'S LABOUR'S LOST, 1598. Shakespeare Quarto Facsimiles, edited by W. W. Greg. *Modern Language Review,* 53 (1958), 235–236

Shakespeare, THE TRUE TRAGEDY OF RICHARD DUKE OF YORK, 1595. Shakespeare Quarto Facsimiles, edited by W. W. Greg. *Modern Language Review,* 54 (1959), 297

Thomas J. Wise and the Pre-Restoration Drama, by D. F. Foxon. *Times Literary Supplement,* June 2, 1959, p. 344

The Copy for the Folio Text of RICHARD III, by J. K. Walton. *Shakespeare Quarterly,* 10 (1959), 91–96

Samuel Johnson: Diaries, Prayers, and Annals, edited by E. L. McAdam, Jr., with Donald and Mary Hyde. *Journal of English and Germanic Philology,* 58 (1959), 132–137

The Business of Criticism, by Helen Gardner. *Virginia Quarterly Review*, 36 (1960), 151–154

The Early Collected Editions of Shelley's Poems, by Charles H. Taylor, Jr. *The Keats-Shelley Journal*, 9 (1960), 35–38

Printing in London from 1476 to Modern Times: Competitive Practice and Technical Invention, by P. M. Handover. *Modern Language Quarterly*, 32 (1961), 214

W. W. Greg: Collected Papers, edited by J. C. Maxwell. *Times Literary Supplement*, Sept. 28, 1967, p. 924

Charles Dickens, OLIVER TWIST, edited by Kathleen Tillotson. *Nineteenth-Century Fiction*, 23 (1968), 226–239

Walt Whitman's Blue Book: The 1860–61 LEAVES OF GRASS, edited by Arthur Golden. *Journal of English and Germanic Philology*, 68 (1969), 316–320

Thomas Dekker: A Bibliographical Catalogue, by A. F. Allison. *Times Literary Supplement*, Nov. 17, 1972, p. 1404

Sir William Davenant: THE SIEGE OF RHODES, *A Critical Edition*, by Ann-Mari Hedbäck. *Svensk Tidskrift för Bibliografi och Textkritik*, 1 (1974), pp. 41–44

Miscellaneous Contributions

Editor of *English Studies in Honor of James Southall Wilson, University of Virginia Studies*, 4 (1951)

Editor of *Studies in Bibliography*, 1 (1948) to date

Textual Principles and Procedures, *John Dewey: The Early Works, 1882–1898* (Carbondale: Southern Illinois Press, 1967–72) I (1969), ix–xix; II (1967), ix–xx; III (1969), l–lx; IV (1971), xli–li (revised), etc. Consulting Textual Editor for this edition.

The Wesleyan Edition of the Works of Henry Fielding. (Middletown, Conn.: Wesleyan University Press) JOSEPH ANDREWS, edited by M. C. Battestin (1967) [Textual Introduction by Fredson Bowers, pp. xxxix–xlvii]; *Miscellanies*, vol. I, edited by H. K. Miller (1972) [Textual Introduction by Fredson Bowers, pp. l–lv]. General Textual Editor for this edition.

The Textual Introduction to THE VIRGIN MARTYR, reprinted from *The Dramatic Works of Thomas Dekker*, III (1958), 367–375, in *Evidence for Authorship: Essays on Problems of Attribution*, edited by D. V. Erdman and E. G. Fogel (Ithaca, N.Y.: Cornell University Press, 1966), pp. 224–228

Excerpt from *Elizabethan Revenge Tragedy 1587–1642* (1940), pp. 177–179, reprinted in *Twentieth Century Interpretations of* THE DUCHESS OF MALFI, edited by N. Rabkin (Englewood Cliffs, N.J.: Prentice-Hall, 1958), pp. 100–101

Excerpt from *Elizabethan Revenge Tragedy 1587–1642* (1940), pp. 228–234 reprinted as "Elizabethan Revenge Tragedy and THE CARDINAL," in *Shakespeare's Contemporaries*, edited by Max Bluestone and Norman Rabkin (Englewood Cliffs, N.J.: Prentice Hall, 1961), pp. 295–300; 2nd edition (1970), pp. 406–411

Bibliographical Introduction, in *Robert Frost: A Descriptive Catalogue of Books and Manuscripts in the Clifton Waller Barrett Library, University of Virginia*, compiled by Joan St. C. Crane (Charlottesville: University Press of Virginia, 1974), pp. xxi–xxii

Chronology

1905	Born New Haven, Connecticut, 25 April
1917–21	Hillhouse High School, New Haven
1921–25	Brown University, Ph.B. 1925
1924	Phi Beta Kappa
1926–36	Instructor in English and Tutor in the Modern Languages, Harvard University
1934	Ph.D., Harvard University
1936–38	Instructor in English, Princeton University
1938–46	Assistant Professor of English, University of Virginia
1942–45	Commander, U.S.N.R., Naval Communications, Washington, D.C.
1946–48	Associate Professor of English, University of Virginia
1948–57	Professor of English, University of Virginia
1948–	Editor, *Studies in Bibliography*
1949–59	Professorial Lecturer in English, University of Chicago
1952–53	Fulbright Fellow for Advanced Research in the United Kingdom
1954	Rosenbach Lecturer in Bibliography
1954–58	Regional Chairman, Woodrow Wilson National Fellowship Foundation
1957–68	Alumni Professor of English, University of Virginia
1958–59	Guggenheim Fellowship
1958	Sandars Reader in Bibliography, Cambridge University
1959	James Lyell Reader in Bibliography, Oxford University
1961–68	Chairman, Department of English, University of Virginia
1961–62	Phi Beta Kappa Visiting Scholar
1962–78	Shakespeare Variorum Committee, Modern Language Association of America
1962–66	Executive Council, Modern Language Association of America
1964	Bicentennial Medal, Brown University
1966–68	English Advisory Committee, Modern Language Association of America
1968–75	Linden Kent Memorial Professor of English, University of Virginia
1968	Corresponding Fellow, The British Academy
1968	Gold Medal, The Bibliographical Society, London

1968–69	Dean of the Faculty, University of Virginia
1969	President, South Atlantic Modern Language Association
1970	Doctor of Letters, Clark University
1970	Doctor of Letters, Brown University
1971	Research Scholar, Villa Serbelloni Research Center, Bellagio, Italy
1971–72	Guggenheim Fellowship
1971	Thomas Jefferson Award, University of Virginia
1972	Fellow, American Academy of Arts and Sciences
1972	Visiting Fellow, All Souls College, Oxford
1972	Research Scholar, Villa Serbelloni Research Center, Bellagio, Italy
1973	Doctor of Humane Letters, University of Chicago
1974	Visiting Fellow, All Souls College, Oxford
1975–	Emeritus Linden Kent Memorial Professor, University of Virginia
1975	Fellow Commoner, Churchill College, Cambridge